THE LAW OF SUCCESSION

AUSTRALIA
The Law Book Company
Brisbane ● Sydney ● Melbourne ● Perth

CANADA
Carswell
Ottawa ● Toronto ● Calgary ● Montreal ● Vancouver

Agents:
Steimatzky's Agency Ltd., Tel Aviv;
N.M. Tripathi (Private) Ltd., Bombay;
Eastern Law House (Private) Ltd., Calcutta;
M.P.P. House, Bangalore;
Universal Book Traders, Delhi;
Aditya Books, Delhi;
MacMillan Shuppan KK, Tokyo;
Pakistan Law House, Karachi, Lahore

PARRY & CLARK

THE LAW OF SUCCESSION

Tenth Edition

by

Roger Kerridge, M.A., LL.B.

Solicitor, Senior Lecturer in Law;
University of Bristol

LONDON
SWEET & MAXWELL
1996

First Edition 1937
Second Edition 1947
Third Edition 1953
Fourth Edition 1961
 Second Impression 1963
 Third Impression 1965
Fifth Edition 1966
Sixth Edition 1972
 Second Impression 1976
Seventh Edition 1977
Eighth Edition 1983
Ninth Edition 1988
Tenth Edition 1996

Published in 1996 by Sweet & Maxwell Limited of
South Quay Plaza, 183 Marsh Wall,
London E14 9FT
Computerset by Wyvern Typesetting, Bristol
Printed in England by
Clays Ltd, St Ives plc

The index was prepared by Jeanne Bradbury

No natural forests were destroyed to make this product;
only farmed timber was used and replanted

A CIP catalogue record for this book is available from the British Library

ISBN 0 421 489 006

Preface

Professor D.H. Parry wrote the preface to the first edition of his book on the *Law of Succession* nearly 60 years ago, in March 1937. He died, Sir David Hughes Parry, aged 80, in 1973, having produced six editions. The seventh to ninth editions were edited by Professor J.B. Clark. Sadly, he died in 1992, when he would have been just about to take on the production of this edition.

I am mindful that this was originally designed to be, and remains, a book primarily for undergraduate law students. I hope that those taking the professional examinations, and practitioners themselves, will continue to use it; but this edition places slightly greater emphasis than the last on the Law of Wills and Intestacy, and slightly less on Administration and Probate.

One problem with a book on succession is its division into topics. Professor Clark arranged the last edition in such a way that it contained 15 chapters, all of approximately equal length. This edition has been re-arranged so that it has 21 chapters of varying length. What has been lost in neatness has, I hope, been compensated for in ease of use. There is no universally agreed order, and teachers of the subject approach topics in different ways. The new division is designed to give both teachers and students more freedom of choice and, it is to be hoped, to make the general scheme of the law of succession a little easier to follow. Some of the chapters have been significantly rewritten and there is a completely new chapter on Tax; I can only hope that it will not be out of date before the book is published. I would welcome comments and criticisms from readers not only as to the order, but as to what has, or has not, now been included in the book. The subject matter is a constant reminder that we are all mortal, so I expect the book to survive me, as it has survived the original author and his successor as editor.

In working on this edition, I have received help and encouragement from a number of colleagues (and ex-colleagues) at Bristol. Stephen Cretney, David Clarke, Nigel Furey, Keith Stanton and Chris Willmore all gave encouragement and/or assistance while Andrew Borkowski read and commented on most of the earlier chapters. But special thanks must go to Alastair Brierley who read and commented on the whole book, helped with the re-arrangement of the order of topics, supplied the draft will and even suggested the picture for the front cover. Having done all this, he decided that academic life was so stressful that he wanted to return to private practice! Thanks are also due to a number of secretaries, but in particular to Rachel Nee, for helping to type the various drafts; and to the Publishers for their assistance and forbearance, and, in particular, for arranging the preparation of the tables of statutes and cases, and the index.

This edition was originally completed, as is appropriate, on St David's

Day, March 1, 1995, but it was possible to make a number of additions and amendments at proof stage and so it is substantially up to date to the end of August 1995. I have even included in the text references to the Law Reform (Succession) Act 1995 which has not, at the time of writing, had its third Commons reading. This is on the basis that I am almost certain that it will get its third reading and receive the Royal Assent in November, just before publication.

Roger Kerridge
St Aidan's Day
August 31, 1995

Contents

TABLE OF CASES

TABLE OF CASES

TABLE OF STATUTES

TABLE OF RULES AND ORDERS

TABLE OF RULES THE SUPREME COURT

CHAPTER 1

THE NATURE OF WILLS AND OTHER DISPOSITIONS TAKING EFFECT AT DEATH

I. WILLS

A. A WILL IS INTENDED TO TAKE EFFECT ONLY AT DEATH

A will is the expression by a person of wishes which he[1] intends to take effect only at his death. In order to make a valid will, a testator must have a testamentary intention, *i.e.* he must intend the wishes to which he gives deliberate expression to *take effect only at his death*. It is not, however, necessary that the testator should intend to make, or be aware that he is making, a will.[2]

A will is ambulatory

A will has no effect until the testator dies.[3] This is the basic characteristic of a will and it is usually expressed by saying that a will, by its very nature, is ambulatory until the testator's death. Thus a will cannot confer benefits whilst the testator is still alive. If a testator makes a will giving his house Blackacre to James, James takes no interest in Blackacre until the testator's death. A will does not limit the testator's rights of ownership and accordingly he remains free to sell, give away, or otherwise dispose of,[4] Blackacre during the rest of his lifetime.

A document intended to take effect only at death is a will

A document intended by a person to be his will is usually worded so as to describe itself as his "will." If the document is intended to be

---

[1] "He" in this context is, of course, shorthand for "he or she". Whenever there is a reference in this book to someone who may be male or female (a testator, a beneficiary, a witness etc.) he or she is referred to as "he". Some may think this old-fashioned, but the alternatives all seem to be inelegant and/or ungrammatical.

[2] *Milnes v. Foden* (1890) 15 P.D. 105; *Re Stable* [1919] P. 7 (soldier's privileged will): see *post* pp. 56 and 89–90.

[3] But revocation of a previous will by another will or codicil takes effect when the latter is executed if the testator's intention to revoke is absolute; see *post*, pp. 104 and 107.

[4] He may want to mortgage Blackacre, or to create a lease over it—in these cases, he may be disposing of part of his interest in it; the fact that he has given Blackacre to James in his will, in no way restricts his freedom of action in relation to these transactions.

supplementary to a will it is usually worded so as to describe itself as a "codicil." Indeed, a professional draftsman invariably inserts words describing the document as a will or a codicil at the beginning, in order to make the nature of the document clear immediately.[5] But it is not necessary for a document which is intended to operate as a will or codicil to describe itself as such. Whatever form it takes, any document can be proved[6] as a will or codicil if (i) the person executing it intended it to take effect only at his death and (ii) it was duly executed. To be duly executed, normally a document must have been signed and witnessed in accordance with the formalities required by the Wills Act 1837.[7] As Lord Penzance put it in *Cock v. Cooke*,[8] "It is undoubted law that whatever may be the form of a duly executed instrument, if the person executing it intends that it shall not take effect until after his death, and it is dependent upon his death for its vigour and effect, it is testamentary." Thus a document duly executed by a person who intended it to take effect only at his death can be admitted to probate as a will or codicil even though in form it appears to be instructions for a will,[9] a cheque,[10] a letter,[11] a deed,[12] or a statutory nomination.[13]

Ascertaining intention

In deciding whether a document can be proved as a will or codicil, the court ascertains the intention of the person who executed it, both from the language of the document and from extrinsic evidence.

If the document appears on its face to be testamentary, a rebuttable presumption arises that the deceased intended it to take effect only at his death. Clearly, this presumption arises if a document describes itself as a will or codicil. It has been suggested that the presumption arises if the document, whatever its form, has been signed and witnessed in accordance with the formalities required by the Wills Act 1837.[14] An unusual example of the application of the presumption was in *Re Berger*,[15] where a Hebrew manuscript, a "zavah", which had been duly executed in accordance with the Wills Act, was admitted to probate. The presumption may be rebutted by cogent extrinsic evidence proving that

---

[5] Two alternative forms of commencement of a will in common use are: "This is the last Will and Testament of me John Smith . . ." or "I John Smith of (address and description) hereby revoke all former wills and testamentary dispositions made by me and declare this to be my last Will . . ."

[6] *Post*, pp. 320 *et seq.*

[7] *Post*, p. 76. Exceptionally, a privileged testator may make an informal will without any formalities; see *post*, p. 87.

[8] (1866) L.R. 1 P. & D. 241, 243: see *Robertson v. Smith* (1870) L.R. 2 P. & D. 43; *In the Goods of Coles* (1871) L.R. 2P. & D. 362.

[9] *Torre v. Castle* (1836) 1 Curt. 303; *Godman v. Godman* [1920] P. 261, 281 *et seq.*, (reviewing the authorities); *Re Meynell* [1949] W.N. 273 (where the testator's instructions to his solicitor for his will were duly executed with the required formalities because the testator's physical condition made him liable to die suddenly).

[10] *Bartholomew v. Henley* (1820) 3 Phill. 317.

[11] *In the Goods of Mundy* (1860) 2 Sw. & Tr. 119.

[12] *In the Goods of Morgan* (1866) L.R. 1 P. & D. 214.

[13] *In the Goods of Baxter* [1903] P. 12: see *post* p. 18.

[14] *Per* Barnard J. in *Re Meynell* [1949] W.N. 273

[15] [1990] Ch 118; Court of Appeal, affirming the decision of Warner J.

the document was not intended to take effect at death. Thus the court refused probate of a will on proof that the deceased made it in jest as a specimen of a will made in as few words as possible.[16]

Conversely, if a document does not appear to be testamentary on its face, the burden of proving that the maker of the document intended it to take effect only at his death lies on those seeking probate of it.[17] This burden can be discharged by extrinsic evidence. Thus in *Jones v. Nicolay*,[18] where an order on a banker to pay £4,000 to X at 12 days' sight was signed by its maker T and attested by two witnesses, extrinsic evidence was admissible to prove that this was done when T knew he was dangerously ill and that he intended the order to be a codicil to his will.

Comparison with an *inter vivos* disposition by deed

Unlike a will, an *inter vivos* disposition of property by deed takes effect forthwith; or, if the deed is executed by the grantor conditionally on the occurrence of some event other than his own death, it takes effect on the occurrence of that event. If, however, the condition is that the deed shall take effect only at the death of the grantor, it cannot take effect as a disposition *inter vivos*[19] but operates as a will or codicil if it was duly executed. In *In the Goods of Morgan*[20] the deceased, during his lifetime, executed three deeds of gift conveying property to trustees for the benefit of his children: each deed of gift contained a clause directing that it was not to take effect until after his death. The court held that the three deeds of gift together contained the will of the deceased and granted probate of them, as they had been signed and witnessed in accordance with the appropriate formalities. In the absence of such a clause in each deed of gift showing the deceased's intention, the result would have been the same if extrinsic evidence had proved that the deceased intended these deeds to take effect only at his death.[21] On the other hand, if these deeds had not been signed and witnessed in accordance with the formalities required by the Wills Act 1837, they would not have constituted a valid will unless the deceased was privileged and so entitled to make a will without any formalities.[22]

A settlement of property does not become a will merely because it postpones the possession of property by, or even the vesting of property in, a beneficiary until the death of the settlor. For instance, a settlor may execute a settlement by deed of Whiteacre on the settlor for life, with remainder to X in fee simple if X survives the settlor. Under this settlement, X's interest only vests in him in possession if he survives the settlor. Nevertheless, provided that the settlor intended the settlement to

---

[16] *Nichols v. Nichols* (1814) 2 Phill. 180 ("I leave my property between my children; I hope they will be virtuous and independent; that they will worship God, and not black coats"); see *Lister v. Smith* (1865) 3 Sw. & Tr. 282 (sham codicil).

[17] *King's Proctor v. Daines* (1830) 2 Hagg.Ecc. 218.

[18] (1850) 2 Rob. 288.

[19] *Governors and Guardians of the Foundling Hospital v. Crane* [1911] 2 K.B. 367.

[20] (1866) L.R. 1 P. & D. 214.

[21] *In the Goods of Slinn* (1890) 15 P.D. 156.

[22] *Post*, p. 87.

take effect forthwith, or on the occurrence of some event other than his own death, the settlement constitutes an *inter vivos* disposition.

B.   A WILL IS REVOCABLE UNTIL DEATH

Another important characteristic is that a will, by its very nature, is revocable by the testator until his death. A testator cannot make his will irrevocable during his lifetime. Thus a declaration by a testator in his will that it is irrevocable does not prevent him from subsequently revoking it.[23]

Joint wills

If two or more persons duly execute the same document as the will of both of them, it constitutes a joint will and is treated as the separate will of each of them.[24] Each is therefore free to revoke or vary the joint will so far as it applies to him at any time, whether or not the other person is still alive.[25] If one dies leaving the joint will unrevoked, probate will be granted of the joint will as the will of the deceased testator.[26] If the other dies leaving the joint will unrevoked, probate will be granted of the joint will as the will of the other deceased testator. Joint wills are rarely made: their sole merit is that a joint will can effectively exercise a power[27] given to two persons jointly to appoint by will,[28] but the cases where such a power is given are extremely rare.

C.   A TESTATOR CAN ONLY LEAVE ONE WILL

A testator may leave more than one expression of his testamentary intentions: he may, for instance, leave several documents worded so as to describe themselves as his will or as codicils to his will. But as the Privy Council pointed out in *Douglas-Menzies v. Umphelby*,[29] however many testamentary documents a testator may leave,

> "it is the aggregate or the net result that constitutes his will, or, in other words, the expression of his testamentary wishes. The law, on a man's death, finds out what are the instruments which express his last will. If some extant writing be revoked, or is inconsistent with a

---

[23] *Vynior's Case* (1609) 8 Co.Rep. 81b; *In the Estate of Heys* [1914] P. 192, 197.

[24] *Re Duddell* [1932] 1 Ch. 585.

[25] *Hobson v. Blackburn and Blackburn* (1822) 1 Add. 274.

[26] The practice, adopted in *In the Goods of Piazzi-Smyth* [1898] P. 7 of proving only that part of the joint will which becomes operative upon the death of the first to die, is not now followed. The Principal Registry maintains an index of joint wills which have been proved in respect of one of the testators.

[27] For a general explanation of powers, see Hanbury and Martin, *Modern Equity* (14th ed., 1993), Chapter 6.

[28] *Re Duddell, supra.*

[29] [1908] A.C. 224, 233.

later testamentary writing, it is discarded. But all that survive this scrutiny form part of the ultimate will or effective expression of his wishes about his estate. In this sense it is inaccurate to speak of a man leaving two wills; he does leave, and can leave, but one will."[30]

This case concerned two testamentary documents, one disposing of the testator's estate in Great Britain and the other disposing of his estate in Australia. Accordingly, the Privy Council did not advert to the possibility of an oral expression of testamentary intentions by a privileged testator. To take account of this possibility, it may be better to say that a testator can only leave one will which is the net result of every valid expression of his testamentary intentions during his lifetime. This is the strict meaning of the word "will."

Frequently the word "will" is used in a different sense, to denote a particular expression by a testator of his testamentary intentions—e.g. "the deceased made a formal will in England and later made an informal privileged will whilst serving as a soldier in Northern Ireland."

D. CONDITIONAL WILLS

A testator may state in his will that he intends it to take effect only if some specified condition is satisfied: for example, "If I survive my wife and inherit under her will . . ."[31]; or ". . . in case anything should happen to me during the remainder of the voyage."[32] If the specified condition is not satisfied, the will does not take effect.

It is not necessary for the condition to appear on the face of the will. Extrinsic evidence may be admitted to show that a will, although not expressed to be conditional, is in fact conditional.[33]

On the other hand, a testator may refer in his will to a possible future event merely in order to show his reason for making his will. An instance is *In the Goods of Dobson*[34] where the will began with the words, "In case of any fatal accident happening to me, being about to travel by railway, I hereby leave . . ." The testator survived his railway journey; and on his death Lord Penzance held that the will was not conditional, saying "the testator's meaning seems to me to have been this: 'My mind is drawn to the consideration that all railway travelling is attended with danger, and therefore I think that I had better make my will'."[35]

It is a question of construction whether words used (i) show that the testator intended the will to take effect only if a specified condition is satisfied (a conditional will), or (ii) refer to a possible future event in order to show the testator's reason for making his will (an unconditional will). When deciding this question the court considers the provisions of

---

[30] Quoted and applied by Sir Denys Buckley in *Re Berger* [1990] Ch. 118.
[31] *In the Estate of Thomas* [1939] 2 All E.R. 567.
[32] *In the Goods of Robinson* (1870) L.R. 2 P.&D. 171.
[33] *Corbett v. Newey* [1994] Ch. 388, where extrinsic evidence was admitted to prove both the existence and the fulfilment of the condition.
[34] (1866) L.R. 1 P.&D. 88: see *Burton v. Collingwood* (1832) 4 Hagg. 176 ("lest I should die before the next sun").
[35] (1866) L.R. 1 P.&D. 88, 89.

the will, read as a whole in the light of the surrounding circumstances in which it was made.[36] In *In the Goods of Cawthorn*[37] a testator wrote out but did not execute his will, which began with the words, "In the prospect of a long journey, should God not permit me to return to my home, I . . . make this my last will." Some months after returning home from this journey he executed his will in the presence of two witnesses. Extrinsic evidence proved that he was not then contemplating any journey and the court held that the will was unconditional and therefore admissible to probate.

If a conditional will contains a clause revoking a previous will but the specified condition is not satisfied, the conditional will is entirely inoperative and the previous will remains unrevoked.[38] However, a conditional codicil which referred to a previous will was admitted to probate, even though the specified condition was not satisfied, on the ground that it would have the effect of republishing the earlier will, or of making the earlier will valid if it had not been duly executed.[39]

A conditional will must be distinguished from a conditional gift in a will. For instance, a gift by will of "£200 to X if he swims the English Channel" is a conditional gift: if X does not satisfy the specified condition, the gift to him fails; but the will as a whole still takes effect.

E.   CONTENTS OF A WILL

The main function of most wills is to dispose of the testator's property after his death. By his will the testator may make gifts, either directly to a person beneficially or to trustees upon trust. Another important function of most wills is to appoint one or more executors to administer the testator's estate after his death.[40] Sometimes wills deal with various other matters in addition to (or instead of) disposing of the testator's property or appointing executors.

The testator's body

The law recognises no property in the dead body of a human being. It follows that a testator cannot by will dispose of his dead body: a direction in a will to executors to deliver the testator's dead body to another person is therefore void.[41] The executors are entitled to the custody and possession of the testator's dead body until it is buried, and the duty of

---

[36] *In the Goods of Spratt* [1897] P. 28 (where many of the cases are considered); *Re Govier* [1950] P. 237 (joint will; "in the event of our two deaths"). For admissible extrinsic evidence see *post*, pp. 187 *et seq.*

[37] (1863) 3 Sw. & Tr. 417 (the journey was from Bideford to Shrewsbury).

[38] *In the Goods of Hugo* (1877) 2 P.D. 73; *In the Estate of O'Connor* [1942] 1 A11 E.R. 546.

[39] *In the Goods of Mendes da Silva* (1861) 2 Sw. & Tr. 315; *In the Goods of Colley* (1879) 3 L.R.Ir. 243: but see *Parsons v. Lanoe* (1748) 1 Ves.Sen. 189, 190. For republication see *post*, p. 118.

[40] *Post*, pp. 294 *et seq.*

[41] *Williams v. Williams* (1882) 20 Ch.D. 659.

disposing of the body falls primarily on them, at any rate if the testator leaves assets sufficient for this purpose.[42]

If a deceased has expressed wishes during his lifetime as to the disposal of his body, either in his will or otherwise, these wishes are generally not legally enforceable against his personal representatives, though they may well have effective moral force. For instance, wishes expressed in favour of, or against, cremation have no legal but only moral force.[43] Certain wishes, however, have some legal effect. Thus, under the Human Tissue Act 1961, if a person, either in writing at any time or orally in the presence of two witnesses during his last illness, requests that his body or some specified part be used after his death for therapeutic purposes or for purposes of medical education or research, the person lawfully in possession of his body after his death may authorise this.[44] In the absence of such a request, he may authorise this if, having made such reasonable inquiry as may be practicable, he has no reason to believe that the deceased had expressed an objection to his body being so dealt with after his death.[45]

A testator needs to ensure that his wishes as to the disposal of his body are quickly brought to the notice of the person in possession of it after his death: indeed minutes count if his body is to be used for the purposes of a transplant. If he merely expresses his wishes in his will, there is a danger that no one will read it and learn of his wishes until after his funeral, particularly if the will is deposited for safe custody with a solicitor or bank. If the testator is unwilling to make his wishes known openly in his lifetime, he needs to inform his executors and any persons who are likely to be with him at his death that his will contains these wishes. Alternatively he can express these wishes in a letter left with his executors and to be opened immediately after his death.[46]

Appointment of testamentary guardians[47]

The law in relation to guardianship was modified and simplified by the Children Act 1989.[48] A parent who has parental responsibility for his child may appoint another individual to be the child's guardian in the event of his death[49]; and a guardian may appoint someone else to take

---

[42] *Rees v. Hughes* [1946] K.B. 517, 524 and 528. For the payment of funeral expenses see *post*, pp. 411–412.

[43] Until 1965, reg. 4 of the Cremation Regulations 1930 (S.R. & O. 1930 No. 1016) made it unlawful to cremate the remains of any person who was known to have left a written direction to the contrary: this was revoked by the Cremation Regulations 1965 (S.I. 1965 No. 1146), reg. 7(a).

[44] Human Tissue Act 1961, s.1(1).

[45] *ibid*. s.1(2): he must also have no reason to believe that the surviving spouse or any surviving relative of the deceased objects. As to a request by a person for anatomical examination of his body, see Anatomy Act 1984, s.4(1) and (2). For the removal of eyes see also Corneal Tissue Act 1986.

[46] H.M.S.O. issue a Kidney Transplant Donor Card which is intended to be kept with the donor at all times in a place where it will be found quickly.

[47] See S.M. Cretney and J.M. Masson, *Principles of Family Law* (5th ed., 1990) pp. 507 *et seq*.

[48] The Act followed *Law Com No. 172* (1988); the Law Commission's Report on *Family Law, Child Law, Guardianship and Custody*.

[49] Children Act 1989 s.5(3).

his place in the event of his own death[50]; *but* the guardian's appointment normally takes effect only when the child no longer has a parent who has parental responsibility for him.[51] In other words, the first parent to die may appoint a guardian, but the appointment is only effective on the death of the second parent.[52] The appointment of a guardian may be made by will or in writing, signed and dated.[53] If an appointment is by will, it is revoked by revocation of the will[54] but an appointment by will will also be revoked by a later written appointment.[55]

Exercise of testamentary powers of appointment

By his will the testator may exercise any power of appointment conferred on him and exercisable by will.[56] For instance, he may under a settlement have a life interest and a power to appoint the remainder interest in the settled property by will among his children or remoter issue.

The testator may exercise a testamentary power of appointment either (i) by a will made in writing and duly executed in accordance with the formalities required by the Wills Act 1837[57] or (ii) by an informal will if the testator is privileged.[58] Occasionally, the instrument creating a power of appointment by will purports to require special formalities to be observed when the power is exercised; such as three witnesses to the will instead of the two required by the Wills Act 1837. To deal with this, section 10 of the Act provides that, despite this special requirement, an appointment made by a will which is in writing and duly executed in accordance with the formalities required by the Act shall be valid "so far as respects the execution and attestation thereof." Section 10 thus makes it unnecessary to observe special formalities concerning execution and attestation; but any other requirements must be observed, otherwise an appointment is void.[59] However, even special formalities concerning execution and attestation must be observed in an informal will, to which section 10 is not applicable.

F. SOLICITOR'S DUTY OF CARE IN PREPARATION OF A WILL

Solicitor's duty to client

If a testator employs a solicitor to prepare a will for him containing a gift to a beneficiary and, owing to the solicitor's negligence, the gift to

---

[50] *ibid.* s.5(4).

[51] *ibid.* s.5(8).

[52] Before the 1989 Act came into force, the guardian normally acted jointly with the surviving parent.

[53] Children Act 1989 s.5(5). Before 1989 the appointment had to be by *deed* or will.

[54] Children Act 1989 s.6(4).

[55] *ibid.* s.6(1).

[56] For the rules of construction governing the exercise of powers of appointment see *post*, pp. 211 *et seq.*

[57] Wills Act 1837, s.10: see also *Re Barnett* [1908] 1 Ch. 402.

[58] *Re Wernher* [1918] 2 Ch. 82 (general power); *Re Earl of Chichester's W.T.* [1946] Ch. 289 (special power over personalty: *obiter* as to special power over realty).

[59] *Cooper v. Martin* (1867) 3 Ch.App. 47 (requirement as to time of appointment). A requirement that the consent of a specified person be obtained to the appointment must, for instance, be observed.

the beneficiary is void, the solicitor is liable in damages to the testator both in contract and in tort.[60] If the testator discovers during his lifetime that the gift to the beneficiary is void, the damages recoverable by the testator are the costs of making a new and valid will or otherwise putting matters right.[61] But if the discovery is made after the testator's death, it seems that T's estate would recover only nominal damages.[62]

Solicitor's duty to beneficiary under will

In *Ross v. Caunters*[63] the testator's solicitors sent him his will for execution, but failed to warn him that the execution should not be witnessed by the spouse of a beneficiary. The execution of the will was then witnessed by the husband of one of the beneficiaries. The testator afterwards returned the will to the solicitors who failed to notice that there was anything wrong. Two years later, T died. Section 15 of the Wills Act 1837 made the gift to the beneficiary whose husband had witnessed the will's execution "utterly nul and void".[64] The solicitors had clearly been negligent but they argued that their duty of care had been owed only to their client, the testator, and not to the beneficiary. Sir Robert Megarry V.-C. held that the beneficiary was entitled to recover from the solicitors by way of damages the value of the gifts to which she would otherwise have been entitled under T's will.

The issue of a solicitor's liability to intended beneficiaries was raised again in the recent case of *White v. Jones*, this time it was taken to the House of Lords.[65] In *White v. Jones* the solicitors' negligence[66] consisted of failing to comply with instructions to prepare a new will. Had the solicitors proceeded with the preparation of a new will within a reasonable timescale, the new will would have been executed before the testator's death. As it was, the new will was not prepared and the prospective beneficiaries under it, the testator's daughters, took no benefit. An earlier will which disinherited them, and which the testator had decided to revoke, took effect on his death. *White v. Jones* is not an easy case. Turner J. at first instance, found in favour of the defendant solicitors. He thought that to find for the plaintiffs in this case would be to extend *Ross v. Caunters* from an act to an omission and he also thought that the damage was too speculative and uncertain in extent to be recoverable. The Court of Appeal unanimously reversed Turner J.'s decision, applying *Ross v. Caunters*. The House of Lords, by a bare majority,[67] affirmed

---

[60] *Ross v. Caunters* [1980] Ch. 297, 306–308; *White v. Jones* [1995] 2 W.L.R. 187, 201: see also *Henderson v. Merrett Syndicates Ltd.* [1994] 3 W.L.R. 761, 766, 773, 778, 789, 800. Whether a solicitor has a duty to draw his client's attention to the effect of marriage on a will (*post*, p. 94) depends on the circumstances, *Hall v. Meyrick* [1957] 2 Q.B. 455, 475–476 and 482.

[61] *Ross v. Caunters* [1980] Ch. 297, 303.

[62] *Ross v. Caunters* [1980] Ch. 297, 302; *White v. Jones* [1995] 2 W.L.R. 187, 201.

[63] [1980] Ch. 297.

[64] For Wills Act 1837, s. 15 (which deprives an attesting witness and his spouse of any benefit under the will which he attests) see *post* pp. 232 *et seq.*

[65] [1995] 2 W.L.R. 187.

[66] It was the negligence of their clerk.

[67] Lord Goff of Chieveley, Lord Browne-Wilkinson and Lord Nolan held that the beneficiaries had a remedy against the solicitors; Lord Keith of Kinkel and Lord Mustill dissented.

the decision of the Court of Appeal, but on different grounds, not by applying *Ross v. Caunters*.

The problem with this branch of the law is that, as was said by Steyn L.J. in the Court of Appeal in *White v. Jones* "It lies at the interface of what has traditionally been regarded as the separate domains of contract and tort."[68] Two pages of Lord Goff's speech in the House of Lords are devoted to "The German experience".[69] This is clearly a compliment to the influence of academic commentators, but, given that the German solution to this problem is to extend the benefit of a contractual cause of action, whereas the English solution appears to be based on tort, there is a danger that the discussion of concepts will not assist Succession practitioners in calculating the extent of their liability.

The reasoning of the majority of the members of the House of Lords in *White v. Jones* is based on *Hedley Byrne v. Heller*,[70] the case which established tortious liability for some forms of negligent misrepresentation and which now seems capable, in some circumstances, of supporting the recovery in tort of financial losses caused by negligent acts.[71] But in *Hedley Byrne v. Heller* information had been sought from the defendants by the plaintiffs and the defendants knew that reliance was being placed, by the plaintiffs, on the defendants' skill and judgment. It is not entirely clear to what extent, if at all, there was any need for reliance, by the plaintiffs, in *White v. Jones*. Lord Goff, one of the majority, expressed it as follows:

> "In my opinion, therefore, your Lordships' House should in cases such as these extend to the intended beneficiary a remedy under the *Hedley Byrne* principle by holding that the assumption of responsibility by the solicitor towards his client should be held in law to extend to the intended beneficiary who (as the solicitor can reasonably foresee) may, as a result of the solicitor's negligence, be deprived of his intended legacy in circumstances in which neither the testator nor his estate will have a remedy against the solicitor."[72]

It could be suggested that the reasoning adopted by the majority in the House of Lords in *White v. Jones*, based on *Hedley Byrne*, based on an assumption of responsibility, on reliance, and on knowledge of reliance, could be restricted to cases where there is a direct link between the plaintiffs and the defendants. In *White v. Jones* itself, the plaintiff daughters did come into contact with the solicitors. One of them had telephoned the solicitors with her father's instructions and had later attempted to arrange an appointment for the execution of the will. It could be suggested that if the gift in the will had been to a stranger, someone who had never come into contact with the solicitors, someone who knew nothing about the prospective will (for example, a charity), the result might have been different. But *White v. Jones* was not argued on this basis[73] and it would be rash of any solicitor, or will draftsman,

---

[68] [1993] 3 W.L.R. 730, 750.
[69] [1995] 2 W.L.R. 187, 201–203.
[70] *Hedley Byrne & Co. Ltd v. Heller & Partners Ltd.* [1964] A.C. 465.
[71] *Henderson v. Merrett Syndicates Ltd.* [1994] 3 W.L.R. 761.
[72] [1995] 2 W.L.R. 187, 206–207.
[73] Lord Mustill, dissenting, considered the hypothetical case of a gift to a charity, the charity having no knowledge of the testator's intention. He did not see how the *Hedley Byrne* principle could be applied to such a case. He did not think it appropriate to distinguish

to assume that such a suggestion would find favour. Lord Browne-Wilkinson implied[74] that a solicitor, by accepting instructions to draw a will, comes into a special relationship with anyone who is intended to benefit under it, while Lord Goff thought that the boundaries to the availability of the remedy "will have to be worked out in the future, as practical problems come before the courts."[75]

It was held in *Clarke v. Bruce Lance & Co*,[76] a case decided after *Ross v. Caunters* but before *White v. Jones*, that a solicitor would not be liable to a beneficiary if there were a conflict between the duty owed to the client and the duty owed to the beneficiary. In *Clarke v. Bruce Lance*, solicitors prepared a will for the testator and this will devised some land to the testator's son. The solicitors later acted for the testator in relation to a lease of the land and, later still, they acted for him when he granted the tenant a fixed price option to purchase the land. The grant of the option was clearly not in the son's interest, but this was a case where there was a clear potential conflict between the testator's interest and his son's interest. Where this conflict existed, the solicitors' duty was to the testator. The principle that where there is a conflict between the testator's interest and the interest of a beneficiary under his will, the solicitors must heed the testator's interest is, almost certainly, still good law.[77]

Another decision which will have survived *White v. Jones* is *Kecskemeti v. Rubens Rabin & Co*[78] where a solicitor was held to owe a duty of care to a beneficiary who failed to obtain a benefit under the testator's will because the testator's property was held as a joint tenant with his widow and so passed to her under the right of survivorship.

G.   CONTRACT TO MAKE, OR NOT TO MAKE, A WILL

Validity of contract[79]

A contract by which T promises P to leave to P by will specific property[80] (such as T's house), a pecuniary legacy,[81] or the whole or a specified

between the hypothetical case and facts of *White v. Jones* because *White v. Jones* had been argued throughout "on the basis of a stark choice between a duty of general application or no duty at all" [1995] 2 W.L.R. 187, 228.

[74] [1995] 2 W.L.R. 187, 214.

[75] [1995] 2 W.L.R. 187, 208.

[76] [1988] 1 W.L.R. 881.

[77] It *is* still good law *but* it has to be said that its application to the facts of *Clarke v. Bruce Lance* is not quite as straightforward as might, at first sight, appear; for a further discussion of *Clarke v. Bruce Lance* (within the context of the doctrine of ademption) see Chapter 11 pp. 251–252.

[78] *The Times*, December 31 1992, decision of Macpherson of Cluny J.

[79] For a remedy under the doctrine of proprietary estoppel see *Snell's Equity* (29th ed., 1990) pp. 573 *et seq.*; Gray *Elements of Land Law* (2nd ed. 1993) Chap. 11; *Griffiths v. Williams* (1977) 248 E.G. 947; *Jones (A.E.) v. Jones (F.W.)* [1977] 1 W.L.R. 438; *Greasley v. Cooke* [1980] 1 W.L.R. 1306; *Re Basham* [1986] 1 W.L.R. 1498 (P acted to detriment, relying on belief, encouraged by D, that P would receive D's property on D's death: held P entitled to whole of D's estate) see commentary and criticism by Sherrin in [1987] All E.R. Annual Review at pp. 263 and 264.

[80] *Synge v. Synge* [1894] 1 Q.B. 466 (to leave P life interest in house); *Parker v. Clark* [1960] 1 W.L.R. 286 (to leave house and contents to P, Q and R jointly).

[81] *Hammersley v. De Biel* (1845) 12 Cl. & F. 45; *Graham v. Wickham* (1863) 1 De G.J. & Sm. 474.

share of his residuary estate, is valid. Of course, under general principles of contract law, such a promise must either be supported by valuable consideration or be made by deed[82]; there must be an intention to create legal relations,[83] and the terms of the contract must not be uncertain.[84] Moreover, if the contract relates to land and was made after September 26 1989 it is void if it is not in writing.[85] If it was made before September 27 1989 it is not enforceable unless there is a signed memorandum satisfying section 40 of the Law of Property Act 1925,[86] or the equitable doctrine of part performance applies.[87]

Similarly, a contract by which T promises P not to revoke or alter T's existing will, or a particular gift in it, is valid.[88] Such a contract is construed as prohibiting intentional revocation by T[89] but not automatic revocation of his will if T marries[90]: thus if T marries, thereby automatically revoking his will, T does not commit any breach of contract.[91] A contract not to revoke may be drafted in such wide terms as to purport to prohibit automatic revocation by marriage as well as intentional revocation. In so far as it operates in restraint of marriage, however, such a prohibition is void on grounds of public policy.[92]

Remedies for breach

If T commits a breach of his contract with P to leave specific property, a pecuniary legacy, or the whole or part of his residuary estate to P, after T's death P is entitled to recover damages from T's estate for loss of the promised benefit.[93] In appropriate circumstances in an action for specific performance of the contract, the court may order T's personal representatives to transfer the property bound by the contract (e.g. T's house) to P.[94]

T commits a breach of his contract with P not to revoke T's existing will if T intentionally revokes it.[95] P cannot stop T from revoking this

[82] At common law, deeds had to be executed under seal, but this requirement was abolished by the Law of Property (Miscellaneous Provisions) Act 1989, s.1(2).

[83] *Parker v. Clark* [1960] 1 W.L.R. 286, 292–294 (not a mere family arrangement).

[84] *MacPhail v. Torrance* (1909) 25 T.L.R. 810 (to make ample provision: too vague).

[85] Law Reform (Miscellaneous Provisions) Act 1989, s.2(1).

[86] *Maddison v. Alderson* (1883) 8 App.Cas. 467; *Re Gonin* [1979] Ch. 16. But T's estate may be liable on a *quantum meruit* to P for services rendered to T, *Deglman v. Guaranty Trust Co. of Canada* [1954] 3 D.L.R. 785.

[87] *Wakeham v. MacKenzie* [1968] 1 W.L.R. 1175 (T promised to leave house and contents to P if P gave up her flat and moved in and looked after him for life; P did so: held part performance): see *Re Gonin* [1979] Ch. 16, 30–31; Pettit (1968) 32 Conv. (N.S.) 384.

[88] *Robinson v. Ommanney* (1882) 21 Ch.D. 780; (1883) 23 Ch.D. 285.

[89] Intentional revocation occurs where the revocation is effected by destruction, another will or codicil, or duly executed writing; see *post*, pp. 99 *et seq.*

[90] *Post*, p. 94.

[91] *Re Marsland* [1939] Ch. 820.

[92] *Robinson v. Ommaney*, *supra*, where the contract not to revoke was held to be divisible, and valid in so far as it prohibited intentional revocation.

[93] *Hammersley v. De Biel* (1845) 12 Cl. & F. 45 (legacy); *Schaefer v. Schuhmann* [1972] A.C. 572, 585 *et seq.*

[94] *Re Edwards* [1958] Ch. 168, 175–176 (contract to devise house to P): see *Coverdale v. Eastwood* (1872) L.R. 15 Eq. 121 (contract to settle all T's property on P in strict settlement). The court may order any person holding the asset as T's successor in title to transfer it (*Synge v. Synge* [1894] 1 Q.B. 466, 471) unless he is a purchaser without notice or protected by the registration provisions applicable to interests in land, see *Snell's Equity* (29th ed., 1990), pp. 45 *et seq.*

[95] *Robinson v. Ommanney* (1882) 21 Ch.D. 780; (1883) 23 Ch.D. 285.

will by bringing an action for specific performance or an injunction, but P is entitled to recover damages from T, or after his death from T's estate, for loss of the promised benefit under this will.[96]

Testator's duty during his lifetime

If T contracts with P to leave *specific* property to P, and later T during his lifetime disposes of the property to Q, T thereby repudiates the contract. P may at once sue T for damages which are assessed subject to a reduction for the acceleration of the benefit and also, if the benefit of the contract is personal to P, subject to a reduction for the contingency of his failing to survive T.[97] If P can intervene before a purchaser for value obtains an interest in the property, P can obtain a declaration of his right to have it left to him by will and an injunction to restrain T from disposing of it in breach of contract.[98]

On the other hand, a contract by T to leave by will *all* his assets (or a share of them) at his death to P does not impose on T a duty not to dispose of any of his assets during his lifetime, unless the contract contains a term to this effect. The contract does, however, impose on T a more limited duty not to make *inter vivos* dispositions which in substance have a testamentary effect, such as a voluntary settlement whereby T settles property on himself for life, remainder to Q.[99]

Effect of lapse

Normally a gift by T's will to P fails by lapse if P predeceases T.[1] It is a question of construction of the contract between T and P whether (i) the benefit of the contract is personal to P, who takes the risk of lapse, so that T is discharged from liability if P predeceases T[2]; or whether (ii) the benefit of the contract is not personal to P but accrues for the benefit of P's estate, so that T ought to make provision in his will against lapse.[3]

Effect of insolvency

A contract to leave by will specific property or a pecuniary legacy to P may merely impose an obligation on T to make a will containing such a gift; in that case P, like any other beneficiary under a will, takes the risk that T's estate may turn out to be insolvent, or insufficient to satisfy the gift; if it does, P takes nothing, or a reduced benefit.[4] Such a contract

---

[96] *ibid*.: probably in appropriate circumstances the court may order T's personal representatives to transfer the promised asset to P.

[97] *Synge v. Synge* [1894] 1 Q.B. 466; *Schaefer v. Schuhmann* [1972] A.C. 572, 586: see *Parker v. Clark* [1960] 1 W.L.R. 286.

[98] *Synge v. Synge, supra* at p. 471; *Schaefer v. Schuhmann, supra.*

[99] *Jones v. Martin* (1798) 5 Ves.Jun. 266; *Fortescue v. Hannah* (1812) 19 Ves.Jun. 67; *Logan v. Wienholt* (1833) 1 Cl. & F. 611; *Re Bennett* [1934] W.N. 177 (Q the ostensible owner but T retained the income): cf. *Palmer v. Bank of New South Wales* (1975) C.L.R. 150 (opening joint bank account with Q not testamentary).

[1] *Post*, p. 234.

[2] *Re Brookman's Trust* (1869) L.R. 5 Ch.App. 182; *Schaefer v. Schuhmann* [1972] A.C.572, 586: see *Jones v. How* (1848) 7 Hare 267; *Needham v. Smith* (1828) 4 Russ. 318.

[3] See *Re Brookman's Trust, supra,* 191. See W.A. Lee (1971) 87 L.Q.R. 358, 361–362.

[4] See *Graham v. Wickham* (1863) 1 D.J. & S. 474, 484–485; *Eyre v. Monro* (1857) 3 K. & J. 305, 308.

is, however, more likely to impose an obligation on T to make the gift effective; in that case, T commits a breach of contract if T's estate is insolvent, or insufficient to satisfy the gift, and P is entitled to be treated as a creditor for the value of the property[5] or the amount of the legacy,[6] and to rank for payment with T's other creditors of the same degree.[7] Thus the effect of insolvency depends on the extent of the obligation imposed on T by the contract.

A contract by T to leave by will the whole or a specified share of his residuary estate to P is different because T's residuary estate available for distribution is only ascertained after T's debts and funeral and testamentary expenses have been paid. P takes the risk that T's estate may turn out to be insolvent; if it does, P takes nothing and has no claim as a creditor for breach of contract.[8]

H. MUTUAL WILLS

The Court of Chancery created the doctrine of mutual wills[9] in order to remedy the unconscionable revocation of a will in certain circumstances. There are three requirements which must be satisfied for the doctrine to apply.

1. Mutual wills made pursuant to an arrangement

The first requirement of the doctrine is that two or more persons make an arrangement as to the disposal of some or all of their property on death and execute wills pursuant to the arrangement.[10] The persons are often husband and wife but the principle is not restricted to husbands and wives. The mutual wills may take the form of a joint will or separate wills.[11] Usually, each of the mutual wills makes provision for the other person in some way. A relatively straightforward arrangement will be where each will gives the other person a life interest, with remainder to the same beneficiary.[12] Sometimes, each will gives the other person an absolute interest, with an alternative gift in case the other dies first.[13] But it is not essential that the other person receives a benefit. In the recent case of Re Dale[14] Morritt J. held that if two testators, e.g. husband and wife, agreed that each should leave his or her property to particular beneficiaries, e.g. their children, the surviving testator's property would

---

[5] Schaefer v. Schuhmann [1972] A.C. 572, 586.
[6] Graham v. Wickham (1863) 1 D.J. & S. 474; Eyre v. Monroe (1857) 3 K. & J. 305.
[7] For the order of priority of T's debts see post, pp. 441 et seq.
[8] Jervis v. Wolferstan (1874) L.R. 18 Eq. 18, 24; Schaefer v. Schuhmann [1972] A.C. 572, 586.
[9] See generally R. Burgess (1970) 34 Conv.(N.S.) 230; J.D.B. Mitchell (1951) 14 M.L.R. 136; T.G. Youdan (1979) U. of Toronto L.J. 390.
[10] Probably it would suffice if the first to die executes a mutual will and dies believing that the survivor has done so.
[11] Re Hagger [1930] 2 Ch. 190 (joint will); Re Green [1951] Ch. 148 (separate); Re Cleaver [1981] 1 W.L.R. 939 (separate).
[12] Re Hagger, supra.
[13] Re Green, supra; Re Cleaver, supra: cf. Re Oldham [1925] Ch. 75, 84 and 87–88.
[14] Re Dale [1994] Ch. 31. See A.H.R. Brierley (1995) 58 M.L.R. 95.

be subject to a trust[15] for the beneficiaries named in the wills.[16] There is also no reason why remainders to different, but agreed, beneficiaries in the two wills should not suffice if this is the arrangement.[17]

2. Agreement for survivor to be bound

The second requirement is that the parties agree that the survivor shall be bound by the arrangement. This requirement normally takes the form of an agreement by the parties not to revoke their mutual wills. For instance, in *Re Hagger*[18] a husband and wife made a joint mutual will which contained a declaration by them that it should not be altered or revoked save by their mutual agreement: it was implicit in this declaration that the parties agreed that the survivor should be bound by this arrangement. This requirement can also be satisfied by an agreement to leave property by will. Thus in *Re Green*[19] a husband and wife made mutual wills which recited an agreement between them that, if the survivor had the use of the other's property for life without any liability to account, the survivor would provide by will for the carrying out of the wishes expressed in the other's will.

The agreement by the parties that the survivor shall be bound by the arrangement can be proved by declarations to this effect in the mutual wills, or by clear and satisfactory extrinsic evidence.[20] A "mere honourable engagement" between the parties does not suffice.[21] In order to bring the agreement to the knowledge of any interested beneficiary and to facilitate proof of it in the future, it is advisable for the mutual wills to contain declarations that they are mutual or for the parties to hand to any interested beneficiary a signed declaration of their agreement.

The fact that the parties agreed to make, and did make, wills at the same time and in substantially identical terms is not sufficient to establish that they agreed that the survivor should be bound. In *Re Oldham*[22] a husband and wife made their wills on the same day, each giving the other an absolute interest with the same alternative gift in case the other died first. The husband died first and the wife took her husband's property under his will. She later remarried and died, having made a new will which provided for her second husband and which departed entirely from the terms of her earlier will. Astbury J. held that the doctrine of mutual wills was not applicable and upheld the wife's new will, saying that "the fact that the two wills were made in identical terms

---

[15] Morritt J. called it an "implied trust"; but "constructive trust" seems more appropriate.
[16] This is phrased hypothetically, "if two testators . . . etc." because the matter was raised as a preliminary issue. There was no decision as to whether there *was* an agreement which was intended to be binding and irrevocable.
[17] *Snell's Equity* (29th ed., 1990), p. 190, n. 79.
[18] [1930] 2 Ch. 190.
[19] [1951] Ch. 148.
[20] *In the Estate of Heys* [1914] P. 192. *Re Cleaver* [1981] 1 W.L.R. 939 (proof on balance of probabilities). And *quaere* whether the agreement, if made after September 26, 1989, will be void if it relates to land and is not in writing and signed by each of the parties— Law Reform (Miscellaneous Provisions) Act 1989, s. 2(1).
[21] *Re Cleaver, supra*, at pp. 945, 947–948.
[22] [1925] Ch. 75: see also *Gray v. Perpetual Trustee Co. Ltd.* [1928] A.C. 391; *Re Cleaver, supra*.

does not necessarily connote any agreement beyond that of so making them."[23]

3. Binding event occurs

There was, until recently, considerable controversy as to when the binding event occurred. It was suggested[24] that there were four possibilities: (i) when the agreement was made; (ii) when the first party died leaving his mutual will unrevoked; (iii) when the survivor received a benefit under the first will; or (iv) when the survivor died. Of these four possibilities, there were strong arguments against the first and the fourth but almost equal support, based on *dicta*,[25] for the second and the third. But Morritt J.'s recent decision in *Re Dale*,[26] to the effect that the doctrine of mutual wills may apply even where the survivor receives no benefit under the will of the first party to die, implies that the binding event *must* be the death of the first party, *i.e.* the second possibility suggested above.

Clearly, this third requirement is not satisfied if the first testator dies having revoked his mutual will before his death.[27] Again, it is not satisfied if the first testator dies knowing that the agreement to be bound no longer stands because the other has already repudiated it. To quote Lord Camden in *Dufour v. Pereira*,[28]

"A mutual will is a revocable act. It may be revoked by joint consent clearly. By one only, if he gives notice, I can admit. But to affirm that the survivor (who has deluded his partner into this will upon the faith and persuasion that he would perform his part) may legally recall his contract, either secretly during the joint lives, or after at his pleasure, I cannot allow."

Each is under an obligation not to revoke his will without giving notice to the other during the other's lifetime.[29]

Remedy of constructive trust

If the three requirements are satisfied equity enforces the arrangement against the survivor by treating him as holding the property concerned on a constructive trust, to apply it in accordance with his mutual will.[30] To quote Lord Camden again,[31]

"he, that dies first, does by his death carry the agreement on his part into execution. If the other then refuses, he is guilty of a fraud, can never unbind himself, and becomes a trustee of course. For no man shall deceive another to his prejudice. By engaging to do something

[23] [1925] Ch. 75, 88–89.
[24] See J.D.B. Mitchell (1951) 14 M.L.R. 136 at p. 137.
[25] See Parry and Clark (9th ed.) p. 13 n. 94 for details.
[26] [1994] Ch. 31.
[27] *Stone v. Hoskins* [1905] P. 194. And see C.E.F. Rickett (1991) 54 M.L.R. 581.
[28] (1769) 1 Dick. 419; the quotation is from 2 Hargr. Jurid. Arg. 304, 308.
[29] *Birmingham v. Renfrew* (1937) 57 C.L.R. 666, 682.
[30] *Birmingham v. Renfrew* (1937) 57 C.L.R. 666; *Re Cleaver* [1981] 1 W.L.R. 939.
[31] *Dufour v. Pereira*, 2 Hargr. Jurid. Arg. 304, 310.

that is in his power, he is made a trustee for the performance, and transmits that trust to those that claim under him."

This constructive trust takes effect when the binding event occurs.[32] Hence a beneficiary under the mutual wills, who survives the first but predeceases the second testator, does not lose his benefit by lapse. In *Re Hagger*[33] a husband H and wife W made a joint mutual will by which they gave their properties at Wandsworth (held by them jointly) to trustees upon trust for the survivor for life, and after the survivor's death to divide the proceeds of sale of the properties among certain named beneficiaries including P. The will included a declaration that it should not be altered or revoked save by their mutual agreement. The arrangement between them was incompatible with the right of survivorship applicable to their joint tenancy; accordingly the arrangement severed their joint tenancy and henceforth they held the Wandsworth properties as tenants in common.[34] W died in 1904 and H accepted his life interest under the will in her share of the properties. P died in 1923; and H died in 1928, having made a different will in 1921. Clauson J. decided that from W's death H held his share of the Wandsworth properties "on trust to apply it so as to carry out the effect of the joint will"[35]; thus from W's death P was entitled to a vested interest in remainder in H's share (as well as W's share) of these properties and there was no lapse by reason of P's death in H's lifetime.

This constructive trust does not stop the survivor from revoking his mutual will which, like any other will, is by its very nature revocable until his death. If the mutual will of the survivor is revoked and he makes a new will, any appointment of executors in his new will is effective (even if the executors are not the executors named in his mutual will), and on his death the new will must be admitted to probate.[36] But the survivor's personal representatives take the property concerned subject to the constructive trust, and to that extent the new will is ineffective.[37] In short, equity does not prevent, but frustrates, the unconscionable revocation of a mutual will.

Where the equitable doctrine of mutual wills applies, it has the considerable merit of making the arrangement enforceable by any beneficiary under the constructive trust: a contract not to revoke is, by contrast, only enforceable by the contracting parties.

Property bound

The property which is bound by the constructive trust depends on the construction of the arrangement embodied in the mutual wills. The

---

[32] *i.e.* when the first party dies; see *supra*.
[33] [1930] 2 Ch. 190.
[34] *Re Wilford's Estate* (1879) 11 Ch.D. 267; *In the Estate of Heys* [1914] P. 192; *Szabo v. Boros* (1967) 64 D.L.R. (2nd) 48.
[35] [1930] 2 Ch. 190, 195.
[36] *In the Estate of Heys, supra.*
[37] *Re Cleaver* [1981] 1 W.L.R. 939. The doctrine of mutual wills applies where the survivor's mutual will is revoked by his marriage, *Re Green* [1951] Ch. 148; but see Law Reform Committee's 22nd Report, *The making and revocation of wills*, Cmnd. 7902 (1980), p. 26.

arrangement may only apply to certain identified property. Or it may apply to a part,[38] or the whole,[39] of each person's residuary estate.

If the constructive trust applies to a part, or the whole, of each person's residuary estate, the question then arises as to the extent to which the survivor is free to dispose, during his lifetime, of (i) the other's property and (ii) the survivor's own property (including his after-acquired property). As regards the other's property, this question only arises if the survivor took an absolute interest, as opposed to a life interest, under the other's will. In the Australian case of *Birmingham v. Renfrew*[40] Dixon J. suggested that often the purpose of such an arrangement is to allow the survivor full enjoyment of both the capital and income of the property for his own benefit during his lifetime, though subject to his not making *inter vivos* gifts calculated to defeat the intention of the arrangement. "I do not see any difficulty in modern equity in attaching to the assets a constructive trust which allowed the survivor to enjoy the property subject to a fiduciary duty which, so to speak, crystallised on his death and [during his lifetime] disabled him only from voluntary dispositions *inter vivos*'"[41] which were calculated to defeat the intention of the arrangement.[42] This floating constructive trust finally attaches to such property as the survivor leaves at his death.

It is rarely sensible for persons to make mutual wills.[43] If they insist on doing so, they ought carefully to consider what provision should be made in their arrangement for possible future events, such as the remarriage of the survivor or the birth of children to the survivor. Again, mutual wills ought clearly to define the property of each person which is intended to be bound by the arrangement and the powers which are intended to be conferred on the survivor to dispose of such property during his lifetime.

II. NOMINATIONS

A. STATUTORY NOMINATIONS

Several statutes permit a person entitled to certain funds or investments to dispose of them by a written nomination operating at his death. Instances include a sum payable by a Friendly Society,[1] Industrial and

---

[38] *Re Green* [1951] Ch. 148, 156. See also *Re Gillespie* (1968) 69 D.L.R. (2d) 368 (assets of H and W at death of first to die held bound).

[39] *Re Cleaver, supra.*

[40] (1937) 57 C.L.R. 666. See J. D. B. Mitchell (1951) 14 M.L.R. 136 and R. Burgess (1970) 34 Conv.(N.S.) 230, 240 *et seq.*

[41] *Birmingham v. Renfrew, supra,* at pp. 689–690; approved in *Re Cleaver* [1981] 1 WLR 939, 945–947.

[42] *Re Cleaver, supra,* at p. 947 ("No objection could normally be taken to ordinary gifts of small value").

[43] See Law Reform Committee's 22nd Report, *The making and revocation of wills,* Cmnd.7902 (1980), p. 26; D.W. Fox (1975) 119 S.J. 380.

[1] Friendly Societies Act 1974, ss. 66 and 67.

Provident Society,[2] and Trade Union[3]: in each case the sum nominated cannot exceed £5,000.[4]

National Savings Certificates[5] and savings in the National Savings Bank[6] also pass under a nomination if it was made before May 1, 1981: in these cases no monetary limit applies.

Comparison with a gift by will

A statutory nomination, like a will, has no effect until the nominator dies and is, therefore, ambulatory during the nominator's lifetime.[7] It follows that the nominee takes no interest in the nominated funds or investments so long as the nominator is still alive; during his lifetime the nominator remains free to deal with the nominated funds or investments as he pleases. Again, if the nominee predeceases the nominator, the nomination fails.[8] Similarly, a gift by will normally fails by lapse if the beneficiary predeceases the testator.[9]

In several other respects, however, a statutory nomination differs from a will:

(i) A person who has attained 16 years of age can make a statutory nomination but normally a person must attain 18 years before he can make a valid will.[10]

(ii) The formal requirements are different. In the case of money payable by a Friendly Society, for instance, a statutory nomination must be by writing under the nominator's hand, delivered at or sent to the registered office of the society or branch, or made in a book kept at that office.[11] In the case of National Savings Certificates and savings in the National Savings Bank, signature by the nominator in the presence of an attesting witness was[12] also required.[13] The formal requirements as to signature and witnesses are different for a will, and a testator is not required to deposit his will anywhere but may retain possession of it during his lifetime.[14]

[2] Industrial and Provident Societies Act 1965, ss. 23 and 24.

[3] Trade Union and Labour Relations Act 1974, Sched.1, para.31 (as amended by Employment Protection Act 1975, Sched.16, Pt. III, paras.31 and 32); Trade Union (Nominations) Regulations 1977 (S.I. 1977 No. 789) and 1984 (S.I. 1984 No. 1290).

[4] Administration of Estates (Small Payments) Act 1965, ss. 2 and 6; Administration of Estates (Small Payments) (Increase of Limit) Order 1984 (S.I. 1984 No. 539), para.2.

[5] National Debt Act 1972, s. 11; Savings Certificates Regulations 1972 (S.I. 1972 No. 641), regs. 13–18 (as amended by S.I. 1981 No. 486).

[6] National Savings Bank Act 1971, ss. 2 and 8(2); National Savings Bank Regulations 1972 (S.I. 1972 No. 764), regs. 33–38 (as amended by S.I. 1981 No. 484).

[7] *Ante*, p. 1.

[8] *Re Barnes* [1940] Ch. 267; see also Savings Certificates Regulations 1972, reg. 16(1); National Savings Bank Regulations 1972, reg. 35(1); Trade Union (Nominations) Regulations 1977, reg. 3(1).

[9] For lapse, and the exceptions to lapse, see *post*, pp. 234 *et seq.*

[10] Exceptionally, an infant who is a privileged testator can make a valid will: see *post*, p. 90.

[11] Friendly Societies Act 1974, s. 66(1).

[12] "*Was*'" because no further nominations are possible under these provisions.

[13] Savings Certificates Regulations 1972, reg. 14; National Savings Bank Regulations 1972, reg. 33(2).

[14] s. 126 of the Supreme Court Act 1981 makes provision for the *voluntary* deposit of a will in the Court's custody by a testator during his lifetime: very few wills are so deposited:

(iii) Although the marriage of the nominator or testator automatically revokes both a statutory nomination[15] and a will,[16] the other rules governing revocation are different. A statutory nomination may be revoked by a notice complying with the same formal requirements as a statutory nomination but (unlike a will) cannot be revoked by a will or codicil.[17]

A person can, and often does, dispose of such funds or investments by will instead of employing a statutory nomination. Indeed, if a person contemplates making a will, it is usually better for him to dispose of all his assets by the will and not to employ a statutory nomination. He can then, if he wishes, revoke or vary any of its provisions by a subsequent will or codicil. A statutory nomination, once made, tends to be forgotten. The risk of this occurring is a major disadvantage because the nomination will not be revoked or varied by any subsequent will or codicil. On the whole, the changes which stop savings in the National Savings Bank and National Savings Certificates from being disposed of by new nominations in the future are to be welcomed. A nomination of such assets made before the relevant closing date is not, of course, affected.

B. PENSION SCHEME NOMINATIONS

An insurance policy on a person's life may belong to him and the proceeds of the policy will then, on his death, fall into his estate and be disposed of by his will; but the policy may not be his and in that case it will not be so disposed of. So, for example, a policy effected under the Married Women's Property Act 1882 is not the deceased's policy but is held on trust. The same principle will apply if an express trust has been created over the policy. But apart from cases of MWPA policies and policies held under express trusts, it is necessary to consider lump sum payments—which may be of substantial value—linked with pension schemes.

Contributory pension schemes often provide that if an employee, who would have received a pension on retirement, dies before reaching retirement age, the pension fund's trustees will make a lump sum payment,[18] a form of insurance. The pension scheme's rules will indicate to whom the payment is to be made. There is usually provision in the scheme's rules for the employee to nominate the person or persons to whom he would like the payment to be made. The question then arises as to

---

for the deposit procedure see the Wills (Deposit for Safe Custody) Regulations 1978 (S.I. 1978 No. 1724). Ss. 23–25 of the Administration of Justice Act 1982 (when brought into operation) make provision for voluntary deposit in the custody of the Principal Registry of the Family Division, which is to register any will so deposited and function as the national body for the purposes of the Council of Europe Convention on the Establishment of a Scheme of Registration of Wills, Cmnd. 5073 (1972).

[15] See, *e.g.* Friendly Societies Act 1974 s. 66(7).

[16] For the two exceptions to the general rule that a will is revoked by the marriage of the testator see *post*, pp. 95 *et seq*.

[17] See *ante*, nn. 1–6; *Bennett v. Slater* [1899] 1 Q.B. 45. For the effect of divorce on a gift by will to the former spouse see *post*, p. 243.

[18] Often called a "death in service payment."

whether, when there is such a nomination, it is a testamentary disposition. The answer seems to be that it depends in each case on the provisions of the individual pension scheme.[19] In the Canadian case of *Re MacInnes*[20] an employee's contributions to a contributory savings fund were held in such a way that during the employee's lifetime he had an absolute beneficial interest in his share of the fund. He was, therefore, in effect, the owner of his share and it could pass only under a document which complied with the formality rules applicable to testamentary dispositions.[21]

This case can be contrasted with two more recent decisions where, in the light of the rules applicable to the pension schemes in question, it was held that nominations were not testamentary dispositions. These two cases are *Re Danish Bacon Co Ltd Staff Pension Fund Trusts*,[22] a decision of Megarry J. and the Privy Council case of *Baird v. Baird*.[23] The reasoning in these cases may be faultless[24] but the result, particularly in the *Baird* case, could be thought to be unfortunate. "Non-statutory nominations are odd creatures"[25] and these two cases decided that the deceased employees, under the applicable rules, did *not* have beneficial interests in the pension funds but powers, under the funds' rules, to nominate beneficiaries to receive benefits payable on their deaths. This meant that in neither case was a nomination a testamentary disposition. So, in the *Danish* case, the nomination was not subject to the Wills Act formality rules and in *Baird* the testator's marriage did not revoke it. By contrast, a will is revoked by marriage[26] and so are *statutory* nominations.[27] A well-drawn pension scheme should make provision for what will happen if the nominator marries after making a nomination or, at the very least, the nominator should be warned that his nomination may be treated differently from a testamentary disposition.

III. DONATIONES MORTIS CAUSA[1]

A *donatio mortis causa* is "a singular form of gift"[2] derived in part from civil law. It is not a gift *inter vivos* nor is it a gift by will. It has its own distinct requirements which are:

[19] *Baird v. Baird* [1990] 2 AC 548 at 561.
[20] [1935] 1 DLR 401.
[21] For formalities see *post*, p. 76.
[22] [1971] 1 WLR 248.
[23] [1990] 2 AC 548.
[24] Though Megarry J's decision in the *Danish Bacon Pension Fund* case was criticised by Chappenden in 1972 JBL 20. In *Baird* the deceased's interest was non-assignable and the trustees had to approve the making, and revocation, of a nomination; it is not easy, therefore, to see how, on these facts, the court could have decided the case any other way.
[25] Megarry J in the *Danish Bacon Pension Fund* case *supra* at p. 256.
[26] This is the general rule—for further details see *post* pp. 94–99.
[27] See, for example, Friendly Societies Act 1974 s.66(7).
[1] The Latin expression *donatio mortis causa* (of which the plural is *donationes mortis causa*) translates literally as "gift by cause of death"; though a rough translation might simply be "deathbed gift."
[2] *Per* Buckley J. in *Re Beaumont* [1902] 1 Ch. 889, 892. He continued, "It may be said to be of an amphibious nature, being a gift which is neither entirely *inter vivos* nor testamentary."

(1) It must be intended by the donor to be conditional on his own death.
(2) It must be made by the donor in contemplation of death.
(3) Before his death the donor must part with dominion over the subject matter of the *donatio*.
(4) Finally, the subject matter must be capable of passing by *donatio mortis causa*.

The burden of proof of these requirements lies on the donee. A *donatio mortis causa* may be established by the sole evidence of the donee if the court, after sifting it carefully, considers his evidence trustworthy.[3]

A. REQUIREMENTS OF A DONATIO MORTIS CAUSA

1. Intended to be conditional on death

The donor must intend the gift to become absolute only at his own death. Meanwhile the gift is revocable. There must be "a clear intention to give, but to give only if the donor dies, whereas if the donor does not die then the gift is not to take effect and the donor is to have back the subject matter of the gift."[4]

(1) *PROOF OF INTENTION.* The donor need not express this intention in words; it may be inferred from the circumstances in which the gift was made. In *Gardner v. Parker*[5] X, who was seriously ill and confined to his bed, gave to Y a bond for £1,800, saying, "There, take that and keep it." X died two days later. Leach V.-C. held that this was a valid *donatio mortis causa*, inferring from the circumstances that X intended the gift to be conditional on his own death. Even if the donor knows that he is certain to die within a short time, there seems no reason why he should not show the necessary intention that the gift should become absolute only at his own death.[6]

(2) *OTHER FORMS OF INTENTION.* There can be no *donatio mortis causa* if the donor intends to make an immediate gift *inter vivos*. In that case the gift stands or falls as an ordinary gift *inter vivos*[7]: if it is invalid as a gift *inter vivos*, it may become effective after the donor's death under the rule in *Strong v. Bird* which is considered later.[8]

Again, there can be no *donatio mortis causa* if the donor intends to make a gift by will, *i.e.* intends the wishes he expresses to take effect at his death but does not intend to part with dominion over the asset during his life.[9] In order to make a valid *donatio mortis causa*, the donor must

---

[3] *Re Dillon* (1890) 44 Ch.D. 76, 80; *Re Farman* (1887) 57 L.J.Ch. 637.
[4] *Re Craven's Estate (No.1)* [1937] Ch. 423, 426.
[5] (1818) 3 Madd. 184; see also *Re Lillingston* [1952] 2 All E.R. 184 and *Re Mustapha* (1891) 8 T.L.R. 160.
[6] See *Wilkes v. Allington* [1931] 2 Ch. 104, 111.
[7] *Edwards v. Jones* (1836) 1 My. & Cr. 226; *Tate v. Hilbert* (1793) 2 Ves Jun. 111.
[8] See Chap. 13.
[9] Solicitor to the *Treasury v. Lewis* [1900] 2 Ch. 812; *cf. Re Ward* [1946] 2 All E.R. 206.

part with dominion over the asset in his lifetime, which involves a mental intention on his part to do so.

2. Contemplation of death

This peculiar requirement is home-grown English law and is not derived from civil law. Of course, the donor cannot form the necessary intention that the gift should become absolute only at his own death without contemplating death. But it is not sufficient for the donor to contemplate the possibility of death at some vague time in the future. This second requirement is only satisfied if he contemplates death "within the near future, what may be called death for some reason believed to be impending."[10] He need not, however, contemplate immediate death or be on his death bed when he makes the *donatio mortis causa*. In *Wilkes v. Allington*[11] this requirement was satisfied because, at the time of the *donatio*, the donor knew that he had cancer and believed himself to be a doomed man: he did not know how long he had to live but he was satisfied that he did not have long to live. A month later he caught a chill on a bus journey on his way home from market and died from pneumonia. The court held that the *donatio mortis causa* was valid because it was not conditional on his death from the particular cause contemplated by him.

Would it suffice if the donor *mistakenly* believed that he was suffering from a serious illness and was a doomed man? Probably it would, because the second requirement appears to be concerned with the donor's subjective assessment of his situation.[12] Again, it would probably suffice if the donor contemplated death from some dangerous mission which he was about to undertake.[13] Contemplation of death by suicide may also suffice as suicide is no longer a crime.[14]

3. Parting with dominion[15]

Before his death the donor must part with dominion over the subject matter of the *donatio*. Two elements are required—(a) the donor's intention to part with dominion; and (b) a sufficient delivery or transfer of the subject matter of the gift, or of something representing it, to the donee.

(1) *THE DONOR'S INTENTION.* The donor must intend to part with dominion over the asset to the donee.[16] In *Reddel v. Dobree*[17] X, when in

---

[10] *Re Craven's Estate (No. 1)* [1937] Ch. 423, 426.
[11] [1931] 2 Ch. 104; see also *Re Richards* [1921] 1 Ch. 513 (contemplation of death from critical operation but died without operation: *d.m.c.* held valid).
[12] *Cf. Thompson v. Mechan* [1958] O.R. 357 (donor regarded air travel as perilous) where the Ontario Court of Appeal adopted an objective assessment: see (1965) 81 L.Q.R. 21.
[13] *Agnew v. Belfast Banking Co.* [1896] 2 I.R. 204, 221.
[14] Suicide Act 1961, s. 1. Before this Act, contemplation of death by suicide did not suffice, *Re Dudman* [1925] Ch. 553; *Agnew v. Belfast Banking Co., supra.* See also *Mills v. Shields* [1948] I.R. 367.
[15] See W.H.D. Winder (1940) 4 Conv. (N.S.) 382.
[16] *Birch v. Treasury Solicitor* [1951] Ch. 298, esp. at pp. 304–306; *Hawkins v. Blewitt* (1798) 2 Esp. 662.
[17] (1834) 10 Sim. 244.

declining health, delivered a locked cash box to Y, telling her that the box contained money for her, that he wanted the box from her every three months whilst he lived, and that at his death Y was to go to his son for the key. The court held that there was no *donatio mortis causa*. X intended to retain dominion over the contents of the box during his lifetime: he had kept control of the key and had reserved to himself in advance the right to deal with the contents. Again, there is no *donatio mortis causa* if X merely intends Y to have custody of a locked box and its key in her capacity as X's housekeeper.[18]

The donor may, however, have the requisite intention to part with dominion even though he imposes on the donee a trust; for instance, a trust to make a certain payment to another person, or to pay the donor's funeral expenses.[19]

(2) *DELIVERY*. There must be a sufficient delivery in the donor's lifetime.[20] If the donor does not part with dominion in his lifetime the *donatio mortis causa* fails. In *Bunn v. Markham*[21] C, believing himself near death, directed that the words, "For Mrs. and Miss C" should be written on sealed parcels containing money and securities, and declared that the parcels were to be delivered to Mrs. and Miss C after his death. C then directed that the parcels should be put back in his iron chest of which he kept the keys. Following C's death the court held that there was no *donatio mortis causa* because there had been no act of delivery and the donor had never parted with dominion over the parcels in his lifetime.

Delivery in the donor's lifetime is essential but it does not matter whether the delivery is made before, or after, the donor expresses his intention to make the *donatio*. For instance, in *Cain v. Moon*[22] a daughter delivered a deposit note to her mother for safe custody. Two years later when the daughter was seriously ill she told her mother, "the bank-note is for you if I die." The court held this to be a valid *donatio mortis causa*: the antecedent delivery sufficed, and it was not necessary for the mother to hand back the note and for the daughter to re-deliver it when she expressed her intention to make the *donatio*.

(a) *Parties to the delivery*. The delivery may be made by the donor or by his duly authorised agent,[23] and it may be made to the donee or to an agent for the donee.[24] But delivery by the donor to his own agent

---

[18] *Trimmer v. Danby* (1856) 25 L.J.Ch. 424 (box contained X's securities, including bonds indorsed by X as belonging to Y: no *d.m.c.* as no delivery of bonds to Y); *Wildish v. Fowler* (1892) 8 T.L.R. 457 ("Take care of this" by sick lodger to landlady: no *d.m.c.*).

[19] *Hills v. Hills* (1841) 8 M. & W. 401; *Hudson v. Spencer* [1910] 2 Ch. 285; *Birch v. Treasury Solicitor* [1951] Ch. 298, 304.

[20] *Ward v. Turner* (1752) 2 Ves.Sen. 431; *Cant v. Gregory* (1894) 10 T.L.R. 584 (no delivery of mortgage deed as donee refused to accept it).

[21] (1816) 7 Taunt. 224: see also *Hardy v. Baker* (1738) West t. Hard. 519 (donor told his servant to deliver property to donee after donor's death: no *d.m.c.*); *Bryson v. Brownrigg* (1803) 9 Ves. 1 (donor told his wife to move securities intended for his daughter to another drawer in his bureau: no *d.m.c.*); *Miller v. Miller* (1735) 3 P.Wms. 356 (oral gift of coach and horses to wife but no delivery: no *d.m.c.*); *Re Miller* (1961) 105 S.J. 207.

[22] [1896] 2 Q.B. 283: see also *Re Weston* [1902] 1 Ch. 680.

[23] *Re Craven's Estate (No. 1)* [1937] Ch. 423.

[24] *Moore v. Darton* (1851) 4 De G. & Sm. 517, 520 (*sed quaere* whether on the facts the donor's lady's maid was the donee's agent).

does not suffice.[25] If the donor intends to make a *donatio* to two donees, H and W, jointly, delivery may be made to W both for herself and as agent for H.[26]

(b) *Delivery of a chattel.* There must either be actual delivery of a chattel (*e.g.* the donor hands his watch to the donee) or delivery of the means of obtaining the chattel (*e.g.* the donor hands to the donee the key of the box which contains the watch)[27]: the latter suffices because the donor thereby parts with dominion over the chattel. A merely symbolic delivery, such as the delivery of a watchstrap as a symbol for the watch, does not suffice.[28] Handing over the key to the box which contains the watch is sufficient even though the donor does not hand over the box itself.[29] On the other hand, it probably does not suffice if the donor delivers to the donee one of two keys to the box but keeps the other key,[30] or delivers the box but keeps the only key to it,[31] because such conduct generally indicates that the donor does not intend to part with dominion. In the recent case of *Woodard v. Woodard*[32] the Court of Appeal upheld a decision that there had been a valid *donatio* where one set of car keys had been handed over and the whereabouts of the duplicate set was unknown. The case appears to be close to the borderline.[33]

In *Re Lillingston*[34] L, in contemplation of death, handed to P a packet of jewellery and the keys to her trunk, telling her that the trunk contained the key to her Harrods safe deposit, which in turn contained the key to her city safe deposit. L said that she wished P to have all her jewellery and that after L's death P could go and get the jewellery in these safe deposits. L and P agreed that the packet of jewellery should be kept in the trunk, which was in L's room, and P placed the packet in the trunk. L then said, "Keep the key: it is now yours." The court held that there had been a valid *donatio mortis causa* of the packet of jewellery and of the jewellery in the two safe deposits. As Wynn-Parry J. put it, it did not matter "in how many boxes the subject of a gift may be contained or that each, except the last, contains a key which opens the next, so long as the scope of the gift is made clear."[35] Again, it did not matter that, under the terms of the contract between L and Harrods, P also needed L's signed authority to withdraw the jewellery from the Harrods

---

[25] *Farquharson v. Cave* (1846) 2 Coll.C.C. 356, 367; *Powell v. Hellicar* (1858) 26 Beav. 261; *Re Kirkley* (1909) 25 T.L.R. 522.
[26] *Birch v. Treasury Solicitor* [1951] Ch. 298, esp. at pp. 303–304.
[27] See generally A.C.H. Barlow (1956) 19 M.L.R. 394, where the *d.m.c.* cases are discussed.
[28] *Ward v. Turner* (1752) 2 Ves. Sen. 431.
[29] *Re Craven's Estate (No. 1)* [1937] Ch. 423, 428. The delivery of the means of obtaining the chattel suffices even though the chattel is not bulky and is capable of manual delivery; *Jones v. Selby* (1710) Prec.Ch. 300 (key delivered to trunk containing government tally); *Re Mustapha* (1891) 8 T.L.R. 160.
[30] *Re Craven's Estate (No. 1), supra*, at p. 428.
[31] *Re Johnson* (1905) 92 L.T. 357.
[32] This is a 1991 Case, but reported [1995] 3 All E.R. 980.
[33] The Court of Appeal appeared not to want to encourage any further litigation in a case where both parties were legally aided and the value of the chattel in dispute (the car) was not great.
[34] [1952] 2 All E.R. 184.
[35] *ibid.* p. 191: see also *Re Mustapha* (1891) 8 T.L.R. 160 (key delivered to wardrobe which contained key to safe which contained bonds).

safe deposit—L had transferred partial dominion to P and this sufficed.[36]

(c) *Delivery or transfer of a chose in action.* Similar rules apply if the subject matter of a *donatio* is a chose in action which is transferable by delivery. Thus, in the case of bearer bonds, there must be either actual delivery of the bonds to the donee or delivery of the means of obtaining them, such as the key of the box which contains the bonds.[37]

If the chose in action is not transferable by delivery there must be either a valid transfer[38] or the delivery of a document which amounts to a transfer[39] In *Birch v. Treasury Solicitor*[40] B, in contemplation of death, handed to H and W her Post Office Savings Bank book, London Trustee Savings Bank book, Barclays Bank deposit pass book, and Westminster Bank deposit account book, intending that the money in these banks should belong to H and W in the event of her death. The Court of Appeal held that this was sufficient delivery to establish a *donatio mortis causa* of each of these bank accounts. The test to apply was to ask "whether the instrument 'amounts to a transfer' as being the essential indicia or evidence of title, possession or production of which entitles the possessor to the money or property purported to be given."[41] This test was satisfied because in the case of each bank the production of the bank book was necessary upon any withdrawal from the account. It was, however, held to be unnecessary for the document to express the terms of the contract out of which the chose in action arose, *i.e.* in this case the terms of the contract between B and each bank.

4. Property capable of passing by donatio mortis causa

In general, most, if not all, pure personalty is capable of being the subject matter of a *donatio*. Thus bonds,[42] an insurance policy,[43] a banker's deposit note,[44] and savings certificates[45] have all been held capable of

---

[36] See also *Re Wasserberg* [1915] 1 Ch. 195.

[37] *Re Wasserberg, supra* (key to bank box containing bearer bonds); *Re Harrison* [1934] W.N. 25 (delivery of key but no intent to part with dominion).

[38] *Staniland v. Willott* (1850) 3 Mac. & G. 664 (*d.m.c.* by valid legal transfer of shares in public company). For the requirements for a valid transfer *inter vivos* see *Re Rose* [1949] Ch. 78.

[39] The phrase used by Lord Hardwicke L.C. in the leading case of *Ward v. Turner* (1752) 2 Ves. Sen. 431, 444.

[40] [1951] Ch. 298: see also *Re Dillon* (1890) 44 Ch.D. 76 (delivery of banker's deposit note) and *Moore v. Darton* (1851) 4 De G. & Sm. 517.

[41] [1951] Ch. 298, 311; *cf. Delgoffe v. Fader* [1939] Ch. 922 (production of bank book unnecessary for withdrawal: no *d.m.c.* by delivery of book).

[42] *Snellgrove v Baily* (1744) 3 Atk. 214 (donor delivered bond to donee saying, "in case I die it is yours": held *d.m.c.*); *Gardner v. Parker* (1818) 3 Madd. 184 (bond for £1,800); *Re Wasserberg* [1915] 1 Ch. 195 (bearer bonds).

[43] *Witt v. Amis* (1861) 1 Best & Sm. 109 (insurance policy on donor's life); *Amis v. Witt* (1863) 33 Beav. 619.

[44] *Re Dillon* (1890) 44 Ch.D. 76: *cf. Re Mead* (1880) 15 Ch.D. 651.

[45] *Darlow v. Sparks* [1938] 2 All E.R. 235 (war and national savings certificates); *Beatrice Finch* (1958) in Lawton's *Guide to the Law of Trustee Savings Banks* (3rd ed., 1962), p. 1026 (*d.m.c.* of premium savings bond). See also *Re Lee* [1918] 2 Ch. 320 (registered Exchequer bond: *d.m.c.* by delivery of Exchequer bond deposit book) and *Re Richards* [1921] 1 Ch. 513 (*d.m.c.* of registered Victory Bonds), and distinguish *Re Andrews* [1902] 2 Ch. 394.

passing by *donatio mortis causa*. The following categories of property need separate consideration:

(1) *LAND*. In *Duffield v. Elwes*[46] Lord Eldon held that a mortgage can be the subject of a *donatio* by delivery of the mortgage deed: the mortgage debt passes under the *donatio* and it carries the mortgage security with it.[47] Nevertheless, he seemed to take the view *obiter* that land itself could not be the subject of a *donatio*[48]; and for more than a century and a half this view was generally assumed to be correct.[49] But in 1991, the Court of Appeal in *Sen v. Headley*,[50] decided that land can be the subject matter of a valid *donatio*. In this case the plaintiff had visited the deceased in hospital and the deceased told her that his house and its contents were hers. The deceased went on to say that the deeds to the house were in a steel box to which the plaintiff had the keys. She later found that the deceased had slipped the keys to the box into her handbag. The Court of Appeal thought that the doctrine of *donatio mortis causa* was anomalous but that "anomalies do not justify anomalous exceptions."[51] In the case of land the doctrine would operate by way of constructive trust. The Appeal Committee of the House of Lords gave leave to appeal against the Court of Appeal's decision but the parties then came to terms and so the appeal was not heard. There is still no case where the House of Lords has had to pronounce on this issue.[52]

(2) *CHEQUES AND PROMISSORY NOTES* A cheque or promissory note drawn by a third party may pass by *donatio*: this is so even though it is not transferable at law by delivery, having been made payable to the donor and not having been indorsed by him.[53] But a cheque drawn by the donor upon his own bank cannot be the subject of a *donatio* because it does not constitute property, but is merely an order to his bank which is revoked by the donor's death.[54] Similarly, there cannot be a *donatio* of a promissory note drawn by the donor himself because it does not constitute property but is merely a promise to pay money.[55] There may, however, be a valid *donatio* if the donee receives payment on the cheque from the bank in the donor's lifetime[56] (or even afterwards before the bank is

---

[46] (1827) 1 Bli.N.S. 497, 542–543.
[47] (1827) 1 Bli.N.S. 497, 541, quoting Lord Mansfield in *Martin v. Mowlin* (1760) 2 Burr. 969, 979.
[48] *Duffield v. Elwes* (1827) Bli NS 497 at 530 and 539.
[49] See casenote by C.E.F Rickett in (1989) 53 Conv 184 where he discusses the position in the Commonwealth.
[50] [1991] Ch. 425.
[51] [1991] Ch. 425, 440.
[52] See casenote by P.V.B. in (1993) 109 L.Q.R. 19.
[53] *Veal v. Veal* (1867) 27 Beav. 303 (*d.m.c.* of unindorsed promissory notes payable to donor or order); *Re Mead* (1880) 15 Ch.D. 651 (*d.m.c.* of unindorsed bills of exchange payable to donor or order); *Clement v. Cheesman* (1884) 27 Ch.D. 631 (*d.m.c.* of unindorsed cheques payable to donor or order). The Cheques Act 1992 does not appear to make any difference here.
[54] *Re Beaumont* [1902] 1 Ch. 889: see also *Re Swinburne* [1926] Ch. 38, 47.
[55] *Re Leaper* [1916] 1 Ch. 579.
[56] *Bouts v. Ellis* (1853) 17 Beav. 121, affirmed 4 De G.M. & G. 249; it suffices if the bank accepts the cheque during the donor's lifetime. *Re While* [1928] W.N. 182; *Re Beaumont* [1902] 1 Ch. 889, 895 (may be sufficient if bank gives undertaking to donee to hold amount of cheque for donee).

apprised of the donor's death[57]), or if the donee negotiates the cheque for value in the donor's lifetime.[58]

(3) *COMPANY SHARES.* In *Ward v. Turner*[59] Lord Hardwicke held that the delivery of receipts for the purchase price of South Sea annuities was not a sufficient delivery of the annuities to the donee by way of *donatio.* He said that a *donatio mortis causa* of company stock could not be made "without a transfer, or something amounting to that," and the receipts were "nothing but waste paper."[60] He certainly never suggested, however, that company stock was incapable of passing by *donatio.* In *Staniland v. Willott*[61] the donor, in contemplation of death, made a valid legal transfer of company shares to the donee and the Lord Chancellor held that this constituted a *donatio mortis causa,* which had been revoked by the donor's recovery from his illness.

Unfortunately, in *Moore v. Moore*[62] the court misunderstood the effect of *Ward v. Turner* and held that railway stock could never be the subject of a *donatio.* This decision was followed in *Re Weston*[63] where the court held that building society investment shares could not be the subject of a *donatio.* The decision in *Staniland v. Willott* was not cited in either *Moore v. Moore* or *Re Weston,* and both these first instance decisions must be regarded as of doubtful authority. Probably, company and building society investment shares are capable of passing by *donatio mortis causa* if the donor makes a valid transfer of them to the donee or, perhaps, delivers a document which amounts to a transfer.

B. EFFECT OF A DONATIO MORTIS CAUSA

Revocable until death

A *donatio mortis causa* is revocable until the death of the donor. Revocation is automatic if the donor recovers from the illness from which he contemplated death.[64] Alternatively, the donor may expressly revoke the *donatio* by resuming dominion over the property[65] or, perhaps, by merely informing the donee of the revocation.[66] There is, however, no revocation if the donor resumes possession of the property in order to hold it in safe custody for the donee but does not resume dominion over it.[67] Again, the donor cannot revoke a *donatio* by his will.[68]

---

[57] *Tate v. Hilbert* (1793) 2 Ves.Jun. 111, 118.
[58] *Rolls v. Peare* (1877) 5 Ch.D. 730.
[59] (1752) 2 Ves.Sen. 431.
[60] *ibid.* at pp. 443–444.
[61] (1850) 3 Mac. & G. 664: see also *Re Craven's Estate (No. 1)* [1937] Ch. 423 (*d.m.c.* of shares transferred to donee).
[62] (1874) L.R. 18 Eq. 474.
[63] [1902] 1 Ch. 680: see also *Griffiths v. The Abbey National B.S.* (1947) [1938–1949] Reg.Rep. 14 (delivery of building society shares pass book; held *d.m.c.* by Registrar of Friendly Societies).
[64] *Staniland v. Willott* (1850) 3 Mac. & G. 664.
[65] *Bunn v. Markham* (1816) 7 Taunt. 224: see also *In the Estate of Mulroy* [1924] 1 I.R. 98.
[66] *Jones v. Selby* (1710) Prec.Ch. 300, 303.
[67] *Re Hawkins* [1924] 2 Ch. 47 (*d.m.c.* by delivery of envelope containing money to donee; envelope then placed in donor's deed box for safe custody).
[68] *Jones v. Selby, supra.*

If the *donatio* transferred the donor's title to the property to the donee, then, on revocation, the donee holds the property on trust for the donor and must re-transfer it to the donor.[69]

Death of the donor

Assuming there has been no revocation, on the death of the donor the *donatio* becomes absolute.

Often a *donatio* vests the donor's title to the property in the donee. This occurs where the donor makes a "complete" delivery or transfer, such as would suffice in the case of a gift *inter vivos*. In this case the donee's title becomes unconditional at the donor's death and no action on the part of the donor's personal representatives is needed to perfect the donee's title. But there may be a valid *donatio* even though the delivery or transfer does not vest the donor's title in the donee. In the case of a chattel or a chose in action transferable by delivery, the donor may make a delivery which suffices for a *donatio mortis causa* but would not suffice in the case of an *inter vivos* gift.[70] Again, a *donatio* of a chose in action not transferable by delivery may be made by the delivery of a document which amounts to a transfer, even though it does not effectively transfer the donor's title to the donee. For instance, a valid *donatio* may be made by the delivery to the donee of a mortgage deed, even though the legal title to the mortgage debt and the mortgage security remains vested in the donor.[71] The same principle will apply to a *donatio* of land. Where the donor makes a *donatio* by an "incomplete" delivery or transfer, the donor's personal representatives hold the legal title on a trust imposed by law for the donee. If need be, the donee is entitled to require the personal representatives to lend their names to any necessary action, on receiving an appropriate indemnity from the donee.[72] In short, if the requisites for a valid *donatio* are satisfied, equity perfects an incomplete delivery or transfer to the donee after the donor's death. "The [equitable] principle of not assisting a volunteer to perfect an incomplete gift does not apply to a *donatio mortis causa*."[73]

Comparison with a legacy

The basic differences between a *donatio mortis causa* and a legacy given by will are that a *donatio* must be made by the donor in contemplation of death, whereas a will can be made at any time; and that a *donatio* requires the donor to part with dominion over its subject matter before his death which is not the case with a will. There are also some subsidiary differences: for instance, the methods of revocation are different; and if the *donatio* vested the donor's title to the property in the donee, no action on the part of the donor's personal representatives is needed to

---

[69] *Staniland v. Willott* (1852) 3 Mac. & G. 664.
[70] *Re Wasserberg* [1915] 1 Ch. 195.
[71] *Duffield v. Elwes* (1827) 1 Bli.N.S. 497.
[72] *Duffield v. Elwes, supra; Re Wasserberg, supra; Re Lillingston* [1952] 2 All E.R. 184.
[73] *Per* Lindley L.J. in *Re Dillon* (1890) 44 Ch.D. 76, 83.

perfect the donee's title.[74] In some respects, however, a *donatio mortis causa* resembles a legacy:

(i) A *donatio* fails if the donee predeceases the donor[75]: similarly a legacy normally fails by lapse if the legatee predeceases the testator.[76]

(ii) Property given by *donatio* is liable for the debts of the donor, but only on a deficiency of the assets of his estate.[77]

(iii) In general, a *donatio mortis causa* is subject to the rules of satisfaction. A *donatio* may therefore be satisfied by a legacy given to the donee by the donor's later will if the donor intended the legacy to be in satisfaction of the *donatio*.[78] It has been held that the mere fact that the legacy is of an amount equal to the *donatio* does not raise a presumption that the donor intended it to be in satisfaction of the *donatio*.[79]

---

[74] As to the rules of private international law governing the validity of a *d.m.c.* see *Re Korvine's Trust* [1921] 1 Ch. 343 (*cf. Re Craven's Estate (No. 1)* [1937] Ch. 423) and Dicey and Morris, *The Conflict of Laws* (12th ed., 1993), p. 968.

[75] *Tate v. Hilbert* (1793) 2 Ves.Jun. 111, 120; *Walter v. Hodge* (1818) 2 Swans. 92, 99.

[76] *Post* p. 234.

[77] *Smith v. Casen* (1718) 1 P.Wms. 406; *Ward v. Turner* (1752) 2 Ves.Sen. 431, 434; *Tate v. Leithead* (1854) Kay 658, 659; *Re Korvine's Trust* [1921] 1 Ch. 343, 348; *cf.* Warnock-Smith [1978] Conv. 130: see *post*, p. 428. As to the liability for debts of general and specific legacies see *post*, pp. 253–256 and 420 *et seq.*.

[78] *Jones v. Selby* (1710) Prec.Ch. 300; *Hudson v. Spencer* [1910] 2 Ch. 285: for satisfaction see *post*, pp. 224 *et seq.*

[79] *Hudson v. Spencer, supra* (delivery of £2,000 deposit notes to housekeeper; two days later donor made will giving £2,000 legacy to her: held she took both *d.m.c.* and legacy).

CHAPTER 2

INTESTACY[1]

Intestacy is either total or partial.[2] There is a total intestacy where the deceased does not effectively dispose of any beneficial interest in any of his property by will.[3] There is a partial intestacy where the deceased effectively disposes of some, but not all, of the beneficial interest in his property by will.[4]

The main rules relating to intestacy are contained in Part IV of the Administration of Estates Act 1925 which has been amended by the Intestates' Estates Act 1952, the Family Provision Act 1966, the Family Law Reform Act 1969, the Administration of Justice Act 1977, the Family Law Reform Act 1987 and the Law Reform (Succession) Act 1995. All references in this chapter to the Administration of Estates Act 1925 are to this Act as thus amended.

I. TOTAL INTESTACY

A. ADMINISTRATION OF ASSETS

Part III of the Administration of Estates Act 1925 deals with the administration of assets before distribution.

A Trust for sale and conversion

Section 33(1) of the Act provides that the personal representatives of an intestate shall hold all his property, whether real[5] or personal, which

---

[1] For a fuller account of the law relating to intestacy, see Sherrin and Bonehill, *The Law and Practice of Intestate Succession* (2nd ed., 1994).

[2] For the rules of private international law governing intestate succession, see Dicey and Morris, *The Conflict of Laws* (12th ed., 1993), pp. 1023 *et seq.; Theobald on Wills* (15th ed., 1993), pp. 7–8; *Re Collens* [1986] Ch. 505.

[3] Re Skeats [1936] Ch. 683 (total intestacy where will appointed an executrix but made no disposition of property: intestacy rules applied).

[4] *Post,* p. 47.

[5] The rules of inheritance applicable to realty under the general law in force before 1926 still apply (i) to an unbarred entail (Law of Property Act 1925, s. 130(4); Administration of Estates Act 1925, ss. 45(2) and 51(4)), and (ii) on the death of a person who was a lunatic of full age at the end of 1925, and who dies without recovering testamentary capacity, as regards realty as to which he died intestate (Administration of Estates Act 1925, s. 51(2) and see *Re Bradshaw* [1950] Ch. 582 and *Re Sirret* [1969] 1 W.L.R. 60). For these rules of inheritance see Megarry and Wade, *The Law of Real Property* (5th ed., 1984), pp. 539 *et seq.*

does not consist of money, upon trust for sale and conversion into money. The personal representatives have power to postpone sale and conversion for as long as they think proper. This duty to sell and convert is qualified by section 33(1) in two respects:

(i) Any reversionary interest of the intestate must not be sold until it falls into possession, unless the personal representatives see "special reason" for sale. A reversionary interest means "a future interest vested in the intestate at the moment of his death in some specific property, which at that moment is in the possession or enjoyment of some other person."[6] For instance, if at his death the intestate is entitled to his deceased father's estate subject to the prior life interest of his mother who is still living, the intestate's reversionary interest must not be sold until it falls into possession on the death of his mother, unless the personal representatives see special reason for sale.

(ii) Personal chattels[7] of the intestate must not be sold except for "special reason", unless required for purposes of administration owing to want of other assets.

The provisions of section 33(1) correspond to the trust for sale and conversion inserted in many wills. The only unusual feature is the second qualification, dealing with personal chattels; but in a will the testator can, of course, insert a specific gift disposing of any personal chattels he wishes to exclude from a trust for sale and conversion.

Payment of debts and expenses

The personal representatives must pay the intestate's funeral, testamentary and administration expenses, debts and other liabilities out of the net money arising from the sale and conversion of his property and his ready money.[8] They have power during the minority of any beneficiary or the subsistence of any life interest to invest any money held by them.[9]

Residuary estate defined

The "residuary estate of the intestate", which is distributable among the persons beneficially entitled on intestacy under Part IV of the Act, means (i) the residue of the said money and any investments for the time being representing it, and (ii) any part of the intestate's estate retained unsold and not required for administration purposes.[10]

---

[6] *Per* Bennett J. in *Re Fisher* [1943] Ch. 377, 383 (moneys payable by instalments after the intestate's death under an insurance policy are not a reversionary interest).

[7] Defined in Administration of Estates Act 1925, s. 55(1)(x); for definition, and entitlement of surviving spouse, see *post*, pp. 34 *et seq.*; for enjoyment by an infant contingently entitled see s. 47(1)(iv).

[8] Administration of Estates Act 1925, s. 33(2); s. 33(5) does not exclude the application of the rule in *Allhusen v Whittell* (1867) L.R. 4 Eq.295, for which see *post* p. 466.

[9] Administration of Estates Act 1925, s. 33(3).

[10] *Ibid.* s. 33(4).

B. THE SURVIVING SPOUSE

How long the intestate's spouse must survive him, to take a beneficial interest

How long the intestate's spouse[11] must survive the intestate, in order to take any beneficial interest on his intestacy, depends on when the intestate dies.

(1) *INTESTATE DIES ON OR BEFORE DECEMBER 31, 1995.* If the intestate dies on or before December 31, 1995, it does not matter that the spouse survives the intestate only for a very short time. Provided the spouse survives the intestate, he takes a beneficial interest.

But where the intestate and his spouse die on or after January 1, 1953 and on or before December 31, 1995, in circumstances rendering it uncertain which of them survived the other, the general presumption in section 184 of the Law of Property Act 1925[12] that the younger survived the elder does not apply. Instead, the younger spouse is presumed not to have survived the elder intestate.[13] It follows that, if a husband aged 60 and his wife aged 59 both die intestate, in December 1995, in circumstances rendering it uncertain which of them survived the other, neither takes on the other's intestacy. This is an exception to the general presumption which applies where, after 1925, two or more persons have died in circumstances rendering it uncertain which of them survived the other or others. Thus if their child also dies and it is uncertain whether he survived them, the child, being younger, is presumed to have survived each of them.

(2) *INTESTATE DIES ON OR AFTER JANUARY 1, 1996.* If the intestate dies on or after January 1, 1996, then, in order to take any beneficial interest on his intestacy, his spouse must survive him by 28 days. This reform follows one of the recommendations in the Law Commission's report *Distribution on Intestacy*[14] and was enacted by section 1(1) of the Law Reform (Succession) Act 1995, which inserts a new subsection (2A) into section 47 of the Administration of Estates Act 1925.

Effect of judicial separation

If either spouse dies intestate while a decree of judicial separation is in force and the separation is continuing, the surviving spouse is treated as already dead and takes no beneficial interests on intestacy.[15]

---

[11] See *Re Seaford* [1968] P. 53 (no divorce after death).

[12] See *post*, pp. 237–239.

[13] Administration of Estates Act 1925, s. 46(3), added by the Intestates' Estates Act 1952 s. 1(4). S. 46(3) applies to intestates dying on or after January 1, 1953 and on or before December 31, 1995.

[14] Law Com. No. 187. In fact, the Law Commission recommended a 14-day survivorship period (para. 57 of the report), but the 14 days were extended to 28 days by an amendment tabled by Lord Mishcon, a practicing solicitor, when the Bill was at committee stage in the House of Lords (Hansard, February 27, 1995). Twenty-eight days is likely to be the minimum survivorship period inserted in a will.

[15] Matrimonial Causes Act 1973, s. 18(2). The surviving spouse may nevertheless apply to the court for reasonable provision under the Inheritance (Provision for Family and Dependants) Act 1975, see Chap. 6.

1. Beneficial interest if intestate leaves issue

The beneficial interest of a surviving spouse in the residuary estate varies in extent according to the state of the intestate's family at or after his death. Three different situations are dealt with in section 46 of the Act. The first is where the intestate leaves issue (*i.e.* children, grandchildren or remoter lineal descendants) who attain the age of 18 years or marry under that age.[16] Under this head a surviving spouse takes the following interests:

(1) *THE PERSONAL CHATTELS ABSOLUTELY.* The detailed definition of this expression in section 55(1)(x) of the Act reads as follows:

> "'Personal chattels' mean carriages, horses, stable furniture and effects (not used for business purposes), motor cars and accessories (not used for business purposes), garden effects, domestic animals, plate, plated articles, linen, china, glass, books, pictures, prints, furniture, jewellery, articles of household or personal use or ornament, musical and scientific instruments and apparatus, wines, liquors and consumable stores, but do not include any chattels used at the death of the intestate for business purposes nor money or securities for money."

Broadly, this definition includes all articles of personal use or ornament and all the contents of the home, but excludes money, securities for money, and chattels used at the death of the intestate for business purposes. A motor car used for both business and private purposes by, for instance, a doctor or solicitor appears to fall outside the definition of personal chattels.

Usually, in applying this definition, the only question is whether an article comes within the ordinary meaning of the word used[17]—*e.g.* horses,[18] furniture,[19] and jewellery.[20] But user is sometimes relevant because the article must not be used for business purposes[21] and because articles of household or personal use or ornament fall within the definition.[22] The phrase "articles of. . .personal use" has been held to include a 60-foot motor-yacht used by the deceased for pleasure[23] and a stamp collection made by the deceased as a hobby.[24] In *Re Crispin's Will Trusts* the Court of Appeal held that a valuable collection of watches fell within the phrase. Russell L.J., in delivering the judgment of the court, said:[25] "A watch is in its nature an article of personal use: and in the present

---

[16] *ibid.* s. 46(1)(i) and (4) and s. 47(1)(i) and (2)(c).
[17] *Re Crispin's W.T.* [1975] Ch. 245 at 251.
[18] *Re Hutchinson* [1955] Ch. 255 ("horses" included 12 racehorses used by intestate for recreation by racing them).
[19] *Re Crispin's W.T.* [1975] Ch. 245 ("furniture" included collection of clocks, whether used or stored or on loan to a museum, and whether bought or inherited).
[20] *Re Whitby* [1944] Ch. 210 ("jewellery" included unmounted cut diamonds).
[21] *Re Ogilby* [1942] Ch. 288 (intestate's herd of cattle held not to be personal chattels as used for farming purposes, though at a loss): see R.E.M. (1966) 82 L.Q.R. 18.
[22] *Re Crispin's W.T.* [1975] Ch. 245 at 251.
[23] *Re Chaplin* [1950] Ch. 507: see *Re White* [1916] Ch. 172.
[24] *Re Reynolds' W.T.* [1966] 1 W.L.R. 19: and *cf. Re Crispin's W.T.* [1975] Ch. 245 at 251–252 and R.E.M. (1966) 82 L.Q.R. 18.
[25] [1975] Ch. 245 at 252.

case we regard the cherishing [by the deceased] by eye and hand of the collection as well as the wearing of selected items from time to time as bringing them within the definition."

The statutory definition of "personal chattels" has been criticised[26]: obviously the opening reference to "carriages, horses, stable furniture and effects" has less relevance now than in 1926. On the whole, however, the definition seems to work reasonably well and it is quite common for a testator by his will to make a gift of "all my personal chattels as defined by section 55(1)(x) of the Administration of Estates Act 1925."[27]

(2) *THE FIXED NET SUM WITH INTEREST.* If the intestate dies after November 30, 1993 the fixed net sum is £125,000.[28] It is payable free of death duties[29] and costs, with interest at the specified rate (6 per cent per annum since October 1983[30]) from the date of death until it is paid.[31] The payment of both the fixed net sum and the interest is charged on the residuary estate but the interest is primarily payable out of the income of the residuary estate. The fixed net sum is often referred to as the *statutory legacy*: it bears a close resemblance to a general pecuniary legacy given to a surviving spouse by will, with a direction in the will that it is to be paid immediately after the testator's death.

(3) *A LIFE INTEREST IN ONE-HALF OF THE BALANCE OF THE RESIDUARY ESTATE, i.e.* the balance after withdrawing the personal chattels and providing for the fixed net sum with interest.[32]

2. Beneficial interest if intestate leaves no issue, but leaves a specified relative

This head applies if the intestate leaves no issue who attain the age of 18 years or marry under that age, but leaves one or more of the following

---

[26] *Re Chaplin, supra,* ("an omnium gatherum . . . The enumeration of specific articles in the definition is neither happy nor clear"); *Re Reynolds' W.T., supra,* ("the curious collection of terms I find in the definition"). As to chattels subject to hire-purchase agreements see Bicknell, (1966) 116 New L.J. 1287.

[27] A recent example of a reported case where the testatrix made a gift in her will of her personal chattels is *Re Beatty* [1990] 1 W.L.R. 1503.

[28] Family Provision (Intestate Succession) Order 1993 (S.I. 1993 No. 2906). This order was made by the Lord Chancellor pursuant to his power to fix the amount of the fixed net sum from time to time by statutory instrument under s. 1 of the Family Provision Act 1966. From 1925 to 1952 the fixed net sum was £1,000, irrespective of whether or not the deceased had left issue. From 1952 onwards, it varied according to whether or not he had left issue. Where the deceased left issue, it was £5,000 from 1953 to 1966; £8,750 from 1967 to 1972; £15,000 from 1972 to 1977; £25,000 from 1977 to 1981; £40,000 from 1981 to 1987 and £75,000 from 1987 to 1993.

[29] The term "death duties" is used in Administration of Estates Act s. 46(1)(2) and now means inheritance tax; it previously covered other taxes. Property passing from one spouse to another, whether *inter vivos* or on death, is, in any event, exempt from inheritance tax, see Chapter 12.

[30] Intestate Succession (Interest and Capitalisation) Order 1983 (No. 1374). The Lord Chancellor has power to specify the rate by statutory instrument under s. 46(1)(i) and (1A) of the Administration of Estates Act 1925. The rate was 4 per cent before 1977 and 7 per cent from 1977 to 1983.

[31] Paid or appropriated.

[32] Subject to the beneficial interest of the surviving spouse, the residuary estate is held on the statutory trusts for the issue of the intestate, see *post,* p. 40.

specified relatives, *i.e.* a parent, or a brother or sister of the whole blood, or issue of a brother or sister of the whole blood who (in the case of the brother or sister or issue) attain the age of 18 years or marry under that age.[33] Under this head a surviving spouse takes the following interests:

(1) *THE PERSONAL CHATTELS ABSOLUTELY.* The surviving spouse has the same entitlement to the personal chattels, whether or not there are issue.

(2) *THE FIXED NET SUM WITH INTEREST.* In this case the fixed net sum is £200,000 if the intestate dies after November 30, 1993.[34] Interest is payable, as under head 1 above.

(3) *ONE-HALF OF THE BALANCE ABSOLUTELY.* Under head 1 above (where there is a surviving spouse and there are issue) the surviving spouse is entitled for life to the income from one-half of the balance of the residuary estate, whereas under this head, head 2, (where there is a spouse, there are no issue, but there is a specified relative) the surviving spouse is entitled to the *capital* of one-half of the balance.[35]

3. Beneficial interest if intestate leaves no issue and no specified relative

If the intestate leaves no issue who attain the age of 18 years or marry under that age and no specified relative (as described above), the surviving spouse takes *the entire residuary estate absolutely.*[36]

The extent of the beneficial interest of a surviving spouse may depend on events after the intestate's death. If the intestate leaves at his death an only child aged six years and an only nephew (the son of the intestate's deceased brother of the whole blood) aged four years, but no other relatives, whether head 1 (spouse and issue), head 2 (spouse, no issue, but specified relative), or head 3 (spouse, no issue and no specified relative) applies, depends on future events. At the least the surviving spouse must take the interests set out under head 1. If the child dies unmarried under the age of 18 years, the surviving spouse takes the larger interests set out under head 2. If the nephew also dies unmarried under the age of 18 years, the surviving spouse takes the entire residuary estate absolutely under head 3.

Often the statutory legacy under heads 1 or 2 exhausts the residuary estate of the intestate and in consequence the surviving spouse alone benefits on intestacy, even though head 3 is not applicable.

Election to have life interest redeemed

A surviving spouse who is entitled to a life interest in part of the residuary estate under head 1 may elect to have it redeemed and to

---

[33] Administration of Estates Act 1925, ss. 46(1)(i) and 47(2)(a), (b) and (4).

[34] It would have been £1,000 if he had died before 1953; £20,000 between 1953 and 1966; £30,000 between 1967 and 1972; £40,000 between 1972 and 1977; £55,000 between 1977 and 1981; £85,000 between 1981 and 1987; and £125,000 between 1987 and 1993.

[35] The specified relatives are entitled to the other half in the order set out, *post*, pp. 43–44.

[36] Administration of Estates Act 1925, ss. 46(1)(i) and 47(2)(b) and (4).

receive its capital value from the personal representatives.[37] If that part of the residuary estate includes any property not in possession, the right to elect for redemption is only exercisable in respect of the life interest in the property in possession.[38] The capital value is to be reckoned by reference to published tables, which take into account the age of the surviving spouse and the prevailing yield on medium-term Government Stocks.[39]

The surviving spouse must elect for redemption within 12 months from the first general grant of representation[40] to the intestate's estate (unless the court extends this time limit)[41] by giving written notice to the personal representatives[42] or, if the surviving spouse is the sole personal representative, to the Senior Registrar of the Family Division of the High Court.[43]

Redemption frees the residuary estate from the surviving spouse's life interest but diminishes the residuary estate by the capital value of the life interest and the costs of the transaction. The surviving spouse receives capital instead of income.[44] The same result can be achieved by agreement between the surviving spouse and the intestate's issue (assuming that all parties are *sui juris*) without observing the statutory requirements.

Acquisition of the matrimonial home

The Second Schedule to the Intestates' Estates Act 1952 contains three different provisions which make it easier for the surviving spouse of an intestate to acquire "the matrimonial home."[45] The Act uses this expression in an unusually wide sense. All three provisions apply to the intestate's interest in a dwelling-house[46] in which the surviving spouse was resident at the intestate's death, without any requirement as to residence by the intestate.

(1) *POWER OF APPROPRIATION ENLARGED.* Personal representatives have a statutory power to appropriate any asset of a deceased's estate in or towards satisfaction of any interest in his estate.[47] This statut-

---

[37] Administration of Estates Act 1925, s. 47A: the personal representatives also pay the costs of the transaction. For the effect of election on inheritance tax see Inheritance Tax Act 1984, s. 145.

[38] s. 47A(3) and see s. 49(4).

[39] s. 47A(3A) and (3B); Intestate Succession (Interest and Capitalisation) Order 1977 (S.I. 1977 No. 1491).

[40] s. 47A(9).

[41] s. 47A(5).

[42] s. 47A(6).

[43] s. 47A(7) as amended by Administration of Justice Act 1970, Sched. 2, para. 4 and Supreme Court Act 1981, Sched. 5. In this case, the form of notice is prescribed and must be filed in the Principal Registry or in the district probate registry from which the grant issued (N.C.Prob. Rules 1987, r. 56).

[44] A surviving spouse who is an infant may elect, but the capital value is not to be paid to the infant, s. 47A(8); see *post*, p. 474.

[45] Intestates' Estates Act 1952, s. 5.

[46] This includes part of a building occupied as a separate dwelling, Sched. 2, para. 1(5); see also Sched. 2, para. 7(1).

[47] Administration of Estates Act 1925, s. 41: see *post*, p. 475.

ory power cannot, however, be used if the value of the asset to be appropriated exceeds the beneficiary's interest in the estate. The Second Schedule creates a limited exception by permitting the appropriation of an interest in a dwelling-house in which the surviving spouse was resident at the intestate's death, partly in satisfaction of an interest of the surviving spouse in the intestate's estate, and partly in return for the payment of "equality money" by the surviving spouse to the personal representatives.[48]

(2) *RIGHT TO APPROPRIATION OF MATRIMONIAL HOME.* Normally a beneficiary who wishes to take a particular asset of the estate cannot require the personal representatives to exercise the statutory power of appropriation in his favour. The Second Schedule gives the surviving spouse a special right to *require* the personal representatives to appropriate the intestate's interest in a dwelling-house in which the surviving spouse was resident at the intestate's death: the appropriation is to be made in or towards satisfaction of any absolute interest[49] of the surviving spouse in the intestate's estate, or partly in satisfaction of that interest and partly in return for the payment of equality money by the surviving spouse.[50] Thus this special right applies, whether the value of the intestate's interest in the dwelling-house is equal to, or is worth less, or more, than that absolute interest of the surviving spouse.[51]

(a) *Interest in dwelling-house.* The intestate's interest in the dwelling-house may be freehold or leasehold. This special right does not apply, however, to a tenancy which would expire, or be determinable by the landlord by notice, within two years from the intestate's death unless the surviving spouse would be entitled to acquire the freehold or an extended lease under the Leasehold Reform Act 1967.[52] Normally the consent of the court to the exercise of this special right is not required.[53]

(b) *Time limit and mode of exercise.* This special right must be exercised within 12 months from the first general grant of representation to the

---

[48] Sched. 2, para. 5(2): see *Re Phelps* [1980] Ch. 275, 278 ("a transaction which in essence is partly appropriation and partly sale becomes an appropriation").

[49] This includes the fixed net sum and the capital value of a life interest which the surviving spouse has elected under s. 47A to have redeemed, Sched. 2, para. 1(4).

[50] *Re Phelps* [1980] Ch. 275.

[51] *ibid.* at p. 279.

[52] Sched. 2, para. 1(2); Leasehold Reform Act 1967, s. 7(8): the enfranchisment rights under the 1967 Act have been extended by the Leasehold Reform, Housing and Urban Development Act 1993, s. 63–68. The personal representatives *may* appropriate a short tenancy to which this special right does not apply, but cannot be required to do so.

[53] In four cases the surviving spouse may not exercise the special right without an order of the court, which must be satisfied that its exercise is not likely to diminish the value of the other assets in the residuary estate or make them more difficult to dispose of. The four cases are where the dwelling-house (i) forms part of a building the whole of which is comprised in the residuary estate, or (ii) is held with agricultural land which is so comprised, or (iii) as to the whole or part was at the intestate's death used as a hotel or lodging house, or (iv) as to part was at the intestate's death used for non-domestic purposes; Sched. 2, paras. 2 and 4(2).

intestate's estate (unless the court extends this time limit)[54] by giving written notice to the personal representatives.[55] It cannot be exercised after the death of the surviving spouse.[56] During this period of 12 months the personal representatives must not without the written consent of the surviving spouse sell or otherwise dispose of the intestate's interest in the dwelling-house, unless this is necessary for the purposes of administration owing to want of other assets.[57] Prior to appropriation, however, this special right does not give the surviving spouse any equitable interest in the dwelling-house.[58]

(c) *Valuation.* Before deciding whether to exercise this special right the surviving spouse may require the personal representatives to have the intestate's interest in the dwelling-house valued and to inform the surviving spouse of the result of the valuation.[59] It is the normal practice to have such a valuation made for the purposes of an appropriation. The intestate's interest in the dwelling-house is to be appropriated at its value at the time of appropriation, and not at the time of the intestate's death.[60]

(3) *PURCHASE OF MATRIMONIAL HOME.* Normally a purchase of an asset from the estate by a personal representative is voidable at the instance of any beneficiary.[61] The Second Schedule creates a limited exception by providing that this rule shall not prevent a surviving spouse, who is one of two or more personal representatives, from purchasing from the estate an interest in a dwelling-house in which the surviving spouse was resident at the intestate's death.[62] The exception does not apply if the surviving spouse is the sole personal representative.[63]

C. The Issue

Subject to the beneficial interests of the surviving spouse (if any), the residuary estate is held on the "statutory trusts" for the intestate's issue.[1]

---

[54] Sched. 2, para. 3(1)(a) and (3).
[55] Sched. 2, para. 3(1)(c). If the surviving spouse is one of the personal representatives, notice must be given to the other personal representative(s): if the surviving spouse is the sole personal representative no notice is required.
[56] Sched. 2, para. 3(1)(b).
[57] Sched. 2, para. 4(1), (3) and (5). The restriction on sale does not apply if the surviving spouse is a personal representative.
[58] *Lall v. Lall* [1965] 1 W.L.R. 1249: see also Sched. 2, para. 4(5) which protects a purchaser from the personal representatives even though the spouse has not given consent.
[59] Sched. 2, para. 3(2): see also Administration of Estates Act 1925, s. 41(3).
[60] *Re Collins* [1975] 1 W.L.R. 309 (value of house was £4,200 at intestate's death in 1971 and £8,000 at hearing of case in 1974).
[61] See *Snell's Equity* (29th ed., 1990), pp. 249 *et seq.*
[62] Sched. 2, para. 5(1).
[63] Where the exception is not applicable, the surviving spouse needs the leave of the court for the purchase: alternatively the surviving spouse may purchase the interests of the other beneficiaries from them if they are *sui juris*. The surviving spouse may well prefer to exercise the power of, or the right to, appropriation.
[1] ss. 46(1) and 47(1).

The statutory trusts

Under the statutory trusts such of the children of the intestate as are living[2] at the intestate's death are beneficially entitled, if more than one in equal shares, subject to three qualifications:

  (i) *subject to representation, i.e.* subject to the rule that such of the issue of a deceased child as are living[3] at the intestate's death take that child's share, if more than one in equal shares, *per stirpes*[4]; and

 (ii) *subject to the rule that no child or other issue is entitled to a vested interest until he or she attains the age of 18 years or marries under that age*; and

(iii) where the intestate dies on or before December 31, 1995, *subject to hotchpot.*[5]

Consider an example:

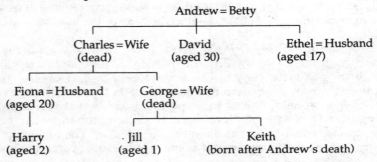

Andrew = Betty

Charles = Wife (dead) David (aged 30) Ethel = Husband (aged 17)

Fiona = Husband (aged 20) George = Wife (dead)

Harry (aged 2) Jill (aged 1) Keith (born after Andrew's death)

Andrew died intestate on January 1, 1995, leaving a widow, Betty, an adult son, David, and a daughter, Ethel. Andrew's other son Charles and Andrew's grandson George had predeceased him, but he was survived by Charles's daughter Fiona and George's daughter Jill. George's son Keith was *en ventre sa mere* at Andrew's death and is accordingly treated as then living.[6] Under the intestacy rules Andrew's residuary estate is distributed or held in trust as follows:

  (i) His surviving spouse Betty takes the personal chattels absolutely, £125,000 with interest, and a life interest in one-half of the balance of the residuary estate. Unless Betty's life interest is redeemed, one-half of the balance of the residuary estate must be held by the personal representatives upon trust for Betty during her life. Subject to Betty's life interest, the balance of the residuary estate is held on the statutory trusts for Andrew's issue.

 (ii) Under the statutory trusts David (having attained 18 years) and Ethel (having married) each take vested one-third shares. Fiona, Jill and Keith take Charles's one-third share *per stirpes*, with the

---

[2] References to a child (or issue) living at the intestate's death include a child (or issue) *en ventre sa mere* at the death, s.55(2).

[3] See *supra*, n.2.

[4] *Per stirpes* means through each stock of descent. No issue take whose parent is living at the intestate's death and so capable of taking, s.47(1)(i).

[5] *Post*, p. 41.

[6] See *supra*, n.2.

result that Fiona takes a vested one-sixth share, and Jill and Keith (taking in place of George) will each take a vested one-twelfth share if each attains the age of 18 years or marries under that age.[7] If Jill and Keith both die unmarried under that age, Fiona will take the whole of Charles's one-third share. Harry takes nothing because his mother Fiona is living at Andrew's death and so is herself capable of taking.[8]

Hotchpot: where intestate dies on or before December 31, 1995

Where an intestate dies on or before December 31, 1995, the hotchpot rule in section 47(1)(iii) of the Administration of Estates Act 1925 requires certain benefits conferred on his *child* by the intestate during his lifetime to be brought into account on the division of his residuary estate into shares under the statutory trusts. For example, if during his lifetime the intestate gave £40,000 to his elder child on marriage, and then dies a widower, leaving a residuary estate worth £160,000 which is divisible between his two children (both of full age) under the statutory trusts, under section 47(1)(iii) the elder child receives £60,000 and the younger child £100,000. The benefit is to be "brought into account" but there is no obligation to refund it to the estate. If the intestate had given £200,000 to his elder child on marriage, the younger child would receive the entire £160,000 on intestacy but the elder child would be entitled to retain the £200,000.

(1) *BENEFITS TO BE BROUGHT INTO HOTCHPOT*[9]. Section 47(1) (iii) applies to "any money or property[10] which, by way of advancement or on the marriage of a child of the intestate, has been paid to such child by the intestate or settled by the intestate for the benefit of such child (including any life or less interest and including property covenanted to be paid or settled)." Property transferred directly to a child by the intestate (*e.g.* a gift of a house on marriage) falls within this definition despite the omission of any reference to property being "transferred" to the child.[11]

To satisfy this definition the payment or settlement must be made by the intestate on the marriage of his child or "by way of advancement," *i.e.* for the purpose of establishing his child in life or of making a permanent provision for him. Payments made for establishing a child in a profes-

---

[7] Subject to Betty's prior life interest in one-half, the income and half the capital of the respective shares of Jill and Keith may be applied during infancy for their respective benefit under the statutory powers of maintenance and advancement: s.47(1)(ii); Trustee Act 1925, ss.31 and 32 (s.31 as amended by Family Law Reform Act 1969, s.1(3) and (4), Sched. 1, Pt. I and Sched. 3, para. 5(1)): for these powers see *Snell's Equity* (29th ed., 1990), pp. 276 *et seq.*

[8] *supra*, n.4.

[9] See also *post* pp. 226–227.

[10] "Property" includes a thing in action and any interest in real or personal property, Administration of Estates Act 1925, s.55(1)(xvii).

[11] *Hardy v. Shaw* [1976] Ch. 82 (gift of company shares by mother to two of her adult children: "it is common ground that a transfer of [company] shares is within the expression 'money or property ... paid' ": see also E.C. Ryder, (1973) 26 C.L.P. 208, 209; *Re Reeve* [1935] Ch. 185, 188.

sion or in business are made by way of advancement.[12] On the other hand, payments made for education, or maintenance, or by way of temporary assistance are not so made.[13] In the absence of evidence as to the purpose for which a payment was made, a gift to a child of a sum sufficiently substantial in itself to be in the nature of a permanent provision is prima facie an advancement.[14] In *Hardy v. Shaw*[15] a transfer by a mother of valuable company shares to two of her adult children, giving them effective control of the family business, constituted an advancement because it made permanent provision for them; it was immaterial that they were already well established in the family business and were not in any particular need. The onus of proving that a payment or transfer was "by way of advancement" lies on the party who asserts this.[16]

In the case of a settlement, where the child is a beneficiary, the benefit to be brought into hotchpot should be the child's interest under the settlement. So, if the child has a life interest under the settlement, this requires that such an interest should be valued according to the relevant actuarial considerations and such an interest cannot be brought into hotchpot as if it were equivalent to an absolute interest in the capital.[17]

(2) *AGAINST WHAT SHARE ON INTESTACY*. Such benefits are brought into account against the child's share "or the share which such child would have taken if living at the death of the intestate."[18] A deceased child's issue must therefore bring into hotchpot benefits conferred on the child by the intestate. If, for instance, in the example already considered[19] the elder child had predeceased the intestate, the elder child's issue[20] would receive £60,000 and the younger child £100,000. It should, however, be noted that the deceased child's issue do *not* have to bring into hotchpot benefits conferred on *them*, the issue, by the deceased during his lifetime. The hotchpot rule on total intestacy only applies to benefits conferred on a *child*. Had the £40,000 been an *inter vivos* gift to a grandchild, there would have been no question of hotchpot. A different rule applies on a partial intestacy.[21]

---

[12] *Taylor v. Taylor* (1875) L.R. 20 Eq. 155 (payment of admission fee to Inn of Court for intending barrister and for purchase of mining plant for son's business held advancements).

[13] *Taylor v. Taylor, supra*, (payment of fee to special pleader for intending barrister to read in chambers, payments made to curate to assist him in his living expenses, and payment of army officer's debts held not advancements); *Hatfield v. Minet* (1878) 8 Ch.D. 136 (annuities paid to daughters for maintenance held not advancements).

[14] *Re Hayward* [1957] Ch. 528 (nominations amounting to £507 in favour of son aged 43; held not prima facie an advancement).

[15] [1976] Ch. 82.

[16] *Hardy v. Shaw, supra* at p. 87.

[17] *Per* Danckwerts J. (*obiter*) in *Re Morton* [1956] 1 Ch. 644, 649. The opposite view seems to be expressed (also *obiter*) by Pennycuick J. in *Re Grover's W.T.* [1971] Ch. 169, 174. Both these cases are concerned with hotchpot on a *partial* intestacy, where different considerations apply. See *post* pp. 51–54. It is submitted that the correct approach on a total intestacy is to bring into hotchpot only the value of the child's life interest.

[18] s. 47(1)(iii).

[19] *Ante*, p. 40.

[20] *i.e.* issue entitled who attained the age of 18 years or married under that age.

[21] For the rule on a partial intestacy, see *post* pp. 51–54.

(3) *AT WHAT VALUATION.* The value of such benefits is "to be reckoned as at the death of the intestate."[22] Probably the intestate's residuary estate is also to be valued for this purpose as at the death of the intestate, for the sake of consistency: the amount actually available at distribution can then be distributed in the proportions calculated by reference to a notional distribution at death.[23]

(4) *CONTRARY INTENTION.* This hotchpot rule is excluded by "any contrary intention (on the part of the intestate) expressed or appearing from the circumstances of the case."[24] The test of contrary intention "is not objective—that is, if the intestate had thought of everything, what would her intention be likely to have been—but *subjective*, that is, looking at all circumstances, do they require an inference that her intention was that the gift should not be brought into hotchpot" on her death?[25] The onus of proving a contrary intention on the part of the intestate lies on the party who asserts it.[26]

(5) *ABOLITION OF THE HOTCHPOT RULES.* The hotchpot rules have long been unpopular and there was some surprise that they survived the 1925 reforms. The Law Commission, in their report *Distribution on Intestacy*,[27] recommended that the hotchpot rules[28] should be repealed. This recommendation has been carried into effect by section 1(2) of the Law Reform (Succession) Act 1995 which will apply to all intestates dying on or after January 1, 1996. No hotchpot rule will apply on the death of any intestate dying on or after January 1, 1996.

D.   THE OTHER RELATIVES

If no issue of the intestate attains a vested interest, then, subject to the beneficial interests of the surviving spouse (if any), the residuary estate of the intestate is held in trust for the relatives of the intestate in the order set out below.[29] Any person who takes a vested interest under a particular paragraph excludes any person falling within a subsequent paragraph.

1.   Parents

Surviving parents take in equal shares absolutely; if only one survives the intestate, that parent takes absolutely

---

[22] s. 47(1)(iii): see *Re Reeve* [1935] Ch. 110 (intestate's life interest surrendered to children: its value at his death was nil): J.T. Farrand (1961) 25 Conv. (N.S.) 468, 478.

[23] See *Re Hargreaves* (1903) 88 L.T. 100; J.T. Farrand, *ibid.* at pp. 480–489 (giving examples).

[24] s. 47(1)(iii).

[25] *Per* Goff J. in *Hardy v. Shaw* [1976] Ch. 82, 89.

[26] *Hardy v. Shaw, supra,* at p. 87.

[27] Law Com. No. 187.

[28] There are further hotchpot rules applicable to partial intestacies. All hotchpot rules, applicable to total or partial intestacies, are repealed as respects persons dying wholly or partially intestate on or after January 1, 1996. For hotchpot on partial intestacies see *post* pp. 51–54.

[29] s.46(1).

2. Brothers and sisters of the whole blood of the intestate, on the statutory trusts

The statutory trusts applicable under this paragraph (and also under paragraphs 3, 5 and 6 below) are the same as those for the intestate's issue[30] except that the hotchpot rule does not apply.[31] The result under this paragraph is (i) that such of the issue of a deceased brother or sister as are living at the intestate's death take the deceased brother's or sister's share, if more than one in equal shares, *per stirpes*, and (ii) that no brother or sister, or issue of a deceased brother or sister, is entitled to a vested interest until he or she attains the age of 18 years or marries under that age.

The specified relatives[32] end at this point. Relatives within paragraphs 1 and 2 may take even though the intestate left a surviving spouse,[33] but relatives within any of the later paragraphs take nothing if the intestate left a surviving spouse.

3. Brothers and sisters of the half blood[34] of the intestate, on the statutory trusts

4. Grandparents

Surviving grandparents take in equal shares absolutely; if only one survives the intestate, that grandparent takes absolutely.

5. Uncles and aunts of the whole blood, on the statutory trusts

Such an uncle or aunt must be a brother or sister of the whole blood of a parent of the intestate: thus an uncle's, or aunt's, spouse is excluded, although usually called aunt or uncle.

6. Uncles and aunts of the half blood, on the statutory trusts

Such an uncle or aunt must be a brother or sister of the half blood of a parent of the intestate.

E.   BONA VACANTIA

If the intestate leaves no surviving spouse, and no issue or other relative of the intestate attains a vested interest under the rules set out above,

---

[30] s.47(3); *ante* p. 40.
[31] *Ante*, p. 41.
[32] *Ante*, p. 35.
[33] If the intestate left a surviving spouse the other half of the balance of the residuary estate (*ante*, p. 35) is held in trust for relatives within paras. 1 or 2 in that order.
[34] Brothers and sisters of the *whole* blood have the same father *and* mother; brothers and sisters of the *half* blood have the same father *or* mother, *i.e.* they have one parent in common.

the Crown[35] takes the residuary estate of the intestate as *bona vacantia*.[36] The Crown in its discretion may provide out of the estate for dependants of the intestate, whether or not related to him, and for other persons for whom the intestate might reasonably have been expected to make provision.[37]

F.   Adopted, Legitimated and Illegitimate Children, Children Born by Artificial Insemination

Adopted child

Under the Adoption Act 1976 an adopted child is treated for purposes of intestacy as the legitimate child of the married couple who adopted him (or, in any other case, as the legitimate child of his adopter), and not as the child of his natural parents.[38] A child adopted by a married couple is therefore treated as the brother or sister of the whole blood of any other child, or adopted child, of both the spouses. In any other case, the adopted child is treated as the bother or sister of the half blood of any other child, or adopted child, of the adopter. The Act applies to an adoption order made by a court in any part of the United Kingdom, the Isle of Man or the Channel Islands,[39] and to certain overseas adoptions.[40]

Legitimated child

Under the Legitimacy Act 1976 a legitimated person[41] (and any other person) is entitled to take any interest on intestacy as if the legitimated person had been born legitimate.[42]

Illegitimate child

An illegitimate child has always taken on the intestacy of his spouse or legitimate issue and similarly his spouse or legitimate issue have always taken on his intestacy. But, at common law, as regards ancestors

---

[35] Or Duchy of Lancaster, or Duchy of Cornwall.
[36] s. 46(1)(vi).
[37] s. 46(1)(vi): see generally, Ing, *Bona Vacantia*.
[38] s. 39: as to adoption by one of the child's natural parents see s. 39(3), and as to protection of personal representatives see s. 45. In the case of a death intestate before January 1, 1976, the Adoption Act 1958, ss. 16 and 17 and provisions containing references to those sections continue to apply, Sched. 2, para. 6.
[39] The Adoption Act 1958, ss. 16 and 17 only applied to an adoption order made in the Isle of Man or Channel Islands on a death intestate after July 15, 1964.
[40] ss. 38(1) and 72(2): for the relevant rules of private international law see Dicey and Morris, *The Conflict of Laws* (12th ed., 1993), pp. 885 *et seq*.
[41] A legitimated person is one whose parents were married to one another after he was born.
[42] Legitimacy Act 1976, ss. 5(1)–(4) and 10(1): as to posthumous legitimation see s. 5(6) and as to protection of personal representatives see s. 7. In the case of a death intestate before January 1, 1976, the Legitimacy Act 1926, ss. 3–5 continues to have effect, Legitimacy Act 1976, Sched. 1, para. 2(1). For the relevant rules of private international law see Dicey and Morris, *op. cit.* pp. 860 *et seq*.

and collaterals, an illegitimate child was not put on the same footing on intestacy as a legitimate child.[43]

Then, under section 14 of the Family Law Reform Act 1969, on a death intestate after 1969:

(i) An illegitimate child (or his legitimate issue if he was dead) took on the intestacy of each of his parents as if he had been born legitimate.[44] For this purpose he was put on an equal footing with the legitimate issue of each of his parents.

(ii) Each of his parents took on the intestacy of the illegitimate child as if he had been born legitimate.

Both these rights of intestate succession depended solely on proof of parentage[45] and it was, for instance, immaterial that the father never supported or recognised the illegitimate child as his before either of them died. These rights of intestate succession under section 14 were limited in their scope. Thus an illegitimate child did not take on the intestacy of his brothers or sisters, grandparents, or uncles or aunts, and none of them took on his intestacy: if an illegitimate child died intestate without leaving a surviving spouse, issue or parent, his estate passed as *bona vacantia* to the Crown.[46]

Section 18 of the Family Law Reform Act 1987 then reversed the common law rule if the intestate dies after April 3, 1988.[47] Under section 18, references to any relationship between two persons are to be construed without regard to whether the father and mother of either of them (or of any person through whom the relationship is deduced) were married to each other at any time. Thus, on a death after April 3, 1988, an illegitimate child is entitled to take on the intestacy of his brothers or sisters, grandparents, and uncles or aunts, and likewise they are entitled to take on the intestacy of the illegitimate child.[48]

Artificial insemination

Section 27 of the Family Law Reform Act 1987 states that where a child is born to a married woman as the result of artificial insemination, the child will be treated as the child of the woman and her husband *unless* it is proved that the woman's husband did not consent to the insemination.

The Human Fertilisation and Embryology Act 1990 covers the case where an embryo, or a sperm and eggs, are placed in a woman who then gives birth to the child. Section 27 of this Act states that the woman

---

[43] Legitimacy Act 1926, s. 9 (now repealed) gave *limited* rights of intestate succession between a mother and her illegitimate child on deaths before 1970.

[44] For succession to an entail see *post*, pp. 199–200.

[45] Family Law Reform Act 1969, s.14(4) raises a presumption that an illegitimate child was not survived by his father unless the father proves the contrary: see also s.17 for special protection of personal representatives. For proof of parentage see *Re Trott* [1980] C.L.Y. 1259.

[46] *Ante*, p. 44.

[47] Family Law Reform Act 1987 (Commencement No. 1) Order 1988 (S.I. 1988 No. 425).

[48] Family Law Reform Act 1987, s.18(2) raises a presumption that an illegitimate child was not survived by his father, or by any person related to the child only through his father, unless the contrary is shown: see also s.20 (no special protection for personal representatives).

who carries the child is to be treated as the child's mother and section 28 says that her husband will be treated as the child's father unless it is shown that he did not consent to the placing.[49]

II. PARTIAL INTESTACY

A partial intestacy arises where the deceased effectively disposes of some, but not all, of the beneficial interest in his property by will. A partial intestacy differs from a total intestacy in two main respects:

A. The intestacy rules take effect subject to the provisions contained in the will. Thus the will prevails over the intestacy rules.
B. If someone dies partially intestate on or before December 31, 1995, two more hotchpot rules apply. These hotchpot rules require a surviving spouse and any issue of the deceased to bring into hotchpot beneficial interests acquired under his will.

A. THE WILL PREVAILS OVER THE INTESTACY RULES

1. Rules as to administration on intestacy

Section 33(7) of the Administration of Estates Act 1925 provides that section 33 "has effect subject to the provisions contained in the will."

(1) *TRUST FOR SALE AND CONVERSION.* Section 33(1) enacts that "on the death of a person intestate as to any real or personal estate" such estate shall be held by his personal representatives upon trust for sale and conversion into money.[1] The section imposes an immediate trust for sale at the death of the deceased.

Section 33(1) does not apply to an asset of the deceased's estate if the deceased effectively disposes of some beneficial interest (*e.g.* a life interest) in the whole of that asset by his will.[2] Again section 33(1) does not apply to an asset held upon an express trust for sale imposed by the deceased's will: this express trust for sale excludes the statutory trust for sale imposed by section 33(1) because there cannot be two subsisting trusts for sale at the same time.[3]

On the other hand, section 33(1) applies to an asset if the deceased dies wholly intestate as to that asset. Section 33(1) also applies to a share in an asset of the deceased's estate if the deceased dies wholly intestate

---

[49] If the sperm is that of the woman's husband, he will *be* the child's father—this is covered by s.28(2)(b).
[1] For the sale of reversionary interests and personal chattels see *ante*, p. 32.
[2] *Re McKee* [1931] 2 Ch. 145, 159, 160 and 165; *Re Plowman* [1943] Ch. 269.
[3] *Re McKee, supra*, esp. at pp. 159 and 165–166; *Re Taylor's Estate* [1969] 2 Ch. 245; see *post*, pp. 449–450.

as to that share and no trust for sale is imposed on that asset by the will.[4]

In *Re McKee*[5] the deceased by his will made certain bequests and gave his residuary estate to his trustee upon trust for sale and conversion, and after payment of his funeral and testamentary expenses, debts and legacies, directed him to stand possessed of the net residue upon trust for his wife for life and after her death for his brothers and sisters who survived his wife. None of his brothers or sisters did survive his wife and there was a partial intestacy. The Court of Appeal held that section 33 did not apply to any asset of the deceased's estate because the deceased had by his will effectively disposed of a life interest for his wife in his entire estate. Alternatively, the express trust for sale in the will excluded the statutory trust for sale imposed by section 33(1).

(2) *PAYMENTS OF DEBTS, EXPENSES AND LEGACIES.* Section 33(2) directs the personal representatives to pay all such funeral, testamentary and administration expenses, debts and other liabilities as are properly payable under the rules of administration contained in Part III of the Act, out of the deceased's ready money and out of the net money arising from the sale and conversion directed by section 33(1); and then directs them to set aside out of the residue of the money a fund sufficient to provide for any pecuniary legacies given by the will. The provisions of the will may exclude or vary this rule. Its effect is considered later.[6]

2. Rules as to distribution on intestacy

Where there is a partial intestacy section 49(1) makes Part IV of the Act applicable to any of the deceased's property (or interest in that property[7]) not effectively disposed of by his will, subject (1) to the provisions contained in the will[8] and (ii) to the two additional hotchpot rules.

Part IV, of course, includes sections 46 and 47,[9] which specify the persons beneficially entitled on a total or partial intestacy. The personal representative of the deceased, subject to his rights and powers for the purposes of administration, is a trustee of such undisposed of property for the persons beneficially entitled on intestacy.[10]

Section 49(1) operates as if the legislature had inserted at the end of every deceased's will an ultimate gift of any undisposed of property (or interest in property) in favour of the persons beneficially entitled on

---

[4] *Re Berrey's W.T.* [1959] 1 W.L.R. 30 (gift of residue by T to A, B, C and D equally; B predeceased T, causing B's share to lapse and go as on T's intestacy: held s. 33(1) applied to B's share). A gift of land by will to persons as tenants in common imposes a statutory trust for sale, Law of Property Act 1925, s. 34(3).

[5] [1931] 2 Ch. 145.

[6] As to expenses, debts and liabilities see *post*, pp. 408 *et seq.* and as to legacies see *post*, p. 448.

[7] "Property" in s. 49(1) includes any interest in real or personal property, s. 55(1)(xvii): see *Re McKee, supra,* at pp. 161 and 163.

[8] *Post*, p. 49.

[9] The reference to "intestate" in ss. 46 and 47 include a person who leaves a will but dies intestate as to some beneficial interest in his real or personal estate, s. 55(1)(vi).

[10] s. 49(1)(b), which adds the qualification "unless it appears by the will that the personal representative is intended to take such part beneficially." The word "expressly" in s. 49(1)(b) may be a misprint for "effectively."

intestacy.[11] Section 49(1) is always applicable on a partial intestacy, whether the deceased dies wholly intestate as to a particular asset or intestate as to some beneficial interest in that asset. Thus section 49(1) applies irrespective of whether section 33(1) imposes a statutory trust for sale.

In *Re Bowen-Buscarlet's Will Trusts*[12] the deceased by his will directed his trustees to hold his residuary estate upon trust for his widow during her life, but failed to direct what was to happen thereafter. Accordingly there was a partial intestacy. The deceased died in 1967 leaving his widow and a married daughter. As the deceased left issue, under the intestacy rules the widow was entitled to the personal chattels absolutely, the statutory legacy with interest, and a life interest in one-half of the balance of the residuary estate.[13] This life interest under the intestacy rules failed, however, because the widow could not enjoy it after her own death when her life interest under the will would end.[14] Disregarding the personal chattels,[15] the deceased's residuary estate was therefore held:

   (i) *under the will*, upon trust for the widow during her life, and, subject to her life interest,
   (ii) *under the intestacy rules*, subject to providing for the payment of the statutory legacy[16] with interest to the widow, on trust for the daughter who was absolutely entitled under the statutory trusts for the intestate's issue.

Goff J. held that the widow was entitled to *immediate* payment of the statutory legacy[16] with interest, because her interests in it under (i) and (ii) merged.[17] Subject to this payment, the income of the remainder of the residuary estate was payable under the will to the widow during her life. Subject to the widow's life interest, the daughter was absolutely entitled under the intestacy rules to the remainder of the residuary estate.

Re Bowen–Buscarlet's Will Trusts shows how capital undisposed of by the will passes to the persons beneficially entitled on intestacy. Income undisposed of by the will similarly passes to those persons.[18]

3. Subject to the provisions contained in the will

Both section 33 and section 49(1) take effect "subject to the provisions contained in the will." This qualification refers to effective provisions and not to provisions which become inoperative for any reason.[19]

[11] *Re McKee, supra,* at p. 161.
[12] [1972] Ch. 463: see *Re Buttle's W.T.* [1977] 1 W.L.R. 1200.
[13] *Ante,* pp. 34–35.
[14] *Re McKee, supra,* at p. 162.
[15] The report does not state whether the deceased specifically disposed of his personal chattels by his will. If he did, the personal chattels would not pass under the intestacy rules. If he did not, the wife in *Re Bowen–Buscarlet's W.T.* would have been entitled to immediate delivery of the personal chattels, see *Re Douglas' W.T.* [1959] 1 W.L.R. 744, 748.
[16] As reduced (under the hotchpot rule) by the actuarial value of her life interest in the residuary estate, valued as at the date of the deceased's death, *post,* p. 51.
[17] Goff J. followed *Re Douglas' W.T., supra,* and rightly rejected the unsatisfactory decision of the C.A. on this point in *Re McKee, supra,* where the point was not argued.
[18] *Re Plowman* [1943] Ch. 269 (undisposed of income of residuary estate).
[19] *Re Thornber* [1937] Ch. 29.

(1) *INOPERATIVE PROVISION.* A provision in a will does not take
effect if the gift in the will to which it is ancillary fails. In *Re Thornber*[20]
the deceased by his will directed his trustees to pay an annuity to his
wife out of the income of his residuary estate, and to accumulate any
surplus income for 21 years from his death or until his wife's earlier
death, and at the expiration of the accumulation period to hold his residuary estate and the accumulations upon trust for his children. The
deceased died childless in 1933. The Court of Appeal held that the direction to accumulate surplus income was inoperative because the trust of
the accumulations for the children had failed. Under section 49(1) the
surplus income passed to the persons beneficially entitled on intestacy
free from the inoperative provision for accumulation.

A provision may become inoperative by disclaimer. In *Re Sullivan*[21]
the deceased by his will gave his residuary estate to his trustees upon
trust to pay the income to his widow during her life and after her death
upon trust for his children. The deceased owned the musical copyrights
of Sir Arthur Sullivan; and the will contained a provision that any royalties received by his trustees should be treated as capital and not as
income. The deceased died childless in 1928. Under the intestacy rules
then in force, the widow was entitled to the personal chattels absolutely,
a statutory legacy with interest, and a life interest in the whole of the
balance of the residuary estate. Moreover, under the intestacy rules, royalties are treated as income and not as capital.[22] Maugham J. decided that,
if the widow disclaimed her life interest under the will, the provision in
the will as to royalties would become inoperative as the deceased had
died childless. He said:

> "In the present case the provision as to royalties was inserted in the
> will in order to diminish the widow's life interest for the benefit of
> children who, in the event, do not exist. It was clearly not inserted in
> order to determine the nature of interests to be taken in property in
> respect of which he died or might die intestate."[23]

The provision as to royalties would therefore not apply to the life interest
taken by the widow on intestacy under section 49(1) if she disclaimed
her life interest under the will.

(2) *PROVISION INTENDED TO OPERATE ON INTESTACY.* A
deceased may insert in his will a provision intended to operate on his
intestacy. Romer L.J. suggested a suitable clause in *Re Thornber,*[24] "In the
event of any of my property being undisposed of by this my will and
the provisions of section 49 taking effect I direct that any such property
shall be dealt with" in a particular way. In *Re Sullivan* the deceased could
have inserted such a clause in his will so as to make the provision as to

---

[20] *ibid.*
[21] [1930] 1 Ch. 84.
[22] Administration of Estates Act 1925, s. 33(5), which excludes apportionment of income
under the rule in *Howe v. Earl of Dartmouth* (1802) 7 Ves. 137, but see *Re Fisher* [1943]
Ch. 377.
[23] *Re Sullivan, supra,* at p. 87.
[24] [1937] Ch. 29, 36–37.

royalties applicable on his intestacy, irrespective of whether he left any children benefiting under the will.

B. Deaths on or Before December 31, 1995: Hotchpot on a Partial Intestacy

In addition to the hotchpot rule in section 47(1)(iii), which applies (where the intestate dies on or before December 31, 1995) to certain benefits conferred by him during his lifetime on his *child*,[25] two more hotchpot rules apply (again, where the intestate dies on or before December 31, 1995) on a partial intestacy.

1. The surviving spouse

Under section 49(1)(aa) of the Administration of Estates Act 1925 a surviving spouse who acquires any beneficial interests under the deceased's will[26] (other than personal chattels specifically bequeathed[27]) is not entitled to the full amount of the fixed net sum with interest thereon under the intestacy rules.[28] Instead, the surviving spouse takes the fixed net sum *less* the value at the deceased's death of such beneficial interests, with interest on this reduced sum. Two examples will illustrate the rather arbitrary operation of this hotchpot rule.

(i) First, the case of a general or specific legacy[29] to a surviving spouse. The deceased by his will gives to his widow his personal chattels as defined in section 55(1)(x) and a general legacy of £100,000 payable immediately after his death (or, alternatively, a specific legacy of company shares which are valued at £100,000 at his death). The deceased dies intestate as to his residuary estate on January 1, 1995, leaving children of full age. Under the intestacy rules, instead of taking £125,000 with interest thereon, the widow takes £25,000 with interest thereon. If the will had given her a legacy of £140,000, the widow would not have taken any fixed net sum with interest, but she would still have been entitled to a life interest in one-half of the residuary estate under the intestacy rules. This hotchpot rule reduces the amount of the fixed net sum with interest, but not the other beneficial interests of a surviving spouse under the intestacy rules.

(ii) Next, the case of a residuary gift. The deceased by his will gives to his widow his personal chattels as defined in section 55(1)(x) and a life interest in one-half of his residuary estate, and gives the other half of his residuary estate to his children absolutely. The will does not dispose of the beneficial interest in remainder in the first half of his resid-

---

[25] *Ante*, pp. 41–43.
[26] Including any acquired by virtue of the exercise by the will of a general power of appointment (including the statutory power to dispose of entailed interests), but not of a special power of appointment, s.49(2). S.49(1) applies to beneficial interests in foreign property, *Re Osoba* [1978] 1 W.L.R. 791, 796–797; [1979] 1 W.L.R. 247, 255.
[27] *Ante*, p. 34.
[28] *Ante*, p. 35.
[29] *Post*, pp. 170 *et seq.*

uary estate. Again the deceased dies on January 1, 1995, leaving children of full age. The widow's fixed net sum of £125,000 must be reduced by the value, at the deceased's death, of her life interest in one-half of his residuary estate under the will. On a *total* intestacy the widow would have taken both the fixed net sum of £125,000 *and* a life interest in one-half of the balance of the residuary estate. In some circumstances it may be better for the widow to disclaim[30] her life interest under the will.

2. Issue

Section 49(1)(a) requires beneficial interests acquired by any *issue* of the deceased under his will[31] to be brought into hotchpot on a partial intestacy. The section is badly drafted[32] and is not easy to construe. Section 49(1)(a) provides that the requirements of section 47(1)(iii)[33]:

> "as to bringing property into account shall apply to any beneficial interest acquired by any issue of the deceased under the will of the deceased, but not to beneficial interests so acquired by any other persons."

Thus, section 49(1)(a) defines the subject matter to be brought into account by reference to section 47(1)(iii), but as section 47(1)(iii) covers advancements to *children* and not advancements to *issue*, the two sections do not fit well together. Furthermore, section 49(1)(a) says that the beneficial interests of any issue are to be brought into account; it does not say by whom or against what shares.[34]

(1) *CONSTRUCTION.* Two different constructions of section 49(1)(a) have been suggested. The first is the *stirpital* construction, which reads section 49(1)(a) as saying that "'issue' must mean children or remoter issue," and that "any member of the family belonging to a certain branch must bring in everything that has been taken or acquired under the will by that branch."[35] The other construction is what may be called the *per capita* construction.

> "Any descendant of the testator who acquires a beneficial interest under his will brings that interest, and nothing more, into account against his share under the partial intestacy. So, for instance, a child of the testator would bring into account any beneficial interest acquired by that child under the will, but nothing more, and similarly a grandchild of the testator would bring into account any beneficial interest taken by that grandchild."[36]

[30] *Post*, p. 261.

[31] *Ante*, n. 26.

[32] "As bad a piece of draftmanship as one could conceive, in many respects," *per* Danckwerts J. in *Re Morton* [1956] Ch. 644, 647: "great difficulties of language," *per* Pennycuick J. in *Re Grover's W.T.* [1971] Ch. 168, 174.

[33] *Ante*, pp. 41 *et seq.*

[34] See E.C. Ryder (1973) 26 C.L.P. 208 at 210.

[35] *Re Young* [1951] Ch. 185. *per* Harman J. at pp. 189–190: see also *Re Grover's W.T., supra*, at p. 176 where Pennycuick J. referred to this statement of Harman J. as being "in extremely wide terms."

[36] *Per* Pennycuick J. in *Re Grover's W.T., supra*, at p. 174. He was describing the *per capita* construction, but did not apply it.

The conflict between the two constructions has been considered in three, essentially similar, first instance cases. The three cases were all decided the same way, in favour of the stirpital construction. The three cases concerned property which was left by the deceased's will in trust for the deceased's child and the child's issue.[37] In each case, the deceased died partially intestate, survived by the child and the child's brothers or sisters. So the child clearly inherited under the deceased's intestacy and had, therefore, to bring something into account under hotchpot. But what had he to bring into account? Did he have to bring into account only the beneficial interest which he, the child, had received under the will, *i.e.* his life interest, or did he also have to bring into account the beneficial interests of his own children, the deceased's grandchildren? The issue was presented starkly in *Re Young*, because the child himself died less than a month after his father; the value of his life interest was negligible in comparison with the capital value of the property in which he had the life interest. Harman J., deciding in favour of the stirpital construction, decided that the whole capital value came into hotchpot. *Re Young* was then followed in *Re Morton*[38] and *Re Grover's Will Trusts*,[39]

The stirpital construction appears to be consistent with the basic structure of sections 49(1)(a) and 47(1)(iii). Section 47(1)(iii) requires property to be brought into hotchpot against a child's share, irrespective of whether the child, or the child's issue representing him, takes that share on intestacy. Having said this, the three cases just referred to are all first instance decisions which, directly at least, deal only with the question of what happens where a child of the deceased survives the deceased and is a life tenant under a settlement under which his own children have interests in remainder.

There are all sorts of other possible problems in this area. The cases decide that a child has to account for his own children's interests in remainder under a trust under which he has a life interest, but does he also have to account for *other property* bequeathed to his children under the deceased's will? Does the deceased's grandchild, if he takes in the child's place, have to account for property bequeathed to the child, his parent?[40] Does one grandchild have to account for property bequeathed to another grandchild, his brother or sister? The stirpital construction, taken to its logical conclusion, seems to indicate that the answer is always "yes."[41]

(2) *AT WHAT VALUATION.* Section 49(1)(a) does not alter the rule in section 47(1)(iii) that the value of interests brought into hotchpot is "to

---

[37] The facts of the three cases differ in that other persons (other than the child and his issue) were also interested in the trusts in two of the three cases—but this should make no difference to the way the cases were decided.

[38] [1956] Ch. 644 ("each child ought to bring into hotchpot the value of the interest . . . taken by such child or his or her issue": Danckwerts J., at p. 649. But there are some passages in the judgement which seem more consistent with the *per capita* construction.)

[39] [1971] Ch. 168, though Pennycuick J. in *Grover* showed limited enthusiasm for the *stirpital* construction; had there been no earlier authority, he might not have adopted it.

[40] If property is bequeathed to the child and the child predeceases his parent, the property will pass to the grandchild by virtue of Wills Act 1837, s. 33, see *post*, pp. 240–243.

[41] And, for this reason, Ryder, *op. cit.*, at p. 222, thinks that it would be better to adopt the *per capita* construction.

be reckoned as at the death of the intestate."[42] In order to produce equality so far as possible, the method of valuation to be used depends on the circumstances, and events occurring after the intestate's death may be considered in deciding which method of valuation to adopt.[43]

(3) *CONTRARY INTENTION*. The application of this hotchpot rule is excluded by a contrary intention on the part of the deceased, "expressed or appearing from the circumstances of the case."[44]

3. Repeal of the hotchpot rules

Like the hotchpot rule applicable on a total intestacy, the hotchpot rules applicable on a partial intestacy will cease to have effect as respects persons dying on or after January 1, 1996.

III. REFORM OF THE INTESTACY RULES

The rules which govern intestacy were radically reformed in 1925 and were then modified in 1952.[1] Before 1926, the rules which governed the devolution of *real property*, properly termed rules of *inheritance*, were completely different from the rules which governed the devolution of *personalty*. Real property passed to the heir, the eldest son if there was one.[2] A married man's personalty passed to his personal representatives and was divided between his widow and children; a married woman's personalty passed to her husband. The effect of the 1925 property legislation was to abolish the distinctions which related to the devolution of real property and personalty and to cease to differentiate between males and females. Widows generally benefited; eldest sons were the losers.

Criticism of the present rules

A number of criticisms can be levelled at the way in which the intestacy rules now operate. In many, probably most, cases of intestacy today, a surviving spouse will inherit the whole estate because the personal chattels and the statutory legacy will exhaust it. Nevertheless, the operation of the rules may appear arbitrary. The amount of the statutory legacy is uprated periodically by statutory instrument and appears in recent years vaguely to have reflected the price of an average house. Even so, the adjustments, when they have occurred, have been quite dramatic. In 1987 the statutory legacy for a surviving spouse, in a case

---

[42] In *Re Grover's W.T., supra,* at p. 179 Pennycuick J. suggested *obiter* that "in certain circumstances" it may be necessary to depart from this rule. As to valuation of the intestate's estate, see *ante,* p. 43.

[43] *Re Young, supra,* at p. 190.

[44] s. 47(1)(iii); see *ante,* p. 43.

[1] The 1952 changes followed a Report by the Morton Committee—*Report of the Committee on Intestate Succession* (1951) Cmd. 8310. For an account of the 1952 reforms, see article by S.M. Cretney, [1994] Denning Law Journal.

[2] If there was no son, the intestate's daughters, if any, inherited as coparceners; *i.e.* they held in undivided shares but without any right of survivorship.

where the deceased left issue, was raised from £40,000 to £75,000; and in 1993 it was raised to £125,000. Thus, a widow whose husband died on June 1, 1987[3] would have received £35,000 more than one whose husband died the day before; and one whose husband died on December 1, 1993 would have received £50,000 more than one whose husband died the day before. Again, the spouse takes the statutory legacy whether or not the deceased owned a house; so the amount of the statutory legacy may be linked vaguely to house prices but not to whether the deceased as an individual owned a house nor to what it was worth. Furthermore, the surviving spouse takes the statutory legacy irrespective of whether any property passes to him as a surviving joint tenant.

In 1988 the Law Commission published a working paper[4] which was followed by a survey of public opinion and then, in 1989, by a report.[5] The report made three proposals for reform of the intestacy rules, together with a further set of proposals to provide for cohabitants.[6]

The three proposals for reform of the intestacy rules were:

(i) that the statutory hotchpot rules should be repealed;
(ii) that a spouse should only inherit under the intestacy rules if he or she survived the intestate for 14 days;
(iii) that (subject to (ii) above) a surviving spouse should in all cases take the intestate's whole estate.

The first two of these proposals were relatively uncontroversial but the third was not. The suggestion that the whole estate should pass to a surviving spouse may operate with particular unfairness in cases where the deceased has re-married and is married at the time of his death to someone who is not the parent of his children.[7] The first two of these proposals have now been enacted by the Law Reform (Succession) Act 1995.[8] The third proposal has not been enacted, though there is likely to be further discussion in future as to what *is* appropriate provision for a widow or widower.[9]

---

[3] The day when the 1987 S.I. first came into force.
[4] Working Paper No. 108, *Distribution on Intestacy*.
[5] Law Com. No. 187, *Distribution on Intestacy*.
[6] The proposals relating to cohabitants are discussed in Chapter 6, *post* pp. 141–142 and 149–150.
[7] See R. Kerridge [1990] 54 Conv 358.
[8] The 14-day survivorship period became 28 days. See *ante* p. 33 n. 14.
[9] See S.M. Cretney (1995) 111 L.Q.R. 77.

CHAPTER 3

THE MAKING OF WILLS
CAPACITY—THE MIND OF THE TESTATOR

I. INTRODUCTION

In the past, aliens, traitors, felons, and married women were all subject to special rules restricting their right to make wills. All of them are now able to make valid wills.[1] The only class of people now generally unable to make wills are infants.

Until 1837, an infant could make a valid will of personal estate at 14 if a boy or at 12 if a girl. The Wills Act 1837, section 7, enacted that no will should be valid if made by a person under 21. This was reduced to 18 for wills made on or after January 1, 1970[2]; and section 11 of the Wills Act[3] qualifies section 7 by excepting wills made by infant soldiers in actual military service or by infant seamen at sea.

It is sometimes said that a testator must intend to make a will. Strictly, this is inaccurate, though it is a convenient way of stating the basic requirement that a testator must have a testamentary intention, *i.e.* must intend the wishes he expresses to *take effect only at his death*. If a person intends a duly executed[4] document to take effect only at his death, it can be admitted to probate as his will whether or not he intended to make, or was aware that he was making, a will.[5] Similarly, a privileged testator[6] must give deliberate expression to his wishes in the event of his death but he need not know that he is making a will.[7]

A testator must be mentally capable of making a will, he must know and approve of its contents; and he must not make it as a result of the undue influence or fraud of another person. For over 100 years, the rules governing contentious probate cases were the Contentious Probate Rules 1862 and, although they have been repealed,[8] they continue to exercise considerable influence over the way in which questions about a testator's

---

[1] For the history of the position of married women and criminals—see Theobald (13th ed, 1971) paras 103–105. As to aliens, see Theobald 14th ed. (1982) p. 29 n. 6.

[2] Family Law Reform Act 1969, s. 3(1)(*a*).

[3] As explained and extended by the Wills (Soldiers and Sailors) Act 1918—and see below, Chap. 4.

[4] For an explanation of "duly executed" see Chap. 4.

[5] *Milnes v. Foden* (1890) 15 P.D.105.

[6] Privileged testators are those who may make informal wills—see Chap. 4.

[7] *Re Stable* [1919] P. 7.

[8] They were repealed in 1964.

56

capacity—and matters related to capacity—are raised or formulated. Under the 1862 Rules a will could be challenged on the basis:

(1) that the testator had not been of sound mind, memory and understanding; and/or
(2) that the testator had not known or approved the contents of his will; and/or
(3) that he had been subject to undue influence; and/or
(4) that there had been fraud.[9]

Issues of mental capacity, knowledge and approval, undue influence and fraud, often merge into one another.[10] If a testator's understanding is limited, that may affect his knowledge or approval; it may also make it easier to exercise undue influence over him, or to make him the victim of fraud. An illustration is *Barry v. Butlin*[11] where the testator, a widower, "a person of slender capacity, ... indolent habits ... addicted to drinking, ... singular in his appearance, ... and ... childish in his amusements,"[12] disinherited his son, his only surviving child, and left his estate to be divided between his butler, his solicitor and a friend. The son challenged the will—pleading, expressly or impliedly, *all four grounds*—but he lost the case. How plaintiffs are best advised to plead cases like this will depend, to some extent, on the burden of proof and on questions relating to costs.[13]

Burden of proof

The *legal* (or persuasive) burden of proof that a testator had testamentary capacity at the time of execution,[14] and that he knew and approved the contents of his will, always lies on the person propounding it. He must "satisfy the conscience of the Court that the instrument so propounded is the last Will of a free and capable testator."[15] If the person propounding the will fails to discharge this burden, the will is not admissible to probate.[16] The *evidential* burden of proof of capacity or knowledge and approval may shift from one party to another in the course of a case.[17]

The legal burden of proof of undue influence or fraud always lies on the person alleging it.[18] That person must prove that the will (or such part of it as he alleges to be invalid) was made as a result of the undue influence or fraud of another person.

[9] See P.S.A. Rossdale *Probate and the Administration of Estates* (1991) p. 65.
[10] Per Scarman J. in *In the Estate of Fuld (dec'd) (No 3)* [1968] P. 675, 722 where he quotes Lord Penzance.
[11] (1838) 2 Moo P.C. 480.
[12] *Barry v. Butlin, supra* at p. 487.
[13] It was suggested in *In the Estate of Fuld, supra*, that positive charges of fraud and undue influence would not feature as largely in the pleadings of probate cases after the decision in *Wintle v. Nye (post* pp. 67–68) as they had before it. It was further suggested that it would be better if they did not.
[14] *Barry v. Butlin, supra* at p. 481.
[15] *Barry v. Butlin, supra* at p. 482; *Cleare v. Cleare* (1869) L.R. 1.P.&D. 655.
[16] *Wood v. Smith* [1993] Ch. 90.
[17] *Waring v. Waring* (1848) 6 Moo P.C. 341, 355 and see *post* p. 61.
[18] *Boyse v. Rossborough* (1857) 6 H.L.C. 2, 49; *Craig v. Lamoureux* [1920] A.C. 349.

Information available to parties

A person seeking to attack a will may have little information as to the precise circumstances in which it was made. Thus he may have no reasonable grounds for pleading undue influence or fraud, but he may nevertheless be able to establish evidence relevant to a plea of want of knowledge and approval.

Costs

The practice as to costs in a probate action (which is considered later)[19] is also relevant to any decision as to whether to challenge a will on the basis of alleged lack of capacity, want of knowledge and approval or of undue influence or fraud.[20]

II. THE TESTATOR'S UNDERSTANDING

A. TESTAMENTARY CAPACITY

Test of testamentary capacity[1]

A classic statement of the test to be applied is contained in the judgment of Cockburn C.J. in *Banks v. Goodfellow*:[2]

"It is essential . . . that a testator shall understand the nature of the act and its effects; shall understand the extent of the property of which he is disposing; shall be able to comprehend and appreciate the claims to which he ought to give effect; and, with a view to the latter object, that no disorder of the mind shall poison his affections, pervert his sense of right, or prevent the exercise of his natural faculties—that no insane delusion shall influence his will in disposing of his property and bring about a disposal of it which, if the mind had been sound, would not have been made."

This test requires the testator to understand three matters:

(i) the effect of his wishes being carried out at his death, although he need not understand their precise legal effect[3];

(ii) the extent of the property of which he is disposing, although he is not required to carry in his mind a detailed inventory of it[4]; and

---

[19] *Post* pp. 360–362.

[20] *Barry v. Butlin, supra,* is a good example of a case where, if the plaintiff (the son) had contented himself with alleging lack of capacity, costs would have been paid from the estate. But he also alleged undue influence and fraud and so, being unsuccessful, he was ordered to pay the costs.

[1] For capacity to make a gift *inter vivos* see *Re Beaney* [1978] 1 W.L.R. 770, and to consent to a marriage see *In the Estate of Park* [1954] P. 112, 120–122, 131–133 and 135–136.

[2] (1870) L.R. 5 Q.B. 549, 565.

[3] *Banks v. Goodfellow, supra,* at p. 567.

[4] *Waters v. Waters* (1848) 2 De G. & Sm. 591, 621 ("*generally* the state of his property and what it consists of"): see *Re Beaney* [1978] 1 W.L.R. 770, 773.

(iii) the nature of the claims on him.

In the recent case of *Wood v. Smith*,[5] the testator told someone, at the time he was making his will, that he had investments worth £17,000, whereas the actual value of his investments was in excess of £105,000. This showed that he was "seriously confused as to the extent of his assets",[6] and the trial judge decided that this was consistent with such confusion of mind as to indicate that the deceased lacked testamentary capacity.[7]

The testator must have "a memory to recall the several persons who may be fitting objects of the testator's bounty, and an understanding to comprehend their relationship to himself and their claims upon him."[8] In *Harwood v. Baker*[9] a will executed by a testator on his deathbed, giving all his property to his wife was held invalid because, owing to his illness, the testator was unable to comprehend and weigh the claims upon him of his relatives. It did not suffice that the testator knew that he was giving all his property to his wife and excluding all his relatives: he must also be "capable of recollecting who those relatives were, of understanding their respective claims upon his regard and bounty, and of deliberately forming an intelligent purpose of excluding them from any share of his property."[10]

A will is not invalid merely because, in making it, the testator is moved by capricious, frivolous, mean or even bad motives. If he satisfies this test of testamentary capacity he "may disinherit ... his children, and leave his property to strangers to gratify his spite, or to charities to gratify his pride."[11]

The same test applies whether the testator has been subnormal from birth or has suffered impairment of the mind during his lifetime, whether through injury, physical or mental illness, senility or addiction.

Effect of delusions

A delusion in the mind of a testator deprives him of testamentary capacity if the delusion influences, or is capable of influencing, the provisions of his will.[12] A testator suffers from a delusion if he holds a belief on any subject which no rational person could hold, and which cannot be permanently eradicated from his mind by reasoning with him.[13] In *Boughton v. Knight*, Sir James Hannen told a jury to put to themselves:

[5] [1993] Ch. 90.

[6] [1993] Ch. 90, 114

[7] The Court of Appeal upheld the trial judge's decision that the onus of establishing testamentary capacity had not been discharged.

[8] Per Sir James Hannen in *Boughton v. Knight* (1873) L.R. 3 P. & D. 64, 65–66.

[9] (1840) 3 Moo.P.C. 282: see *Battan Singh v. Amirchand* [1948] A.C. 161.

[10] *Harwood v. Baker, supra*, at p. 290.

[11] Per Sir James Hannen in *Boughton v. Knight, supra* at p. 66. The will is not invalid, but it may be open to someone to make a claim for family provision—see Chap. 6.

[12] *Dew v. Clark* (1826) 3 Add. 79, 5 Russ. 163 (father's insane aversion to only daughter); *Smee v. Smee* (1879) 5 P.D. 84 (delusion son of George IV); *Re Bellis* (1929) 141 L.T. 245 (delusion T had already benefited one daughter far more than the other); *Battan Singh v. Amirchand* [1948] A.C. 161 (delusion T had no relatives); *Re Nightingale* (1974) 119 S.J. 189 (delusion son attempted to shorten his life).

[13] *Dew v. Clark* (1826) 3 Add. 79, 90.

"this question, and answer it; can I understand how any man in possession of his senses could have believed such and such a thing? And if the answer you give is, I cannot understand it, then it is of the necessity of the case that you should say the man is not sane,"[14]

In practice, it may be difficult to distinguish between grave misjudgement and delusion, particularly in relation to a testator's assessment of the character of a possible beneficiary under his will. Certainly a parent is not incapacitated from making a will because he has formed an unduly harsh view of his child's character. But if the parent's misjudgment really stems from an irrational aversion towards his child, amounting to a delusion, then the parent lacks testamentary capacity.[15]

A delusion in the mind of a testator does not deprive him of testamentary capacity if it cannot have had any influence upon him in making his will. In *Banks v. Goodfellow*[16] the testator suffered from the delusion that he was pursued and molested by a certain man, who was already dead and who was in no way connected with the testator, and by devils or evil spirits whom the testator believed to be visibly present. Nevertheless the court held that the testator had testamentary capacity because the delusions were not capable of having had any influence on the provisions of his will.

Time for satisfying the test

The testator must have testamentary capacity at the time when he executes the will. Alternatively, it suffices if the testator has testamentary capacity at the time when he gives instructions to a solicitor for the preparation of the will provided (i) the will is prepared in accordance with his instructions and (ii) at the time of execution he is capable of understanding, and does understand, that he is executing a will for which he has given instructions. This alternative is useful in cases where a testator's capacity deteriorates after giving instructions. This happened to the testatrix in *Parker v. Felgate*[17] but her will was upheld because, on being roused from a partial coma at the time of execution, she was capable of understanding, and did understand, that she was executing a will for which she had given instructions. It was immaterial that, at the time of execution, she was incapable of remembering her instructions, or even of understanding each clause of the will if it had been put to her.

In *Parker v. Felgate* the testatrix had given her instructions directly to her solicitor. In *Battan Singh v. Amirchand*[18] the Privy Council said that the principle enunciated in *Parker v. Felgate* should be applied with the greatest caution where the testator gives instructions to a lay intermediary who repeats them to the solicitor:

"The opportunities for error in transmission and of misunderstanding and of deception in such a situation are obvious, and the court ought

---

[14] (1873) L.R. 3 P. & D. 64, 68.
[15] *Dew v. Clark, supra; Boughton v. Knight*, (1873) L.R. 3 P. & D.64.
[16] (1870) L.R. 5 Q.B. 549.
[17] (1883) 8 P.D. 171: see also *Perera v. Perera* [1901] A.C. 354, 361–362.
[18] [1948] A.C. 161.

to be strictly satisfied that there is no ground for suspicion, and that the instructions given to the intermediary were unambiguous and clearly understood, faithfully reported by him and rightly apprehended by the solicitor."[19]

Evidential burden of proof of capacity

It was said above[20] that the *evidential* burden of proof may shift from one party to another in the course of a case.[21]

The following rebuttable presumptions may apply.

(1) *WILL RATIONAL.* If a duly executed will is rational on the face of it, a presumption arises that the testator had testamentary capacity.[22] The person challenging the will may rebut this presumption by evidence to the contrary.

(2) *CONTINUANCE OF MENTAL ILLNESS.* If, during a period prior to the execution of his will, the testator suffered from serious mental illness, a presumption arises that it continued and that the testator lacked testamentary capacity.[23] The person propounding the will may rebut this presumption by establishing that the testator made the will during a lucid interval[24] or after recovery from the illness.

If there is any reason at all to anticipate that a will about to be executed may be challenged in the future on the ground that the testator lacked testamentary capacity, it is a useful precaution to arrange for the presence of at least one experienced medical practitioner so that he may examine the testator's state of mind at the time when he executes the will and, if he is satisfied, be a witness to the will.[25] This precaution should always be observed in the case of an aged testator or a testator who has suffered a serious illness. In cases of senility there may be marked variations in mental capacity from time to time.

Consequences of incapacity

A will or codicil is wholly invalid if executed at a time when the testator lacked testamentary capacity. But there may be a limited exception to this rule where only part of a will is affected by a delusion. In *In the*

---

[19] *ibid.* at p. 169.

[20] *Ante*, p. 57.

[21] *Waring v. Waring* (1848) 6 Moo P.C. 341, 355.

[22] *Symes v. Green* (1859) 1 Sw.& Tr. 401; *Sutton v. Sadler* (1857) 3 C.B.(N.S.) 87,98. As to a will which appears irrational on its face, see *Arbery v. Ashe* (1828) 1 Hagg. Ecc. 214; *Austen v. Graham* (1854) 8 Moo. P.C. 493.

[23] *Groom v. Thomas* (1829) 2 Hagg. Ecc. 433; *Bannatyne v. Bannatyne* (1852) 2 Rob. 472; *Banks v. Goodfellow* (1870) L.R. 5 Q.B. 549, 570.

[24] *Cartwright v. Cartwright* (1793) 1 Phill. 90; *Bannatyne v. Bannatyne, supra; Nichols v. Binns* (1858) 1 Sw. & Tr. 239.

[25] *Kenward v. Adams, The Times,* Nov. 29, 1975 (medical practitioner should record his examination of the testator and his findings); *Re Simpson* (1977) 121 S.J. 224; see Law Reform Committee's 22nd Report, pp. 7–8 where it noted that a "solicitor is often placed in an extremely difficult situation if he has any reason at all to doubt the testamentary capacity of the testator". But some medical practitioners may be reluctant to act as witnesses, as they may think that they, too, are placed in a difficult situation.

Estate of Bohrmann[26] a testator made a will which included gifts to English charities. He later developed an insane delusion to the effect that the London County Council was persecuting him. He then executed a codicil to his will, one clause of which substituted United States charities for the equivalent English charities. Langton J. decided that the relevant clause in the codicil was affected by the delusion and he upheld the validity of the original will and the codicil *with the exception of the clause in the codicil which substituted the U.S. charities for the English charities.* This is the only reported case in which a court has treated a testator as having testamentary capacity to make part, but not the whole, of a will or codicil. In taking this approach, Langton J. relied by way of analogy on the court's practice of deleting from testamentary instruments anything not brought to the knowledge and approval of the testator.[27] The scope of this exception to the general rule remains unsettled but it is probably narrow. In fact there are doubts about both the exception itself and the analogy.[28]

B. "STATUTORY" WILLS

Since 1970[29] it has been possible for the Court of Protection[30] to order the execution of a will for an adult patient whom the Court has reason to believe is incapable of making a valid will for himself. This power is now contained in section 96 of the Mental Health Act 1983. Such wills are commonly referred to as "statutory" wills[31] and may make any provision which the patient could have made if he had not been mentally disordered. The power is exercised by one of the nominated judges of the Court of Protection, or, more usually, by the master.[32]

A statutory will must be executed with the formalities specified in section 97 of the Mental Health Act 1983, which requires a statutory will to be:

(i) expressed to be signed by the patient acting by the person authorised by the Court of Protection to execute the will for the patient (such person will usually be the patient's receiver[33]);

---

[26] [1938] 1 All E.R. 271.

[27] *Post,* p. 71.

[28] See C.A. Wright (1938) 16 Can.Bar Rev. 405, 410–411; R.F. Cross (1950) 24 A.L.J. 12.

[29] "Statutory wills" were introduced by the Administration of Justice Act 1969 s. 17.

[30] The Court of Protection used to be known as the Office of the Master in Lunacy. For a description of its work, see an article by the master of the Court of Protection in (1984) 128 S.J. 571 and 590. See also an article by the Official Solicitor in (1990) 20 Fam. Law 53 where he describes his work and also refers (at p. 55) to statutory wills. See also Heywood and Massey, *Court of Protection Practice,* (12th ed., 1991) at pp. 191–196.

[31] C.H. Sherrin, in an article in (1983) 13 Fam. Law 135 suggests that it would be better to call them "judicial" wills. But the term "statutory" wills is now in general use.

[32] The master will normally hear and decide an application for a statutory will, unless the master decides to refer it to one of the nominated judges of the Court. See Practice Note [1983] 1 W.L.R. 1077. Applications are usually heard in chambers.

[33] A patient's receiver is the person appointed under s. 99 of the Mental Health Act 1983; the receiver's main function is to receive the patient's income but he may be empowered to do all that is necessary in the proper conduct of the patient's affairs. See Heywood and Massey, *Court of Protection Practice,* (12th ed., 1991) at p. 4.

    (ii) signed by the authorised person with the name of the patient, and with his own name, in the presence of two or more witnesses present at the same time;

    (iii) attested and subscribed by those witnesses in the presence of the authorised person;[34] and

    (iv) sealed with the official seal of the Court of Protection.[35]

The Court will, broadly speaking, attempt to make for the patient the will it supposes he would, had he not been incapable, have made for himself. In Re D(J)[36] Megarry V.-C. said that there were a number of factors to be considered. The Court should assume that the patient is having a brief lucid interval during which he has a full knowledge of the past and a realisation that he will relapse into incapacity as soon as the will is executed. The actual, and not a hypothetical, patient must be considered, he must be envisaged as being advised by competent solicitors and to be taking a broad brush approach to claims on his bounty.

A recent illustration of the operation of the statutory will provisions is Re C[37] where a statutory will was made for a woman who was aged 75, had been mentally handicapped since birth and who had been in hospital since she was 10. She had inherited property from her parents which was, at the time of the application to the Court, worth more than £1,500,000. If she died intestate, her property would pass to her family, few members of which seem to have been aware of her existence and none of whom was in regular contact with her. Hoffmann J. ordered immediate gifts[38] to be made to the family and to a charity linked with the hospital where the patient lived, and then authorised a statutory will under which, apart from two relatively small specific legacies to persons whom the patient would be presumed to have wished to benefit, the residue of her estate was to be divided equally between her family and mental health charities. The effect of this statutory will was, effectively, to give a substantial benefit to the mental health charities which would have received nothing had the patient died intestate.

An unusual case, illustrating the use to which the statutory will procedure can be put, is Re Davey.[39] At the age of 92, O, an unmarried woman, went to live in a nursing home and shortly afterwards, in September 1979, she made an apparently rational will leaving her property to various members of her family. During the course of October and November she was examined by two consultant psychiatrists who thought that she was suffering from mental deterioration and that she was, by then, incapable of managing her affairs. There was a brief delay while her family and her solicitors discussed who should be appointed

---

[34] The formalities for statutory wills may be compared and contrasted with the formalities applicable under section 9 of the Wills Act; see Chap. 4 pp. 77 et seq.

[35] See Re H.M.F. [1976] Ch 33, as to who should be made parties to an application for a statutory will; and see Re B [1987] 1 W.L.R. 552, as to who should be notified of an application.

[36] [1982] Ch 237.

[37] [1991] 3 All E.R. 866.

[38] The jurisdiction to order immediate gifts is outside the scope of this work, but the object of making the lifetime gifts would have been to avoid inheritance tax—see Chap. 12.

[39] [1981] 1 W.L.R. 164.

her receiver, the person who would look after her affairs.[40] Papers were
filed with the Court of Protection in support of an application for the
appointment of a receiver but no receiver had been appointed when, on
Monday December 17, the Court of Protection received a letter informing
the Court that, unbeknown to O's family or solicitors, O had, at the end
of October, gone through a Register Office ceremony of marriage with
D, a male nurse from the nursing home where she lived. As her marriage
would revoke any previous will,[41] this meant that if O were now to die
she would die intestate and a substantial part of her estate would pass
to the man to whom she had been married for less than two months.[42]
On Tuesday, December 18, the day after the letter about the marriage
was received, the Court made an order appointing the Official Solicitor
as O's receiver. Two days later, on December 20, the penultimate day of
the legal term, the newly appointed receiver applied to the deputy
master of the Court of Protection for the execution of a statutory will.
No notice of this application was given to D or to any member of O's
family. The statutory will which the receiver applied for was in the same
terms as the September will. The deputy master ordered the execution
of the will and execution took place on December 21. O died six days
later. D then appealed against the order and sought to have the will set
aside. Fox J. dismissed his appeal. The course taken by the deputy master
had given the best prospect of a just result because, had O lived longer,
D could have applied for a further statutory will, and now that she had
not survived, D could make an application under the Family Provision
legislation.[43]

III. LACK OF KNOWLEDGE AND APPROVAL AND MISTAKE

A testator must know and approve the contents of his will. Cases
where there is an allegation of lack of knowledge and approval tend to
fall into two broad groups, although there is overlap between them. On
the one hand, there are cases where an alleged lack of knowledge and
approval is linked with problems about the testator's mental capacity
and/or with the possibility of allegations of undue influence or fraud.
On the other hand there are cases where the alleged lack of knowledge
and approval results from a mistake made by a testator without there
being any question about his mental capacity or any suggestion that a
third party has not behaved properly.

A. LACK OF KNOWLEDGE AND APPROVAL

If a testator says to another person, "I will execute any will you draw
up for me," and a will is drawn up and the testator executes it in ignor-

---

[40] For a reference to the appointment and duties of receivers, see n. 33, *supra*.
[41] See Chap. 5.
[42] For the applicable intestacy rules, see Chap. 2. Her marriage may have been voidable,
but once she was dead it would be too late to obtain a decree of annulment; see Chap.
5 pp. 94–95.
[43] See *post* Chap. 6.

ance of its contents, the will is invalid.[1] A valid will must be the result of a testator's own intelligence and volition, although the contents of the will need not originate from the testator provided he understands and approves them.[2]

Time of knowledge and approval

The normal rule is that the testator must know and approve of the contents of his will at the time when he executes it.[3] But, in *In the Estate of Wallace*[4] Devlin J. held valid a will which the testator executed on the day before his death; even though the testator did not know or approve its contents at the time of execution.[5] The will was held valid on the basis that the testator understood that he was executing a will which had been prepared in accordance with instructions which he had given earlier to his solicitor. This case follows the principle laid down in relation to testamentary capacity in *Parker v. Felgate*[6]; and it is logical that the same rule should apply in relation to knowledge and approval.

Evidential burden of proof of knowledge and approval

In the type of case where questions of lack of knowledge and approval may overlap with questions of lack of capacity and/or with questions of undue influence or fraud, the burden of proof may be important. The *legal* (or persuasive) burden of proof always lies upon the person who is propounding a will to prove that the testator knew and approved of its contents. The propounder must "satisfy the conscience of the Court that the instrument so propounded is the last Will of a free and capable Testator."[7]

(1) *PRESUMPTION IN ORDINARY CIRCUMSTANCES.* On proof that the testator was of testamentary capacity and that he duly executed the will, a rebuttable presumption arises, in ordinary circumstances, that he knew and approved of its contents.[8] The *evidential* burden of proof then shifts to the person opposing the will to rebut this presumption. If he does so, the person propounding the will must produce affirmative proof of the testator's knowledge and approval so as to satisfy the legal burden of proof.

(2) *AFFIRMATIVE PROOF.* Affirmative proof of the testator's knowledge and approval may take any form but it must be strong enough to satisfy the court in the circumstances of the particular case.

---

[1] *Hastilow v. Stobie* (1865) L.R. 1 P. & D. 64.

[2] *Constable v. Tufnell* (1833) 4 Hagg. Ecc. 465, 477. A testator does not need to know or approve of the contents of a "statutory" will.

[3] *Hastilow v. Stobie* (1865) L.R. 1 P & D. 64; *Guardhouse v. Blackburn* (1866) L.R. 1 P.D. 109, 116.

[4] [1952] 2 T.L.R. 925; see also *Re Flynn* [1982] 1 W.L.R. 310, 319–320.

[5] Because, at the time of execution, the testator had not read the will or had it read to him.

[6] *Ante*, p. 60. But if the testator gives instructions to a lay intermediary who repeats them to the solicitor, great caution is needed, see *Battan Singh v. Amirchand, ante*, p. 47.

[7] *Barry v. Butlin* (1838) 2 Moo. P.C. 480, 482; *Cleare v. Cleare* (1869) L.R. 1 P. & D. 655.

[8] *Barry v. Butlin, supra*, at p. 484; *Cleare v. Cleare, supra*, at p. 658.

(3) *FORMS OF PROOF.* One form of affirmative proof is to establish that the will was read over by, or to, the testator when he executed it. If a testator merely casts his eye over the will, this may not be sufficient.[9] If it is read over to the testator, this must be done in a proper way so that the testator hears and understands what is read.[10] Another form of affirmative proof is to establish that the testator gave instructions for his will and that the will was drafted in accordance with those instructions.[11]

(4) *READING OVER IS NOT CONCLUSIVE.* There used to be a rule of evidence that a competent testator who had read a will, or had it read over to him, and had executed it, must be taken to have known and approved of its contents unless fraud had been practised on him.[12] Over the years the rigidity of this rule has gradually been eroded and it has been suggested that nowadays the rule "does not survive in any shape or form."[13] The fact that the will was read over by, or to, the testator must be given the weight appropriate to it in all the circumstances of the case, but it is not conclusive.[14]

Suspicious circumstances

The presumption which applies in ordinary circumstances—that the testator who was of testamentary capacity and who duly executed his will knew and approved of its contents—does not apply if the will was prepared and executed under circumstances which raise a well-grounded suspicion that the will, or some provision in it, did not express his mind. In that event the will (or the provision in it) is not admissible to probate unless the suspicion is removed by affirmative proof of the testator's knowledge and approval.[15]

In *Barry v. Butlin*, Parke B. referred to the classic instance of suspicious circumstances:

"If a party writes or prepares a will, under which he takes a benefit, that is a circumstance that ought generally to excite the suspicion of the Court, and calls upon it to be vigilant and jealous in examining the evidence in support of the instrument, in favour of which it ought not to pronounce unless the suspicion is removed, and it is judicially satisfied that the paper propounded does express the true Will of the deceased."[16]

If, however, the benefit taken by the person who has prepared the will is small in relation to the size of the estate, this does not, of itself, raise a suspicion.[17]

---

[9] *Re Morris* [1971] P. 62.
[10] *Garnett-Botfield v. Garnett-Botfield* [1901] P. 335.
[11] *Fincham v. Edwards* (1842) 3 Curt. 63, 4 Moo P.C. 198.
[12] *Guardhouse v. Blackburn* (1866) L.R. 1 P. & D. 109, 116.
[13] Per Latey J. in *Re Morris* [1971] P. 62, 79, where the authorities are reviewed at pp. 75–79.
[14] Per Sachs J. in *Crerar v. Crerar* (1956) 106 LJ 694: see *Re Morris, supra,* at p. 78.
[15] Per Davey L.J. in *Tyrell v. Painton* [1894] P. 151, 159: see *In the Estate of Fuld (No. 3)* [1968] P. 675, 712.
[16] (1838) 2 Moo P.C. 480, 482.
[17] *Barry v. Butlin* pp. 484–485.

Another example of suspicious circumstances is where a person takes an active part in obtaining a will under which he obtains a substantial benefit[18] by, for instance, suggesting the terms of the will to the testator and then taking the testator to a solicitor whom he has chosen himself.

Tyrrell v Painton[19] provides another instance. A testatrix who was ill made a will in favour of her cousin, Mrs Tyrell. This will was executed in the presence of the testatrix's vicar, her doctor and her solicitor. Two days later, Tom Painton brought the testatrix another will which he, Tom Painton, had prepared and which was in favour of his father, John Painton. The testatrix executed this will in the presence of Tom Painton and one of Tom's friends. No one else was present and Tom kept the existence of this will secret until after the testatrix's death. The Court of Appeal held that the circumstances raised a well-grounded suspicion and that John Painton had failed to remove that suspicion by proving affirmatively that the testatrix knew and approved of the contents of the will in his favour.

Circumstances only raise a ·suspicion of a lack of knowledge and approval if they are "circumstances attending, or at least relevant to, the preparation and execution of the will itself."[20] Thus there was no suspicion of want of knowledge and approval where an executrix learnt of the death of the testatrix but took no steps to prove the will (under which the executrix's daughter was the sole beneficiary), possession of which she retained until her own death 16 years later.[21]

Affirmative proof where there are suspicious circumstances

The greater the degree of suspicion, the stronger must be the affirmative proof required to remove it.[22]

The leading case is *Wintle v. Nye*.[23] The testatrix, a rich spinster described by her doctor as being "not very intelligent", died leaving a complex will and a codicil both of which had been prepared by her solicitor and under which the greater part of her estate passed to him. The testatrix's sole next-of-kin was her sister who did not attempt to challenge the will. But the sister died intestate a year after the testatrix and her estate then passed to a number of cousins, one of whom assigned his interest in the sister's estate, and therefore any interest the sister might have in the testatrix's estate, to Colonel Alfred Wintle. Colonel Wintle was himself a cousin but too distant to be entitled on the sister's intestacy. His essential complaint was that the testatrix had intended to make provision in her will for his sister and that the testatrix had lacked knowledge and approval of the will which she had executed. He did not allege that the testatrix lacked testamentary capacity; nor did he allege undue influence or fraud. Because there was no allegation of undue

---

[18] *Fulton v. Andrew* (1875) L.R. 7 H.L. 448, 471–472; *Brown v. Fisher* (1890) 63 L.T. 465; *Re Ticehurst, The Times*, March 6, 1973.

[19] [1894] P. 151.

[20] *Per* Willmer J. in *Re R.* [1951] P. 10, 17.

[21] *In the Estate of Musgrove* [1927] P. 264.

[22] *Fulton v. Andrew* (1875) L.R. 7 H.L. 448, 463 and 472.

[23] [1959] 1 W.L.R. 284.

influence or fraud, the burden of proof remained on the solicitor who had propounded the will.[24]

The case came before Barnard J., sitting with a jury, which found in the solicitor's favour. The Colonel appealed. The Court of Appeal found against him, but only by a majority. Sellers L.J., dissenting, thought that the trial judge had misdirected the jury in relation to the burden of proof in a case where there were suspicious circumstances. The Colonel appealed to the House of Lords which decided, unanimously, that there had been a misdirection. As Viscount Simonds put it:[25]

"It is not the law that in no circumstances can a solicitor or other person who has prepared a will for a testator take a benefit under it. But that fact creates a suspicion that must be removed by the person propounding the will. In all cases the court must be vigilant and jealous. The degree of suspicion will vary with the circumstances of the case. It may be slight and easily dispelled.[26] It may, on the other hand, be so grave that it can hardly be removed. In the present case the circumstances were such as to impose on the respondent as heavy a burden as can well be imagined. Here was an elderly lady who might be called old, unversed in business, having no one upon whom to rely except the solicitor who had acted for her and her family; a will made by him under which he takes the bulk of her large estate; a will made, it is true, after a number of interviews extending over a considerable time, during which details of her property and of her proposed legacies and annuities were said to have been put before her, but in the end of a complexity which demanded for its comprehension no common understanding: on her part, a wish disclosed in January, 1937, to leave her residuary estate to charity which was by April superseded by a devise of it to him, and, on his part, an explanation of the change which was calculated as much to aggravate as to allay suspicion: the will retained by him and no copy of it given to her: no independent advice received by her, and, even according to his own account, little pressure exercised by him to persuade her to get it: a codicil cutting out reversionary legacies to charities allegedly for the benefit of annuitants but in fact, as was reasonably foreseeable, for the benefit of the residuary beneficiary. All these facts and others that I do not pause to enumerate demanded a vigilant and jealous scrutiny by the judge in his summing-up and by the jury in the consideration of their verdict."

One result of the publicity surrounding *Wintle v. Nye* was that the Law Society laid down new standards of professional conduct for solicitors who might take interests under wills which they had prepared.[27] The

---

[24] It was clear that Colonel Wintle took a dim view of the way in which the solicitor had behaved. He de-bagged him. But he did *not*, in the course of the proceedings, allege undue influence or fraud.

[25] [1959] 1 W.L.R. 284, 291.

[26] Parke B. in *Barry v. Butlin* (1838) 2 Moo. P.C. 480 at 485, gave as an example the case of a man of acknowledged business competence with an estate of £100,000, leaving all his property to his family except £50 to his solicitor who prepared the will.

[27] See *Cordery on Solicitors* (8th ed.) pp. 18–19 and *The Guide to the Professional Conduct of Solicitors* published by The Law Society (6th ed., 1993) para. 15.08.

stringency of these standards was shown in *Re A Solicitor*[28] where the Court of Appeal upheld the decision of the Disciplinary Committee of the Law Society in striking off the roll two solicitor-beneficiaries who had failed to advise their clients to obtain independent advice before making wills in the solicitors' favour.

Presumption where testator is dumb, blind or illiterate

If the testator could not speak or read and write and if he gave instructions for his will by signs, the court requires evidence as to the signs used, establishing that the testator understood and approved of the contents of his will.[29] Similarly, the knowledge and approval of a blind or illiterate testator must be proved, *e.g.* by evidence that the will was read over to him before execution.[30] The same rule applies if the will was signed by some person on the testator's behalf.[31]

B. MISTAKE

A testator's lack of knowledge and approval of the whole, or part, of the contents of a will which he executes may be due to his own inadvertence; or it may be due to a mistake on his part, or to a mistake on the part of the draftsman employed by him.

(1) *MISTAKE AS TO THE WHOLE WILL.* A testator does not know and approve of a will if he does not intend to execute it as his will. In *In the Goods of Hunt*[32] a lady, who resided with her sister, prepared two wills for their respective execution and by mistake she executed the will prepared for her sister. The court refused probate because the deceased did not know and approve of any part of the contents of the will which she had executed—"if she had known of the contents she would not have signed it."[33]

---

[28] [1975] 1 Q.B. 475. The Law Society now insists that a solicitor must renounce any significant benefit under a will unless the client *has taken* separate advice; it is not sufficient that the solicitor has advised the client to take separate advice.

[29] *In the Goods of Geale* (1864) 3 Sw.& Tr.431 (testator deaf and dumb and illiterate: detailed evidence as to signs by which testator communicated); *In the Goods of Ouston* (1862) 2 Sw. & Tr. 461 (testator deaf and dumb and illiterate); *In the Estate of Holtam* (1913) 108 L.T. 732 (testatrix unable to speak or write due to stroke).

[30] *Fincham v. Edwards* (1842) 3 Curt. 63, 4 Moo. P.C.198 (proof by other evidence than reading over suffices): see N.C. Prob. Rules 1987, r.13. The attestation clause for the witnesses in the will of a blind or illiterate testator should include a statement that the testator signed the will "after the same had first been read over to him in our presence and had appeared to be perfectly understood and approved by him in the presence of us both . . ."

[31] See N.C. Prob. Rules 1987, r.13. The attestation clause in a will signed by an amanuensis for the testator should include a statement similar to that appropriate to the will of a blind or illiterate testator.

[32] (1875) LR 3 P & D 250: see also *In the Estate of Meyer* [1908] P. 353 (lady executed codicil meant for her sister: probate refused). The Commonwealth courts take a different view, see Hardingham, *The Law of Wills* (1977), p. 64.

[33] (1875) LR 3 P & D 250, 252.

(2) *MISTAKE BY TESTATOR AS TO PART OF WILL.* If, by mistake, a testator includes words in his will, intending to have written other words, he does not know and approve of the words he included.[34] Again, if a testator inadvertently fails to delete a printed clause from a will form, he does not know and approve of the clause. This occurred in *Re Phelan*[35] where the testator executed a home-made will in favour of his landlady and her husband. He then conceived the notion that his three holdings in unit trusts had to be disposed of by separate wills and he executed three more wills in their favour, each will made on a will form at the same time and each disposing of a separate holding. Unfortunately, each will contained a printed revocation clause which the testator did not delete. Stirling J. said that "the Court . . . can omit words which have come in by inadvertence or by misunderstanding . . ."[36] He accordingly admitted all four wills to probate, but with the omission of the revocation clause in the three later wills.

(3) *MISTAKE BY DRAFTSMAN AS TO PART OF WILL.* If by a slip or a clerical error the draftsman inserts in the will words contrary to the testator's instructions, the testator does not know and approve of these words unless the discrepancy comes to his notice.[37] The same principle applies if by a slip or a clerical error the draftsman omits words from the will contrary to the testator's instructions, thereby altering the sense of other words in the will.[38] Again the same principle ought to apply if the draftsman misunderstands the testator's instructions and in consequence inserts in the will words contrary to his instructions.[39]

(4) *MISTAKE AS TO THE WORDS USED, NOT AS TO THEIR LEGAL EFFECT.* Whoever makes the mistake, whether it is the testator or the draftsman employed by him, it must relate to the words used in the will and not to their legal effect. If the testator knows and approves of the words used in his will, it does not matter that he or his draftsman is mistaken as to their legal effect; the words must be admitted to probate.[40] In *Collins v. Elstone*[41] the testatrix executed a will on a printed will form which a friend had obtained for her. The printed will form contained a

---

[34] See *In the Goods of Swords* [1952] P. 368 (mistake in codicil as to numbering of clauses in will).

[35] [1972] Fam. 33: the revocation clause formed part of each printed will form, see [1971] 3 All ER 1256: see also *In the Goods of Moore* [1892] P. 378. Cf. *Collins v. Elstone* [1893] P. 1.

[36] [1972] Fam. 33, 35.

[37] *In the Goods of Oswald* (1874) 3 P. & D. 162 (revocation clause included *per incuriam* without instructions); *Morrell v. Morrell* (1882) 7 P.D. 68 (T intended to give all his shares; counsel wrote "40" by mistake); *In the Goods of Boehm* [1891] P. 247 (T intended to give legacies to Georgiana and Florence; counsel wrote Georgiana twice and omitted Florence); *In the Goods of Walkeley* (1893) 69 L.T. 419 (error in house number in engrossing will from draft); *Smith v. Thompson* (1931) 47 T.L.R. 603; *Re Morris* [1971] P. 62 (mistake in codicil as to numbering of clause in will).

[38] *Re Reynette-James* [1976] 1 W.L.R. 161 (33 words omitted by typist in engrossing will).

[39] *Re Morris* [1971] P. 62, 79–81 (law not settled). The following appear to be cases of want of knowledge and approval where the draftsman misunderstood his instructions, *Morrell v. Morrell, supra*; *Brisco v. Baillie-Hamilton* [1902] P. 234: see also Hardingham, *The Law of Wills* (1977), pp. 55 *et seq.*

[40] In *In the Estate of Beech* [1923] P. 46, 53.

[41] [1893] P. 1.

clause which revoked all previous wills. The testatrix read this and asked her friend what it meant but was assured (incorrectly) that the effect of the clause would not be to revoke a previous will she had made. It was held that, given that she had executed the will knowing that the clause was in it, she was bound by the clause even though she misunderstood its effect. This was not a case of fraud; it was a misunderstanding. Furthermore, the testator is deemed to know and approve of technical language used by his draftsman if the testator adopts it as his own after the draftsman has deliberately chosen it: such language must be admitted to probate even though the draftsman was mistaken as to its legal effect.[42]

The testator cannot approve the words used in his will subject to a condition that they have the legal effect he desires: if he approves the words, it is immaterial that the condition is not satisfied.[43]

Powers of court to alter words

There are three limited powers to alter the words in a will:

(a) A court of probate can *omit* from the will words of which the testator did not know and approve.

(b) A court of equity can order *rectification* of the will, if the testator dies after December 31, 1982.

(c) A court of construction can *construe* the will as if certain words had been inserted, omitted or changed, if it is clear from the will itself both that an error has been made in the wording and what the substance of the intended wording was. This demanding requirement is considered later.[44]

(1) *OMISSION OF WORDS FROM PROBATE.* If a testator died before 1983, the court had no power, when admitting the will to probate, to *add* to it words intended by the testator.[45] In this respect the court was "enslaved" by the formalities required for a will by the Wills Act 1837.[46] A probate court had power only to *omit* from the will words of which the testator did not know and approve, leaving a blank space in the probate copy.

No problem was caused by omitting words of which the testator did not know and approve, provided their omission did not alter the sense of the rest of the will.[47] Thus the court would order the omission of a

---

[42] *Re Morris* [1971] P. 62, 79–81; *Re Horrocks* [1939] P. 198 (use of word "or", instead of "and", in gift of residue to "charitable or benevolent" objects was solicitor's deliberate choice under a mistake as to its legal effect and not typist's error).

[43] *In the Estate of Beech, supra.*

[44] *Post,* pp. 184–185.

[45] *Harter v. Harter* (1873) 3 P. & D. 11, 19; *Morrell v. Morrell* (1882) 7 P.D. 68; *In the Goods of Schott* (1901) P. 190 ("I can strike out words, but I cannot insert anything"); *Re Horrocks* [1939] P. 198, 216 (rule is "elementary"); *In the Goods of Swords* [1952] P. 368; *Re Morris* [1971] P. 62, 75 (rule can possibly be changed by appellate court); *Re Reynette-James* [1976] 1 W.L.R. 161, 166. *Cf. In the Goods of Bushell* (1887) 13 P.D. 7 and *In the Goods of Huddleston* (1890) 63 L.T. 255 (intended words added): but see *In the Goods of Schott, supra* (these decisions "heretical").

[46] *Re Reynette-James, supra:* see also *Harter v. Harter, supra; Re Horrocks, supra.*

[47] *Rhodes v. Rhodes* (1882) 7 App. Cas. 192, 198.

"self-contained" part of the will, such as a revocation clause[48] or the residuary gift in a will.[49] The court also omitted a house number from the devise of a dwelling-house[50] and the word "forty" from a bequest of "the forty ... shares ... in John Morrell & Co. Limited," so that all the testator's 400 shares passed under the bequest as he intended.[51] Again the court ordered the omission of the name of a legatee on whom a legacy was settled[52]; it was immaterial that the effect of this omission might be to render that clause in the will ambiguous or even meaningless.[53]

Sometimes the court had to choose the omission which most nearly gave effect to the testator's intentions. In *Re Morris*,[54] T, by clause 7 of her will, gave 20 pecuniary legacies numbered 7(i) to (xx). She wished to revoke the legacy in clause 7(iv). Owing to a slip by her solicitor she executed a codicil revoking clause 7 of the will but did not notice the discrepancy. She died in 1963. Latey J. held that the codicil should be admitted to probate with the omission of the numeral "7" because this omission got nearest to T's intentions: at that date the court had no power to *add* the missing number "(iv)" to the codicil, so as to give entire effect to T's intentions.

It was, however, held that, where the testator died before 1983, the court would not order the omission of words, of which the testator did not know and approve, if this would alter the sense of the rest of the will.[55]

(2) *RECTIFICATION OF WILL.* If the testator dies after December 31, 1982, section 20 of the Administration of Justice Act 1982 empowers the court to order that a will shall be rectified so as to carry out the testator's intentions.[56] Such an order may be made only if the court is satisfied that the will is so expressed that it fails to carry out the testator's intentions in consequence (i) of a clerical error or (ii) of a failure to understand the testator's instructions. A clerical error is an error of a clerical nature and not an error made only by a clerk; so a testator can make a clerical error in his home-made will.[57] If the court orders rectification under section 20, it may, of course, *add* to the will words intended by the testator.

---

[48] *In the Goods of Oswald* (1874) 3 P. & D. 162; *In the Goods of Moore* [1892] P. 378; *In the Goods of Swords* [1952] P. 368 (words revoking particular clauses in will); *Re Phelan* [1972] Fam. 33, see *ante*, p. 70; see also *Smith v. Thompson* (1931) 47 T.L.R. 603.

[49] *In the Goods of Duane* (1862) 2 Sw. & Tr. 590; *Fulton v. Andrew* (1875) 7 H.L. 448; *Wintle v. Nye* [1959] 1 W.L.R. 284.

[50] *In the Goods of Walkeley* (1893) 69 L.T. 419.

[51] *Morrell v. Morrell* (1882) 7 P.D. 68. See also *In the Goods of Schott* [1901] P. 190 (omission in residuary clause preserved the sense); *Brisco v. Baillie-Hamilton* [1902] P. 234.

[52] *In the Goods of Boehm* [1891] P. 247.

[53] *ibid.* at p. 251.

[54] [1971] P. 62; see also *Re Reynette-James* [1976] 1 W.L.R. 161; see Ryder (1976) 40 Conv. (N.S.) 312.

[55] *Re Horrocks* [1939] P. 198; *Rhodes v. Rhodes* (1882) 7 App.Cas. 192, 198. For cogent criticism of the latter part of the judgment in *Re Horrocks* (on assumption "or" was inserted by a typist's error) see Hardingham, *op. cit.* pp. 65–67; W.A. Lee (1969) 33 Conv.(N.S.) 322, 329–334.

[56] Administration of Justice Act 1982, ss. 73(6) and 76(11); see N.C. Prob. Rules 1987, r. 55; R.S.C. Ord. 76, r. 16. In the High Court rectification is assigned to the Chancery Division, Supreme Court Act 1981, s. 61(1) and Sched. I.

[57] *Re Williams* [1985] 1 W.L.R. 905, 912.

The recent case of *Wordingham* v *Royal Exchange Trust Co Ltd*[58] is a good example of the operation of the section. The testatrix's solicitor was instructed by her to draft a will which was to be based on an earlier will, but was to contain some alterations. He failed to include a clause which had been included in the earlier will and which he should have included. This was an error made in recording the intended words of the testatrix (she intended the clause to be included in her will) and *was* a clerical error. Had the testatrix died before 1983, her will could not have been rectified to include the clause, but under section 20, the clause could be inserted.

If, on the other hand, the will fails to carry out the testator's intentions in consequence of some other cause (for instance, the draftsman understood his instructions but deliberately omitted an intended legacy), section 20 does not apply. In such a situation the court has power only to *omit* words, of which the testator did not know and approve, from the probate copy of the will; in this respect the power is narrower than the remedy of rectification applicable to other documents.[59]

An application for rectification must not be made later than six months from the date on which a grant of probate or letters of administration to the deceased's estate[60] is first taken out; the court has, however, an unfettered discretion to extend this time limit.[61] The purpose of this short time limit is to enable the personal representatives safely to distribute the estate to the beneficiaries entitled under the unrectified will as soon as six months have passed without any application having been made.[62]

Of course, neither the power to rectify nor the power to omit provides any remedy for (i) the testator's failure to appreciate the legal effect of the words used in his will, or (ii) uncertainty as to the meaning of his intended wording,[63] or (iii) a lacuna in the will, because he never had any intention relevant to the events which actually occurred.

IV. UNDUE INFLUENCE AND FRAUD

A will must not be made as a result of either the undue influence or the fraud of another person.[1]

---

[58] [1992] Ch. 412. *Re Segelman* [1995] 3 All E.R. 676 is a case where the section was used to effect a deletion.

[59] See Law Reform Committee's 19th Report, *Interpretation of Wills*, Cmnd. 5301 (1973), pp. 5–13 and particularly the recommendation at p. 23.

[60] *Post*, p. 320 *et seq*.

[61] Administration of Justice Act 1982, s. 20(2). A grant limited to settled land or trust property is disregarded and so is a grant limited to real or personal estate unless a grant limited to the remainder of estate has previously been made or is made at the same time, see s. 20(4): see *post*, p. 320/pp. 124–125.

[62] For protection of the personal representatives in case the time limit is extended see *ibid.*, s. 20(3).

[63] This is a question of construction; see Chap. 8.

[1] Undue influence and fraud are separate pleas—see *Parfitt v. Lawless* (1872) L.R. 2 P. & D. 462, 470 and 471; *White v. White* (1862) 2 Sw. & Tr. 504, and R.S.C., Ord. 18, rr. 8(1) and 12(1). So is a plea of want of knowledge and approval, *Re Stott* [1980] 1 W.L.R. 246.

1. Undue influence

In a court of probate undue influence means coercion,[2] *i.e.* the testator is coerced into making a will (or part of a will) which he does not want to make.[3] Undue influence may take many forms. At one extreme there may be force, *i.e.* actual violence to the testator. At the other extreme the pressure exerted by talking insistently to a weak and feeble testator in the last days of his life may so fatigue his brain that he may be induced, for quietness' sake, to give way to the pressure.[4]

Whatever form undue influence takes, the test is always whether the testator was coerced.

> "Persuasion, appeals to the affections or ties of kindred, to a sentiment of gratitude for past services, or pity for future destitution, or the like,—these are all legitimate, and may be fairly pressed on a testator. On the other hand, pressure of whatever character, whether acting on the fears or the hopes, if so exerted as to overpower the volition without convincing the judgment, is a species of restraint under which no valid will can be made ... In a word, a testator may be led but not driven; and his will must be the offspring of his own volition, and not the record of someone else's."[5]

An immoral influence exercised over the testator by another person does not constitute undue influence in the absence of coercion. A man's mistress may make use of her unbounded influence to induce him to make a will in her favour to the exclusion of his wife and children but in the absence of coercion this does not constitute undue influence.[6] To quote Sir James Hannen in his charge to the jury in *Wingrove v. Wingrove*,[7] "It is only when ... a testator is coerced into doing that which he or she does not desire to do, that it is undue influence."

2. Fraud

Fraud intentionally misleads a testator whereas undue influence coerces him. A very plain instance of fraud is a false representation concerning a person's character or conduct, made to the testator for the purpose of inducing him to revoke a gift made to that person in his existing will.[8]

3. Burden of proof

The legal burden of proof of both undue influence and fraud always lies on the person alleging it.[9]

---

[2] *Per* Hannen P. in *Wingrove v. Wingrove* (1885) 11 P.D. 81, 82.

[3] *Hall v. Hall* (1868) L.R. 1 P. & D. 481, 482.

[4] *Per* Hannen P. in *Wingrove v. Wingrove, supra,* at pp. 82–83; *Lamkin v. Babb* (1752) 1 Lee 1 (wife's pressure).

[5] *Per* Lord Penzance in *Hall v. Hall, supra,* at p. 482.

[6] Though the excluded wife and children may apply for provision to be made for them under the Family Provision legislation. See Chap. 6.

[7] (1885) 11 P.D. 81, 82.

[8] *Per* Lord Lyndhurst in *Allen v. M'Pherson* (1847) 1 H.L.C. 191, 207: see also *In the Estate of Posner* [1953] P. 277 (gift by will to my wife X void if X procured the gift by fraudulently misrepresenting herself as his wife).

[9] *Boyse v. Rossborough* (1857) 6 H.L.C. 2, 49; *Craig v. Lamoureux* [1920] A.C. 349.

In equity, a rebuttable presumption of undue influence arises where a donee stands in a confidential relationship to a donor, *e.g.* a father benefiting from a gift by his child or a solicitor from his client.[10] This rebuttable presumption applies to *inter vivos* transactions but is not applicable to the making of a will.[11] Thus in *Parfitt v. Lawless*[12] no presumption of undue influence arose where a testatrix made a will leaving her residuary estate to a Roman Catholic priest who was her domestic chaplain and confessor.

4. Consequences of undue influence or fraud

A will made by a testator as a result of the undue influence or fraud of another person is invalid. If only part of the will was made as a result of undue influence or fraud, that part may be rejected and the remainder admitted to probate.[13] On the other hand, where a beneficiary under the will of a testator prevents him by undue influence or fraud from altering the will, or making a new will, in favour of other persons, probably the court will impose a trust on the beneficiary for those other persons.[14] In that situation an equitable remedy is needed because no remedy is available in a court of probate.

---

[10] See *Snell's Equity* (29th ed., 1990) pp. 551 *et seq.*
[11] There may be no presumption of *undue influence* by solicitors, *but* a solicitor who takes a benefit under a will he has prepared for a client may be guilty of professional misconduct; see *ante* p. 68 n. 27 and p. 69 n. 28.
[12] (1872) L.R. 2 P. & D. 462: see also (1970) 86 L.Q.R. 447.
[13] *Allen v. M'Pherson* (1847) 1 H.L.C. 191, 209; *In the Goods of Boehm* [1891] P. 247, 251 (*obiter* as to effect of fraud on part of a will).
[14] *Betts v. Doughty* (1879) 5 P.D. 26; *Allen v. M'Pherson, supra,* at p. 214.

CHAPTER 4

FORMALITIES

I. FORMAL WILLS

A. INTRODUCTION

The formalities prescribed for making a will provide some sort of safe-guard not only against forgery and undue influence but also against hasty or ill-considered dispositions[1]: the formalities emphasise the importance of the act of making a will and serve as a check against inconsiderate action. In general, formalities can be justified by the need to provide reliable evidence of a person's testamentary intentions, which may have been expressed many years before his death.

Before the coming into force of Section 9 of the Wills Act 1837, there were different formalities for wills relating to different sorts of property. For example, the formalities required for a will intended to devise free-holds were different from the formalities required for a will intended to bequeath leaseholds. There "were ten different laws for regulating the execution of wills under different circumstances".[2]

It was, therefore, quite possible that a pre-1838 will would be held invalid in relation to one type of property while it was valid in relation to other property. The idea behind the enactment of section 9 was that all wills should be executed according to one form which could be easily and generally understood.[3]

The original section 9, first enacted in 1837,[4] was amended by the Wills Act Amendment Act 1852.[5] Section 17 of the Administration of Justice

---

[1] Law Reform Committee's 22nd Report, *The making and revocation of wills*, Cmnd. 7902 (1980), p. 3.

[2] See the Fourth Report of the Real Property Commissioners (1833) p. 12 and Holdsworth, *A History of English Law* Vol XV p. 172.

[3] The recommendations contained in the Fourth Report of the Real Property Commissioners (1833) led to the enactment of section 9 of the Wills Act 1837.

[4] As originally enacted, section 9 of the Wills Act read: "And be it further enacted, That no will shall be valid unless it shall be in Writing and executed in manner hereinafter mentioned; (that is to say,) it shall be signed at the Foot or End thereof by the Testator, or by some other Person in his Presence and by his Direction; and such Signature shall be made or acknowledged by the Testator in the Presence of Two or more Witnesses present at the same Time, and such Witnesses shall attest and shall subscribe the Will in the presence of the Testator, but no Form of Attestation shall be necessary."

[5] Otherwise known as *Lord St. Leonards' Act*. The original section 9, as amended in 1852, applies to any testator who died before January 1, 1983.

Act 1982 then substituted a new section 9. But the change from the original section 9 to the substituted section was more a change of form than of substance. The similarities of substance (between the original section and the substituted section) are much more marked than the differences.

If a testator dies after December 31, 1982, the substituted section 9 provides that:

"No will[6] shall be valid unless—
  (a) it is in writing, and signed by the testator, or by some other person in his presence and by his direction; and
  (b) it appears that the testator intended by his signature to give effect to the will; and
  (c) the signature is made or acknowledged by the testator in the presence of two or more witnesses present at the same time; and
  (d) each witness either—
    (i) attests and signs the will; or
    (ii) acknowledges his signature, in the presence of the testator (but not necessarily in the presence of any other witness), but no form of attestation shall be necessary."

Section 9 applies to all wills required to be executed in accordance with English internal law,[7] except wills of privileged testators and "statutory" wills of mentally disordered patients.[8]

The court has no power to admit to probate an authentic will which is invalid under section 9.[9]

B.   REQUIREMENTS OF SECTION 9

Section 9 has five requirements:

1.   The will must be in writing

Under section 9 a will must be in writing but there are no restrictions as to the materials[10] on which, or by which, it may be written, or as to what language[11] may be used. It may be handwritten or typed and a

---

[6] "Will" includes a testament, a codicil, an appointment by will or by writing in the nature of a will in exercise of a power, and any other testamentary disposition; Wills Act 1837, s. 1. A nomination under a pension scheme is not a testamentary disposition, *Re Danish Bacon Co. Staff Pension Fund Trusts, ante* p. 21.

[7] For the rules of private international law governing the formal validity of wills see Dicey and Morris, *The Conflict of Laws* (12th ed., 1993), pp. 1028 *et seq.; Theobald on Wills* (15th ed., 1993), Chap. 1. For the Convention on International Wills see ss. 27, 28 and 76(5) and (6) of the Administration of Justice Act 1982–ss. 27 and 28 are *not* yet in force.

[8] For privileged testators see *post*, p. 87. Statutory wills are covered by section 97 of the Mental Health Act 1983; see *ante* pp. 62 *et seq.*

[9] See Law Reform Committee's 22nd Report, *The making and revocation of wills*, Cmnd. 7902 (1980), pp. 3–4: for reform see *post* pp. 85 *et seq.*

[10] *Hodson v. Barnes* (1926) 43 T.L.R. 71 (writing on empty egg shell).

[11] *Whiting v. Turner* (1903) 89 L.T. 71 (will written in French language); *Kell v. Charmer* (1856) 23 Beav. 195 (sums bequeathed represented in letters using jeweller's private code).

printed form[12] may be used; many "home-made" wills are made by filling up the spaces on printed will forms in the testator's handwriting. No particular form of words needs to be used: "all for mother" has been held to be a valid will.[13]

A will may be made in pencil or in ink or in a combination of the two, but there is a presumption that the pencil writing in such a combination was only deliberative and it will be excluded from probate unless the court decides that it represented the testator's definite intention.[14]

2. The will must be signed

(1) *METHODS OF SIGNATURE BY THE TESTATOR.* Instead of signing his name[15] the testator may sign by marking the will in some way intended by him as his signature. Thus initials,[16] a stamped signature,[17] or a mark such as a cross, or an inked thumb mark,[18] or a mark of any shape,[19] are all sufficient if intended by him as his signature. A mark suffices even though the testator's hand was guided by another person[20] and it is immaterial whether the testator could write or not. A mark is a useful method of signature for illiterates and those suffering from severe physical disability, although it is desirable for the attestation clause to state that the testator signed with his mark.[21]

In *In the Goods of Chalcraft*[22] the testatrix was dying and signed a codicil "E. Chal" but was unable to complete her signature: this was held to be a sufficient signature on the ground that what she wrote was intended by her to be the best that she could do by way of writing her name. In another case[23] the will began "I, Emma Cook" and the testatrix wrote the words "Your loving mother" at the end: the court admitted the will to probate, being satisfied that the testatrix meant the words "Your loving mother" to represent her name.

(2) *SIGNATURE ON THE TESTATOR'S BEHALF.* The will may be signed by some other person in the testator's presence and by his direction. The person signing may be one of the attesting witnesses[24] and he may sign his own name instead of that of the testator.[25]

---

[12] Interpretation Act 1978, s. 5 and Sched. 1.
[13] *Thorn v. Dickens* [1906] W.N. 54 ("probably the shortest will ever known").
[14] *In the Goods of Adams* (1872) L.R. 2 P. & D. 367.
[15] Signing in an assumed name suffices: *In the Goods of Redding* (1850) 2 Rob. Ecc. 339.
[16] *In the Goods of Savory* (1851) 15 Jur. 1042.
[17] *In the Goods of Jenkins* (1863) 3 Sw. & Tr. 93.
[18] *In the Estate of Finn* (1935) 105 L.J.P. 36 ("merely a blot" as his thumb slipped and the mark smudged).
[19] *In the Estate of Holtam* (1913) 108 L.T 732 ("a sort of broken line"); *In the Goods of Kieran* [1933] I.R. 222. A seal intended as his signature probably suffices, *In the Estate of Bulloch* [1968] N.I. 96, 99.
[20] *Wilson v. Beddard* (1841) 12 Sim. 28.
[21] To make it clear that the mark is intended by the testator to be his signature.
[22] [1948] P. 222; *cf. Re Colling* [1972] 1 W.L.R. 1440.
[23] *In the Estate of Cook* [1960] 1 W.L.R. 353.
[24] *Smith v. Harris* (1845) 1 Rob. Ecc. 262.
[25] *In the Goods of Clark* (1839) 2 Curt. 329. If someone signs on the testator's behalf, the attestation clause should record this.

(3) *CONNECTION OF SIGNATURE WITH PAGES OF WILL*. If a will is written on more than one page, of which only the last is duly executed, all the pages ought to be attached in some way at the time of execution so as to constitute a single testamentary document. In order to reduce the risk of fraud or accidental loss it is desirable that the pages should be securely attached—for instance, sewn together with lawyers' green tape. It suffices, however, if at the time of execution the pages are held together by the testator's finger and thumb[26] or pressed together on a table by the testator with his hand.[27] Moreover, the Irish courts have even suggested that it suffices if at the time of execution the pages, though not touching, are all in the same room and under the control of the testator.[28]

(4) *POSITION OF SIGNATURE*. The original section 9 required that the testator's signature had to be "at the foot or end" of the will. The courts interpreted this strictly.[29] The Wills Act Amendment Act 1852[30] attempted to undo the effects of this strict interpretation by setting out an exhaustive—if verbose—definition of the meaning of "at the foot or end". Essentially, the 1852 Act provided that it did not matter if there was a blank space between the end of the will and the signature; and it did not matter that the signature was placed on a page on which no part of the will was written: but, (under the 1837 Act as amended in 1852) the signature could never operate to give effect to any part of the will which was underneath it or which followed it. The provisions of the 1852 Act were applied with reasonable leniency—although the attitude of the courts seemed sometimes to vary.[31]

The significant change made by the Administration of Justice Act 1982 related to the position of the signature. The substituted section 9 (applicable to a death on or after January 1, 1983) does not require the signature to be at the foot or end of the will. The change was illustrated by the recent case of *Wood v. Smith*[32] where the testator made a holograph will[33] which began with the words "My will by Percy Winterbone . . ." but did not sign the will anywhere else. The Court of Appeal, upholding the trial judge,[34] held that when the testator wrote his name at the head of the document, this was his signature; once this was established, there could be no problem about its position.[35]

---

[26] *Lewis v. Lewis* [1908] p. 1.

[27] *In the Estate of Little* [1960] 1 W.L.R. 495.

[28] *In the Goods of Tiernan* [1942] I.R. 572; *Sterling v. Bruce* [1973] N.I. 225.

[29] *e.g. Smee v. Bryer* (1848) 1 Rob. Ecc. 616 (will held invalid because the signature of the testatrix was not placed in eight-tenths of an inch left blank at the bottom of a page but on the next page).

[30] Otherwise known as *Lord St. Leonards' Act*. The original section 9, as amended in 1852, applies to any testator who died before January 1, 1983.

[31] It was probably not possible to reconcile all the cases, but this is now of largely historical interest. For further details of the pre-1983 postion, see the 9th (1988) edition of this book pp. 32 and 33.

[32] [1993] Ch. 90.

[33] A holograph will is a will in the testator's handwriting.

[34] Mr David Gilliland Q.C. (sitting as a deputy judge of the High Court).

[35] See also *Weatherhill v. Pearce*, [1995] 1 W.L.R. 592.

3. The testator must intend by his signature to give effect to the will

Under the substituted section 9 a will is invalid unless "it appears that the testator intended by his signature to give effect to the will."

The original section 9[36] did not expressly state that the signature had to have been written with intention to give effect to the will; but the requirement was implied.[37]

The substituted section 9 states that it must *appear* that the testator intended by his signature to give effect to the will; but it does not *require* the intention to appear *from the will*. It often appears presumptively from an attestation clause that a testator intended by his signature to give effect to the will, but such a clause is neither necessary nor conclusive.

Before 1983, it was possible to call extrinsic evidence[38] as to the words and actions of the testator in order to ascertain what he intended by his signature. It is still possible to call such evidence in relation to *post* 1982 deaths and this is again illustrated by *Wood v. Smith*,[39] the case where the testator began his holograph will with the words "My Will by Percy Winterbone . . ." but did not sign it again. Once it was established that the words "Percy Winterbone" *were* a signature, there could be no probem about the signature's position because the testator died after 1982. But two questions remained. Could the signature give effect to the words of the will (the dispositive contents) which were written after it in time? And; could extrinsic evidence be admitted as to whether the testator had intended by his signature to give effect to the will? The trial judge admitted evidence from the witnesses[40] that the testator had told them that by writing his name he intended to give testamentary effect to the document he was writing. On the basis of this evidence, the Court of Appeal held that the testator's signature could give effect to dispositive provisions written after it, provided that the signing and the writing of the will were "all one operation."[41]

The test of "all one operation" was itself derived from the slightly earlier case of *Re White*[42] where the testator made a will in 1981 and altered it in 1984. He did not sign or initial the alterations, but they were initialled by witnesses. It was suggested on behalf of those who would benefit from the 1984 alterations in *Re White* that the testator's 1981 signature could give effect to the 1984 alterations, as though the altered (1984)

---

[36] As amended by Lord St Leonards' Act.
[37] *In the Estate of Bean* [1944] P. 83: see also *Re Beadle* [1974] 1 W.L.R. 417: but contrast *In the Goods of Mann* [1942] P. 146.
[38] *Extrinsic evidence* is evidence not contained in the will itself.
[39] [1993] Ch. 90 *ante* p. 79.
[40] This was, of course, extrinsic evidence; it was not contained in the will itself.
[41] There was no problem as to the admissibility of the extrinsic evidence. The Court of Appeal overruled the trial judge in deciding that the testator's signature *did* give effect to words which were written after it. The idea of "all one operation" appears to come originally from Andrew Park Q.C.'s judgment in *Re White, infra*, it may well cause problems in the future. In any case, probate of the will in *Wood v. Smith* was refused (trial judge affirmed) because the testator lacked capacity; see *ante* p. 59.
[42] [1991] Ch 1.

will was a newly executed will. This was not accepted.[43] In this case the signature and the writing of the alterations were clearly not all one operation.[44]

4. The testator's signature must be made or acknowledged in the presence of witnesses

The signature of the testator must either be made or acknowledged by the testator in the presence of two witnesses present at the same time.
This requirement has not changed since 1837.

(1) *SIGNATURE MADE IN THEIR PRESENCE.* The witnesses need not know that the document is a will.[45] It is sufficient that the witnesses see the testator in the act of writing his signature, although they never see the signature and do not know what he is writing.[46] But if a witness, although present in the same room, is not aware that the testator is writing, this does not suffice.[47] Furthermore, if a witness leaves before the testator completes his intended signature, this does not suffice.[48]

(2) *SIGNATURE ACKNOWLEDGED IN THEIR PRESENCE.* If the signature on the will was not made in the simultaneous presence of two witnesses, the signature must subsequently be acknowledged by the testator in their simultaneous presence. There are three requisites for a valid acknowledgment:

(i) The will must already have been signed before acknowledgment.
(ii) At the time of acknowledgment the witnesses must see the signature or have the opportunity of seeing it. If at that time the signature is covered by the folding of the will,[49] or with blotting paper,[50] there can be no valid acknowledgment: it does not suffice that the testator would have uncovered the signature and allowed the witnesses to see it had he been asked.[51]
(iii) The testator must acknowledge the signature by his words or conduct.

An express acknowledgment by the testator is desirable[52] but not essential; no particular form of words is required. The testator may acknowledge his signature by gestures.[53] Indeed it is sufficient that he (or someone in his presence and on his behalf) simply requests the witnesses to sign the document before them, without telling them that

[43] By Andrew Park Q.C. sitting as a deputy judge of the High Court.
[44] See *post* p. 113. *Wood v. Smith* and *Re White* are easily reconciled, though the Court of Appeal in *Wood v. Smith* expressed reservations about *obiter dicta* in *Re White*.
[45] *In the Estate of Benjamin* (1934) 150 L.T. 417.
[46] *Smith v. Smith* (1866) L.R. 1 P. & D. 143.
[47] *Brown v. Skirrow* [1902] P. 3.
[48] *Re Colling* [1972] 1 W.L.R. 1440 *post*, p. 84.
[49] *Hudson v. Parker* (1844) 1 Rob. Ecc.
[50] *In the Goods of Gunstan* (1882) 7 P.D. 102.
[51] *Re Groffman*, [1969] 1 W.L.R. 733, *post*, p. 86.
[52] By saying "this is my signature" or words to that effect.
[53] *In the Goods of Davies* (1850) 2 Rob. Ecc. 337.

it is his will.[54] As Cotton L.J. summed up the position in *Daintree v. Butcher*[55]:

"When the paper bearing the signature of the testatrix was put before two persons who were asked by her or in her presence to sign as witnesses that was an acknowledgment of the signature by her. The signature being so placed that they could see it, whether they actually did see it or not, she was in fact asking them to attest that signature as hers."

(3) *WHO CAN BE WITNESSES*. A blind person is incapable of being a witness to a will because it cannot be signed in his "presence" and he cannot be a "witness" to a visible act such as signing for the purposes of section 9.[56] Moreover the requirement that the signature shall be made or acknowledged in the "presence" of two witnesses needs their mental as well as their bodily presence. As Dr. Lushington put it in *Hudson v. Parker*[57]:

"What could possibly be the object of the Legislature, except that the witnesses should see and be conscious of the act done, and be able to prove it by their own evidence: if the witnesses are not to be mentally, as well as bodily, present, they might be asleep, or intoxicated, or of unsound mind."

Obviously it is desirable to choose literate witnesses of sound mental capacity and of fixed residence, in case they may later be required to give evidence as to the validity of the will.

The Wills Act 1837 contains other provisions which are relevant to who can be witnesses. Section 15 deprives a witness and his or her spouse of any benefit under the will[58] but allows such a witness to give evidence as to whether or not the will is valid. Thus a beneficiary under a will, or the spouse of a beneficiary, is technically a good attesting witness. Similarly section 16 allows a creditor (whose debt is charged on any property by the will) or his or her spouse to be a witness, and section 17 specifically states that the executor of a will is competent to witness its execution.

5. The witnesses must sign or acknowledge

(1) *PRESENCE OF THE TESTATOR*. The witnesses need not sign in one another's presence.[59] But each witness must sign (or acknowledge

---

[54] *Daintree v. Butcher* (1888) 13 P.D. 102: see also *Gaze v. Gaze* (1843) 3 Curt. 451. But if the testator is acknowledging a signature made by another person on his behalf, it appears not to be sufficient for someone in his presence and at his request to ask witnesses to sign whilst the testator remains passive, *In the Goods of Summers* (1850) 2 Rob. Ecc. 295.

[55] (1888) 13 P.D. 102, 103.

[56] *In the Estate of Gibson* [1949] p. 434; however at pp. 437 and 440 Pearce J. left open the possibility that "in peculiar circumstances" a blind man can be a witness to a will: perhaps a blind person can witness a will written and signed in braille if the testator acknowledges his signature, see (1949) 23 A.L.J. 360.

[57] (1844) 1 Rob.Ecc. 14, 24.

[58] *Post*, p. 232.

[59] This has been the rule since 1837; it is *not* a 1982 change.

his signature, if the testator dies after 1982) ''in the presence of the testator.'' The testator must be mentally, as well as physically, present: if the testator becomes insensible before both witnesses have done this, the will is invalid.[60] If a witness signs, the testator must either see the witness sign, or have the opportunity of doing so if he had chosen to look[61] or had not been blind.[62]

(2)   METHODS OF SIGNATURE BY WITNESSES. Instead of signing his name, a witness may sign by marking the will in some way intended by him as his signature.[63] The words ''Servant to Mr. Sperling'' have been held a sufficient signature by a witness, being intended as an identification of himself as the person attesting.[64] The witness must himself sign,[65] although his hand may be guided by another witness or a third person.

(3)   POSITION OF SIGNATURES OF WITNESSES. The position upon the will of the signatures of the witnesses is immaterial provided they intend by their signatures to attest[66] the testator's operative signature.[67] But their signatures, if not on the same sheet of paper as the will, must be on a sheet of paper physically connected with it.[68] If the testator signs the will and the witnesses sign a duplicate, the will is invalid.[69]

(4)   ATTESTATION AND SUBSCRIPTION (DEATH BEFORE 1983). The original section 9 required the witnesses to *attest, i.e.* bear witness that the signature had been made or acknowledged by the testator in their simultaneous presence,[70] and to *subscribe* the will, *i.e.* sign it at the foot or end. Thus the witnesses had to intend by their signatures to attest the due execution of the will by the testator. If a person signed without any intention to attest, his signature was excluded from probate.[71] The witnesses had to attest the testator's operative signature. If the testator signed his will both at the top and at the bottom, and the witnesses saw

---

[60] *Right v. Price* (1779) 1 Doug. 241; *In the Goods of Chalcraft* [1948] P. 222.
[61] *Casson v. Dade* (1781) 1 Bro.C.C. 99 (testatrix in her carriage able to see witnesses signing in attorney's office through the windows); *Tribe v. Tribe* (1849) 1 Rob.Ecc. 775 (testatrix unable to turn herself in bed to see witnesses sign; will held invalid); *Newton v. Clarke* (1839) 2 Curt. 320.
[62] *In the Goods of Piercy* (1845) 1 Rob.Ecc. 278. A blind testator's ''presence'' is different from a blind witness's ''presence,'' see *In the Estate of Gibson* [1949] P. 434 *ante*, p. 82.
[63] *In the Goods of Ashmore* (1843) 3 Curt. 756; *In the Estate of Bulloch* [1968] N.I. 96 (rubber stamp). A seal is insufficient unless intended as his signature, *In the Estate of Bulloch, supra.*
[64] *In the Goods of Sperling* (1863) 3 Sw. & Tr. 272.
[65] *In the Estate of Bulloch, supra.*
[66] For the meaning of ''attest'' see *infra.*
[67] *In the Goods of Braddock* (1876) 1 P.D. 433; *In the Goods of Streatley* [1891] P. 172; *In the Estate of Denning* [1958] 1 W.L.R. 462 (*post*, p. 355). A witness who acknowledges his signature under the substituted s. 9 is not required to attest.
[68] *In the Goods of Braddock, supra* (witnesses to codicil signed on back of will to which codicil was pinned: codicil held valid).
[69] *In the Goods of Hatton* (1881) 6 P.D. 204.
[70] *Hudson v. Parker* (1844) 1 Rob. Ecc. 14 at p. 26.
[71] *In the Goods of Sharman* (1869) L.R. 1 P. & D. 661 (three signatures, two attesting and the third as residuary legatee: the third was excluded from probate).

the top signature but not the bottom signature which was covered by blotting paper, the will was invalid.[72]

The original section 9 set out the required order of events. Before either witness signed, the testator had first to make or acknowledge his signature in their simultaneous presence. If that was not done, the will was invalid.[73] In *Re Colling*[74] the testator, who was in hospital, started to sign his will in the presence of a nurse and of another patient as witnesses. Before he had completed his intended signature, the nurse was called away to attend to another patient. During her absence the testator completed his signature and the other witness signed. When the nurse returned, both the testator and the other witness acknowledged their signatures and the nurse signed the will. The will was held invalid because the testator neither made nor acknowledged his signature in the presence of both witnesses before both signed it. If, after the testator acknowledged his signature in the presence of both of them, the other witness had signed the will again, it would have been valid.

(5) *ATTESTATION AND SIGNATURE, OR ACKNOWLEDGEMENT (DEATH AFTER 1982).* The substituted section 9 requires each witness either (i) to attest and sign the will or (ii) to acknowledge[75] his signature. This amendment to section 9 reverses the effect of *Re Colling*. After 1982 one or both witnesses may sign the will, the testator may then make or acknowledge his signature in their simultaneous presence and each witness may then attest or sign the will, or acknowledge his previous signature, in the presence of the testator. The will is then valid. There is still a required order of events under the substituted section 9, but the amendment means that an acknowledgement by a witness of his previous signature has the same effect as his actual signature. It is a relatively minor change and it is unlikely that there will be many cases like *Re Colling* which will be affected by it.

6. Attestation clause

Section 9 provides that no form of attestation is necessary. Nevertheless an attestation clause[76] is highly desirable because it facilitates the grant of probate.

    (i) In the absence of an attestation clause, a district judge or registrar must, before granting probate in common form, require the due execution of the will to be established by affidavit evidence.[77]

---

[72] *In the Estate of Bercovitz* [1962] 1 W.L.R. 321; *Re Beadle* [1974] 1 W.L.R. 417. Note that in post 1982 cases the operative signature need not be at the foot or end of the will.

[73] *Wyatt v. Berry* [1893] P. 5: see also *Hindmarsh v. Charlton* (1861) 8 H.L.C. 160; *In the Estate of Davies* [1951] 1 All E.R. 920.

[74] [1972] 1 W.L.R. 1440.

[75] For the nature of an acknowledgement see *ante*, p. 81.

[76] An example reads, "Signed by the said X in our joint presence and then by us in his." Other forms of attestation clause are available for illiterate or blind testators and for wills signed by an amanuensis for the testator, see *ante*, p. 69, nn. 30 and 31.

[77] N.C. Prob. Rules 1987, r. 12: r. 12 does not apply to wills of privileged testators (r. 17): for probate in common form see *post*, p. 326 and for an affidavit of due execution see *post*, p. 354.

(ii) An attestation clause raises a stronger presumption that the will was duly executed than if no such clause was present.[78] Moreover this presumption *omnia praesumuntur rite ac solemniter esse acta* applies with more force in the case of a formal than an informal attestation clause.[79] The presumption becomes important in cases where, for example, witnesses are dead or cannot be traced or where the memory of witnesses is defective.

C. REFORM OF THE FORMALITIES RULES[80]

Unfortunately some authentic wills, which unquestionably represent the true intention of the testator, fail for non-compliance with the prescribed formalities. The number of wills which are submitted to probate and rejected for non-compliance with these formalities is relatively small; most of them are home-made wills.[81] However, as a result of legal advice, most defectively executed wills are never submitted to probate so there are no reliable statistics to indicate the true extent of the problem.[82]

The Law Reform Committee in their Twenty-second Report[83] considered two proposals for legislative reform:

(1) *CONFER DISPENSING POWER ON COURT.* The first proposal was to confer on the court a dispensing power to admit a will to probate if the court were satisfied that, notwithstanding its defective execution, it was genuine. Such a dispensing power has been given to the courts of South Australia where a judge must be satisfied "that there can be no reasonable doubt that the deceased intended the document to constitute his will"[84]: this requirement imposes a high standard of proof; but the minimum formality for the exercise by the court of its dispensing power is simply an unsigned document.[85] In Queensland the minimum formality for the exercise of the dispensing power is stricter: the document must have been executed in "substantial compliance" with the prescribed formalities.[86]

The Law Reform Committee rejected the proposal that there should be a dispensing power on the ground that such a power might create

---

[78] *Post,* p. 355.

[79] *Vinnicombe v. Butler* (1864) 3 Sw. & Tr. 580.

[80] See generally Miller (1987) I.C.L.Q. 559; Miller, *The Machinery of Succession* (1977), pp. 147 *et seq.*: Langbein (1975) 88 Harv.L.R. 489; Davey [1980] Conv. 64 and 101.

[81] In a three-month survey by the Family Division Principal Registry in 1978, 40, 664 wills were admitted to proof and 97 wills were rejected, 93 of them for non-compliance with the s. 9 formalities; of the 97 rejected wills, 91 were home-made and six professionally drawn, see Law Reform Committee's 22nd Report, p. 31.

[82] See memorandum submitted to Law Reform Committee in May 1978 on behalf of the Law Society, p. 5.

[83] Law Reform Committee's 22nd Report, *The making and revocation of wills,* Cmnd. 7902 (1980).

[84] Wills Act Amendment Act (No. 2) 1975, s. 9 inserting a new s. 12 in the Wills Act 1936–1975 (S.A.).

[85] *In the Estate of Williams* (1984) 36 S.A.S.R. 423: see Miller (1987) I.C.L.Q. 559 at pp. 567–573.

[86] Queensland Succession Act 1981, s. 9: see Miller, *loc. cit.,* at pp. 566–567.

more problems than it would solve. The Committee considered that, by making it less certain whether a defectively executed will was capable of being admitted to probate, such a power could lead to litigation, expense and delay and this burden would tend to fall on small estates disposed of by home-made wills.[87]

(2) *RELAX FORMALITIES RULES.* The second proposal was to relax the formalities prescribed by section 9.

This was the proposal favoured by the Law Reform Committee which recommended the two changes which were, in substance, enacted by the Administration of Justice Act 1982. The Committee recommended that:

(i) A will should be admitted to probate if it was apparent "on its face" that the testator intended his signature to validate it, regardless of where on the will the signature was placed.[88] The amendment made in 1982 (by substituting the new version of section 9) differs very slightly from the Law Reform Committee's recommendation, in that it does not require the testator's intention to appear on the face of the will.

(ii) An acknowledgment of his signature by an attesting witness should have the same effect as his actual signature.[89]

The two amendments made to section 9 of the Wills Act by the Administration of Justice Act 1982 amounted to little more than minor tinkering. On balance the more radical proposal—the introduction of a dispensing power—would seem to be desirable. It might lead to litigation, but at least such litigation would ensure that an authentic will did not fail for non-compliance with the prescribed formalities and the county court would, in any event, have jurisdiction in the case of small estates.

An example of a case where a will would certainly have been saved, had there been a dispensing power, is that of *Re Groffman*[90] to which the Law Reform Committee made no reference. In *Re Groffman*, the testator had been married twice and had adult children by his first marriage. He wanted to make a will the purpose of which was to ensure that some of his property passed to his children by his first marriage and that it did not all pass to his second wife. The testator went to a solicitor and arranged for his will to be drafted and engrossed. The solicitor then sent the will to the testator with instructions as to how it was to be executed. The testator knew that he had to sign or acknowledge the will in the presence of two independent witnesses, so one evening he took the will, which he had already signed, to a social function where he knew that he would find two suitable people. If he had then acknowledged his signature in the presence of the two witnesses who signed the will in his presence there would have been no problem. But that did not happen. Having arrived at the function, the testator chose two friends as witnesses and indicated to them that he had his will with him and that he wanted them to witness his signature. At this point, the will was still in his pocket. He then went with one of the witnesses into an adjoining

---

[87] Law Reform Committee's 22nd Report at pp. 3–4.
[88] Law Reform Committee's 22nd Report, pp. 4–5 and 27.
[89] *Ibid.* at pp. 5–6 and 27.
[90] [1969] 1.W.L.R. 733.

room, took his will from his pocket, acknowledged his signature in the presence of this witness who then signed and the witness then left the room just as the second witness entered it. The testator then acknowledged his signature in the presence of the second witness who then signed. It was held by Simon P. that the will had not been properly executed. As he said[91]" . . . I have been satisfied that the document does represent the testamentary intentions of the deceased, I would very gladly find in its favour; but I am bound to apply the statute, which has been enacted by Parliament . . ."

The amendments made in 1982 would have no effect on a case like this. Were the facts of this case to recur, the testator's will would again be declared invalid. It is not easy to justify this result.

II. PRIVILEGED WILLS

Roman Law gave a privilege to legionaries by exempting them from the ordinary formality rules applicable to the execution of wills. Originally, this privilege lasted throughout military service, but Justinian limited it to the time when the legionary was *in expeditione*, when he was in actual service with the colours.[1] English law followed suit and The Statute of Frauds[2] enabled soldiers and sailors to make informal wills disposing of their personalty. Section 11 of the Wills Act 1837 took its wording from the Statute of Frauds and provides "that any soldier being in actual military service, or any mariner or seaman being at sea, may dispose of his personal estate" without any formalities whatever. The Wills (Soldiers and Sailors) Act 1918 extended this privilege to realty[3] as well as to personalty if the testator died after February 5, 1918, and widened the scope of the privilege in other respects.

1. Privileged testators

There are three categories of privileged testators.

(1) *A SOLDIER IN ACTUAL MILITARY SERVICE.* In this context "soldier" includes a member of the Air Force,[4] a female army nurse,[5] and a member of the W.A.A.F.[6] In the leading case of *Re Wingham*[7] Denning L.J. said that it "includes not only the fighting men but also those who serve in the Forces, doctors, nurses, chaplains, W.R.N.S., A.T.S., and so forth."

To be privileged a soldier is required by section 11 to be "in actual

---

[91] At p. 737. Contrast Judge Kolbert's approach in *Weatherhill v. Pearce* [1995] 1 W.L.R. 592.
[1] See W.W. Buckland, *A Text-Book of Roman Law* (3rd ed.) by P.G. Stein p. 361.
[2] The Statute of Frauds 1677, s. 23.
[3] s. 3: this section embraces the privileged testator's realty and realty over which he has a general or special power of appointment exercisable by will, *obiter* in *Re Earl of Chichester's W.T.* [1946] Ch. 289
[4] Will (Soldiers and Sailors) Act 1918, s. 5(2).
[5] *In the Estate of Stanley* [1916] P. 192.
[6] *In the Estate of Rowson* [1944] 2 All E.R. 36.
[7] [1949] P.187, 196.

military service" when he makes his will. In *Re Wingham* the Court of Appeal held that a member of the Royal Air Force undergoing training as a pilot in Canada in 1943 was privileged and therefore entitled to make an informal will, because he was liable at any time to be ordered to proceed to some area in order to take part in active warfare. The test adopted by the Court of Appeal is that a soldier is in actual military service if he is actually serving with the armed forces "in connection with military operations which are or have been taking place or are believed to be imminent."[8] A soldier employed in internal security operations against terrorists in Northern Ireland in 1978 was held in *Re Jones*[9] to be in actual military service. On the other hand, a soldier serving in England or abroad in peacetime when military operations are not imminent is not privileged.[10]

A soldier is in actual military service from the time he receives orders in connection with a war believed to be imminent.[11] Long after fighting has ceased a soldier may still be in actual military service as a member of an army of occupation.[12]

To be privileged, a soldier need not be so circumstanced that he would have been privileged as a legionary who was *in expeditione* under Roman law,[13] or be in danger from enemy action, or be cut off from skilled advice. The privilege was borrowed from Roman law and these factors explain the reasons for its existence; but they do not determine its limits, which depend on the construction of section 11 of the Wills Act 1837 and the Wills (Soldiers and Sailors) Act 1918.[14]

(2) *A MARINER OR SEAMAN BEING AT SEA.* Mariner or seaman includes all ranks of Her Majesty's naval or marine forces[15] and of the merchant service, and has even been held to extend to a woman typist employed aboard a liner.[16]

The words "being at sea" in section 11 have been liberally construed. The privilege has been held applicable to a seaman who made his will while serving in a ship permanently stationed in Portsmouth harbour.[17]

---

[8] [1949] P. 187, 196 and see p. 192; at p. 196 Denning L.J. said, "Doubtful cases may arise in peacetime when a soldier is in, or is about to be sent to, a disturbed area or an isolated post, where he may be involved in military operations. As to these cases, all I say is that, in case of doubt, the serving soldier should be given the benefit of privilege": see also *Re Jones* [1981] Fam. 7, 10.

[9] [1981] Fam. 7 (soldier shot on patrol said, "If I don't make it, make sure Anne gets all my stuff"; held valid will).

[10] *In the Estate of Grey* [1922] P. 140.

[11] *Gattward v. Knee* [1902] P. 99; *Re Rippon* [1943] P. 61 (Territorial officer under orders to join unit).

[12] *In the Estate of Colman* [1958] 1 W.L.R. 457 (soldier on leave in England in 1954 from British Army of the Rhine held privileged): see also *Re Limond* [1915] 2 Ch. 240.

[13] See *ante* p. 87.

[14] *Re Wingham* [1949] P. 187: see also *Re Booth* [1926] P. 118 and *In the Goods of Hiscock* [1901] P. 78, 80.

[15] Wills (Soldiers and Sailors) Act 1918, s. 2.

[16] *In the Goods of Hale* [1915] 2 I.R. 362 (typist on the Lusitania): see *In the Estate of Knibbs* [1962] 1 W.L.R. 852 (barman on liner); *Re Rapley* [1983] 1 W.L.R. 1069, 1073 (nature of service must be sea service but immaterial in what capacity).

[17] *In the Goods of M'Murdo* (1868) L.R. 1 P. & D. 540: see also *In the Goods of Austen* (1853) 2 Rob.Ecc. 611 (Admiral on board ship in Rangoon river on a naval expedition

Moreover a seaman is regarded as constructively "at sea" if he makes his will on land in the course of a voyage[18] or whilst under orders to join a ship. In *In the Goods of Newland*[19] a seaman who made his will in England during his leave ashore between voyages, whilst under orders to rejoin his ship a few days later, was held privileged.

(3) *ANY MEMBER OF HER MAJESTY'S NAVAL OR MARINE FORCES SO CIRCUMSTANCED THAT IF HE WERE A SOLDIER HE WOULD BE IN ACTUAL MILITARY SERVICE.*[20] Such a person is privileged even though not at sea.[21]

2. Extent of the privilege

A testator who falls within one of the above three categories at the time of making his will is privileged in certain respects.

(1) *INFORMAL WILL.* The testator can make a will without any formalities whatever. It may be written, whether signed or witnessed or not, or it may be nuncupative, *i.e.* oral.[22]

The testator must, however, intend deliberately to give expression to his wishes in the event of his death, although he need not know that he is making a will: in this respect there is no difference between an informal and a formal will.[23] In *In the Estate of Beech*[24] the testator executed a formal will in 1917, disposing in detail of his property. Later, whilst on active service in France in 1918, he wrote two letters to his son referring to dispositions which he had already made by his will. The Court of Appeal held that the letters were not admissible to probate as an informal will, because the testator did not intend what he wrote to be remembered as an expression of his wishes in the event of his death: he was merely giving his son a summary of his existing will. Again, in *In the Estate of Knibbs*[25] a barman on a liner (whilst privileged as a mariner at sea) said to the head barman in the course of a conversation about their families' affairs, "If anything ever happens to me, Iris will get anything I have got." The court held that this statement did not constitute an

---

privileged) and *In the Goods of Patterson* (1898) 79 L.T. 123 (master on board ship lying in the Thames before starting ocean voyage held privileged).

[18] *In the Goods of Lay* (1840) 2 Curt. 375 (shore leave).

[19] [1952] P. 71: see also *In the Goods of Wilson* [1952] P. 92 (merchant navy officer in England on leave and whilst under orders to join another ship three days later held privileged); *cf. Re Rapley, supra,* (apprentice seaman on leave and not under orders to join another ship not privileged).

[20] Wills (Soldiers and Sailors) Act 1918, s. 2.

[21] See *In the Estate of Anderson* [1916] P. 49, 52; *In the Estate of Yates* [1919] P. 93 (s. 2 applied to sailor who made his will before, but died after, the 1918 Act came into operation).

[22] *Re Stable* [1919] P. 7 (oral statement, "If I stop a bullet everything of mine will be yours," by soldier to fiancee; held a valid will): see also *In the Estate of Yates, supra,* (farewell words by Navy officer to son at railway station); *Re Jones* [1981] Fam. 7.

[23] *Re Stable, supra; In the Goods of Spicer* [1949] P. 441.

[24] [1923] P. 46: see also *In the Estate of MacGillivray* [1946] 2 All E.R. 301 and *In the Estate of Donner* (1917) 34 T.L.R. 138 (deceased stated he was content not to make a will owing to his (incorrect) belief that all his estate would pass to his mother on intestacy).

[25] [1962] 1 W.L.R. 852.

informal will in favour of his sister Iris because it was merely imparted as a matter of interest in an exchange of family gossip.

An informal will made when the testator was privileged remains valid until revoked, notwithstanding that the testator ceases to be privileged.[26]

(2)   *INFANT*. A person under the age of 18 years can make a will whilst privileged,[27] and, if he does so, can subsequently revoke it whether or not he is still privileged and able to make a will.[28]

As a result of the Wills (Soldiers and Sailors) Act 1918 an infant, whilst privileged, could make a will disposing of realty as well as personalty. However, section 51(3) of the Administration of Estates Act 1925 provides that where an infant, who dies after 1925 without having been married, is at his death equitably entitled under a settlement[29] to a fee simple estate in land, he is deemed to have had an entailed interest. Probably a privileged testator, who dies after 1925 still an infant and without having been married, cannot dispose by will of a fee simple estate to which he is entitled at his death because he must be deemed to have had an entailed interest[30] which terminates on his death.[31]

3.   Should the privilege be retained?

It is easy to understand why it was thought reasonable to grant privileges to soldiers in the seventeenth century when "servicemen were . . . likely to be engaged in long campaigns abroad and thus cut off from the facilities for making a will"[32] but it is not easy to justify the need for, or the scope of, the privilege as it exists more than 300 hundred years later. The Latey Committee on the Age of Majority, reporting in 1967, thought that the distinction between what was and was not "actual military service" had become "blurred to the point of extinction by long-range weapons and informal hostilities"[33] and it recommended that the privilege should be extended to all members of the armed forces of any age whether or not in actual military service. Nothing has been done about this recommendation. The Law Reform Committee noted in their Twenty-second report that the evidence submitted to them on the question of retention of the privilege was divided. The Law Reform Committee appeared to be swayed by the fact that the Ministry of Defence was

---

[26] *Re Booth* [1926] P. 118 (informal will made on actual military service in 1882 admitted to probate after testator's death in 1924). For revocation or alteration by a privileged testator see *post*, pp. 106–107 and 113.

[27] Wills (Soldiers and Sailors) Act 1918, s.1 (as amended by Family Law Reform Act 1969, s.3(1)(*b*)) which overrode the decision in *Re Wernher* [1918] 1 Ch. 339.

[28] Family Law Reform Act 1969, s.3(3); *semble* an infant who is no longer privileged cannot revoke by an informal instrument.

[29] Defined by the Settled Land Act 1925, ss.1(1) and 117(1)(xxiv); Administration of Estates Act 1925, s.55(1)(xxiv). The settlement may arise under a pre-1926 intestacy, *Re Taylor* [1931] 2 Ch. 242.

[30] An infant cannot bar an entail by will, Law of Property Act 1925, s.176

[31] See Megarry and Wade, *The Law of Real Property* (5th ed., 1984), pp. 1018—1019.

[32] Law Reform Committee's 22nd Report, *The making and revocation of wills* (1980) Cmnd.7902 at p. 9.

[33] See C.E. Wright, *Succession; Cases and Materials* (1986) p. 116.

strongly in favour of the retention of the privilege and so recommended that it should be retained in its present form.[34]

The arguments for retention do not appear to be strong. Serving members of the armed forces are *more* rather than less likely than average members of the public to be able to obtain legal advice and so be able to make valid formal wills. And all the arguments in favour of the need for formalities—in particular, those which relate to hasty or ill-considered dispositions—apply equally strongly to members of the armed forces as they do to anyone else. The privilege is not directly linked to the imminence of death. It has been applied to some people who have never been at high risk; furthermore, a privileged will remains valid after the person who made it has ceased to be privileged.[35] It seems odd that someone who made a privileged will while he was a serving soldier, during the War, in 1944, may die more than 50 years later and that such a privileged will may then be granted probate. Contrast this with the accident victim who is not a serviceman but who wants to make an informal will just before he dies. He is accorded no privilege. It is not easy to see why the soldier should be treated differently from the accident victim.

III.   INCORPORATION OF DOCUMENTS

A testator may incorporate in his will a document which has not been duly executed by him and so make that document part of his will.

1.   Requirements for incorporation

This doctrine of incorporation by reference applies if the following three requirements are satisfied. However, a document referred to in a will is not incorporated if the testator directs in his will that it is not to form part of the will.[1]

(1) *DOCUMENT ALREADY IN EXISTENCE.* The document must already be in existence when the will is executed.[2] The onus of proving this lies on the person seeking to rely on the doctrine. If the document comes into existence after the will is executed, but before the execution of a codicil republishing the will, this first requirement is satisfied because the will is treated as having been re-executed at the date of execution of the codicil.[3]

[34] Law Reform Committee's 22nd Report, *The making and revocation of wills* Cmnd. 7902 (1980) p. 19: *cf.* Davey [1980] Conv. 70—72; Cole [1982] Conv. 185.
[35] In Roman Law, a privileged will remained valid for a maximum of one year after discharge from military service. Buckland *op. cit.* p. 361.
[1] *Re Louis* (1916) 32 T.L.R. 313.
[2] *Singleton v. Tomlinson* (1878) 3 App.Cas. 404.
[3] *In the Goods of Lady Truro* (1866) L.R. 1 P. & D. 201: for republication see *post*, p. 118, and for revival which has the same effect see *post*, p. 115.

(2)   REFERRED TO IN THE WILL AS ALREADY IN EXISTENCE. The
will must refer to the document as being already in existence when the
will is executed. If the will refers to "a memorandum *already* written by
me" this requirement is satisfied. On the other hand a reference in a will
to such articles "as may be described in a paper in my own handwriting,"[4] or to friends "to be named in a letter addressed to X,"[5] does not
satisfy this requirement. If a will refers to an already existing document
"or any substitution therefor or modification thereof," again this requirement is not satisfied and there is no incorporation even of the existing
document.[6]

If the will is republished by a codicil and the document comes into
existence between the execution of the will and the codicil, this second
requirement is only satisfied if the will refers to the document as
being already in existence. In *In the Goods of Smart*[7] the testatrix by
her will directed her trustees to give specified articles "to such of my
friends as I *may* designate in a book or memorandum that will be
found with this will." Three years later she made the memorandum
and afterwards she executed a codicil to her will. The court held that
the will (though speaking from the date of execution of the codicil)
still referred to a future document and did not refer to the memorandum as being already in existence at the date of execution of the
codicil, when the will must be treated as having been re-executed. If,
instead, the will had read "as I *have* designated," this second requirement would have been satisfied.[8]

(3)   *IDENTIFIED IN THE WILL.* The document must be sufficiently
described in the will to enable it to be identified.[9] If the description in
the will is so vague as to be incapable of being applied to any document
in particular, it does not suffice.[10] This third requirement applies even
though both the will and the document are written on the same piece of
paper: the document is not incorporated if the will contains no reference
to it.[11]

2.   Effects of incorporation

(1)   *ADMISSIBLE TO PROBATE.* A document incorporated in a duly
executed will is admissible to probate as part of the will.[12] The incorpor-

---

[4] *In the Goods of Sutherland* (1866) L.R. 1 P. & D. 198.
[5] *In the Goods of Reid* (1868) 38 L.J.P. & M. 1: see *The University College of North Wales v.
     Taylor* [1908] P. 140.
[6] *Re Jones* [1942] Ch. 328, but see p. 331. If an existing settlement is incorporated in a will,
     a power to vary conferred on the testator by the settlement is invalid when incorporated,
     Re Edwards' W.T. [1948] Ch. 440; *Re Schintz's W.T.* [1951] Ch.870.
[7] [1902] P. 238: see also *Durham v. Northen* [1895] P. 66.
[8] *In the Goods of Lady Truro* (1866) L.R. 1 P. & D. 201.
[9] *In the Goods of Garnett* [1894] P. 90: *In the Estate of Mardon* [1944] P. 109.
[10] *Allen v. Maddock* (1858) 11 Moo. P.C. 427, 454. It is submitted that *In the Estate of Saxton*
     [1939] 2 All E.R. 418 was wrongly decided (will, "I give and bequeath . . . among the
     following persons": lists found with will held to be incorporated despite absence of any
     other means of identification in the will).
[11] *In the Goods of Tovey* (1878) 47 L.J.P. 63; *In the Estate of Bercovitz* [1962] 1 W.L.R. 321.
[12] In special circumstances the incorporated document (or an examined copy) will not be
     required to be filed in the registry, *In the Goods of Balme* [1897] P. 261 (lengthy library

ated document is then open to inspection by the public. If a testator wishes to avoid this he can employ a secret trust.[13]

(2) *TESTAMENTARY EFFECT.* The incorporated document operates as part of the will and is subject to the ordinary rules—such as lapse and ademption—applicable to wills.[14]

(3) *INCORPORATION OF INVALID WILL IN DULY EXECUTED CODICIL.* If the requirements for incorporation are satisfied, a testator may incorporate an invalidly executed will or codicil in a subsequent duly executed codicil.[15] For instance, in *In the Goods of Heathcote*[16] a testatrix made an invalid will and later duly executed a codicil describing itself as "a codicil to the last will and testament of me ...". On proof that she had made no other will, the court held that the invalid will was sufficiently described in the codicil to enable it to be identified and it could be admitted to probate as incorporated in the codicil. In *In the Goods of Almosnino*[17] a woman drew up a paper in her own handwriting, signed it and put it in an envelope which she sealed; on the envelope she wrote "I confirm the contents written in the inclosed document"; she then signed the envelope and her signature was witnessed in accordance with section 9 of the Wills Act. The court held that the paper was incorporated in the memorandum and both were admissible to probate.[18]

3. Statutory Will Forms 1925[19]

Section 179 of the Law of Property Act 1925 authorises the Lord Chancellor to publish these forms which a testator may incorporate in his will in any manner indicating an intention to do so. By incorporating one or more of these forms in his will a testator may reduce the length of his will. The forms are, however, seldom used in practice owing to the inconvenience of having to refer to the relevant forms in order to understand the will.

catalogue incorporated, but filing not required); *In the Goods of Sibthorp* (1866) L.R. 1 P. & D. 106 (third party in possession of incorporated document: filing not required).
[13] See *Snell's Equity* (29th ed., 1990), pp. 108 *et seq.*
[14] *Bizzey v. Flight* (1876) 3 Ch. 269.
[15] *Allen v. Maddock* (1858) 11 Moo. P.C. 427.
[16] (1881) 6 P.D. 30.
[17] (1859) 29 L.J.P. 46.
[18] *In the Goods of Almosnino* (1859) 29 L.J.P. 46: see *Re Nicholls* [1921] 2 Ch. 11.
[19] (S.R. & O. 1925, No. 780) (L. 15); see *Hallett's Conveyancing Precedents* (1965), pp. 994 *et seq.*

CHAPTER 5

REVOCATION, ALTERATION, REVIVAL AND REPUBLICATION OF WILLS

I. REVOCATION

A will is, by its very nature, revocable by the testator until his death.[1] There are four methods of revocation. A will or codicil may be revoked by marriage, destruction, another will or codicil, or duly executed writing declaring an intention to revoke. The *legal* burden of proof of revocation lies on the party alleging it.[2]

The effect of divorce or annulment of marriage on a will is considered later.[3]

A. MARRIAGE

1. The general rule

As a general rule, marriage automatically revokes any will made by either party before the marriage. It is immaterial whether the party intends the will to be revoked by the marriage. This rule is enacted both by the original section 18 of the Wills Act 1837 (which, together with section 177 of the Law of Property Act 1925, is applicable if the will was made before January 1, 1983) and by the new section 18 as substituted by the Administration of Justice Act 1982 (which is applicable if the will was made after December 31, 1982).[4]

2. Void and voidable marriages

A *void* marriage is treated as never having taken place and so it does not revoke any will already made by either party.[5] But a *voidable* marriage does revoke any will already made by either party and this is so

---

[1] *Ante*, p. 4.
[2] *Harris v. Berrall* (1858) 1 Sw. & Tr. 153; *Sprigge v. Sprigge* (1868) L.R. 1 P. & D. 608; *Benson v. Benson* (1870) L.R. 2 P. & D. 172. For rebuttable presumptions see *post*, p. 102.
[3] *Post*, Chap. 11 pp. 243 *et seq.*
[4] Administration of Justice Act 1982, ss. 18(1), 73(7), 75(1), 76(11) and Sched. 9, Pt. I.
[5] *Mette v. Mette* (1859) 1 Sw. & Tr. 416: see also *Warter v. Warter* (1890) 15 P.D. 152.

whether the voidable marriage is subsequently annulled or not.[6] The position where a marriage is voidable on the ground of absence of consent may now be rather unsatisfactory. Before 1971, lack of consent made a marriage void.[7] But the Nullity of Marriage Act 1971[8] enacted that the effect of absence of consent was, from August 1, 1971, to make a marriage voidable not void. This means that it is now possible for someone who lacks testamentary capacity to contract a voidable marriage which will revoke a will he made when he had capacity.[9] A graphic illustration of this is the case of *Re Davey*,[10] the case of the 92-year-old woman who married the nurse from the nursing home where she lived.[11] In that case the problem was solved, just in time, by the execution of a statutory will; but the woman died within a week of the execution of that will and not all such cases will be dealt with in this way. The Law Reform Committee in their Twenty-second Report[12] considered various suggestions and concluded that the preferred solution would be that, where a deceased person had entered into a marriage while incapable through mental disorder of managing and administering his property and affairs, the court should have a discretion under the Family Provision legislation to make provision for persons who would have benefitted under any will which was revoked by the marriage. This proposal has not been implemented.

3. Exceptions to the general rule

There are two exceptions to the rule that marriage revokes any will already made by either party. The first exception relates to wills made in contemplation of marriage and the second exception to certain appointments made by will. The scope of each of the two exceptions depends on whether the will was made before 1983 or after 1982.

(1A) *FIRST EXCEPTION TO THE GENERAL RULE—WILL MADE BEFORE 1983—WILL EXPRESSED TO BE MADE IN CONTEMPLATION OF A MARRIAGE.* Where a will is made after 1925 and before 1983, the relevant section is section 177 of the Law of Property Act 1925 which provides that "a will expressed to be made in contemplation of a marriage shall . . . not be revoked by the solemnisation of the marriage contemplated." Whether this exception applies depends on the true construction of the will.[13]

---

[6] This is the position since August 1, 1971. Before the enactment of the Nullity of Marriage Act 1971, the effect of a decree of annulment on a voidable marriage was to deem it never to have existed. The 1971 Act did *two* things. It reclassified marriages where there was absence of consent as voidable rather than void *and* it enacted that a voidable marriage which was annulled should henceforth be treated as having existed during the period between the ceremony and the decree absolute of nullity.

[7] *In the Estate of Park deed.* [1954] P. 112.

[8] Subsequently re-enacted in the Matrimonial Causes Act 1973.

[9] *Re Roberts* [1978] 1 W.L.R. 653.

[10] [1981] 1 W.L.R. 164.

[11] For a more detailed account see *ante* pp. 63–64.

[12] *The making and revocation of wills*—Cmnd 7902 (1980) pp. 16–18; (1981) 125 S.J. 317.

[13] *Re Coleman* [1976] Ch. 1, 11: for the admission of extrinsic evidence see *post*, Chap. 8 pp. 187. *et seq.*

(1) *Contemplation of the particular marriage.* The will must be expressed to be made in contemplation of the particular marriage which is later celebrated. If the testator makes a will giving his entire estate to a named beneficiary referred to in the will as "my fiancee" X, or X "my future wife," this suffices and the will is not revoked by his subsequent marriage to her,[14] although it would be revoked by his subsequent marriage to anyone else. If, on the other hand, the testator merely declares in his will "that this will is made in contemplation of marriage," this does not suffice to save the will from revocation by his subsequent marriage because it refers to marriage generally and not to a particular marriage.[15]

In *Pilot v. Gainfort*[16] a testator made a will by which he gave "to Diana Featherstone Pilot my wife all my worldly goods." At that time he was living with her and later he married her. Lord Merrivale P. decided that the will was not revoked by this marriage because the will "practically" expressed contemplation of his marriage to her. The decision has been questioned on the ground that the will did not express that the marriage was in contemplation but implied that it had already taken place.[17]

(2) *Will expressed to be made.* A clause in a will stating "This will is made in contemplation of my marriage to X" satisfies section 177.[18] But need the whole will be expressed to be made in contemplation of the particular marriage? In *Re Coleman*[19] the testator made a will giving his personal chattels, his stamp collection, £5,000 and his dwelling-house to "my fiancee" X, and giving his residuary estate to Y and Z equally. Two months later the testator married X and a year later the testator died. Megarry J. held that the will had been revoked by the testator's subsequent marriage. He construed section 177 as requiring the will as a whole (and not merely particular gifts in it) to be expressed to be made in contemplation of the particular marriage. He said that it would suffice if each beneficial disposition made by the will was expressed to be made in contemplation of the testator's marriage to X. But he decided that section 177 did not apply where only some parts of the will were expressed to be made in contemplation of the particular marriage, even if those parts were substantial, unless they amounted to substantially the whole of the beneficial dispositions made by the will.[20]

It seems unlikely that the decision in *Re Coleman* will be followed. This construction of section 177 by Megarry J. was criticised as "unduly

---

[14] *In the Estate of Langston* [1953] P. 100 ("I give . . . unto my fiancee Maida Edith Beck . . ."); *Re Knight*, unreported but mentioned in *In the Estate of Langston*, p. 103 ("to E.L.B. my future wife"); *Re Coleman* [1976] Ch. 1, 6–8 and 10–11. Cf. *Burton v. McGregor* [1953] N.Z.L.R. 487 ("my fiancee" a mere word of description, and no intent that will should operate after marriage): followed in *Public Trustee v. Crawley* [1973] 1 N.Z.L.R. 695 and *Re Whale* [1977] 2 N.Z.L.R. 1.

[15] *Sallis v. Jones* [1936] P. 43.

[16] [1931] P. 103: not followed in *Re Taylor* [1949] V.L.R. 201. See also *In the Estate of Gray* (1963) 107 S.J. 156 and *Re Coleman, supra*, at pp. 5–6.

[17] *Theobald on Wills* (15th ed., 1993), p. 71.

[18] *Re Coleman* [1976] Ch. 1, 8.

[19] [1976] Ch. 1.

[20] *ibid.* at pp. 8–11 and 12. At p. 10 Megarry J. referred to *Re Chase* [1951] V.L.R. 477 (gift by will of two-thirds of the testator's estate to X "my fiancee": held will expressed to be made in contemplation of particular marriage) and questioned whether the will as a whole was expressed to have been made in contemplation of the marriage.

narrow" by the Law Reform Committee,[21] which suggested (i) that the
courts in practice usually treat the words "in contemplation of a marriage" as equivalent to "with the intention that the will should survive
the impending marriage"[22]; (ii) that if a gift in a will is made in contemplation of a marriage (in the sense of intending that it should survive
the marriage), it seems illogical to suppose that the testator did not
intend the will to survive the marriage, for the gift cannot survive unless
the will survives; and (iii) that the use of the word "fiancee" ought not
to be conclusive. Thus, a will ought not to be construed as expressed to
be made in contemplation of a marriage if it contains only one trivial
gift to "my fiancee" X.[23]

(1B) *FIRST EXCEPTION TO THE GENERAL RULE—WILL MADE
AFTER 1982—WILL (OR DISPOSITION) NOT INTENDED TO BE
REVOKED BY PARTICULAR MARRIAGE.* Where a will is made after
1982, the relevant provisions are contained in subsections 18(3) and (4)
of the Wills Act 1837 as substituted by section 18 of the Administration
of Justice Act 1982. These provisions give effect to the recommendations
of the Law Reform Committee[24] and are a great improvement on Section
177 of the Law of Property Act. The substituted subsections 18(3) and
(4) apply if it appears from a will (i) that at the time it was made the
testator was expecting to be married to a particular person, and (ii) that
he intended that the will,[25] or a disposition in the will,[26] should not be
revoked by the marriage. If the two requirements of subsection 18(3) are
satisfied, the will is not revoked by his marriage to that person. If the
two requirements of subsection 18(4) are satisfied, that disposition takes
effect notwithstanding the marriage, and so does any other disposition
in the will unless it appears from the will that the testator intended the
disposition to be revoked by the marriage. Whether these two requirements are satisfied depends on the true construction of the will.

(2A) *SECOND EXCEPTION TO THE GENERAL RULE – WILL MADE
BEFORE 1983 – CERTAIN APPOINTMENTS BY WILL.* Under the original section 18 of the Wills Act 1837, which applies to wills made before
1983, an appointment made by will is not revoked by the subsequent
marriage of the testator if:

> "the real or personal estate thereby appointed would not in default of
> such appointment pass to his or her heir, customary heir, executor, or
> administrator, or the person entitled as his or her next of kin under
> the statute of distributions."

The underlying purpose of Section 18 was to allow the appointment by

---

[21] Law Reform Committee's 22nd Report, pp. 14–16. See also R.J. Edwards and B.F.J. Lang-
staff (1975) 39 Conv.(N.S.) 121.
[22] See *Burton v. McGregor* [1953] N.Z.L.R. 487; *Public Trustee v. Crawley* [1973] 1 N.Z.L.R.
695; *Re Whale* [1977] 2 N.Z.L.R. 1: cf. *Re Coleman, supra,* at p. 10.
[23] See *Public Trustee v. Crawley, supra,* at p. 700.
[24] Law Reform Committee's 22nd Report, pp. 16 and 27: see also G.M. Bates (1979) 129
New.L.J.547.
[25] Subs. 18(3).
[26] Subs. 18(4).

will to be revoked by the testator's subsequent marriage only in circumstances where the testator's new family might benefit under the gift in
default of appointment.[27] In order to determine whether this exception
applies it is necessary to ascertain who would take in default of the
appointment made by the will. The appointment is not revoked by the
subsequent marriage if persons taking in the specified capacities would
not in any event be entitled in default of the appointment.[28]

(1) *Taking in the specified capacities.* Apart from the testator's executor
or administrator, the other specified capacities all refer to succession on
a death intestate before 1926 when realty passed to the heir, copyhold
land to the customary heir, and personalty to the next of kin under the
Statutes of Distribution 1670 and 1685.[29]

Ought the phrase "next of kin under the statute of distributions" in
section 18 to be construed since 1925 as referring to the persons entitled
on intestacy under the Administration of Estates Act 1925?[30] It seems
that the Interpretation Act may have updated section 18 in this way,[31]
but the position remains uncertain.

(2) *Remainder of will revoked.* Where this exception applies it saves the
appointment, but not the remainder of the will, from revocation by the
testator's subsequent marriage.[32]

(2B) *SECOND EXCEPTION TO THE GENERAL RULE – WILL MADE
AFTER 1982 – CERTAIN APPOINTMENTS BY WILL.* Section 18(2) of the
Wills Act 1837 as substituted provides that:

"a disposition in a will in exercise of a power of appointment shall
take effect notwithstanding the testator's subsequent marriage unless
the property so appointed would in default of appointment pass to
his personal representatives."

The substituted subsection updates this exception, so that it no longer
refers to the pre-1926 intestacy rules, and saves an appointment by will
from revocation by subsequent marriage unless the property appointed
would in default of appointment pass to the testator's estate.[33]

4. Pension scheme nominations

It will be recalled that[34] a nomination in respect of a lump sum benefit
under a pension scheme may, in the light of the rules applicable to the

---

[27] See *In the Goods of Fitzroy* (1858) 1 Sw. & Tr. 133; *In the Goods of McVicar* (1869) 1 P. &
D. 671; *In the Goods of Russell* (1890) 15 P.D. 111; *Re Paul* [1921] 2 Ch. 1.
[28] *In the Goods of Fenwick* (1867) L.R. 1 P. & D. 319; *In the Goods of Worthington* (1872) 20
W.R. 260.
[29] As to the rules governing succession on a death intestate before 1926 see Megarry and
Wade, *The Law of Real Property* (5th ed., 1984), pp. 539 *et seq.*
[30] For the modern code of intestacy see Chap. 2.
[31] See M.J. Russell (1952) 68 L.Q.R. 455, referring to the Interpretation Act 1889, s. 38(1),
from which the Interpretation Act 1978, s. 17(2) is now derived.
[32] *In the Goods of Russell* (1890) 15 P.D. 111.
[33] See Law Reform Committee's 22nd Report, pp. 13–14.
[34] See *ante* pp. 20–21.

scheme in question, not be a testamentary disposition.[35] Marriage will not revoke such a nomination.

B. DESTRUCTION

Under section 20 of the Wills Act 1837 the whole or any part of a will or codicil is revoked:

> "by the burning, tearing, or otherwise destroying the same by the testator, or by some person in his presence and by his direction, with the intention of revoking the same."

Two distinct elements are required: an act of destruction and an intention to revoke. "All the destroying in the world without intention will not revoke a will, nor all the intention in the world without destroying: there must be the two."[36] Moreover both elements are required for the revocation of each will or codicil. The revocation of a will by destruction does not revoke a codicil to the will.[37]

1. An actual act of destruction

There must be an actual, and not merely a symbolic, "burning, tearing, or otherwise destroying." Cancelling a will by striking the body of it through with a pen and crossing out the name of the testator is not an act of destruction.[38] In *Cheese v. Lovejoy*[39] a testator drew his pen through some lines of his will, wrote on the back of it, "All these are revoked," and threw it among a heap of waste paper in the corner of his sitting room. His housemaid retrieved it and kept it in the kitchen until the testator's death seven years later. The Court of Appeal held that the will was not revoked as there was no act of destruction.

(1) *EXTENT OF DESTRUCTION.* In order to revoke it entirely the whole will need not be destroyed, but there must be a destruction of so much of it as to impair the entirety of the will.[40] Accordingly it suffices if the signature of the testator is cut out,[41] or the signatures of the testatrix and attesting witnesses scratched away with a penknife[42] or scored out with a ball-point pen[43] so that it is impossible to see that they are signa-

---

[35] *Baird v. Baird* [1990] 2 A.C 548.
[36] Per James L.J. in *Cheese v. Lovejoy* (1877) 2 P.D. 251, 253, quoting Dr. Deane in the court below.
[37] *In the Goods of Savage* (1870) L.R. 2 P. & D. 78; *In the Goods of Turner* (1872) L.R. 2 P. & D. 403 (codicil not revoked by destruction of will, although codicil gave legacy to be held under conditions stated in will). Cf. *In the Goods of Bleckley* (1883) 8 P.D. 169 (both on same piece of paper).
[38] *Stephens v. Taprell* (1840) 2 Curt. 459: see also *In the Goods of Brewster* (1859) L.J.P. 69 ("cancelled" written across signature: no revocation).
[39] (1877) 2 P.D. 251. See Law Reform Committee's 22nd Report, pp. 22–23.
[40] *Hobbs v. Knight* (1838) 1 Curt. 768, 778.
[41] *Hobbs v. Knight, supra; In the Goods of Gullan* (1858) 1 Sw. & Tr. 23.
[42] *In the Goods of Morton* (1887) 12 P.D. 141.
[43] *Re Adams* [1990] 1 Ch. 601.

tures. It appears to suffice if the signatures of the attesting witnesses are destroyed by any of these methods.[44] It will be noted that all these cases relate to the *destruction* of the testator's and/or witnesses' signature(s). There will be no revocation where, for example, the signature has been scratched but remains legible.[45] It was suggested *obiter* in *Hobbs v. Knight*[46] that it would suffice if the testator's signature were burnt or torn off and this is almost certainly correct.

The testator must complete all he intends to do by way of destruction. In *Doe d. Perkes v. Perkes*[47] the testator, being angry with a devisee named in his will, began to tear it up with the intention of revoking it, and tore it into four pieces before he was stopped, partly by a bystander who seized his arms and partly by the apologies of the devisee. The testator then became calm and fitted the pieces together saying, "It is a good job it is no worse." The court held that the will had not been revoked because the testator had not completed all that he originally intended to do by way of destruction. On the other hand, if the testator's original intention·had been to tear the will into four pieces, it would have been revoked.

(2) *DESTRUCTION BY ANOTHER PERSON.* The act of destruction must be carried out by the testator himself or by another person in his presence[48] and by his direction.[49] If a testator instructs his solicitor by telephone to destroy his will as he wishes to make a new one, and the solicitor does so in the testator's absence, the will is not revoked.[50] A will destroyed by another person in the testator's presence but without the testator's direction to do so is not revoked even if the testator subsequently ratifies the destruction.[51]

2.   Intention to revoke[52]

The testator must have the intention of revoking the whole, or part, of the will whilst the act of destruction is carried out.

(1) *MENTAL CAPACITY TO REVOKE.* Destruction whilst the testator is of unsound mind does not revoke a will.[53] The same standard of

---

[44] *Hobbs v. Knight, supra,* at p. 781 (*obiter* as to erasure); *In the Goods of Dallow* (1862) 31 L.J.P.M. & A. 128 (torn off).
[45] *In the Goods of Godfrey* (1893) 69 L.T. 22.
[46] *Supra.*
[47] (1820) 3 B. & Ald. 489: see also *Elms v. Elms* (1858) 1 Sw. & Tr. 155.
[48] *In the Goods of Dadds* (1857) Dea. & Sw. 290.
[49] *Gill v. Gill* [1909] P. 157 (will torn up in testator's presence by his wife in a fit of temper: no revocation as not done by his direction).
[50] *In the Estate of de Kremer* (1965) 110 S.J. 18 ("considerable professional error" of solicitor). The solicitor in *Re Adams* [1990] 1 Ch. 601 acted correctly in *not* complying with his client's telephoned instructions to destroy her will.
[51] *Mills v. Millward* (1890) 15 P.D. 20, 21; *Gill v. Gill, supra; Re Booth* [1926] P. 118, 132 and 133.
[52] For conditional revocation see *post,* pp. 107–110.
[53] *Brunt v. Brunt* (1873) 3 P. & D. 37 (delirium tremens); *In the Goods of Hine* [1893] P. 282 (softening of the brain); *In the Goods of Brassington* [1902] P. 1 (drunk).

mental capacity is required for revocation by destruction as for the making of a will.[54]

(2) *ACCIDENT OR MISTAKE.* A will destroyed by accident is not revoked.[55] Again, there is no revocation if the act of destruction is done with the intention of destroying but not of revoking the will. Thus a will was not revoked where it was destroyed under the mistaken belief that it was invalid,[56] or that it was useless,[57] or that it had already been revoked.[58] The testator

"may have merely torn it up, thinking that it was no longer worth the paper it was written upon. For myself, in those circumstances, I should have thought the right inference to draw was that he did not intend to revoke it at all; he was merely disposing of what he thought was rubbish."[59]

(3) *WHETHER INTENTION TO REVOKE WHOLE OR PART.* It is necessary to decide whether the testator intended to revoke the whole or, alternatively, only a particular part of a will. There may be evidence of his expressed intention. If need be, the court infers the testator's intention from the state of the will after the act of destruction. If, for instance, the testator's signature is destroyed, this raises an inference that the testator intended to revoke the whole will.[60] If a portion of the will not necessary to its validity as a testamentary instrument is destroyed, the question arises whether the portion destroyed is so important as to raise the inference that the rest cannot have been intended to stand without it.[61] Thus, destruction of a clause at the commencement of a will, or cutting out various legacies, or a clause appointing executors, does not revoke the rest of the will.[62] Again, cutting away half a page, which contained details of the residuary trust, only revoked that part of the will, because sufficient remained to lead to the inference that the testator intended that what remained should be effective.[63] On the other hand, where the first two sheets of a will made on five sheets of paper had been destroyed, it was inferred that the testator intended to revoke the

---

[54] *Re Sabatini* (1969) 114 S.J. 35; see *ante*, pp. 58 *et seq.*
[55] *Burtenshaw v. Gilbert* (1774) 1 Cowp. 49, 52; *In the Goods of Taylor* (1890) 63 L.T. 230.
[56] *Giles v. Warren* (1872) 2 P. & D. 401; *In the Goods of Thornton* (1889) 14 P.D. 82.
[57] *Beardsley v. Lacey* (1897) 78 L.T. 25; *Stamford v. White* [1901] P. 46.
[58] *Scott v. Scott* (1859) 1 Sw. & Tr. 258; *Clarkson v. Clarkson* (1862) 2 Sw. & Tr. 497 (in both cases mistaken belief that later will had already revoked it).
[59] *Per* Buckley L.J. in *Re Jones* [1976] Ch. 200, 205.
[60] *Hobbs v. Knight* (1838) 1 Curt. 768 (T's signature cut out: whole will revoked); *In the Goods of Gullan* (1858) 1 Sw. & Tr. 23; *Bell v. Fothergill* (1870) 2 P. & D 148; *In re Adams* [1990] 1 Ch. 601: *cf. Christmas v. Whinyates* (1863) 3 Sw. & Tr. 81 (only part revoked, though signature cut off, due to manner in which cut).
[61] *Clarke v. Scripps* (1852) 2 Rob. 563 (part only); *Re White* (1879) 3 L.R.Ir. 413 (whole); *Leonard v. Leonard v. Leonard* [1902] P. 243 (whole).
[62] *In the Goods of Woodward* (1871) 2 P. & D. 206; *In the Goods of Nelson* (1872) 6 I.R. Eq. 569; *In the Goods of Maley* (1887) 12 P.D. 12 P.D. 134; *In the Goods of Leach* (1890) 63 L.T. 111; *In the Estate of Nunn* (1936) 154 L.T. 498 (strip in middle of will cut out and remainder stitched together: only strip revoked).
[63] *Re Everest* [1975] Fam. 44.

whole will, because the last three sheets were practically unintelligible in the absence of the first two sheets.[64]

3. Presumptions

Two rebuttable presumptions may apply.

(1) *WILL MISSING AT DEATH.* A will last known to be in the testator's possession but which cannot be found at his death is presumed to have been destroyed by the testator with the intention of revoking it.[65] But the strength of the presumption varies according to the security of the testator's custody of the will: the safer the security, the stronger the presumption. The presumption may be rebutted by evidence of non-revocation, such as evidence that the will was destroyed by enemy action or accident, or by evidence showing the testator's intention to adhere to the will. The contents of the missing will may be proved by means of a draft or copy or by oral evidence.[66]

The leading case is *Sugden v. Lord St Leonards.*[67] Lord St. Leonards, the former Lord Chancellor, died in 1875 aged 93. He had made a holograph will in 1870 and had then made eight codicils to it between 1870 and 1873. The will and codicils were kept in a deed box in Lord St. Leonards' sitting room; the box was locked but there was a spare key to it and the spare key was not kept securely; almost anyone in the house could have obtained access to the deed box. During Lord St. Leonards' final illness, his daughter, who lived with him, removed the deed box to her room, for safekeeping. After his death the box was opened: the codicils were in the box but the will was missing. There was no copy of the will, but the daughter had read it over to her father on a number of occasions and was able to give a reasonably full account of its contents. The case raised two questions: first, whether there was a presumption on these facts that Lord St. Leonards had destroyed his own will, with the intention of revoking it; and secondly, if there were no such presumption, whether the court could accept evidence from the daughter who was herself a beneficiary under the will. Sir James Hannen P. had no hesitation in finding that there was no presumption, on these facts, that Lord St. Leonards had destroyed his own will. No careful Chancery lawyer would be likely to destroy his will without destroying the codicils to it and without making another will. As to the daughter's evidence, it was entirely consistent with the codicils and was accepted. Sir James Hannen's judgment was upheld by a unanimous Court of Appeal.[68] Neither Sir James Hannen nor the members of the Court of Appeal chose to speculate on what had happened to the will, which remains a mystery.[69]

---

[64] *Leonard v. Leonard* [1902] P. 243: see also *Treloar v. Lean* (1889) 14 P.D. 49; *In the Estate of Green* (1962) 106 S.J. 1034; *Re White* (1879) 3 L.R.Ir. 413.

[65] *Eckersley v. Platt* (1886) L.R. 1 P & D. 281; *Allan v. Morrisson* [1900] A.C. 604.

[66] *Re Webb* [1964] 1 W.L.R. 509; *In the Estate of Yule* (1965) 109 S.J. 317: see *post*, pp. 553 *et seq.*

[67] (1876) 1 P.D. 154.

[68] Some great lawyers thought, at the time, that the court would not grant probate to a will thus proved; *i.e.* proved on the basis of secondary evidence of contents given by an interested witness. See Holdsworth, *A History of English Law Vol XVI* p. 46.

[69] They did not speculate, but the judgments hint at what they thought. The will was probably removed from the deed box, while the box was in Lord St. Leonards' sitting

(2)   WILL FOUND MUTILATED AT DEATH. A will, which has been in the testator's possession but which is found to be torn or mutilated at his death, is presumed to have been torn or mutilated by the testator with the intention of revoking it in whole or in part.[70] Again the presumption may be rebutted by evidence to the contrary.[71]

If the testator executed the will whilst of sound mind but was insane during any part of the period when the will was in his possession, there is no presumption that the destruction, or the tearing or mutilation, was carried out by the testator at a time when he was of sound mind. Unless the party alleging revocation proves that the testator was of sound mind (and thus capable of revoking the will) at the time of destruction, the will is admissible to probate.[72]

C.   WILL OR CODICIL

Under section 20 of the Wills Act 1837, the whole or any part of a will may be revoked by another duly executed will or codicil.[73]

1.   Express revocation by will or codicil

Most wills contain a revocation clause in general terms by which the testator expressly revokes "all wills codicils and other testamentary dispositions heretofore made by me." Such a revocation clause normally operates to revoke all previous testamentary instruments[74] just as if they had never existed, and it will therefore revoke an appointment made by the testator in a previous will or codicil.[75] The advantage of inserting such a revocation clause is that it makes it unnecessary to consider whether, or to what extent, an earlier will or codicil is revoked by implication. A revocation clause may be much narrower in its ambit. Thus, in a codicil, a revocation clause commonly revokes a single clause, or even a single word, in a previous will or codicil. No particular form of words is required for express revocation. However, the usual form of commencement of a will—"This is the last will and testament of me . . ."—is not construed as an express revocation of previous wills.[76]

On its proper construction a revocation clause in general terms may

room, by a servant who wanted to know what provision it made for the servants. When Lord St. Leonards' daughter took the box to her room, the servant could not replace the will, and so destroyed it. But this is only speculation.
[70] *Lambell v. Lambell* (1831) 3 Hag.Ecc. 568; *Bell v. Fothergill* (1870) L.R. 2 P. & D. 148.
[71] *In the State of MacKenzie* [1909] P. 305; *Re Cowling* [1924] P. 113.
[72] *Harris v. Berrall* (1858) 1 Sw. & Tr. 153 (tearing); *Sprigge v. Sprigge* (1868) L.R. 1 P. & D. 608 (destruction).
[73] For conditional revocation see *post*, pp. 107 *et seq.* For the rules of private international law governing revocation by will or codicil see Dicey and Morris, *The Conflict of Laws* (12th ed., 1993), pp. 1049 *et seq.*; *Theobald on Wills* (15th ed., 1993), Chap. 1.
[74] But not statutory nominations, see *ante*, p. 20.
[75] *Sotheran v. Dening* (1881) 20 Ch.D. 99 (general power); *Re Kingdon* (1886) 32 Ch.D. 604 (special power); *Cadell v. Wilcocks* [1898] P. 21, 26.
[76] *Cuttc v. Gilbert* (1854) 9 Moo.P.C. 131; *Lemage v. Goodban* (1865) L.R. 1 P. & D. 57; *Simpson v. Foxon* [1907] P. 54 ("This is the last and only will and testament of me" not an express revocation); *Kitcat v. King* [1930] P. 266.

not revoke all previous testamentary instruments. In *Re Wayland*[77] a testator made a will in accordance with the law of Belgium dealing only with his Belgian property. Later he made a will in England which contained a revocation clause but which declared that "this will is intended to deal only with my estate in England." The court construed the revocation clause to mean that the testator revoked all former wills dealing with English property and admitted both the Belgian and the English wills to probate.

A revocation clause does not operate at all if:

(i) the clause is contained in a conditional will which is inoperative owing to the specified condition not being satisfied;[78]

(ii) the clause is rejected for want of knowledge and approval by the testator.[79] The clause is not admitted to probate if the testator did not know and approve of it,[80] but the clause must be admitted even if it was included as a result of a mistake as to its legal effect;[81]

(iii) the clause itself is subject to a condition which is not satisfied.[82]

2.   Implied revocation by will or codicil

A prior will or codicil is impliedly revoked by a later will or codicil so far as the latter contains provisions inconsistent with or merely repeating the former. If the provisions of the later will or codicil are wholly inconsistent or repetitive, the prior will or codicil is completely revoked.[83] If they are only partially inconsistent or repetitive, those parts of the prior will or codicil not affected by the inconsistency or repetition remain unrevoked. The question to ask is not which of his wills or codicils did the testator desire to be admitted to probate: the true question is which provisions did the testator intend to take effect at his death.[84] This is a question of construction.[85]

3.   Proof of revocation

---

[77] [1951] 2 All E.R. 1041; *Gladstone v. Tempest* (1840) 2 Curt. 650; *Denny v. Barton* (1818) 2 Phill. 575.

[78] *In the Goods of Hugo* (1877) 2 P.D. 73; *In the Estate of O'Connor* [1942] 1 All E.R. 546: see *ante*, p. 5.

[79] *Ante*, pp. 64, *et seq.*; see C.H. Sherrin (1972) 122 New L.J. 6.

[80] *Re Phelan* [1972] Fam. 33, see *ante* p. 69; *In the Goods of Oswald* (1874) L.R. 3 P. & D. 162 (included *per incuriam* without instructions); *In the Goods of Moore* [1892] P. 378; *Smith v. Thompson* (1931) 47 T.L.R. 603 and *cf. Lowthorpe-Lutwidge v. Lowthorpe-Lutwidge* [1935] P. 151 (no evidence of want of knowledge and approval of revocation clause); *In the Goods of Swords* [1952] P. 368.

[81] *Collins v. Elstone* [1893] P. 1 (T knew that her will contained revocation clause, but had been wrongly advised that would not revoke her previous will).

[82] This is considered later, *post*, pp. 109–110.

[83] *In the Estate of Bryan* [1907] P. 125 (wholly inconsistent even though later will did not dispose of residue); *In the Goods of Howard* (1869) L.R. 1 P. & D. 636.

[84] *Lemage v. Goodban* (1865) L.R. 1 P. & D. 57; *In the Goods of Petchell* (1874) L.R. 3 P. & D. 153.

[85] *Post*, p. 186.

(1) *BY LOST WILL OR CODICIL.* Revocation of an earlier will or codicil by a later will or codicil takes effect when the latter is executed, and it is immaterial that the latter is not forthcoming at the testator's death.[86] But in order to establish revocation by a will or codicil which has been lost or destroyed, it is necessary to prove (i) that the later will or codicil was duly executed and (ii) that by its contents it did expressly or impliedly revoke the earlier will or codicil. The second requirement may be proved by production of a copy or written instructions, or by clear and satisfactory oral evidence.[87]

(2) *BY WILL OR CODICIL INADMISSIBLE TO PROBATE.* In *Re Howard*[88] a testator first executed a will leaving his estate to his son and later executed two wills on the same day, one in favour of his wife and the other in favour of his son. Each of these two wills contained a revocation clause in general terms. The court held that these two wills were effective to revoke the earlier will. However neither of them could be admitted to probate as they were inconsistent and there was nothing to indicate the order in which they were executed. The deceased therefore died intestate.

D.   DULY EXECUTED WRITING DECLARING AN INTENTION TO REVOKE

Under section 20 of the Wills Act 1837 the whole or any part of a will may be revoked by "some writing declaring an intention to revoke the same" and duly executed in the same manner as a will.

A statement at the foot of an obliterated codicil, "We are witnesses to the erasure of the above," signed by the testator and attested by two witnesses, was held to be a "writing declaring an intention to revoke."[89] Again, in *Re Spracklan's Estate*[90] the Court of Appeal held this requirement to be satisfied by the words, "will you please destroy the will already made out," in a letter signed by the testatrix and duly attested, and addressed to the manager of a bank having custody of her will. The will was therefore revoked as soon as the letter was duly executed.

[86] *Brown v. Brown* (1858) 8 E. & B. 876; *Wood v. Wood* (1867) L.R. 1 P. & D. 309.
[87] *Cutto v. Gilbert* (1854) 9 Moo.P.C. 131 ("oral evidence ought to be stringent and conclusive"); the ordinary standard of proof applies, *i.e.* a reasonable balance of probabilities, *Re Wipperman.* [1955] P. 59: evidence it was solicitor's usual practice to insert a revocation clause is insufficient by itself; *Re Wyatt* [1952] 1 All E.R. 1030 (contents of later will unknown; it had been drawn by a solicitor whose usual practice was to insert revocation clause: earlier will held not revoked); *Re Rear* [1975] 2 N.Z.L.R. 254, 267; *cf.* *In the Estate of Hampshire* [1951] W.N. 174.
[88] [1944] P. 39.
[89] *In the Goods of Gosling* (1886) 11 P.D. 79.
[90] [1938] 2 All E.R. 345, following *In the Goods of Durance* (1872) L.R. 2 P. & D. 406, where Lord Penzance said at p. 407, "If a man writes to another 'Go and get my will and burn it,' he shows a strong intention to revoke his will."

E.   AN ALTERATION IN CIRCUMSTANCES DOES NOT REVOKE

The general rule that marriage revokes a will ensures that a testator starts married life with a clean slate.[91] Apart from marriage, no other alteration in circumstances, such as the birth of children, revokes a will.[92]

F.   REVOCATION BY A PRIVILEGED TESTATOR

The four methods of revocation already considered apply to a privileged testator subject only to the differences arising from his ability to make an informal will.[93]

Marriage

In the Estate of Wardrop[94] Shearman J. decided that the will of a privileged testator was revoked by his subsequent marriage. He said that section 18 (which provided that "every will made by a man or woman shall be revoked by his or her marriage") was "a very sweeping enactment and it must be held to apply to soldiers' and sailors' wills." The two exceptions to the rule that marriage revokes a will also apply in the case of a privileged testator.

Destruction

This method is applicable to an informal will[95] unless it was made orally so that destruction is impossible.

Will or codicil

A privileged testator may revoke any previous will (whether or not made when he was privileged) by an informal will or codicil.[96]

---

[91] See Law Reform Committee's 22nd Report, pp. 11–18, recommending no change in the general rule.

[92] See Wills Act 1837, s. 19. For the effect of divorce or annulment of marriage see *post*, pp. 243 *et seq.*

[93] *In the Estate of Gossage* [1921] P. 194 (the misleading headnote states the *ratio* of Younger L.J., and not that of the majority of the Court of Appeal).

[94] [1917] P. 54: this decision has been doubted on the ground that *In the Estate of Gossage, supra*, by implication overrules it (see Williams, Mortimer and Sunnucks, *Executors, Administrators and Probate* (17th ed. 1993), p. 225, n. 14) but it is only the judgment of Younger L.J. which may carry this implication.

[95] *In the Estate of Gossage, supra*, at p. 196, Bailhache J. at first instance apparently decided that a privileged will had been revoked by its destruction by another person in the testator's absence: no member of the Court of Appeal relied on this ground and the majority treated s. 20 as applicable.

[96] Wills Act 1837, ss. 11 and 20: Wills (Soldiers and Sailors) Act 1918: see *In the Goods of Newland* [1952] P. 71.

Writing declaring an intention to revoke

A privileged testator may revoke any previous will by informal writing declaring an intention to revoke.[97] There is a dictum that such informal writing does not revoke a formal will made when not privileged,[98] but it ought to be irrelevant whether the previous will was made when privileged.[99]

II. CONDITIONAL REVOCATION

Revocation of the whole or part of a will or codicil by destruction, or by another will or codicil or by duly executed writing, requires an intention to revoke. The testator's intention to revoke may be absolute or conditional. If it is absolute, revocation takes place immediately. If it is conditional, revocation does not take effect unless the condition is fulfilled. Often the condition makes revocation dependent upon the validity of another will or codicil and this particular type of conditional revocation has in the past been referred to as the doctrine of dependent relative revocation. It seems preferable, however, to use the less cumbersome term *conditional revocation* in all cases.[1]

Whether the testator's intention to revoke was conditional is a question of fact where revocation was by destruction[2] and evidence as to the testator's declarations of intention is therefore admissible.[3] On the other hand it is a question of construction where revocation was by another will or codicil[4] or by duly executed writing. As will be explained later,[5] this means that extrinsic evidence of the testator's intention is only admissible to assist in the interpretation of the document.[6]

1. Conditional revocation by destruction

The testator's intention to revoke by destruction may have been absolute (in the sense that the testator intended the revocation to take effect at once) or conditional (in the sense that he intended the revocation to

---

[97] *In the Estate of Gossage* [1921] P. 194 (letter from privileged soldier in South Africa to sister in England asking her to burn will "for I have already cancelled it": held letter revoked his previous will).

[98] *In the Estate of Gossage, supra*, at pp. 201–202 (writing must be "executed in the manner . . . required for the execution of the will which it is intended to revoke").

[99] Wills Act 1837, s. 20 refers to the manner in which "a will," not the will, is hereinbefore required to be executed.

[1] "The name of this doctrine seems to me to be somewhat overloaded with unnecessary polysyllables. The resounding adjectives add very little, it seems to me, to any clear idea of what is meant. The whole matter can be quite simply expressed by the word 'conditional,' " per Langton J. in *In the Goods of Hope Brown* [1942] P. 136, 138; *Re Jones* [1976] Ch. 200, 212; Law Reform Committee's 22nd Report, p. 24.

[2] *Dixon v. Solicitor to the Treasury* [1905] P. 42; *Re Jones, supra*, at pp. 215 and 218.

[3] *Powell v. Powell* (1866) L.R. 1 P. & D. 209.

[4] *Att.-Gen. v. Lloyd* (1747) 1 Ves.Sen. 32, 34.

[5] Chap. 8.

[6] *Post*, pp. 187 *et seq.*

take effect only if some condition were fulfilled). To consider some instances:

(1) *CONDITIONAL UPON DUE EXECUTION OF NEW WILL OR CODICIL.* If T formed the intention of making a new will in favour of B, and T destroyed his old will in favour of A, T's intention to revoke his old will may have been absolute or conditional. This is a question of fact to be decided after T's death upon all the evidence before the court. Evidence that T had formed the intention of making a new will does not, of itself, necessarily lead to the conclusion that T's intention to revoke was conditional.[7] For instance, the court may infer that T said to himself, "I cannot get on with making a new will in favour of B until my solicitor returns next week, but at least I will here and now get rid of this one, so that A shall not benefit". If, as in this instance, T's intention to revoke was absolute, T's destruction of his old will would have revoked it immediately.[8] It is irrelevant that this results in an intestacy which it is difficult to believe T intended.[9] On the other hand, the court may infer that T said to himself, "I believe that it is necessary for me to revoke my old will before I can make a new will". If, as in this instance, T's intention to revoke was conditional on his duly executing his new will, T's destruction of his old will would not have revoked it unless the condition was fulfilled.[10]

Similarly, if T believed that he had already made a new will (but had not done so because the "new will" had not been properly executed) and he then destroyed his old will, T's intention to revoke his old will might have been absolute (in which case his old will would have been revoked immediately)[11] or conditional on his new will having been duly executed (in which case his old will would not have been revoked unless the condition was fulfilled).[12] Alternatively, T may have had no intention to revoke, because he mistakenly believed his old will was useless or had already been revoked; in these cases his old will would not be revoked.[13]

(2) *CONDITIONAL UPON REVIVAL OF FORMER WILL.* A will which has been revoked by a later will cannot be revived by the subsequent revocation of that later will.[14] It follows that if the testator destroys the later will, intending to revoke it conditionally on the revival of the former will, the revocation of the later will is ineffective.[15]

---

[7] *Re Jones* [1976] Ch. 200.
[8] *ibid.* at pp. 219–220.
[9] *ibid.* at pp. 213–214 and 217–218.
[10] *Dixon v. Solicitor to the Treasury* [1905] P. 42: see *In the Estate of Bromham* [1952] 1 All E.R. 110. For evidence of conditional revocation of a will missing at death see *post*, p. 354.
[11] See *In the Estate of Green* (1962) 106 S.J. 1034.
[12] *Dancer v. Crabb* (1873) L.R. 3 P. & D. 98; *In the Estate of Davies* [1951] 1 All E.R. 920; *Sterling v. Bruce* [1973] N.I. 255.
[13] *Ante,* pp. 100–102.
[14] *Post,* pp. 115–116.
[15] *Powell v. Powell* (1866) L.R. 1 P. & D. 209; *Cossey v. Cossey* (1900) 82 L.T. 203; *In the Estate of Bridgewater* [1965] 1 W.L.R. 416.

(3) *CONDITIONAL UPON PARTICULAR DEVOLUTION ON INTEST-ACY*. In *In the Estate of Southerden*[16] a testator made a will giving all his property to his wife. Later he burnt it, intending to revoke it conditionally on his wife being entitled to all his property on his death intestate. This condition was not satisfied and the Court of Appeal held that the will had not been revoked and its contents were admissible to probate.

The doctrine of conditional revocation is not confined to these instances. It is of general application and applies if the testator's intention to revoke is conditional on the existence, or future existence, of a particular fact: if this condition is not satisfied, the will is not revoked by destruction.[17]

2. Conditional express revocation by will or codicil

A revocation clause may be subject to an express condition. If, for example, a testator inserts in a codicil a revocation clause expressed to take effect conditionally on his wife predeceasing him, the clause does not operate if she survives him.

Even in the absence of an express condition, a revocation clause may be construed as conditional. An early instance is the decision in *Campbell v. French*[18] where the testator by his will gave legacies to his sister's grandchildren living in America and then by a codicil revoked the legacies "they being all dead." In fact they were still alive. Lord Loughborough held that the revocation was ineffective as it was conditional on the legatees being dead. A recent instance is *Re Finnemore*[19] where a testator made three wills in succession. In each of the three wills the testator gave his house, the contents of his house, and three-quarters of his residuary estate to C. The three wills differed as to the way in which they disposed of the other quarter of the residuary estate. The two later wills contained standard clauses revoking all previous wills. Unfortunately, the gifts to C in the second and third wills were void because C's husband was an attesting witness to both of these wills.[20] Judge Micklem[21] held that the revocation clauses in the two latter wills were conditional on the gifts to C in those wills being valid. As the gifts were void, the revocation clauses would not take effect insofar as they purported to revoke dispositions contained in the first will which gave benefits similar to those contained in the later wills.[22] The revocation clause in the last will was construed distributively, so that it was effective in revoking the parts of the earlier wills which dealt with the quarter of the residue

---

[16] [1925] P. 177.

[17] *In the Estate of Southerden* [1925] P. 177; *Re Jones* [1976] Ch. 200, 213 and 216: see *Re Carey* (1977) 121 S.J. 173 (conditional on fact he had nothing to leave by will).

[18] (1797) 3 Ves. 321: see also *Doe d. Evans v. Evans* (1839) 10 Ad. & El. 228; *Re Plunkett* [1964] I.R. 259: contrast *Re Feis* [1964] Ch. 106.

[19] [1991] 1 W.L.R. 793.

[20] *Post*, pp. 232–234.

[21] Sitting as a Judge of the High Court.

[22] See also *In the Goods of Hope Brown* [1942] P.136: *In the Estate of Cocke* [1960] 1 W.L.R. 491; *In the Estate of Crannis* (1978) 122 S.J. 489; see R.G. Henderson (1969) 32 M.L.R. 447; *cf. Re Luck* [1977] WAR 148.

which did not pass to C; that quarter of the residue passed under the provisions of the last will.

3.   Conditional implied revocation by will or codicil

Where a testator by a will or codicil gives property to X, and by a later will or codicil gives the same property to Y, the gift to X is impliedly revoked. But does this occur if for some reason the gift to Y fails? In that event it is a question of construction whether the testator has shown an intention to revoke the gift to X in any event (in which case X does not take) or conditionally on the gift to Y taking effect (in which case X does take on the failure of the gift to Y).[23] The answer therefore depends on the proper construction of the later will or codicil.

The decision in *Re Robinson*[24] is a useful illustration. In that case the testatrix by will gave her estate upon trust to pay an annuity to her son H and after his death to divide her estate equally between her grandchildren who attained 21 years of age. By a later will she gave her whole estate to H absolutely. This was another case where the disposition was void as H's wife was an attesting witness.[25] The court held that the testatrix had not shown an intention to revoke the earlier will in any event. The later will contained no revocation clause and the only indication in it of an intention to revoke was in the disposition which had failed; the earlier will had therefore not been revoked. The intention to revoke was conditional on the absolute gift to H taking effect and this condition was not satisfied.

III.   ALTERATION

Section 21 of the Wills Act 1837 lays down the rule for any alteration in a will:

> "No obliteration, interlineation, or other alteration made in any will after the execution thereof shall be valid or have any effect, except so far as the words or effect of the will before such alteration shall not be apparent, unless such alteration shall be executed in like manner as hereinbefore is required for the execution of the will . . ."

In considering the effect of section 21 three main questions may arise and they should be considered in turn:

A. Was the alteration made before the execution of the will? If so, the alteration is valid and section 21 does not apply.
B. Was the alteration duly executed? If so, it is valid.
C. Has the alteration made any part of the will not "apparent"? If it

---

[23] *Ward v. Van der Loeff* [1924] A.C. 653 (gift in later codicil void for remoteness: gift in earlier will held not revoked).
[24] [1930] 2 Ch. 332: see also *Re Davies* [1928] Ch. 24.
[25] See *Re Finnemore supra* and *post* pp. 232–234.

is not apparent and the testator intended to revoke it, that part is revoked.

A.   Alteration Made Before Execution of Will

An alteration made in a will before the will is executed by the testator is valid if the testator intends the alteration to form part of the will when it is executed. Thus the alteration is not valid if it was merely deliberative and not final. A rebuttable presumption arises that an alteration in pencil is merely deliberative and that an alteration in ink is intended to be final.[1]

1.   Presumption as to time of alteration

There is a rebuttable presumption that an unattested alteration was made after the execution of the will[2] or any subsequent codicil.[3] This presumption may be rebutted by evidence, which may be internal evidence from the will itself or extrinsic evidence or both. If the alterations are trifling and of little consequence, the presumption may be readily rebutted.[4]

The presumption has been rebutted by internal evidence from the will itself where the alterations were made to supply blanks left in the will by the draftsman,[5] and again where interlineations written with the same ink as the rest of the will completed the otherwise unintelligible sentences of the will.[6]

Extrinsic evidence rebutting the presumption may take different forms, for instance evidence from the draftsman of the will[7] or an attesting witness, or declarations by the testator showing that he made the alterations before executing the will.[8] The court considers all the evidence, both internal and extrinsic, in deciding whether the presumption is rebutted.

A different presumption applies if the will was made by the testator whilst privileged. In that case a rebuttable presumption arises that the

---

[1] *Hawkes v. Hawkes* (1828) 1 Hagg. Ecc. 321 (each presumption is stronger if both ink and pencil alterations); *In the Goods of Adams* (1872) L.R. 2 P. & D. 367.

[2] *Cooper v. Bockett* (1846) 4 Moo. P.C. 419; *In the Goods of Adamson* (1875) L.R. 3 P. & D. 253.

[3] *In the Goods of Sykes* (1873) 3 P. & D. 26, 27–28; *Lushington v. Onslow* (1848) 6 N. of C. 183.

[4] *In the Goods of Hindmarsh* (1866) 1 P. & D. 307 (testator a lawyer, alterations trifling and apparently written with same pen and ink as rest of will, and not very strong evidence of writing expert: presumption rebutted).

[5] *Birch v. Birch* (1848) 1 Rob. Ecc. 675 (blanks left for amounts of legacies); *Greville v. Tylee* (1851) 7 Moo. P.C. 320, 327.

[6] *In the Goods of Cadge* (1868) 1 P. & D. 543.

[7] *Keigwin v. Keigwin* (1843) 3 Curt. 607.

[8] Until the Civil Evidence Act 1968, such declarations were not admissible if made by the testator after the execution of the will.

alteration was made whilst the testator was still privileged and therefore entitled to make informal alterations.[9]

2.   Effect of republication

The republication[10] of a will by its re-execution with the proper formalities validates an alteration made in the will after it was executed but before it was republished, if the testator intends the alteration to form part of the will when it is republished.[11] The same result follows if, after the alteration is made, the will is republished by a duly executed codicil containing some reference to the will.[12] But the alteration is not validated by republication of the will if the alteration was merely deliberative and not final,[13] or if the codicil shows that the testator was treating the will as unaltered.[14]

As already explained,[15] the presumption is that an unattested alteration to the will was made, not only after the execution of the will, but also after the execution of the codicil.[16] Accordingly, unless this presumption is rebutted by evidence showing that the unattested alteration was made before the execution of the codicil,[17] the alteration is not validated by the republication of the will by the codicil.

B.   ALTERATION DULY EXECUTED

1.   Formalities

If the alteration was duly executed with the formalities required for the execution of the will, the alteration is valid. In this connection section 21 of the Wills Act 1837 provides that the signatures of the testator and the witnesses may be made "in the margin or on some other part of the will opposite or near to such alteration, or at the foot or end of or opposite to a memorandum referring to such alteration, and written at the end or some other part of the will." Accordingly an alteration is valid if the testator signs by writing his initials in the margin against the alteration, and the testator either makes or acknowledges this signature in the sim-

---

[9] *In the Goods of Tweedale* (1874) L.R. 3 P. & D. 204 (soldier's will); *In the Goods of Newland* [1952] P. 71 (seaman's will).

[10] *Post*, p. 118: revival has the same effect, *post*, p. 118.

[11] *In the Goods of Shearn* (1880) 50 L.J.P. 15 (alteration after execution: alteration invalid as will not properly re-executed): *cf. In the Goods of Dewell* (1853) 1 Sp.Ecc. & Ad. 103, which was wrongly decided.

[12] *In the Goods of Sykes* (1873) L.R. 3 P. & D. 26.

[13] *In the Goods of Hall* (1871) L.R. 2 P. & D. 256 (pencil alterations).

[14] *Re Hay* [1904] 1 Ch. 317 (three legacies in will struck out by unattested alteration, later codicil revoked only one of them: held the other two stood, as testatrix was confirming her will without the alterations).

[15] See *ante* p. 111.

[16] *In the Goods of Sykes*, *supra*, at pp. 27–28; *Lushington v. Onslow* (1848) 6 N. of C. 183.

[17] *In the Goods of Heath* [1892] P. 253 (wording of codicil showed interlineation in will had already been made).

ultaneous presence of two witnesses, who then both sign in the presence of the testator by writing their initials in the margin.[18]

In the recent case of *Re White*[19] the testator made a valid will in 1981, but in 1984 he decided that he wanted to alter it. A friend made alterations to the original will, in the testator's presence and at his dictation. The alterations were initialled by two witnesses, but the testator, who had signed the will in 1981, did not sign or initial any of the alterations in 1984. The alterations could not be held valid by virtue of section 21 and the *original* will was admitted to probate.[20]

An alteration is valid if a duly executed memorandum refers to the alteration.[21]

Two precautions are advisable in practice in connection with alterations:

    (i) Unless the testator is *in extremis*, it is advisable to restrict alterations to the correction of small errors, such as the misspelling of a name, and to give effect to all other alterations by the execution of a new will or a codicil. This reduces the likelihood that there will be problems of construction.[22]

    (ii) All alterations whenever made should be duly executed. This is advisable even though the alteration was made before the execution of the will, because it makes it unnecessary to rebut the presumption that an unattested alteration was made after the execution of the will.

2. Privileged testator

A testator who has made a will whilst privileged may make alterations to it without any formalities whilst still privileged[23] because no formalities are required for due execution under section 11.

C. PART OF WILL NOT APPARENT

An alteration after execution which makes any part of the will not "apparent" revokes that part if the testator has an intention to revoke it. Probate of the will must be granted with a blank space for the part not apparent.

1. The test of being not apparent

"Apparent" in section 21 means optically apparent on the face of the will itself.[24] A word in a will is not apparent if it cannot be deciphered

---

[18] *In the Goods of Blewitt* (1880) 5 P.D. 116 (initials suffice).
[19] [1991] Ch. 1.
[20] See also *ante* pp. 80–81.
[21] *In the Goods of Treeby* (1875) 3 P. & D. 242.
[22] Alterations and codicils both have the potential disadvantage that someone who has lost a benefit, or who has had a benefit reduced, will find out that this has happened.
[23] *In the Goods of Tweedale* (1874) L.R. 3 P. & D. 204.
[24] *Townley v. Watson* (1844) 3 Curt. 761, 768; *In the Goods of Itter* [1950] P. 130, 132: see Law Reform Committee's 22nd Report, pp. 23–24 (recommending no change).

by any "natural" means, such as holding the paper up to the light with a frame of brown paper around the portion attempted to be read[25] or by using magnifying glasses.[26] In determining whether a word is apparent, it is not permissible to ascertain the word by the use of extrinsic evidence,[27] or by physically interfering with the will by using chemicals to remove ink-marks, or removing a slip of paper pasted over the word,[28] or by making another document, such as an infra-red photograph.[29] If the word can only be ascertained by these "forbidden" methods it is not apparent.

2.   Intention to revoke

The testator must make the alteration which renders part of the will not apparent with an intention to revoke that part.[30] A testator who accidentally obliterates part of his will by spilling ink over it does not, therefore, revoke it.

3.   Conditional obliteration[31]

If the testator's intention to revoke is conditional, revocation does not take place despite the obliteration unless the condition is fulfilled. If the condition is not fulfilled, the word obliterated must be ascertained so that it can be admitted to probate. For this purpose the court has recourse to any means of legal proof, including any of the above "forbidden" methods,[32] because the question to be answered is not whether the word is apparent but, rather, whether the obliterated word can be ascertained.

Usually the condition relates to the validity of a legacy of a different amount which the testator attempts to substitute in place of the original amount which he obliterates. For instance, T by his will gives to X a legacy of "one hundred and fifty pounds": later T obliterates the words "one hundred and fifty" (making them not apparent) and writes the words "two hundred" in their place. If, at the time he carries out this obliteration, T intends to revoke the original amount only if the new amount is effectually substituted, T's intention to revoke is subject to a condition which is not fulfilled (unless the alteration is duly executed or T later republishes his will): accordingly the original amount is admissible to probate.[33] But if T merely obliterates the words "and fifty,"

---

[25] *Ffinch v. Combe* [1894] P. 191 (slips of paper pasted over words in will after execution).

[26] *In the Goods of Brasier* [1899] P. 36.

[27] *Townley v. Watson* (1844) 3 Curt. 761, 768 (evidence of draftsman not admissible to prove what obliterated words were).

[28] *In the Goods of Horsford* (1874) L.R. 3 P. & D. 211 (the same will came before the court in *Ffinch v. Combe, supra*). But a slip of paper may be removed in order to ascertain whether it covers words of revocation which took effect before being covered: *In the Goods of Gilbert* [1893] P. 183.

[29] *In the Goods of Itter* [1950] P. 130.

[30] *Townley v. Watson, supra*, at p. 769.

[31] For conditional revocation by destruction see *ante*, pp. 107–109.

[32] *In the Goods of Horsford, supra* (strips of paper pasted over amount of legacy in codicil ordered to be removed as condition of revocation not fulfilled); *In the Goods of Itter, supra*; *Sturton v. Whetlock* (1883) 52 L.J.P. 29 (evidence of draftsman as to original words).

[33] *In the Goods of Itter* [1950] P. 130; *In the Goods of Horsford, supra*. As to other conditions see *In the Goods of McCabe* (1873) 3 P. & D. 94 (T gave to niece X, believing X's mother

intending to revoke them but not to substitute any new words, his intention to revoke is absolute: probate must be granted with a blank space for the words "and fifty" if these words are not apparent.[34] And the same result follows even though T later changes his mind and attempts to substitute new words. Thus if T first obliterates the words "and fifty," intending to revoke them but not to substitute any new words, and later changes his mind and writes the words "and ninety" in their place, probate must be granted with a blank space for the words "and fifty."[35]

Whether the testator's intention to revoke was conditional is a question of fact and evidence as to the testator's declarations of intention is therefore admissible.[36] If the testator attempts to substitute a legacy of a different amount, but leaves the name of the legatee untouched, the court may infer from this that his intention to revoke was conditional on the validity of the substituted amount.[37]

IV. REVIVAL AND REPUBLICATION

A. REVIVAL

A testator may revive a will or codicil, or any part thereof, which has been revoked. He cannot, however, revive a will or codicil which is no longer in existence: once it has been destroyed it cannot be revived[1] and the testator must execute a new will or codicil in order to give effect to its provisions.

1. Two methods of revival[2]

Section 22 of the Wills Act 1837 provides that a will or codicil which has been wholly or partly revoked may be revived only (i) by its re-execution with the proper formalities, or (ii) by a duly executed codicil showing an intention to revive it.

(1) *REVOCATION OF REVOKING WILL CANNOT REVIVE.* No other methods of revival are available. Thus a will which has been revoked by a later will cannot be revived by the subsequent revocation of that

---

Y was dying, and later substituted Y for X after Y's recovery: held conditional obliteration of X, and "X" admitted to probate); *Sturton v. Whetlock, supra,* (gifts to grandchildren at age of twenty one years; "one" erased and "five" substituted: held conditional obliteration).

[34] *In the Goods of Nelson* (1872) 6 I.R. Eq. 569; *In the Goods of Hamer* (1944) 113 L.J.P. 31.

[35] *In the Goods of Itter, supra,* at p. 133.

[36] *In the Goods of McCabe, supra,* at pp. 96–97; *In the Estate of Zimmer* (1924) 40 T.L.R. 502: see conditional revocation by destruction, *ante,* pp. 107–109.

[37] *In the Goods of Itter, supra.*

[1] *Rogers v. Goodenough* (1862) 2 Sw. & Tr. 342; *In the Goods of Steele* (1868) L.R. 1 P. & D. 575, 576–577; *In the Goods of Reade* [1902] P. 75. *Quaere* whether a testator may revive a will which has been destroyed without his knowledge.

[2] See Law Reform Committee's 22nd Report, p. 25 (recommending no change).

later will. In *In the Goods of Hodgkinson*³ a testator first made a will giving all his property to X and later made a second will giving his realty to Y: the second will impliedly revoked the first will as regards the testator's realty. Subsequently the testator revoked the second will by destruction. The Court of Appeal held that as regards the testator's realty the first will was not revived by the revocation of the second will: the first will disposed of the testator's personalty but his realty passed on intestacy.⁴

(2) *REVIVAL BY CODICIL SHOWING AN INTENTION TO REVIVE.* The second method of revival requires the testator to execute, with the proper formalities, a codicil showing an intention to revive the revoked will or codicil. Whether a codicil shows the necessary intention to revive is a question of construction. The intention must

"appear on the face of the codicil, either by express words referring to a will as revoked and importing an intention to revive the same, or by a disposition of the testator's property inconsistent with any other intention, or by some other expressions conveying to the mind of the Court, with reasonable certainty, the existence of the intention in question."⁵

In construing a codicil, the normal rules as to the admission of extrinsic evidence apply.⁶ For instance, evidence of the surrounding circumstances may be admissible under the "armchair principle" so that the court may ascertain the intention of the testator as expressed in the codicil when it is read in the light of the surrounding circumstances in which it was made.⁷

*In the Goods of Davis*⁸ is a useful illustration. The testator made a will giving all his estate to Ethel Phoebe Horsley. A year later he married her, thereby revoking the will. Subsequently he wrote on the envelope containing the will, "The herein named Ethel Phoebe Horsley is now my lawful wedded wife," and this writing was duly signed and attested. As evidence of the surrounding circumstances, an affidavit by Ethel's sister was admitted; proving that shortly before the testator wrote on the envelope the sister had pointed out to him that the will had been revoked by his marriage. The court held that the writing on the envelope was a codicil showing the testator's intention to revive the will because it conveyed to the mind of the court with reasonable certainty the existence

---

³ [1893] P. 339: see also *Major v. Williams* (1843) 3 Curt. 432; *In the Goods of Brown* (1858) 1 Sw. & Tr. 32.
⁴ The result would have been different if the testator had destroyed his second will, intending to revoke it *conditionally* on the revival of his first will as regards his realty— the condition would not have been fulfilled and the revocation of his second will would not have been effective, see *ante*, p. 108.
⁵ *In the Goods of Steele, supra*, at p. 578. A codicil does not show an intention to revive a revoked will if it is merely attached to it by a piece of tape; *Marsh v. Marsh*, (1860) 1 Sw. & Tr. 528.
⁶ *Post*, pp. 187 *et seq.*
⁷ *In the Goods of Steele, supra*, at p. 576; *In the Goods of Davis* [1952] P. 279.
⁸ [1952] P. 279: see also *In the Goods of Terrible* (1858) 1 Sw. & Tr. 140.

of this intention, and both the will and the envelope were accordingly admitted to probate.

(3) WHEN A CODICIL REFERS TO A REVOKED WILL BY ITS DATE. Suppose the following sequence of events:

(i) will A is dated January 1, 1988;
(ii) will B is dated June 30, 1992 and expressly revokes all former wills;
(iii) codicil "to my will dated January 1, 1988 . . .";
(iv) death of testator.

If the codicil merely describes itself as a codicil to the testator's last will, but gives the date of will A, it does not revive will A or revoke will B: the reference in the codicil to the date of will A does *not* show an intention to revive will A.[9] The cases which decide this may be supported on the ground that the description of the will by the codicil is ambiguous; will A is not the testator's last will, or his will at all, as it has been revoked.[10]

If, on the other hand, the codicil not only refers to will A by date but also refers to the provisions of will A, the codicil shows an intention to revive will A.[11] Probate is granted of will A and the codicil, and also of will B, unless will B was revoked by the codicil or by will A. In doubtful cases, the question of the extent to which will B was revoked may be left to a court of construction. Will B may be revoked expressly by a revocation clause in the codicil, or in will A (which operates as if executed at the time of revival);[12] or impliedly by provisions in the codicil and will A which are inconsistent with the provisions in will B.[13] If the codicil shows an intention to revive part, but not the whole, of will A, probate is granted of that part of will A and the codicil, and also of will B, unless will B is revoked by the codicil or the revived part of will A.[14]

Usually a codicil refers to a revoked will by its date as the result of a blunder.[15] This could have been avoided by proper precautions if:

(i) after will B was executed, will A had been clearly marked to show it had been revoked by will B; and
(ii) the draftsman of the codicil had insisted on having the testator's last will before him.

---

[9] *In the Goods of May* (1868) L.R. 1 P. & D. 575; *In the Goods of Gordon* [1892] P. 228; *Jane v. Jane* (1917) 33 T.L.R. 389; *Goldie v. Adam* [1938] P. 85
[10] *In the Goods of Whatman* (1864) 34 L.J.P.M. & A. 17.
[11] *In the Goods of Stedham* (1881) 6 P.D. 205; *In the Goods of Dyke* (1881) 6 P.D. 207; *In the Goods of Chilcott* [1897] P. 223.
[12] *Re Pearson* [1963] 1 W.L.R. 1358: but see *Re Rear* [1975] 2 N.Z.L.R. 254, 264 (*quaere* from what date revocation clause speaks): for the effect of republication of a will containing a revocation clause see *post*, pp. 119–120.
[13] *Re Baker* [1929] 1 Ch. 668; *In the Goods of Reynolds* (1873) 3 P. & D. 35.
[14] *In the Estate of Mardon* [1944] P. 109.
[15] "If experience had not shown the fact, it would be almost incredible that mistakes should occur so constantly as they do in so simple a matter as reciting the true date of a will," *per* Lord Penzance in *In the Goods of Steele, supra*, at p. 580.

2.   Effects of revival

Under section 34 of the Wills Act 1837 a revived will is deemed for the purposes of the Act to have been made at the time of its revival.[16] A revived will operates as if it had been executed at that time.[17]

(1)   *WILL REVOKED IN STAGES.* Section 22 provides that if a will or codicil is first partly revoked and later wholly revoked, but is subsequently revived, the revival does not extend to the part first revoked unless an intention to the contrary is shown.

(2)   *ALTERATION AND INCORPORATION.* Revival may validate an unattested alteration made to the will or codicil before its revival.[18] Similarly, revival of a will or codicil may incorporate a document which came into existence prior to its revival, but which was not in existence when the will or codicil was first executed.[19]

B.   REPUBLICATION

A testator may "republish" a will or codicil.[20] The term "republication" has been an anachronism since section 13 of the Wills Act 1837 made publication[21] of a will unnecessary. It might be better if the term "confirmation" came into general use instead, because this is the sense in which republication has been used since 1837.[22]

The difference between revival and republication is that revival revives a revoked will or codicil, whereas republication confirms an unrevoked will or codicil.

1.   Two methods of republication

A will or codicil may be republished only (i) by its re-execution with the proper formalities[23] or (ii) by a duly executed codicil containing some reference to it.[24] The codicil need not show an intention to confirm the previous will or codicil in the sense in which a codicil is required by section 22 to show an intention to revive a revoked will or codicil. In

---

[16] s. 34 may on its proper construction merely refer to the commencement of the Act (*Re Elcom* [1894] 1 Ch. 303, 309) but in *Goonewardene v. Goonewardene* [1931] A.C. 647 the Privy Council treated it *obiter* as having general application.

[17] Republication generally has the same effect, *post*, p. 119.

[18] *Neate v. Pickard* (1843) *Notes of Cases* 406. Revival, like republication, does not validate a merely deliberative alteration; again the reviving codicil may show the testator was treating the revived will or codicil as unaltered; see *ante*, p. 112.

[19] Republication has the same effect, *ante*, p. 92.

[20] See generally, J.D.B. Mitchell (1954) 70 L.Q.R. 353.

[21] Publication was a declaration by the testator in the presence of witnesses that the instrument produced to them was his will.

[22] *Berkeley v. Berkeley* [1946] A.C. 555–576.

[23] *Dunn v. Dunn* (1866) L.R. 1 P. & D. 277.

[24] *Re Smith* (1890) 45 Ch.D. 632 (duly executed paper made no reference to previous will: no republication).

order to republish a will, a codicil need only contain some reference to the will. Thus a will is republished by a codicil which describes itself as "codicil to my will."[25] From such a brief reference the inference is drawn that, when executing the codicil, the testator considered the will as his will and thereby confirmed it. This has been termed constructive republication. It has the same effect as if the testator expressly confirmed the will, *e.g.* by using the phrase usually found at the end of a codicil, "In all other respects I confirm my will."

2. Effects of republication

Section 34 of the Wills Act 1837 applies to republication as well as to revival.[26] In general, a republished will operates as if it had been executed at the time of its republication.[27]

(1) *REPUBLICATION MUST NOT DEFEAT INTENTION.* The doctrine of republication is not applied so as to defeat the testator's intention by, for instance, invalidating a gift which was valid at the date of the will.[28] As Barton J. put it in the Irish case of *Re Moore.*[29]:

"The authorities . . . lead me to the conclusion that the courts have always treated the principle that republication makes the will speak as if it had been re-executed at the date of the codicil not as a rigid formula or technical rule, but as a useful and flexible instrument for effectuating a testator's intentions, by ascertaining them down to the latest date at which they have been expressed."

(2) *REPUBLICATION OF WILL CONTAINING REVOCATION CLAUSE.* The sequence of events in *In the Goods of Rawlins*[30] was:

(i) execution of a will which contained a revocation clause in general terms;
(ii) execution of a codicil to the will;
(iii) the testator deleted one clause in the will and then re-executed it.

The court held that the codicil was not revoked by the republication of the will containing the revocation clause. The will was re-executed so as to give effect to the deletion and it was not the testator's intention to

---

[25] *Re Taylor* (1880) 57 L.J. Ch. 430, 434: see also *Skinner v. Ogle* (1845) 1 Rob.Ecc. 363; *Serocold v. Hemming* (1758) 2 Lee 490 (revival prior to Wills Act 1837, and cited in *Re Smith, supra*); *Re Harvey* [1947] Ch.285 (where Vaisey J. said "a codicil described as a codicil to a particular will republishes that will").

[26] See *ante,* p. 118 n. 16.

[27] For the effect of republication of a will which contains an appointment under a special power, which becomes exercisable after the will but before republication, see *Re Blackburn* (1890) 43 Ch.D. 75. For the exception relating to an illegitimate child see *post,* pp. 198–199, and for the exception relating to the age of majority see *post,* p. 200.

[28] *Re Moore* [1907] 1 I.R. 315; *Re Heath's W.T.* [1949] Ch. 170; *Re Park* [1910] 2 Ch. 322.

[29] [1907] 1 I.R. 315, 318: see also *Re Hardyman* [1925] Ch. 287, 291.

[30] (1879) 48 L.J.P. 64: see also *Wade v. Nazer* (1848) 1 Rob. 627. If a will is republished by codicil, any alteration already made to the will by codicil between the execution and republication of the will stands (*Crosbie v. MacDoual* (1799) 4 Ves. 610; *Green v. Tribe* (1878) 9 Ch.D. 231) unless the republishing codicil shows an intention to revive a revoked part of the will (*McLeod v. McNab* [1891] A.C. 471).

revoke the codicil—"prima facie the re-execution of the will is a con-firmation and not a revocation of the codicil, which became part of the instrument."[31]

(3)   *ALTERATION AND INCORPORATION.* The effect of republication on an unattested alteration already made to the will or codicil,[32] and on the incorporation of a document which came into existence prior to republication,[33] has already been considered.

(4)   *INVALID GIFT TO WITNESS OR SPOUSE OF WITNESS.* Section 15 of the Wills Act 1837 deprives an attesting witness and his or her spouse of any benefit under a gift in the will. But if the will is republished by a codicil not attested by that witness, this validates the gift.[34]

(5)   *LAPSE AND ADEMPTION.* The effect of republication on a gift which has lapsed,[35] or been adeemed,[36] is considered later.

(6)   *DATE FROM WHICH A WILL SPEAKS.* Again the effect of repub-lication on the date from which a will speaks is considered later.[37]

---

[31] (1879) 48 L.J.P. 64, 65.
[32] *Ante*, p. 112.
[33] *Ante*, p. 92.
[34] *Post*, pp. 233–234.
[35] *Post*, pp. 236–237.
[36] *Post*, pp. 252–253.
[37] *Post*, p. 223.

Chapter 6

PROVISION FOR THE DECEASED'S FAMILY AND DEPENDANTS[1]

I. INTRODUCTION

From the sixteenth century onwards, there was near total testamentary freedom[2] in England and Wales and in 1891, with the enactment of the Mortmain and Charitable Uses Act, this freedom became total. This meant that a testator could do whatever he liked with his property[3] and a millionaire could, if he wanted, on his death, leave his family destitute.[4] These four hundred years of testamentary freedom came to an end with the enactment of the Inheritance (Family Provision) Act 1938, the start of family provision legislation in England and Wales.

Testamentary freedom is a concept which seems natural to lawyers brought up in the Common Law, as opposed to the Civil Law, tradition. Those accustomed to systems based on Roman Law are more likely to assume that the deceased must pass at least part of his property on to his descendants or to other members of his family. Such property is called in French Law the *réserve légale*[5] and in Scottish Law *legitim*[6].

The Inheritance (Family Provision) Act 1938 enabled four classes of "dependants" of a deceased person to apply to the court for a discretionary order for maintenance out of his estate. The four classes were the deceased's (i) wife or husband, (ii) unmarried or incapacitated daughter, (iii) infant son, (iv) incapacitated son. The 1938 Act applied only where the deceased had left a *will* but it was extended by the Intestates' Estates Act 1952 to intestacies. The Matrimonial Causes (Property and Maintenance) Act 1958, gave *former spouses* rights equivalent to those enjoyed by the four original classes.[7]

---

[1] There are a number of monographs on Family Provision. See, *e.g.* Ross Martyn, *Family Provision: Law and Practice* (2nd ed., 1985); or Tyler's *Family Provision* (2nd ed., by R.D. Oughton, 1984).

[2] Freedom to dispose of personalty at death dated back to the mid-fifteenth century. Freedom to dispose of realty derived from the Statute of Wills 1540. See also Williams, Mortimer and Sunnucks, *Executors, Administrators and Probate* (17th ed., 1993), p. 758.

[3] This refers, of course, to *his* property and not to property held in trust.

[4] Though it should not be forgotten that the widespread use of strict settlements and entails operated in such a way as to ensure that property stayed in the family.

[5] *Code Civil* Arts. 913 and 914.

[6] Walker, *Principles of Scottish Private Law*, Vol. IV (4th ed., 1989). For a comparative study of the law in the United Kingdom and the Republic of Ireland see C.H. Sherrin (1980) 31 N.I.L.Q. 21.

[7] s. 3 of the 1958 Act, which became s. 26 of the Matrimonial Causes Act 1965.

In 1973 the Law Commission produced a report, *Family Law: First Report on Family Property. A New Approach*,[8] in which it considered the possibility of introducing a system under which a surviving spouse would have had a legal right to inherit part of the estate of a deceased spouse. Such a right would not have depended on the court's discretion. The Law Commission concluded, however, that it was neither necessary nor desirable to introduce such a principle; but it decided that, in so far as it was practicable in the differing circumstances, the claim of a surviving spouse upon the family assets should be at least equal to that of a spouse on a divorce.[9] This led, the following year, to a further Law Commission report, *Family Law: Second Report on Family Property. Family Provision on Death*,[10] which in turn resulted in the enactment of the Inheritance (Provision for Family and Dependants) Act 1975.[11]

In 1989, another Law Commission report, *Distribution on Intestacy*[12] considered, *inter alia*, whether cohabitants should be provided for under the intestacy rules. The report recommended that cohabitants should not be provided for under the intestacy rules but that they should, instead, be provided for under the family provision legislation. In accordance with this recommendation, section 2 of the Law Reform (Succession) Act 1995 amended the 1975 Act by adding cohabitants as a further class of applicants. They may apply where the deceased dies on or after January 1, 1996.

The 1975 Act applies on the death of any person after March 31, 1976. Any of the following persons may apply for provision:

"(a) the wife or husband of the deceased;
(b) a former wife or former husband of the deceased who has not remarried;
(c) a child of the deceased;
(d) any person (not being a child of the deceased) who, in the case of any marriage to which the deceased was at any time a party, was treated by the deceased as a child of the family in relation to that marriage;
(e) any person (not being a person included in the foregoing paragraphs of this subsection) who immediately before the death of the deceased was being maintained, either wholly or partly, by the deceased."[13]

And where someone dies on or after January 1, 1996, application may also be made by:

"(ba) any person who was living in the same household as the deceased, and as the husband or wife of the deceased, during the whole of the period of two years ending immediately before the date when the deceased died."[14]

---

[8] Law Com. No. 52: H.C. 274.
[9] Law Com. No. 52: para 61.
[10] Law Com. No. 61: H.C. 324.
[11] For a more detailed history see K Green (1988) 51 M.L.R. 187, 190–195.
[12] Law Com. No. 187.
[13] 1975 Act, s. 1. Each category of applicant is considered more fully, *post*, pp. 135 *et seq*.
[14] Law Reform (Succession) Act 1995, ss. 2(2) and 2(3).

The 1975 Act made a number of important changes to the 1938 legislation. It added to the classes of applicants; it increased and amended the standard of provision for spouses; it added to the orders the court could make; it added to the property out of which financial provision could be ordered; and it introduced anti-avoidance provisions. Cases decided under the 1938 Act represent a continuing body of case law and should not be ignored[15]; but the earlier authorities should be approached with caution because of the substantial changes which have occurred in the legislation.[16]

II. DOMICILE, JURISDICTION, TIME LIMIT AND PROTECTION FOR PERSONAL REPRESENTATIVES.

1. Domicile

The 1975 Act applies only if the deceased died domiciled in England and Wales.[1] The legal burden of proof that the deceased died so domiciled lies on the applicant.[2]

2. Jurisdiction

An application under the Act may be made either to the Chancery Division or to the Family Division of the High Court, which has unlimited jurisdiction; or to the county court which now also has unlimited jurisdiction as a result of the High Court and County Courts Jurisdiction Order 1991.[3] Chancery masters in the High Court and district judges in the county court commonly hear applications; so the distinction between trial in the High Court and in the county court is not as significant as it might otherwise be.[4] As to the choice between the Chancery Division and the Family Division, some applications fall more conveniently within one jurisdiction and some within the other. If, for example, an application under the 1975 Act arises in relation to an estate where there is also a dispute over the construction of the deceased's will, it is best that the application be dealt with immediately after the construction summons

---

[15] *Re Coventry* [1980] Ch. 461, 474 and 487.

[16] *Moody v. Stevenson* [1992] Ch. 486, 502.

[1] 1975 Act, ss. 1(1) and 27(2): for domicile see Dicey and Morris, *The Conflict of Laws* (12th ed., 1993), pp. 115 *et seq.*; Theobald on Wills (15th ed., 1993), pp. 3–7. For forceful criticism of domicile as the sole basis of jurisdiction see J.H.C. Morris (1946) 62 L.Q.R. 170, 178–179; see also Law Com. No. 61, paras. 258–262, which recommended no change.

[2] *Mastaka v. Midland Bank Executor and Trustee Co. Ltd* [1941] Ch. 192. Under the Domicile and Matrimonial Proceedings Act 1973, a married woman can now acquire a domicile independent of her husband.

[3] S.I. 1991 No. 724.

[4] The guidelines for the allocation of proceedings contained in paras. 7 and 9 of the High Court and County Courts Jurisdiction Order 1991 indicate that claims worth less than £25,000 should be tried in the county court and those worth more than £50,000 should be tried in the High Court. Unless the application is obviously simple and modest, the best course is usually to start in the High Court, but to be alert to the possibility of an order for trail in the county court if it will save time and money. See Williams, Mortimer and Sunnucks, *Executors, Administrators and Probate* (17th ed., 1993), pp. 817–818.

by the same judge in the Chancery Division.[5] If, on the other hand, the application relates to the estate of someone who was previously subject to an order under the Matrimonial Causes Act, it may be convenient to deal with it in the Family Division.[6]

3.   Time limit for application

An application under the Act must be made no later than six months from the date on which a valid grant of probate or letters of administration to the deceased's estate[7] is first taken out.[8] The court has, however, an unfettered discretion to extend this time limit. In *Re Salmon*[9] a widow's application for an extension was refused by Sir Robert Megarry V.-C. where her claim was more than four and a half months out of time and the fault was wholly on the widow's side.[10] The Vice Chancellor laid down the following "guidelines":

- (i) the discretion must be exercised judicially;
- (ii) the onus lies on the applicant to make out a substantial case for its being just and proper for the court to exercise its discretion to extend the time. He thought that the court should consider;
- (iii) how promptly, and in what circumstances, the applicant applied to the court for an extension (and how promptly the applicant warned the defendants of the proposed application);
- (iv) whether negotiations commenced within the time limit (if so, and time ran out while they were proceeding, this is likely to encourage the court to extend the time);
- (v) whether the estate had been distributed before a claim under the Act was made or notified; and
- (vi) whether a refusal to extend the time would leave the applicant without redress against anybody or, alternatively, whether she might have a claim against her own solicitors for negligence.[11]

It seems that it may not be possible to make an application *before* a grant of representation is taken out.[12] This may create difficulties where the deceased was a joint tenant of property which passes by

---

[5] Similarly, if there is a claim by the applicant that he has an interest under a constructive (or resulting) trust and is seeking an order under L.P.A. 1925, s. 30.

[6] See Williams, Mortimer and Sunnucks, *Executors, Adminitrators and Probate* (17th ed., 1993), pp. 809 *et seq*.

[7] See *post*, pp. 320 *et seq*. A grant limited to settled land or trust property is disregarded, and so is a grant limited to real or personal estate unless a grant limited to the remainder of the estate has previously been made or is made at the same time, s. 23; *Re Miller* [1969] 1 W.L.R. 583 (representation is first taken out on grant in common form, though affirmed in solemn form later); *Re Freeman* [1984] 1 W.L.R. 1419 (time only runs from a valid grant of representation).

[8] s. 4. An application is made when the summons is issued, and not when it is served: *Re Chittenden* [1970] 1 W.L.R. 1618. For a standing search for a grant see *post*, p. 348.

[9] [1981] Ch. 167. *Cf. Stock v. Brown* [1994] 1 F.L.R. 840.

[10] The fault lay with the widow herself *or* her solicitors.

[11] Applicant must also show he has an arguable case, *Re Dennis* [1981] 2 All E.R. 140.

[12] *Re McBroom* [1992] 2 F.L.R. 49.

survivorship[13] and nobody applies for a grant of probate or letters of administration.[14]

4. Protection of personal representatives

The personal representatives may safely pay the deceased's funeral, testamentary and administration expenses, debts and liabilities before the six months' time limit has expired, irrespective of whether any application under the Act has been made.[15]

After this time limit has expired, if no application under the Act has been made, the personal representatives may safely distribute the estate to the beneficiaries under the deceased's will or intestacy. The time limit is short so as not unduly to impede distribution by the personal representatives. The Act provides that after this time limit has expired the personal representatives can distribute without taking into account the possibility that the court might (i) extend the time limit or (ii) vary its original order for the making of periodical payments to an applicant,[16] but this protection for the personal representatives does not prejudice any power to recover, by reason of the making of an order under the Act, any part of the estate so distributed.[17]

If an applicant does apply to the court, there is no rigid rule that the personal representatives must preserve the entire net estate intact until the pending application has been heard by the court. Whether it is safe for the personal representatives to make any distribution depends on the circumstances. It may be safe, for instance, for them to pay a legacy to the applicant who is seeking more provision under the Act, or to some other legatee if there is no risk of the court directing that any part of any provision ordered for the applicant should fall on the legacy because, for example, the legacy is trifling in comparison with the size of the estate, or because the legatee has a high moral claim on the testator's bounty and is in need of the money. If in doubt, personal representatives can seek the consent of the interested parties to such a payment being made and, if consent is not forthcoming, apply to the court for leave to make the payment.[18]

III. THE TEST OF REASONABLE FINANCIAL PROVISION

The court may order provision to be made under the Act for an applicant only if it "is satisfied that the disposition of the deceased's estate

---

[13] The deceased's net estate, may, if the court so orders, include his severable share of any property of which he was a beneficial joint tenant immediately before his death, see *post*, pp. 151–152.

[14] *Re McBroom, supra*; but *cf. Re Searle* [1949] Ch 73. If the decision in *Re McBroom* is good law (and it is suggested that it may not be), the applicant needs to persuade someone to apply for letters of administration—these may be limited to the proceedings—see p. 346.

[15] See definition of the deceased's net estate, *post*, pp. 150 *et seq*. As to the power of a personal representative to postpone performance of a contract which the personal representative has reason to believe the deceased entered into with the intention of defeating an application for financial provision under the Act, see *post*, pp. 163–164.

[16] *Post*, p. 157.

[17] s. 20(1).

[18] *Re Ralphs* [1986] 1 W.L.R. 1522, 1525 where Cross J. gave helpful guidance.

effected by his will or the law relating to intestacy, or the combination of his will and that law, is not such as to make reasonable financial provision for the applicant."[1] Exactly the same test applies whether the deceased died testate or wholly or partly intestate.[2]

1.   Two standards of reasonable financial provision

Section 1(2) of the 1975 Act sets two different standards of reasonable financial provision, which may be called "the surviving spouse standard" and "the maintenance standard."

(1)   *THE SURVIVING SPOUSE STANDARD.* Reasonable financial provision at the surviving spouse standard means "such financial provision as it would be reasonable in all the circumstances of the case for a husband or wife to receive, whether or not that provision is required for his or her maintenance."[3] In short, the standard is reasonable provision *in all the circumstances*, and not (as it was under the 1938 Act) reasonable provision for the *maintenance* of the husband or wife.[4] In setting this new surviving spouse standard "the legislature had in mind a very much wider approach" than under the 1938 Act.[5] The Law Commission justified the introduction of this new standard on the ground that the claim of a surviving spouse upon the family assets should be at least equal to that of a divorced spouse, and the court's powers to order provision for a surviving spouse should be as wide as its powers to order financial provision on a divorce.[6]

This surviving spouse standard is applicable on any application by the deceased's wife or husband,[7] including a person who in good faith entered into a void marriage with the deceased,[8] but excluding a spouse who is judicially separated from the deceased at the latter's death.

(2)   *DISCRETION TO APPLY SURVIVING SPOUSE STANDARD.* The court may in its discretion apply the surviving spouse standard on an application by a judicially separated spouse[9] or a former spouse who has not remarried[10] if (i) the deceased died within 12 months of the decree of judicial separation, or of the decree absolute of divorce or nullity of marriage (as the case may be), and (ii) at the deceased's death no order making (or refusing) provision for such spouse had been made in the matrimonial proceedings.[11] In this exceptional situation the court has a

---

[1] s.2(1): see *Rajabally v. Rajabally* [1987] 2 F.L.R. 390 (widow's application not defeated by unenforceable assurances by beneficiaries not to insist on their rights under will).
[2] *Re Coventry* [1980] Ch. 461, 488–489: see also s. 24.
[3] s.1(2)(a)
[4] *Re Besterman* [1984] Ch. 458, 465–466 and 470: see *post*, pp. 137–138.
[5] *Re Coventry* [1980] Ch. 461, 468 and 484–485.
[6] Law Com. No. 61, paras. 12–18 and 26–30.
[7] s. 1(2)(a): see *post*, p. 135.
[8] s. 25(4): see *post*, p. 136.
[9] *i.e.* a spouse whose marriage with the deceased was the subject of a decree of judicial separation and at the date of death of the deceased the decree was in force and the separation was continuing, s. 1(2)(a).
[10] 1(1)(b): see *post*, p. 139.
[11] s. 14: no financial provision order or property adjustment order under ss. 23 and 24 of the Matrimonial Causes Act 1973 must have been made or refused; it is immaterial that maintenance pending suit under s. 22 has been ordered or refused.

discretion to apply the surviving spouse standard. The Law Commission recommended this, in order to cope with cases where the death of the deceased has caused the judicially separated or former spouse to miss the opportunity to obtain a fair share of the family assets in the matrimonial proceedings.[12] This is the only situation in which the court has any discretion as to which standard of reasonable financial provision to apply.

(3) *THE MAINTENANCE STANDARD.* Reasonable financial provision at the maintenance standard means "such financial provision as it would be reasonable in all the circumstances of the case for the applicant to receive for his maintenance."[13] The same standard was applicable to all applications under the 1938 Act.

Reasonable provision for maintenance does not mean, on the one hand, merely the provision of the bare necessities of life, so as to keep an applicant at subsistence level[14]; on the other hand, it does not mean "anything which may be regarded as reasonably desirable for his general benefit or welfare."[15] In *Re Coventry*[16] Buckley L.J. suggested it means "such financial provision as would be reasonable in all the circumstances of the case to enable the applicant to maintain himself in a manner suitable to those circumstances." In *Re Dennis*[17] Browne-Wilkinson J. said that "'maintenance' connotes only payments which, directly or indirectly, enable the applicant in the future to discharge the cost of his daily living at whatever standard of living is appropriate to him."[18] The case concerned an application by an able-bodied adult son for £50,000 from the estate of his rich father, so that the applicant son could pay capital transfer tax on a lifetime gift[19] of £90,000 which his father had made to him and which the son had dissipated in spendthrift living. The son claimed that he could not otherwise pay the £50,000 tax and, if he did not pay it, he would be made bankrupt by the Inland Revenue. Browne-Wilkinson J. held that payment of the capital transfer tax would not, directly or indirectly, contribute to the son's living expenses and so

[12] Law Com. No. 61, paras. 59–63.
[13] s. 1(2)(b).
[14] *Re Coventry* [1980] Ch. 461, 485 and 494; *Re E.* [1966] 1 W.L.R. 709, 715 (the purpose of the 1938 Act was not to require the deceased to keep applicants "above the breadline").
[15] Per Goff L.J. in *Re Coventry* [1980] Ch. 461, 485. In *Re Christie* [1979] Ch. 168, 174 the deputy judge said that maintenance "refers to no more and no less than the applicant's way of life and well-being, his health, financial security and allied matters such as the well-being, health and financial security of his immediate family for whom he is responsible": but in *Re Coventry, supra,* at p. 471 Oliver J. expressed reservations as regards this "very broad interpretation of the word 'maintenance' which seems to me to come dangerously near to equating it simply with 'wellbeing' or 'benefit' ". In *Re Jennings* [1994] Ch. 286, 298 the Court of Appeal held that discharging the applicant's mortgage might be for the applicant's general benefit or welfare but that it was *not* reasonably required for his maintenance.
[16] *Re Coventry, supra,* at p. 494: see also *Re Borthwick* [1949] Ch. 395, 401 (a widow's application to which the surviving spouse standard would now be applicable); *Millward v. Shenton* [1972] 1 W.L.R. 711, 715 (married son suffering from a progressive illness: a lump sum to enable him to have a television set, or a car, or even a better house); *Malone v. Harrison* [1979] 1 W.L.R. 1353, 1361.
[17] [1981] 2 All E.R. 140.
[18] [1981] 2 All E.R. 140, 145.
[19] For a brief explantion of capital transfer tax, see Chap. 12.

an application for payment of the tax was not an application for maintenance.[20]

The maintenance standard is applicable on an application by a judicially separated spouse or a former spouse who has not remarried, unless the court has,[21] and exercises, the discretion to apply the surviving spouse standard. The maintenance standard is always applicable on an application by a child of the deceased,[22] by a person treated by the deceased as a child of the family,[23] by a dependant of the deceased,[24] or by a cohabitant.[25]

2. No provision ordered unless test satisfied

The court cannot order provision to be made under the Act for an applicant unless it is satisfied that the disposition of the deceased's estate is not such as to make reasonable financial provision for the applicant, measured by the surviving spouse or maintenance standard as appropriate.[26] "It clearly cannot be enough to say that the circumstances are such that if the deceased had made a particular provision for the applicant, that would not have been an unreasonable thing for him to do and therefore it now ought to be done. The court has no carte blanche to reform the deceased's dispositions or those which statute makes of his estate [on his intestacy] to accord with what the court itself might have thought would be sensible if it had been in the deceased's position."[27] Again, it is not the proper test to ask "how the available assets should be fairly divided?"[28]

3. The test is objective

The vital question whether the disposition of the deceased's estate is not such as to make reasonable financial provision for the applicant (measured by whichever standard is appropriate) is to be answered objectively from the point of view of the court and not subjectively from the point of view of the deceased.[29] As Megarry J. put it in *Re Goodwin*,[30] "The statutory language is ... wholly impersonal." Accordingly it is irrelevant to consider whether the deceased acted unreasonably in

---

[20] The son's application was out of time, he needed to show that he had an arguable case that he was *entitled* to financial provision, see *ante* p. 124; he failed to show this.

[21] See *ante* p. 126.

[22] s. 1(1)(c).

[23] s. 1(1)(d): see *post*, p. 144 *et seq.*

[24] s. 1(1)(e): see *post*, p. 145.

[25] s. 1(1)(ba), inserted by ss. 2(2) and 2(3) of the Law Reform (Succession) Act 1995.

[26] s. 2(1); *Re Coventry* [1980] Ch. 461, 474–475 and 494–495; Re Fullard [1982] Fam. 42, 46 and 50 ("condition precedent").

[27] *Re Coventry, supra*, at p. 475.

[28] *Re Coventry, supra*, at pp. 486 and 493.

[29] ss 1(1) and 2(1); *Re Coventry; supra*, at pp. 474–475 and 488–489 ("any view expressed by a deceased person that he wishes a particular person to benefit will generally be of little significance, because the question is not subjective but objective"): *cf. Re Christie* [1979] Ch. 168, 174.

[30] [1969] 1 Ch. 283, 287 (on the similar language of the 1938 Act): see also *Re Shanahan* [1973] Fam. 1, 8.

making no provision, or no larger provision, for the applicant.[31] The question whether the deceased stands convicted of unreasonableness does not arise.[32]

This objective approach makes it irrelevant to consider whether the deceased knew of all the material facts. On an application by a former wife, for instance, there may well be some material fact which is proved in evidence but which was not known to the deceased. For example, though the deceased does not know it, his former wife may have fallen on ill-health or other ill-fortune and be no longer capable of self-support.[33] The court has regard to all the material facts irrespective of whether they were known to the deceased. Indeed, the court even takes into account material facts which occurred after the death of the deceased before the court hears the application.[34]

4. Two stages of an application

The court considers an application under the Act in two stages, because the court has to decide two key questions in turn.[35]

(1) *FIRST STAGE*. The court first decides whether it is satisfied that the disposition of the deceased's estate effected by his will or the law relating to intestacy, or the combination of his will and that law, is not such as to make reasonable financial provision for the applicant, measured by the surviving spouse or the maintenance standard as appropriate. If the court decides that the disposition does make reasonable financial provision, the application fails at the first hurdle.[36] Thus if the will,[37] or the law relating to intestacy,[38] makes no provision at all for the applicant, but the court decides that reasonable financial provision is nil, the application fails. On the other hand, if the court is satisfied that the disposition is not such as to make reasonable financial provision for the applicant, the court proceeds to the second stage. This first stage involves a "value judgment, or a qualitative decision" by the trial judge.[39]

(2) *SECOND STAGE*. If the application passes the first hurdle, the court next decides, in the exercise of its discretion, whether, and in what manner, it shall order provision to be made for the applicant.[40] This is a question of discretion.[41] At this second stage the court quantifies the

---

[31] *Re Coventry* [1980] Ch. 461, 474.
[32] *Re Goodwin* [1969] 1 Ch. 283, 288. *Moody v. Stevenson* [1992] Ch. 486.
[33] *Re Shanahan, supra*, at p. 4. See also *Re Franks* [1948] Ch. 62 (son born two days before death of mother who had no chance to change her will and provide for him: held provision should be made for son).
[34] s. 3(5).
[35] ss. 2(1) and 3(1): *Re Coventry, supra*, at pp. 469 and 486–487; *Re Sivyer* [1967] 1 W.L.R. 1482, 1486–1487.
[36] *Re Coventry, supra; Re Fullard* [1982] Fam. 42.
[37] *Re Fullard* [1982] Fam. 42 (former wife): see *post*, p. 140.
[38] *Re Coventry, supra*, (adult child): see *post*, p. 143.
[39] *Re Coventry, supra*, at pp. 487 and 495.
[40] s. 2(1) and 3(1); *Re Coventry, supra*, at p. 469 and 486; *Re Rowlands* (1984) 5 F.L.R. 813 (whether and in what manner poses two questions): for the orders which the court may make see *post*, pp. 150 *et seq.*
[41] *Re Coventry, supra*, at p. 487.

provision to be ordered for the applicant by reference to the test of reasonable financial provision, measured by the surviving spouse or the maintenance standard as appropriate.[42]

5. Facts as known to the court at the date of hearing

At both these stages, section 3(5) of the Act directs the court to take into account the facts as known to the court at the date of the hearing.[43] Thus the court must take into account events which occurred after the death of the deceased before the hearing of the application. For instance, the value of the deceased's net estate may have risen or fallen since his death and at both stages the court considers the value of the deceased's net estate at the date of the hearing. Again, if an applicant, who at the deceased's death was poor and had good prospects of making a successful application, shortly afterwards wins a fortune on the football pools, the court takes this into account at the hearing and the application must fail because reasonable provision for the applicant is nil.[44]

6. The general guidelines[45]

At both stages of an application, section 3 of the Act requires the court to have regard to (i) general guidelines, which are applicable on any application, and (ii) particular guidelines, which are specified for each different category of applicant. The particular guidelines are considered later.[46]

(1)–(3) *FINANCIAL RESOURCES AND NEEDS.* The first three general guidelines are the financial resources and financial needs which (a) the applicant, (b) any other applicant for any order under the Act, and (c) any beneficiary[47] has or is likely to have in the foreseeable future.

In considering any person's financial resources, the court must take into account his earning capacity,[48] and not just his, perhaps low, current earnings.[49] Again, the court takes into account a person's pension, whether from the state or from former employment.[50] Other forms of

---

[42] *Re Besterman* [1984] Ch. 458: see *post,* pp. 137–138.

[43] See *Re Coventry, supra,* at pp. 491 and 493.

[44] *Quaere* whether the court will extend the six months' time limit in a case where the applicant relies for his success on an event which occurred after this time limit had expired—for instance, the sudden onset of a disability which made the applicant permanently unfit for work; see *post,* p. 133.

[45] The term "guidelines" was used in Law Com. No. 61, paras. 31–36, 52–54, 81–84, and 96–98: the 1975 Act does not use this term, but refers to them as "matters."

[46] *Post,* p. 135 *et seq.*

[47] *i.e.* a person beneficially interested under the deceased's will or intestacy, or a person who takes under a statutory nomination or a *donatio mortis causa* made by the deceased, s. 25(1).

[48] s.3(6).

[49] *Re Ducksbury* [1966] 1 W.L.R. 1226, 1233: see also *Malone v. Harrison* [1979] 1 W.L.R. 1353, 1359 and 1364–1365 (woman's earning capacity until age of 60).

[50] *Re Catmull* [1943] Ch. 262 (widow's pension); *Re Charman* [1951] 2 T.L.R. 1095 (bank's voluntary pension unlikely to be withdrawn); *Re Clayton* [1966] 1 W.L.R. 969 (prospect of future pension from employer); *Re Crawford* (1983) 4 F.L.R. 273 (widow's pension).

state aid may also be relevant,[51] although the fact of state aid does not preclude consideration of whether reasonable financial provision has been made.[52]

A person's financial resources include his capital assets, such as his house or flat, company shares and money in the bank, and also the damages he has received for personal injuries.[53] It would, however, generally not be right to treat the value of a person's home as expendable capital which he should spend in maintaining himself.[54] The reference in the guideline to the financial resources which a person is likely to have in the foreseeable future covers, for instance, assets which he is likely to inherit under an the will of an elderly relative.[55]

In considering any person's financial needs the court must take into account his financial obligations and responsibilities.[56] Again the guideline refers both to present financial needs and to needs which a person is likely to have in the foreseeable future.[57]

(4) *OBLIGATIONS AND RESPONSIBILITIES OF THE DECEASED.* The fourth general guideline is "(d) any obligations and responsibilities which the deceased had towards any applicant ... or towards any beneficiary."[58] Whether the deceased had any obligations and responsibilities towards an applicant or a beneficiaciary depends on all the circumstances.[59] Before the 1975 Act, these obligations and responsibilities were sometimes referred to as a moral claim on the deceased's bounty.

In the recent case of *Re Jennings*[60] the Court of Appeal held that it was not possible to construe general guideline (d) in such a way as to include legal obligations and responsibilities which the deceased had owed to his son during the son's minority, many years earlier, but which the deceased had failed to discharge. In this case, the applicant son had had

---

[51] *Re E.* [1966] 1 W.L.R. 709; *Re Clayton* [1966] 1 W.L.R. 969; see *post*, p. 133.

[52] *Re Collins* [1990] Fam 56, 61.

[53] *Daubney v. Daubney* [1976] Fam. 267.

[54] *Malone v. Harrison* [1979] 1 W.L.R. 1353, 1365. A house may yield income from lodgers, *Re E., supra.*

[55] See *Morgan v. Morgan* [1977] Fam. 122.

[56] s.3(6).

[57] *Re Clayton, supra,* (provision for crippled widower as employment might end); *Re Ducksbury* [1966] 1 W.L.R. 1226, 1233 (future needs when no longer able to earn her living).

[58] *Ante,* n. 47.

[59] See cases cited *infra*, nn. 63–64; *Re Simson* [1950] Ch. 38, 40 (housekeeper, as beneficiary); *Re Andrews* [1955] 1 W.L.R. 1105 (father owed no moral obligation to daughter incapable of maintaining herself, who left home 42 years before to live with a married man): cf. *Millward v. Shenton* [1972] 1 W.L.R. 711 (son aged 52 incapacitated from earning by progressive illness): *Re Clarke* [1968] 1 W.L.R. 415 (moral claims of applicant wife, and deceased's elderly mother as beneficiary, on his bounty: distant relatives no such claims); *Re Coventry* [1980] Ch. 461, 475–477, 487–490 and 494–495 (father owed no moral obligations to adult son); *Re Fullard* [1982] Fam. 42 (no obligations to former wife); *Re Besterman* [1984] Ch. 458 (duty to wife but not to main beneficiary Oxford University); *Re Rowlands* (1984) 5 F.L.R. 813 (some small moral obligation owed to wife despite 43 years' separation); *Re Debenham* (1986) 7 F.L.R. 404 (mother's moral obligation to unwanted daughter, aged 58 and epileptic). See also *Re Harker–Thomas* [1969] P. 28, 31 where Latey J. said "the ties of blood and, indeed, the rights and benefits which the law itself provides on intestacy ... amount to a claim": *sed quaere* in what sense.

[60] [1994] Ch. 286.

no contact at all with the deceased from the time when the applicant was two years old and his parents were divorced. He was 45 years old when his father died. It was argued, on his behalf, that his father's failure to discharge legal obligations owed to the applicant during the applicant's minority formed the basis for a claim on the estate. The Court of Appeal[61] held that, as a general rule, guideline (d) refers only to obligations and responsibilities which the deceased had immediately before his death. It neither revives defunct obligations and responsibilities as a basis for a claim for financial provision, nor does it turn the blood relationship between father and son into a continuing moral obligation which then forms the basis for an order under the 1975 Act.

The deceased's estate may be large enough to satisfy all his obligations and responsibilities;[62] but, if it is not, the court may have to weigh in the balance the respective obligations which the deceased had towards each applicant and beneficiary in order to adjudicate on the conflicting claims of, for instance, a widow and a woman with whom the deceased was living at the time of his death,[63] or a widow and a former wife,[64] or a wife and the children of another marriage.[65] In doing so, the court considers all the circumstances, including such factors as each person's resources and needs,[66] and the source of the deceased's assets. It may be material that one of the claimants had helped the deceased build up his business,[67] or that most of the deceased's assets had been inherited by him from the mother of one of the claimants.[68]

Two of the particular guidelines—which apply where an application is made by a person treated by the deceased as a child of the family, or by a dependant of the deceased—refer specifically to the assumption by the deceased of responsibility for the applicant's maintenance. These particular guidelines are considered later.[69]

(5) *SIZE AND NATURE OF THE ESTATE.* The fifth general guideline is "(e) the size and nature of the net estate[70] of the deceased." If the deceased left a large net estate, reasonable financial provision for an applicant may well be considerably more than would be appropriate, or indeed possible, from a smaller net estate.[71]

---

[61] Reversing the judge at first instance.

[62] *Malone v. Harrison* [1979] 1 W.L.R. 1353, 1364.

[63] *Re Joslin* [1941] Ch. 201 (T's moral obligation to woman with whom he was living at the time of his death and infant children by her); *Re E.* [1966] 1 W.L.R. 709; *Re Thornley* [1969] 1 W.L.R. 1037. *Jessop v. Jessop* [1992] 1 F.L.R. 591.

[64] *Re Talbot* [1962] 1 W.L.R. 1113; *Roberts v. Roberts* [1965] 1 W.L.R. 560 (moral claims of applicant first wife, and widow as beneficiary, on T's bounty).

[65] *Re Sivyer* [1967] 1 W.L.R. 1482 (applicant child, and third wife entitled on intestacy, had calls upon deceased's bounty); *Re Bellman* [1963] P. 239 (claims of applicant former wife, and sons as beneficiaries, on T's bounty); *Re Ducksbury* [1966] 1 W.L.R. 1226 (applicant daughter aged 29, and second wife as beneficiary).

[66] *Re Joslin, supra,* (applicant widow of small means; common law wife and children by her penniless); *Re Sivyer, supra: Re E., supra.*

[67] *Re Thornley, supra:* see also *Re E., supra,* at p. 714.

[68] *Re Sivyer, supra,* at pp. 1488–1489; *Re Styler* [1942] Ch. 387, 390: see *Re Canderton* (1970) 114 S.J. 208; *Jelley v. Iliffe* [1981] Fam. 128: see *post,* p. 134.

[69] *Post,* pp. 144 and 145.

[70] For the meaning of net estate see *post,* p. 150.

[71] *Re Inns* [1947] Ch. 576, 581; *Re Borthwick* [1949] Ch. 395; *Malone v. Harrison* [1979] 1 W.L.R. 1353, 1364; *Re Besterman* [1984] Ch. 458 (£378,000 provision ordered for widow of millionaire).

The 1975 Act does not impose any minimum limit on the value of the net estate in respect of which an application may be made. "The smallness of the estate neither excludes jurisdiction nor full consideration."[72] Nevertheless the smallness of the estate may be significant in three different ways.

(i) It may be reasonable to make no provision for a needy applicant out of a small estate if the only effect of making provision would be to relieve the state from having to pay means tested benefits.[73]

(ii) Again it may be reasonable to make no provision if the maintenance standard is applicable and the estate is too small to make an effective contribution to the applicant's maintenance, having regard to his means and standard of living. Where the maintenance standard is applicable, the purpose of the 1975 Act is to provide maintenance and not just a small windfall legacy for an applicant.[74] It may, however, be appropriate for maintenance to be ordered by way of a small lump sum payment to an applicant.[75]

(iii) "Claims in cases where the costs of establishing claims leave virtually nothing significant for the claimant deprive the claim of substance, and are to be discouraged."[76] One form of discouragement is for the court to make an order for costs against the claimant.[77]

(6) *DISABILITY OF ANY APPLICANT OR BENEFICIARY.* The sixth general guideline is "(f) any physical or mental disability" of any applicant or any beneficiary.[78] Such a disability may reduce the earning capacity and increase the financial needs of an applicant[79] or beneficiary (which is relevant under general guidelines (a), (b) and (c)). Again such a disability may give rise to, or strengthen, the obligations and responsibilities which the deceased had towards an applicant[80] or beneficiary (which is relevant under general guideline (d)). Thus in *Millward v. Shenton*[81] the Court of Appeal held that a mother's will giving her whole estate to cancer research did not make reasonable provision for the maintenance of her married son, who was aged 52, and incapacitated from earning by a progressive illness.

The availability of state aid, such as free hospital accommodation, is a factor to be taken into account. It has been held reasonable to make only limited provision for a daughter incapable of maintaining herself by reason of mental disability, because the daughter could be maintained

---

[72] *Per* Ungoed-Thomas J. in *Re Clayton* [1966] 1 W.L.R. 969, 971.

[73] *Re E.* [1966] 1 W.L.R. 709, 715; *Re Clayton, supra,* at pp. 971 and 974.

[74] *Re Clayton, supra,* at pp. 971–972; see also *Re Vrint* [1940] Ch. 920, 925–926.

[75] *Re Clayton, supra,* (£400 lump sum from £1,271 estate).

[76] *Per* Ungoed-Thomas J. in *Re Clayton, supra,* at p. 972; see *Re Coventry* [1980] Ch. 461, 486.

[77] *Re Vrint, supra,* (net estate £138: widow's application dismissed with costs): see *Re Fullard* (1982) Fam. 42, 46.

[78] *i.e.* a person beneficially interested under the deceased's will or intestacy, or a person who takes under a statutory nomination or a *donatio mortis causa* made by the deceased, s. 25(1).

[79] *Re Clayton* [1966] 1 W.L.R. 969 (widower crippled in both legs); *Millward v. Shenton* [1972] 1 W.L.R. 711.

[80] *Re Clayton, supra, Millward v. Shenton, supra: cf. Re Andrews* [1955] 1 W.L.R. 1105.

[81] [1972] 1 W.L.R. 71 (estate £3,144: lump sum of eleven-twelfths of estate awarded to son): see also *Re Pointer* [1941] Ch. 60.

free of charge in a state mental hospital.[82] However, in such a case it may be unreasonable to make no provision for pocket money, so as to enable the applicant to buy extra comforts not provided by the state.[83]

(7) *CONDUCT AND ANY OTHER MATTER.* The last general guideline is "(g) any other matter, including the conduct of the applicant or any other person, which in the circumstances of the case the court may consider relevant."

This reference to conduct is in wide terms.[84] It covers the conduct of the deceased[85] as well as that of an applicant or beneficiary. The court has considered, for instance, whether an applicant was a good and loving wife,[86] a deeply affectionate mistress,[87] or a dutiful child.[88] Again the court has considered to what extent an applicant widow and a mistress (who was a beneficiary under the will) each helped the deceased in his business.[89]

Another matter which the court may consider relevant is the source of the deceased's assets. Thus it was material that the deceased earned a death grant (the main asset in his estate) whilst living with his common law wife, to whom he gave the whole of his estate by his will.[90]

THE DECEASED'S REASONS. The 1938 Act required the court to have regard to the deceased's reasons for not making any provision for the applicant. The 1975 Act makes no such requirement. This is because it is based on the principle that what matters is not whether the deceased acted reasonably, or whether he believed himself to have acted reasonably: what has to be judged is not the deceased himself, but the disposition of his estate.[91] In *Williams v. Johns*[92] the deceased left a statement with her will explaining why she had made no provision for the applicant, her adopted adult daughter, who had been independent of her for some years and was now impecunious. Judge Micklem[93] attached little significance to the deceased's recorded reasons, but he held that the applicant, to succeed in her claim, needed to establish some sort of obligation to

---

[82] *Re Watkins* [1949] 1 All E.R. 695; *Re E.* [1966] 1 W.L.R. 709, 714–715 ("something might have been provided for comforts").

[83] *Re Pringle* [1956] C.L.Y. 9248 (£2,291 net estate: 10s. per week ordered for mentally defective son resident in state mental hospital).

[84] *Per* Hollings J. in *Malone v. Harrison* [1979] 1 W.L.R. 1353, 1364.

[85] *Re Thornley* [1969] 1 W.L.R. 1037, 1042 (deceased manic-depressive and violent in drink: "human behaviour (and particularly the domestic variety) is contrapuntal. It is impossible to form a fair or intelligent view of the conduct of either party in a domestic or social relationship without also considering how the other behaved").

[86] *Re Morris* [1967] C.L.Y. 4114 (applicant did not intend to carry out her responsibilities as a wife when she married and never did so); *Re Borthwick* [1949] Ch. 395 (wife not at fault); *Re Blanch* [1967] 1 W.L.R. 987; *Re Thornley, supra.* (gravely wronged wife); *Re Snoek* (1983) 13 Fam. Law 18 (wife's atrocious and vicious behaviour): see *post*, p. 138.

[87] *Malone v. Harrison* [1979] 1 W.L.R. 1353.

[88] *Re Cook* (1956) unreported but referred to in 106 L.J. 466; *Re Ducksbury* [1966] 1 W.L.R. 1226, 1233.

[89] *Re Thornley* [1969] 1 W.L.R. 1037.

[90] *Re E.* [1966] 1 W.L.R. 709 (widow's application dismissed): for other instances see *ante*, p. 132.

[91] See Law Com. No. 61, para. 105 and *ante*, pp. 128–129.

[92] [1988] 2 F.L.R. 475.

[93] Sitting as an additional judge of the High Court.

be maintained by the deceased, or at the expense of her estate, beyond the mere fact of an adoptive relationship. As she had failed to establish such an obligation, there was no foundation for her claim. The disposition of the deceased's estate was objectively reasonable.

Having said that the Act does not *require* the court to have regard to the deceased's stated reasons, it may well be prudent to record them. In *Williams v. Johns*[94] the applicant had, by her behaviour, caused the deceased distress. If the deceased's reasons for failing to make provision for the applicant are good reasons, based on truth, the court has regard to them under guideline (g) or possibly one of the other guidelines. If they are bad or false reasons, the court disregards them.[95] The 1975 Act makes a statement made by the deceased, whether orally or in a document or otherwise, admissible under the Civil Evidence Act 1968 as evidence of any fact stated in it.[96]

THE DECEASED'S STATE OF MIND. The deceased's testamentary capacity is determined in probate proceedings and cannot be put in issue in an application under the 1975 Act.[97] The deceased's state of mind may, however, be a relevant matter to be considered. It may, for example, be relevant to the deceased's obligations that an applicant, or beneficiary, cared for the deceased during a long period of mental illness.[98]

IV. PERSONS WHO MAY APPLY AND THE PARTICULAR GUIDELINES

Each of the following persons who survived the deceased[1] may apply to the court for an order under the 1975 Act.[2]

1. The deceased's wife or husband[3]

The burden of proof lies upon an applicant under this head to prove that at the deceased's death the applicant was the deceased's spouse by a subsisting marriage.[4]

A judicially separated spouse falls within this category,[5] and so does a party to a voidable marriage which has not been annulled prior to the

---

[94] *Supra.*
[95] Re Borthwick [1949] Ch. 395; *Re Clarke* [1968] 1 W.L.R. 415; *Re Coventry* [1980] Ch. 461, 488–489.
[96] s. 21.
[97] *Re Blanch* [1967] 1 W.L.R. 987.
[98] *ibid.* at pp. 991–992.
[1] If the applicant dies before an order is made, the application cannot proceed, *Whytte v. Ticehurst* [1986] Fam. 64 (widow); *Re R. (Deceased)* (1986) 16 Fam. Law 58 (former wife).
[2] s.1(1).
[3] See Miller (1986) 102 L.Q.R. 455.
[4] *Re Peete* [1952] 2 All E.R. 599; *Re Watkins* [1953] 1 W.L.R. 1323.
[5] But a judicially separated spouse may be barred from applying for provision by an order of the court made on the application of the other spouse on or after the decree of judicial separation, s.15(1) and (4), as amended by Matrimonial and Family Proceedings Act 1984, s.8: for similar order following overseas legal separation see s.15A as amended by 1984 Act, s.25(3).

deceased's death. A party to a polygamous marriage falls within this category.[6]

A person who in good faith entered into a void marriage with the deceased falls within this category unless during the deceased's lifetime (i) the marriage was dissolved or annulled or (ii) the person entered into a later marriage.[7] Such a person cannot now recover damages for breach of promise of marriage against the deceased's estate;[8] but, instead, is treated as the deceased's wife or husband for the purpose of an application under the 1975 Act.

(1) *THE SURVIVING SPOUSE STANDARD* is applicable on any application by the deceased's wife or husband, including a person who in good faith entered into a void marriage with the deceased, but excluding a spouse who is judicially separated from the deceased at the latter's death, to whom the maintenance standard is applicable (unless the court has, and exercises, the discretion to apply the surviving spouse standard).[9]

The same standard of provision and the same guidelines apply whether the applicant is a man or a woman. In *Re Clayton*[10] Ungoed-Thomas J. (referring to the 1938 Act) said, "I certainly do not see in the Act a greater onus of proof on the surviving husband than on the surviving wife."

(2) *THE PARTICULAR GUIDELINES* to which the court must have regard on an application by the deceased's wife or husband are[11]:

(a) the age of the applicant and the duration of the marriage[12];
(b) the contribution made by the applicant to the welfare of the deceased's family, including any contribution made by looking after the home or caring for the family[13]; and
(c) the provision which the applicant might reasonably have expected to receive if, on the day on which the deceased died, the marriage, instead of being terminated by death, had been terminated by a decree of divorce. This is the "imaginary divorce" guideline.

This last guideline (c) does not apply on an application by a spouse who is judicially separated from the deceased at the latter's death unless

---

[6] *Re Sehota* [1987] 1 W.L.R. 1506.
[7] s.25(4).
[8] Law Reform (Miscellaneous Provisions) Act 1970, s.1 (agreement to marry not enforceable). Before 1971, the remedy *was* damages for breach of promise—see *Shaw v. Shaw* [1954] 2 Q.B. 429.
[9] *Ante*, pp. 126 *et seq.*
[10] [1966]1 W.L.R. 969, 972 (widower crippled); *Re Wilson* [1969] 113 S.J. 794: provision for a widower was also ordered in *Re Lawes* (1946) 62 T.L.R. 231, *Re Bonham* (1962) 112 L.J. 634 and *Moody v. Stevenson* [1992] Ch. 486.
[11] s. 3(2).
[12] See *Re Pugh* [1943] Ch. 387 (two-and-a-half years' marriage); *Re Clarke* [1968] 1 W.L.R. 415, 425 (seven months together): a period of pre-marital cohabitation does not lengthen the duration of a marriage, *Campbell v. Campbell* [1976] Fam. 347, 352, but see *Kokosinski v. Kokosinski* [1980] Fam. 72, 83–88; *Foley v. Foley* [1981] Fam. 160: and for an application by a dependent mistress see *post*, pp. 145 *et seq.*
[13] See *H. v. H.* [1975] Fam. 9, 16 (contribution made but job unfinished); *Re Rowlands* (1984) 5 F.L.R. 813.

the court has, and exercises, the discretion to apply the surviving spouse standard.[14]

(3) *THE IMAGINARY DIVORCE GUIDELINE.* Guidelines (a) and (b) set out factors to which the court must also have regard in applications under the Matrimonial Causes Act 1973.[15] The introduction of the imaginary divorce guideline (c) was recommended by the Law Commission so as to enable the court "to adopt an approach similar to that adopted in divorce proceedings."[16] Unfortunately, the guideline does not set out all the hypothetical circumstances of the imaginary divorce and it is open to the criticism that it ignores an essential distinction between divorce proceedings and family provision proceedings: in the latter the deceased is dead and so has no future needs or future earnings. In *Re Bunning*[17] Vinelott J. calculated that the maximum provision which the widow would have received in matrimonial proceedings would have been £36,000; yet on an application under the 1975 Act he awarded her £60,000. An award made on divorce would have had regard to the husband's likely future needs and would not have left him with insufficient funds to continue living in the former matrimonial home. As he was dead, and the former matrimonial home had been sold, the court could more easily calculate the widow's entitlement to a reasonable degree of financial security.

Another distinction between divorce and death is that on divorce the courts usually prefer the finality of a "clean break".[18] It avoids bitterness. There is, however, not the same need for a clean break on death; so an appliction by a widow who has been granted, by the deceased's will, a life interest in the residue of his estate, may be dismissed on the basis that the life interest *was* reasonable provision.[19]

The 1975 Act does not require the court to treat the imaginary divorce guideline as decisive, or as laying down a minimum, or maximum[20] provision for the applicant. It is one guideline out of a number of general and particular guidelines, to all of which the court must have regard[21] and which are not ranked in any order of priority. The key questions must be decided by applying the test of reasonable financial provision, measured by the surviving spouse standard. Thus "the overriding consideration is what is 'reasonable' in all the circumstances."[22]

(4) *PROVISION MEASURED BY THE SURVIVING SPOUSE STANDARD.* In *Re Besterman*[23] a wife, W, applied for provision to be made

---

[14] s. 14: see *ante*, pp. 126–127.
[15] Matrimonial Causes Act 1973, s. 25(1)(d) and (f) as amended by 1984 Act: for the case law on these guidelines under the Matrimonial Causes Act 1973 see Cretney, *Principles of Family Law* (5th ed., 1990), pp. 390 *et seq.*
[16] Law Com. No. 61, paras. 33–34: see also paras. 16–18.
[17] [1984] Ch. 480.
[18] *Minton v. Minton* [1979] A.C. 593.
[19] *Davis v. Davis* [1993] 1 F.L.R. 54, see comment by S.M. Cretney in [1993] Fam Law 59.
[20] *Re Bunning* [1984] Ch. 480: but see *Stephens v. Stephens* (1985) Transcript on Lexis.
[21] Per Oliver L.J. in *Re Besterman* [1984] Ch. 458, 469.
[22] *ibid.*
[23] [1984] Ch. 458; see also *Re Bunning, supra; Stephens v. Stephens, supra; Stead v. Stead* [1985] 6 F.L.R. 16.

for her out of the estate of her deceased husband, H. They had been married for 18 years and W had been a faithful and dutiful wife. W was 66 years of age and she had only a widow's pension of £400 per annum. By his will H gave W his personal chattels and a yearly income of £3,500 for life. H left a net estate of over £1.4 million. Oxford University, the major beneficiary under his will, acknowledged that H's provision for W was not a reasonable provision for a millionaire's widow accustomed to a high standard of living. The key question for the court was the amount of the provision to be ordered for W. The trial judge treated the maintenance of W as the paramount factor in fixing this amount, referring to the cost of purchasing an annuity sufficient to maintain W's standard of living, and awarded W a lump sum of £238,000 from H's estate. The Court of Appeal increased the lump sum to £378,000 because reasonable financial provision for W had to be measured by the surviving spouse standard (*i.e.* reasonable provision for W in all the circumstances) and not by the maintenance standard (*i.e.* reasonable provision for W's maintenance). Moreover the sum awarded by the trial judge bore little relation to the sum which W might reasonably have expected to receive on divorce[24], under the imaginary divorce guideline; and took no real account of the need to cushion W against possible future contingencies, such as ill health.

In the case of an estate of more modest size there is inevitably less available from which the court is able to make provision over and above what is required for the maintenance of the applicant spouse.[25]

(5) *RELEVANCE OF CONDUCT.* In what circumstances is the conduct of the applicant, or of the deceased, likely to be considered "relevant" by the court under general guideline (g)?[26] Under the 1938 Act the court was required to have regard to the conduct of the applicant in every case.[27] Under general guideline (g) of the 1975 Act, the court is to have regard to "any other matter, including the conduct of the applicant or any other person which in the circumstances of the case the court may consider relevant." The court may also need to consider conduct under other guidelines. The conduct of an applicant or beneficiary may be relevant to the deceased's obligations and responsibilities under general guideline (d). Again some aspects of an applicant's conduct may be relevant in considering the applicant's contribution to the welfare of the deceased's family under particular guideline (b).[28]

If at the deceased's death the marriage with the applicant had broken down, the court usually considers that the conduct of the parties which led to the breakdown is irrelevant.[29] This is the view adopted by the

---

[24] The sum which W might reasonably have expected to receive on divorce was a "matter of speculation" but counsel suggested £350,000 and Oliver L.J. thought that this was "not . . . excessive," [1984] Ch. 458, 478.

[25] *Stead v. Stead, supra.*

[26] *Ante*, p. 134.

[27] Inheritance (Family Provision) Act 1938, s. 1(6).

[28] See *H. v. H.* [1975] Fam. 9, 16

[29] The Law Commission hoped the court would take this view, see Law Com. No. 61, paras. 35–36. For applications under the 1938 Act see *Re Borthwick* [1949] Ch. 395 (husband deserted wife); *Re Thornley* [1969] 1 W.L.R. 1037 (husband's cruelty); *Re Clarke* [1968] 1 W.L.R. 415 (husband's desertion); *Re Gregory* [1970] 1 W.L.R. 1455 (husband's

court in applications for financial provision in divorce proceedings[30] and a lengthy post-mortem to ascertain who was responsible for the breakdown of the marriage seems even less appropriate in family provision proceedings, after one party to the marriage has died.[31] It is open to the court to take the same view in family provision proceedings because general guideline (g) (unlike the other guidelines) requires the court to have regard to conduct only if it considers it a relevant matter in the circumstances of the case. But, as in divorce proceedings,[32] there will still be a minority of cases where the applicant's conduct is relevant because it would be inequitable to disregard it, so that reasonable financial provision for the applicant is either nothing at all or a reduced amount. Thus in *Re Snoek*,[33] where the wife's atrocious and vicious conduct towards her husband during the latter part of the marriage did not quite cancel out her contribution to the welfare of the family in the early part of the marriage when she managed the home and brought up their children, the court awarded her only a "modest" lump sum of £5,000 out of her husband's £40,000 estate.

Again it is possible that the deceased's conduct may be relevant. For instance, the deceased may have attacked and injured the applicant, disabling the applicant from working again, and this may justify an increased amount of financial provision.[34]

2.   The deceased's former wife or husband who has not remarried[35]

A former wife or husband means a person whose marriage with the deceased was dissolved or annulled during the deceased's lifetime *either* (i) by a decree of divorce or nullity granted under the law of any part of the British Islands *or* (ii) overseas by a divorce or annulment recognised as valid by English law.[36] The deceased must, however, have died domiciled in England and Wales.[37]

A former wife or husband may be barred from applying under the 1975 Act by an order of the court made on the application of the other spouse on or after the decree of divorce or nullity.[38]

desertion); 42 years' separation and virtually no payment of maintenance: wife's application failed).

[30] *Wachtel v. Wachtel* [1973] Fam. 72: see generally Cretney, *op. cit*, pp. 402 *et seq.*

[31] *Re Bunning* [1984] Ch. 480, 489.

[32] Matrimonial Causes Act 1973, s.25(2)(g), as amended by 1984 Act; *Watchel v. Watchel, supra,* at p. 90: *per* Cairns L.J. in *Harnett v. Harnett* [1974] 1 W.L.R. 219, 224, "Where there is something in the conduct of one party which would make it quite inequitable to leave that out of account having regard to the conduct of the other party as well in the course of the marriage"; *Bateman v. Bateman* [1979] Fam. 25; *Robinson v. Robinson* [1983] Fam. 42; *Kyte v. Kyte* (1987) Transcript on Lexis.

[33] (1983) 13 Fam. Law 18.

[34] See *Jones (M. A.) v. Jones (W.)* [1976] Fam. 8 (divorce: "conduct of such a gross kind that it would be offensive to a sense of justice that it should not be taken into account").

[35] Remarriage includes a marriage which is by law void or voidable and it is immaterial that the previous marriage was void or voidable, s. 25(5).

[36] s. 25(1) as amended by 1984 Act, s. 25(1) and (2): British Islands means the United Kingdom, Channel Islands and Isle of Man, Interpretation Act 1978, s. 5 and Sched. 1.

[37] *Ante,* p. 123.

[38] s. 15 as amended by 1984 Act, s. 8: for similar order following overseas divorce or annulment see s. 15A as amended by 1984 Act, s. 25(3). For an instance see *Kokosinski v. Kokosinski* [1980] Fam. 72, 88: see also *Re Fullard* [1982] Fam. 42, 49–50; *Whiting v. Whiting*

(1) *THE MAINTENANCE STANDARD* is applicable on an application by the deceased's former wife or husband unless the court has, and exercises, the discretion to apply the surviving spouse standard.[39]

(2) *THE PARTICULAR GUIDELINES* to which the court must have regard are those applicable on an application by the deceased's wife or husband, except that the imaginary divorce guideline (c) does not apply unless the court has, and exercises, the discretion to apply the surviving spouse standard.[40]

(3) *RELEVANCE OF FINANCIAL PROVISION IN MATRIMONIAL PROCEEDINGS.* Any financial provision made in the matrimonial proceedings, whether by order of the court or by agreement between the parties, is a matter to which the court must have regard under the general guideline (g). In view of the court's powers to make appropriate capital adjustments between spouses in matrimonial proceedings, there will be comparatively few cases where a former wife or husband will succeed in an application under the 1975 Act. In *Re Fullard*,[41] the applicant obtained a divorce from her husband and the parties settled their financial arrangements on the basis that the applicant paid £4,500 to her husband for the transfer to her of his share in the former matrimonial home. The husband moved out of the home and, about six months later, he died, leaving his entire estate (which consisted, for the greater part, of the £4,500 which the applicant had paid to him) to a friend. The applicant's appeal against a refusal to award her financial provision from her husband's estate was dismissed by the Court of Appeal. Had the applicant succeeded in her claim, she would, in effect, have been getting back the money she had paid to buy her husband's share in the former matrimonial home. It was not reasonable to expect a husband, with assets of this kind, who had made arrangements with his former wife which settled their financial affairs, to make further provision for her out of his estate.

This is not to say that no application by a former spouse will ever succeed. Such an application may succeed, for instance, where the deceased made periodical payments to the former spouse for a long time and leaves a reasonable amount of capital,[42] or where a substantial capital sum, such as the the payment of an insurance policy, is unlocked by the death of the deceased.[43] It has been doubted whether the mere accretion of wealth by the deceased after the dissolution of the marriage would of itself justify such an application.[44] Again an application succeeded where the deceased died intestate less than a year after an order

---

[1988] 1 W.L.R. 565, 577–578. Apart from s. 15, *semble* the court's jurisdiction under the 1975 Act cannot be ousted by agreement with the deceased during his lifetime, see *Re M.* [1968] P. 174.

[39] *Ante*, pp. 126–127.
[40] ss. 3(2) and 14: see *ante*, pp. 126–127.
[41] [1982] Fam. 42: see also *Brill v. Proud* [1984] 14 Fam. Law 59.
[42] *Re Crawford* (1983) 4 F.L.R. 273. For the relevance of a secured periodical payments order see *Re Eyre* [1968] 1 W.L.R. 530: for the court's powers to vary or discharge such an order see *post*, p. 130, n. 50.
[43] *Re Fullard*, *supra*, at pp. 49 and 52.
[44] *Ibid.* at p. 52: but see *Re Eyre*, *supra*, at p. 543.

in divorce proceedings to make periodical payments to his former spouse. The court decided that the lack of provision for the former spouse under the intestacy rules did not make reasonable financial provision for her, having regard to the fact that the periodical payments order ran for such a short time.[45]

(4) *RELEVANCE OF CONDUCT.* Probably the court will consider the conduct of the parties which led to the breakdown of the marriage to be irrelevant except in a minority of cases where it would have been relevant in an application for financial provision in divorce proceedings.[46]

3. A cohabitant

If the deceased dies on or after January 1, 1996, application may be made by any person (not being the deceased's wife or husband, or former wife or husband who has not remarried, *i.e.* categories 1 and 2 above) who, during the whole period of two years ending immediately before the date when the deceased dies, was living in the same household as the deceased and as the deceased's husband or wife.

(1) *THE MAINTENANCE STANDARD* applies on an application by a cohabitant.

(2) *THE PARTICULAR GUIDELINES* to which the court must have regard are[47]:

   (a) the age of the applicant and the length of the period during which the applicant lived as the deceased's husband or wife and in the same household as the deceased; and

   (b) the contribution made by the applicant to the welfare of the deceased's family, including any contribution made by looking after the home or caring for the family.

Guideline (a) is a slightly amended version of guideline (a) for wives, husbands and former wives and former husbands. Guideline (b) is identical with guideline (b) as applied to wives, husbands and former wives and former husbands. Guideline (c) for wives and husbands, the imaginary divorce guideline, is, of course, inapplicable to cohabitants.

(3) *LIVING AS THE HUSBAND OR WIFE OF THE DECEASED.* The expression "living as the husband or wife of the deceased" is, following the Law Commission's recommendation,[48] similar to the definition of cohabitant used in section 1(3)(b) of the Fatal Accidents Act 1976. There appears to be no case law on the meaning of the phrase[49] and it is not entirely clear what it is supposed to mean.[50]

---

[45] *Re Farrow* [1987] 1 F.L.R. 205.
[46] *Ante*, p. 138.
[47] s. 3(2A), inserted by the Law Reform (Succession) Act 1995 s. 2(4).
[48] Law Com. No. 187 pp. 15 and 16.
[49] But see A.H.R. Brierley [1995] Conv. 114 and 224.
[50] It has been suggested that the purest test of "living together as husband and wife" is that one party completes the other's tax return, without charging for the service. It is reasonable to assume that this is not what the Law Commission intended.

(4) *IMMEDIATELY BEFORE THE DATE WHEN THE DECEASED DIED.* The applicant must show that he was living in the deceased's household, and as the deceased's husband or wife, during the whole of the period of two years ending immediately before the date when the deceased died. This is, in effect, similar to the condition which applies to dependants and the interpretation of the phrase *"immediately before the death of the deceased'"*, as applied to them, is discussed further below.[51]

4. A child of the deceased

This category includes a child of the deceased *en ventre sa mere* at the deceased's death,[52] an illegitimate child,[53] and a child adopted by the deceased.[54] But it does not include a child who was born to the deceased but has since been adopted by someone else.[55]

(1) *THE MAINTENANCE STANDARD* is applicable on an application by a child of the deceased.[56]

(2) *THE PARTICULAR GUIDELINE* to which the court must have regard is "the manner in which the applicant was being or in which he might expect to be educated or trained."[57]

(3) *APPLICATION BY ADULT SON OR DAUGHTER.* Under the 1938 Act, a son who had attained the age of 21 years and a daughter who had been married were not eligible to apply for provision to be made for their maintenance out of the deceased's estate unless, by reason of some mental or physical disability, they were incapable of maintaining themselves.[58] Under the 1975 Act, there is no age limit or requirement that an applicant must not have been married.[59] In what circumstances is an application by an adult son or daughter appropriate under the 1975 Act?[60]

The particular guideline points to one such situation—the deceased dies whilst supporting his adult son or daughter in the process of acquiring some educational or occupational qualification.[61] General guideline (f)[62] points to another: by reason of physical or mental disability the applicant cannot maintain himself or herself,[63] or, perhaps, is seriously

---

[51] pp. 147–148.
[52] s. 25(1).
[53] *Ibid.*
[54] Adoption Act 1976, s. 39.
[55] *Re Collins* [1990] Fam. 56, where the adoption took place after the deceased had died, but before the application.
[56] *Ante*, p. 127. For an instance see *Re Chatterton*, unreported but referred to in [1980] Conv. 150 (daughter aged five, whom deceased had never seen).
[57] s. 3(3).
[58] 1938 Act, s. 1(1).
[59] See Law Com. No. 61, paras. 71–79.
[60] See G. Miller [1995] Conv. 22.
[61] *Re Coventry* [1980] Ch. 461, 469–470 and 476.
[62] *Ante*, p. 133.
[63] *Re Wood* (1982) 79 L.S. Gaz. 774 (daughter mentally disabled, residing in hospital: £15,000 ordered for extra comforts such as electric wheelchair, outings and holidays); *Re Debenham* (1986) 7 F.L.R. 404 (married daughter, 58, with epilepsy); *Re Pointer* [1941] Ch. 60; *Millward v. Shenton* [1972] 1 W.L.R. 711 (see *ante*, p. 133): *cf. Re Andrews* [1955] 1 W.L.R. 1105 (father owed no moral obligation to daughter incapable of maintaining herself, who left home 42 years before to live as common law wife).

handicapped in earning capacity.[64] Again the deceased may have obligations and responsibilities under general guideline (d) towards an applicant who gives up work in order to care for the deceased during illness
or old age,[65] or to a daughter who is a widow with young children and
who has not been provided for by her deceased husband.[66]

In *Re Coventry*[67] Oliver J. commented that applications for maintenance
under the 1975 Act "by able-bodied and comparatively young men in
employment and able to maintain themselves must be relatively rare and
need to be approached ... with a degree of circumspection."[68] In that
case a son who was 46 years old, in good health and working as a chauf-
feur, applied for provision to be made for him out of his father's £7,000
net estate. His financial resources left him little or no margin for expenditure on anything other than the necessities of life. The father had died
intestate, leaving his widow, who was 74 years old, solely entitled under
the intestacy rules. She had lived apart from the deceased without any
maintenance from him for 19 years. During that time, the son had lived
rent free with his father but had provided his father's food and contrib-
uted to the household outgoings. The Court of Appeal, affirming the
decision of Oliver J., held that it was reasonable that the disposition of
the deceased's estate effected by the intestacy rules made no provision
for the son's maintenance and the son's application therefore failed at
the first hurdle.[69] There was no "special circumstance" (such as moral
obligation upon the deceased to make such provision for the son) which
made this unreasonable.[70]

An application by an adult daughter, who has no disability and is able
to maintain herself, will similarly fail at the first hurdle in the absence
of any special circumstance.[71] The same is true of an application by a
married daughter whose husband is supporting her.[72]

---

[64] See *Re Clayton* [1966] 1 W.L.R. 969 (widower crippled in both legs: maintained himself
but handicapped in earning capacity and in looking after himself).

[65] *Re Coventry* [1980] Ch. 461, 476–477: see *Re Cook* (1956) unreported but referred to in 106
L.J. 466.

[66] Law Com. No. 61, para. 78.

[67] [1980] Ch. 461.

[68] *Ibid.* at p. 465. But there is no "especially heavy burden on a male applicant of full age
beyond that which must, as a practical matter, necessarily exist when a person who
applies to be maintained by somebody else is already capable of adequately maintaining
himself," *ibid.* at p. 474: see also *Re Dennis* [1981] 2 All E.R. 140, 145.

[69] *Ante*, p. 129.

[70] [1980] Ch. 461, 187–489 and 494–495. *cf. Re Christie* [1979] Ch. 168 (adult son took half
T's £13,000 estate, under T's will: held not reasonable provision and T's £9,000 house
should be transferred to son): this was a hard case but the decision was unsatisfactory
because (i) no evidence son was in any need (he already owned £14,000 house subject
to £6,000 mortgage), (ii) deputy judge defined maintenance too widely, *ante*, p. 127, n.
15, and (iii) applied subjective test and relied on T's non-testamentary intention to give
house to son, *ante*, p. 128: for criticism see *Re Coventry* [1980] Ch. 461, 471–472 and 490.

[71] *Williams v. Johns* [1988] 2 F.L.R. 475. Applications under the 1938 Act succeeded in *Re
Borthwick* [1949] Ch. 395 (modest salary; £130,000 net estate); *Re Ducksbury* [1966] 1
W.L.R. 1226 (daughter, part-time art student aged 30, earned meagre living in part-time
employment: order to help provide for future needs when no longer able to earn own
living); *Re Sivyer* [1967] 1 W.L.R. 1482 (daughter aged 13 living with foster parents): and
failed in *Mastaka v. Midland Bank Executor and Trustee Co. Ltd* [1941] Ch. 192 (daughter
aged 19; ordinary relationship of mother and daughter did not exist); *Re Andrews* [1955]
1 W.L.R. 1105 (see *ante*, n. 63). The applicant succeeded in *Re Leach* [1986] Ch. 226 (adult
child of the family, employed but near retirement, and had relied on deceased's stated
intention to make provision by will).

[72] *Re Rowlands* (1984) 5 F.L.R. 813: see Law Com. No. 61, paras 74 and 78.

5.   A person treated by the deceased as a child of the family

Any person (not being a child of the deceased) who was treated by
him as a child of the family in relation to any marriage to which the
deceased was a party.

(1)   *THE MAINTENANCE STANDARD* is applicable on an application
by such a person.[73]

(2)   *THE PARTICULAR GUIDELINES* to which the court must have
regard are "the manner in which the applicant was being or in which
he might expect to be educated or trained" (this is the particular guideline which operates where there is an application by a child of the
deceased)[74] and *also* the following three guidelines[75]:

   (a) whether the deceased had assumed any responsibility for the
       applicant's maintenance and, if so, the extent to which and the
       basis upon which the deceased assumed that responsibility and
       the length of time for which the deceased discharged that
       responsibility[76];
   (b) whether in assuming and discharging that responsibility the
       deceased did so knowing that the applicant was not his own child;
       and
   (c) the liability[77] of any other person to maintain the applicant.

(3)   *APPLICATION BY AN ADULT STEP-CHILD.* Obviously this category covers a young step-child whose mother or father married the
deceased and who was brought up by the deceased as a child of the
family after the marriage. This category is not, however, restricted to
minor or dependent children. In *Re Callaghan*[78] the successful applicant
was 35 years of age and living with his wife in their own home when
his mother married the deceased. The deceased treated the applicant as
a child (albeit an adult child) of the family in relation to this marriage
by acknowledging his own role of grandfather to the applicant's
children, placing confidences as to his property and financial affairs in
the applicant, and depending upon the applicant to care for him in his
last illness.[79] The deceased died intestate and the court held that the
absence of provision for the applicant, under the intestacy rules, did not

---

[73] *Ante*, p. 127.
[74] *Ante*, p. 142. *Re Andrews* [1955] 1 W.L.R. 1105.
[75] s. 3(3): these three guidelines correspond to those applicable on an application by such
   a child in matrimonial proceedings, Matrimonial Causes Act 1973, s. 25(4) as amended
   by 1984 Act.
[76] Under this guideline the assumption by the deceased of responsibility for the applicant's
   maintenance is not essential for success, *Re Beaumont* [1980] Ch. 444, 454–455; *Re Leach*
   [1986] Ch. 226, 231: *cf.* the wording of the particular guideline applicable on an application by a dependant, *post*, p. 146.
[77] This means any liability enforceable at law, whether or not an order has been made,
   Roberts v. Roberts [1962] P. 212.
[78] [1985] Fam. 1: see *Re Leach* [1986] Ch. 226 (step-daughter was 32 when her father married
   the deceased).
[79] *Per* Booth J. in *Re Callaghan* [1985] Fam. 1 at p. 6. *Quaere* whether treatment of the applicant as a child of the family before the marriage suffices, *ibid.*

make reasonable financial provision for his maintenance; especially as the deceased's assets were derived from the applicant's mother who had herself derived them by way of gift from the applicant's paternal grandfather after the applicant's father had been killed on active service.[80]

Treatment of a person as a child of the family refers to the behaviour of the deceased towards that person. The mere display of affection, kindness, or hospitality by a step-parent towards a step-child does not by itself constitute such treatment.[81] The deceased must, as wife or husband (or widow or widower[82]) under the relevant marriage, expressly or impliedly, assume the position of a parent towards the applicant, with the attendant responsibilities and privileges of that relationship.[83] Normally the privileges of the quasi-parent tend to increase and the responsibilities to diminish as the years go by. In *Re Callaghan* the privileges of the elderly quasi-parent were more important than the responsibilities.[84]

6. A dependant of the deceased

This category covers any person "who immediately before the death of the deceased was being maintained, either wholly or partly, by the deceased."[85] Section 1(3) provides that a person shall be treated as being so maintained by the deceased only[86] "if the deceased, otherwise than for full valuable consideration, was making a substantial contribution in money or money's worth towards the reasonable needs of that person." The Law Commission, in 1974, recommended the introduction of this category of applicant,[87] whom it is convenient to call a dependant of the deceased.[88] Obviously this category is not confined to relatives of the deceased or to members of the deceased's household, and it covers persons who had no right to maintenance enforceable against the deceased during his lifetime.[89]

---

[80] *Ibid.* at p. 7 (lump sum payment of £5,000 ordered from £31,000 estate to enable applicant to buy his council house). But one of the things that this case demonstrates is that the intestacy rules do not work well where there is a second marriage without issue, but surviving issue from a first marriage. See R. Kerridge [1990] 54 Conv. 358.

[81] *Re Leach* [1986] Ch. 226, 235.

[82] Treatment of the applicant as a child of the family *after* the marriage has ended by the death of the other spouse is a relevant factor if the treatment stems from the marriage, *ibid.* at pp. 233–235 (giving an example). If treatment occurs, it need not continue until the deceased dies, *ibid.* at p. 233.

[83] *ibid.* at p. 237.

[84] *ibid.*

[85] s.1(1)(e). See generally Cadwallader [1980] Conv. 46; Naresh (1980) 96 L.Q.R. 534.

[86] s.1(3) is to be construed as if the word "only" was inserted in it, so that s.1(3) qualifies s.1(1)(e) and does not provide an alternative to it, *Re Beaumont* [1980] Ch. 444, 450–451; *Jelley v. Iliffe* [1981] Fam. 128.

[87] Law Com. No. 61, paras. 85–98.

[88] Because of the introduction of this category, a popular newspaper described the 1975 Act as a "mistress's charter"; see Green (1988) 51 M.L.R. 187, 195.

[89] See *Re Wilkinson* [1978] Fam. 22 (sister acting as companion); *Re Viner* [1978] C.L.Y 3091 (poor widowed sister); *Malone v. Harrison* [1979] 1 W.L.R. 1353 (mistress); *Re C.* (1979) 123 S.J. 35 (common law wife); *Jelley v. Iliffe, supra* (common law husband); *Harrington v. Gill* (1983) 4 F.L.R. 265 (common law wife); *Williams v. Roberts* [1984] Fam. Law 210; *Bishop v. Plumley* [1991] 1 W.L.R. 582 (common law wife).

(1) *THE MAINTENANCE STANDARD* is applicable on an application by a dependant.[90]

(2) *THE PARTICULAR GUIDELINE* to which the court must have regard is "the extent to which and the basis upon which the deceased assumed responsibility for the maintenance of the applicant and . . . the length of time for which the deceased discharged that responsibility."[91] No minimum period of dependence on the deceased is prescribed but the length of this period is a matter to which the court must have regard.

(3) *BURDEN OF PROOF.* The burden of proof lies upon an applicant[92] under this category to prove that immediately before the death of the deceased:

> (i) the deceased was making a substantial contribution in money or money's worth towards the reasonable needs of the applicant;[93] and
>
> (ii) the deceased was doing so otherwise than for full valuable consideration.[94]

In *Re Wilkinson*[95] the deceased provided board and lodging for her sister, the applicant, who did a share of the light housework and cooking, helped the deceased to dress, and acted as companion to her. Arnold J. held that requirements (i) and (ii) were satisfied because the sister did not do enough to provide full valuable consideration for her board and lodging.

Does requirement (ii) mean full valuable consideration *under a contract*? Arnold J. answered no: the applicant's services had to be valued in order to decide whether they constituted full valuable consideration, irrespective of whether there was a contractual duty to provide those services.[96] Megarry V.-C. took the same view in *Re Beaumont*[97] and so did the Court of Appeal in *Jelley v. Iliffe*.[98]

(4) *DECEASED'S ASSUMPTION OF RESPONSIBILITY.* In *Re Beaumont*[99] Megarry V.-C. held that an applicant must also prove that before his death the deceased had assumed responsibility for the applicant's maintenance. He arrived at this conclusion because the particular guideline applicable to a dependant ("the extent to which and the basis upon which the deceased assumed responsibility for the maintenance of the

---

[90] *Ante,* p. 127.
[91] s. 3(4).
[92] *Re Wilkinson, supra,* at p. 23.
[93] *Re Wilkinson, supra,* (board and lodging); *Re Viner, supra,* (£5 per week); *Malone v. Harrison, supra,* (all living expenses paid; also flats in England and Malta in joint names, a car, £15,000 shares, and £5,500 furs and jewellery); *Re C., supra,* (lived as his wife); *Jelley v. Iliffe* [1981] Fam. 128 (rent-free accommodation); *Harrington v. Gill, supra,* (lived as his wife).
[94] Valuable consideration does not include marriage or a promise of marriage, s. 25(1).
[95] [1978] Fam. 22.
[96] *ibid.* at p. 25: this view was criticised in (1978) 94 L.Q.R. 175 and (1978) 41 M.L.R. 352.
[97] [1980] Ch. 444, 453–454 and 456–457.
[98] [1981] Fam. 128.
[99] [1980] Ch. 444.

applicant . . .") makes an implicit assumption that the deceased had done so, unlike the particular guideline applicable to a person treated by the deceased as a child of the family.[1] An applicant does not, however, need to prove that the deceased had assumed responsibility for the applicant's maintenance *after the death of the deceased*.[2]

In *Jelley v. Iliffe*, however, the Court of Appeal decided that, as a general rule, proof that the deceased was maintaining the applicant raises a presumption that the deceased had assumed responsibility for the applicant's maintenance.[3] There need be no other overt act to demonstrate the deceased's assumption of responsibility[4]: by making a substantial contribution in money or money's worth towards the reasonable needs of the applicant the deceased both assumed, and discharged, responsibility for the applicant's maintenance. Thus the requirement that before his death the deceased had assumed responsibility for the applicant's maintenance does not in general increase the burden of proof upon an applicant.

Under the particular guideline, it is obviously material for the court to have regard to the extent to which, and the basis upon which, the deceased assumed responsibility for the applicant's maintenance. At one extreme the deceased may have assumed this responsibility for the rest of the applicant's life,[5] and at the other the deceased may have disclaimed any further responsibility beyond the contribution he made.[6] Again the deceased may have assumed responsibility for the applicant's complete maintenance on a generous scale,[7] or (on the other hand) grudgingly assumed responsibility for the applicant's partial maintenance.[8]

(5) *IMMEDIATELY BEFORE THE DEATH OF THE DECEASED.* Requirements (i) and (ii) of the burden of proof must be satisfied "immediately before the death of the deceased."[9] What if the situation immediately before the death differs from normal? For instance, C, who normally lives with and is fully maintained by D, falls ill and enters a NHS hospital for investigation: D dies whilst C is still in hospital. If only the abnormal situation at the instant before D's death is to be considered, C

---

[1] *ibid.* at pp. 454–456: see *ante*, p. 144.

[2] *Jelly v. Iliffe* [1981] Fam. 128.

[3] [1981] Fam. 128: *Re Beaumont* [1980] Ch. 444, 457–458 is overruled on this point. It may be that the presumption can be rebutted by circumstances, including a disclaimer of any intention to maintain, *per* Stephenson L.J. in *Jelley v. Iliffe, supra,* at p. 137.

[4] *Per* Griffiths L.J. in *Jelley v. Iliffe, supra,* at p. 142.

[5] *Malone v. Harrison* [1979] 1 W.L.R. 1353, 1358 and 1364–1365 (cable to mistress, "I say to you you will have happiness and contentment with security for ever").

[6] See *Re Beaumont* [1980] Ch. 444, 458 ("it may be that would-be benefactors who wish to protect their families ought to obtain from anyone to whose maintenance they propose to contribute an acknowledgment that they are undertaking no responsibility for his or her [future] maintenance"): Law Com. No. 61, para. 97.

[7] *Malone v. Harrison, supra,* (at least £4,000 per annum, plus furs and jewellery and two flats in joint names).

[8] *Re Viner* [1978] C.L.Y. 3091 (£5 per week paid for six months before death: provision ordered restricted to that made by deceased).

[9] s. 1(1)(e): see *Layton v. Martin* [1986] 2 F.L.R. 227 (mistress dismissed two years before death of deceased: not dependent at death).

is not a dependant of D.[10] In *Re Beaumont* Megarry V.-C. held that the court should consider the settled basis or arrangement at D's death, under which C was fully maintained by D, rather than any temporary variation owing to C's being in hospital.[11] In *Jelley v. Iliffe*[12] the Court of Appeal took the same view: if, for example, D has been making regular payments to the support of C, an old friend, C's claim to be a dependant is not defeated if those payments cease during D's terminal illness because D is too ill to make them.[13] In *Kourkey v. Lusher*[14] the applicant had been the deceased's mistress on an intermittent basis for about 12 years. She was not living with the deceased at the time of his death, nor had she been living with him for a few weeks before his death. Her claim for provision failed, but not simply on the basis that she was not living with the deceased for a matter of weeks, it failed because there had never been any settled pattern of dependence and there had always been a reluctance by the deceased to commit himself financially to the plaintiff during their relationship. In this case, there was no settled basis or arrangement to support her claim.

(6)   *WEIGHING THE CONTRIBUTION OF EACH TO THE OTHER'S NEEDS.* If C and D live together and each of them makes some contribution towards the other's reasonable needs, on D's death C can claim as a dependant if D's contribution was substantially greater than C's.[15] But if the contributions were broadly equal, or C's contribution was greater than D's, C cannot claim.[16]

The court takes a broad common-sense view of the issue whether C was a dependant of D: the right question to ask is whether C was dependent on D for maintenance during D's lifetime, or did C give as good as C got?[17] In striking a balance between their respective contributions:

"the court must use common-sense and remember that the object of Parliament in creating this extra class of persons who may claim benefit from an estate was to provide relief for persons of whom it could truly be said that they were wholly or partially dependent on the deceased. It cannot be an exact exercise of evaluating services in pounds and pence. By way of example, if a man was living with a woman as his wife, providing the house and all the money for their living expenses, she would clearly be dependent upon him, and it would not be right to deprive her of her claim by arguing that she was in fact performing the services that a housekeeper would perform

[10] For this and other examples see *Re Beaumont* [1980] Ch. 444, 451–453.
[11] [1980] Ch. 444, 452–453: similarly, services rendered temporarily by C to D, such as nursing D during D's last illness, do not debar C from being a dependant because the court considers the settled arrangement, *ibid*. See also *Bishop v. Plumley* [1991] 1 W.L.R. 582.
[12] [1981] Fam. 128.
[13] *Per* Griffiths L.J. in *Jelley v. Iliffe*, *supra*, at p. 141.
[14] (1982) 12 Fam. Law 86.
[15] *ibid*.
[16] *Per* Stephenson L.J. in *Jelley v. Iliffe*, *supra* at pp. 138–139: see *Re Kirby* (1981) 11 Fam. Law 210.
[17] *Per* Stephenson L.J. in *Jelley v. Iliffe*, *supra* at p. 139.

and it would cost more to employ a housekeeper than was spent on her and indeed perhaps more than the deceased had available to spend upon her."[18]

In *Bishop v. Plumley*[19] the deceased and the applicant cohabited for about ten years. For most of this time they pooled their modest resources; neither was maintained by the other. The deceased then inherited a substantial legacy and he bought a house in which he and the applicant went to live. Shortly after they moved into the house, the deceased became ill and the applicant looked after him. He died less than a year later. It was held by the Court of Appeal that the provision of the house *was* a substantial contribution and it was not balanced or cancelled out by care and attention, even of an exceptional kind, shown to the deceased by the applicant during the deceased's final illness. The care and attention could not be assessed in isolation from the mutual love and support of a couple living together.

V. REFORM OF THE LAW—ADDING TO THE CLASSES OF APPLICANTS

1. Cohabitants

The case of *Bishop v. Plumley*[1] highlighted a dilemma. Even if the deceased had been making a substantial contribution to the applicant's reasonable needs, this *might*, depending on the circumstances, be cancelled out by the applicant's contribution to the deceased's needs. So the more the applicant had done for the deceased, the harder it might be to make a claim as a dependant. In *Bishop v. Plumley* itself, one of the factors raised by the deceased's children against the applicant's claim was that her care for the deceased during his final illness had been above and beyond the call of duty. It does seem odd that an applicant who claims to have been a dependant will benefit from demonstrating that he or she was slothful and uncaring.

The Law Commission in their report *Family Law: Distribution on Intestacy*[2] considered whether cohabitants should be included as beneficiaries within the intestacy rules. The Commission decided that they should not be so included *but* went on to recommend that cohabitants should be included in the family provision legislation. The Law Commission recommended that this class should cover those cohabitants who are already entitled to bring actions under the Fatal Accidents Act 1976.[3]

---

[18] *Per* Griffiths L.J. in *Jelley v. Iliffe, supra* at p. 141.
[19] [1991] 1 W.L.R. 582.
[1] *Supra.*
[2] Law Com. No. 187 (1989).
[3] Section 1(3)(b) of the Fatal Accidents Act 1976 covers any person who:

    (i) was living with the deceased in the same household immediately before the date of death; and

    ii) had been living with the deceased in the same household for at least two years before that date; and

    iii) was living for the whole of that period as the husband or wife of the deceased.

There appears to be no case law on the meaning of the phrase "living . . . as . . . husband

The implementation of the Law Commission's recommendation has certainly solved one problem—although it could be suggested that it has created another. A cohabitant will not have to present herself as slothful and uncaring, but a relative, say a sister, who lived with the deceased, may complain that she is now being treated less generously than a cohabitant—and she may think that this is neither logical nor fair.

2. Beneficiaries under the Wills of Testators who become mentally disordered and who then marry

The Law Reform Committee in their 22nd Report, *The making and revocation of wills*,[4] considered, *inter alia*, the problem of the testator who married while he was mentally disordered. They recommended that where a testator entered into a marriage while incapable through mental disorder of managing and administering his property and affairs, the court should have a discretion to make financial provision for anyone who could show that he would have been a beneficiary under a will which was revoked by the marriage *and* that he was someone for whom the deceased might have been expected to provide by will if the deceased had not been mentally disordered.[5] There is, at the time of writing, no indication that any steps are being taken to implement this recommendation.

VI. ORDERS WHICH THE COURT MAY MAKE

1. The deceased's net estate

The deceased's "net estate", from which the court may order provision to be made for an applicant, is widely defined in the 1975 Act.

(1) *PROPERTY ALWAYS INCLUDED IN THE NET ESTATE*. The deceased's net estate always includes the following property[1]:

(a) All property of which the deceased had power to dispose by his will[2] (except by virtue of a special power of appointment) less the amount of his funeral, testamentary and administration expenses, debts and liabilities, including any inheritance tax payable out of his estate on his death. This category does not include property nominated under a pension fund trust deed[3] or benefits arising under assurance policies on

---

or wife" and it is not at all clear what it is supposed to mean. But see A.H.R. Brierley, [1995] Conv. 114, and 224.
[4] Cmnd. 7902 (1980).
[5] Law Reform Committee's 22nd Report: para 3:25; and see *ante* p. 95.
[1] s. 25(1): "property" includes any chose in action, *ibid*. *cf.* the property which constitutes assets for the payment of the deceased's debts and liabilities, see *post*, pp. 408 *et seq*.
[2] Or would have had power to dispose by will if he had been of full age and capacity, s. 25(2): it is immaterial that the estate passes as *bona vacantia* on the death of the deceased intestate, s. 24. Probably property, or a debt, subject to the Rule in *Strong v. Bird* (*post*, Chap. 13) falls within category (a).
[3] *Jessop v. Jessop* [1992] 1 F.L.R. 591.

the life of the deceased if the benefits are payable direct to a beneficiary and not to the deceased's estate.[4]

(b) Any property in respect of which the deceased held a general power of appointment (not exercisable by will) which has not been exercised. This category does not apply if it has been exercised.[5] If the general power was exercisable by will, the property falls within category (a), whether or not the deceased exercised the power.

(c) Any sum of money or other property nominated to any person by the deceased under a *statutory* nomination[6] or received by any person from the deceased as a *donatio mortis causa*,[7] less any inheritance tax payable in respect thereof and borne by the nominee or donee.[8] The legislation does not, however, permit the court to order provision from property nominated under a pension fund trust deed.[9]

(2) *PROPERTY INCLUDED IF THE COURT SO ORDERS.* The deceased's net estate also includes property in each of the following two categories if the court so orders:

(d) The deceased's severable share of any property of which he was a beneficial joint tenant immediately before his death.[10] If the deceased and X were beneficial joint tenants of (say) a house or a chose in action (such as a bank account) immediately before the deceased's death, X becomes absolutely entitled by operation of the right of survivorship at the deceased's death. But the court nevertheless has power to order that the deceased's severable share shall, to such extent as appears just in all the circumstances and having regard to any inheritance tax payable in respect of that share, be treated as part of the deceased's net estate.[11] Such an order may be made only if an application is made to the court for an order under the 1975 Act within the six months' time limit[12]: if

[4] But category (e) may be applicable, see *post*, p. 152. For occupational pension benefits see *Re Cairnes* (1983) 4 F.L.R. 225; Rosettenstein (1979) 123 S.J. 661.
[5] Again category (e) may be applicable.
[6] For statutory nominations see *ante*, pp. 18–20.
[7] For *donationes mortis causa* see *ante*, pp. 21 *et seq.*
[8] ss. 8 and 25(1): s. 8 protects a person who pays money or transfers property in accordance with the nomination or *donatio mortis causa*. If any such inheritance tax is repaid in consequence of an order making provision for an applicant, it forms part of the deceased's net estate, Inheritance Tax Act 1984, s. 146(1), (4), (5) and (7): see *post*, pp. 155–156.
[9] *Jessop v. Jessop* [1992] 1 F.L.R. 591—provision may not be ordered *from* such property, but the property may be relevant as a financial resource of a beneficiary of the deceased's estate (if provision is ordered from *other* property.)
[10] ss. 9 and 25(1). For instances see *Re Crawford* (1983) 4 F.L.R. 273 (building society and bank accounts held jointly by deceased and second wife) and *Jessop v. Jessop* [1992] 1 F.L.R. 591 (house in joint names of deceased and cohabitee—cohabitee ordered to pay £10,000 to widow.)
[11] Value is to be determined immediately before the death of the deceased, s. 9(1). It is determined immediately before the death because this is the last moment at which the deceased could have severed the joint tenancy; *but*, in order to value the severable share, the court does have regard to the imminence of death, *i.e.* an insurance policy will be valued as having, effectively, the same value as at death, *Powell v. Osbourne* [1993] 1 F.L.R. 1001.
[12] s. 9(1): see *ante*, p. 124. Any person is protected for anything done by him before an order is made, s. 9(3); *e.g.* the bank is protected if it pays the surviving joint tenant. If any inheritance tax borne by the surviving joint tenant is repaid in consequence of the order, it forms part of the deceased's net estate, Inheritance Tax Act 1984, s. 146(1), (4), (5) and (7): see *post*, pp. 155–156.

no application is made within this time limit, X cannot be deprived in this way of the benefit of the right of survivorship because this category of property is not available on an application made out of time with the court's permission.

Of course, if the deceased and X were beneficial tenants in common, the deceased's undivided share falls within category (a).

(e) Any sum of money or other property which the court directs to be provided by any person under its powers to prevent evasion of the 1975 Act.[13] These powers are considered later.[14]

2. Forms of provision ordered for applicant

If the court is satisfied that the disposition of the deceased's estate is not such as to make reasonable financial provision for the applicant, measured by the surviving spouse or maintenance standard as is appropriate, the court may, in the exercise of its discretion, make any one or more of the following orders.[15]

(1) *PERIODICAL PAYMENTS. i.e.* an order for the making of periodical payments to the applicant out of the deceased's net estate. Such an order may provide for periodical payments:

    (i) of a specified amount[16] (*e.g.* £50 per week); *or*
    (ii) equal to the whole, or a specified part, of the income of the net estate (*e.g.* one-half of the income of the net estate); *or*
    (iii) equal to the whole of the income of such part of the net estate as the court directs to be set aside or appropriated.[17]

Alternatively such an order may provide for the amount of the periodical payments to be determined in any other way the court thinks fit.[18] The 1975 Act does not limit the maximum amount which may be awarded by way of periodical payments by reference to the estimated income of the net estate.[19] In practice the court has regard to the amount of this estimated income, but the court has power to order periodical payments in excess of this amount so that some capital has to be used.

Periodical payments are payable for the period specified by the court in the order.[20] Usually such payments are ordered to run from the death of the deceased (the court fixes the commencing date at its discretion)[21]

---

[13] ss. 10, 11 and 25(1).
[14] *Post,* pp. 159 *et seq.*
[15] s. 2(1).
[16] In that case the court may direct that a sufficient, but not excessive, part of the net estate be set aside or appropriated to meet the payments out of its income, s. 2(3).
[17] s. 2(2).
[18] *ibid.*
[19] See *Re Blanch* [1967] 1 W.L.R. 987, 992.
[20] s. 2(1)(a): *Re Blanch, supra* at pp. 992–993.
[21] See *Askew v. Askew* [1961] 1 W.L.R. 725 (former wife had received national assistance payments since death of former husband: order ran from death despite possible repayment); *Re Goodwin* [1969] 1 Ch. 283, 292: *cf. Re Lecoche* (1967) 111 S.J. 136 (order from date of judgment to avoid sale of house); *Re Eyre* [1968] 1 W.L.R. 530, 544 (date of summons); *Lusternik v. Lusternik* [1972] Fam. 125 (late application and proceedings over four years); *Re Debenham* (1986) 7 F.L.R. 404 (date of order, plus small lump sum to obviate need to backdate order as applicant had received social security).

and invariably the payments are ordered to terminate, at the latest, at the death of the applicant. An order for the making of periodical payments to a judicially separated spouse or former spouse of the deceased terminates automatically on the remarriage of that spouse.[22] The 1975 Act does not, however, specify any other event on which an order for periodical payments terminates. It follows that periodical payments continue to be payable to the widow or widower of the deceased[23] despite remarriage, unless the court has otherwise ordered.[24] Similarly, periodical payments continue to be payable to a child of the deceased despite attainment of full age or marriage, unless the court has otherwise ordered.[25]

(2) *LUMP SUM PAYMENT.* The court may order a lump sum to be paid to the applicant out of the deceased's net estate. The amount of the lump sum is specified in the order and may extend to the entire net estate.[26] The lump sum may be made payable by instalments and the court may subsequently vary the number of instalments payable, and the amount, and date of payment, of any instalment but not the amount of the lump sum itself.[27] In the case of a small estate, a lump sum payment may well be the only practicable order.

(3) *TRANSFER OF PROPERTY.* The court may order the transfer to the applicant of specified property comprised in the deceased's net estate.[28] This may be preferable to an order for a lump sum payment if the latter would necessitate an improvident sale of assets.

(4) *SETTLEMENT OF PROPERTY.* The court may order the settlement for the applicant's benefit of specified property comprised in the deceased's net estate.[29]

(5) *ACQUISITION OF PROPERTY FOR TRANSFER OR SETTLEMENT.* The court may also order the acquisition of specified property (for instance, a house) out of assets comprised in the deceased's net estate, and either the transfer of the acquired property to the applicant or the settlement of it for his benefit.

---

[22] s. 19(2); but any arrears are still payable, *ibid.*

[23] And also to a person who in good faith entered into a void marriage with the deceased, see *ante* p. 136.

[24] Or unless the court varies its order, see *post*, p. 157. See generally Law Com. No. 61, paras. 37–43.

[25] Or unless the court varies its order, see *post*, p. 157.

[26] s. 25(3).

[27] s. 7; see *Re Besterman* [1984] Ch. 458, 478 (if lump sum, court should take account of contingencies and inflation). Application for variation may be made by the person to whom the lump sum is payable, the personal representatives of the deceased, or the trustees of the property out of which the lump sum is payable, s. 7(2).

[28] *e.g.* a house, *Re Christie* [1979] Ch. 168. A weekly contractual tenancy is "property", *Hale v. Hale* [1975] 1 W.L.R. 931 (private landlord); *Thompson v. Thompson* [1976] Fam. 25 (local authority landlord).

[29] And confer on the trustees of the property such powers as appear to the court to be necessary or expedient, s. 2(4)(c): see, *e.g. Harrington v. Gill* (1983) 4 F.L.R. 265 (house to be settled on applicant for life).

(6)   *VARIATION OF MARRIAGE SETTLEMENT.* Finally, the court may order a variation of any ante-nuptial or post-nuptial settlement (including one made by will) made on the parties to a marriage to which the deceased was one of the parties.[30] The variation must be for the benefit of the surviving spouse of that marriage, or any child of that marriage, or any person who was treated by the deceased as a child of the family in relation to that marriage. This form of provision is restricted to these particular applicants.

3.   Quantum of provision ordered

If an application passes the first hurdle, the court determines whether it shall order provision to be made for an applicant; and if so, in what manner. The only express requirement is that, in doing so, the court must have regard to the general and particular guidelines.[31] But it seems implicit that the court should use the surviving spouse, or maintenance, standard of reasonable financial provision (applicable at the first stage of the application) as a measure of the provision to be ordered for the applicant at the second stage.[32]

If the surviving spouse standard is applicable and the court orders a lump sum payment, in fixing the amount of that payment the court does not start with a bias against making a provision which may, ultimately, enable the applicant to make provision for somebody else who is not an applicant. That possibility is inherent in a lump sum order under the surviving spouse standard.[33] But the position is different if the maintenance standard is applicable because maintenance of the applicant is then a limiting factor.[34] In fixing the amount of a lump sum payment under the maintenance standard the court assumes that the applicant will have to spend capital as well as income on maintenance during the period for which provision is being made.[35] Generally, however, it would not be right to treat the value of an applicant's home as expendable capital.[36] The possibility of marriage may also be a relevant factor in fixing this amount.[37]

4.   Consequential and supplemental provisions

An order of the court may contain such consequential and supplemental provisions as the court thinks necessary or expedient for the pur-

---

[30] Settlement has a wide meaning in this context but does not cover an absolute, unqualified and immediate transfer of property, see *Prinsep v. Prinsep* [1929] P. 255, 232; *Prescott v. Fellowes* [1958] P. 260.

[31] s. 3(1).

[32] See *Malone v. Harrison* [1979] 1 W.L.R. 1353, 1365 (maintenance standard); *Re Besterman* [1984] Ch. 458 (surviving spouse standard).

[33] *Re Besterman, ibid.* at pp. 466 and 470.

[34] *ibid.:* see *Re Debenham* (1986) 7 F.L.R. 404 (periodical payments for applicant but not her husband).

[35] *Malone v. Harrison, supra,* (period of applicant's actuarial expectation of life, with possibility of marriage; "it is not my duty to provide for the beneficiaries under her will": estate large and multiplier calculation used to fix amount): for criticism of the multiplier calculation see Bryan (1980) 96 L.Q.R. 165 and *cf. Re Brown* (1955) 105 L.J. 169 ("a judge . . . should not condescend to an analytical statement of how he has arrived at that figure").

[36] *ibid.*

[37] *ibid.:* see also *Re Sivyer* [1967] 1 W.L.R. 1482, 1487–1488 (under 1938 Act).

pose of (1) giving effect to the order, or (2) securing that it operates fairly as between the beneficiaries.[38]

(1) *GIVING EFFECT TO THE ORDER*. In particular the court has power to order any person who holds any property which forms part of the deceased's net estate to make such payment, or to transfer such property, as is specified in the order.[39] This power is useful because the deceased's net estate may include property held by persons other than the deceased's personal representatives—for instance, property nominated by the deceased under a statutory nomination and (if the court so orders) the deceased's severable share of property of which he was a beneficial joint tenant.[40]

(2) *INCIDENCE AS BETWEEN THE BENEFICIARIES*. The incidence of the provision ordered is of vital importance to the beneficiaries.[41] The court has power to vary the disposition of the deceased's estate effected by his will or the law relating to intestacy in such manner as the court thinks fair and reasonable, having regard to the provisions of the order and all the circumstances of the case.[42] Thus, if the court makes an order for the transfer to the applicant of property which was specifically given to a beneficiary by the will, the court may vary the disposition of the deceased's estate so as to make some other provision for that beneficiary. Again, if the court makes an order for periodical payments or a lump sum payment to an applicant, the court may direct from which part of the net estate this provision is to be made and which of the beneficiaries are to bear the burden of it. For example, the court may throw the burden of an order for periodical payments on to specific gifts and pecuniary legacies as well as on to residuary gifts,[43] or the burden of a lump sum payment on to the residuary beneficiaries in proportions different from their respective shares of residue.[44] The court has an unfettered discretion and is not bound by a direction in a will as to the incidence of any provision which may be ordered.[45]

5. Effect of an order

If the court makes an order making provision for an applicant, then for all purposes (including the inheritance tax legislation) the deceased's will or the law relating to intestacy (or both) shall be deemed to have

---

[38] *ibid*. s. 2(4). For the court's powers to vary or discharge a secured periodical payments order made under the Matrimonial Causes Act 1973, and to vary or revoke a maintenance agreement, see 1975 Act, ss. 16 and 17: see also Matrimonial Causes Act 1973, ss. 31 (as amended by Administration of Justice Act 1982, s. 51 and 1984 Act, s. 6) and 36 (as amended by 1975 Act, s. 26(1)) and 1975 Act, s. 18. See generally Law Com. No. 61, paras. 263–276.

[39] s. 2(4)(a). But it appears that the court has no power to order a settlement of the applicant's own property, *Malone v. Harrison* [1979] 1 W.L.R. 1353, 1366.

[40] *Ante*, p. 151.

[41] *i.e.* a person beneficially interested under the deceased's will or intestacy, or a person who takes under a statutory nomination or a *donatio mortis causa* made by the deceased, s. 25(1).

[42] s. 2(4)(b): see also s. 24.

[43] *Re Simson* [1950] Ch. 38: see also *Re Jackson* [1952] 2 T.L.R. 90.

[44] *Re Preston* [1969] 1 W.L.R. 317.

[45] *ibid*.

had effect as from the deceased's death subject to the provisions of the order.[46] An order for a lump sum payment therefore makes the applicant "the equivalent of a beneficiary under the will"[47] or intestacy, and entitled to enforce the order by administration proceedings.[48]

6. Interim order

The court has power to make an interim order in favour of an applicant.

(1) *TWO REQUIREMENTS.* There are two requirements. It must appear to the court:

> (i) that the applicant is in immediate need of financial assistance, but it is not yet possible to determine what final order (if any) should be made; and
> (ii) that property forming part of the deceased's net estate is or can be made available to meet the need of the applicant.[49]

In determining what interim order (if any) to make the court must have regard, so far as the urgency of the case admits, to the general and particular guidelines.[50]

(2) *FORM OF INTERIM ORDER.* By an interim order the court orders payment to the applicant out of the deceased's net estate of such sum or sums, and (if more than one) at such intervals, as the court thinks reasonable.[51] Such an order may impose conditions or restrictions[52] and may contain consequential and supplemental provisions.[53]

By its final order making provision for the applicant the court may direct to what extent any sum paid to the applicant under the interim order is to be treated as having been paid on account of any payment provided for by the final order.[54]

(3) *PROTECTION OF PERSONAL REPRESENTATIVE.* A personal representative who makes a payment under an interim order does not incur any liability by reason of the net estate not being sufficient to make that payment unless at the time of the payment he has reasonable cause to believe that the estate is not sufficient.[55] This protection for the personal

---

[46] s. 19(1): see also as to inheritance tax, Inheritance Tax Act 1984, s. 146. And see *post,* pp. 287.

[47] *Re Jennery* [1967] Ch. 280, 286: see also *Re Pointer* [1946] Ch. 324.

[48] *ibid.* For administration proceedings see *post,* pp. 503 *et seq.*

[49] s. 5(1).

[50] s. 5(3).

[51] s. 5(1). For instances see *Re Besterman* [1984] Ch. 458 (£75,000 capital for widow to buy house and £11,500 income for her maintenance); *Stead v. Stead* (1985) 6 F.L.R. 16.

[52] *ibid.* and see *Re Ralphs* [1968] 1 W.L.R. 1522, 1524 (interim order directed payment of £10 per week to widow, to be brought into account against income to which entitled under will).

[53] s. 5(2); see *ante* p. 154: the provisions as to periodical payments in s. 2(2) and (3) are also applicable.

[54] s. 5(4).

[55] s. 20(2).

representative is necessary in case a payment made by him under an interim order leaves insufficient assets (as events turn out) to pay the deceased's funeral, testamentary and administration expenses, debts and liabilities in full.

VII. VARIATION OR DISCHARGE OF A PERIODICAL PAYMENTS ORDER

Under section 6 of the 1975 Act the court has a wide power to vary or discharge any order already made for the making of periodical payments to an applicant.[1] The court exercises this power by making a new order, which it is convenient to call a variation order. On the other hand, apart from its power to vary the instalments by which a lump sum has been made payable,[2] the court has no power to vary an order making any other form of provision for an applicant. This is in the interests of finality and certainty in the administration of an estate.

1. The relevant property

A variation order may only affect "relevant property."[3] There are two alternatives to consider:

(i) The variation order is made *before* the periodical payments have ceased to be payable under the original order. In that case the relevant property means property the income of which is applicable wholly or in part for the making of the periodical payments at the date of the variation order.[4] The extent of this property depends on the terms of the original order. For instance, the original order may have directed part of the deceased's net estate to be set aside or appropriated and the periodical payments made out of its income: in that case the relevant property is that part of the deceased's net estate which has been set aside or appropriated.

(ii) The variation order is made *after* the periodical payments have ceased to be payable under the original order, *i.e.* after the occurrence of a terminating event specified in the original order[5] (*e.g.* the death of the applicant), or after the expiration of the period of payment so specified (*e.g.* the period during which the applicant was receiving full-time instruction at an educational establishment). In that case the relevant property means property the income of which was applicable wholly or in part for the making of periodical payments immediately before the occurrence of that event or the expiration of that period.[6] But this alter-

---

[1] This power to vary applies to a periodical payments order made under the 1938 or 1965 Act, as well as one made under the 1975 Act, s. 26(4): see *Re Fricker* (1981) 11 Fam. Law 188.

[2] *Ante*, p. 153.

[3] s. 6(6).

[4] s. 6(6)(a).

[5] Other than the remarriage of a former wife or former husband, s. 6(3): for the meaning of former wife or former husband see s. 25(1) and *ante*, p. 139.

[6] s. 6(6)(b).

native applies only if application for a variation order is made within six months from the date of the occurrence of that event[7] or the expiration of that period.[8]

This rule that a variation order may affect only relevant property imposes a time limit beyond which a variation order either cannot be made (in alternative (i)), or cannot be applied for (in alternative (ii)).

2. Applicants for variation order

Any of the following persons may apply for a variation order:

(a) a person who either did apply (whether successfully or not), or would but for the time limit be entitled to apply, for an original order[9];
(b) the deceased's personal representatives;
(c) the trustees of any relevant property; and
(d) any beneficiary[10] of the deceased's estate.[11]

The applicant to whom the periodical payments are payable under the original order may apply for a variation order under category (a); such a person is referred to as "the original recipient."

3. Powers of the court

In exercising its powers the court must have regard to all the circumstances of the case, including any change affecting any of the general and particular guidelines which were applicable when the original order was made.[12]

By making a variation order the court may vary or discharge the original order, or suspend any provision of it temporarily, or revive the operation of any suspended provision.[13] The court may also provide for the making of periodical payments after the occurrence of a terminating event specified in the original order (other than the remarriage of the deceased's former wife or husband) or after the expiration of a period so specified.[14]

Instead of (or in addition to) ordering periodical payments to be made, a variation order may direct the payment of a lump sum or the transfer of all or a specified part of the relevant property.[15] Moreover, a variation order is not restricted to making provision for the original recipient: it

---

[7] Other than the remarriage of a former wife or former husband, s. 6(3): the remarriage of a judicially separated spouse is not referred to in s. 6(3), though it is in s. 19(2).

[8] s. 6(3).

[9] s. 6(5)(a): see also s. 26(4) for an order made under the 1938 or 1965 Act.

[10] *i.e.* a person beneficially interested under the deceased's will or intestacy, or a person who takes under a statutory nomination or a *donatio mortis causa* made by the deceased, s. 25(1).

[11] s. 6(5).

[12] s. 6(7): see also s. 26(4) for an order made under the 1938 or 1965 Act.

[13] s. 6(1): for the power to give consequential directions see s. 6(8).

[14] s. 6(10): for the meaning of former wife or former husband see s. 25(1) and *ante*, p. 139: again the remarriage of a judicially separated spouse is not referred to in s. 6(10), though it is in s. 19(2).

[15] s. 6(2): see also s. 6(9).

may provide for any person who either applied (whether successfully or not), or would but for the time limit have been entitled to apply, for an original order.[16] But, whatever new provision is ordered, a variation order may affect only the relevant property.[17]

Prior to the variation order the periodical payments may already have ceased to be payable to the original recipient: in that case any new provision made by the variation order cuts down the interest of the beneficiaries in the relevant property. On the other hand, if the periodical payments had not ceased to be payable to the original recipient but the variation order makes new provision for another person, both the original recipient and the beneficiaries may be adversely affected.

4. Subsequent variation

The court has power subsequently to vary a variation order in so far as it provides for the making of periodical payments.[18]

VIII. PREVENTION OF EVASION

1. Methods of evasion

Under the 1938 Act the court could order provision to be made for an applicant out of the deceased's net estate.[1] In order to avoid the Act, a person only needed to reduce the value of his net estate at his death— the smaller the value of his net estate, the less the provision which could be ordered by the court. Basically there were two methods of reducing the value of his net estate at his death:

(1) *REDUCTION BY THE DECEASED OF THE PROPERTY OF WHICH HE HAD POWER TO DISPOSE BY HIS WILL.* This could be done by means of dispositions made during his lifetime. For instance, he might make a gift of property to a donee whom he wished to benefit, or settle property on the donee, retaining for himself the income from the settled property until his own death[2]

(2) *INCREASE BY THE DECEASED OF THE DEBTS AND LIABILITIES PAYABLE OUT OF HIS ESTATE ON HIS DEATH.* This could be done by means of contracts made during his lifetime. For instance, he might enter into a contract by deed with a "donee" to pay to the donee at his own death a sum of money large enough to exhaust his assets. Alterna-

---

[16] s. 6(2).
[17] s. 6(2) and (6).
[18] s. 6(4).
[1] Under the 1938 Act (and also the 1965 Act) the deceased's net estate meant all the property of which the deceased had power to dispose by his will (except by virtue of a special power of appointment) less the amount of his funeral, testamentary and administration expenses, debts and liabilities and estate duty (or capital transfer tax) payable out of his estate on his death, 1938 Act, s. 5(1) and 1965 Act, s. 26(6).
[2] But possibly a fraudulent transfer of property might be set aside so far as necessary to give relief against damage suffered from loss of a chance of obtaining relief under the 1938 Act, *Cadogan v. Cadogan* [1977] 1 W.L.R. 1041.

tively, he might enter into a contract with the "donee" to leave by his will a particular asset, or a pecuniary legacy, to the donee. If he failed to do so, the donee was entitled to damages for breach of contract against his estate.[3] If he duly did so, in all probability the court had no power to throw the burden of a family provision order on to that particular asset.[4]

2.   Anti-evasion orders

The 1975 Act confers powers on the court in order to stop the evasion of just claims for provision by either of the methods outlined above. An applicant, who applies to the court for an order making provision for him, may also apply in the same proceedings for an anti-evasion order compelling the "donee" under such a disposition or contract to provide money or other property for the purpose of making financial provision for the applicant.[5] Such an anti-evasion order may also be made against the donee's personal representative or a trustee.

Before the court may make an anti-evasion order the court must be satisfied on four matters[6] and these are considered first.

3.   Four requirements for the making of an anti-evasion order

(1)   *DISPOSITION OR CONTRACT MADE BY THE DECEASED.* First, a disposition or contract must have been made by the deceased since the Act came into force: the Act does not apply to any disposition or contract made before April 1, 1976.[7]

(a)   *Disposition.* A disposition means any *inter vivos* disposition of property made by the deceased except an appointment made under a special power of appointment. The disposition may be a payment of money, including the payment of a premium under an assurance policy, and it is immaterial whether it was made by any instrument or not.[8] In *Clifford v. Tanner*[9] the deceased owned a house in which he and his (second) wife lived. In 1977, the deceased transferred the title to the house to his daughter by his first marriage,[10] but subject to a covenant by the daughter to permit the deceased and his wife to continue living in the house for the rest of their lives. In June 1983, the deceased began divorce pro-

---

[3] Or specific performance in appropriate circumstances, see *ante,* p. 11.

[4] *Schaefer v. Schuhmann* [1972] A.C. 572, esp. at pp. 585 and 587 (P.C. in N.S.W. appeal), not following *Dillon v. Public Trustee of New Zealand* [1941] A.C. 294 (P.C. in N.Z. appeal): see also *Re Brown* (1955) 105 L.J. 169.

[5] ss. 10–13: an application for such an order against a donee cannot be made in proceedings for variation of a periodical payments order. If an application for an anti-evasion order is made in relation to a disposition, the donee under that disposition (or his personal representative) or any applicant for provision may seek an anti-evasion order in relation to any other disposition made by the deceased, ss. 10(5) and 12(4). See generally Sherrin [1978] Conv. 13.

[6] ss. 10(2) and 11(2).

[7] ss. 10(8), 11(6) and 27(3).

[8] s. 10(7).

[9] [1987] C.L.Y. 3881.

[10] This *may* (depending on the size of his estate) have been a tax-effective move, it was effected during the capital transfer tax regime; see Chap. 12.

ceedings and in July he released his daughter from her covenant to permit his wife to live in the house. He died in September. The Court of Appeal held that the release, by the deceased, of his daughter from the covenant to permit her stepmother live in the house (effectively, until the stepmother's death) was a disposition. The deceased was giving up a valuable right.[11]

(b) *Contract.* The Act applies to any contract by which the deceased agreed either to leave by his will a sum of money or other property to any person, or that a sum of money or other property would be paid or transferred to any person out of his estate.[12]

A disposition must have been made less than six years before the deceased's death[13] but no such time limit is applicable to a contract. It follows that a disposition (but not a contract) made at least six years before death remains an effective means of avoiding the 1975 Act. For example, a settlement made at least six years before death effectively avoids the 1975 Act even though the settlor retains for himself both the income from the settled property until his death and a special power of appointment exercisable by deed or will over the settled property.[14] Such a settlement needs to contain an ultimate trust for one or more beneficiaries absolutely in default of appointment: any beneficial interest retained by the settlor which continues after his death falls within his net estate.

(2) *INTENTION OF DEFEATING AN APPLICATION FOR PROVISION.*
The deceased must have made the disposition or contract with the intention of defeating an application for financial provision under the Act.[15] This requirement is satisfied if the court is of the opinion that, on a balance of probabilities, the deceased's intention (though not necessarily his sole intention) was to prevent an order for financial provision being made or to reduce the amount of the provision which might otherwise be ordered.[16]

A special rule applies to a contract made by the deceased for which no valuable consideration was provided by any person, *e.g.* a contract by deed or a contract where the only consideration provided was marriage or a promise of marriage, which is not valuable consideration for this purpose.[17] In that case a rebuttable presumption arises that the deceased made the contract with the required intention of defeating an application for financial provision under the Act.[18]

[11] But neither a statutory nomination nor a *donatio mortis causa* constitutes a disposition, s. 10(7).

[12] s. 11(2)(a).

[13] s. 10(2)(a). See Law Com. No. 61, para. 211 (which recommended this time limit so that the court would not need "to investigate a man's intentions at remote periods of time") and *cf.* para. 237 (no time limit for contract).

[14] Though such a settlement may not be very attractive from the tax viewpoint (looked at both in terms of income tax and inheritance tax), see Chap. 12. For special powers see definition of net estate in s. 25(1) and definition of disposition in s. 10(7). But for the position at common law see *Cadogan v. Cadogan* [1977] 1 W.L.R. 1041.

[15] ss. 10(2) and 11(2)(b).

[16] s. 12(1): see *Re Kennedy* [1980] C.L.Y. 2820.

[17] s. 25(1).

[18] s. 12(2).

(3) *FULL VALUABLE CONSIDERATION NOT GIVEN.* The third requirement is that full valuable consideration for the disposition or contract must not have been given by the "donee" or any other person.[19] "The donee" means the person to whom the disposition, or with whom the contract, was made or for whose benefit the disposition, or contract, was made.[20] Marriage or a promise of marriage is not regarded as valuable consideration for this purpose.[21]

(4) *FACILITATE FINANCIAL PROVISION FOR APPLICANT.* The last requirement is that an anti-evasion order would facilitate the making of financial provision for the applicant.[22]

A disposition is widely defined in the first requirement but the second and third requirements are demanding and very much restrict the number of dispositions open to review after the deceased's death. The class of contracts is narrowly defined in the first requirement and is further restricted by the second and third requirements.

4. Anti-evasion order against the donee

If the court is satisfied as to these four requirements, the court in the exercise of its discretion may make an anti-evasion order against the donee. In deciding what order (if any) to make the court must have regard to the circumstances in which the disposition or contract was made, any valuable consideration which was given for the disposition, the relationship (if any) of the donee to the deceased, the conduct and financial resources of the donee and all the other circumstances of the case.[23]

(1) *DONEE UNDER A DISPOSITION.* The court may order the donee under a disposition to provide a specified sum of money or other property for the purpose of making financial provision for the applicant.[24] But the amount of the sum of money, or the value of the property, which the donee is ordered to provide must not exceed the statutory limit on the donee's liability. This statutory limit is:

  (i) if the disposition consisted of the payment of money to or for the benefit of the donee, the amount of the payment made by the deceased *less* any inheritance tax borne by the donee in respect of the payment[25];

  (ii) if the disposition consisted of the transfer of other property to or

---

[19] ss. 10(2)(b) and 11(2)(c): s. 11(2)(c) provides that when the contract was made, full valuable consideration for that contract must not have been "given or promised" by the donee or any other person. See, *e.g.* Re Dawkins (1986) 2 F.L.R. 360, *post,* p. 163.

[20] *ibid*

[21] s. 25(1).

[22] ss. 10(2)(c) and 11(2)(d).

[23] ss. 10(6) and 11(4): valuable consideration does not include marriage or a promise of marriage, s. 25(1). For the effect of valuable consideration given for the contract see *post,* p. 163.

[24] s. 10(2).

[25] s. 10(3). If any such inheritance tax is repaid in consequence of the order it forms part of the deceased's net estate, Inheritance Tax Act 1984, s. 146(1)-(3), (5) and (7).

for the benefit of the donee, the value at the deceased's death of such property *less* any inheritance tax borne by the donee in respect of the transfer.[26]

The payment by the deceased of a premium due under an assurance policy on his life (of which the benefits are payable to another person X) is an example of a disposition consisting of the payment of money for the benefit of X. Say the deceased pays the premiums due under this policy during the last 10 years of his life. Assuming that the four requisites are satisfied in respect of each of the premiums paid by the deceased less than six years before his death, the statutory limit on X's liability is the amount of these premiums less any inheritance tax borne by X in respect of these payments.[27]

Re Dawkins[28] is an example of a disposition by the transfer of property. The deceased died insolvent having sold his house worth £27,000 to the daughter of his previous marriage for £100. He did this 15 months before his death with the intention of defeating an application under the 1975 Act. His second wife applied under the 1975 Act and the court ordered the daughter to provide £10,000 for the purpose of providing a lump sum for the applicant.

The donee does not escape liability if before the deceased's death he spends all the money paid to him, or the proceeds of sale of other property transferred to him, by the deceased.[29] However, in deciding what order (if any) to make, the court has to consider the donee's financial resources and the court is unlikely to make any order against a donee who has meagre financial resources when the application is heard.

(2) *DONEE UNDER A CONTRACT.* By the time the application is heard the deceased's personal representatives may already have paid or transferred money or other property to or for the benefit of the donee in accordance with the contract. If so, the court may order the donee to provide a specified sum of money or other property for the purpose of making financial provision for the applicant.[30] The court may also order the personal representatives to make no, or no further, payment or transfer of property or only a reduced payment or transfer[31]; of course such an order increases the value of the deceased's net estate from which provision may be directed for the applicant.

Again there is a statutory limit. The court may exercise its powers only to the extent of the gift element in the contract, *i.e.* to the extent that the court considers that the amount of any money or the value of any property payable or transferable in accordance with the contract exceeds the value of any valuable consideration given or to be given for the contract.[32]

If the personal representatives have reason to believe that the deceased

---

[26] s. 10(4); if such property has been disposed of, the value is taken at the date of disposal and not at the deceased's death, *ibid*. As to inheritance tax, see *supra*, n. 25.
[27] See Law Com. No. 61, paras. 203–206.
[28] (1986) 7 F.L.R. 360.
[29] s. 10(2).
[30] s. 11(2).
[31] *ibid*.
[32] s. 11(3): property must be valued as at the date of the hearing, *ibid*.

entered into such a contract with the intention of defeating an application for financial provision under the Act, the personal representatives have power to postpone the payment or transfer of money or property under the contract until the six months' time limit for the making of an application has expired or until any application made within that time limit has been determined.[33]

(3) *CONSEQUENTIAL DIRECTIONS.* The court has a wide power to give consequential directions for the purpose of giving effect to its order or securing a fair adjustment of the rights of the persons affected by it.[34] For example, if the court orders the personal representatives to make no transfer of property to the donee in accordance with the contract, the court may direct a smaller money payment to be made to the donee out of the net estate by way of fair adjustment.

5. Anti-evasion order against donee's personal representative

If the donee has died, the court may make an order against the donee's personal representatives. The court must not, however, make an order in respect of any property forming part of the donee's estate which has been distributed by the personal representatives.[35]

6. Anti-evasion order against trustees

The deceased may have settled property less than six years before his death with the intention of defeating an application for financial provision under the Act: in that case an order may be made against the trustees for the time being of the settlement in respect of the disposition to the original trustees.[36] But any order against a trustee (whether or not he was an original trustee under the disposition) is subject to a special limit. A trustee is liable only to the extent of the value of the relevant assets in his hands at the date of the order, *i.e.* the assets which consist of, or represent or are derived from, the money or other property paid or transferred under the disposition.[37] Similar provisions apply in respect of any payment made or property transferred to trustees in accordance with a contract made by the deceased.[38]

---

[33] s. 20(3).
[34] ss. 11(5) and 12(3).
[35] s. 12(4): the donee's personal representative is not liable for having distributed before he has notice of the making of an application on the ground that he ought to have taken into account the possibility that such an application would be made, *ibid.*
[36] s. 13(1) and (3).
[37] s. 13(1): a trustee is not liable for having distributed on the ground that he ought to have taken into account the possibility that such an application would be made, s. 13(2).
[38] s. 13.

CHAPTER 7

THE CONTENTS OF A WILL

I. A WILL PRECEDENT

The reader may find it helpful at this point to look at a specimen will.[1]

THIS IS THE LAST WILL AND TESTAMENT of me EDWARD BURTENSHAW of 1 Sugden Street St. Leonards Sussex journalist and author.

1. **I HEREBY REVOKE** all former Wills codicils and testamentary dispositions made by me.

2. **I DESIRE** that my body may be buried.

3. **I APPOINT** my wife Sophia Burtenshaw to be the sole executrix and trustee of this my Will but if she shall die in my lifetime or before proving this my Will or shall renounce probate or for any reason be unable or unwilling to act then **I APPOINT** my brother Henry Richard Burtenshaw of 2 Copley Street Lyndhurst and my son Frank Burtenshaw of 3 Smith Street Birkenhead to be the executors and trustees of this my Will in her place and they or my said wife or other the trustee or trustees for the time being of this my Will are hereinafter referred to as "my Trustees".

4. **IN** the event of my said wife dying in my lifetime **I APPOINT** my said brother Henry Richard Burtenshaw to be the guardian of my infant children.

5. **I GIVE** (free of all duties and taxes) the following specific bequests absolutely:-

    (a) To my godson Stephen Lushington of 4 Rolfe Avenue Cranworth my collection of stamps together with all albums catalogues accessories loose stamp covers and other material relating to it

    (b) To my goddaughter Caroline Wilde of 5 Thomas Street Truro my late mother's diamond engagement ring and my mahogany framed Speed map of the County of Cornwall.

---

[1] All persons and places referred to in the will are, of course, fictitious.

6.   I GIVE (free of all duties and taxes) to my said son Frank Burten-shaw absolutely all my ordinary shares now standing in my name in Chancellors Limited and I declare that if at my death the said shares shall by virtue of any amalgamation reconstruction or reorganisation of the capital of the said company's business be represented by a different capital holding to which I am entitled or which I possess at my death then the said bequest shall take effect as if it had been a bequest of the capital holding or holdings which took the place of such shares.

7.   I GIVE to my daughter Henrietta Brougham of Vaux Hall Bedford the sum of Five thousand pounds (£5,000) to be paid out of the money standing to my credit at the Caldecote Building Society at the date of my death and I declare that if this is insufficient the balance of the said sum shall be paid out of my residue.

8.   I GIVE (free of all duties and taxes) the following pecuniary legacies absolutely:-

    (a) To my said brother Henry Richard Burtenshaw the sum of One thousand pounds (£1,000) if he acts as an executor and trustee hereof.

    (b) To my said son Frank Burtenshaw the sum of Two thousand pounds (£2,000) whether or not he acts as an executor and trustee hereof.

    (c) To the Retired Barbers, Benevolent Association of Sweeney Street Todley the sum of Two thousand pounds (£2,000) in memory of my late father for its general charitable purposes and I declare that the receipt of the person who is or professes to be the treasurer or other proper officer for the time being thereof shall be a full and sufficient discharge to my Trustees.

9.   I GIVE (free of all duties and taxes) the freehold dwelling-house and premises situate and known as The Thatched Cottage Wood Lane Hatherley in which my sister Augusta Burtenshaw is now living (or such other freehold or leasehold dwellinghouse bungalow or flat owned by me in which my said sister Augusta is living at the date of my death) to my said sister Augusta absolutely provided that she shall still be living there at the date of my death.

10. (a) **I GIVE** to my daughter Charlotte Burtenshaw for her life an annu-ity of Five thousand pounds (£5,000) free of income tax at the basic rate payable by quarterly instalments from such date as my Trustees may decide but not later than six months from my death and then it shall accrue from day to day

    (b) My Trustees may provide for this gift

        (i) by appropriating a fund of such part of my residue as herein-after defined as they consider appropriate to meet the cost; or

        (ii) by buying an annuity of the equivalent amount from a reput-able insurance company or public company; or

        (iii) with the written consent of my daughter Charlotte by com-muting it for a capital payment out of my residue

(c) If my Trustees provide for this gift as mentioned in paragraph (i) of sub-clause (b) above then
  (i) the powers of investment given to my Trustees by this Will shall apply to the fund;
  (ii) the rest of my estate shall be exonerated from the claims of Charlotte;
  (iii) if the income of the fund is insufficient to meet the annuity my Trustees may resort to the capital thereof;
  (iv) any excess income from the fund shall be applied as income of my residue; and
  (v) after Charlotte's death the fund shall form part of my residue

11. **I GIVE** (free of all duties and taxes) the sum produced by multiplying Ten thousand pounds (£10,000) by the number of my grandchildren living at my death to my Trustees on trust to invest the said sum in any investments authorised by this my Will with power from time to time to vary such investments and to hold the said sum and the investments representing the same and the income thereof **IN TRUST** for such of my grandchildren living at my death as shall attain the age of twenty-five years and if more than one in equal shares absolutely.

12. **SUBJECT** as aforesaid **I GIVE** all my property whatsoever and wheresoever to my said wife Sophia Burtenshaw absolutely if she shall be living on the twenty-eighth day after the date of my death

13. **IF** my said wife shall not be living on the said twenty-eighth day or if the gift to her in the preceding clause hereof shall lapse or for any reason fail to take effect then subject as aforesaid **I GIVE** all my property whatsoever and wheresoever to my Trustees **UPON TRUST** for sale and conversion (with full power to postpone) **AND I DIRECT** that my Trustees shall hold such property and the proceeds of sale thereof **UPON TRUST** to pay my debts and funeral and testamentary expenses and legacies and taxes payable in respect of my estate by reason of my death (including taxes on gifts made free of tax) and subject thereto to hold the same (hereinafter called "my residue") **IN TRUST** for all or any my children or child who attain the age of twenty-one years and if more than one in equal shares absolutely **PROVIDED ALWAYS** that if any child of mine shall die (whether or not in my own lifetime) before attaining a vested interest but leaving issue living at my death or born thereafter who attain the age of twenty-one years such issue shall take per stirpes and if more than one equally between them the share of my residue which such deceased child of mine would have taken had he or she survived me and attained a vested interest

14. **IF** the trusts declared above shall fail or determine then subject to the trusts powers and provisions declared and contained in this Will and to the powers by law vested in my Trustees and to every or any exercise of such powers my Trustees shall hold my residue **IN TRUST** for such of my nephews and nieces who shall be living at the date of such failure or determination and attain the age of twenty-one years and if more than one in equal shares absolutely

(N.B. At this point in a will, there would usually follow a clause containing a wide range of administrative provisions, including authority to the trustees to invest in investments not authorised by the Trustee Investments Act 1961 and (probably) provisions modifying the statutory powers conferred by sections 31 and 32 of the Trustee Act 1925.)[2]

IN WITNESS whereof I have set my hand to this my Will this
     (day)   of   *(month)*   One thousand nine hundred and
ninety-five

SIGNED by the said EDWARD BURTENSHAW ⎫
as and for his last Will and Testament in the ⎪
presence of us both present at the same time who ⎬ *(testator's signature)*
at his request in his presence and in the presence ⎪
of each other have hereunto subscribed our   ⎪
names as witnesses:–   ⎭

(witnesses' signatures, addresses and occupations)

II.   THE CONTENTS OF THE WILL

The will starts with a commencement which identifies the nature of the document.[3] This is not essential to its validity, but it obviously helps to make it clear that the testator knows, when he executes it, that this is his will.[4]

Clause **1** of the will is a revocation clause. It does not revoke a statutory nomination made by the testator.[5] If the testator has foreign property which is disposed of by a foreign will, this general revocation clause is not appropriate.[6]
This will is not made by someone contemplating marriage. If it were made in contemplation of marriage, and the testator wished to insert a declaration that it was not to be revoked by his marriage, such a declaration would be inserted at this point, after the revocation clause.[7]

Clause **2** is an expression of the testator's wishes as to the disposal of his body. It has no legal—merely moral—force[8]; but there is always the danger that the will will not be read until after the funeral. A testator who has strong views as to the disposal of his body should, therefore, make these views widely known in his lifetime.

---

[2] These provisions are outside the scope of this book. For trustee investments and sections 31 and 32 see the standard books on Equity and Trusts, *e.g. Snell's Equity* (29th ed., 1990) or Hanbury and Martin, *Modern Equity* (14th ed., 1993).
[3] *Ante*, p. 1.
[4] *Ante*, pp. 58 *et seq.*
[5] *Ante*, p. 20.
[6] For further discussion of revocation, see Chap. 5.
[7] For further discussion of revocation by marriage, see Chap. 5, pp. 94 *et seq.*
[8] *Ante*, 7.

Clause **3** is the appointment of executors and trustees. Executors are considered further in Chapter 13. The definition of "my Trustees" is inserted to ensure that any powers conferred by the will on "my Trustees" are not construed as personal to the original trustees. If the will contained only immediate absolute gifts, there would be no need to appoint trustees. If a bank is to be appointed, the bank will supply its current recommended form of appointment for use by the draftsman. If a bank, or a professional person, is to be appointed, there needs to be provision for remuneration. It may be a good idea to insert such provision in any case, because it may be appropriate to appoint a professional trustee in the future.

If the testator's wife predeceases him, clause **4** appoints a testamentary guardian for the testator's infant children.[9] The appointment of testamentary guardians was discussed in Chapter 1.[10]

Clauses **5–14** contain the will's dispositive provisions, *i.e.* who is to get what.

Clause **5** contains a number of specific legacies or specific bequests; the terms "legacy" and "bequest" are interchangeable.
The classification of legacies as specific, general and demonstrative is discussed in Part III B of this Chapter. The different effects which follow from the classification are discussed in Part III C.[11]

Clause **6** contains a specific legacy of shares. This specific legacy contains a provision designed to prevent ademption if, for instance, there is a re-construction of the company's share capital or if the company is subject to a take-over before the testator's death. Ademption is discussed in Part III C of this Chapter and in Chapter 11. A direction designed to prevent ademption can give rise to difficulties in identifying which assets represent the original shares at the testator's death.

Clause **7** contains a demonstrative legacy. The advantages of demonstrative legacies to those who are given them are explained in Part III C of this Chapter.[12] Demonstrative legacies are not often encountered in practice.

Clause **8** contains a series of general (pecuniary) legacies. The first is conditional and the third is to a charity.

Clause **9** contains a specific devise. The distinction between legacies and devises is explained in Part III A of this chapter and specific devises are explained in Part III B.[13]

Clause **10** is a gift of an annuity. Annuities are nowadays uncommon.

---

[9] Including children born after the date of the will.
[10] pp. 7–8.
[11] pp. 174 *et seq.*
[12] pp. 174 *et seq.*
[13] p. 173.

They are less popular than they once were because they lose their value with inflation, so an annuitant gradually finds that he has less and less real income as the years pass. Annuities are discussed in further detail in Part IV of this chapter.[14]

Clause **11** creates a (tax-effective) accumulation and maintenance settlement for the benefit of the testator's grandchildren.[15]

Clause **12** is a residuary gift to the testator's widow, provided that she survives him by 28 days.[16] If she does not survive him for that period, the residue passes under Clause **13** to the testator's issue, with stirpital substitution.[17] The stirpital substitution provided for in this will is slightly different from the provision made by section 33 of the Wills Act 1837, which is discussed in Chapter 11.[18] If the will made no express provision for substitution, section 33 would apply.

The final dispositive provision in the will is clause **14** which will apply only if the testator is survived neither by his widow nor by any issue who survive long enough to obtain vested interests. Clause **14** is unlikely ever to come into operation, but is designed to avoid the possibility of the testator's dying wholly or partially intestate.

After the dispositive provisions, there would usually follow a clause containing a wide range of administrative provisions; but this clause has not been reproduced here as many of these provisions are outside the scope of this book.

Finally come the testimonium and attestation clauses; the formal requirements for a valid will, including points relating to attestation, were discussed in Chapter 4.

III. LEGACIES AND DEVISES

A. INTRODUCTION

Legacies in wills may be classified as being either specific, general, or demonstrative.[1]

Devises may be specific or general.

---

[14] pp. 177 *et seq.*
[15] Many of the administrative provisions, which have been omitted, would relate principally to this settlement.
[16] Whether it is tax-advantagous, or tax-disadvantagous, to pass property from one spouse to the other and then on to other beneficiaries, or to pass it direct from the first spouse to other beneficiaries, depends on the sizes of the estates of the two spouses; see Chap. 12. A survivorship clause should be inserted only if there is a tax advantage in passing the property direct to the other beneficiaries—this is not always the case.
[17] *i.e.* if a child does not survive to take his share, his issue will take in his place, etc.
[18] pp. 240 *et seq.*
[1] See generally *Jarman on Wills* (8th ed., 1951), pp. 1036 *et seq.*

In the specimen will set out above, there were specific legacies in Clauses 5 and 6; a demonstrative legacy in Clause 7; general legacies in Clause 8; a specific devise in Clause 9; and Clauses 12–14 contained alternative gifts of residue.

Legacies (or bequests) are gifts of personal or moveable property. Devises are gifts of real property. Real property (or realty) is freehold land and certain rights in land. Leaseholds are personalty, but because of their kinship with realty they are sometimes known as "chattels real".[2] Sometimes the word "legacy" is used loosely to mean any gift by will, *i.e.* to include a devise; but this usage is not followed here. The term "gift" can cover both legacies and devises; and "I give" is quite legitimate shorthand for "I bequeath" or "I devise" or "'I devise and bequeath". The expression "I give" is used in the specimen will.

B. CLASSIFICATION OF LEGACIES AND DEVISES

1. Specific legacies

A specific legacy is a gift by will of specified personal estate: *e.g.* "my collection of stamps" or "all my shares in Chancellors Ltd" or "my late mother's diamond engagement ring" or "my Speed map of the county of Cornwall". The thing given:

(i) must itself be part of the testator's personal property; and
(ii) must be a specified part, so that it is severed or distinguished by the testator from the general mass of his estate.[3]

If the testator uses the word "my" ("*my* shares in Chancellors Ltd"), or any other possessive word, this shows that the subject matter of the gift is itself part of the testator's property. So, too, does a reference to the acquisition by the testator of the subject of the gift, *e.g.* "I give to E the gold watch which my father gave me on my twenty-first birthday." The thing given may be specified in any way which distinguishes it from the remainder of his estate,[4] and it is immaterial whether the time for ascertaining it is the date of the will ("the cars which I own at the date of my will") or the date of death ("the cars which I own at the date of my death").[5]

---

[2] The distinction between real property and personal property is not of great significance since 1925 and the terminology is not always strictly adhered to: but leaseholds are personality, while incorporeal hereditaments, such as easements, are realty: see Megarry and Wade, *The Law of Real Property* (5th ed., 1984) pp. 10 and 11.

[3] *Bothamley v. Sherson* (1875) LR 20 Eq. 304 (a gift of "all my shares or stock in the Midland Railway Company" held specific: a specific legacy must be "what has been sometimes called a severed or distinguished part" of the testator's personal estate); *Robertson v. Broadbent* (1883) 8 App. Cas. 812, 815; *Re Rose* [1949] Ch. 78 (reviewing some of the case law).

[4] Apart from other identical things, *Re Cheadle* [1900] 2 Ch. 620 (gift of "my 140 shares" in C Co.; T had 40 fully paid and 240 partly paid shares: held legatee no right to select but entitled to 140 partly paid shares): see also *Re Tetsall* [1961] 1 W.L.R. 938, 943.

[5] *Bothamley v. Sherson, supra,* at pp. 309–312. For the effect of Wills Act 1837, s.24 see *post,* pp. 215 *et seq.*

Whether a legacy is specific, general, or demonstrative depends on the construction of the particular will. However:

"the court leans against specific legacies, and is inclined, if it can, to construe a legacy as general rather than specific; so that if there is any doubt it should, on the whole, be resolved in favour of the view that the legacy is general."[6]

A gift of "all my shares in Chancellors Ltd" or "my 5,000 shares in Chancellors Ltd" will be a specific legacy, but a gift of "5,000 shares in Chancellors Ltd" will be a general legacy.

2.   General legacies

A general legacy, or general bequest, is a gift, not of any particular thing, but of something which is to be provided out of the testator's general estate. Its subject matter may or may not form part of the testator's property at his death.

"A general bequest may or may not be a part of the testator's property. A man who gives £100 money or £100 stock may not have either the money or the stock, in which case the testator's executors must raise the money or buy the stock; or he may have money or stock sufficient to discharge the legacy, in which case the executors would probably discharge it out of the actual money or stock. But in the case of a general legacy, it has no reference to the actual state of the testator's property, it being only supposed that the testator has sufficient property which on being realised will procure for the legatee that which is given to him."[7]

The classic example of a general legacy is a gift of a sum of money, e.g. "I give £2,000 to my son F." Of course, a gift of a sum of money may be (but in practice seldom is) specific, e.g. "I give all the money in the safe in my study to G"[8] or "I give to H the money now owing to me from J."[9]

Sometimes the term "pecuniary legacy" is used as though it were synonymous with the term "general legacy." This can be confusing. If the term "pecuniary legacy" is used without stating whether the legacy is specific, general, or demonstrative, the sense in which the term is used should be ascertained from its context.[10] The term "pecuniary legacy" is used in the Administration of Estates Act 1925,[11] which provides its own wide definition of the term when used in the Act.[12]

---

[6] *Re Rose, supra,* at p. 82. And see *post,* p. 175.
[7] *Per* Jessel M.R. in *Bothamley v. Sherson, supra* at p. 308.
[8] *Lawson v. Stitch* (1738) 1 Atk. 507 (legacy of sum of money in a particular bag is specific).
[9] *Ashburner v. Maguire* (1786) 2 Bro.C.C. 108; *Chaworth v. Beech* (1799) 4 Ves. 555; *Nelson v. Carter* (1832) 5 Sim. 530; *Davies v. Morgan* (1839) 1 Beav. 405. See also *Re Wedmore* [1907] 2 Ch. 277 ("I forgive my child all debts . . . due from him to me on my death. . ." held a specific legacy—"it really is a gift to the child of what he owes"); *Commissioner of Stamp Duties v. Bone* [1977] A.C. 511, 519—520.
[10] See, *e.g. Re O'Connor's W.T.* [1948] Ch. 628.
[11] s.33(2) and Sched. 1, Pt. II: see *post,* p. 253 (abatement) and *post,* p. 448 (incidence of general legacies).
[12] s.55(1)(ix), which is quoted *post,* p. 425.

A gift of shares in a particular company is a general legacy unless there is something on the face of the will to show that the testator is referring to shares belonging to him

3. Demonstrative legacies

A demonstrative legacy is a hybrid, somewhere between a specific legacy and a general legacy. It is a gift which is in its nature a general legacy, but which is directed to be satisfied primarily out of a specified fund or specified part of the testator's property.[13] Examples include "I give £5,000 to H to be paid out of the money standing to my credit at the Caldecote Building Society" or "I give £1,000 to L out of my 2½ per cent. Consols."[14] But if the gift is directed to be satisfied *only* out of the specified fund or property, it cannot be demonstrative. An essential characteristic of a demonstrative legacy is that it should operate as a general legacy so far as it cannot be satisfied out of the specified fund or property[15]; so a legacy which can be satisfied only out of a particular fund is specific.

4. Specific devises

A specific devise is a gift by will of specified real estate: *e.g.* "I give to my sister Augusta the freehold dwelling-house known as The Thatched Cottage Hatherley" or "I give to M in fee simple my farm Blackacre situated near High Top in the County of Durham," or "all my farms in the County of Durham," or "such of my houses at Sutton in the County of Norfolk as L shall select."[16] As in the case of a specific legacy, the thing given:

    (i) must itself be a part of the testator's real property; and
    (ii) must be a specified part, so that it is severed or distinguished by the testator from the general mass of his estate.

It used to be said that all devises were by their nature specific: that was a loose and inaccurate way of stating that before 1926 specific and residuary devises ranked *pari passu* for the purpose of the payment of the testator's debts.[17] Since 1925 a general or residuary devise no longer ranks *pari passu* with a specific devise.[18]

---

[13] *Per* Lord Thurlow L.C. in *Ashburner v. Macguire* (1786) 2 Bro.C.C. 108, 109, "a demonstrative legacy, that is, a legacy in its nature a general legacy, but where a particular fund is pointed out to satisfy it."

[14] *Kirby v. Potter* (1799) 4 Ves. 748; *Re Webster* [1937] 1 A11 E.R. 602 (I bequeath to K the sum of £3,000 to be paid to him out of my partnership share: held a demonstrative legacy).

[15] *Re O'Connor* [1970] N.I. 159; *Re Culbertson* (1967) 62 D.L.R. (2d) 134.

[16] *Springett v. Jenings* (1871) L.R. 6 Ch.App. 333, 335–336 (gift of particular property in parish of Hawkhurst to X followed by gift of "the rest of my freehold hereditaments situate in the parish of Hawkhurst" to Y: both gifts were specific devises). For the effect of the Wills Act 1837, s.24 see *post*, pp. 215 *et seq.*

[17] *Hensman v. Fryer* (1867) 3 Ch.App. 420; *Lancefield v. Iggulden* (1874) 10 Ch.App. 136.

[18] A general or a residuary devise falls within para. 2 and a specific devise falls within paragraph 6 of the statutory order of application of assets. See *post* p. 421.

C. Different Effects Of Legacies And Devises

The classification of legacies as specific, general and demonstrative; and of devises as specific and general; is important because different rules apply in relation to:

(1) ademption;
(2) abatement;
(3) income and interest; and
(4) expenses.

1. Ademption of a specific legacy or of a specific devise

Ademption is when a specific legacy, or a specific devise, fails because its subject matter is no longer part of the testator's property at the time of his death.[19] For example, T may make a will leaving "the gold pocket watch my father gave me on my twenty-first birthday to A." This is a specific legacy. T has identified a particular pocket watch he owned when he made his will, but if it has been sold, or given away, or stolen, before his death, the gift will be adeemed and A will get no watch.

A specific legacy or specific devise fails by ademption if its subject matter is no longer part of the testator's property at the time of his death.[20] Take, by way of example, the specific legacy of "my 2,000 shares in Marks & Spencer plc to C"; if during his lifetime the testator sells, or otherwise disposes of, his 2,000 Marks & Spencer shares, the specific legacy fails by ademption. Furthermore, C is not entitled to receive the proceeds of sale of these shares, even if the testator set the proceeds apart so that they can be traced at his death: the subject matter of the specific legacy was the testator's 2,000 Marks & Spencer shares, not their proceeds of sale.[21]

Neither a general legacy nor a demonstrative legacy fails by ademption. If the testator gives general legacies of "£2,000 to F" and "5,000 shares in ICI plc to K," it is immaterial whether the testator has, at his death, £2,000 in cash, or 5,000 shares in ICI. The subject matter of a general legacy must be provided by the personal representatives out of the testator's general estate.[22] So the personal representatives may need to realise assets in order to raise the £2,000, or the money needed to buy 5,000 shares in ICI. In *Re O'Connor's W.T.*[23] T by his will bequeathed to his son 10,000 preference shares in a private company. When he died, T held only 9,000 of the shares. There was a dispute as to whether the legacy should be construed as general or specific. It was held that it was a general legacy. As it was a general legacy, T's son was entitled to have 1,000 shares (making up the 10,000) purchased for him

---

[19] *Ashburner v. Macguire* (1786) 2 Bro C.C. 108.
[20] *Ashburner v. Macguire* (1786) 2 Bro. C.C. 108.
[21] *Harrison v. Jackson* (1877) 7 Ch.D. 339. Though the testator may make provision against ademption by, *e.g.* a take-over; see clause 6 of the specimen will and further discussion in Chap. 11, p. 248.
[22] For the incidence of general legacies see Chap. 18.
[23] [1948] Ch. 628; see also *Robinson v. Addison* (1840) 2 Beav. 515.

by T's personal representative within 12 months from T's death: if it was not possible to purchase them in that time, the son was entitled to be paid a sum equal to the market value of 1,000 shares as at the end of 12 months from T's death.[24]

It was said above[25] that a gift of shares in a particular company is a general legacy unless there is something on the face of the will to show that the testator is referring to shares belonging to him. So "I give 5,000 shares in ICI plc to K" is a general legacy, unless there are sufficient indications in the will, construed as a whole in the light of relevant circumstances,[26] that the testator intended to refer to shares belonging to him.[27] The fact that the testator, at the date of his will, held exactly 5,000 shares in ICI is not, by itself, a sufficient indication that he intended to give the particular shares which then belonged to him. In *Re Willcocks*[28] T by her will gave her father £948 3s. 11d. Queensland 3½ per cent. Inscribed Stock. At the time she made her will, T held stock of this description to this exact value. Nevertheless, in the absence of anything in the will to indicate that T intended to give a specific legacy, the court held that this was a general legacy. T's possession of stock to that exact value might have been her motive for fixing the size of the legacy, but T might still have intended to give it in the form of a general legacy.[29] T had sold her stock before she died; so if this had been a specific legacy, it would have been adeemed. As it was held to be a general legacy, it was not adeemed and T's executor was obliged to purchase stock to the value of £948 3s. 11d and to make it over to the legatee, T's father.

Another case which illustrates the court's reluctance to hold that a legacy is specific is *Re Gage*[30] where the will contained the following gifts:

"I give and bequeath to my neice Eleanor R. the sum of £1,150 5% War Loan 1929/47 stock And to Marian G. the sum of £500 New South Wales 5% stock now standing in my name."

At the time when he made his will, the testator had exactly £1,150 5% War Loan 1929/47 stock and had exactly £500 New South Wales 5% Stock. He sold the War Loan before he died and the question was whether the gift of the War Loan was adeemed. The fact that the gift was of an amount of stock which corresponded exactly with the amount he owned when he made his will was not taken to be an indication of a specific legacy, but there was still a problem with the words "now standing in my name". It was held, by Clauson J., that these words qualified only the gift of the £500 New South Wales stock and not the War Loan, so the gift of the War Loan was not adeemed. The result can be justified, technically, by pointing to the capital letter "A" at the start of the word "And", which emphasises the separ-

---

[24] T's son may also have been entitled to interest, see *post*, pp. 460 *et seq*.
[25] *Ante*, p. 173.
[26] "construed as a whole in the light of relevant circumstances" is a reference to the rules of construction. For these rules, see Chap. 8.
[27] *Re Rose* [1949] Ch. 78.
[28] [1921] 2 Ch. 327: see also *Re Gage* [1934] Ch. 536; *Re O'Connor's W.T.* [1948] Ch. 628; *Re Rose, supra.*
[29] *Re Willcocks, supra,* at p. 329.
[30] [1934] Ch 536.

ateness of the two legacies.[31] It can be suggested, therefore, that the final words qualified only the second legacy; but this is a strained interpretation and seems to be carrying the presumption that a legacy is general to its furthest limits.

Although a general legacy is never adeemed, it may fail for uncertainty. Thus, in the case of a general legacy of company shares, if the company is wound up so that it no longer exists at the testator's death, the gift fails for uncertainty because the personal representatives can neither purchase the shares nor ascertain their market value.[32]

A demonstrative legacy is treated as a general legacy so far as it cannot be satisfied out of the specified fund or the specified part of the testator's property primarily designated for its payment. Accordingly, in the case of a demonstrative legacy of "£5,000 to Henrietta to be paid from my account with the Caldecote Building Society"; if T's account with the building society is closed at the date of his death, the demonstrative legacy to Henrietta does not fail by ademption, and Henrietta is entitled to have £5,000 provided for her by the personal representatives out of T's general estate.[33]

Ademption is dealt with further in Chapter 11.

2. Abatement

Abatement concerns the statutory order of application of assets to the payment of expenses, debts and liabilities. General legacies are used to pay expenses, debts and liabilites before resort is made to specific or demonstrative legacies.

From the legatee's point of view, it is better if a legacy is classified as general, rather than specific, if there is any question of its being adeemed, but it will be better if it is classified as specific, rather than general, if the legacy may abate. Someone who is entitled to a demonstrative legacy gets the best of both worlds.[34]

Abatement is dealt with further in Chapter 11.

3. Income and interest

A specific legacy or devise generally carries with it all the income or profits accruing from its subject matter after the death of the testator. A general or demonstrative legacy carries interest at the rate of 6 per cent per annum from the time at which it is payable, i.e. usually from the end of one year (the executor's year) after the testator's death.[35]

Income and interest are dealt with further in Chapter 19.

---

[31] Though there was no full stop before it.
[32] *Re Gray* (1887) 36 Ch.D. 205 (the general legacy "fails, not because of any ademption, but because it has become … utterly impossible to determine what amount of money should be set apart" (for the legatee): *cf. Re Borne* [1944] Ch. 190.
[33] *Mullins v. Smith* (1860) 1 Dr. & Sm. 204, 210; *Fowler v. Willoughby* (1825) 2 Sim. & Stu. 354; *Vickers v. Pound* (1858) 6 H.L.C. 885; *Walford v. Walford* [1912] A.C. 658, 662–663; *Re Webster* (1936) 156 L.T. 128.
[34] *Ante*, p. 174 and *post*, p. 254.
[35] *Post*, pp. 460 *et seq.*

4. Expenses

Unless the testator directs otherwise by his will, any expenses incurred by the personal representatives in the upkeep and preservation of the subject matter of a specific legacy or specific devise during the period between the testator's death and the assent or transfer to the beneficiary must be paid by the beneficiary. In *Re Rooke*[36] T by her will made a specific gift of her freehold house and its contents to her friend M.H.G. and the executors incurred expenses in the upkeep and preservation of the house and contents. Maugham J. held that these expenses were not payable out of T's estate as part of the administration expenses but had to be paid by M.H.G. A specific legatee or devisee is entitled to the income or profits accruing from his legacy or devise from the time of T's death,[37] and so it follows that he ought to be made liable for the upkeep and preservation of the subject matter of the specific gift, also from the time of the death.[38]

By contrast, any expenses incurred by the personal representatives in preserving other assets, *i.e.* those not specifically devised or bequeathed, are payable out of the testator's estate as part of the expenses of administration and are not payable by the general or demonstrative legatees.

IV ANNUITIES

1. Classification of annuities

An annuity given by will is a legacy of money payable by instalments or, more accurately, viewing each instalment of the annuity as a separate legacy, "a series of legacies payable at intervals."[1]

Annuities given by will may be classified under the same three heads as other legacies:

(1) A SPECIFIC ANNUITY, *i.e.* a gift of an existing annuity belonging to the testator at his death[2] (*e.g.* "I give to A the perpetual annuity to which I am entitled under my father's will"), or a gift of an annuity or rentcharge out of specified property belonging to the testator at his death[3] (*e.g.* "I give to B during her life an annuity of £3,000 to be charged upon and payable exclusively out of my farm Blackacre");

---

[36] [1933] Ch. 970; see also *Re Pearce* [1909] 1 Ch. 819 (expenses of upkeep, care and preservation of furniture, horses and carriages, and yacht: held payable by specific legatee); *Re Wilson* [1967] Ch. 53, 65. But if T by his will gives to B such articles of furniture and personal effects as B shall select, the expenses of preservation incurred prior to B's selection are not payable by B, *Re Collins' W.T.* [1971] 1 W.L.R. 37. If a contingent specific gift does not carry intermediate income, it does not bear these expenses prior to the occurrence of the contingency, *Re Eyre* [1917] 1 Ch. 351, 356.

[37] See Chap. 19.

[38] [1933] Ch. 970, 974.

[1] *Re Earl of Berkeley* [1968] Ch. 154, 165.

[2] *Smith v. Pybus* (1804) 9 Ves. 566.

[3] *Creed v. Creed* (1844) 11 Cl. & F. 491; *Long v. Short* (1717) 1 P.Wms. 403; *cf. Re Trenchard* [1905] 1 Ch. 82: see Rentcharges Act 1977, s. 2(3).

(2) A GENERAL ANNUITY, *i.e.* a gift of an annuity to be provided out of the testator's general estate (*e.g.* "I give to C during her life an annuity of £5,000 to begin from my death and to be payable by equal quarterly payments; and

(3) A DEMONSTRATIVE ANNUITY, *i.e.* a gift of an annuity which is in its nature a general annuity, but which is directed to be satisfied primarily out of a specified fund or specified part of the testator's property.[4]

Under each of these three heads, whether an annuity is payable out of the *corpus* or only out of the income of the relevant property depends on the proper construction of the particular will.[5]

Again, the duration of an annuity created by a will depends on the will's proper construction.[6] If, for instance, a testator gives A, an individual, an annuity, prima facie the annuity is only for A's life.[7] If, on the other hand, a testator gives an annuity to a corporation or an unincorporated body capable of existing for an indefinite period of time, the annuity is prima facie perpetual.[8]

The differences in the effects of specific, general, and demonstrative annuities relate to ademption and abatement. In addition it is necessary to consider what provision personal representatives should make for the payment of general annuities, from what date annuities are payable, and whether arrears of an annuity carry interest.

2. Ademption of a specific annuity

Like any other specific legacy, a specific annuity fails by ademption if its subject matter, or the specified property out of which it is payable, has ceased to exist as part of the testator's property at his death.[9]

By contrast, neither a general annuity nor a demonstrative annuity fails by ademption. A demonstrative annuity is treated as a general annuity so far as it cannot be satisfied out of the specified fund or specified part of the testator's property primarily designated for its payment.[10]

3. Providing for payment of general annuities

(1) *APPROPRIATION OF ASSETS.* In the ordinary case, where a general annuity is charged on the whole income, or the whole income and

---

[4] *Mann v. Copland* (1817) 2 Madd. 223; *Livesay v. Redfern* (1836) 2 Y. & C.Ex. 90; *Paget v. Huish* (1863) 1 H. & M. 663, esp. at pp. 667–671; *Re Briggs* (1881) 45 L.T. 249.

[5] See generally *Theobald on Wills* (15th ed., 1993), pp. 538 *et seq.*

[6] See generally *Hawkins and Ryder on the Construction of Wills* (1965), pp. 206 *et seq.*

[7] *Blewitt v. Roberts* (1841) Cr. & Ph. 274, 280: see also *Nichols v. Hawkes* (1853) 10 Hare 342 (Wills Act 1837, s. 28 does not apply to annuity created *de novo* by T's will); *Blight v. Hartnoll* (1881) 19 Ch.D. 294; *cf. Townsend v. Ashcroft* [1917] 2 Ch. 14.

[8] *Re Jones* [1950] 2 All E.R. 239.

[9] *Cowper v. Mantell (No. 1)* (1856) 22 Beav. 223 (T made will, giving a specific annuity to A out of T's leasehold property Blackacre; later T assigned Blackacre to trustees on certain trusts: held annuity was adeemed).

[10] *Mann v. Copland* (1817) 2 Madd. 223 (the annuity "may stand, though the Fund out of which it is directed to be paid does not exist"); *Attwater v. Attwater* (1853) 18 Beav. 330 (T gave X an annuity "from my funded property"; it was insufficient to pay it: held deficiency must be made good from his residuary estate).

corpus, of the residuary estate, the annuitant is entitled to have sufficient assets appropriated to answer the annuity as will make it practically certain that the annuity will be fully paid: subject to this being done, the practice of the court is to direct that the remainder of the residuary estate shall be distributed to the residuary beneficiaries.[11] If the appropriated assets prove insufficient, the annuitant is nevertheless entitled to follow the assets so distributed into the hands of those entitled to them, because they are still subject to the annuity.[12]

(2) *DIRECTION TO PURCHASE AN ANNUITY.* An annuitant for life is generally not entitled to require the capitalised value of his annuity to be paid to him.[13] The will gives him an annuity, not a legacy of a lump sum. But if by his will T directs that an annuity be purchased for A for life, A is entitled to take the purchase-money instead of the annuity.[14] A declaration by T in his will that A shall not be allowed to accept the value of the annuity,[15] or to alienate it,[16] is ineffective unless there is a valid gift over.[17]

If A survives T, but dies before T's personal representatives purchase an annuity for him, A's personal representatives are entitled to take the purchase-money because the right to take it vested in A at T's death.[18]

4. Date from which annuities are payable

An annuity given by will begins to run from the testator's death unless the testator shows a contrary intention in his will.[19] Thus the first payment is to be made (in arrear) at the end of one year from the death, unless the annuity is directed to be paid (say) monthly, in which case the first payment is to be made at the end of one month from the death.[20]

---

[11] *Harbin v. Masterman* [1896] 1 Ch. 351 (annuity payable solely out of income: fund set aside to answer annuity by its income, and remainder of residuary estate ordered to be distributed to residuary beneficiaries); *Re Parry* (1889) 42 Ch.D. 570; *Re Coller's Deed Trusts* [1939] Ch. 277, 284 ("in practice, and as a matter of administration, the distribution of the corpus or the income subjected to the annuity is not held up altogether in cases where the annuitant cannot be prejudiced by a partial distribution").

[12] *Re Evans and Bettell's Contract* [1910] 2 Ch. 438. For the effect of an appropriation under Administration of Estates Act 1925, s. 41, see *post*, p. 477, n. 61.

[13] *Wright v. Callender* (1852) 2 De G.M. & G. 652.

[14] *Stokes v. Cheek* (1860) 28 Beav. 620, 621; *Re Brown's Wills* (1859) 27 Beav. 324 (power for trustees to apply annuity for A's benefit if ill or incapacitated).

[15] *Stokes v. Cheek, supra.*

[16] *Woodmeston v. Walker* (1831) 2 Russ. & M. 197.

[17] See *Hunt-Foulston v. Furber* (1876) 3 Ch.D. 285; *Re Mabbett* [1891] 1 Ch. 707; *Hatton v. May* (1876) 3 Ch.D. 148.

[18] *Re Robbins* [1907] 2 Ch 8 (A died 16 days after T: held A's personal representatives entitled to purchase-money); *Re Brunning* [1909] 1 Ch. 276 (T died on September 21, 1907; T's executors made quarterly payment of annuity to A up to December 20, 1907; A died before purchase of annuity: held A's executors entitled to purchase money required to purchase annuity on December 20, 1907, plus interest from that date).

[19] *Gibson v. Bott* (1802) 7 Ves. 89, 96; *Re Robbins* [1907] 2 Ch. 8; *Pettinger v. Ambler* (1866) 35 Beav. 321 (T by will gave annuity to A to be raised out of a reversionary interest of T: held annuity was payable from T's death).

[20] *Houghton v. Franklin* (1822) 1 Sim. & St. 390. But see *post*, p. 469.

5. Interest on arrears of an annuity

The long-standing general rule is that no interest is payable on arrears of an annuity.[21] Interest is only allowed by the court in exceptional circumstances—for instance, "where the non-payment of the annuity has been the fault of the person out of whose income it would be payable."[22] This general rule is anomalous.[23] Without legislation[24] this rule can only be altered by the House of Lords,[25] but a testator is of course free to override this anomalous rule by a direction in his will that interest is to be paid on arrears of an annuity.

6. Abatement of annuities

The abatement of annuities is discussed in Chapter 11.[26]

---

[21] *Torre v. Browne* (1855) 5 H.L. Cas. 555, esp. 577–580; *Re Berkeley* [1968] Ch. 744, esp. at pp. 760–762.

[22] *Re Berkeley* [1968] Ch. 154, 165. Another instance of exceptional circumstances is "where the annuitant has held some legal security which, but for the interference of the court, he might have made available for the obtaining of interest," *Torre v. Browe, supra,* at p. 578.

[23] *Re Berkeley* [1968] Ch. 154: see also *Re Hiscoe* (1902) 71 L.J. Ch. 347.

[24] The Law Commission have advised that no action be taken on the proposal to abolish this rule; the Commission ascertained that there was a strong body of informed opinion in favour of retaining the rule because to abolish it would create "a disproportionate amount of work and expense": Law Commission, 5th Annual Report (1969–70) Law Com. No. 36, para. 63.

[25] *Re Berkeley* [1968] Ch. 744, 761.

[26] See *post* pp. 255–256.

CHAPTER 8

THE CONSTRUCTION OF WILLS

I. GENERAL PRINCIPLES OF CONSTRUCTION AND ADMISSIBILITY OF EVIDENCE[1]

A. GENERAL PRINCIPLES OF CONSTRUCTION

1. The object is to ascertain the testator's expressed intention[2]

In construing a will, the object of the court is to ascertain the intention of the testator as expressed in his will[3] when it is read as a whole. Sometimes extrinsic evidence, *i.e.* evidence not contained in the will, is admissible to assist in the will's interpretation,[4] but the language of the will is central to its construction because the object is "to discover the meaning of the words as intended by the testator."[5] As Lord Simon L.C. put it in *Perrin v. Morgan*[6]:

"The fundamental rule in construing the language of a will is to put on the words used the meaning which, having regard to the terms of the will, the testator intended. The question is not ... what the testator meant to do when he made his will, but what the written words he uses mean in the particular case—what are the 'expressed intentions' of the testator."

(1) *THE COURT CANNOT REWRITE A WILL*. Apart from its power to rectify a will under section 20 of the Administration of Justice Act 1982[7] and its powers under the Inheritance (Provision for Family and Dependants) Act 1975,[8] the court has no power to rewrite a will for a

---

[1] See *Theobald on Wills* (15th ed., 1993) Chap. 17; *Hawkins and Ryder on the Construction of Wills* (1965) Chap. 1.
[2] For the general principles of construction see Theobald, *op. cit.* pp. 199 *et seq.*
[3] *Per* Knight Bruce L.J. in *Lowe v.* (1854) 5 De G.M. & G. 315, 317, "*the numerous class of persons who, in wills and otherwise, speak as if the office of language were to conceal their thoughts, have no right to complain of being taken to mean what their language expresses.*"
[4] See *post*, pp. 187 *et seq.*
[5] Phipson (1904) 20 L.Q.R. 245, 254.
[6] [1943] A.C. 399, 406.
[7] See *ante* pp. 72–73. The Law Reform Committee's 19th Report *Interpretation of Wills* led to the enactment of s. 20 of the Administration of Justice Act 1982 which deals with *Rectification* and to the enactment of s. 21 which deals with *Interpretation of wills—general rules as to evidence.* See *post* pp. 194–196.
[8] *Ante*, pp. 121 *et seq.*

testator after his death. The function of a court of construction is to con-strue the testator's will, not to make a new will for him.[9] As Jenkins L.J. said in *Re Bailey*[10]:

"... it is not the function of a court of construction to improve upon or perfect testamentary dispositions. The function of the court is to give effect to the dispositions actually made as appearing expressly or by necessary implication from the language of the will applied to the surrounding circumstances of the case.'

(2) *THE COURT DOES NOT GUESS.* Moreover the court does not ascertain the intention of the testator by conjecture or guess-work. Lord Wensleydale warned against this in *Abbott v. Middleton*[11]:

"The use of the expression that the intention of the testator is to be the guide, unaccompanied with the constant explanation that it is to be sought in his words, and a rigorous attention to them, is apt to lead the mind insensibly to speculate upon what the testator may be supposed to have intended to do, instead of strictly attending to the true question, which is what that which he has written means."

2. It is presumed that words are to be given their ordinary meaning

Prima facie the words and phrases used in a will are to be given their ordinary meaning—"' the strict, plain, common meaning of the words themselves."[12] A straightforward example of the operation of this pre-sumption is *Re James's Will Trusts*,[13] where the testator's children took life interests in his residuary estate, each child taking a life interest in an equal share. As each child died, the share in which he had had a life interest passed to his issue, but if a child died without issue his share passed to "my surviving children". The strict and plain meaning of these words was that the share passed to the deceased child's surviving broth-ers and sisters but *not* to the issue of other brothers and sisters who had died before him. The result might well seem harsh and it is probable that the testator, who had begun by adopting a stirpital distribution, would not, had he thought about it, have intended it. Nevertheless, the ordinary meaning of the words was clear and that was the meaning the court gave them.[14]

Sir James Wigram, the author of the classic nineteenth century work on the construction of wills,[15] assumed that every word has one "strict

---

[9] *Scale v. Rawlins* [1892] A.C. 342; *Re Lewis's W.T.* [1985] 1 W.L.R. 102 (T's devise of farm did not pass T's shares in company which owned farm). For rectification of a will see *ante*, pp. 72–73.

[10] [1951] Ch. 407, 421.

[11] (1858) 7 H.L.C. 68, 114: see *Re Rowland* [1963] Ch. 1, 11–12 and 17–18.

[12] *Shore v. Wilson* (1842) 9 Cl. & F. 355, 565: see *Gorringe v. Mahlstedt* [1907] A.C. 225, 227 ("the ordinary and usual meaning of the words").

[13] *Re James's Will Trusts, Peard v. James* [1962] Ch. 226.

[14] See also *Scale v. Rawlings* [1892] A.C. 342.

[15] *The Admission of Extrinsic Evidence in Aid of the Interpretation of Wills* was first published in 1831. The last edition, the 5th, was published in 1914. Sir James Wigram became a Vice-Chancellor in 1841.

and primary" meaning.[16] This is wrong. Some words change their meaning with the passage of time and some words have more than one ordinary meaning. Obviously, the presumption that a word or phrase is to be given its ordinary meaning cannot be applied if the word or phrase has more than one ordinary meaning. For instance, the word "money" has several ordinary meanings, ranging from coin (the narrowest meaning) to the whole of a person's real and personal property (the widest meaning, as used in the phrase, "It's her money he's after").[17] If a word or phrase has more than one ordinary meaning, the court determines the meaning intended by the testator by considering all the provisions of the will,[18] construed with the aid of any admissible extrinsic evidence.[19] Needless to say, a skilled draftsman avoids the use of a word which is as ambiguous as "money."

3. The will must be read as a whole

The testator's intention has to be ascertained from an examination of the whole of his will. "The fundamental and overriding duty binding the court is to ascertain the intention of the testator as expressed in his will read as a whole."[20] The testator's "general" intention, when ascertained with reasonable certainty in this way, "is competent not only to *fix* the sense of *ambiguous* words, but to *control* the sense even of *clear* words, and to *supply* the place of *express* words, in cases of difficulty or ambiguity."[21]

(1) *RESOLVING AMBIGUITY.* If the court is faced with a choice between two (or more) possible meanings of an ambiguous word or phrase (*e.g.* the word "money"), the court determines the meaning intended by the testator by considering all the provisions of the will, construed with the aid of any admissible extrinsic evidence.

(2) *REBUTTING THE PRESUMPTION IN FAVOUR OF THE ORDINARY MEANING—THE DICTIONARY PRINCIPLE.* Apart from the fact that some words have more than one ordinary meaning, the presumption that a word or phrase bears its ordinary meaning may be rebutted under THE DICTIONARY PRINCIPLE.

If it appears, from an examination of all the provisions of a will, that the testator used a word or phrase in a different sense from its ordinary meaning, the word or phrase is to be construed in that different sense. This rule is called the "dictionary principle" because the testator has, in his will, supplied his own dictionary. A testator is free to use words to mean whatever he likes, provided he makes the sense in which he is using them clear *in his will*—he can make "black" mean "white" if he

---

[16] Wigram referred to this meaning as the "strict and primary acceptation."

[17] *Perrin v. Morgan* [1943] A.C. 399, 406–408 ("When Tennyson's Northern Farmer counselled his son not to marry for money, but to go where money is, he was not excluding the attractiveness of private property in land"); *Re Barnes' W.T.* [1972] 1 W.L.R. 587.

[18] *Perrin v. Morgan, supra; Re Whitmore* [1902] 2 Ch. 66, 70; *Re Barnes' W.T., supra.*

[19] *Post,* pp. 187 *et seq.*

[20] Per Ungoed-Thomas J. in *Re Macandrew's W.T.* [1964] Ch. 704, 719.

[21] *Re Haygarth* [1913] 2 Ch. 9, 15, quoting from *Hawkins on Wills* (2nd ed., 1912), p. 6.

makes the dictionary sufficiently clear in his will.[22] Thus the dictionary principle applies if a testator includes a definition clause in his will, stating that a particular word in the will is used in some special sense. And the dictionary principle is equally applicable if the will, construed as a whole, states this indirectly; for example, if the testator uses a word in other parts of his will in a special, though clear, sense. In *Re Davidson*[23] T's residuary gift to "my grandchildren" was held to include the children of T's stepson JF, because T's will described JF as "my son" and also described JF's daughter as "my granddaughter."[24]

But if the presumption in favour of the ordinary meaning is not rebutted, the ordinary meaning of a word or phrase prevails even though it may produce results which appear capricious.[25] To quote Buckley J. in *Re James's Will Trusts*,[26] "a testator is entitled to be capricious or eccentric in his testamentary dispositions if he chooses."

(3) *SUPPLYING, OMITTING OR CHANGING WORDS.* The testator's general intention, ascertained from reading the will as a whole, may even supply by implication words omitted from the will (by, perhaps, the proverbial "blundering attorney's clerk"[27]). But the court exercises great caution over reading words into a will and does so only if it is clear from the will itself, "from the four corners of the document,"[28]:

(i) that something has been omitted from the will; and
(ii) what the omission was.

It is not necessary that the precise words omitted should be clear from the will but the substance of the omission must be clear.[29] In *Re Whitrick*,[30] T, by her will, left her entire estate to her husband and provided that, "in the event of my husband ... and myself both dying at the same time", her estate should be held upon trust for X, Y and Z equally. T's husband predeceased her and consequently, according to the literal meaning of the words used, the gift to X, Y and Z failed and T's entire estate passed as on her intestacy. The Court of Appeal held that it was

---

[22] *Per* Harman J. in *Re Cook* [1948] Ch. 212, 216 (a case on the meaning of technical words), *post*, pp. 185–186.

[23] [1949] Ch. 670; see also *Re Lynch* [1943] 1 All E.R. 168.

[24] See also *Re Helliwell* [1916] 2 Ch 580.

[25] *Gilmour v. MacPhillamy* [1930] A.C. 712: *cf. Bathurst v. Errington* (1877) 2 App. Cas. 698, 709–711 (two possible meanings; court does not adopt capricious meaning).

[26] [1962] Ch. 226, 234: for facts see *ante* p. 182; see also *Hart v. Tulk* (1852) 2 De G.M. & G. 300, 313–314; *Bird v. Luckie* (1850) 8 Hare 301, 306.

[27] *Re Redfern* (1877) 6 Ch.D. 133, 138: attorneys may like to think that the reference should have been to "the attorney's blundering clerk" rather than to "the blundering attorney's clerk." Either way, clerical errors may, if the testator died after December 31, 1982 be cured by *rectification*. See *ante* pp. 72–73.

[28] *Re Whitrick* [1957] 1 W.L.R. 884, 887.

[29] *ibid.* at pp. 892–893: *cf. Re Follett* [1955] 1 W.L.R. 429 (substance of omission not clear).

[30] *Supra*: the court approved the principle stated in *Jarman on Wills* (7th ed., 1930), Vol. I, p. 556, "Where it is clear on the face of a will that the testator has not accurately or completely expressed his meaning by the words he has used, and it is also clear what are the words which he has omitted, these words may be supplied in order to effectuate the intention as collected from the context." See also *Re Smith* [1948] Ch. 49 (implication of gift of residue to husband absolutely); *Re Riley's W.T.* [1962] 1 W.L.R. 344; *Re Doland's W.T.* [1970] Ch. 267.

clear from the will as a whole that T intended, by means of the gift to X, Y and Z, to provide for the contingency of her husband not surviving her. The will was therefore read as if it had directed that X, Y and Z were to take if T's husband predeceased her, as well as if they both died at the same time.

In the same way, the will is read as if certain words were omitted or changed if it is clear from the will itself:

(i) that an error has been made in the wording; and
(ii) what the substance of the intended wording was.[31]

Thus it may be clear from the will itself which of two provisions in the will, which are irreconcilable with each other,[32] ought to be changed, and in what way. Failing this, the court applies the well-established "rule of despair"[33] that the later of the two irreconcilable provisions must prevail because it is the last expression of the testator's wishes.[34]

It must be emphasised that this power of the court to supply, omit or change words, as part of the process of construing a will, is very limited in its scope. The requirement that the substance of the intended wording must be clear from the will itself is particularly demanding. It may be obvious from the will that an error has been made in its wording, but a court of construction cannot supply, omit or change words if the will leaves the substance of the intended wording in doubt. This can, however, be remedied by the rectification of the will if this remedy is available.[35]

4. It is presumed that technical words are to be given their technical meaning

Prima facie, technical legal words and expressions used in a will are to be given their technical meaning.[36] In *Re Cook*[37] T made her will on a printed will form and gave "all my personal estate whatsoever" to her named nephew and nieces. T's estate consisted mainly of realty. Harman

---

[31] *Hart v. Tulk* (1852) 2 De G.M. & G. 300 ("fourth" schedule read as fifth schedule in accordance with general intention); *Key v. Key* (1853) 4 De G.M. & G. 73; *Re Bacharach's W.T.* [1959] Ch. 245 (words of will rearranged in accordance with general intention).

[32] Two gifts of residue, one after the other, are reconcilable by construing the second gift as meant to sweep up any shares of the first residue which fail, and possible lapsed legacies, *Re Isaac* [1905] 1 Ch. 427; *Re Gare* [1952] Ch. 80 See also *Re Alexander's W.T.* [1948] 2 All E.R. 111 (bequest of same bracelet to A and later in will to B: held each entitled to half bracelet).

[33] *Re Potter's W.T.* [1944] Ch. 70, 77.

[34] *Re Hammond* (1938) 54 T.L.R. 903 (I give to X "the sum of one hundred pounds (£500)": held £500).

[35] *Ante*, pp. 72–73.

[36] *Doe d. Winter v. Perratt* (1843) 6 M. & G. 314, 342–343: see also *Re Harcourt* [1921] 2 Ch.491, 503 ("when a testator has used words which have acquired a definite meaning in conveyancing and have for a long time been used in the drafting of wills and settlements and other like documents with that meaning, it requires a very strong case to justify their interpretation in a different sense"); *Falkiner v. Commissioner of Stamp Duties* [1973] A.C. 565, 577–578 (justifying the technical meaning rule).

[37] [1948] Ch. 212: see also *Re Du Cros' S. T.* [1961] 1 W.L.R. 1252, 1256 ("male issue" means male descendants in the exclusively male line) and *cf. Re Drake* [1971] Ch. 179 ("male descendants" not technical expression). For the word "heir" see Theobald (15th ed., 1993) pp. 426 *et seq.*

J. held that T's realty was not disposed of by her will and devolved as on her intestacy. He said[38]:

"It seems unlikely that she intended to dispose only of the personal estate in the lawyer's sense of that word . . . but this is a case where a layman has chosen to use a term of art. The words 'all my personal estate' are words so well-known to lawyers that it must take a very strong context to make them include real estate. Testators can make black mean white if they make the dictionary sufficiently clear, but the testatrix has not done so. It may well be that she thought 'personal estate' meant 'all my wordly goods'; I do not know. In the absence of something to show that the phrase ought not be so construed, I must suppose that she used the term 'personal estate' in its ordinary meaning as a term of art."

The presumption that technical legal words and expressions are to be given their technical meaning may be rebutted in the same way as the presumption in favour of the ordinary meaning. Under *the dictionary principle*, a testator is free to use technical legal words and expressions to mean whatever he wants, provided he makes the sense in which he is using them clear in his will. Thus, he can make the expression "personal estate" include real estate if he makes the dictionary sufficiently clear in his will.[39]

5. An intention to revoke must be as clear as the original gift

It is a "very clear and strong rule"[40] that if a will or codicil contains a gift in clear terms, a later codicil is not construed as revoking the gift unless the intention to revoke is as clear as the original intention to give.[41] In *Re Freeman*[42] T by his will appointed A to be one of his executors and gave him a legacy of £1,000 if he should prove the will, and also gave him a share of residue. By a codicil, T revoked the appointment of A as executor and the legacy of £1,000, appointed B to be an executor in place of A, and declared that his will should be construed as if the name of B were inserted throughout instead of the name of A. The Court of Appeal held that this declaration did not impliedly revoke the gift to A of the share of residue. As Buckley L.J. put it[43]:

"The . . . principle is that a clear gift in a will is not to be cut down by anything subsequent which does not with reasonable certainty

[38] [1948] Ch. 212 at p.216.
[39] In *Lightfoot v. Maybery* [1914] A.C. 782, a unanimous House of Lords, reversing the Court of Appeal, held that the expression "nearest male heir" should be construed to mean "nearest male relative", because the context in which the expression was found made it clear that this is what it meant. The courts were normally reluctant to decide against the heir. Note that this decision must now be read in the light of s. 132 of the L.P.A. 1925.
[40] *Folett v. Pettman* (1883) 23 Ch.D. 337, 342; *Re Resch's W.T.* [1969] 1 A.C. 514, 547–548.
[41] *Doe d. Hearle v. Hicks* (1832) 1 Cl. & F. 20, 24; *Re Stoodley* [1915] 2 Ch. 295 ("a clear unambiguous gift in a will can only be revoked by codicil by words at least equally clear and unambiguous as those of the original gift").
[42] [1910] 1 Ch. 681: see also *Re Percival* (1888) 59 L.T. 21; *Re Wray* [1951] Ch. 425: *cf. Re Crawshay* [1948] Ch. 123.
[43] [1910] 1 Ch. 681 at p. 691.

indicate the intention of the testator to cut it down. If there be a plain gift in a will the Court will not say it is defeated by something ambiguous in a codicil which does not plainly cut down the previous gift."

B ADMISSIBILITY OF EVIDENCE

1. Probate is conclusive as to the words of the will

A grant of probate (or letters of administration with the will annexed) is conclusive as to what the words of the will are. A court of construction must not look at the original will for the purpose of correcting any error alleged to exist in the wording of the probate copy of the will.[44] Extrinsic evidence is not admissible in a court of construction to fill up total blanks in the will.[45] A court of construction may, however, look at the original will for the purpose of considering the manner in which it is set out. Thus the presence (or absence) of marks of punctuation,[46] the use of capital letters, the arrangement of the words,[47] and the presence of blanks[48] or erasures[49] in the original will may be taken into consideration in construing the will, whether or not they appear in the probate copy.[50] Again, if two testamentary documents have been admitted to probate, a court of construction may decide that the earlier document has no operative effect, all its provisions having been revoked or repeated in the later document.[51]

2. Extrinsic evidence is admissible to prove the existence, and the fulfilment, of a condition

In the recent case of *Corbett v. Newey*[52] the question arose, apparently for the first time, as to whether extrinsic evidence could be admitted to show that a will was conditional, even though it was not conditional on its face. All the earlier cases on conditional wills were concerned with wording contained in the will and with the constructional question as

---

[44] *Oppenheim v. Henry* (1853) 9 Hare 802, note (b); *Gann v. Gregory* (1854) 3 De G.M. & G. 777; *Re Cliff's Trusts* [1892] 2 Ch. 229. Such an error can only be corrected by an amendment made to the grant by the Family Division.

[45] *Baylis v Att.-Gen.* (1741) 2 Atk. 239 (to Mr.   ); *Hunt v. Hort* (1791) 3 B.C.C. 311 (bequest to Lady   : court could not supply a total blank by parol evidence): see *post*, p. 194. Cf. a partial blank, *In the Estate of Hubbuck* [1905] P. 129 (*post*, p. 193).

[46] *Houston v. Burns* [1918] A.C. 337 (commas); *Gauntlett v. Carter* (1853) 17 Beav. 586 (commas); *Re Steel* [1979] Ch. 218 (absence of commas); *Child v. Elsworth* (1852) 2 De G.M. & G. 679, 683 (full stop); *Morrall v. Sutton* (1845) 1 Ph. 533, 538 (brackets); *Compton v. Bloxham* (1845) 2 Coll. 201 (colon).

[47] *Re Steel, supra,* (indentation or the lack of it).

[48] *Re Harrison* (1885) 30 Ch.D. 390 ("I know of no rule that for the purpose of construing a will you may not look at the original will itself").

[49] *Re Battie–Wrightson* [1920] 2 Ch. 330 (name of bank erased; later in will legacy to X of balance "at the said bank": held court may look at original will to ascertain name of bank); *Manning v. Purcell* (1855) 24 L.J. Ch. 522.

[50] A photostat copy of the will is annexed to the grant, so that reference to the original will is seldom necessary.

[51] *Re Hawksley's Settlement* [1934] Ch. 384.

[52] [1994] Ch. 388; Eben Hamilton Q.C., sitting as a deputy judge of the High Court.

to whether such wording indicated the imposition of a condition or merely the expression by the testator of the reason for making the will.[53] In this dearth of authority, it was held by analogy and by an extension of the principle that *animus testandi*[54] can be proved by extrinsic evidence (including direct evidence of the testator's intention),[55] that extrinsic evidence could be admitted to show both that the will was subject to a condition and whether the condition had been fulfilled. On the facts, it was held that the will was a valid conditional will and that the condition had been satisfied.[56]

decision appealed decided

3. Extrinsic evidence is admissible to prove the existence of the object or the subject-matter of a gift

Obviously extrinsic evidence is admissible to prove the existence of any person or property described in the will. "You must always, of course, have evidence who are the persons mentioned, and you must also have evidence of what are the things bequeathed."[57] For instance, if by his will T gives to "my nephew John Turner the car which I own at the date of my death" (*or* "at the date of my will"), evidence is admissible to prove the existence of a person who, and of a chattel which, falls within the description used in the will. Such evidence is essential "in order to establish contact between the language in the will and the outside world."[58]

4. There is a distinction between two forms of extrinsic evidence—evidence of surrounding circumstances—and evidence of the testator's intention.

The question now arises—what extrinsic evidence is admissible as an aid in the construction of a will, so as to ascertain the testator's expressed intention? At the outset it is essential to distinguish between, on the one hand, *evidence as to the circumstances surrounding the testator when he made his will* and, on the other, *evidence as to the testator's dispositive intention.* If by his will T gives a legacy of £100 "to Mrs. G.," the fact that T was acquainted with a lady named Mrs. Gregg, to whom he habitually referred as "Mrs. G.," is *evidence as to the circumstances surrounding him when he made his will.*[59] On the other hand, the fact that T told a friend that he intended to give a legacy of £100 to "Mrs. Gregg" is *evidence as to his dispositive intention.* Evidence of any instructions the testator gave for his will and of any declarations made by him as to what he intended

---

[53] The cases were reviewed by Jeune P. in *Re Spratt* [1897] P. 28. See also *ante* p. 6.

[54] The intention to make a will. See *ante* pp. 2 *et seq.*.

[55] See *post* pp. 188–189 for a discussion as to the distinction between direct evidence of the testator's intention and evidence of circumstances surrounding the testator at the time he made his will.

[56] The condition in *Corbett v Newey*, not expressed in the will but proved by extrinsic evidence, was that certain *inter vivos* gifts had to be effected.

[57] *Per* James L.J. in *Sherratt v. Mountford* (1873) 8 Ch. App. 928, 929: see *Sanford v. Raikes* (1816) 1 Mer. 646.

[58] Albery (1963) 26 M.L.R. 353, 359.

[59] See *Abbot v. Massie* (1796) 3 Ves. 148 (the nature of the evidence is not reported).

to do, or had done, by his will also constitutes evidence of his dispositive intention.

If the testator died before January 1, 1983, the admissibility of extrinsic evidence to assist in the interpretation of his will is governed by case law. If the testator dies after December 31, 1982, section 21 of the Administration of Justice Act 1982 applies.[60] The principal change effected by section 21 is to admit evidence of the testator's dispositive intention in instances where it would not previously have been admissible.

5.   Admissibility of extrinsic evidence on a death before 1983.

(1)   *EVIDENCE OF SURROUNDING CIRCUMSTANCES—ADMISSIBLE IN CASES OF UNCERTAINTY OR AMBIGUITY ON A DEATH BEFORE 1983 UNDER THE ARMCHAIR PRINCIPLE.* Evidence as to the circumstances surrounding the testator when he made his will has always been admissible as an aid in construction in cases of uncertainty or ambiguity. This rule is generally referred to as the "armchair principle." "You may place yourself, so to speak, in [the testator's] armchair, and consider the circumstances by which he was surrounded when he made his will to assist you in arriving at his intention."[61]

(a)   *Identity of Beneficiary.* The decided cases usually concern the identity of the beneficiary (the object) or the description of what is given (the subject matter of a gift). In the example of T's gift of a legacy of £100 to "Mrs. G", there was uncertainty because of the description of the beneficiary. Evidence that T was acquainted with a lady named Mrs. Gregg, to whom he habitually referred as "Mrs. G", is therefore admissible as evidence of the circumstances, to help discover T's intended meaning.[62] The case of *Charter v. Charter*[63] is an instance of uncertainty arising from the misdescription of a beneficiary. T, a farmer, by his will appointed "my son, Forster Charter" as his executor and gave him his residuary estate. He also directed him to pay an annuity and allow maintenance to his mother, T's widow, "so long as they reside together in the same house". T had had a son named Forster Charter, but this son had died some years before the testator made his will and he could not have been the son referred to. At the time the will was made, T had two sons, one named William Forster Charter and the other named Charles Charter. Probate was granted to William Forster Charter. Charles applied for revocation of the grant on the ground that he, Charles, was the person named in the will. Lord Penzance, sitting as a judge of the Probate Court, admitted evidence of the surrounding circumstances when T made his will, *i.e.* that Charles was living at home with his parents and working on T's farm, that William had lived away from home for some years and seldom visited T, and that T did not call him "Forster" but always

---

[60]   Administration of Justice Act 1982, ss. 73(6) and 76(11).
[61]   *Per* James L.J. in *Boyes v. Cook* (1880) 14 Ch.D. 53, 56.
[62]   See *Abbott v. Massie* (1796) 3 Ves. 148; *Price v. Page* (1799) 4 Ves. 680 (gift of legacy to
"   Price the son of   Price"); *Re Ofner* [1909] 1 Ch. 60 (single instance of T's
use of wrong name admissible); *Re Tetsall* [1961] 1 W.L.R. 938.
[63]   (1874) L.R. 7 H.L. 364: see also *Doe d. Hiscocks v. Hiscocks* (1839) 5 M. & W. 363; *Bernasconi
v. Atkinson* (1853) 10 Hare 345.

"William" or "Willie." Lord Penzance decided in favour of Charles. William appealed to the House of Lords; the four members were evenly divided. Lord Chelmsford and Lord Hatherley thought that the will was not uncertain or ambiguous. They thought that the reference to "Forster Charter" was a clear reference to William Forster Charter. But Lord Cairns and Lord Selborne upheld the decision of Lord Penzance. They considered that the provision in the will under which the executor was directed to pay the annuity and allow maintenance to T's widow "so long as they reside together in the same house" did not apply to William Forster Charter and so there was uncertainty or ambiguity. Once uncertainty or ambiguity was established, evidence of the circumstances surrounding the testator at the time he made his will could be admitted under the armchair principle and this evidence pointed clearly to Charles.[64]

(b) *Identity of Subject Matter of Gift.* Then there are cases where there is uncertainty as to the identity of the subject matter of the gift. In *Ricketts v. Turquand*[65] T by his will devised "all my estate in Shropshire, called Ashford Hall," and the House of Lords held that evidence was admissible to show the extent of the land in Shropshire which T during his lifetime habitually called his Ashford Hall estate. Again, in *Kell v. Charmer*[66] T, a jeweller, by his will gave "to my son William the sum of i.x.x. To my son Robert Charles the sum of o.x.x." The court held that evidence was admissible that in carrying on his business T used private symbols to denote his prices and that, according to this system, the letters "i.x.x." and "o.x.x." represented £100 and £200 respectively.

(c) *Limits on the Effect of such Evidence.* Evidence of circumstances surrounding the testator at the time he made his will is admitted in cases of uncertainty or ambiguity in order to assist in ascertaining the intention expressed in the will. But such evidence cannot make words in a will bear a meaning which, on the face of the will, they are incapable of bearing.[67] Extrinsic evidence cannot, by itself, make "black" mean "white."

As regards the beneficiary, a "very strong presumption"[68] arises that

---

[64] The case is very borderline. The House was evenly divided—so Lord Penzance's decision at first instance was affirmed. Charles won. But the extrinsic evidence of surrounding circumstances could only be admitted if the provisions of the will were uncertain or ambiguous. There was a gift to "Forster" and this seemed to point to William (whose name was Forster). So the question was whether the words "so long as they reside together in the same house" made the apparent gift to William uncertain or ambiguous. Lords Cairns and Selborne thought that they did, Lords Chelmsford and Hatherley that they did not.

[65] (1848) 1 H.L. Cas. 472: see also *Webb v. Byng* (1855) 1 K. & J. 580 ("all my Quendon Hall estates in Essex"); *Castle v. Fox* (1871) 11 Eq. 542 ("my mansion and estate called Cleeve Court"); *Re Glassington* [1906] 2 Ch. 305 (my "real estate" passed T's interest under a trust for sale of realty as T had no realty at date of will) and *cf. Re Sykes* [1940] 4 All E.R. 10; *Re Lewis's W.T.* [1985] 1 W.L.R. 102.

[66] (1856) 23 Beav. 195.

[67] *Higgins v. Dawson* [1902] A.C. 1; *Re Mulder* [1943] 2 All E.R. 150, 151; *Re Lewis's W.T., supra.*

[68] *National Society for the Prevention of Cruelty to Children v. Scottish National Society for the Prevention of Cruelty to Children* [1915] A.C. 207, 212 and 216.

the person who completely satisfies the description in the will was meant and this presumption cannot be overcome by evidence of surrounding circumstances except in "exceptional circumstances."[69] In *National Society for the Prevention of Cruelty to Children v. Scottish National Society for the Prevention of Cruelty to Children*[70] T gave a legacy "to the National Society for the Prevention of Cruelty to Children," which was the exact name of an English society. T had lived all his life in Scotland and the legacy appeared in his will in the middle of a series of legacies to Scottish charities. The legacy was claimed by the Scottish National Society for the Prevention of Cruelty to Children, and evidence showed that the Scottish N.S.P.C.C. had been brought to T's notice shortly before he had made his will: there was no evidence that T had taken any interest in the English society. The House of Lords decided that the English society was entitled to the legacy. Lord Loreburn said:

"What a man has said ought to be acted upon unless it is clearly proved that he meant something different from what he said . . . I do not think that in this case any ambiguity has been established."[71]

The same rule probably applies, by analogy, with regard to the subject matter of a gift.[72]

(2) *EVIDENCE OF SURROUNDING CIRCUMSTANCES—ADMISS- IBLE ON A DEATH BEFORE 1983 WHERE THE WORDS IN THEIR "STRICT AND PRIMARY" MEANING DO NOT MAKE SENSE.* A will must be read in the light of the circumstances surrounding the testator when it was made. If the ordinary meaning of a word or phrase in the will does not make sense when read in the light of these circumstances, and the word or phrase has a secondary meaning which does make sense when read in this light, the word or phrase may be given this secondary meaning. This rule applies, for example, to words which describe a relationship. In *Re Smalley*[73] a testator left all his property to "my wife Eliza Ann Smalley." There were, however, two women in the testator's life and each claimed to be the one who fitted the description. There was Mary Ann Smalley who was the testator's lawful wife but with whom he had not lived for some years and there was Eliza Ann Mercer with whom he had gone through a ceremony of marriage and who lived with him, believing herself to be his wife. The Court of Appeal decided that Eliza Ann Mercer was entitled: the surrounding circumstances showed that the testator had used the words "my wife" in his will in their sec- ondary meaning of his *reputed* wife. The finding in favour of Eliza Ann Mercer was made possible because the desription in the will did not make sense in the light of the circumstances. The testator's wife was not called Eliza and Eliza was not his wife. The description fitted neither, so it was possible to give the word "wife" a secondary meaning. Had the

[69] *Ibid.* ("in some abnormal case of a special character").
[70] [1915] A.C. 207: see also *Re Satterthwaite's W.T.* [1966] 1 W.L.R. 277; *Re Carlisle* [1950] N.I. 105.
[71] [1915] A.C. 207 at pp. 212–213.
[72] But see *Re Seal* [1984] 1 Ch. 316, 322–323.
[73] [1929] 2 Ch. 112: see *Allgood v. Blake* (1873) L.R. 8 Exch. 160, 163–164; *Re Jebb* [1966] Ch. 666.

testator simply left his property to "my wife" with no further qualification or description, his lawful wife would have taken, there would have been no cause to seek a secondary meaning for the expression.

In the same way, a technical word or expression which does not make sense if read in the light of the circumstances surrounding the testator at the time when he made his will, may be read in a non-technical way if that makes sense. In *Re Bailey*[74] T by her home-made will gave the house in which she lived to X and several pecuniary legacies to persons named, and concluded, "I leave Y as my residuary legatee." T's estate consisted mainly of realty. Romer J. held that there was sufficient context in the will, read in the light of the surrounding circumstances, to show that the technical words "residuary legatee" (prima facie referring to personalty) had been used in the wider sense of "residuary beneficiary," and therefore Y was entitled to T's residuary realty as well.

Admitting evidence of circumsances surrounding the testator when he made his will, in cases where the strict and primary meaning (or the technical meaning) of words does not make sense, differs from the dictionary principle in that, in these cases, the word or phrase must be capable of bearing the secondary meaning to be put on it. Evidence extrinsic to the will cannot make "black" mean "white".

(3) *ADMISSIBILITY OF EXTRINSIC EVIDENCE AS TO THE TESTATOR'S INTENTION ON A DEATH BEFORE 1983.* If the testator died before 1983, extrinsic evidence of his intended meaning, of his actual wishes, was admissible *only* in cases of *equivocation.*[75] Evidence of the testator's intention has always been admissible to rebut equitable presumptions, but they are not rules of construction.[76]

Equivocation. There is an equivocation if a description of the object or the subject matter of a gift in a will is applicable to two or more persons or things. Sometimes the term "latent ambiguity" is used instead of equivocation. The term equivocation is preferable because a description which is equally applicable to two or more persons or things constitutes an equivocation, even though the existence of the two or more persons or things is mentioned elsewhere in the will, so that the ambiguity is not latent.[77]

Here are some examples of equivocation:

  (i) There is an equivocation as to the *object* of a gift if T by his will makes a gift to "my son John," and T has two sons called John;[78]

---

[74] [1945] Ch. 191; *cf. Re Gibbs* [1907] 1 Ch. 465.

[75] *Doe d. Hiscocks v. Hiscocks* (1839) 5 M. & W. 363; *Charter v. Charter* (1874) L.R. 7 H.L. 364 (see *ante*, pp. 189–190); *Re Atkinson's W.T.* [1978] 1 W.L.R. 586, 590: see Phipson (1904) 20 L.Q.R. 245, 252–253 and 268–271. However, T's instructions may be admissible as *circumstantial* evidence of T's intended meaning, *Re Ofner* [1909] 1 Ch. 60 (T gave legacy to grandnephew "Robert": evidence admissible that T wrote "Robert," referring to grand-nephew Richard, in instructions to solicitor).

[76] See *post* p. 225.

[77] See *Doe d. Gord v. Needs* (1836) 2 M. & W. 129 ("George Gord the son of Gord"; George, son of George Gord, and George, son of John Gord, both mentioned elsewhere in will: evidence of T's declarations of intention admissible).

[78] *Lord Cheyney's Case* (1590) 5 Co. 68a, 68b (T supposed elder son John to be dead).

or to "my granddaughter [blank]," when he has three grand-daughters;[79] or to "my nephew Arthur Murphy," where he has more than one nephew called Arthur Murphy;[80] or to "The Clergy Society," if there are several societies popularly so called.[81]

(ii) There is an equivocation as to the *subject* matter of a gift if T by his will makes a gift of his "manor of Dale" and he has two manors of Dale, South Dale and North Dale.[82]

If the will, construed as a whole, with the aid of any evidence as to surrounding circumstances admissible under the armchair principle,[83] shows to which of the two or more persons or things the testator was referring, there is no equivocation.[84] But, if it does not, extrinsic evidence of the testator's dispositive intention, is admissible. This evidence may take the form of the instructions the testator gave for his will or of declarations made by him as to what he intended to do or had done.[85] If the equivocation cannot be resolved, the gift fails for uncertainty.[86]

If part of the description does not apply to any possible person (or thing), it may be rejected, leaving the remainder of the description equivocal. So there is an equivocation if by his will T makes a gift to "my nephew Arthur Charles Brown," and at the date of his will T has two or more nephews named Arthur Brown and no nephew named Charles Brown (or Arthur Charles Brown.)[87] The remainder of the description must, however, be sufficient to describe with legal certainty one of the competing persons (or things) if the other of them did not exist.[88]

If, on the other hand, T has left a legacy to "my nephew Arthur Charles Brown," and at the date of his will T had one nephew named Arthur Brown and another nephew named Charles Brown, this is not treated as an equivocation. This is because part of the description ("Arthur") applies to one person and another part ("Charles") applies to the other person.[89] It must be said that it is not clear why this latter rule became law, it is both artificial and arbitrary.[90] It was by virtue of this rule that Charter v. Charter,[91] referred to above, was dealt with in the House of Lords as a case of uncertainty or ambiguity not equivocation. Lord Penzance, had, at first instance, admitted direct evidence, *i.e.* evidence of declarations made by the testator, of his intention to benefit his son Charles. All four members of the House of Lords agreed that this evidence should not have been admitted because there had been no equivocation. There would only have been an equivocation, in the

---

[79] *In the Estate of Hubbuck* [1905] P. 129: see *Price v. Page* (1799) 4 Ves. 680 ("   Price the son of   Price").

[80] *Re Jackson* [1933] Ch. 237: see *Doe d. Morgan v. Morgan* (1832) 1 C. & M. 235.

[81] *Re Clergy Society* (1856) 2 K. & J. 615.

[82] *Miller v. Travers* (1832) 8 Bing. 244, 248: see *Re Battie-Wrightson* [1920] 2 Ch. 330.

[83] *Ante,* pp. 189–191.

[84] *Doe d. Westlake v. Westlake* (1820) 4 B. & Ald. 57.

[85] *Lord Cheyney's Case, supra; the Estate of Hubbuck, supra,* (T's instructions for her will); *Price v. Page supra.*

[86] *Asten v. Asten* [1894] 3 Ch. 261 (*ante,* pp. 349–350).

[87] *Re Ray* [1916] 1 Ch. 461; *Bennett v. Marshall* (1856) 2 K. & J. 740.

[88] *Re Ray, supra: cf. Miller v. Travers* (1832) 8 Bing. 244.

[89] *Doe d. Hiscocks v. Hiscocks* (1839) 5 M. & W. 363.

[90] See *Charter v. Charter* (1874) L.R. 7 H.L. 364, *ibid.* at p. 383.

[91] (1874) L.R. 7 H.L. 364, *supra.*

narrow technical sense relevant here, if the testator had, at the time when he made his will, had two living sons both called Forster.

Another example of a case where extrinsic evidence of the testator's intention was not admitted, but where the intended legatee was still successful was *Re Feather*.[92] Here the testator left £2,000 to a servant provided he was "still in my employ." In the course of the War, the servant was conscripted for military service but the testator told one of his executors that he regarded him as being still in his employ. The testator died while the servant was still in the army. The statement by the testator to his executor could not be admitted as evidence of the testator's intention, there was no question of equivocation, but it was relevant in that it showed that the testator regarded the servant as being still in his employ. Insofar as there was a doubt about the servant's status, it was relevant evidence.

6. Admissibility of extrinsic evidence on a death after 1982

Section 21 of the Administration of Justice Act 1982, which applies where the testator dies after December 31, 1982, makes extrinsic evidence of the testator's intention admissible where only evidence of surrounding circumstances would have been admissible before. The section makes *both* evidence of the circumstances surrounding the testator at the time of the execution of his will and evidence of his intention admissible to assist in interpretation of a will in three situations:

(1) *IN SO FAR AS ANY PART OF A WILL IS MEANINGLESS.* Thus if T employs in his will a word or symbol which appears to have no meaning,[93] extrinsic evidence both of surrounding circumstances and of the testator's intention is admissible to assist in the interpretation of the word or symbol. For example, such evidence is admissible if T gives to his son "the sum of o.x.x.,"[94] or gives Blackacre "to K. then to L."[95] If T died before 1983, only evidence of surrounding circumstances would have been admissible in these sorts of cases.

Extrinsic evidence is, however, probably not admissible to fill up a total blank in a will[96] ("I give £100 to   "), because there is nothing which the evidence can assist in interpreting. Again, if T's will reads, "I give my son nothing," evidence cannot be admitted that T intended "nothing" to denote £20,000, because this part of the will is not meaningless.

---

[92] [1945] Ch 343.

[93] The section says "is meaningless" but this must mean "appears to be meaningless"; otherwise it seems not to make sense.

[94] See *Kell v. Charmer* (1856) 23 Beav. 195 (before 1983, evidence of surrounding circumstances could include T's use of private symbols in his jeweller's business, see *ante*, p. 190).

[95] See *Clayton v. Lord Nugent* (1844) 13 M. & W. 200 (before 1983, key written on separate card was not admissible as direct evidence): but evidence of surrounding circumstances was admissible, *Abbot v. Massie* (1796) 3 Ves. 148 (*ante*, p. 189).

[96] *Ante*, p. 187.

(2)   *IN SO FAR AS THE LANGUAGE*[97] *USED IN ANY PART OF A WILL IS AMBIGUOUS ON THE FACE OF IT.* A classic instance is a gift by T's will of "my money" or "my effects."[98] If T died before 1983, only evidence of surrounding circumstances would have been admissible: if T dies after 1982, extrinsic evidence both of surrounding circumstances and of the testator's intention is admissible.

(3)   *IN SO FAR AS EVIDENCE, OTHER THAN EVIDENCE OF THE TESTATOR'S INTENTION, SHOWS THAT THE LANGUAGE USED IN ANY PART OF A WILL IS AMBIGUOUS IN THE LIGHT OF SUR-ROUNDING CIRCUMSTANCES.* This obviously applies where there is what, under the old rules, would have been regarded as an equivocation; but it also applies where, although there is no equivocation, there is nevertheless an ambiguity—for instance, where T makes a gift to "my nephew Arthur Charles Brown," and at the date of his will T has one nephew named Arthur Brown and another nephew named Charles Brown. This means that the fine, the almost artificial, line between an equivocation and other forms of ambiguity can, for testators dying after 1982, be regarded as irrelevant.

Having said this, the extrinsic evidence of T's intention is admissible, not to *show* that the language of his will is ambiguous, but to assist in its interpretation if it is shown to be ambiguous in the light of surrounding circumstances. It will now be admissible in a case like *Re Smalley*[99] where the testator left all his property to "my wife Eliza Ann Smalley" and had no wife called Eliza Ann Smalley. But it would not be admissible to show that a gift to "my wife" was really intended for someone other than the testator's wife, if he had a wife at the time when he made his will, for in this case, the language of the will in not ambiguous even when it is read "in the light of the surrounding circumstances".

Furthermore, the function of the evidence, admissible under section 21, is "to assist in . . . interpretation," not to make a new will for the testator. Accordingly, such evidence cannot make "black" mean "white." To quote Nicholls J. in *Re Williams*[100]:

"The evidence may assist by showing which of two or more possible meanings a testator was attaching to a particular word or phrase. . . . That meaning may be one which, without recourse to the extrinsic evidence, would not really have been apparent at all. So long as that meaning is one which the word or phrase read in its context is capable of bearing, then the court may conclude that, assisted by the extrinsic evidence, that is its correct construction. But if, however liberal may be the approach of the court, the meaning is one which the word or phrase cannot bear, I do not see how in carrying out a process of . . . interpretation . . . the court can declare that meaning to be the meaning

---

[97] See *Re Williams* [1985] 1 W.L.R. 905, 912–913 (language includes numerals as much as words or letters, but *quaere* whether it includes a division of legatees in a will into three groups).
[98] *Re Williams*, *supra*, at p. 911 (obvious examples): for gifts of "money" see *ante*, p. 183.
[99] Referred to *supra*; [1929] 2 Ch 112.
[100] [1985] 1 W.L.R. 905, 912.

of the word or phrase. Such a conclusion, varying or contradicting the language used, would amount to rewriting part of the will. . . ."

II. SPECIFIC RULES OF CONSTRUCTION—GIFTS TO CHILDREN—THE AGE OF MAJORITY—ASCERTAINING CLASSES—ABSOLUTE/LIFE GIFTS

A. ADOPTED, LEGITIMATED AND ILLEGITIMATE CHILDREN

The position of adopted, legitimated and illegitimate children for the purposes of intestacy was considered in Chapter 2.[1] Now it is necessary to turn to gifts by will.

1. Adopted child

Under the Adoption Act 1976 an adopted child is treated as the legitimate child of the married couple who adopted him (or, in any other case, as the legitimate child of his adopter),[2] and not as the child of his natural parents.[3] This principle applies to the construction of the will of a testator who dies after December 31, 1975, subject to any contrary indication,[4] and it is immaterial whether the adoption order is made before or after the testator's death.[5] Thus, if T dies in 1976, having by his will given property upon trust for his son X for life and after X's death for X's children in equal shares absolutely, any child adopted by X (whether before or after T's death) will be entitled to take, unless there is a contrary indication in T's will. If X is T's daughter, the same result follows, subject to a curious exception which may be applicable in the case of a child adopted by a woman after she has attained 55 years of age.[6]

---

[1] *Ante*, pp. 45–47.

[2] Adoption Act 1976, s. 39(1), (2) and (4): this rule applies to an adoption order made by a court in any part of the U.K., the Isle of Man or the Channel Islands, and to certain foreign adoptions, (s. 38). For the protection of personal representatives see *post*, p. 472.

[3] *ibid*. s. 39(2); *Re Collins* [1990] 2 W.L.R. 161; as to the effect of adoption by one of the child's natural parents see Adoption Act 1976 s. 39(3) and Legitimacy Act 1976, s. 4 as amended by Adoption Act 1976, s. 73(3) and Sched. 3. The adopted child retains any interest vested in possession in him before the adoption, (s. 42(4).

[4] *ibid*. ss. 42(1), 46(3) and 72(1). In the case of a testator who died before January 1, 1976, the Adoption Act 1958, ss. 16, 17 and provisions containing references to those sections continue to apply, (s. 73(1) and Sched. 2, para. 6).

[5] *ibid*. s. 39(6). If the testator T died before January 1, 1976, the adoption order must have been made before T's death (Adoption Act 1958, s. 16(2) and 17(2)): but if T's will or codicil was executed before April 1, 1959, (i) the adoption order must have been made before its execution, unless it was confirmed by codicil executed after March 31, 1959. Sched. 5, para. 4(3), (4)), and (ii) the adopted child cannot take if T's will or codicil was executed before January 1, 1950 (Sched. 5, para. 4(1), (2)) unless, exceptionally, the child is entitled to take at common law, *Re Fletcher* [1949] Ch. 473; *Re Gilpin* [1954] Ch. 1; *Re Jebb* [1966] Ch. 666, but see J.H.C. Morris (1966) 82 L.Q.R. 196.

[6] Adoption Act 1976, s. 42(5) provides that "where it is necessary to determine for the purposes of a disposition of property effected by an instrument [*i.e.* T's will] whether a woman can have a child, it shall be presumed that once a woman has attained the age

The Adoption Act 1976 sets out two rules of construction (complete with statutory examples) which are applicable to the will of a testator who dies after 1975, subject to any contrary indication. The rules relate to a disposition[7] by will which depends on the date of birth of a child or children. The disposition is to be construed as if:

(i) the adopted child had been born on the date of adoption[8]; and
(ii) two or more children adopted on the same date had been born on that date in the order of their actual births;

but these rules do not affect any reference to the age of a child.[9] To take the statutory example of a gift by T's will to the children[10] of A "living at my death or born afterwards". T dies in 1976 and after T's death A adopts a child, who was born in 1974. This child is entitled to take under the gift as a child of A born (applying rule (i)) after T's death, though the child does not answer to the description of a child of A living at T's death. The second statutory example is another gift by T's will to the children[11] of A "living at my death or born afterwards before any one of such children for the time being in existence attains a vested interest and who attain the age of 21 years." A's adopted child is entitled to take under this gift if he is adopted before any other child attains a vested interest and if he attains the age of 21 years, which is measured from his true date of birth and not from the date of his adoption. Finally, consider a gift by T's will to the eldest son of B. At T's death in 1976 B has a natural son (born in 1974) and an adopted son (born in 1973 and adopted in 1975). If "eldest" is a reference to the age of a child, the adopted son takes; but probably it is not and, if so (applying rule (i)), the natural son takes.

By way of exception, an adoption does not affect the devolution of any property limited (expressly or not) to devolve along with any peerage or dignity or title of honour, unless a contrary intention is expressed in the will.[12]

2. Legitimated child[13]

Under the Legitimacy Act 1976 a legitimated person (and any other person) is entitled to take any interest under the will of a testator who

of 55 years she will not adopt a child after execution of the instrument [this may mean after T's death, s. 46(3)], and, . . .if she does so that child shall not be treated as her child or as the child of her spouse (if any) for the purposes of the instrument." If T's daughter X disclaims or releases her life interest, it may be necessary to determine whether X can have a child: *quaere* in what other circumstances it is "necessary".
[7] See *ibid*. s. 46.
[8] As to the effect of adoption by one of the child's natural parents, see the 1976 Act s. 43 (which sets out a statutory example).
[9] The Adoption Act 1976, s. 42(2).
[10] *Or* grandchildren. Another statutory example is to A for life "until he has a child," and then to his child or children.
[11] *Or* grandchildren.
[12] The Adoption Act 1976, s. 44; adoption does not affect the descent of any peerage or dignity or title of honour.
[13] A legitimated child is one who was illegitmate at the time of his birth, but who becomes legitimate by his parents' subsequent marriage. Legitimation was introduced into English law by the Legitimacy Act 1926.

dies after December 31, 1975 as if the legitimated person had been born legitimate, subject to any contrary indication.[14] As in the case of adoption, it is immaterial whether the legitimation occurs before or after the testator's death.[15] Again, in the case of legitimation, similar rules of construction are applicable to a disposition by will which depends on the date of birth of a child or children as apply (as explained above) in the case of adoption.[16] For instance, if T dies in 1976 having by his will (which was made before 1970) made a gift to the children of C "living at my death or born afterwards," a child of C who is legitimated after T's death by his parents' marriage is entitled to take under the gift as a legitimate child of C born (under the rule of construction) on the date of his legitimation.[17]

3. Illegitimate child

At common law a gift by will to children, or other relations, was prima facie construed as referring only to legitimate children, or persons tracing their relationship exclusively through legitimate links.[18] This rule of construction was reversed by section 15 of the Family Law Reform Act 1969, which applies to a disposition of property by a will or codicil made after December 31, 1969 and before April 4, 1988. If the will or codicil was executed before 1970, it is not, for this purpose, treated as made after December 31, 1969, even if it is confirmed by a codicil executed after that date.[19]

(1) *RULES OF CONSTRUCTION UNDER THE FAMILY LAW REFORM ACT 1969.* Section 15(1) of the Act lays down two rules of construction:

(i) Any reference (express or implied) to the child or children of any person D is to be construed as, or as including, a reference to any illegitimate child of D. If T's will (made after 1969) gives property upon trust for D for life and after D's death for D's children in

---

[14] Legitimacy Act 1976, s. 5(1), (3) and (6) and s. 10. In the case of a testator who died before January 1,1976, the Legitimacy Act 1926, ss. 3 and 5 continue to apply, Legitimacy Act 1976, Sched. 1, para. 2. For the protection of personal representatives see *post* p. 472.

[15] If the testator T died before January 1, 1976, the legitimation must have occurred before T's death, Legitimacy Act 1926, s. 3(1).

[16] Legitimacy Act 1976, s. 5(4), (5): as to the effect of posthumous legitimation see s. 5(6), and as to devolution of property limited to devolve along with any dignity or title of honour see Sched. 1, para. 4.

[17] Legitimacy Act 1976, s. 5(4). If T's will had been made after 1969 an illegitimate child of C would have been entitled to take: s. 5(5) gives statutory examples but in each example legitimation appears to have no practical effect if T's will was made after 1969, because the illegitimate child, or a person related through him, would have been entitled to take anyway, unless a contrary intention appeared in the will, Family Law Reform Act 1969, s. 15; Legitimacy Act 1976, s.6(1), (3).

[18] For this rule, and the exceptions to it, see generally *Hawkins and Ryder on the Construction of Wills* (1965), pp. 131 *et seq.*; *Theobald on Wills* (15th ed., 1993), pp. 366 *et seq.*

[19] Family Law Reform Act 1969, s. 15(8): see also s. 1(7). For the general rule that a republished will or codicil operates as if it had bee made at the time of its republication see *ante*, pp. 119–120.

equal shares absolutely, any illegitimate child of D (whether born before or after T's death[20]) is entitled to take.

(ii) Any reference (express or implied) to a person or persons related in some other manner to any person D is to be construed as, or as including, a reference to anyone who would be so related if he, or some other person through whom the relationship is deduced, had been born legitimate. A gift by T's will (made after 1969) to D's grandchildren therefore includes both the illegitimate child of a legitimate child of D and the legitimate child of an illegitimate child of D.[21]

(2) *EXCEPTIONS.* These rules of construction apply only to references to a child or other relation, where the reference is to a person who is to benefit, or who is capable of benefiting under the disposition; or where (when such person is being designated) someone else is referred to as being someone to or through whom that person is related.[22] So these rules do not apply to a gift to ·E absolutely "if he dies without leaving children"; the word "children" in this case means legitimate children and, if E dies leaving one illegitimate child but no legitimate children, E takes absolutely.[23] Again, these rules of construction do not affect the construction of the word "heir" or "heirs" or of any expression which is used to create an entail,[24] or the devolution of any property which would (apart from these rules) devolve along with a dignity or title of honour.[25]

These rules of construction apply "unless the contrary intention appears." A testator is free to exclude the operation of these rules by his will, *e.g.* by making a gift to D's legitimate children.[26]

(3) *RULES OF CONSTRUCTION UNDER THE FAMILY LAW REFORM ACT 1987.* Section 19 of the Family Law Reform act 1987 changes these rules of construction and abolishes most of these exceptions.[27] It applies to dispositions[28] by will or codicil made after April 3, 1988.[29] Under section 19 references (whether express or implied) to any relationship between two persons are to be construed without regard to whether the father and mother of either of them, or the father and mother of any

---

[20] *ibid.* s. 15(7) abolishes any rule of law that a gift to illegitimate children born after T's death is void as contrary to public policy.
[21] *Quaere* whether it also includes the illegitimate child of an illegitimate child of D, see E. C. Ryder (1971) 24 C.L.P., 163–164; Law Commission Report on Illegitimacy, Law Com. No. 118, p. 104. See also Prichard [1981] Conv. 343 ("as on intestacy" in will).
[22] Family Law Reform Act 1969, s. 15(2).
[23] See E.C. Ryder, *loc. cit.* pp. 164–166.
[24] Family Law Reform Act 1969, s. 15(2).
[25] *ibid.* s. 15(5).
[26] See E.C. Ryder, *loc. cit.* pp. 166–167.
[27] See Law Commission Second Report of Illegitimacy, Law Com. No. 157.
[28] Including an oral disposition, Family Law Reform Act 1987, s. 19(6), *e.g.* a privileged will made orally.
[29] Family Law Reform Act 1987 (Commencement No. 1) Order 1988 (S.I. 1988 No. 425). A will or codicil executed before, but confirmed by codicil executed on or after, April 4, 1988 is not treated as made on or after that date, *ibid.* s. 19(7).

person through whom the relationship is deduced, were married to each other at any time. This new rule of construction applies whether or not the reference is to a person who is to benefit or be capable of benefiting under the disposition. It also applies to the construction of the word "heir" or "heirs" and to any expression which is used to create an entailed interest,[30] but it does not apply to the devolution of any property which would otherwise devolve along with a dignity or title of honour.[31]

The new rule of construction applies "unless the contrary intention appears."

B.   AGE OF MAJORITY

In a will the expressions "full age," "infant," "infancy," "minor," "minority" and similar expressions are to be construed by reference to the provision that a person attains full age on attaining the age of 18.[32] This construction applies, in the absence of a definition or of any indication of a contrary intention, if the will was made after December 31, 1969. A will or codicil executed before 1970 is not treated as made after 1969 although it was confirmed by a codicil executed after 1969.[33]

The construction of any expression specifying a particular age (for example, "twenty-one") is not altered by the Family Law Reform Act 1969.[34]

C.   RULES FOR ASCERTAINING CLASSES

Wills often contain gifts to a class of beneficiaries. For example, T by his will may give:

(i) £100 to each of the children of A (an individual gift to each member of a class, not a class gift in the strict sense);

(ii) £10,000 to the children of B in equal shares absolutely (a class gift in the strict sense, because the size of a child's share depends on the number of children who fall within the class[35]); and

(iii) £10,000 to the children of C who attain the age of 21 years in equal shares absolutely (again a class gift in the strict sense, but subject to a contingency).

In each of these examples the question may arise whether children who come into existence after T's death are eligible to take. Of course, T might have expressed his intention clearly in his will, *e.g.* by giving £100 to

---

[30] Family Law Reform Act 1987, s. 19(2).
[31] *ibid.* s. 19(4).
[32] Family Law Reform Act 1987, s. 1.
[33] *ibid.* s. 1(7): for republication see *ante*, pp. 119–120.
[34] See E.C. Ryder, *loc. cit.* pp. 158–160; Cretney (1970) 120 N.L.J. 144, 145.
[35] *Pearks v. Moseley* (1880) 5 App. Cas. 714, 723. For the nature of a class gift see *post*, pp. 235–236.

each of the children of A "who shall be living at my death." But, if T has not done so, the question must be answered by applying certain rules of construction known as the class-closing rules.[36] Which rule is applicable depends upon whether the gift is:

(1) an individual gift to each member of a class (as in example (i) above); or
(2) a class gift where each member of the class takes a share at birth (as in example (ii) above); or
(3) a class gift where a contingency is imposed on each member of the class (as in example (iii) above).

In the explanation which follows of the class-closing rules reference will be made to persons who are "living" at a particular time or who "come into existence" before a particular time. In applying these rules it is necessary to remember that a child who is *en ventre sa mere* at that time (and who is subsequently born alive) is by a legal fiction treated as already "living," or as having already "come into existence," at that time if the child may thereby become entitled to benefit as a member of the class.[37]

1. Individual gift to each member of a class

In the case of an individual gift to each member of a class, the class closes at the testator's death. If T by his will gives a legacy of £100 to each of the children of A, only children of A living at T's death take under the gift[38]; if no child of A is living at T's death the gift fails.[39] The same rules applies if the gift imposes a contingency on each member of the class, *e.g.* if T gives a legacy of £100 to each of the children of A who attain the age of 21 years or marry. In that case only children of A living at T's death are eligible to take under the gift, although it is immaterial whether each of them satisfies the contingency before or after T's death; if no child of A is living at T's death the gift fails.[40].

The object of this drastic class-closing rule is to enable the personal representatives to distribute T's residuary estate. The rule is a rule of convenience which fixes the maximum number of members of the class at T's death, so that the personal representatives may know the total sum required to meet their legacies and may safely distribute the remainder of T's estate. If the class did not close at T's death, the personal representatives could not safely distribute T's residuary estate until it had become impossible for further children of A to be born.

---

[36] See generally *Hawkins and Ryder on the Construction of Wills* (1965), Chap. 8; J.H.C. Morris (1954) 70 L.Q.R. 61; S.J. Bailey [1958] C.L.J. 39.

[37] *Trower v. Butts* (1823) 1 S. & S. 181 (such a child is "within the reason and motive of the Gift"); *Storrs v. Benbow* (1853) 3 De G.M. & G. 390; *Re Salaman* [1908] 1 Ch. 4 (such a child is treated as born if he thereby takes a direct benefit); *Elliot v. Joicey* [1935] A.C. 209: *cf. Re Corlass* (1875) 1 Ch.D. 460 (child *en ventre* illegitimate, though legitimated before birth). But see *Re Gardiner's Estate* (1875) 20 Eq. 647 (which appears to be wrongly decided)

[38] *Ringrose v. Bramham* (1794) 2 Cox 384.

[39] *Re Belville* [1941] Ch. 414 (T by his will gave £10,000 each to any daughters of X born after the date of his will: held daughter conceived after T's death could not take).

[40] *Rogers v. Mutch* (1878) 10 Ch.D. 25.

The rule is modified if the will postpones payment of the legacies and distribution of the residue until the death of a life tenant, *e.g.* if T gives his estate upon trust for X for life, and after X's death to pay £100 to each of the children of A and to hold the remainder on trust for Y absolutely. In that case the class remains open until the death of the life tenant, X, and therefore embraces children of A who are living at T's death or who come into existence before X's death.[41]

The rule is altogether excluded, so that any children of A coming into existence after T's death may take, if the inconvenience prevented by the rule either does not exist or is expressly contemplated by the testator.[42] An instance of the first exception is where the testator directs a fund of a specified amount to be set aside out of which alone the legacies are made payable.[43] The second exception was held to be applicable in a case where the testator showed a clear intention that the class should include any children coming into existence after his death and directed a sufficient fund to be set aside for this purpose.[44]

2.   Class gift where each member takes a share at birth

Under a class gift in the strict sense the members of the class share the same subject-matter of the gift, whether equally or in specified proportions. If the class has not yet closed, the personal representatives cannot safely distribute a share to a person who is already a member of the class, because the minimum size of that share is not yet fixed. However, the personal representatives can safely distribute the remainder of the testator's estate. As already explained, in the case of an individual gift to each member of a class, the object of the class-closing rule is to enable the personal representatives to distribute the testator's residuary estate. But, in the case of class gifts in the strict sense, the relevant class-closing rules serve a different purpose—to enable the personal representatives to distribute a share of the subject matter of the gift to a person who is already a member of the class.

A class gift where each member takes a share at birth may be (1) immediate or (2) postponed.

(1)   *IMMEDIATE GIFT.* In the case of an immediate gift where each member takes a share at birth, the class closes at the testator's death if any member of the class is then in existence[45]; if no member of the class is then in existence, no class-closing rule applies and the class remains open indefinitely.[46] To consider the gift by T's will of £10,000 to the children of B in equal shares absolutely. If one or more children of B are living at T's death, then the class closes immediately and they alone take

---

[41] *Att.-Gen. v. Crispin* (1784) 1 Bro.C.C. 396.

[42] *Re Belville, supra,* at pp. 418–419.

[43] *Evans v. Harris* (1842) 5 Beav. 45.

[44] *Defflis v. Goldschmidt* (1816) Mer. 417 (court directed master to inquire what would be a sufficient sum to set aside to answer legacies of £2,000 payable to each child of A who might thereafter be born, having regard to A's age): *cf. Butler v. Lowe* (1839) 10 Sim. 317.

[45] *Viner v. Francis* (1789) 2 Cox 190 (£2,000 to the children of my late sister B); *Re Chartres* [1927] 1 Ch. 466, 471; *Re Manners* [1955] 1 W.L.R. 1096.

[46] *Shepherd v. Ingram* (1764) Amb. 448; *Weld v. Bradbury* (1715) 2 Vern. 705; *Harris v. Lloyd* (1823) 1 T. & R. 310; *Re Chartres, supra; Re Bleckly* [1951] Ch. 740, 749.

under the gift. On the other hand, if no child of B is living at T's death, then the class remains open indefinitely and all the children of B born thereafter take under the gift. This rule that the class closes at the testator's death if any member of the class is then in existence applies to an immediate class gift which is vested, even though payment is directed to be postponed until the youngest member of the class attains full age,[47] or even though a member's share is liable to be divested in a certain event (e.g. on his death under 21 years of age[48]).

(2) *POSTPONED GIFT.* A class gift may be postponed by a preceding life or other interest,[49] e.g. a gift by T's will of £10,000 upon trust for X for life and after X's death for the children of B in equal shares absolutely. In this case the class closes at the time when the postponement ends,[50] but if at that time there is as yet no member of the class, no class-closing rule applies and the class remains open indefinitely.[51] Consider this last example of a postponed class gift. If one or more children of B are living at T's death or come into existence before X's death, the class closes at X's death and only embraces children of B who are living at T's death or who come into existence before X's death. If any such child dies after T's death but before distribution of the £10,000, the child's share passes as an asset of his estate to his personal representatives.[52] On the other hand, if no child of B is living at T's death or comes into existence before X's death, then the class remains open indefinitely and all the children of B born thereafter take under the gift. This rule that the class closes at the time when the postponement ends applies to a class gift which is vested, even though payment is directed to be postponed until the youngest member of the class attains full age,[53] or even though a member's share is liable to be divested in a certain event.

Thus the same class-closing rule applies to any class gift where each member takes a share at birth, whether the gift is immediate or postponed, except that the crucial "class-closing time" is the testator's death in the case of an immediate gift, and the end of the period of postponement in the case of a postponed gift. This rule differs in one vital respect

[47] *Re Manners, supra* (gift by T's will to my grandchildren (the children of my son X) "to be administered towards their maintenance and education until the youngest is 21 . . . and then distributed equally among them": held grandchildren alive at T's death alone took): see also *Scott v. Harwood* (1821) 5 Madd. 332.

[48] *Davidson v. Dallas* (1808) 14 Ves. 576; *Scott v. Harwood, supra.*

[49] e.g. a life interest which is determinable or subject to a condition subsequent, *Re Aylwin's Trusts* (1873) L.R. 16 Eq. 585 (life interest determinable on bankruptcy or insolvency): or an absolute interest subject to a gift over, *Ellison v. Airey* (1748) 1 Ves. Sen. 111 (to X absolutely, but if X dies under 21 unmarried, to the children of B). See also *Oppenheim v. Henry* (1853) 10 Hare 441 (gift to all my grandchildren, to be divided among them at the end of 20 years after my death, income to be accumulated meanwhile: held class closed at end of 20 years).

[50] *Ellison v. Airey, supra: Devisme v. Mello* (1782) 1 Bro. C.C. 537; *Ayton v. Ayton* (1787) 1 Cox 327; *Middleton v. Messenger* (1799) 5 Ves 136; *Walker v. Shore* (1808) 15 Ves 122; *Holland v. Wood* (1871) L.R. 11 Eq. 91.

[51] *Chapman v. Blisset* (1735) Cas.t.Talb. 145; *Hutcheson v. Jones* (1817) 2 Madd. 124; *Re Chartres* [1927] 1 Ch. 466, 471–472; *Re Bleckly* [1951] Ch. 740, 749 and 755.

[52] *Devisme v. Mello, supra*: but if the child held as a joint tenant (which is not the case in the example in the text) the right of survivorship operates.

[53] *Smith v. Jackson* (1823) 1 L.J.(O.S.) Ch. 231 (gift to children of T's granddaughters to be paid when youngest attained 21 years).

from the more drastic rule applicable in the case of an individual gift to each member of a class:[54] under this rule, if at the class-closing time there is as yet no member of the class, the class remains open indefinitely.

This class-closing rule, in common with the other rules, is sometimes called a rule of convenience (though it may appear inconvenient to B's children who come into existence after the class has closed). In truth, it is a rule of construction and it is based upon the supposition that T would not wish B's children who are in existence at T's death (or, in the case of a postponed gift, who come into existence before the time when the postponement ends) to have to wait for distribution of the capital until it is no longer possible for further children of B to be born.[55]

(3) ACCELERATION OF A CLASS GIFT BY FAILURE OF A PRECEDING INTEREST. To return to the gift by T's will of £10,000 upon trust for X for life and after X's death for the children of B in equal shares absolutely. If X's life interest fails because (for instance) he predeceases T, the class gift to the children of B is accelerated and becomes an immediate (and not a postponed) gift, so that the crucial class-closing time is the testator's death.[56]

If X survives T, but X disclaims his life interest and thereby accelerates the class gift to the children of B, does this have the same effect on class-closing as if X had predeceased T? Probably the answer is no—the crucial class-closing time is still X's death. In *Re Davies*[57] X (who had three children) disclaimed her life interest under T's will, and Vaisey J. held that the vested class gift in remainder to the issue of X was accelerated, and that X's three children took to the exclusion of any other issue of X who might come into existence prior to X's death. But in *Re Harker's Will Trusts*[58] Goff J. refused to follow *Re Davies*. He decided that, despite the acceleration of the class gift in remainder, the class of beneficiaries must remain open until X's death. It appears likely that the decision in *Re Harker's Will Trusts* will be followed. X, by disclaiming his life interest *after* T's death, cannot change the composition of the class of beneficiaries entitled under the class gift remainder. The class-closing rules are rules of construction and the proper construction of T's will cannot be altered after T's death by X's disclaimer.

3. Class gift where contingency is imposed on each member

To turn to the other type of class gift where a contingency is imposed on each member of the class, *e.g.* a gift by T's will of £10,000 to the

[54] Where the gift fails if there is no class member living at the testator's death.
[55] *Re Ward* [1965] Ch. 856, 865. See generally for the basis of the rules S.J. Bailey [1958] C.L.J. 39, 45–48.
[56] *Sprackling v. Ranier* (1761) Dick. 344: as to T's revocation of X's life interest by a codicil see *Eavestaff v. Austin* (1854) 19 Beav. 591; *Re Johnson* (1893) 68 L.T. 20. For acceleration see *post*, pp. 264–265.
[57] [1957] 1 W.L.R. 922: see also *Re Taylor* [1957] 1 W.L.R. 1043, 1047–1048 and *Re Chartres* [1927] 1 Ch. 466.
[58] [1969] 1 W.L.R. 1124 (X for life, on his death to X's children equally on attaining 21; X surrendered his life interest; later one child of X attained 21: held the remainder was accelerated but the class remained upon until X's death): see also *Re Kebty-Fletcher's W.T.* [1969] 1 Ch. 339.

children of C who attain the age of 21 years in equal shares absolutely. In this case the relevant class-closing rule is known as the rule in *Andrews v. Partington*.[59]

(1) *IMMEDIATE GIFT.* In the case of an immediate gift where a contingency is imposed on each member, the class closes at the testator's death if any member of the class who has satisfied the contingency is then in existence;[60] if not, the class closes as soon as one member satisfies the contingency.[61] Thus, taking this last example, the class closes at T's death if any child of C who has attained the age of 21 years is then in existence; if not, the class closes as soon as a child of C attains the age of 21 years. Once the class closes, any child already in existence may take under the gift if the child subsequently satisfies the contingency, but any child not already in existence is excluded from taking.

(2) *POSTPONED GIFT.* Again the class gift may be postponed by a preceding life or other interest,[62] *e.g.* a gift by T's will of £10,000 upon trust for Y for life and after Y's death for the children of C who attain the age of 21 years in equal shares absolutely. In this case the class closes at the time when the postponement ends if any member of the class who was in existence after T's death has satisfied the contingency[63]; if not, the class closes as soon as one member satisfies the contingency.[64] Applying this rule to this example, the class closes at Y's death if any child of C, who was in existence after T's death, has attained the age of 21 years; if not, the class closes as soon as a child of C attains the age of 21 years.

In short, the same class-closing rule applies to any class gift where a contingency is imposed on each member, whether the gift is immediate or postponed, except that the crucial class-closing time is the testator's death in the case of an immediate gift, and the end of the period of postponement in the case of a postponed gift. The rule differs in one vital respect from both the rules so far considered—under this rule, if at the class-closing time there is as yet no member who has satisfied the contingency, the class does remain open but only until one member satisfies the contingency.

This rule, like the other rules, is a rule of construction[65] and is based

---

[59] (1791) 3 Bro. C.C. 401.

[60] *Picken v. Matthews* (1878) 10 Ch.D. 264; *Balm v. Balm* (1830) 3 Sim. 492.

[61] *Andrews v. Partington, supra*; *Re Mervin* [1891] 3 Ch. 197. It is immaterial that no member of the class is in existence at the testator's death, *Re Bleckly* [1951] Ch. 740, 749–750.

[62] *e.g.* a life interest which is determinable or subject to a condition subsequent, *Re Smith* (1862) 2 J. & H. 594 (life interest determinable on bankruptcy or insolvency); *Re Bleckly* [1951] Ch. 740 (whilst wife or widow of X): or an absolute interest subject to a gift over, *Gilman v. Daunt* (1856) 3 K. & J. 48. As to postponement by a direction to accumulate see *Watson v. Young* (1885) 28 Ch.D. 436; *Re Stephens* [1904] 1 Ch. 322; *Re Watt's W.T.* [1936] 2 All E.R. 1555.

[63] *Re Smith, supra*; *Re Canney's Trusts* (1910) 101 L.T. 905; *Gillman v. Daunt, supra*. See also *Re Faux* (1915) 113 L.T. 81 (one-half of income to A for life and other half to B for life: held postponement did not end at A's death, B still being alive); *Re Paul's S.T.* [1920] 1 Ch. 99.

[64] *Clarke v. Clarke* (1836) 8 Sim. 59; *Re Smith, supra*; *Locke v. Lamb* (1867) L.R. 4 Eq. 372; *Re Emmet's Estate* (1879) 13 Ch.D. 484. It is immaterial that no member of the class comes into existence until after the time when the postponement ends, *Re Bleckly, supra*.

[65] *Re Bleckly, supra*, at pp. 747 and 750.

upon the supposition that T would not wish a child of C who has satisfied the contingency to have to wait for distribution of the capital until it is no longer possible for further children of C to be born.[66]

4. Gift of income to a class

The rules so far considered do not apply to a gift of income to members of a class, *e.g.* a gift by T's will of property upon trust to pay the income thereof to the children of D in equal shares during some defined period. In this case the class does not close and each instalment of income is payable to the children of D for the time being living.[67] For example, if D has three children at T's death, the first instalment of income is payable in third shares to D's three children; if another child of D is then born, the next instalment is payable in quarter shares to D's four children. This rule that the class does not close applies whether the members of the class take a share of income at birth[68] (as in the last example), or on satisfying a contingency[69] (*e.g.* a gift of income to the children of D who attain the age of 21 years in equal shares).

The class-closing rules which apply to gifts of capital are based on suppositions which are not applicable to gifts of income.[70]

5. Class gifts to which class-closing rules apply

The class-closing rules do not, of course, apply to a gift to particular persons individually; for instance, a gift of property by T's will "to be divided equally between the children of A, namely B, C and D" is not a class gift.[71] Again, the class-closing rules do not apply in the case of a gift on trust for X for life and after X's death for X's children, because it is impossible for further children of X to come into existence after X's death: accordingly T cannot be taken to have intended a distribution before all X's children come into existence.[72]

The class-closing rules have been applied to a class gift made by T's will to a *limited* class of relatives, *i.e.* to a class which is not capable of infinite expansion, being limited to one or more particular generations. Instances include class gifts made by T's will to the children of X,[73] T's grandchildren,[74] T's brothers and sisters,[75] the nephews and nieces of X,[76]

---

[66] *Re Ward* [1965] Ch. 856, 865.
[67] *Re Ward* [1965] Ch. 856 (not following *Re Powell* [1898] 1 Ch. 227).
[68] *Re Ward, supra.*
[69] *Re Wenmoth's Estate* (1887) 37 Ch.D. 266.
[70] *Re Ward, supra,* at p. 865.
[71] *Bain v. Lescher* (1840) 11 Sim. 397 (B predeceased T and his share lapsed): see also *Havergal v. Harrison* (1843) 7 Beav. 49 ("my brothers and sisters"): *post* p. 236.
[72] *Re Harker's* W.T. [1969] 1 W.L.R. 1124, 1128; *Re Kebty-Fletcher's* W.T. [1969] 1 Ch. 339.
[73] *Viner v. Francis* (1789) 2 Cox 190 (the children of my late sister X); *Re Bleckly* [1951] Ch. 740 (children of my son X who attain 21).
[74] *Oppenheim v. Henry* (1853) 10 Hare 441 (my grandchildren); *Gimblett v. Purton* (1871) L.R. 12 Eq. 427 (such of my grandchildren as attain 21); *Re Manners* [1955] 1 W.L.R. 1096.
[75] *Re Gardiner's Estate* (1875) L.R. 20 Eq. 647.
[76] *Dimond v Bostock* (1875) L.R. 10 Ch.App. 358 (nephews and nieces of my late husband X, who were living at his death, excepting P and Q).

T's great-nephews and nieces,[77] and T's cousins.[78] On the other hand, the class-closing rules have been held not to apply to a gift by T's will to an unlimited class of relatives, such as the issue (or the descendants) of X who attain the age of 21 years. T cannot have intended all X's issue, born in any generation at any time in the future, to take. Therefore, the question of construction inevitably arises—what class of issue did T intend should take? This question is to be answered without regard to the class-closing rules.[79] If the gift is to all of a limited class of relatives, it only raises the question as to when the gift should be closed as a matter of convenience, and the class-closing rules provide the answer.

6. Rules excluded by contrary intention

The class-closing rules, being rules of construction, are not applicable if the testator has clearly shown a contrary intention by his will. A gift by will to "all or any" the children of C who attain the age of 21 years is not sufficient by itself to indicate a contrary intention.[80] Again, a gift to all the children of C "whether now born or hereafter to be born" does not indicate a contrary intention because the words of futurity are capable of referring only to the period before the application of the relevant class-closing rule would close the class.[81] But the emphatic phrase children of C "whenever born" is a particular reference to the future expressly unlimited in time, and therefore excludes the application of the class-closing rules[82]: it is equivalent to the phrase "at whatever time they may be born," which has the same effect.[83]

D. WHETHER GIFT IS ABSOLUTE OR FOR LIFE

1. Presumption that devise passes fee simple

Section 28 of the Wills Act 1837 enacts that a devise of real estate to any person without any words of limitation shall be construed to pass

---

[77] *Balm* v *Balm* (1830) 3 Sim. 492.

[78] *Baldwin* v *Rogers* (1853) 3 De G.M. & G. 649 (my first cousins by my mother's side).

[79] *Re Cockle's* W.T. [1967] Ch. 690 (gift by T's will upon trust for X for life and after X's death for the issue of X who attain 21 years or being female marry in equal shares absolutely; X had no issue at T's death: held only issue in existence at X's death were intended to take); *Re Deeley's Settlement* [1974] Ch. 454 (again a postponed gift); *Re Drummond* [1986] 1 W.L.R. 1096.

[80] *Re Bleckly* [1951] Ch. 740, 751: see also *Prescott* v *Long* (1795) 2 Ves. 690 ("all and every the child and children of his son"); *Re Canney's Trusts* (1910) 101 L.T. 905; *Re Emmet's Estate* (1880) 13 Ch.D. 484 ("all and every the children" of X).

[81] *i.e.* in the case of an immediate gift, the period until T's death, *Sprackling* v. *Ranier* (1761) 1 Dick. 344; *Dias* v. *De Livera* (1879) 5 App.Cas. 123 (children which may hereafter be procreated): in the case of a postponed gift, the period until the end of the period of postponement, *Scott* v. *Earl of Scarborough* (1838) 1 Beav. 154, 168: see also *Re Chapman's S.T.* [1977] 1 W.L.R. 1163.

[82] *Re Edmondson's* W.T. [1972] 1 W.L.R. 183 (an appointment by deed).

[83] *Re Edmondson's* W.T., *supra*, at p. 188. See also *Scott* v. *Earl of Scarborough*, *supra*, (children of A, B and C "now born or who shall hereafter be born, during the lifetime of their respective parents": class-closing rule excluded); *Re Ransome* [1957] Ch. 348 (such of the children of C as shall be living at time youngest child of C attains 21 years: class-closing rule excluded); *Re Tom's Settlement* [1987] 1 W.L.R. 1021 ("closing date" in deed); *cf. Re*

the fee simple, or other the whole interest of which the testator has power to dispose, unless a contrary intention appears by his will.[84] The section applies to any will made or republished after 1837.[85] Thus, T's devise of Blackacre "to X" passes T's fee simple estate in Blackacre to X, unless a contrary intention is shown by T's will. The rule applies to a devise by T of any *existing* interest, *e.g.* a devise by T "to X" of a rentcharge (which is vested in T in fee simple at his death) passes the rentcharge to X in fee simple, unless a contrary intention is shown. However, the rule is not applicable to a devise by T of a *new* interest created by his will, *e.g.* a devise by T "to X" of a new rentcharge, issuing out of T's land Blackacre, passes a rentcharge to X *for life*, unless a contrary intention is shown.[86] Since 1925 a testator who wishes to create an entail in any real or personal property by his will must employ the formal expressions which were effective to create an entail in a deed before 1926, *i.e.* the word "heirs" followed by words of procreation or the words "in tail."[87]

2. Presumption that bequest is absolute

A bequest by T of personal estate "to X" gives X an absolute interest, unless a contrary intention is shown by T's will. But if T's will also contains a direction that on X's death the same property is to go to Y, this shows T's intention to give X only a life interest.[88]

3. Gift over of what remains

Home-made wills sometimes contain a gift of property "to X," followed by a direction that on X's death *what remains* of the property (or words to that effect) is to go to Y. The decided cases indicate that at least three different constructions are possible:

(i) One construction is that X takes absolutely, and the gift over to Y is void, either because it is repugnant to X's absolute interest[89]

Clifford's S.T. [1981] Ch. 63 (compound class). As to the exclusion of the rules by a power of advancement applicable to vested presumptive shares, see *Re Henderson's Trusts* [1969] 1 W.L.R. 651.

[84] *Gravenor v. Watkins* (1871) L.R. 6 C.P. 500.

[85] Wills Act 1837, s. 34.

[86] *Nichols v. Hawkes* (1853) 10 Hare 342.

[87] Law of Property Act 1925, s. 130(1): see also s. 130(3) and *Re Jones* [1934] Ch. 315. For the effect since 1925 of informal expressions, which would have created an entail in a will before 1926 (*e.g.* "to X and his issue," "to X and his descendants," or "to X and his children"), see Law of Property Act 1925, s. 130(2); *Hawkins and Ryder on the Construction of Wills* (1965), pp. 256 *et seq.* For the effect of a gift to X, but if he die without issue, to Y, see Wills Act 1837, s. 29, and Law of Property Act 1925, s. 134, as amended by Family Law Reform Act 1969, s. 1(3) and Sched. 1, Pt. I; *Hawkins and Ryder, op. cit.* pp. 265 *et seq.*

[88] *Re Russell* (1885) 52 L.T. 559; *Re Houghton* (1884) 53 L.J.Ch. 1018; *Sherratt v. Bentley* (1833) 2 My. & K. 149.

[89] *Perry v. Merritt* (1874) L.R. 18 Eq. 152 (gift of residuary personalty to X "for her own absolute use and benefit": gift over to Y after X's death held void for repugnancy); *Henderson v. Cross* (1861) 29 Beav. 216 (gift to X to spend both principal and interest during his lifetime: gift over to Y should X not spend it held void for repugnancy); *Re Jones* [1898] 1 Ch. 438 (gift to X "for her absolute use and benefit so that during her lifetime for the purpose of her maintenance and support she shall have the fullest power to sell and dispose of my said estate absolutely").

or because, construed as a trust, it fails for uncertainty of subject-matter.[90]

(ii) Another construction is that X takes a life interest, coupled with a power to dispose of capital (perhaps only *inter vivos*, or only by will), and subject thereto Y takes absolutely.[91].

(iii) A third construction is that X takes a life interest and subject thereto Y takes absolutely.[92] This construction treats the gift over to Y of *what remains* of the property as if it were a gift over to Y of all the property.

Obviously each of the decided cases turned on the particular wording in a particular will.[93] The same question arises in each case—what intention did the testator express in his will read as a whole with the aid of any admissible extrinsic evidence?

4. Presumption as to effect of gift to spouse

If a testator dies after December 31, 1982,[94] section 22 of the Administration of Justice Act 1982 provides that a gift by the testator's will to his spouse shall be presumed to be absolute if two requirements are satisfied:

(i) The gift is made to the spouse "in terms which in themselves would give an absolute interest to the spouse,"—for instance, T gives "my house Blackacre to my wife Jane" or "all my property to my husband John." On the other hand this requirement is not satisfied if T's gift is "to my wife Jane (*or* husband John) *for life.*"

(ii) The testator purports by the same instrument to give his issue an interest in the same property—for instance, "after her (*or* his) death I give Blackacre (*or* all my property *or* what remains of all my property) to my children equally." On the other hand this requirement is not satisfied if the gift over is to "my nephew George" or "the Oldcastle Dogs' Home."

If these two requirements are satisfied, under section 22 Jane takes Blackacre (*or* John takes all T's property) absolutely and T's children take nothing. However, section 22 is excluded where a contrary intention is shown—for instance, where T adds, "I direct that my wife Jane shall take only a life interest in Blackacre and after her death I give Blackacre to my children equally."

The purpose of section 22 is to prevent the creation of an "unintended"

---

[90] *Pushman v. Filliter* (1795) 3 Ves. 7; *Bull v. Kingston* (1816) 1 Mer. 314.

[91] *Re Stringer's Estate* (1877) 6 Ch.D. 1; *Re Pounder* (1886) 56 L.J.Ch. 113 (X took for life with power to dispose of capital *inter vivos* but not by will); *Re Sanford* [1901] 1 Ch. 939 (X took for life, with general power of appointment): *cf. Re Jones, supra.*

[92] *Constable v. Bull* (1849) 3 De G. & Sm. 411; *Bibbens v. Potter* (1879) 10 Ch.D. 733 (gift over to Y was by codicil); *Re Sheldon and Kemble* (1885) 53 L.T. 527 (at the decease of X what might remain of my property to go to Y).

[93] *Re Minchell's W.T.* [1964] 2 All E.R. 47, 49 (the will provided "an outstanding example of the toast of the Chancery Bar, 'Here's to the man who makes his own will.'" He plainly did not . . . brood on the rules of construction in his leisure time . . . 'One testator's nonsense is no guide to another testator's nonsense' ").

[94] Administration of Justice Act 1982, ss.73(6) and 76(11).

life interest for the spouse by a home-made will.[95] A testator who makes his own will often assumes (wrongly) that it is possible to give successive absolute interests in property, so that his spouse may first enjoy the full rights of an absolute owner and at her death these rights may pass to another person. Such a testator may well have no conception of the nature of a life interest, but he may nevertheless make his will in language which read as a whole (under the law applicable prior to 1983) expressed an intention to give a life interest, rather than an absolute interest, to his spouse. If the testator dies after December 31, 1982, section 22 applies but (rather oddly) only where the purported gift over is to the testator's issue.

5. The rule in *Lassence v. Tierney*

Under the rule in *Lassence v. Tierney*[96] (more accurately called the rule in *Hancock v. Watson*[97]), "it is settled law that if you find an absolute gift to a legatee in the first instance, and trusts are engrafted or imposed on that absolute interest which fail, either from lapse,[98] or invalidity, or any other reason, then the absolute gift takes effect so far as the trusts have failed to the exclusion of the residuary legatee or next-of-kin as the case may be."[99] The rule applies to an absolute gift of realty as well as of personalty.[1] The rule reconciles two inconsistent provisions in T's will, *e.g.* (i) an initial gift of property to B absolutely, and (ii) a subsequent provision that the property given to B shall be held upon trust for B for life and after his death for B's children absolutely as tenants in common in equal shares. If B dies childless, so that the trust for B's children fails, under the rule the absolute gift to B takes effect; the property therefore passes under B's will or intestacy and does not pass under T's residuary gift or as on T's intestacy. The rule imputes to T an intention to modify the absolute gift to B only so far as is necessary to give effect to the trusts.[2]

(1) INITIAL ABSOLUTE GIFT. The real difficulty usually lies in determining whether there is an initial absolute gift to B; this is a question of construction. If there is, the first requirement of the rule in *Lassence v. Tierney* is satisfied. The rule applies whether the initial gift is made directly to B or to trustees on trust for B.[3] To consider an instance of an initial absolute gift, in *Hancock v. Watson*[4] T by his will gave his residuary personal estate to trustees upon trust for his wife for life and after her death to be divided into five portions, two of which he "gave" to B; his will continued:

---

[95] See Law Reform Committee's, 19th Report, *Interpretation of Wills*, Cmnd. 5301 (1973), paras. 60–62 and 65.
[96] (1849) 1 Mac. & G. 551.
[97] [1902] A.C. 14.
[98] *Post* pp. 234 *et seq.*
[99] *Per* Lord Davey in *Hancock v. Watson, supra*, at p. 22.
[1] *Moryoseph v. Moryoseph* [1920] 2 Ch. 33.
[2] *Fyffe v. Irwin* [1939] 2 All E.R. 271, 282.
[3] *Re Harrison* [1918] 2 Ch. 59 (rule applies to legacy bequeathed to trustees on trust for B).
[4] *Supra.* For the extensive case law see *Theobald on Wills* (15th ed., 1993), pp. 521 *et seq.*

"But it is my will and mind that the two fifth portions allotted to [B] shall remain in trust, and that she be entitled to take only the interest. . .of the shares so bequeathed to her during her natural life"

and after her death be held upon other trusts, which failed. The House of Lords held that there was an initial absolute gift of two-fifth shares to B, because T used the words "I give" and referred to these shares as "allotted" to B. Accordingly, after B's death these two-fifth shares formed part of B's estate.

On the other hand, this first requirement is not satisfied if the words of gift to B run straight on into a whole series of limitations, so as to form one system of trusts under which B takes only a limited interest.[5]

(2) ENGRAFTED TRUSTS FAIL. The other requirement of the rule in *Lassence v. Tierney* is that the trusts engrafted on B's absolute interest in the property do not (in the events which happen) exhaust the whole beneficial interest in the property. These trusts may be declared later in T's will or in a codicil,[6] and the cause of their failure is immaterial.[7] Under the rule the absolute gift to B takes effect so far as the trusts do not exhaust the whole beneficial interest in the property.[8]

III. CONSTRUCTION OF POWERS[1]

1. General powers of appointment to which section 27 applies

Unless a contrary intention appears by T's will, section 27 of the Wills Act 1837 makes a general gift by his will of real or personal estate operate to exercise a power to appoint real or personal property, provided it is a power conferred on T to appoint such property "in any manner he may think proper." If section 27 is applicable, T need not expressly show an intention in his will to exercise the general power. "It has been often said, and is now a platitude, that the object of the section was to abolish the distinction between property and a general power over property, because an ordinary man considers in the latter case that the property is his own."[2]

(1) POWERS WITHIN SECTION 27. Section 27 applies to any power of appointment[3] which satisfies the three following requirements:

[5] *Re Payne* [1927] 2 Ch. 1; *Lassence v. Tierney, supra*: see also *Re Cohen's W.T.* [1936] 1 All E.R. 103 (estate to be equally distributed amongst T's seven named children "subject to the provisions and directions hereinafter contained": held no initial absolute gift to a child).
[6] *Norman v. Kynaston* (1861) 3 De G.F. & J. 29.
[7] *Watkins v. Weston* (1863) 3 De G.J. & S. 434 (B died childless); *Re Coleman* [1936] Ch. 528 (trusts in part void for perpetuity).
[8] *Re Coleman, supra*, (engrafted trusts after B's death were (i) discretionary trusts during life of B's widow and (ii) after her death trust for B's children: discretionary trust void for remoteness, and under rule income during widow's life formed part of B's estate).
[1] For an explanation of powers of appointment, see Hanbury and Martin, *Modern Equity* (14th ed., 1993) p. 171.
[2] *Re Jacob* [1907] 1 Ch. 445, 449.
[3] But not to a power of revocation and new appointment, *Re Brace* [1891] 2 Ch. 671: see also *Re Salvin* [1906] 2 Ch. 459.

(i) At T's death the power must be capable of being exercised by T by his will[4]; section 27 does not apply to a power exercisable by T by deed but not by will.[5] It does not matter whether the power had already been created at the date of the will, because under section 24 of the Wills Act[6] a will speaks from death as to property.[7]

(ii) The terms of the power must not impose any condition incompatible with the operation of section 27.[8]

(iii) T must be entitled to appoint "in any manner he may think proper," i.e. to any objects he may think proper. So section 27 does not apply to a special power of appointment among a limited class of objects, e.g. T's children[9]; and it does not apply to a "hybrid" power to appoint in favour of anyone except one or more excepted persons, e.g. except "her present husband, or any friend or relative of his."[10]

(2)   GENERAL GIFTS WITHIN SECTION 27. Section 27 applies to "a general devise of the real estate of the testator, or of the real estate of the testator in any place or in the occupation of any person mentioned in his will, or otherwise described in a general manner," and to "a bequest of the personal estate of the testator, or any bequest of personal property described in a general manner." The section applies both to residuary gifts of property[11] and to specific gifts of property described in a general manner.[12]

Moreover, section 27 applies to a gift by T of general pecuniary legacies because this constitutes a "bequest of personal property described in a general manner." If and so far as T's own assets are insufficient for their payment,[13] the legacies are payable out of personal property over which T had a general power.[14]

---

[4] *Re Powell's Trusts* (1869) 39 L.J.Ch. 188 (power to appoint to any persons by will only is within s.27); *Hawthorn v. Shedden* (1856) 3 Sm. & G. 293.

[5] *Phillipps v. Cayley* (1890) 43 Ch.D. 222, 232 and 234.

[6] See Chap. 9.

[7] *Boyes v. Cook* (1880) 14 Ch.D. 53; *Airey v. Bower* (1887) 12 App.Cas. 263. But s.27 does not apply to a power created after T's death, *Re Young* [1920] 2 Ch. 427.

[8] *Phillips v. Cayley, supra; Re Tarrant's Trust* (1889) 58 L.J.Ch. 780: see also *Re Davies* [1892] 3 Ch. 63. But a condition imposing special formalities as to execution and attestation need not be observed in a formal will when a power is exercised, Wills Act 1837, s.10: *see ante*, p. 8.

[9] *Cloves v. Awdry* (1850) 12 Beav. 604.

[10] *Re Byron's Settlement* [1891] 3 Ch. 474; but see *Re Harvey* [1950] 1 All. E.R. 491. For an explanation of the difference between general, special and hybrid powers, see Hanbury and Martin, *Modern Equity* (14th ed., 1993) pp. 171–72.

[11] *Re Spooner's Trust* (1851) 2 Sim. (N.S.) 129 ("constituting my son ... my residuary legatee": held s.27 applied).

[12] *Re Jacob* [1907] 1 Ch. 445; *Turner v. Turner* (1852) 21 L.J.Ch. 843: *cf. Re Brown's Trusts* (1855) 1 K. & J. 522. *Re Doherty-Waterhouse* [1918] 2 Ch. 269 ("all my shares in the Halifax Corporation New Market consolidated stock": held s.27 applied.)

[13] For the rules governing the incidence of general legacies see *post*, pp. 446 *et seq.*

[14] *Hawthorn v. Shedden* (1856) 3 Sm. & G. 293; *Re Wilkinson* (1869) L.R. 4 Ch.App. 587; *Re Seabrook* [1911] 1 Ch. 151. An express direction in T's will for the payment of his debts has the same effect, *Laing v. Cowan* (1858) 24 Beav. 112; *Re Davies' Trusts* (1871) L.R. 13 Eq. 163, 166.

(3) CONTRARY INTENTION. The operation of section 27 is excluded if "a contrary intention shall appear by the will," *i.e.* if it appears from the will that T, having the power in mind, did not intend to exercise it.[15] The onus of establishing such a contrary intention from the will lies on those who assert it.[16] In practice such a contrary intention very seldom appears from T's will.[17]

2. Powers of appointment to which section 27 does not apply

Section 27 does not apply to a special power, or to a hybrid power. In order to exercise such a power by will, there must be a sufficient indication in the will of an intention to exercise it.[18] In general, a reference either to the power or to the property subject to it constitutes a sufficient indication for this purpose.[19] The testator's intention is, of course, to be gathered from an examination of the whole of his will, with the aid of any admissible extrinsic evidence.[20]

3. Power to bar entail by will

Under section 176 of the Law of Property Act 1925 a tenant in tail[21] has power to bar his entail in any real or personal property by will, and thus dispose of the fee simple in realty, or absolute interest in personalty, or any lesser interest[22] in such property. A testator may exercise this power to bar his entail if the following requirements are satisfied:

(i) the testator is of full age and holds the entail in possession[23] (not in remainder) at his death;

(ii) his will is executed after 1925 (or republished by a codicil executed after 1925); and

---

[15] *Scriven v. Sandom* (1862) 2 J. & H. 743 (there must be something in T's will inconsistent with the view that the general gift was meant to exercise the power); *Re Thirlwell* [1958] Ch. 146.

[16] *Re Jarrett* [1919] 1 Ch. 366, 370; *Re Thirlwell, supra.*

[17] *Re Jacob* [1907] 1 Ch. 445 ("all stocks, shares and securities which I possess or to which I am entitled": held s.27 applied); *Re Doherty-Waterhouse* [1918] 2 Ch. 269; *Re Spooner's Trust* (1851) 2 Sim. (N.S.) 129.

[18] *Re Ackerley* [1913] 1 Ch. 510 (special power); *Re Lawrence's W.T.* [1972] Ch. 418, esp. pp. 428–432 (hybrid power). If the instrument creating the power lays down any special requirement for its exercise, this must also be complied with, *Re Lawrence's W.T., supra,* at p. 430. But a condition imposing special formalities as to execution and attestation need not be observed in a formal will when a power is exercised, Wills Act 1837, s. 10, and see *ante*, p. 8.

[19] *Re Ackerley, supra,* at pp. 514–515: see also *Re Holford's Settlement* [1945] Ch. 21 (reviewing some of the case law: "the principle . . . is clear. The difficulty lies in the application of it").

[20] *Re Knight* [1957] Ch. 441.

[21] Including an owner of a base fee in possession who has power to enlarge it into a fee simple without the consent of any other person, Law of Property Act 1925, s. 176(3): but not a tenant in tail restrained by statute from barring his entail, or a tenant in tail after possibility of issue extinct, (s. 176(2)).

[22] If he merely disposes of a lesser interest such as a life interest, then, subject to the life interest, the entail devolves in the normal way, *ibid.* ss. 130(4) and 176(1).

[23] See the Law of Property Act 1925, s. 205(1)(xix).

(iii) his will refers specifically *either* to the property (*e.g.* "Blackacre"), or to the instrument under which it was acquired (*e.g.* "the property I acquired under my father's will"), *or* to entailed property generally (*e.g.* "all entailed property").[24]

---

[24] *Acheson v. Russell* [1951] Ch. 67 ("the object of the section . . . must surely be to avoid any risk of a disentail being effected by inadvertence or involuntarily").

CHAPTER 9

THE DATE FROM WHICH A WILL SPEAKS

The question of the date from which a will speaks is a question of construction. It is dealt with here, in a separate chapter, because it is relevant to ademption and so, to some extent, depends on the classification of legacies and devises as specific or general.[1]

A will is normally construed to speak from death when identifying, or describing, property; but from the date when it was made when identifying, or describing, the object of a gift, the legatee or devisee. So, if someone makes a will leaving "my I.C.I. shares to my butler" this will prima facie be construed as a gift of the I.C.I. shares owned by the testator at the time of his death to the person who was his butler at the time the will was made.

A. A WILL SPEAKS FROM DEATH AS TO PROPERTY

Before the Wills Act 1837, it was a rule of law that realty acquired after the date of the will could not be devised. So, until 1837, if an owner of freehold land who had a son and a daughter made a will devising his land to his daughter and then sold the land and bought some more land, the newly acquired land would not pass under his will but would go his heir, in this case his son. If the testator wanted the freehold land he had acquired after he made his will to go to his daughter, he had, until 1837, to make another will. Section 3 of the Wills Act 1837 changed this rule and makes it lawful for a testator to devise his after-acquired realty. Section 24 of the Wills Act 1837 then goes on to provide that:

> "every will shall be construed, with reference to the real estate and personal estate comprised in it,[2] to speak and take effect as if it had been executed immediately before the death of the testator, unless a contrary intention shall appear by the will."

Thus, the description of the subject matter of a gift is prima facie to be construed as comprising all the property which satisfies the terms of the description at the death of the testator, including property acquired by

---

[1] For the classification of legacies as specific or general, see Chap. 7 pp. 170 *et seq.*
[2] *Langdale (Lady) v. Briggs* (1856) L.J. Ch. 27, 49 ("with reference to the real estate and personal estate comprised in it" means "so far as the will comprises dispositions of real and personal estate").

him after he made his will. For example, a devise by a testator of "all my freehold land" prima facie comprises all the freehold land to which the testator is entitled at his death, including any acquired by him between the date when he made his will and his death.[3]

1. General and residuary legacies

If someone leaves a general pecuniary legacy, there is no problem about construing it in terms of time. A legacy of "£10,000" is a legacy of money, which is the same in amount (if not in value) whether calculated at the time of the will or at the time of the death.[4] A gift of residue obviously means residue at the time of death and would have to be so construed even if section 24 had not been enacted. So, it seems at first as though section 24 has no application to general or residuary legacies, apart from stating the obvious. But section 24 does sometimes apply to general legacies. It applies when there is a legacy of, say, "10,000 shares in X.Y.Z. Ltd (a named company)" and the shares in X.Y.Z. Ltd have been reorganised or subdivided. It may be that any shareholder who had one old £1 share will, after a reorganisation or division, have 20 new 5p shares; so a shareholder who had 10,000 old shares will have 200,000 new ones. The effect of section 24 in this case, is, prima facie, to give the legatee 10,000 new shares, not 10,000 old shares.[5] The shares are described as at the date of death.

2. Specific legacies

Section 24 also applies to specific legacies.

Unless a contrary intention appears in his will, a specific legacy by T of "all my shares in Marks & Spencer plc" speaks from T's death and is construed as a gift of all the shares in Marks & Spencer to which T is entitled at his death.[6] Similarly, unless a contrary intention appears in the will, a specific devise by T of "all my lands in the county of Kent" is construed as a gift of all T's lands in the county of Kent at the date of his death.[7] These two examples are, respectively, of a specific generic legacy and a specific generic devise. In each case, the subject matter is described in such a way as to be capable of increase or decrease between

---

[3] *Langdale (Lady) v. Briggs, supra*: and see *Re Kempthorne* [1930] 1 Ch. 268.

[4] This would not be true if the currency were reorganised, so, for example, that ten old pounds became equivalent to one new pound. But this is not a situation which has ever arisen in the United Kingdom (though it has arisen in other countries). If it were to arise, the legislation providing for the reorganisation of the currency would probably make specific provision for pecuniary legacies. If not, the same rule would apply as applies to shares (see *infra*).

[5] *Re Gillins* [1909] 1 Ch. 345.

[6] *Goodlad v. Burnett* (1855) 1 K. & J. 341 (gift of "my New Three-and-a-quarter per Cent. Annuities": held gift passed all Annuities of which T died possessed): see also *Trinder v. Trinder* (1866) L.R. 1 Eq. 695; *Re Bancroft* [1928] Ch. 577.

[7] *Re Evans* [1909] 1 Ch. 784, 786; *Re Davies* [1925] Ch. 642; *Castle v. Fox* (1871) L.R. 11 Eq. 542, *post* p. 220: *cf. Webb v. Byng* (1855) 1 K. & J. 580. Where s.24 applies, a gift only passes after-acquired property which falls within the description of the subject-matter of the gift, *Re Portal and Lamb* (1885) 30 Ch.D. 50 (devise of "my cottage and all my land at S": T later bought large house adjoining his small cottage: held s.24 applied but house did not satisfy description).

the date of the will and the date of T's death. There is no problem about the application of Section 24 to specific generic legacies and devises.

3. Contrary intention

The problem cases in this area are concerned with specific legacies and devises which are not generic and the difficulty is to know when a contrary intention appears from the will. The cases are not easily reconciled.

Some of the cases are concerned with whether or not a specific gift has been adeemed. The doctrine of ademption was explained, in outline, in Chapter 7 and will be discussed in further detail in Chapter 11. Ademption, as has already been explained, occurs when a specific legacy or devise fails because its subject matter is no longer part of the testator's property at the time of his death. Section 24 is concerned with the time at which property is identified and so may be crucial in deciding whether a gift has or has not been adeemed.

Suppose that a testator makes a will leaving "my pocket watch to my nephew X". There can be no problem if the testator owned a pocket watch at the time when he made his will and owns the same pocket watch at the date of his death. The watch will pass. There can also be no problem if the testator owns no pocket watch at the time of his death, for in that case the legacy must be adeemed. But a problem arises if the testator owned a pocket watch at the time he made his will but owns a different pocket watch at the time of his death. Does a "contrary intention" appear by the will in this sort of case?

Section 24 lays down a rule which appears to be generally favourable to a specific legatee. By stating that the description of the subject matter of a gift is to be construed as at the testator's death, it makes it less likely that a legacy will be adeemed. If the testator had two pocket watches, one when he made his will and another when he died, the straightforward application of section 24 will save the gift from ademption, while a finding that there is a contrary intention will cause the gift to be adeemed. It is, therefore, generally, in the legatee's interest to argue that the will shows no contrary intention. So what do the cases decide is a contrary intention?

There are two things in the description of property which appear to indicate a contrary intention under section 24. The first is a reference to the present time, *i.e.* the time when the will was made. The second is a detailed description, indicating a reference to a particular watch, or car, or whatever.

4. Reference in a will to the present time

A devise by a testator of "all my freehold land" prima facie comprises all the freehold land to which he is entitled at his death. But if T by his will devises "all the freehold land of which I am possessed *at the date of this my will*," section 24 is excluded and the devise does not pass any freehold land acquired by T after the date of his will. Some forms of wording are harder to construe. A reference in a will to property *"now"'* or *"at present"'* possessed by the testator may refer to the date of his will, or may refer to the date of his death. Such a reference to the present time makes it necessary to consider the language of T's will, in order to ascertain whether there is a contrary intention.[8] If a reference to the present time is an essential part of the description of the subject matter of a specific gift, a contrary intention appears, section 24 is excluded and the reference is construed as referring to the date of T's will.[9] But if a reference to the present time is not an essential part of the description of the subject matter of the gift; if it is merely intended as an additional form of identification; a contrary intention does not appear, section 24 applies and the reference is construed as referring to the date of death.

The latter construction was adopted in *Re Willis*.[10] In this case, T owned a house and garden and he devised to his wife "all that my freehold house and premises situated at Oakleigh Park, Whetstone . . . and known as 'Ankerwyke,' and in which I now reside." After T had made his will, he bought two further plots of land next to the garden. He treated these two plots as an extension of the garden, so that while he was alive the house, the garden and the plots were all occupied as one unit. The question was whether the devise passed only the house and the original garden or whether it passed the plots as well. The problem lay with the words "and in which I now reside". If they were construed as an essential part of the description of the subject matter of the devise, it would be restricted to the house and the part of the garden owned by the testator at the time he made his will. Eve J. held that the phrase was not an essential part of the description of the subject matter and so the devise passed the house and premises known as "Ankerwyke" at the date of T's death, including the two adjoining plots.

5. Detailed description of property devised or bequeathed

The subject matter of a gift may be described with such particularity as to show that the testator intended to designate an object in existence at the date when he made his will. If this is so, a contrary intention appears in the will and section 24 does not apply. For example, the testator may bequeath "my gold watch, which I bought in Bond Street". If he were to lose that watch before his death and to buy another gold watch, but were not to buy it in Bond Street, the replacement watch would not pass. This is clear because the replacement article does not satisfy the terms of the description of the original article and, the more detailed the description, the more likely it is not to satisfy the description. But, even if the replacement article does satisfy the terms of the description, the fact that the description is especially detailed may indicate a reference to a particular article and so indicate a contrary intention in the context of section 24. In the case of a bequest of "my gold watch, which I bought in Bond Street" if the testator were to lose his original gold watch and replace it with another gold watch, bought in Bond Street (so satisfying the terms of the description of the original article) it may well be that a contrary intention would be found, on the basis that the

[8] *Re Whitby* [1944] Ch. 210; *Cole v. Scott* (1849) 1 Mac. & G. 518; *Hutchinson v. Barrow* (1861) 6 H. & N. 583.
[9] *Re Whitby, supra* (construction of exclusion clause).
[10] [1911] 2 Ch. 563: see also *Re Champion* [1893] 1 Ch. 101 (where North J. adopted this construction and the C.A. relied on republication by codicil); *Re Horton* [1920] 2 Ch. 1.

description is of one particular gold watch. So what if the bequest were simply of "my gold watch"? Would there be a contrary intention in this case too? Or, to put the question another way, can section 24 ever save any specific gift from ademption other than a specific generic gift?

In *Re Gibson*[11] T bequeathed to his son Joseph "my one thousand North British Railway preference shares". He had, at the time he made his will, one thousand shares which fitted the description, but he sold these shares and later acquired some more shares, more than a thousand, which also fitted the description. Page Wood V-C. held that the gift had been adeemed. This was clearly a specific legacy and he held that the gift showed a contrary intention. He seemed to suggest, *obiter*, that section 24 would never apply to save from ademption any specific legacy other than a specific generic legacy.[12] He suggested a hypothetical example:

"Suppose a man to have, at the date of his will, a picture of the Holy Family by some inferior artist, and to give by his will 'my Holy Family.' He afterwards disposes of this picture, and subsequently acquires, by purchase or gift, a very much better one on the same subject, painted by an eminent artist. Would it not be a monstrous construction to hold that the picture . . . in [his] possession at the time of his death would pass."

Page Wood V-C.'s *obiter* view in *Re Gibson* is consistent with the decision of Clauson J. in *Re Sikes*.[13] In this case, a testatrix bequeathed "my piano" to a friend. By the time of her death, the testatrix had sold her original piano and had acquired another piano. Clauson J., in a very brief judgment, held that the bequest did not cover the replacement piano because there was a contrary intention within the terms of section 24. Yet the only indication of a contrary intention appears to be the use of the word "my". So, *Re Gibson* and *Re Sikes* appear to say that no specific legacy, other than a specific generic legacy, will, by virtue of section 24, survive ademption. On their authority, a gift of "my watch" or "my car" will be adeemed whenever the testator has replaced his original watch or car.

Having said this, it is easy to understand why there would be reluctance to apply section 24 in a case where a specific article belonging to the testator had been replaced by another article of similar description but very different value; but it it seems much less probable that there would be reluctance to apply the section if the two articles were of approximately the same value. Page Wood V.-C.'s hypothetical example in *Re Gibson*[14] supposed a replacement picture worth much more than the one it replaced. The facts in *Re Sikes*[15] are also unusual. The testatrix sold her original piano for £5 to the husband of the friend to whom she had bequeathed it in her will. She then bought a replacement piano for £228. Either the original piano was worth much less than the new one, or the friend's husband had a bargain. Either way, it is not hard to see why Clauson J. felt it inappropriate to apply section 24; had he applied

[11] (1866) L.R. 2 Eq 669.
[12] At p. 672.
[13] [1927] 1 Ch 364.
[14] *Supra.*
[15] *Supra.*

it, the friend and her husband would have had two pianos. These cases do not really answer the question as to what would happen if there were a gift of "my watch" or "my car" and the watch or car were to be replaced with something of much the same type and value. Section 24 says nothing about the value, but it is not unreasonable to suggest that the value will be thought significant, certainly in a case which would otherwise be regarded as borderline. And the more commonplace an article, the more general the description of it, the more likely it is that section 24 will be held to apply. There seems to be no case which clearly establishes that a gift of "my watch" or "my car" or "my horse" can survive a change of watch or car or horse, under the terms of section 24; but there is no clear authority that it cannot, and a straightforward reading of section 24 would appear to favour the application of the section in this sort of case. The absence of cases on the point is probably due to a sensible avoidance, by testators, of specific legacies of this kind.

There are two further cases on section 24 which deserve nothing. They are not cases on ademption but they both contain *obiter dicta* relating to ademption and they are not agreed as to what the correct rule should be. In *Castle v. Fox*[16] the testator devised "my mansion and estate called Cleeve Court" and there was a dispute as to whether the devise covered land which was acquired, and added to the estate, after the will was made. A straighforward application of section 24 would say that it did, and Malins V.-C. applied the section straighforwardly. He found no contrary intention. There seems little doubt that the decision is correct. But Malins V.-C. went on to suggest, *obiter*, that a devise of "my house in Grosvenor Square" would not be adeemed if the testator disposed of his house in Grosvenor Square after he had made his will and then acquired another house in the same square.[17] This is not so clear. *Castle v. Fox* may be contrasted with *Re Evans*[18] in which T's will read as follows: "To my wife Agnes Evans I give and bequeath house and effects known as "Cross Villa" situated at Templeton in the County of Pembroke." At the time when the testator made his will, "Cross Villa" consisted of a house with a large garden. T later divided part of the garden from the rest with a hedge and built two more houses in the part of the garden he had divided off. These newly built houses were known as "Ashgrove Villas." T continued to own all three houses. The question in the case was whether the devise passed only the one house known as "Cross Villa" at the time of the testator's death; or whether the devise passed all the land which would have been included within the description "Cross Villa" at the time the testator made his will. On the former construction, the widow would be entitled to one house, on the latter, she would be entitled to three houses. A straightforward reading of section 24 would construe the gift at the time of death and give her one house. Joyce J. held that there was a contrary intention because the description was "so particular and precise." He suggested that the description was just the same as if the testator had used the expression "now known as 'Cross Villa'." This reasoning is not altogether easy to follow. The test-

---

[16] (1871) L.R. 11 Eq. 542.
[17] At p. 551.
[18] [1909] 1 Ch. 784.

ator did not use the expression "now known as Cross Villa"; and even if it is correct that it would have made no difference if he had used it, that does not prove that the addition of the word "now" would show a contrary intention. In *Re Willis*[19] the expression "and in which I now reside" was not taken to indicate a contrary intention within the terms of section 24. In fact, *Re Evans* and *Re Willis* contrast oddly. In the former, the gift was construed as excluding section 24, in spite of the fact that there was no obvious reference to the date of the will; in the latter, section 24 was not excluded, even though there was a reference to the present time. The one thing the two cases have in common—and they share this with *Castle v. Fox*—is that each of them adopts the construction most favourable to the specific devisee.

Castle v. Fox, *Re Evans* and *Re Willis* are all cases where the issue was not ademption, but the extent of the devise. But there are *dicta* in *Castle v. Fox* and in *Re Evans* as to what would happen in cases of possible ademption. It has already been noted that in *Castle v. Fox* Malins V.-C. suggested that a gift of "my house in Grosvenor Square" would carry a house which fitted the description if the testator had sold one house in the Square and had bought another one. In *Re Evans* Joyce J. suggested exactly the same example[20] but thought that the new house would not be covered by the gift. As in the case of a gift of "my gold watch", there appears to be no authoritative ruling.

6. Testator's later acquisition of a different interest

If T by his will makes a gift of "my leasehold house, 54 Narcissus Road," of which T is the lessee at the date of his will, and T later acquires the freehold reversion, it was held in *Re Fleming's Will Trusts*[21] that the gift passes T's entire interest in the property at his death. To quote from Templeman J.'s judgment in this case[22]:

"a gift of property discloses an intention to give the estate and interest of the testator in that property at his death; a mere reference in the will to the estate and interest held by the testator at the date of his will is not sufficient to disclose a contrary intention."

On occasion the same result has been reached in reliance (at least in part) on section 24,[23] but the result is probably best explained as based on the

---

[19] [1911] 2 Ch. 563, see *ante*, p. 218.

[20] [1909] 1 Ch 784 at 786 (except that he changed "Grosvenor Square" to Cavendish Square").

[21] [1974] 1 W.L.R. 1552 (no merger occurred, but T's freehold estate and leasehold interest both passed under the gift): see also *Struthers v. Struthers* (1857) 5 W.R. 809; *Miles v. Miles* (1866) L.R. 1 Eq. 462; *Cox v. Bennett* (1868) L.R. 6 Eq. 422; *Saxton v. Saxton* (1879) 13 Ch.D. 359 (gift of "all my term and interest in the leasehold. . .premises. . .No. 1, Berkeley Gardens. . .subject to the payment of the ground rent and performance of the covenants affecting the same": held subsequently acquired freehold passed). As to renewal of a lease, see *Wedgwood v. Denton* (1871) L.R. 12 Eq. 290.

[22] At p. 1555.

[23] *Miles v. Miles, supra; Saxton v. Saxton, supra*: s.23 of the Wills Act 1837 was relied on (at least in part) in *Struthers v. Struthers, supra, Cox v. Bennett, supra*, and *Saxton v. Saxton, supra*: *sed quaere* whether s.23 is relevant.

testator's intention to pass whatever interest in the property he has at his death.

Similarly, if T by his will makes a gift of his share in a partnership business, in which he has a third share at the date of his will, and T later acquires his two partners' shares and carries on the business as sole owner until his death, the gift passes T's entire interest in the business at his death.[24]

If, however, T by his will shows an intention to give the leasehold interest in Blackacre which he holds at the date of his will, *and nothing else*, his intention must prevail. If at his death T no longer holds this leasehold interest, the gift fails by ademption; such a gift does not pass any other leasehold interest in Blackacre granted to T after the date of his will.[25]

B.   A WILL SPEAKS FROM ITS DATE AS TO THE OBJECT OF A GIFT

Section 24 applies with regard to the subject matter of a gift but it does not in any way affect the construction of a will with regard to the object of a gift.[26] In general, a will speaks from its date as to the object of a gift, unless a contrary intention appears in the will. Accordingly, words in a will indicating an existing person prima facie refer to a person in existence at the date of the will. Thus, where T by his will gave to "Lord Sherborne and his heirs my Oliver Cromwell cup ... for an heir-loom," and the person who was Lord Sherborne at the date of the will died before T, the Court of Appeal held that the gift lapsed[27] and did not take effect in favour of the person who was Lord Sherborne at T's death.[28] Similarly, a gift by T to the "eldest son of my sister Frances" is a gift in favour of the person who answers the description at the date of the will, and the gift lapses if that person dies before T.[29]

The general rule that a will speaks from its date as to the object of a gift is, of course, excluded if a contrary intention appears in the will. For instance, a gift by T of a legacy to "the Lord Mayor of London for the time being" takes effect in favour of the person who holds this office at T's death.[30] And, as was explained earlier, the general rule that a will speaks from its date as to the object of a gift, does not apply to a class gift or to an individual gift to each member of a class.[31]

---

[24] *Re Russell* (1882) 19 Ch.D. 432 (s.23 relied on).
[25] *Cox v. Bennett, supra,* at p. 426; *Re Reeves* [1928] Ch. 351.
[26] *Bullock v. Bennett* (1855) 7 De G.M. & G. 283.
[27] For the doctrine of lapse, see Chap. 11 pp. 234–243.
[28] *Re Whorwood* (1887) 34 Ch.D. 446.
[29] *Amyot v. Dwarris* [1904] A.C. 268: see also *Foster v. Cook* (1791) 3 Bro. C.C. 347 (gift by T's will to the child, wherewith his wife was pregnant; this child was stillborn: held gift did not take effect in favour of another child of which wife was pregnant at T's death); *Re Coley* [1903] 2 Ch. 102 (the wife of my son).
[30] *Re Daniels* (1918) 118 L.T. 435: the general rule may not apply to a gift to the holder of an office, *In the Estate of Jones* (1927) 43 T.L.R. 324.
[31] *Ante,* pp. 200 *et seq.*

C. Effect of republication[32]

1. Subject of a gift

If a will speaks from its date as to the subject matter of a gift (section 24 not being applicable because a contrary intention appears by the will), and later the will is republished by a codicil, the effect is to make the will speak *from the date of the codicil* as to the subject matter of the gift, unless a contrary intention appears. In *Re Reeves*[33] a testator by his will made in 1921 gave to his daughter "all my interest in my present lease" of Blackacre. At the date of his will the testator held a lease granted in 1917 and due to expire in 1924. Later the testator took a new lease for a term of 12 years and by a codicil made in 1926 confirmed his will. The court held that the daughter was entitled to the new lease. The testator had republished his will by confirming it, and the will, speaking as if it had been executed at the date of the codicil, referred to the new, and not to the expired, old, lease. But republication does not make a gift pass property which does not answer the description in the will: if by his will the testator had given "my lease of Blackacre dated September 25, 1917," republication would not have made the will refer to the new lease.[34] Again, republication does not make the will speak from the date of the codicil if a contrary intention appears.[35]

2. Object of a gift

Similarly, if a will speaks from its date as to the object of a gift, and later the will is republished by a codicil, the effect is to make the will speak *from the date of the codicil* as to the object of the gift, unless a contrary intention appears. The decision in *Re Hardyman*,[36] which will be considered in Chapter 11[37] is an example of this.

[32] For the requirements of republication see *ante*, p. 118.
[33] [1928] Ch. 351: see also *Re Champion* [1893] 1 Ch. 101 (land "now in my occupation" included land acquired by T between making and republishing his will); *Re Fraser* [1904] 1 Ch. 726; *Grealey v. Sampson* [1917] 1 Ir. R. 286; *Goonewardene v. Goonewardene* [1931] A.C. 647.
[34] *Re Reeves, supra*, at pp. 357–358.
[35] *Grealey v. Sampson, supra*, at p. 305.
[36] [1925] Ch. 287.
[37] *post*, pp. 236–237.

CHAPTER 10

SATISFACTION

A. SATISFACTION OF A DEBT BY A LEGACY

1. The equitable presumption

If T owes C a debt, and T later makes a will or codicil giving C a pecuniary legacy of an amount equal to, or greater than, the debt, equity presumes that the legacy is intended to satisfy the debt. If at T's death C accepts the legacy, he cannot also claim payment of the debt.[1] And if after he has made his will T pays off the debt, the legacy is adeemed.[2]

(1) *REQUIREMENTS*. This equitable presumption arises only if three requirements are fulfilled:

    (i) T must already owe the debt to C before T makes the will or codicil giving C the pecuniary legacy. No presumption of satisfaction arises if T incurs the debt to C afterwards, because when he made the will or codicil T could not have intended the legacy to satisfy a non-existent debt.[3]

    (ii) T must give C a pecuniary legacy of an amount equal to, or greater than, the debt.[4] A devise of land,[5] or a gift of residue or a share of residue,[6] raises no presumption of satisfaction.

    (iii) The pecuniary legacy must be as beneficial to C as the debt. The presumption is not applicable if the debt is secured but the legacy is not,[7] or if the debt is immediately due at T's death but the legacy is payable at a future time under an express term to this effect in the will.[8]

---

[1] *Talbot v. Duke of Shrewsbury* (1722) Prec. Ch. 394.

[2] *Re Fletcher* (1888) 38 Ch.D. 373 (legacy of same amount as debt).

[3] *Cranmer's Case* (1702) 2 Salk. 508: see also *Horlock v. Wiggins* (1889) 39 Ch.D. 142 (separation deed, containing covenant to pay £100, and will, giving £100 legacy, were contemporaneous: held no presumption of satisfaction).

[4] *Re Manners* [1949] Ch. 613.

[5] *Eastwood v. Vinke* (1731) 2 P.Wms. 613: *Richardson v. Elphinstone* (1794) 2 Ves. 463.

[6] *Barret v. Beckford* (1750) 1 Ves.Sen. 519; *Devese v. Pontet* (1785) 1 Cox C.C. 188.

[7] *Re Stibbe* (1946) 175 L.T. 198: *cf. Re Haves* [1951] 2 All E.R. 928.

[8] *Clark v. Sewell* (1744) 3 Atk. 96 (legacy payable one month after T's death); *Adams v. Lavender* (1824) M'Cle. & Yo. 41 (legacy payable within six months after T's death): see also *Re Van Den Bergh's W.T.* [1948] 1 All E.R. 935 (annuity given by will determinable on attempted alienation).

2. Rebutting the presumption

This "artificial"[9] presumption is not a rule of construction and so has
never been subject to the restrictions on the admissibility of extrinsic
evidence which apply in relation to construction.[10] The presumption may
be rebutted by extrinsic evidence that T did not intend the legacy to
satisfy the debt, but intended to give the legacy regardless of his liability
to pay the debt; direct extrinsic evidence of T's declarations of intention
is admissible for this purpose.[11] The presumption may also be excluded
by T's expression of a contrary intention in a will or codicil made by T
after he incurred the debt to C.[12] In *Chancey's Case*[13] it was held that a
direction in T's will that his debts and legacies should be paid expressed
a contrary intention and so C was entitled to the payment of both the
debt and the legacy. It is now settled that a direction in T's will that his
debts should be paid expresses a contrary intention.[14] As most wills contain such a direction, the presumption is usually excluded.

B. SATISFACTION OF A LEGACY BY ANOTHER LEGACY

Intention of the testator

If a testator gives two general legacies of the same amount to the same
legatee, the question arises whether the legacies are cumulative (so that
the legatee takes both of them) or substitutional (so that he takes only
one of them). T may have expressed his intention to make the legacies
cumulative or (alternatively) substitutional in his will read as a whole.
If not, the following rules apply.

(1) *LEGACIES IN THE SAME INSTRUMENT.* If by the same will (or
the same codicil) T gives two general legacies of the same amount[15] to
the legatee, an equitable presumption arises that the legacies are *substitutional* and that the legatee is intended to take only one of them.[16] Minor
differences in the way in which the two legacies are given do not rebut
this presumption.[17]

(2) *LEGACIES IN DIFFERENT INSTRUMENTS.* If T gives two legacies

---

[9] *Horlock v. Wiggins* (1888) 39 Ch.D. 142, 147: *Re Horlock* [1895] 1 Ch. 516, 518 ("no sooner
was [the rule] established than learned Judges of great eminence expressed their disap-
proval of it, and invented ways to get out of it").
[10] For construction, see Chap. 8; and for admissibility of extrinsic evidence in relation to
construction, see pp. 187 *et seq.*
[11] *Wallace v. Pomfret* (1805) 11 Ves. 542.
[12] *Gaynon v. Wood* (1717) 1 P.Wms. 409n.
[13] (1725) 1 P.Wms. 408.
[14] *Re Manners* [1949] Ch. 613; *Re Huish* (1890) 43 Ch.D. 260: *cf. Re Hall* [1918] 1 Ch. 562.
[15] If the two legacies are of different amounts, they are prima facie cumulative, *Curry Pile*
(1787) 2 Bro.C.C. 225.
[16] *Garth Meyrick* (1779) 1 Bro.C.C. 30 (two legacies of £1,000 old South Sea annuities); *Holford
Wood* (1798) 4 Ves. 76 (two annuities of £30 for life"; *Manning Thesiger* (1835) 3 My. &
K. 29.
[17] *Holford Wood, supra,* ("to B I give an annuity of £30 for his life payable quarterly....I
give to B the butler £30 a year for his life": held B took only one annuity).

of the same amount to B by different instruments (*e.g.* one legacy by a will and the other by a codicil), prima facie the legacies are *cumulative* and the legatee takes both of them.[18] This is a rule of construction and not an equitable presumption. It "rests upon the perfectly sound basis, which is not to be weakened, that a testator intends each and every disposition which he makes to take effect where these are not mutually inconsistent."[19]

(3) *LEGACIES IN DIFFERENT INSTRUMENTS GIVEN FROM THE SAME MOTIVE.* If T gives two legacies of the same amount to one legatee but by different instruments, and T expresses the same motive in each instrument for giving each legacy, an equitable presumption arises that the legacies are *substitutional* and that the legatee is intended to take only one of them.[20] The court raises this presumption only where there is the double coincidence of the same amount and the same motive in each instrument, *e.g.* each instrument contains a legacy of £100 to the legatee "for his trouble as executor."[21]

The equitable presumptions in (1) and (3) above (that the legacies are substitutional) are not rules of construction and so may be rebutted by extrinsic evidence that T intended the legacies to be cumulative; direct extrinsic evidence of T's declarations of intention is admissible for this purpose.[22] But the rule in (2) above (that the legacies are cumulative) is a rule of construction and so direct extrinsic evidence is not admissible on T's death before 1983 to rebut it[23]: on T's death after 1982, section 21 of the Administration of Justice Act 1982 is applicable.[24]

C.   EQUITY LEANS AGAINST DOUBLE PORTIONS

1.   Nature of a portion[25]

Not every gift made by a father or person *in loco parentis* to a child is treated as a portion. A gift constitutes a portion if it is made for the purpose of establishing a child in life or of making a permanent provi-

---

[18] *Hooley Hatton* (1773) 1 Bro.C.C. 390; *Hurst Beach* (1821) 5 Madd. 351, 358; *Roch Callen* (1848) 6 Hare 531; *Re Davies* [1957] 1 W.L.R. 922.

[19] *Re Resch's W.T.* [1969] 1 A.C. 514, 548: see also *Wilson O'Leary* (1872) L.R. 7 Ch. App. 448, 454 (this rule "is not to be frittered away by a mere balance of probabilities"). For a summary of the case law as to what constitutes a clear indication of an intention to make the legacies substitutional see *Theobald on Wills* (15th ed., 1993), pp. 254 *et seq.*

[20] *Benyon Benyon* (1810) 17 Ves. 34 (£100 by will, and £100 by codicil, to B, in each case for his trouble as exector: held substitutional); *Hurst Beach, supra,* at pp. 358–359; *Re Royce's W.T.* [1959] Ch. 626. Cf. *Wilson O'Leary, supra,* at pp. 454–455.

[21] If the instruments merely describe him as "my servant," this is not construed as an expression of T's motive for giving each legacy and the legacies are prima facie cumulative, *Roch Callen* (1848) 6 Hare 531.

[22] *Hurst Beach, supra,* at pp. 360–361; *Hall Hill* (1841) 1 Dr. & War. 94, 124–128.

[23] *Hurst Beach, supra; Hall Hill, supra.*

[24] *Ante,* pp. 194–196.

[25] See Chap. 2. pp. 41–42.

sion for him.[26] Most gifts by will are treated as portions,[27] although a legacy to a daughter of a diamond necklace is not a portion.[28] Similarly, a provision for a child made by a marriage settlement constitutes a portion.[29] Again, payments of money or transfers of property made for establishing a child in a profession or in business constitute portions,[30] but not payments of money made for the child's education or maintenance, or by way of temporary assistance.[31] If there is no evidence as to the purpose for which a payment was made, a gift to a child of a sum sufficiently substantial in itself to be in the nature of a permanent provision is prima facie a portion.[32] But the court does not add up a series of small gifts (such as birthday and Christmas presents) to make a portion.[33]

2. Testator must be father or *in loco parentis*

The equitable presumptions which follow from the principle that equity leans against double portions apply only to portions provided for a child by his father or by some other person who stands *in loco parentis* to the child.[34] The presumptions have been held not to apply to a provision made by the child's mother unless she stood *in loco parentis* to the child.[35] A person stands *in loco parentis* to a child if that person intends to undertake the parental duty of making financial provision for the child.[36] Whether a person intends to undertake this duty is decided from evidence of his general conduct towards the child and particularly from evidence of any financial provision made by him for the child. For instance, an uncle who intends to undertake this duty may put himself *in loco parentis* to his nieces, even though they continue to live with their father,[37] and so may a grandfather to his grandchildren.[38]

---

[26] *Taylor Taylor* (1875) L.R. 20 Eq. 155, 157. This was a decision on the Statute of Distribution 1670 which required an advancement "by portion" to be brought into account by a child on a distribution on intestacy; see also the hotchpot rule in Administration of Estates Act 1925, s.47(1)(iii), for which see *ante*, pp. 41–43.

[27] e.g. *Re Furness* [1901] 2 Ch. 346, 348 (£20,000 legacy to daughter a portion); *Thynne v. Earl of Glengall* (1848) 2 H.L.Cas. 131 (gift of half his residuary personal estate a portion).

[28] *Re Tussaud's Estate* (1878) 9 Ch.D. 363, 367.

[29] *Taylor Taylor* (1875) L.R. 20 Eq. 155, 157.

[30] *Taylor v. Taylor, supra,* (payment of admission fee to Inn of Court for intending barrister and for purchase of mining plant for son's business); *Re George's W. T.* [1949] Ch. 154 (gift *inter vivos* of live and dead farming stock to son to set him up in farming business held a portion); *Hardy v. Shaw* [1976] Ch. 82.

[31] *Taylor v. Taylor, supra,* (payment of fee to special pleader for intending barrister to read in chambers, payments made to curate to assist him in his living expenses, and payment of army officer's debts); *Re Scott* [1903] 1 Ch. 1 (paying off part of son's mortgage debt was by way of temporary assistance and not a portion).

[32] *Re Hayward* [1957] Ch. 528 (nominations amounting to £507 in favour of a son aged 43: held not prima facie an advancement for purposes of hotchpot on intestacy – if son had been 20 years younger the result might have been different); *Hardy, v. Shaw, supra,* at p. 88.

[33] *Schofield v. Heap* (1858) 27 Beav. 93; *Watson v. Watson* (1864) 33 Beav. 574.

[34] *Fowkes v. Pascoe* (1875) 10 Ch.App. 343, 350.

[35] *Re Ashton* [1897] 2 Ch. 574 (reversed on other grounds [1898] 1 Ch. 142). But *quaere* whether the position would be the same today.

[36] *Powys v. Mansfield* (1837) 3 My. & Cr. 359, 367.

[37] *ibid.*

[38] *Pym v. Lockyer* (1841) 5 My. & Cr. 29; *Rogers v. Soutten* (1839) 2 Keen 598 (grandfather to illegitimate grandchild): see also *Booker v. Allen* (1831) 2 Russ. & My. 270 (near relation to child whose father had died).

3. Two applications of the principle that equity leans against double portions

Two applications of the principle that equity leans against double portions need consideration i.e.:

(i) the presumption of the satisfaction of a portion-debt by a legacy; and
(ii) the presumption of the ademption of a legacy by a portion.[39]

The principle that equity leans against double portions imputes to a father an intention to achieve equality amongst his children. In *Re Vaux*[40] Lord Greene M.R. explained the presumption of the ademption of a legacy by a portion as follows:

"The rule against double portions rests upon two hypotheses: first of all, that under the will the testator has provided a portion and, secondly, that by the gift *inter vivos* which is said to operate in ademption of that portion either wholly or *pro tanto*, he has again conferred a portion. The conception is that the testator having in his will given to his children that portion of the estate which he decides to give to them, when after making his will he confers upon a child a gift of such a nature as to amount to a portion, then he is not to be presumed to have intended that that child should have both, the gift *inter vivos* being taken as being on account of the portion given by the will."

(1) *SATISFACTION OF A PORTION-DEBT BY A LEGACY.* If T (a father or person standing *in loco parentis*) incurs a legal obligation to provide a portion for a child C, and later T makes a will or codicil giving a legacy or share of residue (constituting a portion) to C, an equitable presumption arises that the legacy or share of residue is intended to be a complete or partial satisfaction of the portion-debt.[41] Unless this presumption is rebutted, C cannot take both, but he is entitled to elect whether to take the portion-debt or (alternatively) the legacy or share of residue.[42] For instance, if on C's marriage T covenants to pay £10,000 to the trustees of C's marriage settlement, and later T makes a will giving a legacy of £10,000 (or more) to these trustees, an equitable presumption arises that the legacy is intended to be a complete satisfaction of T's obligation under his covenant[43]: if T gives a legacy of £6,000, the presumption is that the legacy is intended to be a partial satisfaction. The

---

[39] The third application of the principle is the satisfaction of a portion-debt by a portion: see generally *Snell's Equity* (29th ed., 1990), pp. 521 *et seq.*

[40] [1939] Ch. 465, 481.

[41] *Weall v. Rice* (1831) 2 Russ. & M. 251; *Warren v. Warren* (1783) 1 Bro.C.C. 305 (partial satisfaction).

[42] *Thynne v. Earl of Glengall* (1848) 2 H.L.C. 131; *Lord Chichester v. Coventry* (1867) L.R. 2 H.L. 71, 87 and 90–94. But if T *provides* the portion for C before making his will, no presumption of satisfaction arises and C takes both provisions, *Taylor v. Cartwright* (1872) L.R. 14 Eq. 167, 176.

[43] If T by his will had given the legacy to C, this would have satisfied C's beneficial life interest in the £10,000 under the settlement, but not the beneficial interests of C's spouse and issue, *Re Blundell* [1906] 2 Ch. 222.

beneficiaries under the settlement are entitled to elect whether to take under the covenant or under the will.

Of course, if T is not the father of (or a person standing *in loco parentis* to) the creditor, or if the debt is an ordinary debt and not a portion-debt, the position is governed by the ordinary rules relating to the satisfaction of a debt by a legacy.[44]

(2) ADEMPTION OF A LEGACY BY A PORTION. If T (a father or person standing *in loco parentis*) makes a will or codicil giving a legacy or share of residue[45] (constituting a portion) to a child C, and later T provides (or incurs a legal obligation to provide) a portion for C, an equitable presumption arises that the later portion adeems the legacy or share of residue, either wholly[46] or partially.[47]

If T is not the father of (or a person standing *in loco parentis* to) the legatee under his will there is generally no presumption that a later *inter vivos* gift by T to that legatee adeems the legacy.[48] The legatee remains entitled to the legacy, despite the later gift, unless (exceptionally) a presumption of ademption arises because both the legacy and the later gift were expressly given for a particular purpose,[49] or pursuant to a specific moral obligation.[50]

4. A stranger cannot benefit

Equity leans against double portions so as to achieve equality amongst children, not to benefit a stranger, *i.e.* a person who is neither a child of T nor a person to whom T stood *in loco parentis*. The presumptions of satisfaction and ademption which arise under this principle must not be applied to benefit a stranger.[51]

5. Rebutting the presumptions

The equitable presumptions of satisfaction and ademption (which follow from the application of the principle that equity leans agains double portions and so which relate to legacies and portions) may be rebutted:

---

[44] See *ante*, pp. 224–225.

[45] *Montefiore v. Guedalla* (1859) 1 De G.F. & J. 93 (share of residue). As to a devise of realty see *Davys v. Boucher* (1839) 3 Y. & C. 397, 411 (of doubtful authority, as revocation of all wills is now governed by Wills Act 1837, s.20).

[46] *Re Pollock* (1885) 28 Ch.D. 552, 555–556; *Re Vaux* [1939] Ch. 465, 481–482. For the effect of inheritance tax see *Re Turner's W.T.* [1968] 1 W.L.R. 227.

[47] *Pym v. Lockyer* (1841) 5 My. & Cr. 29 (ademption may be *pro tanto*).

[48] *Ex p. Pye* (1811) 18 Ves. 140 (the father was not, in 1811, *in loco parentis* to his illegitimate child).

[49] *Re Corbett* [1903] 2 Ch. 326 (legacy to hospital's endowment fund adeemed by later *inter vivos* gift for same purpose); *Re Jupp* [1922] 2 Ch. 359: *cf. Pankhurst v. Howell* (1870) 6 Ch.App. 136.

[50] *Re Pollock* (1885) 28 Ch.D. 552 (legacy by T's will of £500 to X "according to the wish of my late beloved husband": T later gave £300 to X as "legacy" from T's husband: held legacy adeemed to extent of £300): *cf. Re Aynsley* [1915] 1 Ch. 172.

[51] *Meinertzagen v. Walters* (1872) L.R. 7 Ch.App. 670; *Re Heather* [1906] 2 Ch. 230; *Re Vaux* [1938] Ch. 581 (not considered on appeal [1939] Ch. 465).

    (i) by intrinsic evidence from the different nature of the two provisions; or[53]

    (ii) by extrinsic evidence of T's actual intention.[52]

Evidence of T's declarations of intention is admissible as direct extrinsic evidence.[53]

It is easier to rebut the presumption of the satisfaction of a portion-debt by a legacy than the presumption of the ademption of a legacy by a portion.

> "When the will precedes the settlement [which provides the portion] it is only necessary to read the settlement as if the person making the provision had said, 'I mean this to be in lieu of what I have given by my will.' But if the settlement [which creates the portion-debt] precedes the will, the testator must be understood as saying, 'I give this in lieu of what I am already bound to give, if those to whom I am so bound will accept it.' It requires much less to rebut the latter than the former presumption."[54]

It follows that factors which rebut the presumption of satisfaction will not necessarily rebut the presumption of ademption.

The presumption of satisfaction, at any rate, is rebutted by intrinsic evidence if there are substantial differences between the limitations contained in the two provisions; this indicates T's intention to provide a double portion.[55] Moreover each of the presumptions is rebutted if the provisions are not *ejusdem generis*.[56] Thus, a legacy of a sum of money is not adeemed by a later gift *inter vivos* of stock-in-trade,[57] unless T puts a money value on the stock-in-trade at the time when he gives it so that it can be regarded as a gift of money.[58]

---

[52] *Weall v. Rice* (1831) 2 Russ. & My. 251, 267–268.

[53] *Re Tussaud's Estate* (1878) 9 Ch.D. 363 (satisfaction); *Kirk v. Eddowes* (1844) 3 Hare 509 (ademption): see *ante*, p. 225.

[54] Per Lord Cranworth in *Lord Chichester v. Coventry* (1867) L.R. 2 H.L. 71, 87.

[55] *Weall v. Rice, supra*, ("it is not possible to define what are to be considered as slight differences between two provisions"): cf. *Thynne v. Earl of Glengall* (1848) 2 H.L.Cas. 131 (slight differences: presumption of satisfaction applied) and *Lord Chichester v. Coventry, supra*, (substantial differences: presumption of satisfaction rebutted).

[56] *Re Jacques* [1903] 1 Ch. 267.

[57] *Holmes v. Holmes* (1783) 1 Bro.C.C. 555.

[58] *Re George's W.T.* [1949] Ch. 154; *Bengough v. Walker* (1808) 15 Ves. 507.

Chapter 11

FAILURE OF GIFT BY WILL OR OF INTEREST ON INTESTACY

A gift by will may fail for any one or more of the following reasons, which are considered in turn in this Chapter:

(1) The beneficiary or his spouse is an attesting witness.
(2) The beneficiary predeceases the testator, causing the gift to lapse.
(3) The dissolution or annulment of the deceased's marriage to the beneficiary causes the gift to fail.
(4) The gift fails by ademption.
(5) The gift abates.
(6) The gift fails for uncertainty.
(7) The beneficiary is guilty of the murder or manslaughter of the deceased.
(8) The beneficiary disclaims.

This list is not exhaustive. A gift by will may also fail because it infringes some rule of law, such as the rule against inalienability,[1] or is made for a purpose contrary to public policy.[2] Again, a contingent gift by will may fail because the contingency is not satisfied.[3]

Heads 7 and 8 are also applicable to a beneficiary on an intestacy. Head 2 is not applicable on an intestacy but, of course, a person who predeceases an intestate cannot take on intestacy because the intestacy rules require the intestate's spouse or next-of-kin to survive the intestate in order to be eligible to take.[4] Similarly, head 3 is not applicable on an intestacy, but a former spouse, whose marriage to the intestate has been dissolved or annulled, cannot take on intestacy. Again, a contingent interest under the statutory trusts applicable on intestacy may fail

---

[1] Sometimes called the rule against perpetual trusts: for this rule, see Megarry and Wade, *The Law of Real Property* (5th ed., 1984), pp. 296 *et seq.*
[2] See, *e.g. Re Caborne* [1943] Ch. 224 (provision void as tending to encourage break-up of existing marriage); *Re Johnson's W.T.* [1967] Ch. 387.
[3] Sometimes this is referred to as failure by lapse; see, *e.g. Re Parker* [1913] 1 Ch. 162 and *Re Fox's Estate* [1937] 4 All E.R. 664.
[4] See Chap. 2, the intestacy rules include, of course, the rules relating to the statutory trusts, so, *e.g.* if a child of the intstate predeceases the intestate, the child's issue may take in his place: and a child *en ventre sa mere* at the intestate's death is treated as then living, *ante*, p. 40, n. 2.

because the contingency of attaining the age of 18 years or marrying is not satisfied.

The fact that a particular gift in a will fails, does not mean that the will as a whole is no longer valid. The failure of one gift, or of more than one gift, has no necessary effect on other dispositions contained in the will. The effect of the failure of a particular gift is considered at the end of this chapter. So, too, is the effect on an intestacy of failure under heads 7 and 8.

I. BENEFICIARY OR SPOUSE IS AN ATTESTING WITNESS

1. General rule

Section 15 of the Wills Act 1837 deprives an attesting witness[5] and his or her spouse of any benefit under the will which the witness attests: the attestation is valid but any beneficial gift in the will to the witness or his or her spouse is "utterly null and void."[6]

"Every time. . .that a beneficiary [or the spouse of a beneficiary] is an attesting witness, section 15 of the Wills Act 1837, deprives him of his benefit and defeats the testator's intention. This is considered necessary to ensure reliable, unbiased, witness of due execution."[7]

Not surprisingly, critics have questioned whether this drastic rule is really justified.[8]

There are, in any case, several limits to the operation of the rule.

2. Privileged will

The rule does not apply to a will intended to be an informal will and made by a privileged testator, because such a will does not require any attesting witnesses. Thus if a soldier, whilst in actual military service, makes a will intended by him to be an informal will, a gift in it to someone who happens to witness the will is valid.[9]

3. Superfluous attesting witness to a formal will

If the testator dies after May 29, 1968, the Wills Act 1968 provides that the attestation of his will by a beneficiary (or his spouse) is to be disre-

---

[5] Presumably s.15 applies to a witness who acknowledges his signature under the amended s.9 of the Wills Act 1837, though such a witness is not required to attest: see *ante*, p. 84.
[6] The words of s.15.
[7] *Per* Russell L.J. in *In the Estate of Bravda* [1968] 1 W.L.R. 479, 492.
[8] See Law Reform Committee's 22nd Report, *The making and revocation of wills*, Cmnd. 7902 (1980), pp. 6–7 (recommending no change); (1981) 125 S.J. 283; M. Davey [1980] Conv. 64. 75. For an account of the origins of the rule, a discussion of the policy behind it and of its present day utility, see D.E.C. Yale (1984) 100 L.Q.R. 453.
[9] *Re Limond* [1915] 2 Ch. 240.

garded if without him the will is duly executed.[10] It follows that if a will is attested by three witnesses, only one of whom is a beneficiary (or the spouse of a beneficiary), the general rule is excluded and the beneficiary may take his benefit under the will. If, on the other hand, more than one of the three witnesses is a beneficiary (or the spouse of a beneficiary), the general rule is applicable and none of the witnesses (or their spouses) may take any benefit under the will.

4. Beneficiary signed but not as a witness

The general rule does not apply if (which would be very unusual) the beneficiary (or his spouse) signed the will otherwise than as an attesting witness—for example, with the intention of recording his agreement with the gifts made by the testator in the will.[11] There is, however, a rebuttable presumption that any person (except the testator) whose signature appears at the end of a will signed as an attesting witness: so the general rule applies unless this presumption is rebutted.[12]

5. Beneficiary not spouse of witness when will executed

A beneficiary who marries an attesting witness after the execution of the will may take a benefit under it: section 15 only disqualifies a beneficiary who is the spouse of an attesting witness when the will is executed.[13]

6. Gifts on trust

The general rule only applies to beneficial gifts and not to gifts to an attesting witness (or his spouse) as trustee. If T by her will gives £200 to X and "£200 to Brompton Church, to be disposed of as X wishes," and X's wife is one of the two attesting witnesses, the first gift is void but the second gift is valid because X is a trustee for the purpose of directing the disposition of the legacy.[14]

7. Gift made or confirmed by another will or codicil

The general rule does not apply:

(i) if the gift to the beneficiary B is contained in a will or a codicil

---

[10] s. 1. For the formalities required for due execution, see Chap. 4. If the testator died before May 30, 1968, the general rule applies even though there were two other attesting witnesses, *In the Estate of Bravda, supra.*

[11] *In the Goods of Sharman* (1869) L.R. 1 P. & D. 661 (beneficiary's signature omitted from grant as she did not intend to attest testator's signature); *In the Goods of Smith* (1889) 15 P.D. 2 (wife, a beneficiary, signed will to verify its contents: her signature omitted from probate); *Kitcat v. King* [1930] P. 266: but see *In the Estate of Bravda, supra,* at pp. 488, 491 and 493.

[12] *In the Estate of Bravda, supra.*

[13] *Thorpe v. Bestwick* (1881) 6 Q.B.D. 311: see *Re Royce's W.T.* [1959] Ch. 626.

[14] *Cresswell v. Cresswell* (1868) L.R. 6 Eq. 69: see also *Re Ray's W.T.* [1936] Ch. 520 (gift by T's will to the person who should be Abbess at T's death: an attesting witness later became Abbess: held gift was valid as she took in trust for the purposes of the convent— it was immaterial that she might, as a member of the convent, get some benefit in some shape or form out of the administration of the fund).

which was not attested by B or B's spouse, even though some
other document was so attested[15]; or

(ii) if the gift to B is contained in a document which was attested by
B or B's spouse, but this document was confirmed by a will or
codicil not so attested.[16]

Consider situation (i). B is the residuary beneficiary under T's will,
which was not attested by B or B's spouse. By a codicil, T revokes certain
legacies given by his will, thereby swelling his residuary estate. It is
immaterial that B or B's spouse attested this codicil—the general rule is
not applicable because B takes the swollen residuary estate under T's
will and not under the codicil.[17]

But the general rule is applicable if the will or codicil which contains
the gift to B, and each document which confirmed this will or codicil,
was attested by B or B's spouse. In this case B cannot take, because he
cannot point to a document under which he claims which neither he not
his spouse attested.[18]

The application of the doctrine of conditional revocation in *Re Finnemore*,[19] to save a gift in an earlier will from revocation by a later will
(which itself contained a gift which was void because the later will was
witnessed by the beneficiary's husband) was discussed in Chapter 5.[20]

8.   Witness or spouse takes under secret trust

If T by his will gives property to X, and X takes this property on a
secret trust for Y, the general rule does not apply if Y or Y's spouse
attested T's will.[21] This is because Y does not take his beneficial interest
under T's will. He takes it by virtue of the secret trust imposed upon X
who takes under the will.[22]

II. LAPSE

1. Doctrine of lapse[1]

Under this doctrine a gift by will lapses and fails if the beneficiary
dies before the testator.[2] Similarly, a gift by will to a corporate body

---

[15] *Re Marcus* (1887) 57 L.T. 399 (gifts to B and C by T's will; B attested codicils but not the
will and C attested both the will and the codicils: held B could take but C could not);
Gurney v. Gurney (1855) 3 Drew. 208.

[16] *Anderson v. Anderson* (1872) L.R. 13 Eq. 381; *Re Trotter* [1899] 1 Ch. 764 (B, a solicitor,
attested will and second codicil: held B could take benefit of a charging clause in will
under first codicil which confirmed will): *cf. Burton v. Newbery* (1875) 1 Ch.D. 234
(republication of will by second codicil does not validate gift to attesting witness in first
codicil not republished). For confirmation (or republication), see ante, pp. 118 *et seq.*

[17] *Gurney v. Gurney, supra.*

[18] *Re Marcus, supra,* at p. 400.

[19] [1991] 1 W.L.R. 793.

[20] See *ante* p. 109.

[21] *Re Young* [1951] Ch. 344; *O'Brien v. Condon* [1905] 1 I.R. 51. For secret trusts, see *Snell's
Equity* (29th ed., 1990), pp. 108 *et seq.*

[22] *Re Young* [1951] Ch. 344 at p. 350.

[1] See generally H. A. J. Ford (1962) 78 L.Q.R. 88.

[2] *Elliott v. Davenport* (1705) 1 P.Wms. 83; *Maybank v. Brooks* (1780) 1 Bro.C.C. 84 (legacy
given to M, his executors, administrators, or assigns; M predeceased testator: held legacy
lapsed).

lapses if the corporate body is dissolved before the testator's death.[3] The doctrine of lapse is a consequence of the ambulatory character of a will, which has no effect until the testator's death and so confers no benefit on persons who die before him.[4]

(1) *DECLARATION AGAINST LAPSE INEFFECTIVE, BUT SUBSTITU-TIONAL GIFT EFFECTIVE.* A testator cannot exclude the doctrine of lapse by declaring in his will that it is not to apply.[5] But he may provide that, if the original beneficiary predeceases him, the subject matter of a gift shall be given to another beneficiary.[6] So, the testator may provide that if the original beneficiary predeceases him, the subject matter of the gift shall be given to the original beneficiary's personal representatives, to be held as part of the original beneficiary's estate.[7] Or he may direct that if A dies in his lifetime, a gift to A shall operate as if A had survived him and had taken the gift but had died immediately afterwards (which achieves the same result).[8] Again (and this is much more common), the testator may make a gift to A, but if A shall die in his lifetime, he makes a substitutional gift to such of A's children living at his death, as attain the age of (say) 21 years (or marry) in equal shares.[9]

(2) *GIFT TO JOINT TENANTS.* The nature of the gift made by the testator may exclude the doctrine of lapse. Thus if T by his will makes a gift to two or more persons as *joint tenants* (*e.g.* to A, B and C jointly), no lapse can occur unless all the beneficiaries die before the testator. If A and B both die before T, C takes the whole gift if he survives T[10]; but if C also dies before T, the gift lapses. The doctrine of lapse is, however, fully applicable if there are words of severance in T's will, so that the beneficiaries take as *tenants in common* (*e.g.* to X, Y and Z *equally*): in that case, if X dies before T, the gift of a third share to X lapses.[11]

(3) *CLASS GIFT.* The doctrine of lapse does not apply to a class gift

---

[3] *Re Servers of the Blind League* [1960] 1 W.L.R. 564; *Re Stemson's W.T.* [1970] Ch. 16; *Re Finger's W.T.* [1972] 1 Ch. 286. A gift by T's will to a corporation with charitable objects does not fail by lapse owing to its dissolution in T's lifetime if (i) it is really a gift for charitable purposes (unless the gift shows the corporation's continued existence is essential), or (ii) T shows a general charitable intention; see generally *Snell's Equity* (29th ed., 1990), pp. 164 *et seq.*

[4] *Jarman on Wills* (8th ed., 1951), p. 438.

[5] *Re Ladd* [1932] 2 Ch. 219 (T had a general testamentary power of appointment and by her will appointed to her husband "to the intent that this my will shall take effect whether I survive or predecease my husband"; the husband predeceased T: held the appointment to him failed by lapse and his executors did not take); *Browne v. Hope* (1872) L.R. 14 Eq. 343 (declaration that gift to vest on execution of will does not prevent lapse).

[6] *Sibley v. Cook* (1747) 3 Atk. 572; *Re Greenwood* [1912] 1 Ch. 393, 396.

[7] For the consequences see *Re Cousen's W.T.* [1937] Ch. 381: see also (1962) 78 L.Q.R. 88, 90 *et seq.*

[8] *Re Greenwood, supra.*

[9] Alternatively the substitutional gift may be in favour of A's children and remoter issue *per stirpes* in equal shares, so as to include descendants of a deceased child of A.

[10] *Morley v. Bird* (1798) 3 Ves. 629.

[11] *Page v. Page* (1728) 2 P. Wms. 489; *Peat v. Chapman* (1750) 1 Ves. Sen. 542; *Re Wood's Will* (1861) 29 Beav. 236. Of course, T may by his will provide that the gift is to such of X, Y and Z as shall survive him, and if more than one in equal shares, this prevents a lapse.

made to persons who are to be ascertained at the testator's death.[12] It does not matter whether they take as joint tenants or as tenants in common. An instance is a gift by T's will "to all my children as tenants in common in equal shares." This is construed as a gift to all the persons coming within the description at the testator's death; they will take the subject matter of the gift equally. If one of T's children predeceases him, there is no lapse because such child was never a member of the class.[13] A gift may be to a class, even though some individual members of the class are named: thus a gift "to my children including [or excluding] X" is a class gift.[14] But a gift "to Y and the children of Z" is prima facie not a class gift because Y falls outside the general description[15]: however, T's will may, on its proper construction, show that T intended this gift to take effect as a class gift, so that if Y predeceases T there is no lapse.[16]

On the other hand, if T by his will makes a gift "to my three brothers as tenants in common in equal shares," this is a gift to individuals and not a class gift: each brother takes a distinct third share which is quantified from the beginning and which does not vary in size according to the number of the recipients. If one or more of the three brothers predeceases T, the gift to him of a third share lapses.[17] But if the gift is "to such of my three brothers as shall be living at my death as tenants in common in equal shares," there is no lapse if one of them predeceases T, because T has made provision for this event: the other two brothers living at T's death take the subject matter of the gift equally.[18]

(4) *EFFECT OF REPUBLICATION OF WILL.* If T makes his will containing a gift to X, and after X's death T makes a codicil which republishes his will, this does not prevent the gift to X from lapsing or make it take effect as a gift to X's personal representatives.[19] The will is read as if it had been executed at the time of its republication[20] but this makes no difference: there is still a gift to X which fails by lapse.

Occasionally, republication may alter the construction of a will as to the identity of the beneficiary and so save a gift which would otherwise have lapsed. In *Re Hardyman*[21] the testatrix by her will gave a legacy of £5,000 on trust for her cousin for life and then for "his wife" for life with remainders over. The will referred to the cousin's wife living at the date of the will. But this wife died and the testatrix, knowing of her death, made a codicil which republished her will. After the testatrix's death, the cousin married again. Romer J. held that, as a result of its republica-

---

[12] Or *after* the testator's death.
[13] *Doe d. Stewart v. Sheffield* (1811) 13 East. 526; *Shuttleworth v. Greaves* (1838) 4 M. & Cr. 35. For the effect of the original, and the amended, s.33 of the Wills Act 1837 see *post*, p. 242.
[14] *Shaw v. M'Mahon* (1843) 4 D. & War. 431: see *Re Jackson* (1883) 25 Ch.D. 162. There may be a composite class gift—"to the children of A and the children of B."
[15] *Re Chaplin's Trusts* (1863) 33 L.J. Ch. 183; *Re Allen* (1881) 44 L.T. 240.
[16] *Kingsbury v. Walter* [1901] A.C. 187 (a "special" class gift).
[17] *Re Smith's Trusts* (1878) 9 Ch.D. 117.
[18] See *Re Woods* [1931] 2 Ch. 138; *Re Peacock* [1957] Ch. 310 (a gift to a group, having for purposes of lapse the characteristics of a class gift).
[19] *Hutcheson v. Hammond* (1790) 3 Bro.C.C. 127; *Re Wood's Will* (1861) 29 Beav. 236.
[20] See *ante*, p. 118.
[21] [1925] Ch. 287.

tion, the will referred to any lady whom the cousin might marry and not to the dead first wife. As a result of its republication the will, said Romer J., "is a will which the testatrix tells me expressed her wishes as they were at the date of the codicil."[22] The cousin's second wife was therefore entitled to an interest in the legacy. If the will had not been republished, it would have been construed as referring to the first wife and any gift to her would have failed by lapse. Of course, if the will had referred to the first wife by name, any gift to her would have failed by lapse.

2. Presumption where there is uncertainty as to who survived whom

Owing to the doctrine of lapse, the order of deaths of T, a testator, and B, a beneficiary under T's will, is crucial. If B survived T for however short a time, B may take under T's will.[23] But if B predeceased T, the doctrine of lapse applies and B cannot take under T's will unless one of the exceptions to the doctrine of lapse (which have still to be considered) is applicable. The order of deaths may also be crucial (i) on an intestacy, (ii) on the death of joint tenants, in order to ascertain which of them benefits by the right of survivorship, and (iii) under the terms of a gift in a will—for instance, a gift by T "to X if my wife shall die in my lifetime," and T and his wife are both swept off a ship by the same wave and never seen again.[24]

Before 1926, if the evidence left the order in which people had died uncertain, there was no legal presumption that one person had survived another. If any person sought to establish a claim which depended upon B's having survived T, the onus of proof lay on the claimant to establish that fact by affirmative evidence: if he did not do so, his claim failed.[25] Thus if two people died in a shipwreck and the evidence left it uncertain which of them survived the other, a claim by the personal representatives of either of them to benefit under the other's will or intestacy necessarily failed.[26]

(1) *DEATH PRESUMED IN ORDER OF SENIORITY.* Section 184 of the Law of Property Act 1925 now raises a presumption as to the order of deaths by providing as follows:

"In all cases where, after the commencement of this Act, two or more persons have died in circumstances rendering it uncertain which of them survived the other or others, such deaths shall (subject to any order of the court), for all purposes affecting the title to property, be

---

[22] *ibid.* at p. 293.
[23] Provided that the gift is absolute and not contingent, a gift may be made contingent on the beneficiary's surviving the testator by (say) 28 days.
[24] *Underwood v. Wing* (1855) 4 De G.M. & G. 633; *Wing v. Angrave* (1860) 8 H.L.C. 183: see also *Re Rowland* [1963] Ch. 1.
[25] *Underwood v. Wing, supra; Wing v. Angrave, supra; Re Phene's Trusts* (1870) 5 Ch. App. 139 ("the true proposition is, that those who found a right upon a person having survived a particular period must establish that fact affirmatively by evidence").
[26] *Underwood v. Wing, supra; Wing v. Angrave, supra.*

presumed to have occurred in order of seniority, and accordingly the younger shall be deemed to have survived the elder."

Accordingly, where section 184 applies, there is a statutory presumption that the deaths occurred in order of seniority, *i.e.* the eldest died first and the youngest died last. The words in brackets, "subject to any order of the court," appear to be meaningless in this context.[27] They certainly give the court no discretion to disregard the statutory presumption on the ground that it would be unfair or unjust to act upon it.[28]

(2) *UNCERTAINTY AS TO WHO SURVIVED WHOM.* Section 184 applies where it is uncertain which of two or more persons survived the other. It applies when the deaths occurred in a common disaster (the case of *commorientes*, such as a bomb explosion[29] or the sinking of a ship[30]), and it applies when the deaths occurred separately (the husband's ship may disappear at sea on an unknown date and the wife may die at home after the ship has sailed[31]). In *Hickman v. Peacey*[32] five people were killed in the same house by a bomb dropped during a wartime air raid; two of them had made wills in favour of some of the others. The House of Lords held (by a majority) that section 184 was applicable in all cases where it could not be proved that one person had in fact survived the other, and it was immaterial whether the deaths appeared to be simultaneous or consecutive. As Lord Macmillan (speaking for the majority) put it,[33]

"Can you say for certain which of these two dead persons died first? If you cannot say for certain, then you must presume the older to have died first. It is immaterial that the reason for your inability to say for certain which died first is either because you think they both died simultaneously or because you think they died consecutively but you do not know in what sequence."

(3) *EXCLUSION OF THE STATUTORY PRESUMPTION.* By way of exception, the statutory presumption does not apply as between spouses if the older spouse dies *intestate*. Section 46(3) of the Administration of Estates Act 1925, as amended by section 1(4) of the Intestates' Estates Act 1952, states that if an intestate and his younger spouse die in circumstances rendering it uncertain which of them survived the other, the statutory presumption that the younger survived the older does not apply

---

[27] *Per* Lord Simonds in *Hickman v. Peacey* [1945] A.C. 304, 346–347, "I have tried in vain to give any reasonable meaning and effect" to the words. For other explanations see *Re Lindop* [1942] Ch. 377, 382 (words make it clear presumption is rebuttable by evidence); *Re Grosvenor* [1944] Ch. 138, 143 and see 148–149 (words may refer to subsequent orders of the court in the event of fresh evidence becoming available); *Hickman v. Peacey, supra* at p. 316 (words provide for case where insufficient evidence as to respective ages of deceased persons).

[28] *Re Lindop, supra.*

[29] *Hickman v. Peacey* [1945] A.C. 304 (bomb in German air raid). See also *Re Bate* (1947) 116 L.J.R. 1409 (gas poisoning from gas oven in kitchen).

[30] *Re Rowland* [1963] Ch. 1.

[31] *Hickman v. Peacey, supra*, at pp. 314–315.

[32] *Supra.*

[33] *ibid.* at pp. 323–324.

and the younger spouse is presumed not to have survived the older. Section 46(3) applies if the spouses die on or after January 1, 1953 and on or before December 31, 1995. If they die on or after January 1, 1996, a newly inserted Section 46(2A) of the Administration of Estates Act 1925 will provide that an intestate's spouse, in order to benefit on his intestacy, must survive him by 28 days.[34]

Also, the Section 184 presumption, that deaths occurred in the order of seniority, is not applicable for inheritance tax purposes; for inheritance tax, each of the deceased persons is assumed to have died at the same instant.[35] Take the case of T and his child B (aged 20) who are both killed in a road accident, in circumstances rendering it uncertain which of them survived the other: under the statutory presumption, B (the younger) is presumed to have survived T and may therefore take T's estate under T's will or on T's intestacy; but inheritance tax on T's estate is only payable (if at all) in respect of T's death and not, a second time, in respect of B's death.[36] On B's death, inheritance tax would be payable (if at all) in respect of B's property only, ignoring the property inherited from T.

Where it is applicable, the statutory presumption has the merit of providing a definite (though arbitrary) solution, if the order of deaths is uncertain but there is sufficient evidence as to the respective ages of the deceased persons. This solution may, however, sometimes defeat the wishes which a testator would have expressed if he had thought about the problem. For instance, if T by his will gives his entire estate to his daughter D, and T and D die in circumstances rendering in uncertain which of them survived the other, under the statutory presumption D is presumed to have survived T and therefore takes T's estate, which then passes to the beneficiaries entitled under D's will[37] or to D's next-of-kin entitled on her intestacy, possibly her widower. It may well be a better solution for T to provide by his will that D shall take only if she survives T for (say) a period of one month: such a *commorientes* clause prevents D from taking under the statutory presumption and also guards against the possibility that D may only survive T for a very short time.[38]

3. Exceptions to the doctrine of lapse

There are three exceptions to the doctrine of lapse, the first two of which are statutory exceptions under the Wills Act 1837 and the third is based on case law.

(1) *ENTAIL*. By section 32 of the Wills Act 1837[39] there is no lapse if T

---

[34] Law Reform (Succession) Act 1995, s. 1. See Chap. 2.

[35] Inheritance Tax Act 1984, s. 4(2). For a further discussion of the tax position, see Chap. 12.

[36] Under Inheritance Tax Act 1984, s. 4(1) inheritance tax is charged in respect of B's death on the value of B's estate *immediately before B's death*: at that moment T would still be alive and would not have inherited T's estate, s. 4(2).

[37] See *Re Rowland* [1963] 1 Ch. 1.

[38] There can be tax advantages, or disadvantages, depending on the circumstances, in passing property from T to W (who dies shortly after T) and then on to X, rather than directly from T to X. See Chap. 12.

[39] s. 32 is applicable to entails of personalty, Law of Property Act 1925, s. 130(1).

by his will gives property to A in tail,[40] and A predeceases T, but A leaves issue living at T's death capable of inheriting under the entail. The exception applies subject to any contrary intention appearing in T's will.

(2) *GIFT TO THE TESTATOR'S CHILD OR REMOTER DESCENDANT.* Section 33(1) of the Wills Act 1837 provides that:

> "where—
> (a) a will contains a devise or bequest to a child or remoter descendant of the testator; and
> (b) the intended beneficiary dies before the testator, leaving issue; and
> (c) issue of the intended beneficiary are living at the testator's death,
> then, unless a contrary intention appears by the will, the devise or bequest shall take effect as a devise or bequest to the issue living at the testator's death."

This section is quoted as substituted by section 19 of the Administration of Justice Act 1982, and it applies in its substituted form if the testator dies after December 31, 1982.[41] Section 33 in its original form applied if the testator died before January 1, 1983.[42] There are significant differences between the substituted section and the original section.

(a) *The requirements of section 33(1).* For the substituted section 33(1) to apply, T's will must contain a devise or bequest to B, who is T's child or remoter descendant. The original section 33 also required the devise or bequest to be for an interest not determinable at or before B's death, and therefore did not apply to a gift to B of a life interest, or an interest in joint tenancy,[43] or an interest contingent on B's attaining 25 years of age if B died under that age.[44] The substituted section 33(1) does not impose this additional requirement. Neither the substituted nor the original section applies to an appointment by will under a special power,[45] but each of them applies to an appointment by will under a general power.[46]

Both the substituted and the original section require issue of B to be "living" at T's death. For the purposes of the substituted section, any issue of B who is conceived before T's death and is born alive after T's

---

[40] For an explanation of the nature of an entail (or fee tail) see *Megarry's Manual of the Law of Real Property* (7th ed., 1993) pp. 39–46.

[41] Administration of Justice Act 1982, ss. 73(6) and 76(11).

[42] s. 33 in its original form reads, "where any person being a child or other issue of the testator to whom any real or personal estate shall be devised or bequeathed for any estate or interest not determinable at or before the death of such person shall die in the lifetime of the testator leaving issue, and any such issue of such person shall be living at the time of the death of the testator, such devise or bequest shall not lapse, but shall take effect as if the death of such person had happened immediately after the death of the testator, unless a contrary intention shall appear by the will."

[43] *Re Butler* [1918] 1 I.R. 394.

[44] *Re Wolson* [1939] Ch. 780: *cf. Re Wilson* (1920) 89 L.J. Ch. 216.

[45] *Holyland v. Lewin* (1883) 26 Ch.D. 266.

[46] *Eccles v. Cheyne* (1856) 2 K. & J. 676: see Wills Act 1837, s. 27 and *ante*, pp. 211 *et seq.* For an explanation of the difference between special powers and general powers, see Hanbury and Martin, *Modern Equity* (14th ed., 1993) pp. 171–172.

death is treated as living at T's death.[47] This was probably not so under the original section.[48]

For the section to apply, B must leave issue living at B's own death and issue living at T's (later) death. But under neither the original section nor the substituted section do the issue need to be the same people. So, the section applies where T by her will gives all her property to her daughter B, who predeceases T leaving an only child C, who also predeceases T after bearing a child D who survives T.[49] Again, the section applies though B is already dead at the date of T's will.[50]

For the purposes of the substituted section, the illegitimacy of any person is to be disregarded.[51] This was so under the original section if T died after 1969, whenever he made his will.[52]

(b) *The operation of section 33(1).* If the requirements of the original section 33 were satisfied, then, unless a contrary intention appeared by T's will,[53] T's gift to B did not lapse but took effect as if B had died immediately after T. The gift therefore fell into B's estate and had to be administered by B's personal representatives as an asset of B's estate. So, if B's estate was insolvent, the original section 33 increased B's assets and benefited his creditors.[54] If B's estate was solvent, the subject matter of T's gift to him passed to the persons beneficially entitled under B's will[55] or intestacy[56] at the date when he actually died.[57] Thus, though B's issue living at T's death saved the gift to B from lapse, such issue only benefited if they were beneficially entitled under B's will or intestacy. Under the original section 33, B's issue living at T's death did not stand in B's shoes and take the gift in B's place—they merely enabled the gift to him to take effect.

The substituted section 33(1) operates differently. If the requirements of the substituted section 33(1) are satisfied, then, unless a contrary inten-

---

[47] Substituted s. 33(4)(*a*).

[48] *Elliot v. Joicey* [1935] A.C. 209, esp. at pp. 229–233, disapproving *Re Griffith's Settlement* [1911] 1 Ch. 246.

[49] *In the Goods of Parker* (1860) 1 Sw. & Tr. 523: see *Jarman on Wills* (8th ed., 1951), pp. 463–464.

[50] *Mower v. Orr* (1849) 7 Hare 473; *Wisden v. Wisden* (1854) 2 Sm. & G. 396.

[51] Substituted s. 33(4)(*b*).

[52] Family Law Reform Act 1969, s. 16(1). Before this Act, s. 33 applied if B was legitimated, *Re Brodie* [1967] Ch. 818, and this is still so, Legitimacy Act 1976, ss. 1–3 and 5(1) and (3), Sched. I, paras. 1(1) and 2(1): for the status conferred by adoption see Adoption Act 1976, s. 39, and *ante*, p. 196.

[53] *Re Meredith* [1924] 2 Ch. 552.

[54] *Re Pearson* [1920] 1 Ch. 247 (T by his will made a gift to his son B, who predeceased T but left issue living at T's death; B died an undischarged bankrupt: held the gift passed to B's trustee in bankruptcy).

[55] *Johnson v. Johnson* (1843) 3 Hare 157; *Re Hayter* [1937] 2 All E.R. 110 (B by his will gave "everything I die possessed of" to X: held a general residuary gift which included property which passed to B under s. 33 on the later death of T).

[56] *Eager v. Furnivall* (1881) 17 Ch.D. 115: see Ryder (1971) 24 C.L.P. 157, 174–177.

[57] *Re Basioli* [1953] Ch. 367 (reviewing the cases); *Re Hurd* [1941] Ch. 196: see *Re Hone's Trusts* (1883) 22 Ch.D. 663. If T was the person beneficially entitled under B's will (or intestacy), this produced a "circle" which had to be broken at some point: see *Re Hensler* (1881) 19 Ch.D. 612 (T devised Blackacre to son B, who predeceased T but left issue living at T's death; B's will gave his estate to T: held Blackacre did not pass back to T under B's will); *Re Basioli*, at p. 376; Ryder, *loc. cit. pp.* 175–176.

tion appears by T's will, the devise or bequest to B takes effect as a devise or bequest to B's issue living at T's death and B's issue take *per stirpes*, if more than one in equal shares.[58] In other words, under the substituted section 33(1), B's issue stand in his shoes and take the gift in his place. An example will illustrate the operation of the section. Suppose that T's will contains an absolute gift to his child B, who dies before T leaving issue, *i.e.* B's two children C and D. Then D has two children, E and F, and D dies. At T's death, B's issue C, E and F are living. Under section 33(1) the gift to B takes effect as a gift to C (a one-half share), and E and F (a one-quarter share each). The substituted section 33(1) has the merit of operating in the same way as an express substitutional gift in a will commonly operates, *i.e.* benefiting B's issue and not his estate.[59]

(c) *Class gift to testator's children or remoter descendants.* The original section 33 did not apply to a class gift because (as was explained earlier) the doctrine of lapse does not apply to a class gift to persons who are to be ascertained at T's death or subsequently.[60] Consider again the example of a class gift by T's will "to all my children as tenants in common in equal shares." If B, one of T's children, predeceased T but left issue living at T's death, the original section 33 did not apply and B's personal representatives did not take under the gift.[61] This was so even if B was T's only child.[62]

If the testator dies after December 31, 1982, the substituted section 33(2) applies to a class gift to T's children or remoter descendants. The requirements are that:

   (i) T's will contains a devise or bequest to a class of persons consisting of T's children or remoter descendants;
   (ii) a presumptive member of the class[63] dies before T, leaving issue; and
   (iii) issue of that member are living at T's death.

If these requirements are satisfied, then, unless a contrary intention appears by T's will, the devise or bequest takes effect as if the class included the issue of its deceased member living at T's death, and the

---

[58] Substituted s. 33(3), which provides that B's issue take through all degrees according to their stock, in equal shares if more than one, any gift or share which their parent would have taken and so that no issue take whose parent is living at T's death and so capable of taking. If the gift to B was contingent, *quaere* whether B's issue take subject to the same contingency.

[59] *Ante*, p. 235. Given that the substituted s. 33 operates in this way, the reader may wonder whether, since 1983, express provision in the will serves any purpose; the advantage of express provision is that it means that the testator's attention has been drawn to the point, and he may wish a provision to be inserted in his will, the effect of which is not in all respects identical with that of the substituted s. 33.

[60] *Ante*, pp. 235–236.

[61] *Olney v. Bates* (1855) 3 Drew. 319; *Browne v. Hammond* (1858) Johns. 210. The original s. 33 of course applied to a gift to individuals, *Re Stansfield* (1880) 15 Ch.D. 84 (T's will gave "to my nine children as tenants in common in equal shares": held not a class gift and s. 33 applied).

[62] *Re Harvey's Estate* [1893] 1 Ch. 567.

[63] Substituted s. 33(2)(*b*) refers to "a member of the class": in the context this means a *presumptive* member.

issue take the deceased member's share *per stirpes*, if more than one in equal shares.[64]

The substituted section 33(2) does not create an exception to the rule that the doctrine of lapse does not apply to a class gift. But where section 33(2) applies, it adds the issue of a deceased presumptive member to the class eligible to take, in order to give effect to the testator's likely intention, which he did not express in his will.

(3) *GIFT TO DISCHARGE A MORAL OBLIGATION.* If T by his will makes a gift to C in discharge of a moral obligation recognised by T in his will, and which still exists at T's death, the gift does not lapse, though C predeceases T, because the court infers that T intended the gift to pass to C's estate. As Farwell J. put it in *Stevens v. King,*[65]

"I think that the cases. . .have established the rule that, if the Court finds, upon the construction of the will, that the testator clearly intended not to give a mere bounty to the legatee, but to discharge what he regarded as a moral obligation, whether it were legally binding or not, and if that obligation still exists at the testator's death, there is no necessary failure of the testator's object merely because the legatee dies in his lifetime; and therefore death in such a case does not cause a lapse."

This exception to the doctrine of lapse is based on case law and its ambit is uncertain. The exception has been held applicable where T makes a gift in discharge of his own debt which is barred by limitation,[66] or by the law of bankruptcy,[67] or in discharge of his deceased son's debt.[68] It may be that the exception is confined to the express recognition by T in his will of a moral obligation to pay one or more debts, and that it does not extend to the recognition of any other form of moral obligation.

III.   DISSOLUTION OF TESTATOR'S MARRIAGE TO BENEFICIARY

If a testator makes a will, is later divorced and then dies without having remarried[1] and without having made a new will,[2] the rule governing the effect of the divorce on his will varies according to the date of his death. The original rule, which applied until 1982, was that divorce had no effect on a will. The rule for testators dying between 1983 and 1995 was that a gift to the testator's spouse would *lapse*. The rule for

---

[64] Substituted s. 33(3).
[65] [1904] 2 Ch. 30, 33.
[66] *Williamson v. Naylor* (1838) 3 Y. & C. 208.
[67] *Philips v. Philips* (1844) 3 Hare 281; *Re Sowerby's Trust* (1856) 2 K. & J. 630; *Turner v. Martin* (1857) De G.M. & G. 429.
[68] *Re Leach's W.T.* [1948] Ch. 232.
[1] (Re) marriage will revoke the will, see Chap. 5.
[2] The new will will almost always contain a revocation clause.

testators dying from 1996 onwards is that the divorced spouse will, for most purposes, be deemed to have pre-deceased the testator.

1.   Testator dies on or before December 31 1982

The Wills Act 1837, when it was first enacted, contained no provision which attempted to deal with the effect of divorce on wills. There was no need. Before the enactment of the Matrimonial Causes Act 1857, divorce could only be effected by Private Act of Parliament and there were on average about two divorces a year.[3] So, section 18 of the Wills Act 1837 provided that marriage would revoke a will,[4] but divorce had no effect. This remained the position until 1982 and covered all testators who died on or before December 31 1982.

2.   Testator dies on or after January 1 1983 and on or before December 31 1995

The Law Reform Committee's 22nd Report *The making and revocation of wills*[5] (published in May 1980) considered the position and a majority of the Committee's members recommended that the law should be changed so that a divorced spouse should be treated as having pre-deceased the testator. This led to the enactment of the Administration of Justice Act 1982 section 18(2) which inserted section 18A into the Wills Act. This section applies to testators who die on or after January 1 1983 and on or before December 31 1995, the material part reads as follows:

18A.—
   (1) Where, after a testator has made a will, a decree of a court of civil jurisdiction in England and Wales dissolves or annuls his marriage. . .
      (a) the will shall take effect as if any appointment of the former spouse as an executor. . .were omitted; and
      (b) any devise or bequest to the former spouse shall lapse,
      except in so far as a contrary intention appears by the will.
   (3) Where
      (a) by the terms of a will an interest in remainder is subject to a life interest; and
      (b) the life interest lapses by virtue of subsection (1) (b) above,
      the interest in remainder shall be treated as if it had not been subject to the life interest. . ..[6]

The problem with section 18A, as enacted by the Administration of Justice Act 1982, was that it did *not* enact the Law Reform Committee's recommendation, which was that the divorced spouse should be deemed to have pre-deceased the testator. The effect of section 18A(3) was that there was a deemed pre-decease where the divorced spouse was given

---

[3] There were 184 Parliamentary divorces between 1715 and 1852—see Law Reform Committee's 22nd Report para 3.26 footnote 11.
[4] See Chap. 5.
[5] Cmnd. 7902 (1980).
[6] Subs (2) makes it clear that the former spouse retains a right to make an application under the family provision legislation.

a life interest; but in the more usual case, where the divorced spouse was given an absolute interest, section 18A(1)(b) enacted that a devise or bequest to the former spouse should *lapse*.

The difference between the Law Reform Committee's recommendation and section 18A, as enacted by the Administration of Justice Act 1982, became apparent in the case of *Re Sinclair*.[7] Mr Sinclair made a will in which he devised and bequeathed his whole estate to his wife. The will contained the following clause:

> "If my said wife shall pre-decease me. . .then I give. . .the whole of my estate. . .unto the Imperial Cancer Research Fund. . .absolutely."

The Sinclairs were divorced but Mr Sinclair made no new will and did not remarry. He died in October 1983, survived by his former wife. Had Mr Sinclair remarried, his remarriage would have revoked his will. Had Mr Sinclair died before January 1 1983, when section 18A came into force, his former wife would have benefited under his will; but as section 18A had come into force, she did not benefit. The question arose as to who did benefit. It was suggested on behalf of the Imperial Cancer Research Fund that "lapse" could be read to mean "fail with the same consequences as if the former spouse had died in the testator's lifetime", but this was not accepted by the trial judge,[8] and his decision was upheld by a unanimous Court of Appeal. "Lapse" simply meant "fail". The gift to the former spouse failed, but there was nothing in the section to suggest that she was deemed to have pre-deceased the testator. The property which she would have inherited, in this case the whole of the estate, accordingly passed not to the Imperial Cancer Research Fund but, on intestacy, to Mr. Sinclair's brother.

3.   Testator dies on or after January 1, 1996

It was generally agreed that *Re Sinclair* left the law in an unsatisfactory state and the Law Commission were asked to look at the problem. In September 1993 they presented a Report—*Family Law: The Effect of Divorce on Wills*.[9] This Report recommended that the law should be amended so that, where there is a divorce or an annulment, the former spouse should, *for most purposes*, be deemed to have pre-deceased the testator: a *selective* deemed pre-decease rule.

The Law Commission's recommendations have been enacted as sections 3 and 4 of the Law Reform (Succession) Act 1995 which apply to persons dying on or after January 1 1996 (regardless of the date of the will and of the date of the dissolution or annulment of the marriage).

Section 4 is straightforward. It inserts a subsection into section 6 of the Children Act 1989 and the effect of the subsection is to revoke the divorced spouse's appointment as a testamentary guardian of the testator's infant children. This will only apply where the divorced spouse is *not* the children's parent, but is a step parent; if the divorced spouse is the children's parent he will have parental responsibility in any event.

---

[7] [1985] Ch. 446.
[8] Michael Wheeler Q.C., sitting as a deputy High Court judge.
[9] Law Com No 217.

Section 3 of the 1995 Act contains the significant change—though it is not quite as straightforward as it at first sight appears.

The effect of section 3 is to substitute new paragraphs (a) and (b) for the original paragraphs (a) and (b) in section 18A(1). Section 18A(1) as amended (and as applying to testators dying on or after January 1 1996) then reads:

18A.—

(1) Where, after a testator has made a will, a decree of a court of civil jurisdiction in England and Wales dissolves or annuls his marriage . . .

   (a) provisions of the will appointing executors or trustees or conferring a power of appointment, if they appoint or confer the power on the former spouse, shall take effect as if the former spouse had died on the date on which the marriage is dissolved or annulled; and

   (b) any property which, or an interest in which, is devised or bequeathed to the former spouse shall pass as if the former spouse had died on that date;

   except in so far as a contrary intention appears by the will.

The change effected by the substituted 18A(1)(*a*) is to revoke the former spouse's appointment as the donee or appointor of a power of appointment, as well as revoking his appointment as executor or trustee. The substituted subsection also makes it clear that the former spouse is deemed to have pre-deceased the testator, so any appointment of another person which is to take effect on the former spouse's death will be effective.

The substituted 18A(1)(*b*) is the more important subsection, it negatives the effect of *Sinclair*.[10]

All the changes effected by the amendments to section 18A are clear improvements. But what seems slightly confusing about them is that they seem to have been effected in a way that is more complicated than it needs to have been. The changes enact that the former spouse shall be deemed to have pre-deceased the testator *for certain purposes*. So far so good. But why did the Law Commission not suggest, quite simply, that the former spouse should be deemed to have pre-deceased the testator *for all purposes*? Such a rule would have been simpler, what is the advantage of the more complicated formulation? The Law Commission's recommendations, enacted as sections 3 and 4 of the 1995 Act, ensure that the former spouse is not deemed to have pre-deceased the testator for all purposes. For at least two purposes he shall be treated as being still alive. First, the former spouse is treated as being still alive for the purpose of benefiting as an *appointee* under a *special* power of appointment.[11] Second, the former spouse will be treated as being still alive where a gift to a third party is somehow dependent on the former spouse's being alive, for example where a gift to a child is dependent

---

[10] The substituted 18A(1)(*b*) is also wide enough to cover the ground formerly covered by 18A(3), so 18A(3) is repealed; Law Reform (Succession) Act 1995 s. 5 and Sched.

[11] General powers of appointment are covered by 18A(1)(*b*) because "devised or bequeathed" has been held to include the exercise of a general power, but the words do include the exercise of a special power; see Law Commission's Report para 2.11.

on the child's living with the former spouse. Such gifts will be extremely rare.

The amended section 18A is a clear improvement on the original section 18A; but it has been suggested[12] that it would have been better still simply to have enacted that the divorced spouse should have been deemed to have pre-deceased the testator for *all* purposes. The problem with the original section 18A was that it was over-complicated.[13] It was drafted as it was, rather than as the Law Reform Committee recommended, because the draftsmen appear to have thought that a *simple deemed pre-decease formula* would cause complications. In the event, and as *Re Sinclair*[14] showed, the *lapse formula* caused more problems than it solved. The *selective deemed pre-decease formula*, which will apply from 1996, will clearly be an improvement over it *but* not necessarily over a *simple deemed pre-decease formula*.

It is suggested that the best course of action, when a testator is divorced, is to encourage him to make a new will, not to try to guess what he would have put into a will he has not bothered to make.

IV. ADEMPTION

1. Ademption of specific gifts

A specific legacy or specific devise fails by ademption if its subject matter has ceased to exist as part of the testator's property at his death. As was explained in Chapter 7, neither a general legacy nor a demonstrative legacy fails by ademption in this way.

Consider some examples of ademption:

(i) A specific legacy by T of "my 200 shares in X.Y.Z. Ltd. to A"; if T sells or gives away his shares in X.Y.Z. Ltd. during his lifetime, the specific legacy fails by ademption.[1] If T sells his shares, A is not entitled to receive the proceeds of sale, because the subject matter of the gift was the shares themselves and not their proceeds of sale.[2] If T sells or gives away some of his shares, the legacy fails to that extent.[3]

(ii) A specific legacy by T of a chattel, *e.g.* "the gold watch which my father gave me"; if T loses the watch,[4] or destroys it, or sells it, or gives it away, in each case the legacy fails by ademption.

(iii) A specific legacy by T of a debt, *e.g.* "I give to F the money now

---

[12] See R. Kerridge [1995] Conv. 12.
[13] The change from the Law Reform Committee's original suggestion to the wording of section 18A was not the result of an accident. Section 18A was amended as the 1982 Bill was introduced, because it was thought that a deemed pre-decease rule would create problems. But the *Sinclair* case shows that those who drafted section 18A did not take into account the problems *it* would create.
[14] *Supra.*
[1] *Ashburner v. Macguire* (1786) 2 Bro.C.C. 108.
[2] *Harrison v. Jackson* (1877) 7 Ch.D. 339.
[3] *Humphreys v. Humphreys* (1789) 2 Cox. 184.
[4] *Durrant v. Friend* (1851) 5 De G. & S. 343 (specific legacy of chattels; T and the chattels perished together at sea: held adeemed and insurance money for chattels fell into residue).

due to me from G"; if G pays the debt to T during his lifetime, whether voluntarily or under compulsion, again the legacy fails by ademption.[5] If G pays part of the debt to T, the legacy fails to that extent.[6]

(iv) A specific devise by T of "my farm Blackacre to L"; if T sells, or gives away, his farm Blackacre during his lifetime, the specific devise fails by ademption. Again, if T sells Blackacre, L is not entitled to receive the proceeds of sale.[7]

2. Failure of specific gifts speaking from death

A specific gift which speaks from the testator's death[8] is not subject to ademption in the strict sense of the doctrine. Examples include a specific gift of "the cars which I own at the date of my death," or "all shares in X.Y.Z. Ltd. of or to which I may be possessed or entitled at my death." Such a specific gift does, of course, fail if, at his death, the testator has no assets which answer the description in the will.[9] But such a specific gift does not fail under the doctrine of ademption in its strict sense, which applies only where the subject matter of the gift is to be ascertained at some time prior to death (*e.g.* "the cars which I own at the date of my will" or "my 200 shares in X.Y.Z. Ltd."[10]), and has ceased to exist as part of the testator's property at his death.

3. No intention to adeem needed

Ademption occurs whether or not the testator intended ademption to occur.[11] Indeed, the doctrine of ademption may often defeat the intention which a testator would have expressed if he had appreciated how the doctrine operates.[12] A testator may, however, insert a provision against ademption in his will—*e.g.* by a gift of "my 200 shares in X.Y.Z. Ltd. or *the investments representing the same at my death if they shall have been converted into other holdings.*"[13] Such a provision may, however, give rise to difficulties of identification, especially if many years elapse between the will and the death.

4. A change in substance causes ademption, a change in name or form does not

A change in substance in the subject matter of a specific gift causes ademption; a change which is only a change in name or form does not.[14]

---

[5] *Ashburner v. Macguire, supra; Re Bridle* (1879) 4 C.P.D. 336 (specific legacy of mortgage debt which was paid off in T's lifetime: held adeemed and immaterial T kept sum paid by mortgagor separate); *Gardner v. Hatton* (1833) 6 Sim. 93: *Re Robe* (1889) 61 L.T. 497: *Sidney v. Sidney* (1873) L.R. 17 Eq. 65. *Cf. Re Heilbronner* [1953] 1 W.L.R. 1254.

[6] *Aston v. Wood* (1874) 43 L.J.Ch. 715.

[7] *Re Bagot's Settlement* (1862) 31 L.J.Ch. 772, 774.

[8] For specific gifts which speak from the death of the testator under the Wills Act 1837, s.24, see Chap. 9, pp. 215 *et seq.*

[9] *Re Slater* [1907] 1 Ch. 665.

[10] *Re Gibson* (1866) L.R. 2 Eq. 669; some of the *obiter dicta* in *Re Gibson* may be open to question; see the discussion on pp. 218 *et seq.*

[11] *Ashburner v. Macguire* (1786) 2 Bro.C.C. 108; *Stanley v. Potter* (1789) 2 Cox 180.

[12] *Harrison v. Jackson* (1877) 7 Ch.D. 339, 341.

[13] *Re Lewis's W.T.* [1937] Ch. 118.

[14] *Re Slater, supra*, at pp. 671–672.

This principle has been applied in cases where T gives a specific legacy of shares in a particular company and then, after T has made his will but before his death, the shares are altered in the course of an amalgamation or reconstruction.

In *Re Slater*[15] T's will contained, *inter alia*, a specific legacy of his stock in the Lambeth Waterworks Company. Before T died, the Lambeth Waterworks Company was acquired by the Metropolitan Water Board (which also acquired other waterworks companies). Stock in the Metropolitan Water Board was issued to T before his death as compensation for the loss of his Lambeth Waterworks stock. The specific legatee claimed that this was a change only of form, that the Metropolitan Water Board stock was substantially the same investment as the Lambeth Waterworks stock, and that she was entitled to the Metropolitan Water Board stock. Her claim failed. It was held that the Metropolitan Water Board stock differed in substance from the Lambeth Waterworks stock; it was different stock in a different concern operating over a much larger area.[16]

Re Slater may be contrasted with *Re Clifford*[17] in which T by his will gave "twenty-three of the shares belonging to me" in the L Co. Ltd. At the date of his will T held 104 £80 shares in the company and the gift was a specific legacy of 23 of these £80 shares. Before T's death the company changed its name and sub-divided each £80 share into four new £20 shares so that at his death T held 416 new £20 shares in lieu of his 104 original £80 shares. Swinfen Eady J. held that this change had not adeemed the specific legacy because the subject matter remained the same in substance, though changed in name and form: the legatee therefore took 92 of the new £20 shares, which were "identical in all but name and form" with 23 original £80 shares. The same principle was applied in *Re Leeming*[18] where T gave a specific legacy of "my ten shares" in K Co. Ltd.: at the date of his will T held 10 £4 shares in this company. After the date of the will the company went into voluntary liquidation for the purpose of reconstruction as a new company with the same name, and at his death T held 20 £5 ordinary and 20 £5 preference shares in the new company in place of his 10 original £4 shares in the old company. The court held that the specific legacy had not been adeemed: the legatee took all T's shares in the new company because they were really in substance the same as the shares in the old company. In the recent case of *Re Dorman*[19] there was a specific legacy of "the balance of my Barclays higher deposit account No 10327719". After the testatrix had made her will, she gave D a power of attorney[20] and D, not knowing the terms of the will, closed the higher deposit account and opened another account, a capital advantage account, with a different number at the same branch of the same bank. D transferred into the new account all

---

[15] [1907] 1 Ch. 665.
[16] *Re Slater* [1907] 1 Ch. 665, 671–673 and 674–675; the Court of Appeal was affirming the decision of Joyce J. Statutes often provide that specific bequests of, *e.g.* government stock, shall not be adeemed by a conversion offer.
[17] [1912] 1 Ch. 29: see also *Re O'Brien* (1946) 115 L.J. Ch. 340.
[18] [1912] 1 Ch. 828: *cf. Re Kuypers* [1925] Ch. 244 (original shares given still existed though with rights curtailed: new shares issued in compensation for loss of rights did not pass).
[19] [1994] 1 W.L.R. 282.
[20] It was an enduring power of attorney; for enduring powers of attorney, see S.M. Cretney, *Enduring Powers of Attorney* (3rd ed., 1991).

the money which had been in the old account. He opened the new account because a "capital advantage account" paid a higher rate of interest, though it was subject to special conditions as to notice of withdrawal of funds. On these "very unusual facts" and "after considerable hesitation" it was held[21] that the bequest was not adeemed. There can be little doubt that this is what the testatrix would have intended; the problem is that ademption is independent of intention.[22] This having been said, it seems likely that there has been a slight tendency, in borderline cases in recent times, to find that a gift which has changed its form has not been adeemed, because the change is not a change of substance. The line between a change of form and a change of substance has always been a very fine one, and it could be suggested that the legatee in *Re Slater*, the first of the cases referred to above, was rather unlucky.

The problem can, in any event, be avoided by provision in the will. For example, the will can make specific provision for what is to happen where there is a reorganisation of share capital. This will normally provide that ademption shall not occur in such a case.[23]

5. Ademption by contract (made after the will)

If T by his will makes a specific gift of his farm Blackacre to L, and T later enters into a binding contract to sell Blackacre to P, but T dies before completion, this adeems the specific gift to L and L is not entitled to the purchase price payable by P.[24] L is only entitled to enjoy Blackacre or its rents and profits from T's death until the time for completion of the sale to P.[25] This result follows from the doctrine of conversion. Under this doctrine T, by contracting to sell Blackacre, disposes of his beneficial interest in Blackacre except in so far as he remains entitled to enjoy it until the time for completion.

6. Ademption by conditional contract (made after the will)

In *Re Sweeting*[26] it was held that a devise is adeemed by a conditional contract, in the same way that it is adeemed by an unconditional contract; provided, of course, that the condition is fulfilled and the contract is, in due course, completed.

7. Ademption by exercise of an option to purchase (granted after the will was made)

Under the anomalous, but well-settled, rule in *Lawes v. Bennett*,[27] if T by his will makes a specific gift of Whiteacre to L, and then later grants

---

[21] By David Neuberger Q.C. sitting as a deputy High Court judge.

[22] For further discussion, see Williams Mortimer and Sunnucks, *Executors, Administrators and Probate* (17th ed., 1993) p. 942.

[23] See *ante*, p. 248.

[24] *Farrar v. Earl of Winterton* (1842) 5 Beav. 1; *Watts v. Watts* (1873) L.R. 17 Eq. 217; *Re Galway's W.T.* [1950] Ch. 1; *Re Edwards* [1958] Ch. 168; *Re Sweeting* [1988] 1 All E.R. 1016 (conditional contract): *cf. Re Thomas* (1886) 34 Ch.D. 166 (contract not binding as T's title defective). See generally P.H. Pettit (1960) 24 Conv. (N.S.) 47.

[25] *Watts v. Watts, supra.*

[26] [1988] 1 All E.R. 1016.

[27] (1785) 1 Cox 167. See generally *Snell's Equity* (29th ed., 1990), pp. 491 *et seq.*

to O an option to purchase Whiteacre, O's exercise of his option after T's death adeems the specific gift to L. L is not entitled to the purchase price payable by O,[28] he is only entitled to enjoy Whiteacre or its rents and profits from T's death until the option is exercised.[29] In other words, an option to purchase which is exercised after T's death adeems a specific gift in the same way as a binding contract for sale made by T before his death.

In the case of an option to purchase (unlike a binding contract for sale) T is, at his death, still entitled to his beneficial interest in Whiteacre, subject to O's interest which is contingent upon O's exercise of the option. After T's death, his beneficial interest passes to L under the specific gift, and O's subsequent exercise of the option should not, but does, adeem the specific gift retrospectively.

The decision in *Re Carrington*[30] is a classic instance of the application of this rule. T by his will made specific gifts of 420 shares held by him in C Ltd. Later T granted to O an option (exercisable within one month of T's death) to purchase all his shares in C Ltd. T died and O duly exercised the option. The Court of Appeal reluctantly held that the specific gifts of the 420 shares had been adeemed by O's exercise of his option after T's death and that the purchase price payable by O was not payable to the specific legatees but fell into T's residuary estate.

The rule in *Lawes v. Bennett* is anomalous and a potential cause of trouble both for testators and their advisers. It is almost certainly easier to overlook an option than it is to overlook a contract. Most contracts will be completed within a relatively short time scale, whereas it may be many years between the grant of an option and its exercise. In the case of an option, the devisee may well (either as a result of ignorance or as a result of bad faith) fail to hand over the eventual proceeds of sale to the rightful beneficiaries after the option has been exercised.[31]

In *Clarke v. Bruce Lance & Co*[32] a specific devisee attempted to sue a firm of solicitors because they had not warned their client, the testator, about the problems involved in granting to a third party a fixed price option to purchase land which he, the testator, had specifically devised. The devisee's claim was struck out as disclosing no reasonable cause of action. But the devisee appears to have attempted to base his claim on the fact that the solicitors did not warn the testator about the dangers

[28] *Weeding v. Weeding* (1860) 1 J. & H. 424.
[29] *Townley v. Bedwell* (1808) 14 Ves. 591.
[30] [1932] 1 Ch. 1: see also *Re Rose* [1949] Ch. 78.
[31] If an option relates to unregistered land, it is registrable by the option holder against the name of the grantor at the Central Land Charges Registry as an estate contract (a c(iv) land charge; Land Charges Act 1972, s. 2(4)). If the title to the land is registered, the option is registrable by way of a notice/caution against the land at the Land Registry (Land Registration Act 1925, s. 49(1), s. 54) although if the holder of the option to purchase is in actual occupation (as he may well be, if the option is contained in a lease), he will have an overriding interest within the Land Registration Act 1925, s. 70(1)(g), *Webb v. Pollmount, Ltd.* [1966] Ch. 584. But *quaere* how many solicitors carry out a Central Land Charges Search against the deceased before they prepare an assent giving effect to a specific devise, to check whether a testator has granted an option over property which was specifically devised by a will made before the option was granted. The existence of the option should be apparent where the title to the land which is the subject of the specific devise is registered.
[32] [1988] 1 W.L.R. 881.

of a *fixed price* option. Any claim against the solicitors that they should
have warned the testator about the dangers of granting a fixed price
option should have been instituted by the personal representatives, not
by the devisee. As devisee, he had no interest in the amount which
would be paid under the option, because the money would not pass to
him; that is the essence of the rule in *Lawes v. Bennett*. But what if the
devisee had attempted to sue the solicitors for failing to warn the testator
about ademption? The court might well have been sympathetic to such
a claim. The testator himself would have been very likely to have
assumed that if he devised land to the devisee (who was his son) and
later granted an option to a third party, then, if the third party exercised
the option after his death, the purchase money would be paid to his son,
the devisee. Given that this is not what *Lawes v. Bennett* decides, any
solicitor concerned with the grant of an option should consider giving
careful advice on the point. He should either ensure that the property
over which the option is being granted is not already the subject matter
of a specific gift in the will of the person granting the option, or that the
person granting the option fully understands how its excercise will effect
an ademption and so deprive the specific devisee both of the property
and of the proceeds of sale.

8. Will made after contract, conditional contract or option

The rules set out above apply when T enters into the contract, the
conditional contract, or the option, after he has made his will. It will be
different if T first enters into the contract, the conditional contract, or
option and afterwards by his will makes a specific gift of the property,
subject to the contract or option, to L. In this case the gift is generally
construed as passing to L all T's interest, whatever it may be, so that L
is entitled to the purchase price payable by P.[33] The same result follows
if the will is made before the contract or grant of the option, but is confirmed by a codicil which is made after it[34] or substantially contemporan-
eously with it.[35]

9. Effect of republication of will

If a specific gift in a will has been adeemed, and the testator later
makes a codicil which republishes his will, in general this does not save
the specific gift from ademption.[36] For instance, if T by his will makes a
specific gift of Blackacre to L, and T sells Blackacre to P, and later T
makes a codicil which confirms his will, this does not make the specific
gift to L take effect as a gift of the proceeds of sale of Blackacre.

---

[33] *Re Callow* [1928] Ch. 710, esp at p. 714 *Drant v. Vause* (1842) 1 Y. & C.C.C. 580: see
generally *Hawkins and Ryder on the Construction of Wills* (1965), pp. 60 *et seq.*
[34] *Emuss v. Smith* (1848) 2 De G. & Sm. 722: for republication see Chap. 5.
[35] *Re Pyle* [1895] 1 Ch. 724 (T by will made specific devise of Whiteacre; T by codicil confirmed will and on same day granted lease to Q containing option to purchase Whiteacre;
Q exercised option after T's death: held specific devisees took purchase price).
[36] *Drinkwater v. Falconer* (1755) 2 Ves. Sen. 623, 626; *Powys v. Manfield* (1837) 3 My. & Cr.
359, 375–376; *Cowper v. Mantell (No. 1)* (1856) 22 Beav. 223; *Sidney* (1873) L.R. 17 Eq. 65;
Macdonald v. Irvine (1878) 8 Ch.D. 101, esp. at p. 108; *Re Galway's W.T.* [1950] Ch. 1.

Nevertheless, republication may alter the construction of a will as to the subject of a specific gift, and thereby save a gift which would otherwise have failed by ademption. One instance has just been mentioned in relation to a contract of sale or an option to purchase.[37] Another instance is the decision in *Re Reeves*[38] which was discussed in Chapter 9.[39]

10. Ademption of legacies by portions

The ademption of legacies by portions under the principle that equity leans against double portions was considered in Chapter 10.

V. ABATEMENT

1. Introduction

Abatement concerns the statutory order of application of assets to the payment of expenses, debts and liabilities.

The distinction between specific, general and demonstrative legacies was explained in Chapter 7, where it was said that one of the reasons why it was necessary to distinguish between them was that general legacies are used to pay expenses, debts and liabilities before resort is had to specific or demonstrative legacies.

2. The order of abatement

Where the estate of a deceased person is solvent,[1] the burden of his expenses, debts and liabilities as between the beneficiaries is regulated by section 34(3) of the Administration of Estates Act 1925 which enacts that, unless the statutory order is varied by his will, his real and personal estate will be applicable towards the discharge of his funeral, testamentary and administration expenses, debts and liabilities in the order mentioned in Part II of the First Schedule to the Act. This applies on the death of any person after 1925.[2]

The statutory order consists of seven numbered paragraphs, starting with property undisposed of by will and ending with property appointed by will under a general power. The seven paragraphs are set out, and discussed, in detail, in Chapter 17.[3] The property described in each paragraph is to be applied towards the payment of expenses, debts and liabilities before the property described in the following paragraph.[4] The two paragraphs relevant to the present disussion are paragraphs 5

---

[37] *Ante,* pp. 250–252.
[38] [1928] Ch. 351; see also *Re Champion* [1893] 1 Ch. 101. For another instance see *Re Harvey* [1947] Ch. 285, following *Re Warren* [1932] 1 Ch. 42: *cf. Re Newman* [1930] 2 Ch. 409 and *Re Galway's W.T., supra.* And see J. D. B. Mitchell (1954) 70 L.Q.R. 353, 364 *et seq.*
[39] *Ante* p. 223.
[1] For insolvent estates, see *post* pp. 438 *et seq.*
[2] For the special rules applicable to debts charged on the deceased's property and to the incidence of inheritance tax see *post* pp. 428 and 433.
[3] *post* pp. 420 *et seq.*
[4] *post* p. 421.

and 6. Paragraph 5 covers "the fund, if any, retained to meet pecuniary legacies", but the expression "pecuniary legacy" is defined[5] to include a general legacy; so paragraph 5 covers, in effect, the general legacy fund. Paragraph 6 covers "property specifically devised or bequeathed." This means that general legacies abate before specific legacies or devises.

A demonstrative legacy is treated as a specific legacy in so far as it can be discharged out of the designated property: to this extent it falls within paragraph 6.[6] But in so far as it is not discharged out of the specified fund or specified part of the testator's estate primarily designated for its payment: it falls within paragraph 5.[7] The justification for this distinction is that the testator is presumed to have intended the demonstrative legacy to be payable in priority to his general legacies so far as the demonstrative legacy can be satisfied out of the designated property.[8]

Summarising the liability to abatement under the statutory order, property falling within paragraph 5 will be applied towards the payment of expenses, debts and liabilities before resort is made to property in paragraph 6. A general legacy, and a demonstrative legacy so far as it is not discharged out of the designated property, both fall within paragraph 5. On the other hand, a specific legacy, a specific devise, and a demonstrative legacy so far as it can be discharged out of the designated property, all fall within paragraph 6. From the beneficiary's viewpoint, if there is any possibility of abatement, it is to his advantage to be entitled to property in paragraph 6 rather than in paragraph 5.

In relation to ademption and abatement, a demonstrative legacy is said to have "the best of both worlds"[9] because it is immune from ademption (like a general legacy) and, so far as it can be discharged out of the designated property, is preferred (like a specific legacy) on abatement under the statutory order.

3. Gifts in the same class abate rateably

Paragraph 6 of the statutory order provides that property specifically devised or bequeathed is to bear the burden of expenses and debts falling on it "rateably according to value." It follows that any property specifically devised or bequeathed and any demonstrative legacy so far as it can be discharged out of the property primarily designated for its payment must abate rateably.[10] For the purpose of this rateable abatement under paragraph 6, the property affected is valued as at the testator's death.[11]

Paragraph 5 of the statutory order does not refer to rateable abatement but there is a well-settled general rule that all general legacies abate rate-

---

[5] By s. 55(1)(ix) of the Act.
[6] See *Re Turner* [1908] 1 Ir. 274 (T's will gave specific legacies and devises, and demonstrative legacies payable out of specified railway stock held by T; T's other assets were insufficient to pay expenses and debts: held specific legacies and devises and demonstrative legacies so far as they could be satisfied from railway stock must all abate rateably).
[7] Administration of Estates Act 1925 s. 55(1)(ix) defines "pecuniary legacy" to include "a demonstrative legacy so far as it is not discharged out of designated property."
[8] *Acton v. Acton* (1816) 1 Mer. 178; *Creed v. Creed* (1844) 11 Cl. & F. 491, 509; *Livesay v. Redfern* (1837) 2 Y. & C.Ex. 90; *Robinson v. Geldard* (1851) 3 M. & G. 735, 745.
[9] *Snell's Equity* (29th ed., 1990), p. 362.
[10] *Re Turner, supra.*
[11] *Re John* [1933] Ch. 370; *Re Cohen* [1960] Ch. 179: see *post* p. 426.

ably on the principle that "equality is equity."[12] Demonstrative legacies, so far as they cannot be discharged out of the designated property, are treated as, and therefore abate rateably with, general legacies. This general rule applies whenever the property from which general legacies are payable[13] is insufficient to satisfy them in full. For the purpose of this rateable abatement, a general legacy of something other than money (*e.g.* company shares) is valued 12 months after the testator's death.[14]

4. Testator's intention to give priority

The testator may, of course, by his will vary the statutory order or give priority to a particular legacy or devise. For instance, the testator may direct that a particular general legacy (*e.g.* to his wife) shall have priority over any other legacy or devise whatsoever contained in his will (*i.e.* taking priority over specific legacies and devises) or (alternatively) over any other general legacies given by his will.[15]

In order to give priority to a particular legacy or devise the testator must show by his will a clear intention to do so.[16] Thus a direction by a testator that a legacy to his wife was to be paid to her immediately after his decease out of the first money to be received by his executors did not give her priority over the other general legacies, but merely specified the *time* for payment.[17] Again, a legacy given to an executor for his trouble did not take priority over other legacies.[18]

5. Abatement of annuities

(1) *ORDER OF ABATEMENT UNDER THE STATUTORY ORDER.* Under the statutory order of application of assets, both a general annuity and a demonstrative annuity so far as it is not discharged out of the designated property fall within paragraph 5, whereas both a specific annuity and a demonstrative annuity so far as it can be discharged out of the designated property fall within paragraph 6. A demonstrative annuity is payable in priority to general legacies and annuities in so far as the demonstrative annuity can be satisfied out of the designated property.[19]

---

[12] *Miller v. Huddlestone* (1851) 3 Mac. & G. 513, 523. Interest on a legacy is not an additional legacy for the purpose of abatement, *Re Wyles* [1938] Ch. 313.

[13] For the incidence of general legacies see Chap. 18.

[14] *Blackshaw v. Rogers*, cited in *Simmons v. Vallance* (1793) 4 Bro.C.C. 345; *Auther v. Auther* (1843) 13 Sim. 422, 440: see also *Re Hollins* [1918] 1 Ch. 503.

[15] cf. *Marsh v. Evans* (1720) 1 P. Wms. 668. See also *Re Compton* [1914] 2 Ch. 119 (legacies by T of certain company stock "all now standing in my name as general and not as specific legacies": held T intended these specific legacies to be treated as general legacies and they must abate as such).

[16] *Miller v. Huddlestone, supra*. For the case law see Williams, Mortimer and Sunnucks, *Executors Administrators and Probate* (17th ed., 1993), pp. 1005 *et seq.*

[17] *Blower v. Morret* (1752) 2 Ves.Sen. 420; *Re Schweder's Estate* [1891] 3 Ch. 44 (general legacy to be paid to wife within three months after death: no priority); *Cazenove v. Cazenove* (1890) 61 L.T. 115.

[18] *Duncan v. Watts* (1852) 16 Beav. 204. For the effect of a charging clause see *post* p. 404.

[19] *Livesay v. Redfern* (1836) 2 Y. & C.Ex. 90: see also *Creed v. Creed* (1844) 11 Cl. & F. 491 (specific annuity payable in priority to general legacies charged in aid on same property).

(2) *ANNUITIES IN THE SAME CLASS ABATE RATEABLY.* Property falling within paragraph 6 of the statutory order abates "rateably according to value." This includes a specific annuity and a demonstrative annuity so far as it can be discharged out of the designated property.

As to the abatement of general annuities[20] under paragraph 5, if the property from which two general annuities (or a general legacy and a general annuity) are payable is insufficient to satisfy them in full, the general rule applies to the effect that they must abate rateably unless the testator has shown by his will a clear intention to give priority to a particular legacy or annuity.[21] In order to achieve a rateable abatement, the rule of practice is to make an actuarial valuation of each annuity (so that the value can be treated as a legacy of a lump sum) and then abate this value (and also any general legacy) rateably, and pay this abated value to the annuitant.[22] Where this rule of practice applies, each annuitant is entitled to be paid a lump sum, by way of exception to the general rule against this.[23]

VI. UNCERTAINTY

A gift by will is void for uncertainty if, after applying any relevant rules of construction and considering any admissible evidence,[1] it is impossible to identify the subject matter or the object of the gift. Of course, the court tries to put a meaning on the words of a gift rather than "repose on the easy pillow of saying that the whole is void for uncertainty."[2]

1. Uncertainty of subject matter

For instance, gifts by a testator's will of "some of my best linen"[3] and of "a handsome gratuity to be given to each of the executors"[4] have been held void for uncertainty as to their subject matter. In *Asten v. Asten*[5] T, who owned four houses in Sudeley Place, by his will made separate gifts to each of his four sons of "all that newly built house, being No.   , Sudeley Place" (using similar terms for each gift). The court held that the four gifts failed for uncertainty because the will showed that T intended to give a particular house to each of his sons (so the sons were not

---

[20] See generally *Theobald on Wills* (15th ed., 1993), pp. 543 *et seq.*
[21] *Miller v. Huddlestone* (1851) 3 Mac. & G. 513.
[22] *Wright v. Callendar* (1852) 2 De G.M. & G. 652; *Wroughton v. Colquhoun* (1847) 1 De G. & Sm. 357; *Re Cox* [1938] Ch. 556.
[23] For the general rule and for exceptions to it, see *ante*, p. 179.
[1] *Ante*, Chap. 8 pp. 187 *et seq.*
[2] *Per* Jessel M.R. in *Re Roberts* (1881) 19 Ch.D. 520, 529.
[3] *Peck v. Halsey* (1726) 2 P. Wms. 387 (if it were "so much of my bed linen, as they [the legatees] should chuse, or as my executors should chuse for them, this would be good, and by the choice of the legatees or executors is reducible to a certainty").
[4] *Jubber v. Jubber* (1839) 9 Sim. 503.
[5] [1894] 3 Ch. 261.

intended to select in turn), but the will did not indicate which house each was intended to take.[6]

By way of contrast, a direction by will to executors to let X enjoy a flat during her lifetime and "to receive a reasonable income from my other properties" was held valid on the ground that this required an objective assessment of reasonable income, which the court could undertake if need be.[7] In another case T's will read, "I give devise and bequeath unto my brother Mr Harry Pateman [address] Also sister Mrs Jane Slade [address] Also sister Mrs Ethel James [address]." The court inferred that the will was intended to deal with the whole of T's property and held that T's whole estate passed under this gift, even though T had omitted any mention of the subject matter of the gift.[8]

2. Uncertainty of object

The decision in *Re Stephenson*[9] is an example of a gift failing for uncertainty of objects. T by his will gave his residuary estate "unto the children of the deceased son (named Bamber) of my father's sister share and share alike." This sister (as T was aware) had three deceased sons, each with the surname Bamber, and each had left children. The Court of Appeal held that the gift was void for uncertainty as it was impossible to ascertain which son's children were intended to take.

By way of exception to the general rule about uncertainty of objects, "a charitable bequest never fails for uncertainty."[10] This means that if the testator has shown a general charitable intention, a gift does not fail for uncertainty of objects merely because the testator has not indicated which particular charity he wishes to benefit. For instance a gift by will on trust for "the following charitable societies, *viz.*   to be divided in equal shares among them" (the objects not being named) is valid and the court directs a scheme in order to give effect to the gift.[11]

This exception to the general rule is not, however, applicable if the gift is not exclusively charitable.[12] Thus in *Chichester Diocesan Fund and Board of Finance v. Simpson*[13] a testator by his will directed his executors to apply his residuary estate for such "charitable or benevolent" objects

---

[6] *cf. Tapley v. Eagleton* (1879) 12 Ch.D. 683 (T owned three houses in King Street; gift by T's will of "two houses in King Street" to X for life: held X was entitled to select); *Boyce v. Boyce* (1849) 16 Sim. 476 (selector dead); *Re Knapton* [1941] Ch. 428 (T by will gave "one house to each of my nephews and nieces:" held if they disagreed they must choose in turn, the order of the choice to be determined by lot).

[7] *Re Golay* [1965] 1 W.L.R. 969: but see R. E. M. (1965) 81 L.Q.R. 481: see also *Talbot v. Talbot* [1968] Ch. 1 (option by will to purchase farm at "a reasonable valuation": option held valid).

[8] *Re Stevens* [1952] Ch. 323.

[9] [1897] 1 Ch. 75.

[10] *Re White* [1893] 2 Ch. 41, 53.

[11] *Re White, supra*, where the gift was "to the following religious societies. . ."; this was treated as prima facie confined to charities. For application in accordance with the directions of the Crown under the Royal Prerogative where the gift is direct, and not by way of a trust, see *Re Bennett* [1960] Ch. 18.

[12] For qualifications to the "exclusively charitable" requirement, including the Charitable Trusts (Validation) Act 1954, see *Snell's Equity* (29th ed., 1990). pp. 155 *et seq.*

[13] [1944] A.C. 341. For the sequel see *Re Diplock* [1948] Ch. 465, C.A.; and *Ministry of Health v. Simpson* [1951] A.C. 251, H.L.; *post,* p. 511.

in England as they might in their absolute discretion select. The House of Lords held that the gift was void for uncertainty because it was not confined to charitable objects, but extended to objects which were benevolent but not charitable.[14]

In the judgments in the House of Lords in this case there are *dicta* to the effect that a testator may not delegate his testamentary power. To quote, for example, from the judgment of Lord Simonds.[15]

> "It is a cardinal rule, common to English and Scots law, that a man may not delegate his testamentary power. To him the law gives the right to dispose of his estate in favour of ascertained or ascertainable persons. He does not exercise the right if in effect he empowers his executors to say what persons or objects are to be his beneficiaries. To this salutary rule there is a single exception. A testator may validly leave it to his executors to determine what charitable objects shall benefit, so long as charitable and no other objects may benefit."

Such *dicta* seem to go too far. A testator may by his will confer on another person,[16] or on the trustee of his will,[17] a power of appointment and thereby delegate his testamentary power.[18] In *Re Park*[19] T by his will gave his residuary estate to his trustee in trust to pay the income to such person (other than his sister Jane) or charitable institution as his sister Jane should from time to time during her lifetime direct in writing. Clauson J. held that this "intermediate" power (*i. e.* intermediate between a general and a special power) was valid, and he referred in his judgment to "the well settled principle" that a testator by his will may confer on any person a general or a special power.

Re Park was followed in the recent case of *Re Beatty*[20] where the testatrix appointed executors and trustees, vested her personal chattels and cash to the value of £1,500,000 in them and then provided that they should distribute the chattels and cash "among such person or persons (whether individual or corporate) as they think fit," instructing them to observe any wishes as to distribution that she might express and providing that any chattels or cash not distributed within two years were to pass under the residuary gift in her will. Hoffmann J. upheld these provisions and said that a:

> ". . . rule against testamentary delegation, in the sense of a restriction

[14] There are many similar case *e.g. Houston v. Burns* [1918] A.C. 337 (residue to be applied by trustees "for such public, benevolent, or charitable purposes" in connection with named parish as trustees should think proper: held void for uncertainty); *Att.-Gen. v. National Provincial and Union Bank of England* [1924] A.C. 262 (patriotic or charitable purposes void for uncertainty).

[15] [1944] A.C. 341 at p. 371 (and see Viscount Simon L.C., at p. 348, Lord Macmillan, at p. 349, Lord Porter, at p. 364): see also *Houston v. Burns* [1918] A.C. 337, 342 and *Att.-Gen v. National Provincial and Union Bank of England* [1924] A.C. 262, 264 and 268.

[16] *Re Park* [1932] 1 Ch. 580: see also *Re Hughes* [1921] 2 Ch. 208, 212 and *Re Jones* [1945] Ch. 105. *Cf. Re Carville* [1937] 4 All E.R. 464 ("to each of my executors £100. . .The residue to be disposed of as the executors shall think fit": held by Clauson J. residue went as on intestacy).

[17] *Re Abrahams' W.T.* [1969] 1 Ch. 463, 474–476.

[18] See generally D.M. Gordon (1953) 69 L.Q.R. 334.

[19] [1932] 1 Ch. 580.

[20] [1990] 1 W.L.R. 1503.

on the scope of testamentary powers, is a chimera, a shadow cast by the rule of certainty, having no independent existence."

He had no doubt as to the validity of testamentary powers whether special, general or intermediate.[21]

VII. MURDER OR MANSLAUGHTER OF THE TESTATOR OR INTESTATE

1. Introduction

Before 1870, the property of a convicted felon was forfeited to the Crown.[1] Murder and manslaughter were both felonies, so the property of anyone convicted of murder or manslaughter was forfeited. The Forfeiture Act 1870[2] abolished forfeiture to the Crown. A judge-made forfeiture rule,[3] a rule of public policy, then developed to the effect that someone who commits murder[4] or some forms of manslaughter[5] is debarred from taking any benefit under his victim's will or intestacy.[6] The rule does not apply if the killer is insane—*i.e.* if he is found not guilty by reason of insanity.[7]

The problem with the post-1870 forfeiture rule is that its ambit is far from clear. It applies to all murders. It does not apply if the killer is insane. It applies to some cases of manslaughter. It has been applied where the killer has been convicted of manslaughter by reason of diminished responsibility,[8] but it may not apply to all cases of diminished responsibility.[9] In practice, the line between insanity and diminished responsibility has been rather a fine one and a reason for pleading insanity rather than diminished responsibility would, in some instances, have been to avoid forfeiture. It is not clear to what other manslaughter cases the forfeiture rule applies and a complicating factor is that there may be different rules to cover (i) benefits derived under the deceased's will or intestacy; (ii) benefits derived under insurance policies and (iii) state

---

[21] But see J.D. Davies (1991) 107 L.Q.R. 211.

[1] His realty would escheat to his feudal lord, but, by the 19th century, this was equivalent to forfeiture.

[2] An Act to abolish Forfeitures for Treason and Felony: 33 & 34 Vict. Chap. 23.

[3] It may be rather confusing to refer to the *pre*-1870 rule and to the *post*-1870 rule as both being "the forfeiture rule." But that is how they are referred to. The *pre*-1870 rule meant that the felon forfeited all his property to the Crown. The *post*-1870 rule, where it applies, is that the killer does not benefit from his victim's estate—he forfeits what he would have inherited and the property goes to someone else, see *infra*.

[4] *In the Estate of Crippen* [1911] P. 108 (intestacy); *Re Sigsworth* [1935] Ch. 89 (will or intestacy): as to burden of proof see *Re Dellow's W.T.* [1964] 1 W.L.R. 451.

[5] *In the Estate of Hall* [1914] P. 1 (will).

[6] Or statutory nomination or *donatio mortis causa* of his victim. As to joint tenants see *Re K* [1985] Ch. 85, 100 (forfeiture severs a beneficial joint tenancy); see also *Schobelt v. Barber* (1966) 60 D.L.R. (2d) 519; *Re Pechar* [1969] N.Z.L.R. 574, 584–588.

[7] *Re Houghton* [1915] 2 Ch. 173 (insane killer may take on his victim's intestacy); *Re Pitts* [1931] 1 Ch. 546. There is a presumption of sanity, *Re Pollock* [1941] Ch. 219.

[8] *Re Giles* [1972] Ch. 544 (will or intestacy).

[9] See *Re H. (dec'd.)* [1990] 1 F.L.R. 441.

benefits (such as the widow's pension).[10] It is probable, though not certain, that the forfeiture rule does not apply to other cases of unlawful killing, for example, to cases where there is a conviction for causing death by reckless driving.[11]

2. Forfeiture Act 1982

The Forfeiture Act 1982 gives the court the power to modify the effect of the forfeiture rule if the court is satisfied that the justice of the case so requires, having regard to the conduct of the offender and of the deceased and of any other material circumstances.[12] The power to modify the effect of the rule does not apply in the case of someone convicted of murder.[13] Under the power to modify, the court can grant complete or partial relief from the effect of the forfeiture rule.[14]

Again, unless the killer stands convicted of murder, the killer may apply for provision to be made under the Inheritance (Provision for Family and Dependants) Act 1975,[15] but the application must inevitably fail if the deceased's will or intestacy would have made reasonable provision for the applicant if the forfeiture rule had not applied.[16]

The 1982 Act is not well drafted. It is engrafted onto the earlier law and, as the earlier law is uncertain, the present position is uncertain too.[17] The Act does not affect the position in relation to murder, does not affect the position in relation to cases where the killer is insane, probably does not affect the position in relation to cases where there has been a conviction for causing death by reckless driving; so its effect is confined to *some* manslaughter cases. In *Re H (dec'd.)*[18] a husband killed his wife while he was suffering from a form of mental disorder and was convicted of manslaughter by reason of diminished responsibility. Peter Gibson J. held that the forfeiture rule did not apply in this case. He said that the proper test was whether the killer had been guilty of deliberate, intentional and unlawful violence or threats, and that it was for the court to determine, after careful scrutiny of the facts in each particular case, where the line should be drawn. He also went on to hold that, if the

---

[10] *Gray v. Barr* [1971] 2 Q.B. 554, 569 and 581 (manslaughter varies infinitely in its seriousness—but this is an insurance case); *R. v. Chief National Insurance Commissioner, Ex. p. Connor* [1981] Q.B. 758, 765 (this is a state benefit case); *Re K* [1985] Ch. 85, 95–98; *Re H.* [1990] *supra.* See generally Youdan (1973) 89 L.Q.R. 235.

[11] See A.J. Oakley, *Constructive Trusts* (2nd ed., 1988) pp. 25–26.

[12] Forfeiture Act 1982, s.2. If the killer stands convicted, proceedings for modification cannot be brought more than three months after conviction, s. 2(3); *Re Royse* [1985] Ch. 22. Property acquired before October 13, 1982 by a person other than the killer in consequence of the forfeiture rule is protected, s. 2(7); *Re K* [1985] Ch. 85, 98–99, [1986] Ch. 180 (only property actually transferred to other person, not property held by personal representative pending administration).

[13] Forfeiture Act 1982 s. 5.

[14] *ibid.* s. 2(1) and (5); see *Re K* [1985] Ch. 85, [1986] Ch. 180 (probation for H's manslaughter: W granted complete relief from forfeiture of her interests under H's will and in matrimonial home as surviving joint tenant).

[15] *ibid.* ss. 3 and 5.

[16] *Re Royse* [1985] Ch. 22: see *ante,* p. 128.

[17] See S. Cretney (1990) 10 O.J.L.S. 298; P. Matthews (1983) J.S.W.L. 141 "little short of a legislative disaster."

[18] [1990] 1 F.L.R. 441.

forfeiture rule had applied, he would have granted relief from it under the 1982 Act. A similar result was reached by a different route in *Re K*[19] where Vinelott J. held that the forfeiture rule did apply to a wife who had killed her husband with a single shot from a shotgun and who had been convicted of manslaughter.[20] She was granted relief under the Act and was permitted to inherit virtually the whole of her husband's substantial estate.

Given that there appears to be such doubt as to when the forfeiture rule applies in manslaughter cases, it may seem that the safest course for the beneficiary/killer is to apply for relief under the Act. The problem is that this may involve unnecessary legal costs and, even if the applicant obtains relief under the Act, and so is able to inherit all or part of the estate of his victim, he may, by making an application under the Act, provoke potential problems in relation to insurance claims and/or state benefits. The position is not satisfactory and this branch of the law is in need of legislative clarification.

VIII. DISCLAIMER[1]

1. Beneficiary is free to disclaim

A beneficiary under a will may disclaim the gift to him. "The law certainly is not so absurd as to force a man to take an estate against his will."[2] Similarly a beneficiary entitled under the intestacy rules may disclaim his interest on intestacy.[3] The beneficiary may disclaim by a deed of disclaimer[4] or by conduct.

If a beneficiary does disclaim a benefit under a will, he may subsequently retract his disclaimer provided that no one has altered his position in reliance on the disclaimer.[5]

2. Limits on freedom to disclaim

There are, however, certain limits on a beneficiary's freedom to disclaim:

(i) If the beneficiary has already unequivocally accepted the gift, the beneficiary cannot disclaim it.[6]

---

[19] [1985] Ch. 85, Vinelott J; decision affirmed by C.A. [1986] Ch 180.
[20] It is not clear from the report of the case (dealing with the forfeiture) what type of manslaughter the widow had been convicted of; there was a dispute in the forfeiture proceedings as to whether remarks made by the trial judge in the criminal case implied that this was a case of reckless manslaughter, or whether it was a case of an intentional killing which was manslaughter because of provocation. In any event, the distinction, where there has been a shooting, is likely to be a very fine one.
[1] There may be tax advantages in a disclaimer, as there may be in a variation. See Chap. 12, pp. 285 *et seq.*
[2] *Per* Abbot C.J. in *Townson v. Tickell* (1819) 3 B. & Ald. 31.
[3] *Re Scott* [1975] 1 W.L.R. 1260; *cf.* Goodhart (1976) 40 Conv.(N.S.) 292; Oughton (1977) 41 Conv.(N.S.) 260.
[4] *Townson v. Tickell, supra.*
[5] *Re Cranstoun* [1949] Ch. 523: see also *Re Paradise Motor Co.* [1968] 1 W.L.R. 1125, 1143.
[6] *Re Hodge* [1940] Ch. 260; *cf. Re Wimperis* [1914] 1 Ch. 502.

(ii) In general the beneficiary is free to disclaim an onerous gift[7] in a will and accept another beneficial gift in the same will,[8] but occasionally the will requires him to take both or neither of the gifts.[9]

(iii) If a single gift includes two or more different assets, the beneficiary must take all the assets or none of them. For instance, a gift to B by T's will of his leasehold house Blackacre together with its contents constitutes a single gift, and not two separate gifts, and therefore B is not free to disclaim the gift of Blackacre and accept the gift of its contents.[10]

(iv) One of two or more joint beneficiaries cannot disclaim, though he can release his interest to the other joint tenants[11]—"the only disclaimer which can be made by joint tenants is a disclaimer which is made by them all."[12]

IX.   EFFECT OF FAILURE

1.   A legacy or specific devise which fails falls into residue or passes on intestacy

In general, the subject matter of any legacy or specific devise which fails passes under the residuary gift (if any) contained in the testator's will or, if not effectively disposed of by the will, passes on intestacy.[1]

(1)   *RESIDUARY BEQUEST.* Prima facie a residuary bequest includes the subject matter of any legacy which fails for any reason.[2] As Grant M.R. put it in *Leake v. Robinson,*[3]

"I have always understood that, with regard to personal estate, everything which is ill given by the will does fall into the residue ... It is immaterial how it happens that any part of the property is undisposed of ..."

If T by his will gives "my 200 shares in X.Y.Z. Ltd." to A and "all the residue of my personal estate" to B, the word "residue" is *not* construed as referring to all T's personal estate except the 200 shares: instead, if the gift to A fails, the "residue" includes the 200 shares because the gift

---

[7] *e.g.* a gift of a lease with an unduly heavy rent, or a gift subject to a condition imposing an onerous personal obligation, as in *Re Hodge, supra,* (devise of Blackacre to H subject to personal obligation to pay £2 per week to S for life, and if H disposed of Blackacre to invest £2,000 on trust for S for life and after her death for S's children).

[8] *Warren v. Rudall* (1861) 1 J. & H. 1.

[9] *Talbot v. Earl of Radnor* (1834) 3 M. & K. 252; *Fairtlough v. Johnstone* (1865) 16 Ir.Ch. 442.

[10] *Re Joel* [1943] Ch. 311; *Guthrie v. Walrond* (1882) 22 Ch.D. 573 ("all my estate and effects in the Island of Mauritius": held a single gift which could only be disclaimed as a whole).

[11] *Re Schar* [1951] Ch. 280.

[12] *ibid.* at p. 285.

[1] See generally *Hawkins and Ryder on the Construction of Wills* (1965), pp. 64 *et seq.*

[2] *Cambridge v. Rous* (1802) 8 Ves. 12 (lapsed legacies); *Blight v. Hartnoll* (1883) 23 Ch.D. 218 (legacy void for remoteness); *Re Backhouse* [1931] W.N. 168 (disclaimed legacy).

[3] (1817) 2 Mer. 363, 393.

to B is a residuary bequest. The same result follows if T gives "all the rest of," or "all the remainder of," or "all other," his personal estate to B.[4] However, this common law rule that a residuary bequest includes the subject matter of any legacy which fails is not applicable if the will shows a contrary intention. Accordingly, the rule is not applicable if the testator shows an intention to exclude the subject matter of a legacy from his residuary bequest in any event, irrespective of whether the legacy fails: in that event, if the legacy fails, the subject matter passes on intestacy.[5]

(2) *RESIDUARY DEVISE.* Under section 25 of the Wills Act 1837, unless a will shows a contrary intention, a residuary devise[6] includes the subject matter of any specific devise which fails for any reason. Thus, as a result of section 25, a residuary devise operates in the same way as a residuary bequest.[7]

2. A residuary gift which fails passes on intestacy

If a residuary gift in a will fails completely, the residuary estate passes on intestacy. Again, if a gift of a share in the residuary estate fails, prima facie that share passes on intestacy. Accordingly, if T by his will gives his residuary real and personal estate to X and Y absolutely as tenants in common in equal shares, and the gift to X fails for any reason, prima facie X's share goes on T's intestacy and does not pass to Y. A residuary gift sweeps up property not effectively disposed of by any other form of gift, but it does not sweep up property not effectively disposed of by the residuary gift itself.[8] However, this rule is not applicable if the will shows a contrary intention. For instance, T may direct that if the disposition of a share of his residue fails, that share is to accrue to the other share, and under such a direction X's share does pass to Y.[9]

3. Gifts which do not fail

The principles so far considered are not, of course, applicable if the gift (whether a legacy, specific devise or residuary gift) does not fail, even though one or more of the beneficiaries cannot take. This occurs:

[4] *Re Mason* [1901] 1 Ch. 619, 624–625; *Re Barnes' W.T.* [1972] 1 W.L.R. 587.
[5] Re Fraser [1904] 1 Ch. 726; *Wainman v. Field* (1854) Kay. 507, but see *Blight v. Hartnoll*, *supra*, at p. 223. Also the subject matter may, on the construction of the will, fall into a particular residue of that description of property, and not into general residue, *De Trafford v. Tempest* (1856) 21 Beav. 564 and see Hawkins and Ryder, *op. cit.* pp. 66–68.
[6] s. 25 only applies to general residuary devises, *Springett v. Jenings* (1871) L.R. 6 Ch.App. 333: *cf. Re Davies* [1928] Ch. 24.
[7] *Re Mason* [1901] 1, Ch. 619, C.A., [1903] A.C. 1, H.L. (specific devise to attesting witness fell into devise of "all other my freehold messuages and tenements at Wimbledon aforesaid and elsewhere," which was held to be residuary).
[8] *Skrymsher v. Northcote* (1818) 1 Sw. 566, 570.
[9] For examples of contrary intention see *Evans v. Field* (1839) 8 L.J.Ch. 264; *Re Palmer* [1893] 3 Ch. 369 and *Re Allan* [1903] 1 Ch. 276. For the effect of Wills Act 1837, s. 15 see *Re Doland's W.T.* [1970] Ch. 267 (trust of 2 per cent. share of residue for X, whose wife was an attesting witness; proviso that if "any of the trusts ... shall fail" gift to Y and Z equally: held under Wills Act 1837, s. 15 the will must be treated as though it contained no trust in favour of X which could fail—X's share went on intestacy and not under proviso).

    (i) in the case of a gift to A, B and C as joint tenants if A and B both die before the testator, but C survives him and takes the whole by survivorship[10]; and

    (ii) in the case of a class gift to persons who are to be ascertained at the testator's death or subsequently.

If a presumptive member of a class dies in the testator's lifetime,[11] or is incapable of taking by reason of his being an attesting witness,[12] or forfeits because he is guilty of the testator's manslaughter,[13] this does not cause the gift to fail if at least one other member of the class takes. Again, if any property is given by will to X subject to a charge in favour of Y (*e.g.* charged with a legacy of £1,000 for Y), and the gift to Y fails, this causes the charge to fail and X takes the entire property free from the charge.[14] Finally, if any property is given by will to X absolutely and trusts are engrafted on X's absolute interest which fail, under the rule in *Lassence v. Tierney* the absolute gift to X takes effect so far as the trusts have failed. This rule was considered in Chapter 8.[15]

4. Acceleration of subsequent interest

The doctrine of acceleration may be applicable if T by his will gives any real or personal property to X for life and this gift to X fails. It may fail because X or his spouse was an attesting witness, or X predeceased T, or T's marriage to X was dissolved or annulled, or X was guilty of T's murder or manslaughter, or X disclaimed the gift.

(1)   *GIFT IN REMAINDER VESTED.* If after X's life interest there is a vested gift in remainder (*e.g.* a gift in remainder to Y absolutely), the remainder is accelerated and takes effect in possession immediately.[16] "An interest is postponed that a prior interest may be enjoyed. If that prior interest is determined, whether by the death of a prior beneficiary or for any other cause, the reason for postponement disappears and there is no reason why there should not be acceleration."[17] If the gift to Y is expressed to take effect "after the death" of X, this does not prevent acceleration – the gift to Y is construed as a gift taking effect on the death of X *or on any earlier failure or determination of X's interest.*[18] In short, "after his death for Y absolutely" is construed in the same sense as the

---

[10] *Morley v. Bird* (1798) 3 Ves. 629.

[11] *Doe d. Stewart v. Sheffield* (1811) 13 East. 526; *Shuttleworth v. Greaves* (1838) 4 M. & Cr. 35: see also *Re Woods* [1931] 2 Ch. 138 and *cf. Re. Midgley* [1955] Ch. 576.

[12] *Fell v. Biddolph* (1875) L.R. 10 C.P. 701 (the headnote is wrong); *Re Coleman and Jarrom* (1876) 4 Ch.D. 165 ("the true rule is that those members of the class who are at the testator's death capable of taking take, and that those who become incapable of taking— whether by dying in the testator's lifetime, or by attesting the will, or by some other operation of law—do not take").

[13] *Re Peacock* [1957] Ch. 310.

[14] *Tucker v. Kayess* (1858) 4 K. & J. 339.

[15] See *ante*, Chap. 8, pp. 210–211.

[16] *Lainson v. Lainson* (1854) 5 De G.M. & G. 754 (X's life interest revoked by codicil: vested remainder accelerated); *Jull v. Jacobs* (1876) 3 Ch.D. 703 (X an attesting witness: vested remainder accelerated); *Re Flower's Settlement Trusts* [1957] 1 W.L.R. 401, 405.

[17] *Re Hodge* [1943] Ch. 300, 301–302 (X disclaimed: held annuities in remainder accelerated).

[18] *Re Flower's Settlement Trusts, supra.*

useful phrase *"subject as aforesaid for Y absolutely'"*. But T may by his will exclude the doctrine of acceleration by making it plain that the expression "after the death" of X refers to X's death in the literal sense and nothing else.

The doctrine of acceleration applies even though the vested gift in remainder is vested in Y subject to being divested[19] (e.g. a gift in remainder to Y absolutely, but if Y dies before X and leaves issue, to Y's issue absolutely in equal shares *per stirpes*). In this case, under the doctrine of acceleration Y's interest takes effect in possession immediately, but Y's interest nevertheless remains liable to be divested in accordance with the terms of T's will.[20]

(2) *GIFT IN REMAINDER CONTINGENT.* On the other hand, if after X's life interest there is only a contingent gift in remainder (*e.g.* a gift in remainder to the first child of Y absolutely, and at T's death Y has no child), normally the remainder is not accelerated whilst the remainder remains contingent.[21] But if the gift in remainder subsequently becomes vested (*i.e.* in this example, if a child is born to Y), under the doctrine of acceleration the remainder is then accelerated and takes effect in possession.[22]

5. Failure of interest on intestacy

An interest on intestacy may fail because the beneficiary is guilty of the murder or manslaughter of the intestate,[23] or the beneficiary disclaims his interest.[24] At least three different situations may arise.

(1) *INTEREST OF SURVIVING SPOUSE FAILS.* If the surviving spouse is debarred by his murder or manslaughter of the intestate from taking any benefit on intestacy, the intestate's issue take the whole estate.[25] The same result follows if the surviving spouse disclaims his interest on intestacy.

(2) *ANOTHER MEMBER OF THE SAME CLASS TAKES.* In *Re Callaway*[26] T by her will gave her whole estate to her daughter, D, who murdered her and was therefore debarred from taking under her will

---

[19] *Re Taylor* [1957] 1 W.L.R. 1043 (X disclaimed: held vested remainder accelerated but remained liable to be divested); *Re Conyngham* [1921] 1 Ch. 491.

[20] *Re Taylor, supra; Re Conyngham, supra.*

[21] *Re Townsend's Estate* (1886) 34 Ch.D. 357 (X's wife an attesting witness; gift in remainder to X's child or children; X was childless: held no acceleration possible until X has a child—then "the interest of the children in remainder would be accelerated"); *Re Taylor, supra,* at pp. 1045 and 1049; *Re Scott* [1975] 1 W.L.R. 1260. But *cf. Re Dawson's Settlement* [1966] 1 W.L.R. 1456, esp. at pp. 1465–1467 where Goff J. held that a remainder which is contingent may be accelerated if the person contingently entitled is *in esse* and "the contingency is in no way related to the words of futurity or the determination of the prior interest," *e.g.* attaining 21 or marrying: see Prichard [1973] C.L.J. 246.

[22] *Re Townsend's Estate, supra; Re Taylor, supra.* For the effect of acceleration on class closing see *ante*, p. 204.

[23] *Ante,* pp. 259 *et seq.*

[24] *Ante,* p. 261.

[25] *Re Giles* [1972] Ch. 544.

[26] [1956] Ch. 559.

or intestacy. T died a widow and T's issue entitled under the intestacy rules were T's son, S, and her daughter, D. Vaisey J. held that D was disqualified from being counted as a member of the class of issue entitled on intestacy and that accordingly S was solely entitled to T's estate. He rejected the Crown's claim to take (*as bona vacantia*) the half share to which D would have been entitled on intestacy had she not murdered T.[27]

If in this case T had died a natural death but D had disclaimed her interest under both T's will and T's intestacy, the disclaimer would have barred D from being counted as a member of the class of issue entitled on intestacy and again S would have been solely entitled to T's estate.[28]

(3)   *THE NEXT CLASS TAKES.* If all the members of the class of next-of-kin entitled under the intestacy rules are either disqualified by murder or manslaughter or barred by disclaimer, that class is disregarded and the next class of next-of-kin (of which there are members in existence capable of taking) is entitled.[29]

---

[27] But see pp. 563–565 where Vaisey J. stated that, but for case law authority, he would have decided that T's whole estate (or alternatively D's half share on intestacy) was undisposed of and passed to the Crown *as bona vacantia*.

[28] See *Re Scott* [1975] 1 W.L.R. 1260, 1270–1271.

[29] *Re Scott, supra* (brother and sister both disclaimed: next class of next of kin held entitled, not the Crown): see E.C. Ryder (1976) 40 Conv. (N.S.) 85.

CHAPTER 12

TAX

I. INTRODUCTION

This Chapter is not intended to be a detailed account of the various taxes which are, or may be, relevant in relation to Succession. It is merely intended as an outline—an attempt to explain the overall position, to enable the reader to understand how the principal taxes operate in this field and how they interact with one another.

1. Tax avoidance and tax evasion

It may be best to begin by referring to a question of terminology. In everyday English, the words "avoidance" and "evasion" mean approximately the same thing. But in the world of tax they have taken on different meanings. "Tax evasion" is an expression used to refer to conduct which is unlawful. Essentially, it consists in misleading the Revenue as to the facts, either by failing to disclose facts which should be disclosed or by making false disclosures. Failing to declare income which should be declared is tax evasion (evasion of income tax). Informing the Revenue that a deceased person's estate contains jewellery worth £1,000 when the true figure is £10,000 is also tax evasion (evasion—or attempted evasion—of inheritance tax). Tax avoidance is different. It does not consist in misleading the Revenue, it consists in organising the taxpayer's affairs in such a way that, by taking advantage of the tax rules, the taxpayer pays less tax.

Tax avoidance schemes vary in their complexity and sophistication. Some consist in taking advantage of rules which have clearly been inserted into the tax code to encourage taxpayers to act in particular ways. Others sometimes consist in taking advantage of errors made by the Revenue or by the government when tax legislation has been enacted. Some judges[1] have, in recent times, attempted to draw distinctions between "tax avoidance", "tax planning" and "tax mitigation". For the purposes of the present discussion, these distinctions will not be drawn.

---

[1] In particular, Lord Templeman who, in the recent capital transfer tax avoidance case of *Fitzwilliam v. I.R.C.* [1993] 1 W.L.R. 189 described what the taxpayers had done as "no better than attempts to cheat the Revenue" (at p. 1126). But Lord Templeman was dissenting and this does not seem to be the general view. If a distinction can be drawn between "tax avoidance", "tax mitigation" and "tax planning" the present writer would not be sure that he could adequately explain it.

The expression "tax avoidance" will be used to describe the lawful avoidance of tax—no moral, and no political, judgments are made or implied.

II. INHERITANCE TAX

When someone dies, his property will pass, *via* his personal representatives, to someone else. It may pass under his will or by the rules of intestacy and it may pass to one other person or to several other persons. The disposition of the deceased's property effected by the deceased's will or by the rules of intestacy may be altered by the court under the Family Provision legislation.[2]

1. Taxes on death may be of a mutation character or of an acquisition character

If on the death of a testator (or an intestate) his property passes to a number of beneficiaries, some of whom are members of his family and some of whom are not, such property could be charged to tax in one or other of two ways. It could be charged according to its total value, disregarding the way in which it is divided up between the beneficiaries; or it could be charged according to the value of the property acquired by each individual beneficiary. In the former case the tax may be said to be of a *mutation character* while in the latter it may be said to be of an acquisition character.[3] If the tax is a flat rate tax,[4] it will make no difference, but if it is a graduated tax, one where the percentage rate of tax rises as the sum involved gets bigger, it may be important. Suppose that a tax on death is graduated in such a way that the rate is 10 per cent on the first £10,000, 20 per cent on the next £10,000, 30 per cent on the next £10,000 and so on up to a maximum rate of 90 per cent. If the tax is calculated according to the total value of the property left by the deceased and he dies leaving an estate worth £100,000, it will make no difference whether he leaves all his property to one person, or whether he divides it between several members of his family. But if the tax is calculated according to the amount which passes to each beneficiary, it will effect a substantial reduction in tax if the estate is split.

This involves a question of social policy. Does a government want to encourage, does it want to discourage, or is it indifferent to, the splitting up of a deceased person's estate? There is a further, related, choice for those imposing the tax. If tax is to be charged on the beneficiary, rather than on the deceased, it can be imposed at different rates according to the relationship between the deceased and the beneficiary. In other words, there could be lower rates of tax for spouses or children than for beneficiaries who are either not members of, or are more remote mem-

---

[2] See Chap. 6.
[3] *Beattie's Elements of Estate Duty* (8th ed., 1974).
[4] A flat rate tax may also be described as a proportional tax—it is one where the amount paid is a fixed percentage, the percentage does *not* increase as the amount gets bigger.

bers of, the deceased's family. If would be perfectly feasible to adopt a system whereby, for example, a beneficiary paid standard tax on the basis of a relatively steep graduation *but* the deceased's brother or sister might pay half the standard tax, a descendant of the deceased might pay only a quarter of the standard tax and the deceased's spouse might pay a tenth of the standard tax, or possibly, might not pay at all.

There is then a further question. Should the tax be imposed only on property which passes on death or should it be imposed on lifetime gifts as well? It is generally easier for the Revenue to keep a record of property passing on death than it is for them to keep track of lifetime gifts; but if a tax is imposed only on property which passes on death, it will obviously be tempting to avoid the tax by making lifetime gifts.

2. Principal United Kingdom taxes on death have been of a mutation character

The principal United Kingdom taxes on property passing on death have all been, or have all essentially been, of a mutation and not of an acquisition character: they have been charged on the value of the total property passing from the deceased, disregarding how such property has been divided, or not divided, between the beneficiaries. This has certainly led to administrative simplicity. It is clearly easier for the Revenue to calculate and collect one sum of tax from the personal representatives than it is to calculate and collect a number of separate sums from a number of beneficiaries.

The principal United Kingdom tax on succession is now inheritance tax. Inheritance tax is a hybrid, a mixture of two earlier taxes; it is, therefore, easier to understand inheritance tax if something is said about these two earlier taxes.

(1) *ESTATE DUTY.* The main tax on death from 1894 until 1974–1975[5] was estate duty. It was introduced by the Finance Act 1894 and was payable on all property passing on death.[6]

It was a graduated tax levied at increasing rates on successive slices of the deceased's estate. The top rate on the top slice during the final years of estate duty was 75 per cent.

(2) *AVOIDANCE[7] OF ESTATE DUTY.* There was one simple way of avoiding estate duty and that was for the owner of property to dispose of it *inter vivos.* To overcome the problem of avoidance of the tax by deathbed gifts, rules were enacted to the effect that property given away less than a certain time before death would be treated as though made on death and so would be subject to tax. The time limit for this was gradually extended to seven years.[8] That meant that it was still possible to make an absolute gift of property, live for more than seven years and pay no tax at all, no matter how large the gift. But that led to further

---

[5] The changeover from estate duty to capital transfer tax took place over a period between 1974–1975 – it was not an abrupt or overnight change.

[6] It was subject to certain exceptions and modifications.

[7] For the meaning of "tax avoidance" see *supra.*

[8] At a reduced rate if the gift had been effected sometime before the death.

attempted avoidance and further anti-avoidance rules. Suppose someone were to give property to someone else, say his son, and were then to survive for more than seven years after the gift *but* were to benefit in some way from the use of the property *after* giving it away.

Suppose that someone aged 60 owned a house, the only substantial asset in his estate, and that he wanted to pass it on to his son when he died, but wanted to pay as little tax as possible. Suppose that he were to transfer the title to the house to his son while he was still alive but that he then continued to live in the house. If he survived for more than seven years there would, if there were no further anti-avoidance rules, be no tax payable on the house on his death. Provided relations between father and son were good, this was an easy way of avoiding the tax. So, again, rules were enacted to levy estate duty on death on the value of property which had been given away during the deceased's lifetime where the deceased had reserved a benefit in property which he had purported to give away.

Essentially, this is how estate duty operated. It taxed property which passed on death; property given away less than seven years before death; property given away more (or less) than seven years before death if the donor had reserved a benefit in the property. But it did not tax property given away more than seven years before a death if the deceased had reserved no benefit in it. In that sense it was an easy tax to avoid. And avoidance was made easier by the use of discretionary trusts. Property could be transferred into a discretionary trust by someone who had a life expectancy of more than seven years and, provided the settlor had no interest in the settlement, *i.e.* provided he could not benefit from the property he had settled,[9] no estate duty would be payable.[10] It is not hard to see why some people thought that estate duty was a voluntary tax.

(3) *CAPITAL TRANSFER TAX.* The Finance Act 1975[11] abolished estate duty and replaced it with capital transfer tax. It was a radical change. Like estate duty, capital transfer tax was a mutation tax *but* it was *not* a tax on property which passed on death. It was, instead, a tax on *transfers of value* and these included lifetime gifts, death transfers and transfers into settlements. Capital transfer tax was not estate duty with some sort of additional provision for taxing lifetime gifts, but a completely new tax.

As it was originally envisaged, capital transfer tax would have taxed life and death transfers at the same rate; but, by the time the tax was introduced, the original scheme had been modified and some lifetime transfers were taxed at a lower rate than death transfers. Nevertheless, capital transfer tax began life as a tax designed to tax both lifetime and death transfers and to ensure that there would be no substantial tax advantage in giving away property while the donor was alive. Under the estate duty regime, no tax was payable if someone made an absolute

---

[9] In which case he would have fallen foul of the reservation of benefit rules.

[10] There were special anti-avoidance rules for discretionary trusts during the last years of estate duty, but the details are beyond the scope of this account.

[11] Many major tax changes take place in the year after a general election, as 1975 was.

gift of property, with no reservation of benefit, and then survived seven years. Under the capital transfer tax regime, such a lifetime transfer was taxable—or rather, it was, in principle, subject to tax, whether tax would be payable would depend on the size of the transfer.

So, capital transfer tax was generally much harder to avoid than estate duty. But it was not harder to avoid in all circumstances. There were two ways in which capital transfer tax was an even more avoidable tax than estate duty had been. The first related to transfers between spouses. Under the capital transfer tax code, all transfers between spouses, whether lifetime transfers or transfers on death, were exempt from tax. The idea seems to have been that property should be subject to tax approximately once a generation, so it should be taxed as it passed from parents to children but not as it passed between husbands and wives. A husband could make an *inter vivos* gift of property to his wife, or she to him, and such gift would be tax free. Either could leave property to the other on death and that would be tax free too. The exemption carried no upper financial limit, the super rich could claim its full benefit.

The other way in which capital transfer tax was easier to avoid than estate duty had been, was in relation to reservation of benefit; there was no capital transfer tax rule forbidding reservation of benefit. Someone could, therefore, make an *inter vivos* gift of property in which he reserved a benefit, *i.e.* he could give his house to his son but could continue to live in it, and yet he would *not* be taxed on the gift when he died. The theory behind this approach was that it was not necessary to penalise reservations of benefit, because the donor who reserved a benefit in property he had given away would have paid tax on it at the time of the gift. There was no need to require him to pay tax when he died, because he would have paid tax earlier. This would have been perfectly logical if the donor had paid tax on the gift at the time it was made. The problem was that from the inception of capital transfer tax, some lifetime gifts had been subject to tax at different rates from property transferred on death and after 1979[12] the difference between the treatment of lifetime transfers and death transfers became more marked. Under the capital transfer tax regime which existed in the early 1980s, it was possible to make quite large lifetime transfers and to pay no tax. A transfer of the average family home presented no significant problem. So there was nothing to stop a 60-year-old parent from transferring his house to his child but continuing to live in it. That became, for a while, a reasonably easy way of avoiding tax on estates worth between £100,000 and £1,000,000—whether it always avoided family discord is another question.

Capital transfer tax had its own, rather complicated, regime for the taxation of discretionary trusts. Discretionary trusts had been used so effectively for avoiding estate duty that those who devised capital transfer tax were determined to put in place a regime which would ensure that the use of discretionary trusts for the avoidance of this tax would not be possible. The general idea behind the regime was to tax discretionary trusts at 10 yearly intervals at a special rate of tax designed to compensate for the fact that property settled on discretionary trusts would

---

[12] There was a change of government in 1979.

not, once it was settled, become subject to capital transfer tax in the ordinary way. Property not settled on discretionary trusts would, in theory and in the ordinary course of events, become subject to tax approximately once a generation, once every 30 years or so. So property settled on discretionary trusts was subjected to tax at about 30 per cent of the rate it would otherwise have paid—but this 30 per cent was paid once every 10 years. The system was simple in its outline but complicated in detail; the complications arose largely because capital transfer tax was originally a highly graduated tax and it was difficult to translate a system of graduation which applied to individual transferors to trusts and settlements which were treated as having some characteristics derived from their own settlors.

3. Inheritance tax

It was said above[13] that inheritance tax is a hybrid, a mixture of estate duty and capital transfer tax. The change over from estate duty to capital transfer tax had followed a general election and a change of government and was not a surprise.[14] But the changeover from capital transfer tax to inheritance tax followed neither a general election nor a change of government and *was* a surprise.[15] Capital transfer tax had been introduced by the Finance Act 1975 and had then been consolidated in the Capital Transfer Tax Act 1984. When inheritance tax was introduced, in 1986, its introduction did not even merit a fresh consolidation. The Capital Transfer Tax Act 1984 was renamed the Inheritance Tax Act 1984 (meaning that the consolidation act for inheritance tax is two years older than the tax itself) and the new tax was created largely by adding extra sections to the capital transfer tax consolidation to turn what had been capital transfer tax into something much more like estate duty. So inheritance tax has the *form* of capital transfer tax, its consolidation act is the amended capital transfer tax consolidation act, but its substance is more the substance of estate duty.

4. Inheritance tax combines the form of capital transfer tax with the substance of estate duty

The principal difference between estate duty and capital transfer tax was that estate duty taxed any property passing on death whereas capital transfer tax taxed transfers of value. Inheritance tax, the hybrid tax, continues to tax transfers of value, just as capital transfer tax did, *but* it then

---

[13] *Ante* p. 269.
[14] Most major tax changes follow elections—capital transfer tax was introduced in 1975, the year after a general election; capital gains tax (see below) was introduced in 1965, the year after a general election. *Or* they occur because there is an identifiable need to raise extra finance. Estate duty was introduced to pay for extra spending on the navy. Gladstone finally resigned as Prime Minister in 1894 because he did not wish to be associated with the policy. He liked neither military expenditure nor raising taxes.
[15] Days before the budget speech in which the Chancellor of the Exchequer announced that he was abolishing capital transfer tax and replacing it with inheritance tax, there were newspaper advertisements placed by organisations selling life assurance policies to the effect that "CTT is here to stay".

exempts most lifetime transfers. That is how it retains the form of capital transfer tax but with the substance of estate duty.

Even calling the tax "inheritance tax" is confusing. The term "inheritance tax" implies a tax of an *acquisition* character, but this tax is *not* of an acquisition character. When the United Kingdom joined what was then called the European Economic Community (now the European Union) in the early 1970s, consideration was given to scrapping estate duty and to replacing it with an acquisition tax which would have been called "inheritance tax."[16] EEC countries generally favoured acquisition taxes. This is not the place to comment on whether the introduction of an acquisition tax to replace estate duty would or would not have been a good idea, but it is confusing to use the same name for a mutation tax as had earlier been proposed for an acquisition tax. But it is not just the name of the tax which is confusing; because the tax retains the form of capital transfer tax, it also retains its terminology.

5. Transfers on death under inheritance tax

Inheritance tax, like capital transfer tax, taxes transfers of value[17] and the principal charging section for the tax is Section 4 which covers transfers on death. It provides that:

"(1) On the death of any person tax shall be charged as if, immediately before his death, he had made a transfer of value and the value transferred by it had been equal to the value of his estate immediately before his death."

Section 4(2) makes it clear that no tax will be payable as between *commorientes*:

"(2) For the purposes of this section, where it cannot be known which of two or more persons who have died survived the other or others they shall be assumed to have died at the same instant."

So if a parent and child die together in circumstances where it cannot be known who survived whom, the child will, as a question of Succession, be deemed to have survived the parent,[18] but no inheritance tax will be payable on the child's death on property which has passed from the parent to the child.

6. Lifetime gifts under inheritance tax; potentially exempt transfers

To return to the (odd) terminology, the section which now exempts most lifetime gifts from inheritance tax is the Inheritance Tax Act section 3A[19] which states that *potentially exempt transfers* shall not be taxable. A potentially exempt transfer is an *inter vivos* transfer, a lifetime gift, made

---

[16] See "Taxation of Capital on Death: a possible Inheritance Tax in place of Estate Duty" Cmnd. 4934 (1972).

[17] Inheritance Tax Act s. 1, 2 and 3.

[18] L.P.A. s. 184, see Chap. 11, pp. 237–239.

[19] Inserted into the 1984 Act in 1986.

by an individual after March 18, 1986[20] to another individual or to certain favoured trusts.[21] If the donor dies within seven years of the gift, it becomes chargeable to tax, just as it would have done under the estate duty regime. The expression *potentially exempt transfer* is really a misnomer because it is not a potentially exempt transfer. It is a transfer which is exempt from the tax but which may become chargeable *if* the donor dies within the relevant timescale. It would be better described not as a *potentially exempt transfer*, which is what the legislation calls it, but a *potentially chargeable transfer* which is what it really is.[22]

7. Gifts subject to reservation of benefit under the inheritance tax regime

Because inheritance tax reintroduced the principle that a lifetime gift would normally be tax free, it had also to reintroduce the rule that a lifetime gift subject to reservation of benefit would be taxable on the donor's death. Such a rule follows on inevitably from the scheme of exempting lifetime gifts from inheritance tax.[23] So, inheritance tax has the form of capital transfer tax but the substance of estate duty, it taxes transfers on death, it does not, generally tax *inter vivos* transfers, though it does tax, *inter vivos* transfers where the donor has reserved a benefit. Inheritance tax has, however, in addition to its form, retained two substantive rules, or sets of rules, from capital transfer tax. One set of rules retained by inheritance tax from capital transfer tax is concerned with the taxation of discretionary trusts, but the other, and arguably more important rule retained by inheritance tax from capital transfer tax, covers transfers between spouses. Under the estate duty regime, transfers between spouses were taxable, unless they were made more than seven years before the transferor's death. Under capital transfer tax, transfers between spouses, whether *inter vivos* or on death, were tax exempt and they *remain* tax exempt for inheritance tax.[24]

8. Inter-spouse transfers under inheritance tax

Looked at from the viewpoint of the potential taxpayer, inheritance tax combines the estate duty advantage of not taxing lifetime gifts with the capital transfer tax advantage of not taxing inter-spouse transfers. The exemption for inter-spouse transfers is central to much inheritance

---

[20] March 18, 1986 was Budget Day—the day on which the introduction of inheritance tax was announced.

[21] But not to discretionary trusts—see below.

[22] See *Butterworths UK Tax Guide* 37:04. Another condition of being a potentially exempt transfer is that the transfer must not otherwise be exempt. A gift which would be exempt anyway, for example a gift to a spouse or to a charity (see below) cannot be classified as potentially exempt. But the legislation would have been easier to follow if potentially exempt transfers had been called potentially chargeable transfers—then a simple rule could have been enacted that no exempt transfer could become chargeable. The way the rules are set out makes the scheme of the tax *seem* much more complicated than it really is.

[23] Gifts subject to reservation of benefit are dealt with in Finance Act 1986 s. 102 and Sched. 20.

[24] I.H.T.A. s. 18.

tax planning. Anyone who drafts a will for a married man or woman *must* take account of the effect of this exemption.

The point may be made clearer by an example. Suppose that someone dies leaving a will in which he devises and bequeaths most of his property to his wife, his children and his grandchildren. So that the example may remain simple, let it be supposed that he had made no gifts within seven years of his death[25] and that on his death his estate is worth approximately £308,000. Inheritance tax, like estate duty and capital transfer tax before it, is a graduated tax. No tax is payable on the first "slice" of the testator's or intestate's property, which is known as the nil-rate band. Tax then becomes payable. Before 1988 it was payable at different rates on different slices; the larger the estate, the higher the rate. When estate duty was first introduced there were 12 rate bands and by the mid-1930s this had risen to 33 rate bands[26] but in recent years the number of rate bands has gradually decreased and since 1988 there has only been one rate—40 percent.[27] So there is now a nil-rate band, currently £154,000,[28] followed by one rate of tax, which is 40 percent. This has the advantage (for lawyers) of making the calculation relatively easy.

Suppose the testator in the example leaves all his property, worth £308,000 in total, to his children and grandchildren. Tax will be payable. No tax will be payable on the first £154,000—nil-rate band, but then tax will be payable at 40 percent on £154,000, *i.e.* £61,600. Had he left his estate to his widow, he would have paid no tax at all. That makes it look as though he should, to save tax, have left all his property to his widow. Nevertheless, leaving the testator's entire estate to the widow would not necessarily effect a long-term tax saving. There would be no tax payable on the testator's death *but*, if the widow were later to die owning property worth £308,000,[29] tax of £61,600 would then be payable on *her* death. So far so bad. Can anything be done? Of course. There are two escape routes. The first, the simpler, is for the testator to leave property to the value of the nil-rate band, £154,000, to his children and grandchildren and the residue to his widow. No tax will be payable on the testator's death. If his widow has no other property, she can die and if her estate does not exceed the nil-rate band, she pays no tax either. *Or*, the testator can leave more than £154,000 to his widow on the assumption that she will make lifetime gifts to the children and grandchildren more than seven years before her own death. The risk involved in this is that the widow may miscalculate her own life expectancy.

This is only a very simple introduction to planning for inheritance tax but it gives the succession student a flavour. In the example just given, the family can save £61,600 tax on a £308,000 estate, a 20 per cent average rate, simply by arranging how the property passes.

---

[25] If he had made any exempt transfers, they would not count anyway—for a further discussion of exempt tranfers see below.

[26] See *Oxford History of England, Vol XIV* p. 218 n. 1.

[27] There has been only one rate (40 per cent) since 1988. The width of the nil-rate band is index-linked (Inheritance Tax Act 1984 s. 8(4)) but this may be overridden by a Finance Act, as it was, for example, by F.A. 1994 s. 246.

[28] £154,000 is the nil-rate band for the tax year 1995–96. *i.e.* starting on April 6, 1995.

[29] The example assumes the widow has no property of her own, which is unlikely, but it keeps the example simple.

9. Other inheritance tax exemptions

The spouse exemption is not the only exemption from the tax. There are number of other exemptions which operate both for *inter vivos* and death transfers, including transfers to charities,[30] to political parties,[31], for national purposes,[32] and for public benefit.[33] There are then a number of exemptions which operate only for lifetime transfers; these include the annual exemption,[34] the small gifts exemption[35] and the exemption for gifts in consideration of marriage.[36] The exemptions for *inter vivos* transfers are less important under inheritance tax than they were under capital transfer tax because most *inter vivos* gifts will be potentially exempt transfers and so will end up by being exempt from the tax in any case. *But* if an *inter vivos* transfer is covered by an exemption, say the exemption for gifts made in consideration of marriage,[37] the gift will not become taxable even if the transferor dies within seven years.

10. Inheritance tax reliefs

In addition to the *exemptions*, there are *reliefs* from inheritance tax. The technical distinction between exemptions and reliefs is that *exemptions* depend on the identity of the transferor or the transferee – for example the inter-spouse exemption – whereas *reliefs* depend on the nature of the property being transferred. Where exemptions apply, no tax is payable. Where a relief applies, it may be that tax remains payable, but that the amount payable is reduced by a percentage. Having said this, some reliefs now operate at 100 per cent, and a 100 per cent relief may operate in much the same way as an exemption.

(1) *AGRICULTURAL RELIEF AND BUSINESS RELIEF.* The two most important reliefs are the relief for agricultural property[38] and the relief for business property.[39] A working farmer will be entitled to 100 per cent relief on the *agricultural value* of his farm. The relief will not apply if the value of the farm reflects something other than its agricultural value, *e.g.* development potential. An agricultural landlord – as opposed to a working farmer – is entitled to a 50 per cent relief.[40] Owners of relevant business property where the business is a qualifying business, are also entitled to a 100 per cent relief. The 100 per cent relief goes to sole traders, partners, shareholders who control companies *via* unquoted shares and some other shareholders with substantial holdings of

---

[30] s. 23.
[31] s. 24.
[32] s. 25.
[33] s. 26.
[34] s. 19.
[35] s. 20.
[36] I.H.T.A. s. 22.
[37] The exemption for gifts made in consideration of marriage covers, for example, a gift of up to £2,500 made by a parent of a party to the marriage; if there are four living parents they can, between them, make exempt transfers totalling £10,000.
[38] I.H.T.A. ss. 115–124.
[39] I.H.T.A. ss. 103–114.
[40] This is a simplified account – but it is the essential position.

unquoted shares.[41] Those with smaller holdings of unquoted shares and with controlling holdings of quoted shares may be entitled to a 50 per cent relief.[42]

(2) *WOODLANDS AND WORKS OF ART*. There is also a woodlands relief[43] and a works of art and historic buildings relief.[44]

(3) *USE OF THE RELIEFS*. It is, of course, important for someone drafting a will to try to take advantage of these reliefs. It is not generally good tax planning to bequeath a farm to the testator's widow while at the same time devising property which would not be eligible for any relief to his children. Given that any transfer to the widow will be exempt anyway, it is, in tax planning terms, wasteful to give her something also covered by a 100 per cent relief. Imagine the case of a working farmer entitled to 100 per cent relief who is also a partner in a qualifying business,[45] (maybe a business breeding racehorses) and who *also* has a flat in London and some cash in the bank. It will save tax if the farm and the interest in the business are left to the children while the flat and the cash go to the widow. On the supposition that he has made no potentially exempt transfers within the seven years before he dies, it would be possible to pass property to the value of the nil-rate band, plus any property covered by a 100 per cent relief, to persons other than his widow and still pay no tax at all.

There may be all sorts of non-tax reasons for not arranging things in the most tax-effective way. But it would be foolish (and possibly negligent for a professional adviser) not to consider the tax implications of the deceased's dispositions.

11. Payment of inheritance tax—accountability and incidence

Two questions arise in relation to the payment of inheritance tax. First of all, who is responsible for accounting to the Revenue—*i.e.* making payment—for the tax which is due? Second, on whom will the ultimate burden of the tax fall?

The simplest case, the usual case, is that of a person who dies domiciled in the United Kingdom. Inheritance tax is then chargeable on all the property comprised in his estate—it does not matter where such property is situated. If he was not domiciled in the United Kingdom, inheritance tax will be chargeable only on property which *is* situated in the United Kingdom.

Let it be supposed that someone dies domiciled in the United King-

---

[41] 25 per cent may be enough, but there are conditions – see I.H.T.A. s. 105(1A).
[42] The 50 per cent relief may also apply to land, buildings, machinery or plant used for the purposes of a business carried on by a company controlled by the transferor or by a partnership of which he was a partner.
[43] I.H.T.A. ss. 125–130.
[44] In the legislation, the works of art and historical buildings relief is described as a "conditional exemption", I.H.T.A. ss. 30–35, but it operates in very much the same way as the woodlands relief and it would probably be better to describe it as a 100 per cent relief. This all goes to highlight the blurring of the distinction between exemptions and reliefs.
[45] The sort of "business" which will not qualify will be one whose purpose is basically investment.

dom, having made no potentially exempt transfers within the seven years before his death and leaving an estate which exceeds the nil-rate band—this assumes that it exceeds the band after taking account of exempt transfers, they can be ignored, and after taking account of reliefs. Property subject to a 100 per cent relief drops out of account, property subject to a 50 per cent relief is reduced in value before calculating the tax.[46] Let it be supposed that *after* taking account of exemptions and reliefs, the testator has left an estate worth £254,000. Tax will then be payable at 40 per cent on the amount by which it exceeds the nil-rate— band, *i.e.* 40 per cent (£254,000—£154,000 =) £100,000 = £40,000. The responsibility for accounting to the Revenue for this tax on the deceased's free estate in the United Kingdom lies on the personal representatives.[47] Tax has to be paid within six months of the death and, in practice, the personal representatives will need to pay quickly because they must deliver an account and pay the tax *before* they can obtain probate or letters of administration. This means that they must raise the money to pay the tax *before* they can sell any of the deceased's property.[48] In practice, they will borrow the money from a bank or other institution; the interest payable on the borrowing is deductible for income tax purposes.[49]

When the tax has been paid by the personal representatives, the question then arises as to the person upon whom the ultimate burden falls. This should be provided for in the will. If the will makes no provision, tax is treated as part of the general testamentary and administration expenses of the estate[50] and will be payable from residue.[51] This may *not* be what the testator would have wanted, which is why it is preferable that the will should make express provision. A particular danger is that a gift of the residue of an estate to a widow (itself exempt from tax) may be reduced by the tax payable on a specific bequest to someone else. It is usually best to stipulate in a will that a specific bequest bears its own tax. The size of the bequest can be adjusted, at the time when the will is drafted, to take account of the tax which is likely to be paid.[52]

The liability for tax on a potentially exempt transfer, which becomes chargeable because the testator dies within seven years, falls on the donee *both* as a question of accountability[53] and incidence, although the Revenue may be able to recover tax from the personal representatives if they cannot obtain it from the donee.[54] Donees are also liable for tax on gifts subject to reservation. Trustees are generally liable for tax on trusts.[55]

---

[46] Because the 50 per cent relief reduces the value of the transfer.
[47] I.H.T.A. s. 200.
[48] They will need to obtain probate or letters of administration in order to sell.
[49] See below.
[50] I.H.T.A. s. 211.
[51] See Chap. 17 pp. 433 *et seq.* and 420 *et seq.*
[52] The calculation of the tax, made at the time when the will is drafted, may well prove to be out of line with the tax payable at the time of death—but stipulating that specific bequests bear their own tax obviates the risk that the residue is all swallowed up in tax.
[53] I.H.T.A. s. 216.
[54] I.H.T.A. s. 199.
[55] I.H.T.A. s. 201. When a discretionary trust is *created* during the settlor's life, this is *not* a potentially exempt transfer but is a lifetime chargeable transfer—as under capital trans-

III.   CAPITAL GAINS TAX

1.   Outline of capital gains tax

Capital gains tax was introduced in 1965.[1] It is designed to levy tax on profit-making transactions which are somehow not covered by income tax. Someone who is a trader, say a shopkeeper, pays income tax on his trading profits, but someone who cannot be designated as trading for income tax purposes, but who is engaged in profit-making transactions, used to escape tax altogether—before capital gains tax was enacted. Before 1965, someone who bought and sold shares and who made a profit on the buying and selling, or who bought and sold land and who made a profit on the buying and selling, would generally escape tax altogether, unless he could be designated as trading for the purposes of income tax. Capital gains tax was designed to close the gap, but it does it by throwing its net wide. It covers "chargeable gains . . . accruing to a person on the disposal of assets".[2] So it will cover profits made by buying and selling shares or land but it will also cover many other transactions. Nevertheless, there are a number of exemptions and reliefs from the tax and the effect of these exemptions and reliefs is that most transactions subject to capital gains tax will probably relate to shares, commercial land, businesses or farms. There are exemptions or reliefs which cover owner occupied housing,[3] chattels worth less than £6,000,[4] ordinary motor cars[5] and debts.[6] It has to be said that some of these exemptions and reliefs appear to have been included in the capital gains tax regime with the primary object of ensuring that transactions which are likely to be loss-making will not be subject to tax; *i.e.* to disallow potential losses[7] and so to benefit the Revenue. But the effect is that transactions in shares, commercial land, businesses and farms are the ones likely to attract liability to capital gains tax. There is also a capital gains tax retirement relief which may relieve all or a large part of the gain on a business if it is disposed of on the owner's retirement.[8]

2.   Capital gains tax and death

When capital gains tax was first introduced, in 1965, *disposals*, for the purposes of the tax, consisted of sales, gifts and *death*. Capital gains tax

---

fer tax. In this case, the *settlor* is primarily liable for the tax (I.H.T.A. s. 119(1)) but this is outside the scope of this work.

[1] It *was*, like capital transfer tax, introduced in the year following a general election.

[2] Taxation of Chargeable Gains Act 1992 s. 1—the T.C.G.A. 1992 is the latest capital gains tax consolidation.

[3] T.C.G.A. ss. 222–226.

[4] s. 262.

[5] s. 263.

[6] ss. 251–255.

[7] Chattels worth less than £6,000, ordinary motor cars and debts are *all* likely to be loss makers. Owner occupied housing was probably exempted from the tax, in 1965, with a view to ensuring that the tax was acceptable to the middle class voter—political prudence.

[8] T.C.G.A. ss. 163, 164 and Sched 6. This was not inserted into the tax regime to benefit the Revenue.

was chargeable at a flat rate, 30 per cent, and there was no relief for inflation.[9] So if, for example, someone bought some shares for £20,000 and later sold them for £30,000 he would pay tax at 30 per cent on the paper gain—taking no account of inflation. He would be liable to pay tax of £3,000.[10] And it would have been the same if he gave the shares away, or if he died. Sales, gifts and deaths were all disposals; all attracted tax. If capital gains tax were payable on someone's death, it would be paid before calculating the value of the estate for estate duty purposes (estate duty being the death duty then payable) and the amount of capital gains tax payable would be deducted from the estate in calculating its net worth for estate duty. So, if someone died with an estate worth £100,000, but his death meant that there was a £3,000 capital gains tax liability, the capital gains tax would be paid first and estate duty would then be levied on an estate of 97,000. It was suggested by some that this was a form of double taxation; the point is arguable, it could be said that the two taxes were taxing different things. Whether this was, or was not, a form of double taxation; the rules were changed in 1971[11] and, since 1971, death has no longer been a chargeable event for capital gains tax purposes. Death is not ignored for capital gains tax purposes—not at all. Since 1971, death gives a capital gains tax uplift. All gains made by the deceased before he died are freed from tax and the deceased's assets are revalued at his death, so that any future gains are calculated only as from death. The way that this is effected, technically, is by enacting that the personal representatives shall be deemed to have acquired the deceased's assets on his death, for their then market value, *but* that the deceased shall *not* be deemed to have disposed of such assets. There is no disposal and so no liability to tax, but there is an acquisition so there is a new base price. The tax jargon for this is "washing".

The governing section is section 62 of the Taxation of Chargeable Gains Act 1992.

62. Death: general provisions

(1) For the purposes of this Act the assets of which a deceased person was competent to dispose—
  (a) shall be deemed to be acquired on his death by the personal representatives or other person on whom they devolve for a consideration equal to their market value at the date of the death, but
  (b) shall not be deemed to be disposed of by him on his death (whether or not they were the subject of a testamentary disposition).
  . . .
(3) In relation to property forming part of the estate of a deceased person the personal representatives shall for the purposes of this

---

[9] There was a rule whereby small gains made in any one tax year might be wholly or partly relieved from tax.
[10] 30 per cent of (£30,000–£20,000 =) £10,000 is £3,000. There was *no* relief for inflation—the gain might have been entirely due to inflation.
[11] Which *was*, again, the year after a general election.

Act be treated as being a single and continuing body of persons
. . .

(4) On a person acquiring any asset as legatee (as defined in section
64)—

    (a) no chargeable gain shall accrue to the personal representatives, and

    (b) the legatee shall be treated as if the personal representatives' acquisition of the asset had been his acquisition of it.

(5) . . . no chargeable gain shall accrue to any person on his making
a disposal by way of donatio mortis causa.
. . .

(10) In this section references to assets of which a deceased person was
competent to dispose are references to assets of the deceased which
(otherwise than in right of a power of appointment or of the testamentary power conferred by statute to dispose of entailed interest)
he could, if of full age and capacity, have disposed of by his will,
assuming that all the assets were situated in England and, if he
was not domiciled in the United Kingdom, that he was domiciled
in England, and include references to his severable share in any
assets to which, immediately before his death, he was beneficially
entitled as a joint tenant.

The section covers property owned by the deceased and devised or
bequeathed under his will[12]; property which passes on intestacy[13]; property passing by *donatio mortis causa*[14]; property passing on the death of
a joint tenant by survivorship[15]; and property of which the deceased was
able to dispose under a general testamentary power of appointment.[16]

Let us return to the earlier example. Suppose that someone owns property which he bought for £20,000 and which he sells or gives away when
it is worth £30,000; he will prima facie be liable to tax on a gain of
£10,000. If, however, he dies owning the property, there will be no liability to tax, actual or potential; the property will be revalued to its value
at death but there will be no tax liability. So, if the owner of the property
wants to pass it to a member of his family, he will save capital gains tax
by passing it on his death rather than by making an *inter vivos* gift. For
capital gains tax purposes, the passing of the property from the personal
representatives to the beneficiary under the will or intestacy is ignored,[17]
and the beneficiary is deemed to have acquired the property from the
deceased at his death and at its value at the death.

3. Interrelationship between inheritance tax and capital gains tax on death

The negative aspect of escaping capital gains tax on death is that it
seems that the owner of the property will be liable to inheritance tax

---

[12] T.C.G.A. 1992 s. 62(1)(*b*).
[13] T.C.G.A. 1992 s. 62(1)(*b*).
[14] T.C.G.A. 1992 s. 62(5).
[15] T.C.G.A. 1992 S. 62(10).
[16] Whether or nor he *did* so dispose of it – T.C.G.A. 1992 s. 62(10).
[17] T.C.G.A. 1992 s. 62(4).

instead. If that is so, it will seem to be an unattractive exchange. If there is a choice between paying one or other of the two taxes, inheritance tax would seem to be the less attractive option because, disregarding any difference in tax rates, inheritance tax is effectively levied on the *total* value of the property transferred whereas capital gains tax is only levied on any increase in its value since the date of acquisition.

But, does escaping capital gains tax necessarily mean falling into the inheritance tax net? Those who, in 1971, were responsible for enacting the rule that capital gains would be "washed" on death probably assumed that escaping capital gains tax meant paying estate duty instead, and they probably assumed that estate duty was likely to be a heavier imposition than capital gains tax; so they assumed that no tax-payer would *gain* by holding onto property until death rather than giving it away during his lifetime. Generally that was correct, at the time. The only substantial qualification was that someone might die leaving an estate so small that the estate would not be liable to pay estate duty *yet* the deceased might own assets which would have been liable to capital gains tax if the capital gains had not been washed. This could have occurred, but it would not have occurred often, because taxpayers liable to capital gains tax would generally have had, and will still generally have, substantial estates. Capital gains tax has always been a tax paid by the rich or the relatively rich.[18] A taxpayer who was liable to capital gains tax was likely to have had an estate large enough to be liable to estate duty.

That is, however, not the end of the story, which contains an historical twist. When estate duty was replaced by capital transfer tax, capital transfer tax contained an exemption for transfers to the transferor's spouse and this exemption applied both to *inter vivos* transfers and to transfers on death. As explained above, it still applies under the inheritance tax regime, under the hybrid tax. So consider now how capital gains tax and inheritance tax inter-relate. The system appears to have lost all logic. It is possible to pay *one* tax, or the *other* tax, or *both* taxes or *neither* tax. Consider the following possibilities as the rules apply today, under the capital gains tax and inheritance tax regimes. If someone makes an *inter vivos* transfer more than seven years before he dies, with no reservation of benefit, there will be a capital gains tax liability at the time of the gift but no liability to inheritance tax, either at the time of the gift or at the time of death. If someone dies leaving property which passes to his children (under his will, or by way of *donatio mortis causa*, or under the intestacy rules) such property will be subject to inheritance tax but any capital gains on such property will be washed on the death—there will be no capital gains tax liability. So, in the two above mentioned cases one tax *or* the other is payable. How can *both* taxes become payable? They can both become payable if there is a lifetime gift, subject to capital gains tax, followed by the donor's death within seven years. They can both become payable if there is a lifetime gift, subject to capital gains tax, and the donor reserves a benefit in the gift. Reservation of benefit

---

[18] That is largely because of the operation of the reliefs and exemptions, see above, it does not cover owner occupied housing, it tends to cover assets owned by the (relatively) rich.

is to be *avoided*.[19] How can it be arranged that *neither* tax is payable? It can be arranged by transferring an asset to the owner's spouse on death. There will be a capital gains tax uplift combined with an inheritance tax exemption. And since 1992, there has been the same effect where property which is subject to the 100% (inheritance tax) business or agricultural property relief is transferred on death, in this case it does not matter to whom the property is transferred.

4. Planning to avoid a double tax charge

There are two very simple tax-planning rules to be followed when considering the inter-relationship between capital gains tax and inheritance tax. First, avoid reservation of benefit because it leads to a double tax charge.[20] Secondly, attempt to ensure that assets which are likely to attract a liability to capital gains tax, *i.e.* those which have shown substantial increases in value since they were acquired, are retained until the owner's death. They need not necessarily attract a liability to inheritance tax because they may be covered by the spouse exemption, business relief, agricultural relief or the nil-rate-band. Assets given away during the donor's lifetime should *generally* be those which are not going to be subject to capital gains tax, either because they are covered by capital gains tax reliefs or exemptions (*e.g.* owner-occupied houses) or because they have not shown gains which will attract the tax.

5. Allowing for inflation when computing capital gains and calculating the rate of tax

Capital gains tax was originally imposed as a flat rate tax at 30 per cent on paper gains making no allowance for inflation. In 1982, a partial allowance was given for inflation. The rules relating to the effect of inflation on gains were remodelled in 1988, so that, since 1988, only gains made since 1982 have generally been liable to capital gains tax *and*, in calculating these gains, inflation since 1982, or since the date of acquisition if later, is allowed for. So if, for example, someone acquired a block of shares (a chargeable asset for the purposes of capital gains tax) in 1975 and the block of shares was worth £10,000 at the time of acquisition, £20,000 in 1982 and £40,000 in 1995 the capital gains tax calculation, if the shares are disposed of in 1995, will be as follows. The gain will be the difference between the 1982 value and the 1995 value but allowing for inflation between 1982 and 1995. The allowance for inflation is achieved by indexing the acquisition cost (or 1982 value, in the case of an asset acquired before 1982)[21] the indexation from 1982 to 1995 will be approximately 85 per cent.[22] This means that the acquisition cost for capital gains tax purposes will be £20,000 × 185% = £37,000; and the charge-

---

[19] See below under **VI Tax Planning**.

[20] It is generally more difficult to plan that someone shall *not* die within seven years of a gift, though there may be some cases where the donor's death within a short time of a gift is so probable that the making of the gift is almost an invitation to a double tax charge.

[21] T.G.C.A. ss. 53–57.

[22] There are, of course, detailed rules for calculating the indexation.

able gain will be £40,000 – £37,000 = £3,000. The post-1988 calculation for capital gains tax generally gives a much smaller gain than the pre-1988 calculation.[23] An *individual* taxpayer (*i.e.* one who is not a personal representative and not a trustee) is then entitled to an annual exempt amount on which he pays no tax.[24] This now (tax year 1995–96) stands at £6,000.[25] So if his net gains are less than £6,000, he will pay no tax and if they exceed £6,000 he pays tax only on the excess over £6,000. If, for example, his net gains are £10,000 he will pay tax on £4,000.

The rate of tax for an *individual* will then, since 1988, be his *marginal rate of income tax, i.e.* effectively the top rate at which he pays income tax. For most capital gains tax payers that will be the top rate of income tax, *i.e.* 40 per cent.[26]

6. Payment of capital gains tax by personal representatives

For personal representatives the rules are different. The assets they acquire from the deceased are washed at the deceased's death, so there is no capital gains tax liability to the point of death. If an asset is then handed over to a "legatee" (which, for capital gains tax purposes, means a beneficiary under the deceased's will or his intestacy)[27] the legatee is deemed to have acquired the asset at death and no tax is payable at the time of the transfer from the personal representatives to the legatee. The legatee is deemed to have acquired the asset at the time of the death and at the value at death. *But* if the personal representatives sell assets in order to raise money to pay debts, or to pay pecuniary legacies, they will be liable to pay capital gains tax, *but* only on the basis of gains made since the death (and allowing for inflation); *and* they are entitled to an annual exempt amount for the year of death and for the next two tax years—*i.e.* £6,000 worth of tax free gains for three years.[28] If they pay tax, they pay tax at a rate equivalent to the basic rate of income tax, *i.e.* 25 per cent—not 40 per cent. So it may not be bad tax planning for the personal representatives to realise assets by selling them over approximately a three-year period *provided* such assets have risen in value by more than inflation since the deceased's death. This may even give some personal representatives an excuse for delay in winding up an estate.

7. Personal representatives and bare trustees

A last point. There may sometimes be a dispute about the capacity in which personal representatives dispose of assets. Were they acting as personal representatives or as "bare trustees"? The Scottish case of *Cochrane*[29] seems to say that in case of doubt they will be treated as disposing of assets as personal representatives. On the whole, the advantage

---

[23] Though, since 1994, indexation relief cannot turn a gain into a loss—F.A. 1994 s. 93.
[24] T.C.G.A. 1992 s. 3.
[25] It is normally adjusted each year, in line with inflation.
[26] For income tax rates—see below.
[27] Taxation of Chargeable Gains Act 1992 s. 64(2).
[28] "Years" in this context means income tax years not calendar years—the income tax year runs from April 6 to April 5.
[29] *Cochrane v. IRC* (1974) 49 T.C. 299.

lies with the personal representatives. Suppose that the deceased owned shares which have gained considerably in value since the death and some of these shares could be sold to pay debts or pecuniary legacies, or could be appropriated to legatees in satisfaction of their entitlement under the deceased's will or intestacy. The personal representatives can calculate how many shares to sell to use up their annual exempt amount or they can appropriate shares to beneficiaries who are unlikely to dispose of them until their own deaths or who will dispose of them in dribs and drabs, so utilising their annual exemptions. Flexibility is an advantage.

IV. POST DEATH VARIATIONS

An important form of flexibility for the tax planner is to be able to vary dispositions after a death and to backdate the variations so that they are deemed to have been effected at the time of the death—by the deceased. Such variations *are* permitted both for inheritance tax and for capital gains tax, but not for income tax.

1. Inheritance tax variations

If someone dies leaving a will which gives approximately half his estate to his widow and the other half to his children, this may or may not have the effect of minimising his potential liability to inheritance tax; it depends on the size of the estate. On the assumption that he made no transfers in the last seven years of his life and that none of his property is covered by reliefs,[1] the best way to save tax (tax saving being, of course, only one consideration among many) would be to leave property to the value of the nil-rate band, currently £154,000, to his children, and the residue to his wife. If he were to leave a will giving his wife half his property, this might be too much if the estate were small, or too little if it were large. Section 142 of the Inheritance Tax Act[2] allows the beneficiaries to alter the size of their shares after the death; and the variation is then treated, for inheritance tax purposes, as if it had been the deceased's original disposition.

142. Alteration of dispositions taking effect on death

(1) Where within the period of two years after a person's death—
    (a) any of the dispositions (whether effected by will, under the law relating to intestacy or otherwise) of the property comprised in his estate immediately before his death are varied, or
    (b) the benefit conferred by any of those dispositions is disclaimed,
    by an instrument in writing made by the persons or any of the persons who benefit or would benefit under the dispositions, this

---

[1] Agricultural and business property reliefs.
[2] Combined with s. 17.

Act shall apply as if the variation had been effected by the deceased or, as the case may be, the disclaimed benefit had never been conferred.

(2) Subsection (1) above shall not apply to a variation unless an election to that effect is made by written notice given to the Board within six months after the date of the instrument. . .by—

(a) the person or persons making the instrument, and

(b) where the variation results in additional tax being payable, the personal representatives;

but personal representatives may decline to join in an election only if no, or no sufficient, assets are held by them in that capacity for discharging the additional tax.

(3) Subsection (1) above shall not apply to a variation or disclaimer made for any consideration in money or money's worth other than consideration consisting of the making, in respect of another of the dispositions, of a variation or disclaimer to which that subsection applies.

(4) . . .

(5) . . .

(6) Subsection (1) above applies whether or not the administration of the estate is complete or the property concerned has been distributed in accordance with the original dispositions.

Under the provisions of Section 142 the original beneficiaries must *agree* to any change; so if someone is, as a result of a variation, to receive a smaller share of the deceased's estate, that person has to consent. An instrument in writing must be made within two years of the death, and notice of it must be given to the Board (of the Inland Revenue) within six months.[3]

The sort of case where Section 142 is particularly useful is one where, for example, the widow is given what, in inheritance tax terms, is too large a share of the deceased's estate. She may, within two years of the deceased's death, calculate her needs and decide to give the children some property which passed to her under her husband's will or intestacy. She could, as an alternative, transfer property by way of a potentially exempt transfer, but this could result in an inheritance tax charge if she were to fail to survive for seven years; it is a less satisfactory way of proceeding.[4]

Section 143 is a variation on the theme of section 142

143. Compliance with testator's request

Where a testator expresses a wish that property bequeathed by his will should be transferred by the legatee to other persons, and the legatee transfers any of the property in accordance with that wish within the period of two years after the death of the testator, this Act shall have effect as if the property transferred had been bequeathed by the will to the transferee.

[3] There is no need for notice in the case of a *disclaimer* as opposed to a *variation*.
[4] There is also the danger that the law may change.

More significant is section 144 which provides that a distribution from a testamentary discretionary trust within two years of the testator's death will be treated as though it had been made under the testator's will. So the testator can leave his trustees to decide how best to dispose of his property, taking into account the competing claims of the widow and children and all other considerations, including fiscal ones. Some trustees may think that this imposes too great a burden upon them and may be unwilling to act as the trustees of such a discretionary trust unless they have reasonably clear instructions from the testator as to how he would expect them to act in given circumstances.[5]

The next two sections in this part of the inheritance tax consolidation are closely linked with topics ordinarily regarded as a standard part of the Law of Succession. Section 145 states that where an election is made by a surviving spouse under section 47A of the Administration of Estates Act 1925, *i.e.* an election to capitalise the spouse's life interest,[6] such election shall have effect as if the surviving spouse had originally been entitled to the capital sum. The effect is to backdate the election to the death for inheritance tax purposes.

Section 146 deals with orders of the court made under the Inheritance (Provision for Family and Dependants) Act 1975. They are also backdated to the death and any property which passes under such an order is treated, for tax purposes, as if it had devolved in that way on the death. For example, if someone dies and leaves his substantial estate entirely to his mistress, this will result in a liability to inheritance tax. If the court then orders that part of the estate should be transferred to the deceased's widow, such property will be deemed to have been bequeathed to the widow by the deceased; this will reduce the inheritance tax burden because the property passing to the widow will be entitled to the spouse exemption. If property worth £100,000 is transferred from the mistress to the widow, this will effect a tax saving of £40,000. The tax effect is the same as for a variation—this is an involuntary variation.

2. Capital gains tax variations

Just as variations are possible for inheritance tax, so they are possible for capital gains tax. Section 62(6)–(10) of the Taxation of Chargeable Gains Act 1992 is essentially equivalent to section 142 of the Inheritance Tax Act. Dispositions under a will or intestacy may be varied for inheritance tax purposes under the one section[7] and for capital gains tax purposes under the other.[8] Those who effect the variation may want it to take effect for both taxes or only for one. In the ordinary course of events, a variation will be effected for inheritance tax purposes and an equivalent variation will be effected, simultaneously, for capital gains tax purposes. But there may be no need to effect a capital gains tax variation and in some cases a capital gains tax variation may be positively disad-

---

[5] A testator may leave his trustees a "letter of intent" which indicates how he would like them to exercise their powers and discretions. This letter will not be legally binding on them (if it were, the trust would not be discretionary), but will be morally binding.

[6] See *ante* pp. 36–37.

[7] I.H.T.A. 1984 s. 142.

[8] T.C.G.A. 1992 s. 62.

vantageous, it will not then be made. For example, suppose that the variation is that a block of shares in a public company[9] will, for inheritance tax purposes, pass to X and not to Y. The variation will be effected for inheritance tax purposes and the shares will be treated as though the deceased had bequeathed the shares to Y in his will. If the variation is effected also for capital gains tax, the capital gains tax effect will be that Y will be deemed to have inherited the shares from the deceased. If the variation is not effected for capital gains tax, X will be treated, for capital gains tax purposes as having inherited the shares from the deceased and as then having disposed of them to Y. There is a choice. Quite often it is *not* to the parties' advantage to effect a variation for capital gains tax purposes; there will be no point in a variation for capital gains tax purposes if the subject matter of the variation is an asset which is not subject to capital gains tax, such as cash or a motor car[10] and there will also be no point in a capital gains tax variation if the value of the asset has remained stable[11] and, in some cases, a capital gains tax variation will be positively disadvantageous. Suppose that someone dies leaving his entire estate to his widow. The estate consists of a house worth approximately £150,000 and other assets worth a further £200,000. A year after the death, the widow, who has lived in the house since the death, decides to go to live with her sister, so she does not need the house and she decides to give the house to her only daughter. A variation is effected for inheritance tax purposes so that the deceased is deemed to have devised the house to the daughter. This is clearly the correct course, to reduce any liability to inheritance tax on the widow's death. But should there be a variation for capital gains tax? Probably not. There will be *no* liability to capital gains tax if the disposal of the house is treated as being by the widow to the daughter because the widow will be entitled to capital gains tax main-residence relief. But if the daughter is treated as having acquired the house at the time of the death, she will not be entitled to capital gains tax main-residence relief because she was not living in it. Whether this matters will depend on whether the house has risen greatly in value during the year after the death.

Another reason for *not* opting to vary for capital gains tax purposes is that, depending on the sums involved, the gain actually made if the property is treated as passing from the deceased to X and then onto Y *may* be covered by X's annual exempt amount, in which case a variation will *not* be advantageous. So, if the deceased dies, leaving a block of shares to X, and this disposition is varied for inheritance tax purposes, so that the shares pass from the deceased to Y, it may be that the rise in value between the deceased's death and the disposal from X to Y may be (say) £5,000.[12] If X has no other chargeable gains during the tax year, the gain of £5,000 will be covered by his annual exempt amount and so he will pay no tax anyway. It is then better *not* to effect a variation for capital gains tax purposes because, without the variation, Y has a higher

---

[9] *Not* covered by inheritance tax business property relief.
[10] Private cars are not subject to capital gains tax—T.C.G.A. s. 263—see above.
[11] Meaning, in this context, that any increase in value has been equivalent to inflation.
[12] After allowing for inflation.

base price and his own gain will be smaller when, at a later date, he comes to dispose of the shares.

A warning needs to be issued at this point. Some readers may be tempted to think that because wills can be varied after death, there is no need, after all, to bother about planning before death. That is wrong. It is wrong, first of all, because most variations can only take effect with the consent of the beneficiaries, and beneficiaries may well not consent to variations which do not benefit them personally, even if such variations result in tax savings for others. Secondly, it is wrong because there is no guarantee that variations will always be possible. The rules may change. The Revenue do not like post-death variations and the 1989 Finance Bill proposed their abolition; the proposal was subject to much adverse comment[13] and the government were persuaded not to proceed with it. But it is always possible that similar proposals may be introduced at some time in the future and there is no guarantee that they will not then be proceeded with. No will draftsman should assume that, on the death of the testator, it will necessarily be possible, tax effectively, to vary the will he has drawn.

V. INCOME TAX

In the context of the Law of Succession, income tax is less significant than inheritance tax or capital gains tax. It is a tax on income[1] which is levied both on earned income and on income from investments. It is a graduated tax: the more income an individual taxpayer has, in a particular tax year,[2] the more income tax he pays as a percentage of his income. He pays no tax on the first "slice", because of a "personal allowance",[3] then he pays lower rate tax of 20 per cent on a band of income.[4] After this he pays at the basic rate of 25 per cent on the next band[5] and higher rate, now 40 per cent, beyond this.[6]

1. Deduction of income tax at source

Much income tax is collected by deduction at source, at the time when the income is paid over to the taxpayer. This is the case, for example, with most investment income and with employees' earnings.

2. Income tax owed for the period before death

When someone dies, income tax, insofar as it has not been deducted from income at source, may be owed in relation to the period before

---

[13] See [1989] B.T.R. 113 and 211 where the proposal was described as "a mean piece of tinkering".
[1] See Lord Macnaghten in *London County Council v. Attorney General* [1901] AC 26, 35 "Income tax, if I may be pardoned for saying so, is a tax on income . . .".
[2] The income tax year runs from April 6 to April 5, this is historical.
[3] In 1995–96 the personal allowance stands at £3,525.
[4] The width of the band varies but in 1995–96 it stands at £3,200.
[5] Currently, 1995–96, this is the next £21,100, *i.e.* the band from £3,201 to £24,300.
[6] *i.e.* anything over £24,300.

death. This is a debt of the estate.[7] It will be the duty of the personal representatives to submit accounts to the Revenue in order to enable them to calculate the tax owed. From the personal representatives' point of view, the most difficult type of case is probably that of a self-employed sole trader because accounts have to be furnished to calculate the income tax which is a debt of the estate deductible from the gross estate when calculating its net worth for inheritance tax purposes.[8]

3.   Income of the estate

Once the income of the deceased has been calculated, and the tax on it paid, it is then necessary to calculate the income of the estate. This income is generally, though not invariably, investment income. Sometimes, there may be room for argument as to whether income belonged to the deceased or belongs to the estate: the general rule is that income *due* before the death was the deceased's and income *due* after the death is the estate's.

Income of the estate, that is to say income *due* after the death but before the completion of the administration of the estate[9] is taxable in the hands of the personal representatives at the basic rate of income tax, 25 per cent. If and when they pay such income over to the beneficiaries, the tax liability is recalculated to take account of the fact that basic rate tax has already been paid, but the individual beneficiaries may owe tax on the top slice of their income at more or less than the basic rate.[10]

4.   Interest on money borrowed to pay inheritance tax

As was mentioned above,[11] the personal representatives will need to pay inheritance tax *before* obtaining probate or letters of administration. At this stage, when they pay the inheritance tax, they cannot generally sell assets, because they will not be able to prove their title to them, so they will have to borrow the money. Interest on such a borrowing *is*, deductible, for income tax purposes, from the estate income.[12]

VI.   TAX PLANNING

Someone who is drafting a will should bear the tax position in mind—particularly the inheritance tax position. Having said this, it is obviously not appropriate that saving tax should take precedence over everything

---

[7] There was a time when, if the deceased was insolvent, the Revenue were preferential creditors—this is no longer the case.

[8] There is no difference of *principle* between a sole trader and other taxpayers but the self-employed generally present problems—and once a sole trader is dead it may be particularly difficult to calculate his pre-death profits.

[9] I.C.T.A. s. 695.

[10] This *is* a simplified account—but it is hoped that it is sufficient for the Succession student's purposes.

[11] *Ante* p. 278.

[12] I.H.T.A. s. 364.

else. To leave a widow with too little capital because this will save tax is neither fair nor sensible.

This is not the place to go into further detail as to how to avoid tax. What can, however, be said is that the safest forms of tax planning are usually those which are the most straightforward—those which are based on a simple application of the rules.

For example, it is a simple application of the rules for someone who has an estate worth more than the inheritance tax nil-rate band to bequeath property to the value of the nil-rate band to his children and the residue of his estate to his wife. If she were then to leave all her property to the children on her death, it would be difficult to allege any impropriety whether or not her net estate exceeded the nil-rate band at that stage. But not all cases are as simple as this and the Revenue may invoke anti-avoidance rules in cases where they think that tax payers are taking too much advantage.

1. Associated operations

The principle statutory anti-avoidance rule for inheritance tax is concerned with "associated operations". Section 272[1] of the Inheritance Tax Act says that:

"disposition" includes a disposition effected by associated operations"

and section 268(1) says:

268. Associated operations

(1) In this Act "associated operations" means, . . . any two or more operations of any kind, being—
  (a) operations which affect the same property, or one of which affects some property and the other or others of which affect property which represents, whether directly or indirectly, that property, or income arising from that property, or any property representing accumulations of any such income, or
  (b) any two operations of which one is effected with reference to the other, or with a view to enabling the other to be effected or facilitating its being effected, and any further operation having a like relation to any of those two, and so on,
  whether those operations are effected by the same person or different persons, and whether or not they are simultaneous; and "operation" includes an omission.

It is not entirely clear what this section means and, when it was first enacted, in 1975[2] there were apparently contradictory statements made by ministers in parliament[3] as to its intended effect. It probably would apply, for example, where someone dies leaving property to his widow on the understanding that she will transfer this property to the children

---

[1] The interpretations section.
[2] It was part of the original capital transfer tax legislation.
[3] See [1976] L. S. Gaz p. 650.

by way of an *inter vivos* gift. If she makes the transfer without any such prior understanding, that is probably *not* an associated operation, particularly if the transfer takes place some time after the death.

Nevertheless, there is one example of something which the Revenue are understood to *claim* would be an associated operation; though, at the time of writing, the matter has not been litigated. It is where property is left by will to someone other than the testator's spouse, say his adult child, and the child then varies the will to pass the property to the spouse (the child's mother), who then makes an *inter vivos* gift of that same property to the child. This is a scenario to be avoided, although it can be avoided only by pre-death planning.

2.   The "New Approach"

The tax planner also needs to be aware of the "New Approach" to tax planning adopted by the House of Lords in their decision in *Ramsay v. IRC*,[4] extended in *Furniss v. Dawson*[5] and then restricted in *Craven v. White*[6] and *Fitzwilliam v. IRC*.[7] This approach began by deciding that taxpayers could not, in capital gains tax cases, claim artificial losses which had been created by a pre-ordained series of self-cancelling transactions. At one stage it seemed to have been carried much further than this. Now that it appears again to have been limited, it is not clear how far it applies to inheritance tax[8] and it is not entirely clear how the inheritance tax rule about "associated operations" fits in with it.

3.   Contrasting reservation of benefit and "carve out"

A gift subject to a reservation of benefit is subject to inheritance tax on the donor's death even if he dies more than seven years after the gift was made. So it is important to try to ensure that the gift is not subject to reservation of benefit. But there is rather a fine dividing line between, on the one hand, giving something away, yet reserving a benefit in it, and on the other hand, splitting something up and then giving away one part while retaining another. In the latter case there is no reservation of benefit, but what is known as a "carve out".

"... by retaining something which he has never given, a donor does not bring himself within the mischief [of the reservation of benefit rule]. In the simplest analysis, if A gives to B all his estates in Wiltshire except Blackacre, he does not except Blackacre out of what he has given; he just does not give Blackacre".[9]

So, if a farmer owns a farm, including a farmhouse, and he gives the farm, including the farmhouse, to his son, but goes on living in the farmhouse, this *will* constitute reservation of benefit. If, by contrast, he trans-

---

[4] [1982] A.C. 300.
[5] [1984] A.C. 474.
[6] [1989] A.C. 398.
[7] [1993] 1 W.L.R. 1189.
[8] *Fitzwilliam* makes it hard to see how it can be applied to inheritance tax schemes—see R. Kerridge (1994) 110 L.Q.R. 217.
[9] *St Aubyn v. AG* [1952] AC 15, 29, Lord Simonds.

fers the farm *excluding* the farmhouse to his son, *i.e.* makes a gift of the
fields only, and not the house, it will not be reservation of benefit if he
goes on living in the farmhouse, because he has not given the farmhouse
away.

This is a straightforward case; others may be closer to the line.[10] The
best advice will generally be to keep away from the line because any
dispute with the Revenue will occur after the donor's death when it will
be too late to change things.[11]

One final point. Little has been said in this Chapter about the taxation
of trusts and settlements, which clearly overlaps with the taxation of
lifetime and death disposals; but to venture into the territory of the taxation of trusts and settlements would be to stray too far from the law of
Succession.

It is hoped that those readers who have not been put off by what they
have already read about tax in this Chapter will take the time to pursue
the subject further.

---

[10] The reader may think that this is an odd example, given that there will be a 100% agricultural relief and so no inheritance tax anyway—but that is not necessarily correct. Agricultural relief will apply only to the agricultural value—some, or all, of the farm may have
development potential to which the relief will not apply. This said, if the farmhouse is
separated from the farm, the *farmhouse* will lose agricultural relief. The planner needs
to take care.

[11] There are, as yet, no inheritance tax cases on reservation of benefit which are worth
drawing to the student's attention; but there are a number of estate duty cases which
are worth looking at. See, in particular, *Stamp Duties Commissioner of New South Wales
v. Permanent Trustee Co of New South Wales* [1956] A.C. 512; *Chick v. Stamp Duties Commissioner* [1958] A.C. 435; *Munro v. Stamp Duties Commissioner* [1934] A.C. 61 and *A.G. v.
Seccombe* [1911] 2 K.B. 688.

CHAPTER 13

EXECUTORS AND ADMINISTRATORS

The personal representatives of a deceased person are either executors or administrators.[1]

An executor *de son tort* is not a personal representative, but he is liable to creditors and beneficiaries of the deceased as if he were a lawful executor.[2]

I. EXECUTORS

A. APPOINTMENT OF EXECUTORS

Executors may be appointed:

(1) By the testator in his will. This is by far the most common method of appointment of executors.
(2) Under a power conferred by the testator in his will. This method is rarely used.
(3) By the court, which has statutory powers to appoint executors in certain circumstances.

1. By the testator in his will

The appointment of executors by the testator in his will may be express or implied; or, in the case of settled land, statutory.

(1) *EXPRESS APPOINTMENT.* Most wills contain an express appointment of one or more named, or otherwise identified, persons as the "executors" of the will. A typical clause reads "I appoint AB of (address

---

[1] Or, if female, executrices or administratices. See Administration of Estates Act 1925, s. 55(1)(i), (ii) and (xi).

[2] Administration of Estates Act 1925, ss. 28 and 55(1)(xi): *post*, pp. 515 *et seq.*

and description) and CD of (address and description) to be the executors of this my Will."[3]

The appointment of an executor may be absolute, or it may be qualified in one or more respects, for instance:

(i) By a condition precedent or subsequent, *e.g.* "I appoint my nephew EF and also my son GH *if he shall have attained the age of 25 years at the time of my death* to be the executors of this will."[4]

(ii) As to the subject matter of the office, *e.g.* "I appoint my brother IJ to be the executor of this will *as to the business of grocer carried on by me at the date of this will at* (address)." Usually the testator first appoints general executors, *i.e.* appoints persons to be "the executors of this will except as to my business as hereinafter defined."

(iii) As to the time when the person appointed shall begin, or shall cease, to be executor, *e.g.* "I appoint my sister KL to be the executrix of this will *during the minority of my son* MN."

The testator may, and often will, appoint one or more substituted executors to take office on a specified event in place of the first named executors, *e.g.*:

"I appoint my wife PQ to be the executrix of this will *but if she shall die in my lifetime or shall renounce probate or for any other reason she is unwilling or unable to act as such executrix* then I appoint my son RQ to be executor in her place."

The event on which the substitution is to take place should be clearly specified.[5]

(2) *IMPLIED APPOINTMENT.* A person impliedly appointed executor by the testator in his will is usually called "an executor according to the tenor" of the will. A person is an executor according to the tenor if the testator has shown by his will an intention that this person should act as executor of the will, without expressly nominating him as "executor." Whether the testator has shown such an intention by his will is a ques-

---

[3] This form is suitable for a will which contains only absolute immediate gifts. For a will containing any other gifts, where trustees will be needed, it is usual to appoint the same persons "to be the executors *and trustees* of this my Will." A suitable clause for the appointment of the partners in a firm of solicitors reads, "I appoint the partners at the date of my death in the firm of XY & Co. of (address) or the firm which at that date has succeeded to and carries on its practice to be the executors and trustees of this my Will (and I express the wish that two and only two of them shall prove my Will and act initially in its trusts)"; the words in brackets are precatory: see *Re Horgan* [1971] P. 50, 61.

[4] A condition precedent. As to an infant who is appointed executor see *post,* p. 300.

[5] *cf. In the Goods of Foster* (1871) L.R. 2 P. & D. 304 (wife appointed executrix "and in default of her" JK and RF appointed executors; wife took probate and died: held substitution intended in event of wife's death, whether before or after probate); *In the Goods of Betts* (1861) 30 L.J.P.M. & A. 167 (JJ appointed executor "but should he decline or consider himself incapable of acting" EJ appointed executor; JJ died before testatrix: held EJ entitled to probate); *In the Goods of Lane* (1864) 33 L.J.P.M. & A. 185.

tion of construction. The following are examples of the appointment of an executor according to the tenor[6]:

(i) "I appoint my sister AB my executrix, only requesting that my nephews, CD and EF, will kindly act for or with this dear sister." It was held that CD and EF were executors according to the tenor[7]—"they can only act for or with her in the same character as was conferred on her, namely, as executors."[8]

(ii) "I desire GH to pay all my just debts." It was held that GH was an executor according to the tenor.[9] "The essential duties of an executor are to collect the assets of the deceased, to pay his funeral expenses and debts, and to discharge the legacies"[10] and other gifts made by his will.

(iii) "I nominate as trustees to carry out this will JK and LM." It was held that they were executors according to the tenor.[11] The case fell "within the principle that where the direction is to carry out the general provisions of the will, and not to execute a specific trust, the trustees are executors according to the tenor."[12] On the other hand, "I wish PQ to act as trustee to this estate," was not enough to make him executor according to the tenor: the will did not require him to pay the debts and generally to administer the estate.[13]

A person who is the universal devisee and legatee under a will (i.e. the sole beneficiary of the entire estate) is not entitled to probate as an executor according to the tenor unless the will shows an intention that he should act as executor.[14]

As in the case of an express appointment, the appointment of an executor according to the tenor may be absolute, qualified, or substitutional.

(3) *SETTLED LAND.*[15] Section 22 of the Administration of Estates Act 1925 deals with settled land vested in the testator at his death, which

---

[6] For a summary of the case law see Williams, Mortimer and Sunnucks, *Executors, Administrators and Probate* (17th ed., 1993), pp. 29 *et seq.*

[7] *In the Goods of Brown* (1877) 2 P.D. 110 (a combination of express and implied appointments).

[8] *ibid.* at p. 111.

[9] *In the Goods of Cook* [1902] P. 115: see also *In the Estate of Fawcett* [1941] P. 85 ("All else be sold and proceeds after debts, etc., Barclays Bank will do this to Emily Thompson": held Bank was executor according to the tenor).

[10] *In the Goods of Adamson* (1875) L.R. 3 P. & D. 253, 254.

[11] *In the Goods of Russell* [1892] P. 380: see also *In the Goods of Laird* [1892] P. 381; *In the Goods of Way* [1901] P. 345; *In the Goods of Baylis* (1865) L.R. 1 P. & D. 21, where Lord Penzance said at p. 22, "the persons appointed trustees are to get in and receive the whole estate, to pay the debts, and to divide the residue. Now that is the very office of an executor, and therefore it is clear that the trustees are executors according to the tenor."

[12] *In the Goods of Laird, supra.* at p. 381.

[13] *In the Goods of Punchard* (1872) L.R. 2 P. & D. 369: see also *In the Estate of Mackenzie* [1909] P. 305; *In the Goods of Wilkinson* [1892] P. 227; *In the Goods of Jones* (1861) 2 Sw. & Tr. 155.

[14] *Re Pryse* [1904] P. 301; *In the Goods of Oliphant* (1860) 1 Sw. & Tr. 525.

[15] For an explanation as to what "settled land" *is*, see *Megarry's Manual of the Law of Real Property* (7th ed., 1993) Chap. 7.

was settled previously to his death and not by his will, and which remains settled land after his death.[16] The section provides that,

"a testator may appoint, and in default of such express appointment shall be deemed to have appointed, as his special executors in regard to settled land, the persons, if any, who are at his death the trustees of the settlement thereof, and probate may be granted to such trustees specially limited to the settled land."[17]

Thus, in the case of settled land, there is either an *express* appointment or a *deemed* appointment by the testator of the trustees of the settlement as his special executors in regard to settled land. The testator is, of course, free to appoint persons of his own choice to be his general executors in regard to his other assets.[18]

2. Under a power conferred by the testator in his will

The testator may by his will authorise another person to appoint executors of the will after the testator's death. For instance, the testator may by his will authorise his legatees to appoint two executors,[19] or direct that on the death of one of two executors expressly appointed in his will the surviving executor may appoint another executor.[20]

3. By the court

The court has power to appoint executors[21] in the following circumstances:

(1) *SUBSTITUTED PERSONAL REPRESENTATIVE.* The court has a wide power to appoint a substituted personal representative in place of all or any of the existing personal representatives of the deceased. The power is exercisable by the court on an application relating to the deceased's estate made by a personal representative of the deceased or a beneficiary under the deceased's will or intestacy.[22] As from the date of appointment the substituted personal representative becomes an executor if he is appointed to act with one or more existing executors. Otherwise he becomes an administrator.

(2) *MINORITY OR LIFE INTEREST.* If at any time during the minority

---

[16] *Re Bridgett and Hayes' Contract* [1928] Ch. 163.
[17] *See post,* p. 337.
[18] Administration of Estates Act 1925, s. 22(2).
[19] *In the Goods of Cringan* (1828) 1 Hagg. Ecc. 548.
[20] *In the Goods of Deichman* (1842) 3 Curt. 123: see also *In the Goods of Ryder* (1861) 2 Sw. & Tr. 127 (will concluded, "I must beg EC to appoint someone to see this my will executed,: EC appointed himself as executor: probate granted to EC); *Jackson & Gill v. Paulet* (1851) 2 Rob. 344.
[21] In both (2) and (3) below the relevant legislation uses the generic term "personal representative"; see Williams Mortimer and Sunnucks, *Executors, Administrators and Probate* (17th ed., 1993), p. 34, n. 69 (not strictly executors).
[22] Administration of Justice Act 1985, s. 50: for remuneration of the substituted personal representative see *post,* p. 406, and for appointment instead of a judicial trustee see s. 50(4) and *post,* pp. 506–507.

of a beneficiary or the subsistence of a life interest under a will or intestacy there is only one personal representative (not being a trust corporation), the court has power to appoint one or more additional personal representatives to act while the minority or life interest subsists and until the estate is fully administered.[23] The power is exercisable on the application of any person interested, or the guardian or receiver of any such person.[24]

(3) *SETTLED LAND.* The court has power to appoint a special or additional personal representative in respect of settled land on the application of the trustees of the settlement or any person beneficially interested thereunder.[25]

B. Transmission of the Office

In general, an executor cannot assign his office because it is an office of personal trust.[26] Section 7 of the Administration of Estates Act 1925 provides, however, for the automatic transmission of the office on death through proving executors. This important provision must now be considered.[27]

1. Executor by representation

If X is T's sole, or last surviving, executor and X has obtained probate of T's will, then if X dies, having by his will appointed Y to be his executor, and Y obtains probate of X's will, Y will be X's executor and T's *executor by representation.* As section 7(1) puts it, "An executor of a sole or last surviving executor of a testator is the executor of that testator"— subject to the proviso that each executor must have proved the will of his testator.[28]

If Y is unwilling to act as T's executor by representation, he should

---

[23] Supreme Court Act 1981, s. 114(4): for trust corporation see *post,* p. 301, and for the rules governing the number of personal representatives see *post,* pp. 300 and 311.

[24] *Ibid.* See also N.C. Prob. Rules 1987, r. 26.

[25] Administration of Estates Act 1925, s. 23(2)-(5) (as amended by Administration of Justice Act 1970, s. 1 and Sched. 2, para. 3): for an instance see *In the Estate of Clifton* [1931] P. 222.

[26] *In the Estate of Skinner* [1958] 1 W.L.R. 1043.

[27] For another statutory transmission see Public Trustee Act 1906, s. 6(2), which permits transfer of the estate by an executor or administrator to the Public Trustee with the sanction of the court.

[28] It suffices that the original executor obtained probate limited to certain property, *In the Goods of Beer* (1851) 2 Rob. 349: for limited probate see *post,* p. 340. There is no chain of representation through a grant of probate limited to settled land, *Registrar's Direction,* July 21, 1936; or through an additional personal representative appointed under Supreme Court Act 1981, s. 114(4), s. 114(5); or through a substituted personal representative appointed under Administration of Justice Act 1985, s. 50(1) and (2). For Scottish confirmations and Northern Irish grants see *post,* pp. 324–325.

renounce probate of X's will. He cannot both accept office as X's executor and renounce office as T's executor by representation.[29]

2. The chain of representation

The last executor in an unbroken chain of representation is the executor of every preceding testator.[30] So, if Y obtains probate of X's will and later dies, having by his will appointed Z to be his executor, and Z obtains probate of Y's will, Z is the executor of Y and *the executor by representation of both X and T*. But the chain of representation is broken by:

(a) an intestacy, *i.e.* if Y dies intestate in the above example; or
(b) the failure of a testator to appoint an executor, *i.e.* if Y does not appoint an executor; or
(c) the failure to obtain probate of a will, *i.e.* if Y appoints Z to be his executor but Z does not obtain probate of Y's will.[31]

The chain of representation is not, however, broken by a temporary grant of administration to Y's estate if Z subsequently obtains probate of Y's will.[32]

3. Effect of representation

Section 7(4) provides that every executor in the chain of representation to a testator:

(a) has the same rights in respect of the testator's estate as the original executor would have had if living; and
(b) is, to the extent to which the testator's estate has come to his hands, answerable as if he were an original executor.

4. Double probate

Finally, consider the position if T by his will appoints (say) two executors, P and Q, and P alone obtains probate of T's will, power to prove being reserved to Q. P dies, having by his will appointed R to be his executor, and R obtains probate of P's will. R is P's executor and T's executor by representation. But if Q later obtains probate of T's will (called double probate[33]) R will thereupon cease to be T's executor by representation. So, a grant of double probate terminates an executorship by representation.[34]

---

[29] *In the Goods of Perry* (1840) 2 Curt. 655; *Brooke v. Haymes* (1868) L.R. 6 Eq. 25. For possible reform see Law Reform Committee's 23rd Report, *The powers and duties of trustees*, Cmnd. 8733 (1982), pp. 53–54 and 67.
[30] Administration of Estates Act 1925, s. 7(2).
[31] *ibid.* s. 7(3). If the chain of representation is broken, and X's or T's estate has not been fully administered, a grant of letters of administration de *bonis non administratis* with the will annexed is needed to each estate, see *post*, pp. 340–341.
[32] *ibid.* s. 7(3).
[33] See *post*, p. 336.
[34] Administration of Estates Act 1925, s. 7(1).

C.   NUMBER AND CAPACITY OF EXECUTORS

1.   Number of executors

By his will a testator may appoint as many executors as he pleases. What rules govern the number of executors to whom probate may be granted?

(1)   *MAXIMUM NUMBER.* Section 114(1) of the Supreme Court Act 1981 provides that probate or administration shall not be granted to more than four persons in respect of the same part of the deceased's estate. If a testator appoints six executors of the same property, probate can be granted to not more than four of them, though power will be reserved to the others (if they have not renounced) to apply on the occurrence of any vacancy. Section 114(1) does not, however, prohibit probate being granted to four executors in respect of a particular part of the deceased's estate and to four different executors in respect of the remainder of the estate.

(2)   *NO MINIMUM NUMBER.* Probate may be granted to one executor, whether or not there is a minority or a life interest which arises under the deceased's will or intestacy.[35] The rule is different for grants of administration.[36]

2.   Capacity of executors

By his will a testator is free to appoint any persons[37] as his executors, irrespective of their infancy, mental or physical incapacity, insolvency, criminal record, foreign nationality,[38] marital status,[39] or anything else. What rules govern the capacity of a person so appointed to act as executor after the testator's death and to take probate?

(1)   *A MINOR.* A minor who is appointed an executor cannot obtain probate until he attains the age of 18 years.[40] The testator's estate does not vest in the minor and the minor cannot act as an executor for any purpose until he obtains probate.[41]

(2)   *MENTAL OR PHYSICAL INCAPACITY.* A person who is incapable

---

[35] For the court's power to appoint additional personal representatives see *ante*, pp. 297–298.

[36] *Post*, p. 311.

[37] Including a corporation and members of a particular firm, *Re Horgan* [1971] P. 50 (partners in firm of solicitors), *ante*, pp. 294–295.

[38] Status of Aliens Act 1914, s. 17, as amended by British Nationality Act 1948, s. 34 and Sched. 4, Pt. II.

[39] For married women see Law Reform (Married Women and Tortfeasors) Act 1935, s. 1.

[40] N.C. Prob. Rules 1987, rr. 32 and 33; Family Law Reform Act 1969, s.1(3) and Sched. I. For grants of administration for the use and benefit of a minor see *post*, pp. 341–343.

[41] Supreme Court Act 1981, s. 118.

of managing his affairs by reason of mental or physical incapacity cannot act as executor, or take probate, while his incapacity continues.[42]

(3) *A CORPORATION.* Three types of corporation need to be considered. (i) A corporation sole, such as the vicar of a parish, may act as executor and take probate in his own name.[43] (ii) Under section 115(1) of the Supreme Court Act 1981 a trust corporation[44] may also act as executor and obtain probate in its own name, either alone or jointly with another person. (iii) By contrast, a corporation aggregate, such as a company, which is not a trust corporation, cannot take probate in its own name.[45] Letters of administration (with the will annexed)[46] for the corporation's use and benefit may be granted to its nominee or attorney.[47]

D. Passing over an Executor

Factors such as the insolvency or the criminal record of an executor do not disqualify him from acting as executor and taking probate.[48] But under section 116 of the Supreme Court Act 1981 the court has power to pass over an executor and appoint as administrator such other person as it thinks expedient if "by reason of any special circumstances" this appears to be necessary or expedient.[49] The grant of administration may be limited in any way the court thinks fit. Probably the "special circumstances" need not relate to the estate itself, or the administration of it, but

[42] *Evans v. Tyler* (1849) 2 Rob. 128: see also *In the Goods of Galbraith* [1951] P. 422 (probate granted to two executors revoked, as both had became unfit to act in old age owing to physical and mental infirmity); *In the Estate of Shaw* [1905] P. 92; N.C. Prob. Rules 1987, r. 35.

[43] *In the Goods of Haynes* (1842) 3 Curt. 75 (Archbishop of Tuam for the time being): as to the effect of a vacancy in the office see Law of Property Act 1925, s. 180(3).

[44] For the definition of "trust corporation" see Supreme Court Act 1981, s. 128; a trust corporation includes the Public Trustee but also includes companies formed to take on the business of acting as trustees or P.R.s and which have a share capital of at least £250,000. Most trust corporations are, in fact, created by, and are subsidiaries of, the clearing banks. A trust corporation can also act as administrator, Supreme Court Act 1981, s. 115(1).

[45] *In the Estate of Rankine* [1918] P. 134, 139; *In the Goods of Darke* (1859) 1 Sw. & Tr. 516. For a brief period it could do so under the Administration of Justice Act 1920, s. 17 which was repealed by the Administration of Estates Act 1925, s. 56 and Sched. 2, Pt. II.

[46] *Post,* p. 306.

[47] If the corporation is appointed executor jointly with an individual, the latter must be cleared off, see N.C. Prob. Rules 1987, r. 36(4).

[48] *Smethurst v. Tomlin & Bankes* (1861) 2 Sw. & tr. 143 (conviction for felony did not disqualify executor). The court has no power of selection among executors not appointed by the court, as it has among administrators entitled in the same degree, *post,* p. 309. The court does of course refuse probate to any executor who lacks capacity. It is not clear whether the murder or manslaughter of the testator by a sane executor automatically disqualifies him; in practice the court may pass over such an executor, and the issue of automatic disqualification does not arise.

[49] See N.C. Prob. Rules 1987, r. 52, under which applications for passing over may be made to a registrar. In the case of deaths before 1926 the court had power to pass over an executor under the Court of Probate Act 1857, s. 73; before 1982 the court had this power under Judicature Act 1925, s. 162(1), as amended by Administration of Justice Act 1928, s. 9.

may extend to any other circumstances which the court thinks relevant.[50]

This useful power enables the court to pass over an executor where special circumstances exist. For instance, in *In the Estate of S.*[51] the court passed over an executrix who was serving a sentence of life imprisonment for the manslaughter of the testator, her husband; this made it in a practical sense "quite impossible for her to act as executrix."[52] Again, in *In the Estate of Biggs*[53] the court passed over two executors, a husband and wife, both elderly and infirm, and both of whom had steadfastly refused to take out a grant of probate. The husband had intermeddled with the testator's estate and had been cited to take probate,[54] but he had ignored an order of the registrar to do so: he was so violently aggrieved that it was possible that he might go to the length of suffering imprisonment rather than obey this order. The wife had not been cited but she shared the hostility of her husband to undertaking the duty of an executor. In these special circumstances the court exercised its power to pass over the executors and appointed another person as administratrix of the estate, with the will annexed.

E. ACCEPTANCE AND RENUNCIATION

1. Executor may accept or renounce

A person who has been appointed executor is free to accept or renounce the office as he pleases[55]:

"No man has a right to make another an executor without his consent; and even if in the lifetime of the testator he has agreed to accept the office, it is still in his power to recede."[56]

Even persons deemed to have been appointed as special executors in regard to settled land are free to accept or renounce.[57]

---

[50] *Re Clore* [1982] Fam. 113, [1982] Ch. 456 (conduct of executors so far in administration and both executors abroad: passed over): *cf. In the Goods of Edwards-Taylor* [1951] P. 24, 27: both cases were decided under the 1925 Act: *Re Mathew* [1984] 1 W.L.R. 1011.

[51] [1968] P. 302: see also the following cases decided under the 1857 Act; *In the Estate of Crippen* [1911] P. 108; *In the Estate of Drawmer* (1913) 108 L.T. 732 (executor serving 12 months' prison sentence for conspiracy: passed over); *In the Goods of Wright* (1898) 79 L.T. 473 (executor disappeared and warrant for arrest issued on embezzlement charge: passed over) and *In the Goods of Clayton* (1886) 11 P.D. 76.

[52] *In the Estate of S., supra,* at p. 305.

[53] [1966] P. 118: see also *In the Estate of Potticary* [1927] P. 202 (intermeddling and misfeasance: executors passed over under 1857 Act); *In the Goods of Ray* (1927) 96 L.J.P. 37; *In the Estate of Leguia* [1934] P. 80; (1936) 105 L.J.P. 72; *Re D. and B.* (1979) 10 Fam. Law 55.

[54] *Post,* p. 303.

[55] This does not apply to personal representatives after their appointment by the court, see *ante,* pp. 297–298. But see N.C. Prob. Rules 1987, r. 26(1) for prior consent of the person proposed for appointment by the court under Supreme Court Act 1981, s. 114(4); Administration of Estates Act 1925, s. 23(3). The Public Trustee is free to accept or renounce, subject to restrictions imposed by the Public Trustee Act 1906, ss. 2 and 5.

[56] *Per* Lord Redesdale in *Doyle v. Blake* (1804) 2 Sch. & Lef. 231, 239; *Hargreaves v. Wood* (1862) 2 Sw. & Tr. 602.

[57] See the words "if willing to act" in Administration of Estates Act 1925, s. 23(3).

2. Citation to accept or refuse probate

An executor can, however, be compelled to decide whether he will accept office by taking probate. The court has power to summon any person named as executor in a will to prove, or renounce, probate of the will.[58] The court exercises this power by issuing a citation at the instance of any person who would himself be entitled to a grant of letters of administration if the executor renounced.[59] The citation calls on the executor to enter an appearance and accept or refuse probate of the will. If the executor does not appear to the citation or renounces probate, his rights as executor wholly cease.[60] Thus the issue of the citation compels the executor to decide whether to take probate.

In *Re Stevens*, Vaughan Williams L.J. said that he thought "no action would lie for neglect to take out probate—no such action appears ever to have been brought; and I think that plaintiff's only remedy is by citing the executor."[61]

3. Acceptance of office

An executor accepts office (1) by taking probate or (2) by acting as executor.

(1) *BY TAKING PROBATE.* An executor accepts office by taking probate—he has made his choice and cannot renounce after he has taken probate.[62] "By taking probate an executor takes upon himself duties and liabilities which he cannot afterwards shake off."[63] But an executor who has sworn the executor's oath[64] may still renounce if probate has not yet been granted to him.[65]

(2) *BY ACTING AS EXECUTOR.* An executor also accepts office if he does any act or acts in relation to the testator's assets which indicate an intention to take upon himself the executorship. Examples of such acts of inter-meddling include taking possession of the testator's goods, receiving or releasing debts due to the testator,[66] writing to request payment of money due upon an insurance policy on the testator's life,[67] and inserting an advertisement calling upon all persons who had any claim on the testator's estate to send in their accounts and to pay all money

---

[58] Supreme Court Act 1981, s. 112.
[59] N.C. Prob. Rules 1987, r. 47. see *post*, p. 314.
[60] Administration of Estates Act 1925, s. 5. If the executor appears, but does not apply for probate, the citor may apply for a grant of administration to himself, N.C. Prob. Rules 1987, r. 47(7).
[61] [1898] 1 Ch. 162, 177; Chitty L.J. expressed the same view, at p. 174.
[62] *In the Goods of Veiga* (1862) 32 L.J.P.M. & A. 9 ("once an executor, always an executor").
[63] *ibid.* at p. 10.
[64] *Post*, pp. 351 *et seq.*
[65] *Jackson & Wallington v. Whitehead* (1821) 3 Phill. 577; *M'Donnell v. Prendergast* (1830) 3 Hagg. Ecc. 212.
[66] *Pytt v. Fendall* (1754) 1 Lee 553 (executor had released debt due to the testator: held he had accepted office and could not renounce).
[67] *Re Stevens* [1897] 1 Ch. 422.

due to the estate to X and Y "his executors in trust."[68] Whether the executor's acts indicate an intention to take upon himself the executorship depends, however, on all the circumstances. An executor does not accept office if he deals with the testator's assets solely as the agent of another executor to whom probate has been granted.[69] Again, the executor's acts, though technically acts of administration, may be too trivial to indicate an intention on his part to take upon himself the executorship.[70] And section 36(5) of the Trustee Act 1925 provides that a sole or last surviving executor intending to renounce, or all the executors where they all intend to renounce, may appoint new trustees before renouncing probate without thereby accepting the office of executor.

An executor who accepts office by acting as executor cannot thereafter renounce.[71]

4. Citation to take probate

Any person interested in the estate may cite an executor to take probate if he has accepted office by acting as executor. Such a citation may be issued at any time after the expiration of six months from the testator's death unless proceedings as to the validity of the will are pending.[72] After the executor has been cited, the citor may apply for an order requiring the executor to take probate within a specified time,[73] and if the executor fails to do so he becomes liable to a fine and committal to prison for contempt of court.[74] Alternatively, the citor may apply for a grant to himself or some other person, pursuant to the court's power under section 116 of the Supreme Court Act 1981 to pass over an executor where special circumstances exist.[75] By adopting this latter course, the citor may avoid the difficulty and expense which is likely to be incurred in compelling an unwilling executor to take probate.

5. Renunciation

An executor who has not accepted office is free to renounce probate. Once he has done so he may retract his renunciation only with the leave of the court.

(1) *FORM OF RENUNCIATION.* An executor renounces probate in writing signed by him[76] and filed in a probate registry. A renunciation becomes binding on being filed.[77]

---

[68] *Long & Feaver v. Symes & Hannam* (1832) 3 Hagg. Ecc. 771.
[69] *Rayner v. Green (1839)* 2 Curt. 248.
[70] *Holder v. Holder* [1968] Ch. 353, 392, 397 and 401.
[71] *In the Goods of Badenach* (1864) 3 Sw. & Tr. 465; *Re Stevens* [1897] 1 Ch. 422; *Long & Feaver v. Symes & Hannam, supra,* (executors who intermeddled compelled to take probate); *Pytt v. Fendall, supra:* see also *Holder v. Holder, supra.*
[72] N.C. Prob. Rules 1987, r.47(3).
[73] N.C. Prob. Rules 1987, r. 47(5)(c) and (7)(c).
[74] *Mordaunt v. Clarke* (1868) L.R. 1 P. & D. 4592: see Contempt of Court Act 1981, s.14.
[75] N.C. Prob. Rules 1987, r. 47(5)(c) and (7)(c); *In the Estate of Biggs* [1966] P. 118 and see *ante,* pp. 301–302.
[76] Or under seal if a trust corporation.
[77] *In the Goods of Morant* (1874) L.R. 3 P. & D. 151.

(2) *AN EXECUTOR CANNOT RENOUNCE IN PART.* An executor cannot renounce part of his office and accept the other part. "The principle is very plain that a person cannot accept one part of the duties of an executor and refuse the rest."[78] For instance, after the death of X, who is the sole or last surviving executor of T, X's executor, Y, cannot both accept office as X's executor and renounce office as T's executor by representation.[79] There is a single statutory exception to the rule that an executor cannot renounce in part. An executor, who is not a trustee of a settlement which was created before the testator's death and not by his will, may renounce his office in regard to the settled land without renouncing it in regard to other property.[80]

(3) *EFFECT OF RENUNCIATION.* If an executor renounces probate, his rights in respect of the executorship wholly cease.[81] But any right which the executor may have to a grant of administration in some other capacity (whether as a beneficiary or as a creditor) does not cease unless he expressly renounces that right as well.[82]

6. Retracting a renunciation

An executor who has renounced probate may with the leave of the court retract his renunciation and take probate.[83]

(1) *GROUNDS FOR OBTAINING LEAVE.* The court grants leave to an executor to retract his renunciation only if this will be for the benefit of the estate, or for the benefit of those interested under the testator's will. Leave was refused where an executor renounced probate as a result of his solicitor's erroneous advice that he would be put to great trouble in proving the will, and later the executor changed his mind.[84] In another case, leave was granted to an executor to retract his renunciation and take probate because his co-executor had absconded after taking probate.[85]

(2) *EFFECT OF RETRACTION.* Section 6 of the Administration of Estates Act 1925 provides that if an executor is permitted to retract his renunciation and prove the will, the probate shall take effect without prejudice to the previous acts and dealings of, and notices to, any other

---

[78] *Per* Romilly M.R. in *Brooke v. Haymes* (1868) L.R. 6 Eq. 25, 30.
[79] See *ante.* p. 299. Similarly an executor cannot refuse a worthless leasehold interest of the deceased; see *post*, p. 388.
[80] Administration of Estates Act 1925, s.23(1); see *post*, p. 339.
[81] *ibid. s.*5. See *Crawford v. Forshaw* [1891] 2 Ch. 261 (executor who renounces is not entitled to exercise powers conferred on executors as such and not as individuals).
[82] N.C. Prob. Rules 1987, r. 37(1); *cf.* effect of renouncing administration, *post*, p. 315.
[83] *In the Goods of Stiles* [1898] P. 12 (on Court of Probate Act 1857, s.79, the predecessor of Administration of Estates Act 1925, s.5): Administration of Estates Act 1925, s.6, now assumes that an executor may retract. See also N.C. Prob. Rules 1987, r. 37(3); a registrar may give leave, but only "in exceptional circumstances" may leave be given to an executor to retract after a grant has been made to some other person entitled in a lower degree: *Ibid.*
[84] *In the Goods of Gill* (1873) 3 P. & D. 113.
[85] *In the Goods of Stiles*, *supra*.

personal representative who has previously proved the will or taken out letters of administration.

II. ADMINISTRATORS

An administrator is a person to whom the court has granted letters of administration of a deceased's estate.[1] He can only be appointed to his office by the court. There is no transmission of the office on the death of a sole, or last surviving, administrator[2]; if by then the original deceased's estate has not been fully administered, one or more new administrators may be appointed by a grant of letters of administration *de bonis non administratis*[3]

A. ORDER OF PRIORITY TO ADMINISTRATION

The Non-Contentious Probate Rules 1987 regulate the classes of persons entitled to a grant of letters of administration in particular circumstances and the order of priority between them.[4]
Two main heads need to be considered:

(1) Where the deceased left a will. In this case, if no executor takes probate, the court makes a grant of letters of administration with the will annexed.[5]
(2) Where the deceased died wholly intestate. In this case the court makes a grant of letters of administration (or "simple" administration).[6]

The court has power to pass over the person who is entitled to the grant of administration under the normal order of priority: this power is considered later.[7]

---

[1] See *Administration of Estates Act* 1925, s.55(1)(i) and (ii): for a substituted personal representatives see *post*, p. 507.
[2] cf. the automatic transmission of office on death through proving executors, *ante*, pp. 298 *et seq* and see *ante*, p. 298, n. 27 for statutory transmission to the Public Trustee.
[3] *Post*, pp. 340–341.
[4] See Supreme Court Act 1981, s. 127: the N.C. Prob. Rules 1954 were made under s.100 of the Judicature Act 1925 (now repealed). For the rebuttable presumption that the deceased left no surviving relatives who are illegitimate, or whose relationship is traced through illegitimacy, see Family Law Reform Act 1987, s.21 (not applicable on death before April 4, 1988). For the special rules applicable where the deceased died domiciled outside England and Wales see N.C. Prob. Rules 1987, rr. 28(2) and 30.
[5] Supreme Court Act 1981, s.119.
[6] *Post.* p. 309.
[7] *Post*, pp. 312 *et seq*. For settled land and other limited grants see *post*, pp. 307 *et seq*.

1.   Where the deceased left a will

(1)   *THE ORDER OF PRIORITY.* Rule 20 of the Non-Contentious Probate Rules 1987 specifies the order of priority to a grant of probate or administration with the will annexed. The order is as follows:

(a) *The executor.* The executor is, of course, entitled to a grant of probate: a person who falls within any of the later classes is entitled to a grant of administration with the will annexed. The later classes become relevant if, for instance, no executor was appointed, or the executor appointed has died,[8] or has renounced probate, or has not appeared to a citation to accept or refuse probate.[9] If T appoints P and Q to be executors of his will and P alone applies for a grant of probate, with power to prove being reserved to Q (who has not renounced), P must give notice of his application to Q.[10]

(b) *Any residuary legatee or devisee holding in trust for any other person, i.e.* any person to whom the residuary personal or real estate is given by the will upon trust.

(c) *Any other residuary legatee or devisee*[11] *(including one for life) or where the residue is not wholly disposed of by the will, any person entitled to share in the undisposed of residue under the intestacy rules.*[12]
For example, if T by his will gave his residuary real and personal estate to X and Y upon trust for his widow W for life and after her death upon trust for his three nephews A, B and C absolutely in equal shares, then X and Y fall within class (b) and W, A, B and C fall within class (c). If A predeceased T, so that the gift to A lapsed and A's share passed on T's intestacy, the persons entitled to it under the intestacy rules fall within class (c).

(d) *The personal representative of any residuary legatee or devisee (but not one for life, or one holding in trust for any other person), or of any person entitled to share in any residue not disposed of by the will.* For example, if C (in the above example) died soon after T's death, C's personal representative falls within class (d).

(e) *Any other legatee or devisee (including one for life or one holding in trust for any other person) or any creditor of the deceased.*[13]

---

[8] Unless he took probate before his death and the chain of representation continues; *ante*, p. 298.

[9] *Ante,* p. 303.

[10] N.C. Prob. Rules 1987, r. 27(1); a registrar may dispense with the giving of notice if this is impracticable or would result in unreasonable delay or expense, r. 27(3); see *Practice Direction (Probate: Executor, Notice to)* [1988] 1 W.L.R. 195.

[11] Unless a registrar otherwise directs, a residuary legatee or devisee whose legacy or devise is vested in interest is preferred to one entitled on the happening of a contingency, r. 20(c), proviso (i).

[12] Including the Treasury Solicitor (or Solicitor for the affairs of the Duchy of Lancaster and the Solicitor of the Duchy of Corwall) when claiming *bona vacantia* on behalf of the Crown (or Duchy of Lancaster or Duke of Cornwall). For the power of the registrar to disregard the persons entitled as on intestacy where the testator has disposed of the whole or substantially the whole of the known estate see r. 20(c), proviso (ii).

[13] Unless a registrar otherwise directs, a legatee or devisee whose legacy or divise is vested in interest is preferred to one entitled on the happening of a contingency, r. 20(e), proviso.

Class (e) covers all beneficiaries under the will other than residuary beneficiaries who fall within the earlier classes.

A creditor is entitled to a grant notwithstanding that his debt is barred by limitation[14] or was assigned to him after the death of the debtor.[15]

Where a gift by will to a beneficiary is void by reason of his (or his spouse's) having attested the will, the beneficiary has no right to a grant of administration as a beneficiary named in the will, though this does not prejudice his right to a grant in any other capacity, such as a person taking on intestacy or a creditor.[16] Again, a sane person who commits murder or manslaughter is generally debarred by public policy from taking any benefit under the will or intestacy of his victim[17]: if so debarred, the killer is not entitled to a grant of administration of his victim's estate as a person beneficially interested.[18]

(f) *The personal representative of any other legatee or devisee (but not one for life or one holding in trust for any other person) or of any creditor of the deceased.*

(2) *CLEARING OFF.* Any applicant for a grant of administration with the will annexed must "clear off" all persons who have a prior right to a grant.[19] Return to the example of T's will, which gave his residuary real and personal estate to X and Y upon trust for his widow W for life and after her death upon trust for his three nephews A, B and C absolutely in equal shares. If A and B, who fall within class (c), wish to apply for a grant of administration with the will annexed, they must first clear off all persons who fall within classes (a) and (b). If no executor was appointed by or under T's will, no one falls within class (a). If X predeceased T, this clears him off. A and B must also clear off Y, who falls within class (b). Y must either renounce his right to administration[20] (if Y is willing to do so) or A and B must cite Y to accept or refuse a grant of administration. If Y does not appear to the citation, or appears but does not apply for a grant to himself, A and B may themselves apply for a grant of administration with the will annexed.[21]

(3) *PERSONS ENTITLED IN THE SAME DEGREE.* W, A, B and C all fall within class (c) and are therefore entitled to a grant in the same degree. A grant of administration may be made to any person entitled without any notice being given to other persons entitled in the same

---

[14] *Coombs v. Coombs* (1866) L.R. 1 P. & D. 193 and 288.

[15] *In the Goods of Cosh* (1909) 25 T.L.R. 785 (statutory assignment), but see *Macnin v. Coles* (1863) 33 L.J.P.M. & A. 175. See also Companies Act 1985, ss.539(2)(f) and 610 for power of liquidator of company to take a grant of administration to a deceased contributory.

[16] N.C. Prob Rules 1987, r.21

[17] *Ante,* p. 259. For proof of the crime see Civil Evidence Act 1968, s. 11. *Re Raphael* [1973] 1 W.L.R. 998; for relief against forfeiture see Forfeiture Act 1982, *ante,* p. 260.

[18] *In the Estate of G.* [1946] P. 183.

[19] N.C. Prob. Rules 1987, r. 8(4). Alternatively persons having a prior right may be passed over by the court, *post,* p. 312.

[20] *Post,* p. 315.

[21] N.C. Prob. Rules 1987, r. 47: see *post,* p. 314.

degree.[22] Thus A and B do not need to give any notice to C or W. It is, however, open to C or W to enter a caveat which ensures that no grant is sealed without notice to the person entering the *caveat*.[23]

Unless a registrar otherwise directs, administration must be granted:

(i) to a living person in preference to the personal representative of a deceased person; and
(ii) to a person of full age in preference to the guardian of a minor.[24]

If a dispute arises among persons entitled in the same degree as to which of them shall take a grant of letters of administration, the court[25] in its discretion selects the person or persons who are most likely to administer the estate to the best advantage in the interests of the creditors and beneficiaries.[26] Grounds of objection to an applicant include his bad character, bankruptcy or insolvency,[27] or ineptitude for business: an applicant who has an interest which conflicts with the proper administration of the estate will not be selected.[28] If there is no ground of objection to any applicant, the court's usual practice is to select the applicant with the largest interest, or who is supported by those with the largest interest.[29] This practice is, however, not binding on the court.[30]

2. Where the deceased died wholly intestate

(1) *ORDER OF PRIORITY.* Rule 22 of the Non-Contentious Probate Rules 1987 specifies the following order of priority[31] to a grant of administration where the deceased died wholly intestate after 1925:

(1) The person or persons[32] having a beneficial interest in the estate, in the following order of priority:
  (a) The surviving husband or wife.
  (b) The children of the deceased and the issue of any deceased child who died before the deceased.
  (c) The father and mother of the deceased.
  (d) Brothers and sisters of the whole blood and the issue of any deceased brother or sister of the whole blood who died before the deceased.
  (e) Brothers and sisters of the half blood and the issue of any deceased brother or sister of the half blood who died before the deceased.

---

[22] N.C. Prob. Rules 1987, r. 27(4): *cf.* the requirement of notice to another executor, see *ante*, p. 307.
[23] *Post*, p. 347.
[24] N.C. Prob. Rules 1987, r. 27(5). For grants on behalf of minors see *post*. pp. 312 and 341.
[25] On a summons before a registrar, N.C. prob. Rules 1987, rr. 27(6)–(8).
[26] *Warwick v. Greville* (1809) 1 Phill. 123, 125.
[27] *Bell v. Timiswood* (1812) 2 Phill. 22.
[28] *Budd v. Silver* (1813) 2 Phill. 115; *In the Goods of Carr* (1867) 1 P. & D. 291.
[29] *Dampier v. Colson* (1812) 2 Phill. 54 (applicant beneficiary); *In the Goods of Smith* (1892) 678 L.T. 503 (applicant creditor).
[30] *Cardale v. Harvey* (1752) 1 Lee 177, 179 and 180; *In the Goods of Stainton* (1871) L.R. 2 P. & D. 212.
[31] But subject to the court's power to pass over the person entitled under this order of priority, see *post*, p. 312.
[32] For illegitimacy see *ante*, p. 306, n. 4.

(f) Grandparents.

(g) Uncles and aunts of the whole blood and the issue of any deceased uncle or aunt of the whole blood who died before the deceased.

(h) Uncles and aunts of the half blood and the issue of any deceased uncle or aunt of the half blood who died before the deceased.[33]

The personal representative of any person has the same right to a grant as the person whom he represents.[34]

A person must have a beneficial interest in the estate in order to be entitled to a grant under paragraph (1) of this order of priority. For instance, if under the intestacy rules the surviving spouse is beneficially entitled to the whole estate, then the surviving spouse (or his or her personal representative) is the only person entitled to a grant under these paragraphs because no other person has a beneficial interest in the estate. In order to ascertain the person or persons who are entitled to a grant of administration, it is therefore necessary to apply the intestacy rules.[35]

(2) In default of any person having a beneficial interest in the estate, the Treasury Solicitor[36] if he claims bona vacantia on behalf of the Crown.

(3) If all prior persons entitled to a grant have been cleared off, a creditor of the deceased, or the personal representative of such a creditor,[37] or any person who may have a beneficial interest in the event of an accretion to the estate.

(2) *CLEARING OFF.* Any applicant for a grant of "simple" administration to the estate of a deceased who died wholly intestate must clear off all persons who have a prior right to a grant.[38] For example, a creditor who applies for a grant of administration must establish that each of the persons beneficially interested in the estate under the intestacy rules has either renounced his right to administration or has been cited to accept or refuse a grant of administration.[39]

(3) *PERSONS ENTITLED IN THE SAME DEGREE.* The rules and practice already considered in connection with grants of administration with

---

[33] This order corresponds with the order of entitlement on intestacy; see Chap. 2.

[34] Subject to (i) the preference of a living person over the personal representative of a deceased person (*ante*, p. 309), and (ii) the preference of the persons mentioned in classes (b) to (h) over the personal representative of a spouse who has died without taking a beneficial interest in the deceased's whole estate as ascertained at the time of the application for the grant, see r. 22(4).

[35] See *ante*, p. 31 *et seq.*

[36] Including the Solicitor for the affairs of the Duchy of Lancaster and the Solicitor of the Duty of Cornwall, N.C. Prob. Rules 1987, r. 2(1).

[37] Subject to the preference of a living person over the personal representative of a deceased person, r. 27(5).

[38] N.C. Prob. Rules 1987, r. 8(4). Alternatively persons having a prior right may be passed over by the court, *post* p. 312.

[39] If no persons are beneficially interested in the estate under the intestacy rules, the creditor must clear off the Treasury Solicitor who has a prior right to a grant.

the will annexed also apply where two or more persons are entitled in the same degree to a grant of simple administration.[40]

3. Grants to assignees

If all the persons entitled to the deceased's estate under his will or intestacy have assigned their whole interest in the estate, the assignee replaces the assignor (or, if more than one, the assignor with the highest priority) in the relevant order of priority for a grant of administration.[41] If there are two or more assignees, administration may be granted with the consent of the others to any one or more (not exceeding four) of them.[42]

4. Foreign domicile

Rules 20 and 22 of the Non-Contentious Probate Rules 1987 do not normally apply if the deceased died domiciled outside England and Wales.[43]

B. NUMBER AND CAPACITY OF ADMINISTRATORS

1. Number of administrators

(1) *MAXIMUM NUMBER.* Section 114(1) of the Supreme Court Act 1981 provides that probate or administration shall not be granted to more than four persons in respect of the same part of the deceased's estate. This provision has already been considered.[44]

(2) *MINIMUM NUMBER.* Section 114(2) also lays down the important "minimum number" rule. If under a will or intestacy any beneficiary is a minor, or a life interest arises, administration must be granted *either* to a trust corporation (with or without an individual) or to not less than two individuals, *unless* it appears to the court to be expedient in all the circumstances to appoint an individual as sole administrator.[45] For instance, in order to comply with the rule on an intestacy under which a minority or a life interest arises, a grant of administration may be made to the deceased's spouse and child of full age, or (if the deceased's spouse has been cleared off) to two of the deceased's children of full age.[46] The rule, of course, applies to a grant of administration with the will annexed

---

[40] *Ante,* p. 308.
[41] N.C. Prob. Rules 1987, r. 24.
[42] *ibid.* r. 24(2).
[43] *ibid.* r. 28(2): instead r. 30 regulates grants where the deceased died domiciled outside England and Wales.
[44] *Ante,* p. 300.
[45] On an application for administration the oath must state whether any minority or life interest arises under the will or intestacy, N.C. Prob. Rules 1987, r. 8(4), and the court may act on the prescribed evidence, Supreme Court Act 1981, s.114(3).
[46] As to joinder of a second administrator with the person entitled to administration see N.C. Prob. Rules 1987, r. 25.

as well as to a grant of simple administration.[47] On the other hand, the rule does not apply:

    (i) in the case of a grant to an administrator pending suit under section 117 of the Supreme Court Act 1981, which refers to "an administrator" in the singular[48]; and

    (ii) in the case of a grant of administration (whether or not with the will annexed) limited to settled land.[49]

(3) *POWER TO APPOINT ADDITIONAL PERSONAL REPRESENTATIVES.* If, pursuant to the minimum number rule, administration is granted to two individuals and one of them subsequently dies, there is no requirement that a replacement must be appointed and the survivor can continue to act alone. But, if at any time during the minority of a beneficiary or the subsistence of a life interest there is only one administrator (not being a trust corporation), the court has the power to appoint one or more additional personal representatives to act while the minority or life interest subsists and until the estate is fully administered.[50] The power is exercisable on the application of any person interested, or the guardian or receiver of any such person.[51]

2. Capacity of administrators

A minor[52] or a person who is incapable of managing his affairs by reason of mental or physical incapacity[53] cannot take a grant of administration. A trust corporation may take a grant of administration in its own name, either alone or jointly with another person.[54] Any other corporation aggregate cannot take a grant of administration: instead, letters of administration for its use and benefit may be granted to its nominee or attorney.[55] These rules are the same as those governing the capacity of executors.

C. Passing over a Person Entitled to Administration

The power of the court under section 116 of the Supreme Court Act 1981 to pass over an executor has already been considered.[56] The court

---

[47] The rule applies to an insolvent estate, *Re White* [1928] P. 75; and where the court passes over the person otherwise entitled to a grant, *Re Hall* [1950] P. 156: but it may appear expedient to appoint a sole administrator in such circumstances under s.114(2).

[48] *In the Estate of Lindley* [1953] P. 203; *In the Estate of Haslip* [1958] 1 W.L.R. 583 (decided on similar wording in Judicature Act 1925, s.163): for administration pending suit *post*, pp. 344–346.

[49] *Post*, p. 337.

[50] Supreme Court Act 1981, s.114(4), which also applies if there is only one executor, *ante*, p. 298.

[51] *ibid.* See also N.C. Prob. Rules 1987, r. 26.

[52] For grants of administration for the use and benefit of a minor see *post*, p. 341.

[53] N.C. Prob. Rules 1987, r.35 (mental incapacity).

[54] Supreme Court Act 1981, s.115(1): for trust corporation see *ante*, p. 301, n. 44.

[55] N.C. Prob. Rules 1987, r. 36(4); see *ante*, p. 301.

[56] *Ante*, p. 301.

has power under the same provision to pass over the person who would otherwise have been entitled to the grant of administration and to appoint as administrator such other person as it thinks expedient if "by reason of any special circumstances" this appears to be necessary or expedient.[57] The grant of administration may be limited in any way the court thinks fit. Probably the "special circumstances" need not relate to the estate itself, or the administration of it, but may extend to any other circumstances which the court thinks relevant.[58]

The court has used its power to pass over a person entitled to administration in a wide variety of special circumstances[59] of which the following are merely examples.

1. Bad character or other unfitness to act

The deceased's husband has been passed over because he was a man of drunken habits and was mismanaging a public house which was an asset of the estate.[60] A person serving a prison sentence may be passed over on the ground that it is impracticable to carry out the duties of an administrator from a prison cell.[61]

2. Person missing

If the person entitled has been missing for a number of years, he may be passed over.[62]

3. Person entitled abroad

If the person entitled is living abroad he may be passed over, particularly in urgent cases.[63]

4. Death of sole solicitor

If a solicitor in practice on his own dies, the interests of his former clients may be jeopardised if no grant of representation to his estate is obtained within a reasonable time after his death. In these circumstances

---

[57] See N.C. Prob. Rules 1987, r. 52, under which applications for passing over may be made to a registrar: see *ante*, p. 301, n. 49.
[58] *Re Clore* [1982] Fam. 113, [1982] Ch. 456: *cf. In the Goods of Edwards-Taylor* [1951] P. 24, 27; *Re Mathew* [1984] 1 W.L.R. 1011.
[59] For the extensive case law see Williams, Mortimer and Sunnucks, *Executors, Administrators and Probate* (17th ed., 1993), pp. 344 *et seq.*
[60] *In the Goods of Ardern* [1898] P. 147: see also *In the Estate of Paine* (1916) 115 L.T. 935 (widow who had propounded will found to be forged and had made claims against the estate passed over).
[61] See *In the Estate of S.* [1968] P. 302 (executor passed over); see *ante*, p. 302.
[62] *In the Goods of Callicott* [1899] P. 189; *In the Goods of Chapman* [1903] P. 192: see also *In the Goods of Peck* (1860) 2 Sw. & Tr. 506 (uncertain order of deaths); *In the Goods of Harling* [1900] P. 59.
[63] *In the Goods of Cholwill* (1866) 1 P. & D. 192 (deceased a farmer: son in New Zealand passed over and administration granted to deceased's sister limited until son or his attorney obtained administration).

the court may pass over the persons entitled and make a grant to a nominee of the Law Society.[64]

On the other hand, in *In the Goods of Edwards-Taylor*[65] the court refused to pass over a daughter of 21 years of age, who was entitled to administration of her mother's estate as the residuary legatee under her will. The daughter was alleged to be immature and therefore unfit freely to enjoy the estate but the court refused to pass her over merely in order to protect her from herself.

D. ACCEPTANCE AND RENUNCIATION

1. Person entitled to administration may accept or renounce

Like an executor, a person entitled to administration is free to accept or renounce office as he pleases. He cannot be compelled to take a grant of administration.[66]

2. Citation to accept or refuse administration

Again, like an executor, a person entitled to administration may be cited by the court to accept or refuse a grant of administration: such a citation is issued at the instance of any person who would himself be entitled to a grant if the person cited renounced. If the person cited does not appear to the citation, or appears but does not apply for a grant, the citor may himself apply for a grant.[67]

3. Acceptance of office

A person entitled to administration accepts office by taking a grant of letters of administration. But, unlike an executor, he does not accept office as administrator by doing acts in relation to the deceased's assets which indicate an intention to take upon himself the office.[68] "An executor who has intermeddled can be compelled to take probate, but an administrator who has intermeddled cannot be compelled to take a grant."[69] The court has never issued citations to take administration.

In *In the Goods of Davis*[70] administration with the will annexed was granted to X. Afterwards a later will of the deceased was discovered and X was cited to, and did, bring in her grant to the registry so that it might be revoked. The court refused to issue a citation against X to take a grant of administration with this later will annexed, because the court does not compel anyone (even an intermeddler) to take a grant of administration.

---

[64] *Practice Direction* [1965] 1 W.L.R. 552.
[65] [1951] P. 24: *cf. Re Clore* [1982] Fam. 113, 117; [1982] Ch 456.
[66] *In the Goods of Davis* (1860) 4 Sw. & Tr. 213.
[67] N.C.Prob Rules 1987, r.47.
[68] *In the Goods of Davis* (1860) 4 Sw. & Tr. 213; *In the Goods of Fell* (1861) 2 Sw. & Tr. 126: *cf. ante*, p. 303.
[69] *In the Goods of Davis, supra, per* Sir Cresswell Cresswell.
[70] *ibid.*

4. Renunciation

(1) *FORM OF RENUNCIATION.* Like an executor renouncing probate, a person renounces his right to administration in writing signed by him and filed in a probate registry.[71] Unlike an executor, he need not declare that he has not intermeddled in the deceased's estate.[72]

(2) *EFFECT OF RENUNCIATION.* Renunciation of administration in one capacity (*e.g.* as a residuary legatee) precludes the person who has renounced from obtaining administration in some other capacity (*e.g.* as creditor) unless a registrar otherwise directs.[73] But renunciation by a person of administration does not bind that person's personal representatives; after his death they are free to take a grant of administration to the original deceased.

5. Retracting a renunciation.

A renunciation of administration may be retracted with the leave of the court.[74] Retraction is permitted if necessary or expedient.[75]

III. THE RULE IN *STRONG v. BIRD*

A. THE ORIGIN OF THE RULE

1. Forgiveness of a debt

Strong v. Bird[1] was decided in 1874 and concerned the forgiveness of a debt. B borrowed £1,100 from his stepmother, who was living in his house and paying him £212 10s. each quarter for her board. They agreed that B should repay the loan by a deduction of £100 from the stepmother's next 11 quarterly payments. The stepmother deducted £100 from her next two quarterly payments but then refused to make any further deductions and expressly forgave B the debt. She continued to make quarterly payments of £212 10s. to B until her death. By her will she appointed B her sole executor and B proved her will. When she forgave B the debt there was no release of the debt at law because her forgiveness of the debt was not made by deed or supported by valuable consideration.[2] But B, as executor, could not sue himself for the debt and therefore, as from his stepmother's death, B was no longer liable for the

---

[71] *Ante*, p. 304. Again, like an executor, he cannot renounce in part except under Administration of Estates Act 1925, s. 23(1); see *ante*, p. 305.

[72] *In the Goods of Fell, supra.*

[73] N.C. Prob. Rules 1987, r. 37(2): *cf.* effect of renouncing probate, *ante*, p. 305.

[74] N.C. Prob. Rules 1987, r. 37(3); a registrar may give leave, *ibid.*

[75] *In the Goods of Thacker* [1900] P. 15 is an instance.

[1] (1874) L.R. 18 Eq. 315.

[2] *Pinnel's Case* (1602) 5 Co. Rep. 117a; *Foakes v. Beer* (1884) 9 App. Cas 605: in some circumstances the debtor may have a defence under the doctrine of promissory or quasi-estoppel.

debt at common law.[3] Normally equity compels a debtor executor to account for the amount of his debt at the instance of the deceased's creditors or the beneficiaries under the deceased's will or intestacy. Jessel M.R. held, however, that B was not liable to account because his stepmother had a continuing intention to forgive him the balance of the loan. The debt was released at law and there was "no equity against him" to make him pay the debt. So, the stepmother's continuing intention to forgive the debt rebutted the equity of the deceased's creditors or beneficiaries to make him pay the debt.[4]

2. Imperfect gift of property

The rule in *Strong v. Bird* has been extended from the forgiveness of a debt to an imperfect gift of property made by the deceased during his lifetime. In *Re Stewart*[5] a few days before his death, the deceased bought and paid for three bearer bonds through his brokers. He then handed his wife an envelope which contained the brokers' letter announcing the purchase and the bought note, and said to her, "I have bought these bonds for you." The bonds were not, however, delivered to the wife and immediately before his death she had no legal or equitable interest in the bonds. The wife was one of his executors and she and the other executors proved his will. Neville J. held that the wife was beneficially entitled to the bonds under the principle of *Strong v. Bird*, which he stated in this way[6]:

> "Where a testator has expressed the intention of making a gift of personal estate belonging to him to one who upon his death becomes his executor, the intention continuing unchanged, the executor is entitled to hold the property for his own benefit. The reasoning by which the conclusion is reached is of a double character—first, that the vesting of the property in the executor at the testator's death completes the imperfect gift made in the lifetime, and, secondly, that the intention of the testator to give the beneficial interest to the executor is sufficient to countervail the equity of beneficiaries under the will, the testator having vested the legal estate in the executor."

This reasoning is unconvincing. The legal title to the bonds vested in the wife in her *fiduciary* capacity as one of the executors appointed by the deceased, and not as intended donee. Why should this complete the imperfect gift made in the deceased's lifetime? *Re Stewart* has, however, been followed at first instance,[7] has been considered by the Court of Appeal[8] and has never been judicially doubted. In the present state of

[3] *Jenkins v. Jenkins* [1928] 2 K.B. 501.
[4] *Re Applebee* [1891] 3 Ch. 422, 429–430; *Re Pink* [1912] 2 Ch. 529: see also *Re Gonin* [1979] Ch. 16, 34.
[5] [1908] 2 Ch. 251: see also *Re Griffin* [1899] 1 Ch. 408, 412.
[6] [1908] 2 Ch. 251, 254.
[7] *Re James* [1935] Ch. 449 (imperfect gift of a house); *Re Comberbach* (1929) 73 S.J. 403; *Re Nelson* (1947) 91 S.J. 533. See also *Carter v. Hungerford* [1917] 1 Ch. 260: *Re Ralli's W.T.* [1964] Ch. 288; *Re Gonin* [1979] Ch. 16, 35 ("a simple rule of equity").
[8] *Re Freeland* [1952] Ch. 110: see also *Cope v. Keene* (1968) 42 A.L.J.R. 169 (High Court of Australia).

the case law authorities the rule in *Strong v. Bird* is applicable to an imperfect gift of any property, whether real or personal, made by the deceased during his lifetime.

B. REQUIREMENTS OF THE RULE

1. Deceased's intention

For the rule in *Strong v. Bird* to apply, the deceased must show during his lifetime a present intention of forgiving a debt or of making a gift of particular property (as the case may be), and this intention must continue unchanged until his death. It is not enough if the deceased merely intends, or promises, to make a gift on a future occasion.[9]

(1) *NOT A TESTAMENTARY INTENTION.* If the deceased's intention is to forgive the debt, or to make the gift, at his death or by his will, the rule in *Strong v. Bird* does not apply. Such an intention is testamentary and has no effect unless the deceased shows such an intention in his duly executed will. In *Re Hyslop*[10] the deceased by his will appointed X, who owed him £100, to be one of his executors. After his death a letter written by the deceased to X was found; the letter showed that the deceased intended to cancel the debt due from X. The will, but not the letter, was admitted to probate. The court held that X was liable in equity to pay the debt to the deceased's estate. The rule in *Strong v. Bird* did not apply because the deceased's intention to cancel the debt was testamentary. The letter was not duly executed as a will and was, therefore, not admissible in evidence and had to be disregarded.

(2) *NO CHANGE OF INTENTION.* The deceased's intention of forgiving the debt, or of making the gift, must continue unchanged until his death. This requirement is not satisfied if the deceased later takes security from X for the debt which she has previously forgiven,[11] or later lends to Y the car which she previously intended to give to X.[12]

2. Property vests in donee

The other requirement of the rule in *Strong v. Bird* is that the debt, or the subject matter of the gift, must become vested in the intended donee. It suffices if it becomes vested in him as sole executor (as in *Strong v.*

---

[9] *Re Innes* [1910] 1 Ch. 188; *Re Freeland, supra,* (promise to give car when put in running order: rule not applicable); *Cope v. Keene, supra; Simpson v. Simpson* [1992] 1 F.L.R. 601 at 623 (promise to give proceeds of sale of cottage when sold, rule not applicable.)

[10] [1894] 3 Ch. 522: see also *Re Pink* [1912] 2 Ch. 529, 536 and 538–539; *Re Greene* [1949] Ch. 333 and *Brown v. Selwin* (1735) Cas.t.Talb. 240 (also reported in 3 Bro.P.C. 607 *sub nom. Selwin v. Brown*).

[11] *Re Eiser's W.T.* [1937] 1 All E.R. 244.

[12] *Re Freeland, supra,* at p. 121; *Re Wale* [1956] 1 W.L.R. 1346. See Kodilinye [1982] Conv. 14, 26–28.

Bird itself) and in *Re Stewart*[13] it was held that the rule applied to one of several proving executors.[14]

Does it suffice if it becomes vested in him as administrator? In *Re James*[15] it was held to be sufficient that it had vested in the intended donee as one of two administratrices appointed by the court. In that case S became entitled to his father's house on the latter's death intestate. S "gave" the house to his father's housekeeper, handing her the title deeds, but he did not convey the house to her. She occupied the house as donee and S had a continuing intention to give the house to her until his own death intestate nine years later. The housekeeper was appointed to be one of two administratrices of S's estate. The legal estate in the house therefore vested in the housekeeper jointly with the other administratrix. Farwell J. held that under the rule in *Strong v. Bird* this perfected the imperfect gift of the house made by S in his lifetime. But, in *Re Gonin*[16] Walton J. doubted whether the rule ought to apply to an administrator who (unlike an executor) is appointed by the court and not by the deceased: it would seem "an astonishing doctrine of equity" that the gift is perfected if the intended donee manages to obtain a grant of letters of administration, but is not perfected if another person equally entitled to a grant does so.[17]

Several other problems still need to be resolved.[18] For instance, does the rule apply to an executor by representation?[19] And is the rule binding on the deceased's creditors, as well as on the beneficiaries entitled under his will or intestacy? The answer to each of these questions is probably no.

C. AN IMPERFECT RULE

There may be something to be said for not perfecting any imperfect gift made by the deceased in his lifetime—so that at his death all his assets pass under his will or intestacy. There may perhaps be more to be said for perfecting all the imperfect gifts made by the deceased in his lifetime, provided his intention to give continues unchanged until his

---

[13] [1908] 2 Ch. 251.

[14] In *Re Stewart* the other executors took probate and the wife later took a grant of double probate (post, p. 336). In *Simpson v. Simpson* [1992] 1 FLR 601, 623 it was suggested that an intended donee who was not the sole executor could, at least since 1925, not claim the benefit of the rule in *Strong v. Bird*. The point was reserved and did not have to be argued because it was held that there was no intention to make a present gift. In any case *quaere* whether the rule applies if the executor does not prove, see Kodilinye [1982] Conv. 14, 18–19.

[15] [1935] Ch. 449: see also *Re Ralli's W.T.* [1964] Ch. 288 (H made imperfect gift of her interest under T's will to her marriage settlement trustees of whom X was one; later X was appointed trustee of T's will; H died; X held H's interest on the trusts of the marriage settlement).

[16] [1979] Ch. 16, 34–35.

[17] *Ibid.* at p. 35; but see (1977) 93 L.Q.R. 486; Kodilinye [1982] Conv. 14, 16–17. As to persons entitled in the same degree to a grant see *ante* p. 308.

[18] For the effect of the Inheritance (Provision for Family and Dependants) Act 1975, see *ante* p. 150, n. 2.

[19] *Ante*, p. 298.

death; this gives effect to the deceased's intention when he is no longer able to perfect the gifts himself. But what is there to be said for the rule in *Strong v. Bird* under which an imperfect gift (or the forgiveness of a debt) is perfected only if the property (or debt) vests in the donee in a *different capacity*, and in a *fiduciary capacity* at that?

CHAPTER 14

GRANTS OF PROBATE AND LETTERS OF ADMINISTRATION

I. JURISDICTION OVER GRANTS

A. THE COURTS

A grant of probate or letters of administration is an order under seal of the Family Division of the High Court of Justice, which has exclusive jurisdiction in England and Wales to issue a grant.[1] The High Court also has authority to determine all questions relating to the grant or revocation of probate or administration.[2] The county court has jurisdiction (limited in amount) over any contentious matter arising in connection with the grant or revocation of probate or administration but it does not itself issue such a grant.

1. The High Court

Since 1971 the probate jurisdiction[3] of the High Court has been split between the Family Division and the Chancery Division:

(1) non-contentious or common form probate business is assigned to the Family Division; and
(2) all other probate business (termed contentious or solemn form probate business) is assigned to the Chancery Division.[4]

For more than 100 years before 1971, probate business had been dealt with in one court (the Court of Probate from 1858 to 1875) or in one division of the High Court (the Probate, Divorce and Admiralty Division from 1875 to 1971).

(1) *NON-CONTENTIOUS OR COMMON FORM PROBATE BUSINESS* is assigned to the Family Division. The expression has a technical

---

[1] Supreme Court Act 1981, ss. 25, 61(1) and 128, and Sched. 1. para. 3. For recognition of Scottish confirmations and Northern Irish grants of representation see *post*, p. 324.
[2] *ibid.* ss. 19(2), 25 and 128; Judicature Act 1925, ss. 20 and 175(1).
[3] "Probate jurisdiction" includes jurisdiction in relation to letters of administration as well as probates, Supreme Court Act 1981, s. 25(1).
[4] *ibid.* ss. 61(1) and 128, and Sched. 1, paras. 1 and 3.

meaning[5] which is defined in section 128 of the Supreme Court Act 1981:

> " 'non-contentious or common form probate business' means the business of obtaining probate and administration where there is no contention as to the right thereto, including—
> (i) the passing of probates and administrations through the High Court in contentious cases where the contest has been terminated,
> (ii) all business of a non-contentious nature in matters of testacy and intestacy not being proceedings in any action, and
> (iii) the business of lodging caveats[6] against the grant of probate or administration."

The great majority of grants of probate or letters of administration are issued "in common form" without any contention as to the applicants' right to the grant.[7] So a very high proportion of probate business is non-contentious or common form. Moreover, even in contentious cases, once the contest as to (say) the validity of an alleged will has been terminated by an order of the Chancery Division (or the county court) pronouncing for or against the validity of the will, any consequent grant of probate or letters of administration is non-contentious business. It follows that every grant of probate or letters of administration is made by the Family Division of the High Court.

Non-contentious or common form probate business is regulated by the Non-Contentious Probate Rules 1987.[8] Most of this business is dealt with in the Principal Registry of the Family Division in London or in one of the district probate registries.[9] A small part of it may, however, come before a judge of the Family Division by summons or on motion[10]—for instance, an appeal from any decision or requirement of a registrar of the principal or a district probate registry,[11] or a reference to a judge by a registrar who is doubtful whether a will was duly executed.[12]

(2) *CONTENTIOUS OR SOLEMN FORM PROBATE BUSINESS* is assigned to the Chancery Division. A probate action in the Chancery Division begins with the issue of a writ.[13] Probate actions are usually classified in three categories:

> (i) actions seeking a decree pronouncing for or against the validity

---

[5] *Re Clore* [1982] Fam. 113, 116 (matter categorised as non-contentious "could hardly be more contentious").

[6] For *caveats* see *post*, p. 347.

[7] A dispute between persons entitled to a grant in the same degree is determined by a district judge or registrar and is technically non-contentious, N.C. Prob. Rules 1987, r. 27(6). So is a dispute as to passing over, *Re Clore* [1982] Fam. 113, [1982] Ch. 456.

[8] See Supreme Court Act 1981, s. 127.

[9] Supreme Court Act 1981, ss. 104–106; District Probate Registries Order 1982, (S.I. 1982, No. 379). There are at present 11 district probate registries; all except one have one or more sub-registries attached.

[10] Though few probate matters are now heard on motion; the N.C. Prob Rules 1987 make no provision for motions; see Williams Mortimer and Sunnucks, *Executors, Administrators and Probate* (17th ed., 1993) pp. 396–397.

[11] N.C. Prob. Rules 1987, r. 65(1); *Re Clore, supra*, is an instance.

[12] N.C. Prob. Rules 1987, r. 61; *Re Bigger* [1977] Fam. 203 is an instance.

[13] R.S.C., Ord. 76.

    of an alleged will; if the court pronounces for its validity, the will is said to be proved "in solemn form";

(ii) "interest actions" in which the interest alleged by a claimant to a grant of letters of administration is disputed (*e.g.* the dispute may be as to whether the claimant is the child of the intestate); and

(iii) actions for the revocation of a previous grant of probate or letters of administration.

These three categories are not mutually exclusive. A plaintiff may bring a probate action claiming, as the son and only person entitled on intestacy to the deceased's estate, (i) to have the probate of an alleged will of the deceased granted in common form to the defendant as executor revoked, (ii) to have the alleged will pronounced against (*e.g.* on the ground that the deceased lacked testamentary capacity), and (iii) to have a grant of letters of administration of the estate of the deceased. If the defendant denies that the plaintiff is the son of the deceased and seeks to uphold the validity of the will, the action falls within all three categories.

2. The county court

    The county court has jurisdiction over any contentious matter arising in connection with the grant or revocation of probate or administration[14] if the value of the deceased's estate at the time of his death was less than £30,000, exclusive of property of which he was a trustee and after making allowance for funeral expenses, debts and incumbrances.[15] Within this monetary limit the county court has the same function as the Chancery Division in contentious or solemn form probate business.

B. JURISDICTION TO MAKE A GRANT

1. Property in England and Wales

    Until 1932 the court only had jurisdiction to make a grant of probate or letters of administration to a deceased's estate if there was property to be administered within England and Wales.[16] The object of the court in making grants was "to enable the executor or administrator to administer property in this country."[17] It was, however, immaterial whether the property to be administered was situated in England and Wales at the death of the deceased or was brought to this country after his death.[18]

---

[14] *In the Estate of Thomas* [1949] P. 336 (county court may pronounce on validity of a will).

[15] County Courts Act 1984, s. 32 as amended by Administration of Justice Act 1985, s. 51; County Courts Jurisdiction Order 1981, (S.I. 1981 No. 1123). The probate jurisdiction of the county court is not affected by the High Court and County Court Jurisdiction Order 1991.

[16] *In the Goods of Fittock* (1763) 32 L.J.P.M. & A. 157 (letters of administration refused); *In the Goods of Tucker* (1864) 3 Sw. & Tr. 585.

[17] *In the Goods of Coode* (1867) L.R. 1 P. & D. 449 (will disposing only of property in Chile not entitled to probate).

[18] *In the Goods of Coode, supra; Stubbings v. Clunies-Ross* (1911) 27 T.L.R. 127.

2. Discretion of the court

Section 2(1) of the Administration of Justice Act 1932[19] gave the court jurisdiction to make a grant notwithstanding that the deceased left no estate. Thus it is no longer a bar to a grant of representation that there is no property of the deceased to be administered within England and Wales and the court in its discretion may nevertheless make a grant.[20] But there must be sufficient reason for the court to make a grant in such circumstances.[21]

3. Proof of a will

The jurisdiction of the court to admit a will to proof by granting probate, or letters of administration with the will annexed, needs to be considered under two heads.

(1) *PROPERTY IN ENGLAND AND WALES.* Assuming that there is property to be administered within England and Wales, a will is admissible to proof:

- (i) if it appoints one or more executors, even though the appointed executor renounces probate[22]; or
- (ii) if it contains a disposition of property within England and Wales.[23]

In *In the Goods of Coode*[24] the deceased left two wills, one of which disposed of his property in England and the other of his property in Chile. The court admitted the will of his English property to probate but refused probate of the other will because it did not dispose of any property within England and Wales. On the other hand, if in this case either will had incorporated the other will by confirming it, both would have been admitted to probate because together they would have constituted the deceased's will.[25] A later will which merely confirms an earlier will is admissible to probate.[26]

A will or codicil, the whole of which is subject to a condition which has not been satisfied, is not admissible to proof.[27] Again an instrument

---

[19] Now repealed but its effect is preserved by Supreme Court Act 1981, ss. 19(2), 25(2) and 152(4), and Sched. 7.

[20] *Re Wayland* [1951] 2 All E.R. 1041.

[21] See *Aldrich v. Att.-Gen.* [1968] P. 281, 295 ("contrary to principle" for court to make grant to estate of person domiciled abroad, who left no assets in England): but s. 2(1) did not fetter court's discretion by any requirement as to the deceased's domicile.

[22] *In the Goods of Jordan* (1868) L.R. 1 P. & D. 555; *In the Goods of Leese* (1862) 2 Sw. & Tr. 442.

[23] The will need not *effectively* dispose—a will may be admitted to proof even though all the dispositions have failed by lapse, *Re Cuffe* [1908] 2 Ch. 500.

[24] (1867) L.R. 1 P. & D. 449.

[25] *In the Goods of Howden* (1874) 43 L.J.P. & M. 26. If the foreign will is independent of the English will and is not admitted to probate, an attested copy of it is filed and its existence is noted on the probate, *In the Goods of Astor* (1876) 1 P.D. 150.

[26] *Weddall v. Nixon* (1853) 17 Beav. 160.

[27] *In the Estate of Thomas* [1939] 2 All E.R. 567 (codicil inadmissible as conditional on testator surviving his wife, which did not occur); *In the Estate of O'Connor* [1942] 1 All E.R. 546: see *ante*, p. 5.

which does no more than completely revoke the previous will of the deceased is not admissible to proof[28]: of course such a revoking instrument is effective for its purpose and is admissible in evidence in a probate action in order to establish the revocation of the will. On the other hand, an instrument which effected only a partial revocation of the deceased's previous will is admissible to proof.

A will which merely appoints a guardian of the testator's children, but does not appoint any executor or dispose of any property within England and Wales, is not admissible to proof under this head.[29]

(2) *DISCRETION OF THE COURT.* Since the Administration of Justice Act 1932[30] the court may in its discretion admit a will to proof which does not appoint any executor or dispose of any property within England and Wales. In *Re Wayland*[31] the court granted probate both of the deceased's English will and codicil (which dealt with his estate in England) and of his two Belgian wills (which dealt with his Belgian property). The Belgian wills were admitted to probate under the court's discretion in order to obviate "an injustice to the estate in respect of the Belgian property"[32]: if the Belgian wills had not been admitted to probate, duty would have become payable under Belgian law on all the deceased's English and Belgian assets.

Probably, since the Administration of Justice Act 1932, the court may in its discretion admit to proof a will which merely appoints a guardian of the testator's children.[33]

C. RECOGNITION AND RESEALING OF GRANTS

1. Recognition of Scottish confirmations and Northern Irish grants

The Administration of Estates Act 1971 provides for the direct recognition in England and Wales of Scottish confirmations or Northern Irish grants of representation if the deceased died domiciled[34] in the country where the grant was issued.[35] Thus if the deceased died domiciled in Scotland or Northern Ireland leaving assets in England and Wales, the normal practice is for a grant of representation to be taken only in the country where he was domiciled.

---

[28] *In the Goods of Fraser* (1870) L.R. 2 P. & D. 40; *Toomer v. Sobinska* [1907] P. 106: see also *Re Howard* [1944] P. 39. The revoking instrument must be filed in the registry and its existence is noted on the grant of letters of administration.

[29] *In the Goods of Morton* (1864) 3 Sw. & Tr. 422. For the appointment of guardians by will see *ante*, p. 7–8.

[30] *Ante*, n. 19.

[31] [1951] 2 All E.R. 1041.

[32] *ibid.* at p. 1044.

[33] *Ante*, pp. 7–8.

[34] For domicile see Dicey and Morris, *The Conflict of Laws* (12th ed., 1993), pp. 115 *et seq.*; *Theobald on Wills* (15th ed., 1993), pp. 3–7.

[35] Administration of Estates Act 1971, s. 1. Under ss. 2 and 3 English grants of representation are similarly recognised in Northern Ireland and Scotland if the deceased died domiciled in England.

(1) *SCOTTISH CONFIRMATION.* A Scottish confirmation is equivalent to an English grant of probate or letters of administration: a Scottish executor nominate is equivalent to an English executor and a Scottish executor dative to an English administrator. Where a person dies domiciled in Scotland, a Scottish confirmation[36] which notes his Scottish domicile is treated (i) under section 1(2)(*a*) as a grant of probate to the executors named in the confirmation where it appears from the confirmation that they are executors nominate, and (ii) under section 1(2)(*b*) as a grant of letters of administration in any other case.[37]

(2) *NORTHERN IRISH GRANTS OF REPRESENTATION.* Where a person dies domiciled in Northern Ireland, a grant of probate or letters of administration made by the High Court in Northern Ireland and which notes his domicile there is treated as if it had been originally made by the High Court in England and Wales.[38]

(3) *EFFECT OF RECOGNITION ON CHAIN OF REPRESENTATION.* The chain of representation through proving executors under section 7 of the Administration of Estates Act 1925[39] continues through an executor who obtains a Northern Irish grant of probate if the grant is recognised in England and Wales.[40] But section 1(3) of the 1971 Act provides that section 7 of the Administration of Estates Act 1925 shall not apply on the death of a Scottish executor nominate.

2. Resealing of Commonwealth and Colonial grants

A grant of representation made in any country to which the Colonial Probates Act 1892 has been applied may be resealed with the seal of the Family Division of the High Court and thereafter has the same effect as an English grant.[41] The Act has been applied by Order in Council to the great majority of the countries within the Commonwealth.[42] It does not apply to the Republic of Ireland.

The court has a discretion whether to reseal such grants whereas Scottish confirmations and Northern Irish grants receive direct recognition without being resealed. The Colonial Probates Act 1892 does not, however, require the deceased to have been domiciled in the country where the grant was made.[43]

---

[36] Or certificate of confirmation. As to the noting, of property outside Scotland of which the deceased was a trustee, and the inclusion of real estate situate in any part of the U.K. in the inventory of the deceased's estate, see ss. 5 and 6.

[37] *ibid.* s. 1(1) and (2): s. 1 applies to confirmations, probates and letters of administration granted before, as well as after, the 1971 Act, s. 1(6).

[38] *ibid.* s. 1(4): see *Supra* n. 37.

[39] *Ante,* p. 298.

[40] *i.e.* if the deceased (whether the original testator or an executor in the chain) died domiciled in Northern Ireland and the grant notes his domicile there.

[41] Colonial Probates Act 1892, ss. 1 and 2. There is a chain of representation through a resealed probate.

[42] For a list of the countries covered, see Williams, Mortimer and Sunnucks, *Executors, Administrators and Probate,* (17th ed., 1993), p. 379 n. 27.

[43] But see N.C. Prob. Rules 1987, r. 39(3).

II. THE NATURE OF A GRANT

A.   PROOF OF A WILL IN COMMON OR SOLEMN FORM

1. Proof in common form

A will may be proved in common form or in solemn form. A will is proved in solemn form when the court pronounces for the validity of the will in a probate action. Unless the court has done so, a will can only be proved in common form.

If a will is proved in common form, a grant of probate or letters of administration with the will annexed is made in the absence of the interested parties. Indeed if a will contains a proper attestation clause and does not on the face of it give rise to any doubt,[1] the executors need only support their application for probate by their own oath[2] in order to obtain a grant of probate in common form. The executors are not required to give notice of their application for probate to the deceased's next of kin entitled under the intestacy rules.

(1) *REVOCATION OF A GRANT IN COMMON FORM.* Any grant made in common form may later be challenged in an action for revocation of the grant brought by an interested party.[3] Thus one of the next of kin entitled under the intestacy rules may bring an action for revocation of the probate of a will granted in common form to the executors, alleging that the will is invalid for some reason, such as want of due execution, the testator's incapacity, or want of knowledge or approval. If the court decides that the will is invalid, the probate is revoked. It is sometimes said that the next of kin, as interested parties, have a right to have a will proved in solemn form, notwithstanding a previous grant of probate in common form. It seems better to say that the next of kin, by bringing an action for revocation, may insist on the validity of such a will being determined by the court in contentious proceedings. The next of kin cannot compel executors, who have obtained probate of a will in common form, to start an action to establish the validity of the will in solemn form,[4] though the executors are at liberty to do so.

If there is any doubt as to the validity of a will, or any possibility of its validity being challenged in the future, it is advisable for the executors (or the persons entitled to a grant of administration with the will annexed) to prove the will in solemn form, rather than take a grant in common form. Otherwise, there is a risk that the validity of the will may

---

[1] See N.C. Prob. Rules 1987, rr. 12 (doubt as to due execution), 13 (doubt as to testator's knowledge of contents of will at time of execution), 14 (terms, conditions and date of execution of will), and 15 (appearance of attempted revocation); see *post*, pp. 354 *et seq*.

[2] *Post*, p. 351. A personal applicant must also produce a certificate of death, N.C. Prob. Rules, r. 4(5).

[3] Interested parties include any person entitled as on an intestacy and an executor or beneficiary under any other will of the deceased. Only a creditor to whom administration has already been granted may oppose an application for probate, *Menzies v. Pulbrook* (1841) 2 Curt. 845, 851.

[4] *Re Jolley* [1964] P. 262.

be challenged years later when material witnesses have died or cannot be traced.

(2) *EFFECT OF DELAY OR ACQUIESCENCE.* An interested party is not barred from bringing an action for revocation of a grant made in common form by lapse of time,[5] or his acquiescence in the making of the grant,[6] or his acceptance of a legacy under the will he seeks to challenge.[7]

2. Proof in solemn form

It is necessary to consider (1) what persons are bound by an order of the court pronouncing a will valid in a probate action, and (2) on what grounds a person bound by such an order may nevertheless have it set aside.

(1) *PERSONS BOUND.* Such an order of the court pronouncing a will valid is of course binding on the parties to the action.[8] The order is also binding on any person who, being *sui juris*, was aware (i) of the probate action and (ii) of his own interest, which would have enabled him to apply to the court to be added as a defendant.[9] In *Newell v. Weeks*[10] two of the deceased's next of kin, who were aware (i) of a previous suit in which the deceased's will had been unsuccessfully contested by other next of kin and (ii) of their own interest as next of kin, were held bound by the previous decision of the court pronouncing for the validity of the will. As Sir John Nicholl pointed out[11]:

"if they had been dissatisfied, they might have intervened at any moment of the proceedings ... they had not only a right, but it was their duty to intervene if they meant not to abide by the decision— their interests were directly affected; if the will had been set aside,

---

[5] *Re Flynn* [1982] 1 W.L.R. 310 (*obiter*): an action for revocation may be struck out by the court if the claim is frivolous or vexatious or otherwise an abuse of the process of the court, *ibid.* p. 318.

[6] *Bell v. Armstrong* (1822) 1 Add. 365, 373; *Goddard v. Smith* (1873) L.R. 3 P. & D. 7: see also *Williams v. Evans* [1911] P. 175 (next of kin, who as executor of will had obtained probate in common form, may bring action for revocation of probate). Acquiescence in a Chancery inquiry for next of kin has defeated an application for letters of administration made useless by the acquiescence, *Mohan v. Broughton* [1899] P. 211, [1900] P. 56: cf. *Re Coghlan* [1948] 2 All E.R. 68.

[7] *Bell v. Armstrong, supra,* at p. 374 (but the party challenging the will must bring the legacy into court); *Goddard v. Norton* (1846) 5 N.C. 76 (legacy paid to infant).

[8] Under R.S.C., Ord. 35, r. 2 the court has a discretion to set aside an order obtained where one party does not appear at the trial, see *Re Barraclough* [1967] P. 1, 11 (for instance, by unavoidable accident): as to compromise of a probate action see Administration of Justice Act 1985, s. 49; Sunnucks (1987) 137 N.L.J. 721.

[9] This is the modern equivalent of the old right of intervention, under which such a person might apply to the court for leave to "intervene" in the action.

[10] (1814) 2 Phill. 224 (the report refers to citations to see proceedings which are no longer issued; instead a person not joined as a defendant may be served with notice of proceedings, in order that he may be bound by the court's decision): see also *Ratcliffe v. Barnes* (1862) 2 Sw. & Tr. 486, *In the Estate of Langston* [1964] P. 163. As to the effect of a compromise, see *Wytcherley v. Andrews* (1871) 2 P. & D. 327; *Re West* [1948] W.N. 432.

[11] (1814) 2 Phill. 224, 233.

they would have established their claim. The *lis pendens* served as a public notice on which they were bound to act."

On the other hand, a person who is aware of the probate action but is not aware of his own interest in it, is not bound by the order of the court.[12]

The rule applied in *Newell v. Weeks* is a rule of substantive law peculiar to the probate jurisdiction of the court and is derived directly from the law and practice of the Prerogative Court of Canterbury.[13]

(2) *GROUNDS FOR SETTING ASIDE.* Even a person bound by an order of the court in a probate action may have the order set aside on one of the following grounds:

(i) that the order was obtained by fraud[14]—for instance, a "benefi-ciary" propounded a will which he had forged;
(ii) the discovery, after the order was made, of a will or of a later will than that previously pronounced for;
(iii) the discovery, after the order was made, that the will previously pronounced for had been revoked by the marriage of the testator.

A person not bound by an order of the court in a probate action is not restricted to these narrow grounds and may re-open issues already decided in that action. If such an order of the court is subsequently set aside at the instance of a person not bound by it, this enures to the benefit of those persons bound by it who were adversely affected by it because "the will is either good or bad against all the world."[15]

B.   DIFFERENT EFFECTS OF PROBATE AND LETTERS OF ADMINISTRATION

An executor derives his title from the testator's will, whereas an administrator derives his title from the grant to him of leters of adminis-tration. This distinction explains the differences which exist between the effects of probate and of letters of administration.

1.   Source of authority

A grant of probate *confirms* the authority of an executor, whereas a grant of letters of administration *confers* authority on an administrator.

(1) *EXECUTOR.* An executor who is expressly or impliedly appointed by the testator in his will derives his authority from the will and not from a grant of probate.[16] Similarly, a special executor in regard to settled land derives his authority from the will by express or deemed appoint-

---

[12] *Young v. Holloway* [1895] P. 87 (unaware of own interest under another will).
[13] *In the Estate of Langston* [1964] P. 163, 178 and 179.
[14] *Birch v. Birch* [1902] P. 62 and 130.
[15] *ibid.* at p. 138.
[16] *Chetty v. Chetty* [1916] 1 A.C. 603, 608; *Biles v. Caesar* [1957] 1 W.L.R. 156, 159–160.

ment by the testator.[17] Again, an executor appointed under a power conferred by the testator in his will derives his authority from the combined effect of the will and the appointment made under it.[18] In all these cases a grant of probate merely confirms the authority of the executor.[19]

(2) *ADMINISTRATOR.* On the other hand, an administrator derives his authority from the letters of administration which appoint him to his office.[20] This is so whether the letters of administration are granted with the deceased's will annexed or on intestacy.

(3) *PROOF OF AUTHORITY.* In order to prove his title in any court, any personal representative must produce a grant of probate or letters of administration (as the case may be).[21] Even an executor is not permitted to prove his title in any other way.[22]

2. Time at which property vests

(1) *EXECUTOR.* At his death the deceased's real and personal property vests in an executor appointed by him in his will if the executor is of full age.[23] A subsequent grant of probate enables the executor to prove that this has occurred.[24]

(2) *ADMINISTRATOR.* Section 9(1) of the Administration of Estates Act 1925, as substituted by section 14 of the Law of Property (Miscellaneous Provisions) Act 1994[25] provides that:

"Where a person dies intestate, his real and personal estate shall vest in the Public Trustee until the grant of administration"[26]

The original section 9 provided that an intestate's property should vest in the Probate Judge, *i.e.* the President of the Family Divison. This created a potential problem,[27] because the President of the Family Division is not a corporation sole and there could have been difficulties where the

---

[17] *Ante*, pp. 296–297.

[18] *Ante*, p. 297.

[19] By way of exception, an executor appointed by the court under its statutory powers does not derive his authority from the will; see *ante*, pp. 297–298.

[20] *Chetty v. Chetty* [1916] 1 A.C. 603, 609.

[21] For recognition of Scottish confirmations and Northern Irish grants of representation and resealing of Commonwealth and Colonial grants see *ante*, p. 324.

[22] *Chetty v. Chetty, supra,* at pp. 608–609. *cf. Re Crowhurst Park* [1974] 1 W.L.R. 583, 594 (unproved will of realty on death prior to Land Transfer Act 1987 admissible) and *Whitmore v. Lambert* [1955] 1 W.L.R. 495 (unproved will admissible in Rent Act case).

[23] *Woolley v. Clark* (1822) 5 B. & Ald. 744; *Chetty v. Chetty, supra,* (as to personalty); Administration of Estates Act 1925, ss. 1(1) and 3 (as to realty). As to devolution of property on death see *post*, pp. 368 *et seq.*

[24] *Whitehead v. Taylor* (1839) 10 A. & E. 210, 212.

[25] Part II (*i.e.* ss. 14–19) of the Law Reform (Miscellaneous Provisions) Act 1994 is based on the recommendations contained in the Law Commission's Report on *Property Law: Title on Death* (1989), Law Com No 184.

[26] The substitution of the original s. 9 (by s. 14 of the 1994 Act) took effect on July 1, 1995: see Law of Property (Misc. Provs) Act 1994 (Commencement No. 2) Order 1995: (S.I. 1995 No. 1317).

[27] It appears that no problem had ever, in fact, occurred.

holder of the office changed. The Public Trustee *is* a corporation sole and so the vesting of the property in him solves these difficulties.

The Public Trustee has no beneficial interest in, or duties to perform in respect of, property vested in him by section 9,[28] but a notice affecting land, which would have been served on the deceased but for his death, shall be sufficiently served, before a grant has been filed, if it is addressed to "The Personal Representatives of" (the named deceased) and left at or posted to his last known place of residence or business *and* a copy is then served on the Public Trustee.[29]

An example of a recent case where a notice was incorrectly served is *Edwards v. Strong*,[30] where a notice purporting to exercise an option to purchase the deceased's house was served on his daughters as the persons who would be entitled to his estate under the intestacy rules. The service was ineffective. There had been no grant of administration to the deceased's estate and the notice should have been served on the Probate Judge,[31] not on the next-of-kin.

The deceased's property vests in an administrator when letters of administration are granted to him in respect of that property.[32]

Section 9(2) of the Administration of Estates Act 1925, as substituted by section 14 of the Law of Property (Miscellaneous Provisions) Act 1994, also vests property in the Public Trustee where the deceased leaves a will but there is no executor with power to obtain probate. This may happen where the will appoints no executor, or where it appoints an executor but he is an infant or has predeceased the testator. Before the substituted section 9 took effect,[33] the position in these cases was not entirely clear. The substituted section is effectively retrospective[34] so there should now be no problems.

(3) *RELATION BACK.* A doctrine (or fiction) of relation back has been adopted by the courts for the limited purpose of protecting the deceased's estate from wrongful injury in the interval between his death and the grant of letters of administration to his estate. Under this doctrine, the letters of administration relate back to the death of the deceased.

"It is clear that the title of an administrator, though it does not exist until the grant of administration, relates back to the time of the death of the intestate; and that he may recover against a wrongdoer who

[28] Section 9(3), as substituted.

[29] Law Reform (Misc Provs) Act 1994 s. 18. Under s. 17, a notice remains effective where the person serving it has no reason to believe that the deceased has died, and it would have been effective but for the death.

[30] *The Times*, November 8, 1994.

[31] The notice should have been served on the Probate Judge (The President of the Family Division) because the deceased died before July 1, 1995, when the original s. 9 was in force. Had he died on or after July 1, 1995, when the substituted section took effect, service should have been on the Public Trustee. But in neither case should service have been on the next-of-kin.

[32] *Woolley v. Clark, supra*, (as to personalty); Administration of Estates Act 1925, ss. 1(1) and 3 (as to realty).

[33] On July 1, 1995.

[34] 1994 Act s. 14(2).

has seized or converted the goods of the intestate after his death, in an action of tresspass or trover."[35]

The administrator may sue in respect of any wrongdoing to an asset of the deceased's estate during this interval between death and the grant of letters of administration—for instance, in respect of trespass to the deceased's land[36] or breaches of covenant by a lessee of the deceased's land.[37]

This doctrine of relation back does not apply outside the limits of the purpose for which it was created; which was to protect the deceased's estate from wrongful injury during this interval. Administrators cannot invoke the doctrine in order to bring to life a tenancy which was lawfully determined by notice to quit served by the landlord on the Public Trustee during this interval.[38] "The doctrine of 'relation back' cannot breathe new life into a corpse."[39]

An executor appointed by the deceased in his will does not need to rely on this doctrine of relation back, because the deceased's property vests in the executor at death.

3. Litigation before grant

(1) *EXECUTOR.* An executor may begin an action in his representative character before obtaining probate and continue it until such time as he needs to prove his title, but at that stage he must produce a grant of probate.[40] It is immaterial that the defendant to the action is willing to admit the plaintiff's title as executor—the court nevertheless insists that the plaintiff must prove his title by producing a grant of probate, so as to protect the interests of the deceased's creditors and the beneficiaries under his will or intestacy.[41] If the executor brings an action against a defendant, who is willing to pay a debt due to the deceased as soon as the executor can prove his title to receive it, the court does not dismiss the action but stays proceedings in the action until the executor obtains probate.[42]

(2) *ADMINISTATOR.* An administrator, on the other hand, cannot begin any action in his representative character before obtaining letters

---

[35] *Per* Parke B, in *Foster v. Bates* (1843) 12 M. & W. 226, 233; *Thorpe v. Stallwood* (1843) 5 M. & Gr. 760; *Re Pryse* [1904] P. 301, 305.

[36] *R. v. Inhabitants of Horsley* (1807) 8 East 405, 410 (trespass to leaseholds); *Re Pryse, supra,* (trespass to freehold land).

[37] *Fred Long & Son Ltd. v. Burgess* [1950] 1 K.B. 115, 121.

[38] *Fred Long & Son Ltd. v. Burgess, supra.*

[39] *Per* Asquith L.J. in *Fred Long & Son Ltd. v. Burgess, supra,* at p. 121.

[40] *Easton v. Carter* (1850) 5 Exch. 8, 14; *Chetty v. Chetty* [1916] 1 A.C. 603, 608; *Re Crowhurst Park* 1974] 1 W.L.R. 583: see also *Biles v. Caesar* [1957] 1 W.L.R. 156.

[41] *Re Crowhurst Park, supra,* at pp. 590–592.

[42] *Webb v. Adkins* (1854) 14 C.B. 401 (if the defendant "pays money into court, he may be paying it to a person who may never acquire the title of executor; and so he may be forced to pay it over again"): *Tarn v. Commercial Banking Company of Sydney* (1884) 12 Q.B.D. 294.

of administration. In *Ingall v. Moran*[43] the plaintiff issued a writ "as administrator of his son's estate" claiming damages in respect of the son's death intestate in a motor accident caused by the defendant's negligence. The plaintiff did not take out letters of administration to his son's estate until nearly two months after the issue of the writ. The Court of Appeal held that the action must fail because the plaintiff had no title to sue when he issued the writ. The doctrine of relation back did not apply for the purpose of validating the invalid writ. If in this case the son had made a will by which he appointed his father his executor, the son's cause of action would have vested in his father at the son's death and the father would have been entitled to issue the writ as executor before obtaining probate.[44]

(3) *EFFECT OF ACTUAL POSSESSION.* If a plaintiff, whether an executor or an intending administrator, has had actual possession of the property which is the subject of the action before it came to the defendant's hands, the plaintiff may bring an action founded upon his possession—for instance, an action of trespass. In such an action the plaintiff does not need to rely upon his title as personal representative and therefore it is immaterial whether the plaintiff has obtained any grant of probate or letters of administration.[45]

4. Acts of administration before grant

(1) *EXECUTOR.* Before obtaining probate an executor[46] has power to do all the acts which are incident to his office, except those acts for which he needs a grant of probate in order to prove his title.[47] For instance, before obtaining probate an executor may:

(i) Take possession of any of the assets of the testator's estate and receive, or release, debts owing to the estate.[48] But if the holder of any asset refuses to hand it over, or any debtor refuses to pay, the executor cannot prove his title in an action against him without producing a grant of probate.[49] In practice many debtors are

---

[43] [1944] K.B. 160: see also *Chetty v. Chetty, supra; Hilton v. Sutton Steam Laundry* [1946] K.B. 65, and *Finnegan v. Cementation Co. Ltd.* [1953] 1 Q.B. 688 (plaintiff had obtained letters of administration in Eire but had no title to sue in England) and *cf. Stebbings v. Holst & Co. Ltd.* [1953] 1 W.L.R. 603 and *Bowler v. John Mowlem & Co.* [1954] 1 W.L.R. 1445. An administrator with the will annexed, like an administrator on intestacy, cannot commence any action in his representative character before obtaining letters of administration, *Phillips v. Hartley* (1827) 3 Car. & P. 121.

[44] *Ingall v. Moran* [1994] 1 K.B. 160, 167–168 and 170.

[45] *Oughton v. Seppings* (1830) 1 B. & Ad. 241 (money had and received, waiving the trespass).

[46] The executor must be of full age at the testator's death, *ante,* p. 300.

[47] *Re Stevens* [1897] 1 Ch. 422, 429–430, citing *Williams on Executors* (9th ed.), p. 249; *Kelsey v. Kelsey* (1922) 91 L.J.Ch. 382, 384 (notice to be served on "personal representatives" validly served on executors before probate). For appointment of new trustees by an executor before probate see *Re Crowhurst Park* [1974] 1 W.L.R. 583, 593–594: see *post,* p. 395, n. 9.

[48] *Re Stevens, supra.* He may also distrain for rent due to the testator, *Whitehead v. Taylor* (1839) 10 A. & E. 210.

[49] Revenue Act 1884, s. 11 as amended by Revenue Act 1889, s. 19; Administration of Estates Act 1925, s. 2(1).

unwilling to pay their debts before probate is obtained because they cannot be certain that the person claiming to be the executor has been duly appointed.[50]

(ii) Pay, or take releases of, debts owing from the estate.[51]

(iii) Sell and transfer to a purchaser any of the assets of the testator's estate. A conveyance of the testator's land the title to which is unregistered (commonly called unregistered land) by an executor to a purchaser vests the legal title to the land in the purchaser, but the purchaser can only establish the executor's authority to sell and convey by proving that the executor subsequently obtained probate.[52] Accordingly, a purchaser of land invariably insists on the production by the executor of a grant of probate before completion of the sale.[53] A transfer of the testator's land with registered title cannot be registered before probate is granted.[54]

(iv) Pay legacies or transfer property given by the will to the person entitled.[55] Again, the beneficiary can only establish the executor's authority by proving that the executor subsequently obtained probate.[56]

If an executor does any of these acts incident to his office and dies without obtaining probate, such acts "stand firm and good".[57] The death of the executor without obtaining probate determines his executorship,[58] but does not invalidate acts done by him before his death whilst his authority as executor subsisted.[59]

(2) *ADMINISTRATOR.* A person entitled to administration has no power to do anything as administrator before letters of administration are granted to him.[60]

(3) *PROTECTION OF THE ESTATE BEFORE GRANT.* In order to pro-

---

[50] For the protection of persons making payments in good faith to an executor who has obtained probate see *post*, p. 366.

[51] *Re Stevens, supra.*

[52] Or, if (say) the executor died without obtaining probate, by means of a grant to some other person of letters of administration with the will annexed, which establishes the appointment of the executor.

[53] *Newton v. Metropolitan Railway Co.* (1861) 1 Dr. & Sm. 583: for the indorsement on the probate or letters of administration of a notice of an assent or conveyance by a personal representative see Administration of Estates Act 1925, s. 36(5). Or the purchaser requires the vendor's solicitors to hold the sale proceeds to the order of the purchaser's solicitors, pending the issue of the grant.

[54] Land Registration Rules 1925, r. 170(4).

[55] *Re Stevens, supra; Re Crowhurst Park* [1974] 1 W.L.R. 583, 594. 95

[56] *Johnson v. Warwick* (1856) 17 C.B. 516 (*per* Jervis C.J., when a will has been proved (by a grant of probate or letters of administration with the will annexed) "the court has the legal optics through which to look at it"); see, *supra*, n. 52.

[57] *Re Stevens, supra.*

[58] Administration of Estates Act 1925, s. 5.

[59] *Wankford v. Wankford* (1704) 1 Salk. 299, 309.

[60] *Wankford v. Wankford, supra,* at p. 301; *Doe d. Hornby v. Glenn* (1834) 1 A. & E. 49; *Morgan v. Thomas* (1853) 8 Exch. 302; *Holland v. King* (1848) 6 C.B. 727 (notice to be served by administrator of deceased partner: intending administratrix cannot give notice before grant) and *cf. Kelsey v. Kelsey, ante,* n. 47; *Mills v. Anderson* [1984] Q.B. 704 (settlement of claim on behalf of deceased's estate prior to letters of administration not binding).

tect the assets of the estate before a grant of probate or letters of administration is made, the court may appoint a receiver pending the grant.[61] An application to the Chancery Division for the appointment of such a receiver may be made by any person interested, whether a creditor[62] or a beneficiary.[63] For example, the court appointed a receiver where an executor had carried on the deceased's solicitor's practice for three years without taking probate.[64]

5. Period after grant

These differences between the effects of probate and of letters of administration relate to the period between the death of the deceased and the grant of representation to his estate. There is one important difference which relates to the period *after* a grant of representation has been made—the chain of representation through executors is continued by a grant of probate, but is not continued by a grant of letters of administration.[65] Apart from this single difference, section 21 of the Administration of Estates Act 1925 provides that every person to whom letters of administration are granted has[66] the same rights and liabilities, and is accountable in like manner, as if he were the executor of the deceased. Moreover, if letters of administration are granted in respect of a deceased's estate, section 15 provides that no person shall have power to bring any action or otherwise act as executor of the deceased so long as the grant has not been recalled or revoked.

C.   PAYMENTS FOR WHICH A GRANT MAY NOT BE NEEDED

The general rule is that a grant of probate or letters of administration must be produced in order to establish the right to recover or receive any part of the deceased's estate situated in the United Kingdom.[67] There are, however, a large number of provisions, made by statute or statutory instrument, under which payment of particular sums otherwise due to the deceased's estate may be made without the production of any grant of representation to the deceased's estate.[68] Obviously the scope and

---

[61] For grants of administration *pendente lite* and *ad colligenda bona* see *post*, pp. 344–346.
[62] *Re Sutcliffe* [1942] Ch. 453.
[63] *Steer v. Steer* (1864) 2 Dr. & Sm. 311 (receiver and manager of deceased's business appointed); *Re Oakes* [1917] 1 Ch. 230; *Ingall v. Moran* [1944] K.B. 160, 169, 171–172.
[64] *Re Sutcliffe, supra.*
[65] *Ante*, p. 298.
[66] But subject to any limitations contained in the grant: for limited grants see *post*, p. 339.
[67] Revenue Act 1884, s. 11 (personalty) and extended to realty by Land Transfer Act 1897, s. 2(2), now replaced by Administration of Estates Act 1925, s. 2(1).
[68] Instances are: (a) Friendly Societies Act 1974, s. 68: (b) Trade Union and Labour Relations Act 1974, Sched. 1, para. 31 (as amended by Employment Protection Act 1975, Sched. 16, Pt. III, para. 32); Trade Union (Nominations) Regulations 1977 (S.I. 1977 No. 789), reg. 6 (as amended by S.I. 1984 No. 1290): (c) National Savings Bank Act 1971, s. 9; National Savings Bank Regulations 1972 (S.I. 1972 No. 764) reg. 40 (as amended by S.I. 1984 No. 602): (d) National Debt Act 1972, s. 11; Savings Certificates Regulations 1972 (S.I. 1972 No. 641), reg. 20 (as amended by S.I. 1984 No. 603): (e) Building Societies Act 1986, s. 32 and Sched. 7.

effect of each of these provisions depends on its own particular wording but some characteristics are common to most, if not all, of them.[69]

1.   Sum must not exceed £5,000

Almost every such provision specifies that the sum payable must not exceed £5,000. The Administration of Estates (Small Payments) Act 1965 made a £500 limit generally applicable by inserting this £500 limit in almost 50 such provisions listed in the First Schedule to the Act.[70] The Treasury has power to fix a higher limit. In 1975 the Treasury fixed a £1,500 limit on the sum payable and in 1984 increased this to £5,000.[71]

2.   Payment is permissive

These provisions authorise the payer to make the payment without the production of a grant of representation to the deceased's estate, but they do not compel the payer to make payment. The payer may insist on making his payment to the deceased's personal representatives after they have proved their title by production of a grant of representation. For instance, under section 25(1)[72] of the Industrial and Provident Societies Act 1965, if any member of a registered society dies and his property in the society in respect of shares, loans or deposits does not exceed £5,000 and is not the subject of any nomination, the committee of the society *may*, without letters of administration or probate of any will having been obtained, distribute that property among such persons as appear to the committee on such evidence as they deem satisfactory to be entitled by law to receive it. The committee's power to distribute under this provision is entirely discretionary.[73]

These provisions may be contrasted with those applicable to statutory nominations[74]: on the death of a nominator, payment to his nominee is obligatory, subject only to satisfactory proof of the nominator's death.[75]

3.   The payer is protected

Many of these provisions expressly protect the payer against the risk of making a payment to a person who turns out not to be entitled. For instance, section 27 of the Industrial and Provident Societies Act 1965

---

[69] The provision contained in the Revenue Act 1884, s. 11 (as amended by Revenue Act 1889, s. 19) is exceptional: it provides that the production of a grant of representation from a U.K. court shall not be necessary to establish the right to receive money payable in respect of a life assurance policy effected with any insurance company by a person who dies domiciled outside the U.K.; there is no maximum limit on the money payable and payment is obligatory, see *Haas v. Atlas Assurance Co.* [1913] 2 K.B. 209 (foreign executor entitled to judgment for policy money less estate duty).

[70] Administration of Estates (Small Payments) Act 1965, s. 1(12).

[71] *ibid.* s. 6; Administration of Estates (Small Payments) (Increase of Limit) Orders 1975 (S.I. 1975 No. 1137), para. 3, and 1984 (S.I. 1984 No. 539), paras. 2 and 3.

[72] As amended by Administration of Estates (Small Payments) Act 1965; S.I. 1984 No. 539, para. 2.

[73] *Escritt v. Todmorden Co-operative Soceity* [1896] 1 Q.B. 461.

[74] For statutory nominations see *ante*, pp. 18 *et seq.*

[75] See *e.g.* Industrial and Provident Societies Act 1965, s. 24

provides that all payments made by the committee under section 25 to any person appearing to the committee at the time of the payment to be entitled thereunder shall be valid and effectual against any demand made upon the committee or society by any other person.

III. FORMS OF GRANTS

There are three basic types of grant of representation:

(i) probate (which is granted when an executor proves a will);
(ii) administration with the will annexed (which is granted when a person other than an executor proves a will); and
(iii) administration or "simple" administration (which is granted when the deceased died wholly intestate).

Each of these basic types of grant may be general or limited—for instance limited as to the property to which the grant extends or as to the duration of the grant.[1]

A. GENERAL GRANTS

Most grants of probate or administration (whether or not with the will annexed) are general in the sense that the grant is not by its terms limited in any way. A grant may be general even though it was preceded by another grant in respect of the same estate.

1. Double probate

When probate of a will is granted to some but not all of the executors, it is the practice to reserve power to the other executors who have not renounced to apply later for probate. If such an executor later applies for probate, he receives a grant called double probate.[2] If he was a minor when the original grant was made, he must attain 18 years of age before he applies, and if the original grant was made to four executors (the maximum number permitted), he must wait for a vacancy to occur.

A grant of double probate is a general grant which runs concurrently with the original grant. Until the grant of double probate is made, the executors to whom probate was originally granted may exercise all the powers conferred by law on a personal representative.[3]

2. Cessate grant

A grant of probate or administration which is limited as to its duration terminates at the end of its allotted span. For instance, where a minor is

---

[1] Supreme Court Act 1981. s. 113.
[2] Such an executor may be cited to accept or refuse a grant at the instance of the executors who have proved, or the executors of the last survivor of them, N.C. Prob. Rules 1987, r. 47(2).
[3] Administration of Estates Act 1925, s. 8.

the sole executor of a will, administration with the will annexed may be granted to his guardian, limited until the minor attains the age of 18 years[4]: when he attains 18, the grant automatically terminates. On the termination of any grant by the occurrence of the event which limited its duration, a further grant called a cessate grant may be made. In this instance, on attaining full age, the executor may apply for a cessate grant.

B. GRANTS TO SETTLED LAND

1. Settled land grant

A special form of grant known as a settled land grant may be made on the death of a person after 1925 in whom settled land was vested at his death. The land must have been settled previously to his death and not be settled by his will, and it must remain settled land notwithstanding his death.[5] Such a grant is made to the deceased's special personal representatives. Consider an example. Land is settled on A for life, remainder to B for life, remainder to C in fee simple, and the legal estate in the land is vested in A (who is of full age) as tenant for life.[6] At A's death the land remains settled land because it is still limited in trust for B and C by way of succession. Accordingly, on A's death a settled land grant may be made to A's special personal representatives. B (who is of full age) is the next tenant for life and A's special personal representatives convey the land to B.[7] At B's death, however, the land ceases to be settled land if C is then of full age and has not in the meantime settled his interest in remainder. If at B's death the land ceases to be settled land, it vests in B's general personal representatives[8] and they in turn convey the land to C.[9]

2. Special personal representatives

Special personal representatives are either special executors or special administrators.

(1) *SPECIAL EXECUTORS*. Section 22(1) of the Administration of Estates Act 1925 provides that a testator may appoint, and if he does not do so, is deemed to have appointed, as his special executors in regard

---

[4] *Post*, pp. 341–343.
[5] Administration of Estates Act 1925, s. 22(1); N.C. Prob. Rules 1987, r. 29. "Settled land" has the same meaning as in the Settled Land Act 1925, see Administration of Estates Act 1925, s. 55(1)(xxiv): for the requirement that the land must remain settled land notwithstanding his death see *Re Bridgett & Hayes' Contract* [1928] Ch. 163.
[6] Settled Land Act 1925, ss. 1(1) and 19(1).
[7] *ibid.* s. 7(1). The conveyance to B is made by vesting assent or vesting deed, *ibid.* s. 8(1) and (4).
[8] Administration of Estates Act 1925, s. 1(1) and (3); *Re Bridgett & Hayes' Contract, supra*; see *post*, p. 365.
[9] Settled Land Act 1925, s. 7(5). The conveyance to C is made by ordinary assent or conveyance. Conversely, if the land continues to be settled land at B's death, it vests in B's special personal representatives, *In the Estate of Taylor* [1929] P. 260 (settlement by C); *Re Norton* [1929] 1 Ch. 84 (subsisting voluntary rentcharges).

to settled land, the persons (if any) who are the trustees of the settlement at his death, and probate may be granted to such trustees limited to the settled land. Consider again what happens at A's death in the above example; if he leaves a will and at his death S and T are the trustees of the settlement of the land,[10] then they are by express, or deemed, appointment the special executors of A's will in regard to the settled land. S and T may therefore obtain a grant of probate limited to the settled land.

(2) *SPECIAL ADMINISTRATORS.* Rule 29 of the Non-Contentious Probate Rules 1987 provides for a grant of administration limited to settled land to be made to the persons who are the trustees of the settlement at the time of their application for a grant.[11] Unlike special executors, the applicants need not be the trustees of the settlement at the death of the deceased. To continue with the above example, if S and T die without obtaining a grant of probate and new trustees of the settlement are appointed after A's death, the new trustees may obtain a grant of administration with A's will annexed, limited to the settled land. If A leaves no will at his death, the trustees of the settlement may obtain a grant of simple administration limited to the settled land.

(3) *GENERAL GRANT EXCLUDING SETTLED LAND.* A grant of probate or administration made in respect of the deceased's free estate alone must expressly exclude the settled land.[12] But, if the persons entitled to a grant in respect of the free estate are also entitled to a grant of the same nature in respect of settled land, a grant expressly including the settled land may issue to them.[13] This only applies if the applicants are entitled either to probate or to administration in both cases. If the applicants are entitled to probate in one case and administration in the other, separate grants are necessary.

3. Order of priority to settled land grant

The order of priority to a settled land grant is as follows[14]:

  (i) *The special executors* who take a grant of probate limited to the settled land.
 (ii) *The trustees of the settlement at the time of the application for the grant.*
(iii) *The personal representatives of the deceased.* The persons in classes (ii) or (iii) take a grant of administration with the will annexed (if the deceased left a will) or simple administration (if the deceased left no will), in each case limited to the settled land. If the personal representatives of the deceased apply for such a grant, they must clear off the persons who fall within classes (i) or (ii) unless these persons are passed over by the court.[15]

[10] Settled Land Act 1925, s. 30.
[11] For powers to make limited grants see Supreme Court Act 1981, ss.113 and 116; *post*, p. 339.
[12] N.C. Prob. Rules 1987, r. 29(5).
[13] *ibid.* r. 29(4).
[14] *ibid.* r. 29(2) and (3).
[15] *cf. In the Estate of Powell* [1935] P. 114.

A personal representative of the deceased (who is not a trustee of the settlement) is not bound to act in regard to settled land as well as the deceased's free estate. If he is not a trustee of the settlement, he may, before representation has been granted, renounce his office in regard to settled land without renouncing it in regard to other property, and he may, after representation has been granted, apply to the court for revocation of the grant in regard to settled land without applying in regard to other property.[16]

4. Land ceasing to be settled land

The provisions authorising a settled land grant do not apply if the land ceases to be settled land at the deceased's death. In that event the land vests in the deceased's general personal representatives.[17]

5. Position of purchaser

Section 24 of the Administration of Estates Act 1925 provides that the special personal representatives may dispose of the settled land without the concurrence of the general personal representatives, who may likewise dispose of the other property of the deceased without the concurrence of the special personal representatives.

The Settled Land Act 1925 requires every vesting instrument to describe the settled land,[18] so that a purchaser may identify the land without reference to the trust instrument. Unfortunately there is no similar requirement for a settled land grant, which is just as much a document of title to the legal estate.[19]

C. LIMITED GRANTS

1. Powers to make limited grants

Under section 113 of the Supreme Court Act 1981, the court has power to grant probate or administration in respect of any part of the deceased's estate, limited in any way the court thinks fit.[20] This wide power to make limited grants is subject to only one restriction: where the deceased's estate is known to be insolvent,[21] the section forbids severance of the grant of representation to it, except as regards a trust estate in which the deceased had no beneficial interest.

---

[16] Administration of Estates Act 1925, s. 23(1). For the power of the court to appoint a special or additional personal representative in respect of settled land see Administration of Estates Act 1925, s. 23(2)–(5) (as amended by Administration of Justice Act 1970, s. 1 and Sched. 2, para. 3); *In the Estate of Clifton* [1931] P. 222; *In the Estate of James* (1926) 162 L.T.J. 498.

[17] *Re Bridgett & Hayes' Contract* [1928] Ch. 163 (see *post*, p. 365) followed in *In the Estate of Bordass* [1929] P. 107. For grants where the deceased died intestate without known next of kin see *In the Estate of Birch* [1929] P. 164 and *In the Estate of Mortifee* [1948] P. 274.

[18] ss. 5(1) and (2) and 8(4).

[19] See A.H. Withers (1946) 62 L.Q.R. 167, 168 and Settled Land Act 1925, s.110.

[20] See N.C. Prob. Rules 1987, r. 51.

[21] *Post*, p. 438.

Again, if the court exercises its powers under section 116 of the Act to pass over an executor, or to pass over a person who would otherwise have been entitled to the grant of administration, and it appoints some other person as administrator,[22] the court may limit its grant of administration in any way it thinks fit.[23] Thus, on passing over, the power to make a limited grant is not subject to any restriction.

If a grant is first made limited to particular property or a particular purpose, a grant may later be made *caeterorum, i.e.* of all the rest of the estate. If the grants are made in the reverse order, a grant is first made *save and except* the particular property or particular purpose, and a grant limited to that property or purpose may be made later.

2. Limited probate

The appointment by a testator of an executor may be qualified as to the subject matter of his office (an appointment "to be the executor of this will as to the business of grocer carried on by me at the date of this Will"), or as to time (an appointment of an executor "during the minority of my son James").[24] Such an executor may only take a grant of probate limited to the property, or the time, specified in the will.[25]

3. Administration *de bonis non*

A grant of administration *de bonis non administratis* (usually known as a grant *de bonis non*) is made in respect of a deceased's unadministered estate. Such a grant, like a settled land grant, is by its nature limited as to the property to which the grant extends. The purpose of such a grant is to enable the administration of the estate to be completed.

(1) *WHEN MADE.* A grant *de bonis non* is made following the death of a sole, or last surviving, personal representative who died without having fully administered the deceased's estate. Two requirements apply:

    (i) There must have been a prior grant of probate or letters of administration to the personal representative who has died. If, for instance, a sole executor starts to administer the deceased's estate but dies before taking probate, an original grant of administration with the will annexed is made, not a grant *de bonis non*. Again the prior grant must not have terminated by the occurrence of the event which limited its duration; if this happens a *cessate grant*[26] is made.

    (ii) Any chain of representation through proving executors must have been broken.[27] A grant *de bonis non* cannot be made so long as the

---

[22] See *ante*, pp. 301 and 312.
[23] For an instance see *In the Goods of Baldwin* [1903] P. 61 (will only made specific gift to X: next-of-kin passed over and letters of administration (with will annexed) granted to X limited to property specifically given to X by will).
[24] *Ante*, pp. 294–295.
[25] *In the Estate of Falkner* (1915) 113 L.T. 927.
[26] *Ante*, p. 336.
[27] *Ante*, p. 298.

chain of representation through proving executors continues. In *In the Goods of Reid*[28] T died, having by his will appointed X and Y to be his executors. X alone obtained probate of T's will, power to prove being reserved to Y. X died, not having fully administered T's estate. By his will X appointed Z to be his executor and Z proved X's will. Accordingly Z was T's executor by representation.[29] The court therefore refused T's daughter's application for a grant to herself of letters of administration *de bonis non* with T's will annexed.

A grant *de bonis non* is also made following the revocation by the court of a previous grant of probate or administration. For example, in *In the Goods of Galbraith*[30] two elderly executors, to whom probate had been granted six years previously, became unfit to act owing to their physical and mental infirmity. As they had not fully administered the estate of the testatrix, the court revoked the probate and granted to another person letters of administration *de bonis non* with the will annexed.

(2) *TO WHOM MADE.* The rules of priority which govern applications for original grants apply equally to applications for *de bonis non* grants. Thus rule 20 of the Non-Contentious Probate Rules applies to an application for administration *de bonis non* with the will annexed, and rule 22 to an application for simple administration *de bonis non*.[31] An applicant for a *de bonis non* grant must clear off all persons who have a prior right to a grant: alternatively the court may pass them over pursuant to its power under section 116 of the Supreme Court Act 1981.

4. Administration for the use and benefit of a minor

A minor cannot take a grant of probate or letters of administration.[32] If the person to whom a grant of probate or administration would otherwise be made is a minor, administration is granted for the use and benefit of the minor until he attains the age of 18 years.[33] If a grant of probate or administration with the will annexed would otherwise be made, it is a grant of administration with the will annexed: if the deceased left no will, it is a grant of simple administration. This form of grant, formerly known as a grant *durante minore aetate*, is by its nature limited as to its duration and terminates automatically when the minor attains the age of 18 years or dies under this age. When the minor attains the age of 18, probate or administration may be granted to him.

---

[28] [1896] P. 129.

[29] Z may cite Y to accept or refuse probate of T's will, N.C. Prob. Rules 1987, r. 47(2): if Y does not appear to the citation, his rights in respect of the executorship wholly cease, Administration of Estates Act 1925, s.5.

[30] [1951] P. 422; see also *In the Goods of Loveday* [1900] P. 154 (grant to administratrix who could not be traced revoked, and grant *de bonis non* made); *In the Estate of French* [1910] P. 169.

[31] *Ante*, pp. 306 and 309.

[32] *Ante*, pp. 300 and 312. An infant is usually referred to as a minor in probate practice.

[33] N.C. Prob. Rules 1987, r. 32. As an alternative to a grant for the use and benefit of a minor, a trust corporation may sometimes take a limited grant until the minor applies for and obtains a grant, see r. 36(3).

(1) *WHEN MADE.* If the sole executor is a minor, a grant of administration for his use and benefit is made. But if there are two or more executors of whom at least one is not under disability, probate may be granted to any executor not under disability, with power reserved to the executor who is a minor to take probate on attaining full age[34]: in such a case a grant for the use and benefit of the minor cannot be made unless the executors not under disability either renounce or fail to take probate on being cited to accept or refuse a grant.[35]

In determining whether a minor is the person to whom a grant of administration would otherwise be made, rule 27(5) of the Non-Contentious Probate Rules requires administration to be granted to a person of full age entitled thereto in preference to a guardian of a minor, unless a district judge or registrar otherwise directs.

(2) *TO WHOM MADE.* Under rule 32 a grant for the use and benefit of a minor is made to:

(i) *A parent of the minor* who has, or is deemed to have parental, responsibility for him,[36] or *a guardian of the minor* who is appointed, or is deemed to have been appointed, in accordance with section 5 of the Children Act 1989.[37]

There is a single exception to this head (i). If a minor who is sole executor has no interest in the deceased's residuary estate, such a grant is made to the person entitled to the residuary estate, unless a district judge or registrar otherwise directs.[38]

(ii) Any person appointed by a district judge or registrar to obtain administration for the use and benefit of the minor.[39]

The person so appointed may obtain administration for the use and benefit of the minor in default of, or jointly with, or even to the exclusion of, any person falling under head (i). Thus any person falling under head (i) may be passed over.

If any beneficiary is a minor, or a life interest arises under a will or intestacy, administration must be granted either to a trust corporation (with or without an individual) or to not less than two individuals, unless it appears to the court to be expedient to appoint an individual as sole administrator. If there is only one person competent and willing to take a grant under heads (i) and (ii), that person may nominate a suitable person as co-administrator unless a district judge or a registrar otherwise directs.[40]

---

[34] N.C. Prob. Rules 1987, r. 33(1).
[35] *ibid.* r. 33(2).
[36] In accordance with—(i) section 2(1), 2(2) or 4 of the Children Act 1989, (ii) paragraph 4 or 6 of Schedule 14 to that Act, or (iii) an adoption order within the meaning of section 2(1) of the Adoption Act 1976.
[37] Or in accordance with paragraphs 12, 13 or 14 of Schedule 14 to of that Act. R. 32 (1) as amended by The Non-Contentious Probate (Amendment) Rules 1991, S.I.1991, No. 1876; and see Practice Direction [1991] 1 W.L.R. 1069. The amendments followed the enactment of the Children Act 1989.
[38] N.C. Prob Rules 1987, r.32(1) proviso.
[39] Rule 32 (2)
[40] N.C. Prob. Rules 1987, r. 32(3).

(3) *RENUNCIATION.* A minor's right to administration may be renounced only by a person appointed administrator by a registrar and who is authorised to renounce by the registrar.[41]

A minor's right to take probate as executor on attaining the age of 18 years may not be renounced by any person on his behalf.[42]

(4) *ACCOUNTABILITY OF ADMINISTRATOR.* An administrator who takes a grant for the use and benefit of a minor has the same rights and liabilities as an ordinary administrator.[43] "The limit to this administration is no doubt the minority of the person, but there is no other limit. He is an ordinary administrator: he is appointed for the very purpose of getting in the estate, paying the debts . . ."[44] and otherwise carrying out the due administration of the estate.[45] After his grant has terminated, he must account to the person who subsequently obtains a grant of representation to the deceased—often this person is the former minor, who takes probate or administration after attaining full age.[46]

5. Administration during mental incapacity

A person who is incapable of managing his affairs by reason of mental incapacity cannot take a grant of probate or letters of administration. Instead, administration may be granted for his use and benefit, limited until further representation is granted or in such other way as the district judge or registrar may direct.[47] If the deceased left a will, it is a grant of administration with the will annexed—otherwise it is a grant of simple administration.

(1) *WHEN MADE.* Unless a district judge or registrar otherwise directs, no such grant is made unless all the persons equally entitled with the incapable person have been cleared off.[48] As in the case of an infant executor, probate may be granted to any other executor not under disability, with power reserved to the incapable executor to take probate on his disability ceasing. Notice of an intended application for such a grant must be given to the Court of Protection.[49]

(2) *TO WHOM MADE.* Under rule 35 such a grant is made:

(i) to the person authorised by the Court of Protection to apply for a grant;

(ii) where there is no person so authorised, to the lawful attorney of

---

[41] *ibid.* r. 34(2).
[42] *ibid.* r. 34(1).
[43] Administration of Estates Act 1925, s. 21.
[44] *Per* Jessel M.R. in *Re Cope* (1880) 16 Ch.D. 49, 52.
[45] *Harvell v. Foster* [1954] 2 Q.B. 367.
[46] *Fotherby v. Pate* (1747) 3 Atk. 603; *Taylor v. Newton* (1752) 1 Lee 15 (accounting to creditor administrator).
[47] N.C. Prob. Rules 1987, r. 35(2): such a grant was formerly known as a grant *durable dementia*.
[48] *ibid.* r. 35(1).
[49] *ibid.* r. 35(5). For proof of mental incapacity see *Practice Note* [1962] 2 All E.R. 613; *Practice Direction* [1969] 1 All E.R. 494.

the incapable person acting under a registered enduring power of attorney[50];

(iii) where there is no such attorney entitled to act, or if the attorney renounces administration, to the person entitled to the deceased's residuary estate.

If there is only one person competent and willing to take a grant under heads (i), (ii) and (iii), and a grant is required to be made to not less than two administrators, that person may nominate a co-administrator unless a district judge or registrar otherwise directs.[51]

A district judge or registrar may override this order of priority by ordering administration for the use and benefit of the incapable person to be granted to such two or more other persons as he may direct.[52]

6.   Administration *ad colligenda bona*.

A grant of administration *ad colligenda bona* is made to any suitable person for the purpose of preserving the assets of the estate until a general grant is made. Such a grant is useful, for instance, where urgent action is needed and the person entitled to a general grant cannot readily apply for it.[53] A grant *ad colligenda bona* is usually limited to the purpose of collecting, getting in and receiving the estate and doing acts necessary for its preservation, and is always limited until a further grant of representation is made. The grant is one of administration, and the will (if any) of the deceased is not annexed because no distribution to beneficiaries is authorised. A grant *ad colligenda bona* may specifically confer any wider power (such as a power to sell the deceased's farming stock) needed by the administrator. But if wider powers are needed, or it is not clear what action the administrator may have to take, it is preferable to apply for a grant to be made, limited as may be appropriate, under section 116 of the Supreme Court Act 1981.[54]

7.   Administration pending suit

After a probate action has begun[55] the court has power under section 117 of the Supreme Court Act 1981 to grant administration of the deceased's estate to an administrator. Such a grant of administration pending suit is limited to the duration of the probate action and terminates at its

---

[50] For enduring power of attorney see *Practice Direction (Powers of Attorney)* [1986] 1 W.L.R. 419.

[51] N.C. Prob. Rules 1987, r. 35(3).

[52] *ibid*. r. 35(4).

[53] *In the Goods of Bolton* [1899] P. 186 (next of kin in South America, goodwill of deceased's business as a newsagent needed to be sold before it became valueless; grant *ad colligendum* made to deceased's friend); see also *In the Goods of Stewart* (1869) L.R. 1 P. & D. 727; *In the Goods of Schwerdtfeger* (1876) 1 P.D. 424; *In the Goods of Ashley* (1890) 15 P.D. 120; *In the Goods of Roberts* [1898] P. 149; *Re Clore* [1982] Fam. 113, [1982] Ch. 456 (capital transfer tax dispute: Official Solicitor, not executors, appointed): N.C. Prob. Rules 1987, r. 52.

[54] *Ante*, pp. 301 and 312: see *In the Goods of Wyckoff* (1862) 32 L.J.P.M. & A. 214; *In the Goods of Suarez* [1897] P. 82.

[55] *Salter v. Salter* [1896] P. 291 (caveator appearing to warning but no writ issued: no jurisdiction to grant administration *pendente lite*).

conclusion.[56] The person entitled may then take a grant of probate or administration as appropriate.

(1) *WHEN MADE.* A grant of administration pending suit is made if this is proper in all the circumstances. In general a grant is justified if there are assets of the estate to be collected and safeguarded.[57] But in *Mortimer v. Paull*[58] the court refused to make such a grant where a probate action had been begun to determine the validity of a codicil, but the appointment of executors by the deceased's will was not challenged.[59] An application for the appointment of an administrator pending suit may be made by any party to the probate action or by any other interested person, such as a creditor.[60]

(2) *TO WHOM MADE.* Usually such a grant is made to a person unconnected with the action,[61] such as an accountant, and not to a party to the action unless all parties consent.[62] A sole administrator pending suit may be appointed, although there is the possibility of a minority or a life interest arising, because section 117 refers to the appointment of "an administrator" in the singular and an administrator pending suit is under the constant supervision of the court.[63]

(3) *FUNCTION OF ADMINISTRATOR PENDING SUIT.* Section 117 provides that an administrator pending suit shall have all the rights, dutes and powers of a general administrator,[64] subject to an important restriction—he must not make any distribution of the deceased's estate to any beneficiary without the leave of the court.[65] The administrator is subject to the immediate control of the court and acts under its direction[66]: he should, for instance, obtain the directions of the court as to any disputed debt.[67].

The administrator, like a receiver, must lodge his accounts for passing

---

[56] *Weiland v. Bird* [1894] P. 262 (probate action terminates with decree); *Taylor v. Taylor* (1881) 3 P.D. 29 (appeal extends probate action).

[57] *Re Bevan* [1948] 1 All E.R. 271.

[58] (1870) L.R. 2 P. & D. 85.

[59] See also *Horrell v. Witts* (1866) L.R. 1 P. & D. 103 and *In the Estate of Day* [1940] 2 All E.R. 544 (only second codicil disputed: court pronounced for will appointing executors and first codicil, the executors undertaking not to dispose of property dealt with in second codicil pending the probate action).

[60] *In the Goods of Evans* (1890) 15 P.D. 215; *In the Estate of Cleaver* [1905] P. 319. Application is made in the Chancery Division, R.S.C., Ord. 76, r. 15, and after appointment by the Chancery Division the administrator applies to the Principal Registry of the Family Division for a grant.

[61] *Stratton v. Ford* (1755) 2 Lee 216; *Whittle v. Keats* (1866) 35 L.J.P. & M. 54.

[62] *Re Griffin* [1925] P. 38 (plaintiff appointed without defendant's consent as appointment was clearly desirable).

[63] *In the Estate of Lindley* [1953] P. 203; *In the Estate of Haslip* [1958] 1 W.L.R. 583; see *ante*, p. 311.

[64] *Re Toleman* [1897] 1 Ch. 866 (administrator *pendente lite* may be sued by a creditor of the deceased without any leave of the court).

[65] Or in such circumstances as may be prescribed by rules of court, Supreme Court Act 1981, ss. 117(2) and 151(1).

[66] *ibid.* s. 117(2).

[67] *Charlton v. Hindmarsh* (1860) 1 Sw. & Tr. 519.

by the court[68] and he is entitled to such reasonable remuneration as the court thinks fit out of the deceased's estate.[69]

8. Representation in legal proceedings

If there is no personal representative of the deceased and it is necessary for the estate to be represented in legal proceedings, a grant of administration limited to an action (known as a grant *ad litem*) may be made under section 116 of the Supreme Court Act 1981.[70] Such a grant is limited to bringing, defending or being a party to particular legal proceedings. Thus an intending plaintiff, who wishes to bring an action for damages against the deceased's estate in respect of the deceased's negligence in a motor accident, may apply for a grant to be made to the plaintiff's nominee, limited to defending the action.[71]

Since 1971 the Rules of the Supreme Court have provided a simpler alternative procedure, which is applicable where any person against whom an action would have lain has died but the cause of action survives.[72] If no grant of probate or administration has been made, the plaintiff may bring his action against the estate of the deceased (*e.g.* against "the personal representatives of A.B. deceased") and then apply in the action for an order appointing a person to represent the deceased's estate for the purpose of the proceedings.[73] This procedure is likely to be adopted in preference to a grant of administration *ad litem* but it is not applicable to an action to be brought by (and not against) the deceased's estate, or to an action which would not have lain against the deceased, such as an application for family provision on death.

---

[68] R.S.C., Ord. 30, rr. 2–4 and 6 and Ord. 76, r. 15(2); *Practice Direction* [1973] 1 W.L.R. 627.
[69] Supreme Court Act 1981, s. 117(3): see also *Re Howlett* [1950] P. 177. See *post*, p. 406.
[70] *Ante*, pp. 301 and 312.
[71] *In the Estate of Simpson*; *In the Estate of Gunning* [1936] P. 40; *In the Goods of Knight* [1939] 3 All E.R. 928 (grant *ad litem* to Treasury Solicitor); *In the Estate of Newsham* [1967] P. 230.
[72] R.S.C., Ord. 15, r. 6A: Supreme Court Act 1981, s. 87(2) (replacing Proceedings Against Estates Act 1970, s. 2, as amended by Administration of Justice Act 1977, s. 27). As to the County Court, see C.C.R. 1981, Ord. 5, r. 8.
[73] R.S.C., Ord. 15, r. 6A: the deceased driver's insurers may be appointed in a running-down action. As to the appointment of the Official Solicitor see r. 6A(5A); *Re Amirteymour* [1979] 1 W.L.R. 63. See also R.S.C., Ord. 15, r. 15; *Lean v. Alston* [1947] 1 K.B. 467.

CHAPTER 15

THE MAKING AND REVOCATION OF GRANTS

I. THE MAKING OF GRANTS

A. CAVEATS AND CITATIONS

1. Caveats

A *caveat* is a notice in writing to the Family Division of the High Court that no grant is to be sealed in the deceased's estate without notice to the *caveator*, the person who enters the *caveat*.[1] An index of *caveats* entered in any registry is kept and is searched on any application for a grant being made in any registry.[2] Thus the entry of a *caveat* stops the issue of any grant in the deceased's estate (except to the *caveator* himself) until the caveat ceases to be effective. It gives the *caveator* time to take legal advice, or collect evidence, so that he may decide whether to oppose an application by another person for a grant.

(1) *WARNING OF* CAVEAT. When an applicant for a grant finds that a *caveat* has been entered, he may issue a warning in the prescribed form to the *caveator*.[3] A warning states the interest of the applicant (*e.g.* that he is the executor of the will of the deceased, or interested on intestacy) and sets out two alternative courses of action open to the *caveator*:

  (i) To enter an appearance to the warning in the Registry, stating the *caveator's* contrary interest (*e.g.* that he is the executor of a different will of the deceased).[4] If the *caveator* enters an appearance, no

---

[1] *Caveats* are regulated by N.C. Prob. Rules 1987, r. 44.

[2] Supreme Court Act 1981, s. 108; N.C. Prob. Rules 1987, r. 44(4) and r. 44(1): notice of the entry of a *caveat* in the Principal Registry or in a district registry is immediately given to the registry maintaining the current index of grant applications, this is now the Leeds District Probate Registry; a *caveat* does not prevent a grant being sealed on the day the *caveat* is entered. A *caveat* is effective against the resealing of Commonwealth or Colonial grants, but does not stop the issue of a grant *ad colligenda bona*, *Re Clore* [1982] Fam. 113. [1982] Ch. 456.

[3] N.C. Prob. Rules 1987, r. 44(5): any person interested may issue a warning. Since August 1988, the index of *caveats* has been maintained at the Leeds District Probate Registry and so warnings must be lodged at Leeds; see *Practice Direction* [1988] 3 All E.R. 544.

[4] N.C. Prob. Rules 1987, r. 44(10); appearance to a warning must be entered at Leeds, *Practice Direction* [1988] 3 All E.R. 544.

grant can be issued without an order of the court.[5] Often the applicant or the *caveator* commences a probate action at this point in order to obtain the decision of the court as to who is entitled to a grant.

(ii) To issue a summons for directions if the *caveator* has no contrary interest but wishes to show cause against the sealing of a grant to the applicant.[6] The *caveator* and the applicant may, for instance, be entitled to a grant in the same degree.

If the *caveator* does not follow either of these courses of action, the *caveat* ceases to be effective[7] and a grant of probate or administration may be issued to the applicant.

(2) *DURATION OF A* CAVEAT. A *caveat* also ceases to be effective at the expiration of six months beginning with the date on which it was entered.[8] A *caveator* may lodge a written application for its extension during the last month of this six months' period: each time the *caveator* does this, the caveat remains in force for another six months.[9]

A *caveat* ceases to be effective if the *caveator* withdraws it before he enters an appearance to a warning.[10]

(3) *STANDING SEARCH FOR A GRANT*. A person who wishes to commence family provision or other proceedings should not enter a *caveat*.[11] Instead, he should apply for a standing search to be made for any grant of representation to the deceased's estate issued within the previous 12 months or within the following six months.[12]

2. Citations

There are three types of citation.[13] Two have already been considered, namely a citation to accept or refuse a grant[14] and a citation to take probate.[15] The third type is a citation to propound a will.

A person who is interested on intestacy, or under an earlier will of the deceased, may cite the executors and beneficiaries under an alleged will, or an alleged later will, to propound it. If they fail to enter an appearance and propound the alleged will, the citor may apply for an order for a grant in common form as if the alleged will were invalid.[16]

---

[5] N.C. Prob. Rules 1987, rr. 44(13) and 45(3): for the caveator's position in a consequent probate action see *Rose v. Epstein* [1974] 1 W.L.R. 1565: for *caveats* entered by a vexatious litigant see *Re Hancock* [1978] C.L.Y. 1443.

[6] N.C. Prob. Rules 1987, r. 44(6).

[7] *ibid.* r. 44(12); the *caveator* has at least eight days to do so, see r. 44(10) and (6).

[8] *ibid.* r. 44(3a); but see r. 48(8) and (13).

[9] *ibid.* r. 44(3); but see r. 44(4).

[10] *ibid.* r. 44(11).

[11] He will not be objecting to the validity of a will or to the issue of a grant: he will be claiming that the will does not make adequate financial provision for him.

[12] N.C. Prob. Rules 1987, r. 43: for exclusion see r. 43(3).

[13] For the issue of citations see N.C. Prob. Rules 1987, r. 46.

[14] *Ante*, p. 303 (probate) and p. 314 (administration).

[15] *Ante*, p. 304.

[16] N.C. Prob. Rules 1987, r. 48: see also *In the Goods of Morton* (1863) 3 Sw. & Tr. 179; *In the Goods of Dennis* [1899] P. 191; *In the Goods of Bootle* (1901) 84 L.T. 570.

A citation to propound a will is not, however, appropriate if the will in question has already been proved in common form. In this case, the person challenging the will may bring a probate action for the revocation of the previous grant.[17]

This procedure by citation is useful where there is doubt as to the validity of a will.[18] The procedure cannot, however, be invoked by an executor of a will who doubts the validity of a later codicil. In this case the executor should apply for a grant of probate in solemn form and, if he has reason to believe that the codicil is invalid, should adduce evidence of its invalidity.[19]

B.   TIME LIMIT FOR ISSUING A GRANT

1.   Minimum time

Normally no grant of probate or letters of administration with the will annexed may be issued within seven days, and no grant of simple administration within 14 days, of the deceased's death. An earlier grant may be issued with the leave of a registrar.[20]

2.   No maximum time

There is no maximum limit of the time within which a grant must be obtained. But penalties are laid down for administering an estate without obtaining a grant of representation.[21]

C.   LIABILITY OF PERSONAL REPRESENTATIVES FOR INHERITANCE TAX

The overall tax position was discussed in Chapter 12. This part of this Chapter is concerned only with the liability of the deceased's personal representatives for inheritance tax. The incidence of the tax on the beneficial interests under the deceased's will or intestacy is considered later.[22]

1.   Liability of the personal representatives

Under section 200(1) of the Inheritance Tax Act 1984 the deceased's personal representatives are liable for the inheritance tax charged on his death on the value of:

---

[17] *Re Jolley* [1964] P. 262.
[18] *In the Estate of Muirhead* [1971] P. 263, following *In the Goods of Benbow* (1862) 2 Sw. & Tr. 488
[19] *In the Estate of Muirhead, supra,* at p. 270. Cairns J. also suggested *obiter* that his decision might apply in a case where there were two wills with the same executors, the later will if valid revoking the earlier.
[20] N.C. Prob. Rules 1987, r. 6(2); see also r. 6(1) (registrar's inquiries to be answered before grant issued).
[21] Stamp Act 1815, s. 37 as amended by Finance Act 1975, s. 59(5) and Sched. 13 Pt. I; Customs and Inland Revenue Act 1991, s. 40.
[22] *Post,* p. 433.

(i) any property which was not immediately before his death comprised in a settlement; and

(ii) any land in the United Kingdom which immediately before his
death was comprised in a settlement and which devolves upon
or vests in the personal representatives.[23]

Head (ii) is relatively narrow whereas head (i) is very wide, including,
not only the deceased's property which vests in his personal representatives, but also the deceased's severable notional share of property held
jointly, and the deceased's foreign property which does not vest in them.

This liability of a personal representative for inheritance tax under section 200(1) is a personal liability—his own assets are liable to be taken
in execution to satisfy the tax due to the Crown.[24]

2.   Limit on extent of liability.

In order to protect a personal representative section 204(1) imposes a
limit on the extent of his personal liability—he is not liable for tax under
head (i) except to the extent of the assets which he has received as personal representative or might have so received but for his own neglect
or default. This upper limit becomes operative in a case where the tax
payable on the deceased's death (including the tax payable on his foreign
property) exceeds the amount of the assets which the personal representative either received or ought to have received.[25] A similar upper limit
applies under head (ii).

3.   Delivery of Inland Revenue Account

The personal representatives[26] must deliver an account to the Commissioners of Inland Revenue within 12 months from the end of the month
in which the death occurs or (if this is later) within three months from
the date on which they first acted.[27] But normally, no account need be
delivered if the value of the deceased's estate does not exceed £125,000.[28]
The account specifies to the best of their knowledge and belief[29] the
nature and value of all property which formed part of the deceased's

---

[23] For exceptions to the personal representatives' liability under s. 200(1) see ss. 30–35 (as
amended), 125–130, and 207–208; the exceptions include heritage property and woodlands to which special accountability rules apply: for the definition of settlement see s.
43. For the contingent secondary liability of personal representatives to tax in respect of
lifetime transfers see s. 199(2), as amended by Finance Act 1986, Sched. 19, para. 26.

[24] I.R.C. v. Stannard [1984] 1 W.L.R. 1039 (order is in de bonis propriis form).

[25] See Re Clore [1982] Ch. 456.

[26] This means executors, any person by whom or on whose behalf an application for a
grant of administration or for the resealing of a grant made outside the U.K. is made,
and an executor de son tort, see s. 272: as to an executor de son tort see post, pp. 515 et seq.

[27] ss. 216(1) and (6) and 257. For delivery of the account to a probate registry instead see
s. 257(3).

[28] If the deceased dies after 31 March 1991 his estate will be "excepted" when: (i) the gross
value is less than £125,000: (ii) there is no settled property: (iii) not more than £15,000
is property outside the UK: (iv) the deceased died domiciled in the UK and had made
no potentially exempt transfers with seven years of his death: Inheritance Tax (Delivery
of Accounts) Regulations 1991, SI 1991, No. 1248.

[29] I.R.C. v. Stype Trustees (Jersey) Ltd. [1985] 1 W.L.R. 1290.

estate immediately before his death.[30] They may submit a provisional estimate of value if they are unable to ascertain the exact value of any property and undertake to deliver a further account as soon as its value is ascertained. If the personal representatives discover that the account delivered by them is defective, they must deliver a corrective or supplementary account within six months of this discovery.[31] Personal representatives often discover other assets or liabilities of the deceased in the course of administration.

4. No grant before payment of tax

Personal representatives must pay all the tax for which they are liable on delivery of their account, unless they are entitled to, and do, elect to pay by instalments.[32] Although they have 12 months from the end of the month in which the death occurs to deliver their account, interest at the rate of 6 per cent per annum is charged on unpaid tax as soon as six months have passed from the end of the month in which the death occurs.[33]

The High Court cannot make any grant of probate or letters of administration, or reseal any grant made outside the United Kingdom, until the personal representatives have paid any inheritance tax payable on delivery of their account.[34]

Personal representatives find themselves in a practical difficulty over the payment of tax. The difficulty is circular. They cannot generally dispose of the deceased's assets without a grant and they cannot easily raise money without disposing of the deceased's assets. But they cannot obtain a grant without paying the tax and to pay the tax they need money. The standard escape is for them to borrow from a bank the money to pay the tax. One small consolation is that the interest on the bank loan is tax deductible for income tax purposes.[35]

D.   OATH AND OTHER EVIDENCE

Every application for a grant must be supported by an oath sworn by the applicant and by such other papers as the registrar may require.[36]

---

[30] s. 216(3); see also s. 5(1) and (2). A special executor delivers an account specifying the settled land and its value, s. 216(3) and (4). The Revenue may restrict the property to be specified by any class of personal representatives, s. 216(3)(b).

[31] s. 217. For penalties in connection with accounts see ss. 245–253.

[32] s. 226(2). For their election to pay tax by 10 yearly instalments in the case of land, certain company shares or securities, a business or interest in a business, see ss. 227–234.

[33] s. 233: Inheritance Tax and Capital Transfer Tax (Interest on Unpaid Tax) Order 1987 (S.I. 1987 No. 887). Interest payable is not deductible for tax purposes, s. 233(3).

[34] Supreme Court Act 1981, s. 109 as amended by Inheritance Tax Act 1984, Sched. 8: this requirement may be dispensed with by arrangement between the President of the Family Division and the Revenue, s. 109(2) see *Re Clore* [1982] Fam. 113, 117.

[35] *Ante* p. 290.

[36] N.C. Prob. Rules 1987, r. 8(1): the applicant may affirm instead of swearing the oath.

1. The oath

The oath of the applicant is contained in an affidavit sworn by him. The form of oath varies according to the circumstances of the case.[37] For instance, if the application for a grant is made after judgment has been given in a probate action, the oath refers to the judgment. An oath normally includes the following:

(1) *DEATH OF THE DECEASED.* The applicant swears to the death of the deceased, stating the date of death if this is known.[38]

(2) *DOMICILE AT DEATH.* The oath states where the deceased died domiciled[39] and this is noted in the grant.

(3) *WILL OR INTESTACY.* The applicant swears that he believes "the paper writing now produced to and marked[40] by me to contain the true and original last will and testament" of the deceased (on an application for probate or administration with the will annexed), or that the deceased died intestate (on an application for simple administration).

(4) *TITLE OF APPLICANT TO GRANT.* In his oath, the applicant shows his title to the grant for which he is applying—for instance, that he is the sole executor of the will (on an application for probate), the residuary legatee and devisee named in the will (on an application for administration with the will annexed), or the lawful son and one of the persons entitled to share in the estate (on an application for simple administration). On any application for administration (whether or not with the will annexed), the oath must state in what manner all persons having a prior right to a grant have been cleared off, and whether any minority or life interest arises under the will or intestacy.[41]

(5) *SETTLED LAND.* The oath must state whether, to the best of the applicant's knowledge, information and belief, there was land vested in the deceased which was settled previously to his death and not by his will and which remained settled land notwithstanding his death.[42]

(6) *DUTIES OF PERSONAL REPRESENTATIVE.* Section 25 of the Administration of Estates Act 1925[43] summarises the duties of a personal representative as being to:

---

[37] See, *e.g. Practice Direction* [1990] 2 All E.R. 576; where unnamed partners in firm of solicitors are appointed executors, and not all partners wish to apply for probate.

[38] N.C. Prob. Rules 1987, r. 53.

[39] *ibid.* r. 8(2).

[40] The will is "marked" by the signatures of the applicant and the person before whom the oath is sworn, N.C. Prob. Rules 1987, r. 10.

[41] N.C. Prob. Rules 1987, r. 8(4). For the minimum number of administrators see *ante*, p. 311.

[42] *ibid.* r. 8(3) (applicable if the deceased died after 1925); for grants to settled land see *ante*, pp. 176, *et seq.*

[43] As amended by Administration of Estates Act 1971, s. 9; see also *Report on Administration Bonds, etc.*, Law. Com. No. 31 (1970), pp. 5–6.

"(a) collect and get in the real and personal estate of the deceased and administer it according to law;

(b) when required to do so by the court, exhibit on oath in the court a full inventory of the estate and when so required render an account of the administration of the estate to the court;

(c) when required to do so by the High Court, deliver up the grant of probate or administration to that court."

The applicant swears that he will carry out these duties which are set out in the oath.

(7) · *VALUE OF THE ESTATE.* In his oath the applicant states the gross value and net value of the estate passing under the grant to the best of his knowledge, information and belief.[44]

2. Will not available

Normally on an application for probate or administration with the will annexed, the applicant lodges the original will in the registry,[45] where a photostat copy is made and annexed to the grant.[46] Sometimes the original will is not available. It may be in the custody of a foreign court, in which case a duly authenticated copy of the will may be admitted to proof.[47] It may have been lost or destroyed, either during the testator's lifetime (without being revoked) or since his death. In that case, a registrar may make an order admitting to proof the will as contained in a copy or a reconstruction.[48] The registrar may require application to be made to a judge,[49] who in turn may make such an order or, if there is opposition from persons entitled under an intestacy or an earlier will, require the will to be propounded in a probate action. Usually the grant made is limited until the original will or a more authentic copy of it be proved.[50]

An applicant who seeks to prove a will which has been lost or destroyed needs to establish:

(i) That the will was duly executed. This may be proved, for instance, by the evidence of one or more of the attesting witnesses, or by proof that the will contained a proper attestation clause.[51]

---

[44] The fee payable for a grant of probate or administration is assessed on the net value shown in the Inland Revenue account or oath, N.C. Prob. Fees Order 1981 (S.I. 1981 No. 861) as amended by S.I. 1981 No. 1103, S.I. 1983 No. 1180, S.I. 1986 No. 705 and S.I. 1986 No. 2185; *Practice Direction (Probate: Representation Grant)* [1981] 1 W.L.R. 1185.

[45] The original will is then preserved in a place of deposit, Supreme Court Act 1981, s. 124; *Re Greer* (1929) 45 T.L.R. 362 and *cf. In the Estate of White Todd* [1926] P. 173.

[46] For the lodging of an engrossment of the original will where a photographic copy would not be satisfactory, or where the will contains alterations not admissible to proof or has been ordered to be rectified, see N.C. Prob. Rules 1987, r. 11.

[47] N.C. Prob. Rules 1987, r. 54(2).

[48] *ibid.* r. 54(1): the rule also applies to a nuncupative will of a privileged testator.

[49] *ibid.* r. 61(1) and see *In the Estate of Nuttall (Practice Note)* [1955] 1 W.L.R. 847.

[50] *In the Goods of Lemme* [1892] P. 89 (French notary forbidden to part with original will); *In the Goods of Von Linden* [1896] P. 148.

[51] *In the Estate of Phibbs* [1917] P. 93 (proof that will contained a proper attestation clause sufficed though identity of attesting witnesses not known); *Re Webb* [1964] 1 W.L.R. 509 (attestation clause in completed draft); *Harris v. Knight* (1890) 15 P.D. 170 (no attestation

(ii) What the contents of the will were. There may, for instance, be a
copy or draft of the will in existence, or the contents of the will
may be proved by the evidence of a person who read the will
before it was lost.[52]

In addition, if the will was last known to be in the testator's possession
but could not be found at his death so that a presumption of revocation
arises, the applicant needs to rebut this presumption by evidence of non-
revocation,[53] or evidence showing the testator's intention to revoke subject to a condition which is not fulfilled,[54] or proving that the will was
destroyed by enemy action or accident.

Re Webb[55] is an illustration. Shortly before the testatrix's death her
sister found a completed draft of her will in a tin trunk and the testatrix
told her, "Don't throw that away; it's my will." After her death the original will could not be found and the sister (a beneficiary) propounded
the draft in a probate action. Faulks J. held that the presumption of
revocation was rebutted by what the testatrix said to her sister. He found
that the original will had been destroyed by enemy action in 1940[56] and
the completed draft was admissible as secondary evidence to prove its
contents. But had the original will been duly executed? The completed
draft contained an attestation clause. A witness (named as an attesting
witness in the draft) testified that she did not remember signing the will
but she did remember being called by the testatrix to her shop for some
purpose and that "a little man in a homburg hat" was there. There was
a solicitor who was named in the draft as the other attesting witness.
Faulks J. held, applying the *maxim omnia praesumuntur rite esse acta*, that
this attestation clause, which spoke to the regularity of the execution of
the will, was, in the absence of cogent negative evidence, sufficient evidence of due execution. He admitted the completed draft to probate.

3.   Evidence of due execution

An attestation clause raises a presumption that the will was duly
executed.[57] If a will contains no attestation clause or the clause is insufficient, or if it appears to the registrar that there is some doubt about the

---

clause, will signed by testator and two others, maxim *"omnia praesumuntur rite esse acta'"*
applied).
[52] *Re Webb, supra*, (completed draft); *In the Goods of Leigh* [1892] P. 82 (will torn into pieces
and some lost, copy will supplied the missing words); *Sugden v. Lord St. Leonards* (1876)
1 P.D. 154 (oral evidence of daughter who was a beneficiary); *In the Estate of Phibbs,
supra*; *In the Estate of Lintott* [1941] L.T.Jo. 115 (copy will: original destroyed by enemy
action after death of testatrix); *Re Yelland*, (1975) 119 S.J. 562.
[53] *Sugden v. Lord St. Leonards, supra*; *Re Webb, supra*; *In the Estate of Wilson* (1961) 105 S.J.
531.
[54] *In the Estate of Botting* [1951] 2 All E.R. 997 (conditional revocation, though no direct
evidence of destruction of will), explaining *Homerton v. Hewitt* (1872) 25 L.T. 854; *In the
Estate of Bridgewater* [1965] 1 W.L.R. 416; *Sterling v. Bruce* [1973] N.I. 255: for conditional
destruction see *ante*, pp. 107 *et seq.*
[55] *Supra*; see also [1964] 2 All E.R. 91.
[56] The court might have decided that the presumption was also rebutted by the will's
destruction by enemy action.
[57] *Ante*, p. 85.

due execution of a will, he must require an affidavit as to its due execution before admitting the will to probate in common form.[58]

The affidavit of due execution is to be from one or more of the attesting witnesses[59] or, if no attesting witness is available, from any other person who was present when the will was executed.[60] Sometimes both the attesting witnesses are dead or cannot be traced, and so far as is known no other person was present when the will was executed. If no such affidavit can be obtained, the registrar may accept evidence on affidavit from any person to show that the signature on the will is in the handwriting of the deceased, or of any other matter which may raise a presumption in favour of due execution and he may require notice of the application to be given to any person prejudiced by the will.[61] Normally evidence on affidavit as to the deceased's handwriting is accepted if accompanied by the consent of the persons prejudiced (if all are *sui juris*) or by evidence on affidavit as to the handwriting of the witnesses. If after considering the evidence the registrar is doubtful whether the will was duly executed, he may refer the matter to a judge on motion. If he is satisfied that the will was not duly executed he must refuse probate and mark the will "Probate Refused".[62]

The maxim *omnia praesumuntur rite esse acta* may apply if the observance of all the formalities required for due execution is not proved by the evidence of witnesses. To quote Lindley L.J. in *Harris v. Knight*,[63]

"The maxim, '*omnia praesumuntur rite esse acta*,' is an expression, in a short form, of a reasonable probability, and of the propriety in point of law of acting on such probability. The maxim expresses an inference which may reasonably be drawn when an intention to do some formal act is established; when the evidence is consistent with that intention having been carried into effect in a proper way; but where the actual observance of all due formalities can only be inferred as a matter of probability."

The maxim applies with more or less force according to the circumstances of each case; for example, a formal attestation clause in a will which is regular in form raises a strong presumption, but an informal clause,[64] or a formal clause in a will irregular in form,[65] raises a weaker presumption.

The maxim may apply in the absence of any attestation clause. In *In the Estate of Denning*[66] the will consisted of a small sheet of writing paper.

---

[58] N.C. Prob. Rules 1987, r. 12(1): see also r. 16. For proof of a privileged will see rr. 17 and 18.

[59] An attesting witness who refuses to make an affidavit may be required to attend for examination in open court, Supreme Court Act 1981, s. 122; N.C. Prob. Rules 1987, r. 50(1): see *In the Goods of Sweet* [1891] P. 400.

[60] N.C. Prob. Rules 1987, r. 10(2).

[61] *ibid*. r. 12(2).

[62] *ibid*. r. 12(1).

[63] (1890) 15 P.D. 170, 179.

[64] *Vinnicombe v. Butler* (1864) 3 Sw. & Tr. 580

[65] *In the Estate of Bercovitz* [1961] 1 W.L.R. 892, 896.

[66] [1958] 1 W.L.R. 462: see also *In the Goods of Peverett* [1902] P. 205; *Harris v. Knight* (1890) 15 P.D. 170; *Trott v. Skidmore* (1860) 2 Sw. & Tr. 12: *cf. In the Estate of Early* [1980] I.R. 223.

On one side (and occupying the whole of it) was written, "Sept. 3rd. Year of our Lord 1939. I give all I possess to my cousins Mary Jane and John Harnett in Parish of St. Feock, County of Cornwall" followed by the signature of the testatrix. On the other side (turning the paper upside down) two names were written in different hands, "Edith Freeman" and "Dorothy Edwards," one below the other. No person of either of these names could be traced. During her lifetime the testatrix had told John Harnett that she had made a will in favour of him and his sister: at her death no other will had been found. In a probate action Sachs J. held the maxim applicable and declared the will to be duly executed. He said that it seemed to him "that there is no other practical reason why these names should be on the back of the document unless it was for the purpose of attesting the will."

The maxim is not applicable if observance of the formalities is disproved by the evidence.[67]

4. Doubt as to knowledge and approval

If a will appears to have been signed by a blind or illiterate testator, or by another person by the testator's direction, or for any other reason gives rise to doubt as to the testator's having had knowledge of its contents at the time of its execution, the registrar must, before admitting the will to proof, satisfy himself that the testator had such knowledge.[68] He may require affidavit evidence for this purpose.

5. Condition, alteration or attempted revocation of will

(1) *CONDITION.* If a will contains any reference to another document in such terms as to suggest that it ought to be incorporated in the will, the registrar must require the document to be produced and accounted for by evidence.[69]

(2) *ALTERATION.* The registrar must require evidence to show whether an unattested alteration was present in a will when it was executed.[70] There is a rebuttable presumption that an unattested alteration was made after the execution of the will.[71] The registrar also has a useful time-saving power to disregard any alteration which appears to him to be of no practical importance[72]—for instance, an alteration to a gift which has lapsed.

(3) *ATTEMPTED REVOCATION.* Any appearance of attempted revocation of a will by burning, tearing or otherwise must be accounted

---

[67] *In the Estate of Bercovitz* [1961] 1 W.L.R. 892, [1962] 1 W.L.R. 321.
[68] N.C. Prob. Rules 1987, r. 13; for the burden of proof of the testator's knowledge and approval see *ante,* pp. 65 *et seq.* In a professionally drawn will, the attestation clause will be amended to record the circumstances of the attestation.
[69] N.C. Prob. Rules 1987, r. 14(3); see also r. 14(4) if there is doubt as to the date on which the will was executed.
[70] *ibid.* r. 14(1).
[71] *Ante,* p. 111.
[72] N.C. Prob. Rules 1987, r. 14(2).

for to the registrar's satisfaction.[73] The person who found the will may swear an affidavit as to its plight and condition when found.

E. THE SURETY'S GUARANTEE

Until 1972 an administrator was normally required to enter into an administration bond, usually with one or more sureties, for the due performance of his duties. This requirement has been abolished. Instead, since 1971, the court may require a guarantee from one or more sureties as a condition of granting letters of administration.[1] An executor has never been required to enter into a bond or guarantee.

1. When guarantee required

Normally, a surety's guarantee is not required as a condition of granting administration. It seems likely that the court will only require a guarantee in special circumstances.

2. The guarantee and its effect

(1) *FORM OF GUARANTEE.* In the form of guarantee formerly prescribed, a surety entered into a guarantee under seal that he would make good any loss which any person interested in the administration of the deceased's estate might suffer in consequence of the breach by the administrator of his duties.[2]

(2) *EFFECT OF GUARANTEE.* Section 120(2) of the Supreme Court Act 1981 provides that a guarantee shall enure for the benefit of every person interested in the administration of the deceased's estate as if contained in a contract by deed[3] made by the surety with every such person. But no action to enforce a guarantee may be brought without the leave of the court.[4] So a creditor or beneficiary who has suffered loss in consequence of a breach of the administrator's duties has a remedy, not only against the administrator, but also (with the leave of the court) against a surety under his guarantee.

For a surety to be liable under his guarantee, there must be a breach by the administrator of his duties *as administrator* and not of his duties as trustee.[5]

Section 42 of the Administration of Estates Act 1925 provides that

---

[73] *ibid.* r. 15.
[1] Supreme Court Act 1981, s. 120: for the power of the court to require a surety's guarantee as a condition of resealing letters of administration see Administration of Estates Act 1971, s. 11 (as amended by Supreme Court Act 1981, s. 152(1) and Sched. 5). See generally *Report on Administration Bonds, etc.,* Law. Com. No. 31.
[2] Supreme Court Act 1981, s. 120(1); N.C. Prob. Rules 1954, r. 38(3) and Sched. I, Form I.
[3] s. 120(2) said "contract under seal", but this has been amended by The Law of Property (Misc Provs) Act 1989 s. 1(7).
[4] Supreme Court Act 1981, s. 120(3): leave may be given by a registrar, N.C. Prob. Rules 1987, r. 40.
[5] *Harvell v. Foster* [1954] 2 Q.B. 367; *cf. Re Cockburn's W.T.* [1957] Ch. 438.

where an infant is absolutely entitled, either under a will (in which no trustees are appointed of the gift to the infant) or on an intestacy,[6] the personal representatives may appoint a trust corporation or two or more individuals not exceeding four (whether or not including the personal representatives) to be trustees for the infant. On such an appointment being made, the personal representatives are discharged from all further liability.

F. OMITTING WORDS FROM PROBATE

A particular passage or word in an otherwise valid will or codicil is omitted from probate if it was inserted:

(i) owing to an insane delusion on the testator's part[7];
(ii) without the testator's knowledge and approval[8];
(iii) as a result of undue influence or fraud[9];
(iv) as an alteration which was not duly executed by the testator.[10]

The court may also exclude from probate words which have no testamentary value[11] but which are offensive,[12] defamatory[13] or blasphemous. Such words are not expunged from the will itself but are omitted from the probate copy.[14]

G. PROBATE ACTIONS

In general, the same practice and rules of evidence are applicable in a probate action as in other actions. But a few significant differences may be mentioned.

1. Administration pending suit

After a probate action has begun, a grant of administration pending suit limited to the duration of the probate action may be made. This type of grant has already been considered.[15]

---

[6] On a death intestate after 1925 an infant is absolutely entitled in the capacity of surviving spouse, but only a married infant is absolutely entitled under the statutory trusts for the issue of the intestate, see *ante*, p. 40.
[7] *In the Estate of Borhmann* [1938] 1 All E.R. 271; see *ante*, pp. 61–62.
[8] *Ante*, pp. 64 *et seq.*: for rectification see *ante*, pp. 72–73.
[9] *Ante*, p. 73 *et seq.*.
[10] *Ante*, pp. 110 *et seq.*
[11] *In the Estate of Rawlings* (1934) 78 S.J. 338 ("that rascal" her husband relevant to construction).
[12] *In the Goods of Bowker* [1932] P. 93 (offensive directions as to disposal of testator's remains and funeral excluded): *cf. In the Estate of Caie* (1927) 43 T.L.R. 697 (exhortation to become a Freemason not excluded).
[13] *In the Estate of White* [1914] P. 153; *In the Goods of Wortnaly* (1846) 1 Rob. 423; *Marsh v. Marsh* (1860) 1 Sw. & Tr. 528; *In the Goods of Honywood* (1871) L.R. 2 P. & D. 251.
[14] *Re Maxwell* (1929) 45 T.L.R. 215: for the procedure see *Practice Direction* [1968] 1 W.L.R. 987.
[15] *Ante*, pp. 344–346.

If the probate action is for the revocation of a previous grant of probate or letters of administration, the previous grant must be lodged in court after the commencement of the action.[16]

2. Affidavit of testamentary scripts

At an early stage in a probate action, each party must swear and file an affidavit of testamentary scripts of the deceased.[17] A testamentary script means a will or draft will of the deceased, written instructions for a will (*e.g.* a solicitor's attendance note recording the deceased's instructions), and any document purporting to be evidence of the contents, or to be a copy, of a will which is alleged to have been lost or destroyed. The affidavit must describe any testamentary script of which the party has any knowledge. If he has any such script in his possession, he must lodge it in court with his affidavit.

This special procedure ensures that at an early stage in a probate action any testamentary scripts in the possession of the parties are lodged in the safe custody of the court. The procedure is different from discovery of documents, which takes place at a later stage.

3. Evidence of attesting witnesses

The party propounding a will in a probate action must call one of the attesting witnesses to give evidence as to its due execution unless they are all unavailable,[18] *e.g.* dead.

(1) *WITNESS OF THE COURT.* An attesting witness is regarded as the witness of the court. Accordingly (and contrary to the general rule) he may be cross-examined by the party calling him on matters relating to the execution of the will,[19] and no claim of professional privilege may be made in respect of his previous statements to solicitors concerning execution.[20]

(2) *NOT CONCLUSIVE.* The evidence of the attesting witnesses is not conclusive for, or against, the due execution of the will. A formal attestation clause in a will raises a presumption of due execution[21] and the party propounding a will is free to call other evidence that it was duly executed.[22] The court decides whether the will was duly executed having regard to all the circumstances of the case.[23]

---

[16] R.S.C., Ord. 76, r. 4.

[17] *ibid.* r. 5.

[18] *Bowman v. Hodgson* (1867) L.R. 1 P. & D. 362: see Evidence Act 1938, s. 3. The rules in this section doubtless apply to a witness who acknowledges his signature under the amended s. 9 of the Wills Act 1837, *ante*, p. 84.

[19] *Oakes v. Uzzell* [1932] P. 19; *Re Brock; Jones v. Jones* [1908] 24 T.L.R. 839; *Re Webster* [1974] 1 W.L.R. 1641 (party calling attesting witness may cross-examine him on other issues, as well as due execution).

[20] *In the Estate of Fuld* [1965] P. 405.

[21] *Ante*, p. 354.

[22] *Re Vere-Wardale* [1949] P. 395.

[23] *Wright v. Rogers* (1869) L.R. 1 P. & D. 678 (formal attestation clause; memory of attesting witness unreliable).

4. Costs

Costs in a probate action, as in other proceedings in the High Court and Civil Division of the Court of Appeal, are in the discretion of the court.[24] Generally costs follow the event,[25] *i.e.* the losing party is ordered to pay the costs of the successful party.

(1) *NOTICE TO CROSS-EXAMINE.* Order 62, rule 4(3) of the Rules of the Supreme Court imposes a significant restriction on the court's discretion in a probate action. A party who opposes a will in a probate action may give notice with his defence to the party setting up the will that he merely insists upon the will being proved in solemn form and only intends to cross-examine the witnesses produced in support of the will. No order may then be made for him to pay the other side's costs unless the court is of opinion that there was no reasonable ground for opposing the will.[26] This protection may be relied on if the party opposing the will pleads want of due execution, incapacity, or want of knowledge and approval,[27] but not if he pleads undue influence or fraud[28] or claims revocation of probate already granted in common form.[29]

(2) *EXCEPTIONS TO THE GENERAL RULE.* Apart from this important restriction, the court has an unfettered discretion as to costs. The general rule of practice is that costs follow the event, but in special circumstances a different order may be made. The special circumstances justifying a different order may be classified under two heads,[30] *i.e.* (a) fault of the testator or the residuary beneficiary—costs out of the estate, (b) case for inquiry—no order as to costs.[31]

(a) *Costs out of the estate.* If the litigation has been caused by the conduct of the deceased, or of the residuary beneficiaries, the costs of both parties may be ordered to be paid out of the estate. Such an order was made where the litigation was caused by the confusion in which the deceased left his testamentary papers,[32] or by the deceased's habits and mode of life which gave grounds for questioning his testamentary capacity.[33] Again, such an order was made where the residuary beneficiaries were

---

[24] Supreme Court Act 1981, s. 51.

[25] R.S.C., Ord. 62, r. 3(3); *Twist v. Tye* [1902] P. 92.

[26] *Davies v. Jones* [1899] P. 161 (reasonable ground for opposing though opposition failed: no order as to costs); *Spicer v. Spicer* [1899] P. 38 (no reasonable ground: costs follow event).

[27] *Cleare v. Cleare* (1869) 1 P. & D. 655. And see Chap. 3, especially p. 58.

[28] *Ireland v. Rendall* (1866) 1 P. & D. 194; *Harrington v. Bowyer* (1871) 2 P. & D. 264.

[29] *Tomalin v. Smart* [1904] P. 141.

[30] *Spiers v. English* [1907] P. 122; *Mitchell v. Gard* (1863) 3 Sw. & Tr. 275.

[31] *Re Cutcliffe's Estate* [1959] P. 6, 13.

[32] *Jenner v. Ffinch* (1879) 5 P.D. 106 (doubt as to deceased's intention to revoke former will); *Lemage v. Goodban* (1865) L.R. 1 P. & D. 57; *Orton v. Smith* (1873) L.R. 3 P. & D. 23 (testator had patched up his signature); *cf. Re Wynn* [1983] 3 All E.R. 310, 315.

[33] *Davies v. Gregory* (1873) 3 P. & D. 28 (deceased a recluse of strange habits); *Roe v. Nix* [1893] P. 55 (testatrix of unsound mind); see also *Boughton v. Knight* (1873) L.R. 3 P. & D. 64 (testator outwardly capable of managing his affairs); *Larke v. Nugus* (1979) 123 S.J. 337 (solicitor draftsman ought to provide full information as to execution and surrounding circumstances).

active in the preparation of a will in their own favour, thereby raising suspicions by their conduct,[34] and where the residuary beneficiary, despite inquiries, failed to produce the will after administration had been granted to the next of kin.[35]

(b) *No order as to costs.* If the circumstances led reasonably to an inquiry into the issues raised, the losing party is left to pay his own costs but is not ordered to pay the costs of the successful party. It is therefore necessary to consider whether the losing party had reasonable grounds, looking to his knowledge and means of knowledge, for the issues he raised.[36]

No order for costs was made where the next of kin unsuccessfully opposed a will because the deceased's doctor, who was an attesting witness, stated that when the will was read over the testator approved it by gesture only and that he could not swear that the testator was in full possession of his mental faculties.[37]

(3) *PLEAS OF UNDUE INFLUENCE OR FRAUD.* A party ought never to put forward a plea of undue influence or fraud unless he has reasonable grounds upon which to support it.[38] If he does plead undue influence or fraud, and loses the action, he will normally be ordered to pay the costs of the successful party[39] unless special circumstances justify a different order.[40] There are a few reported cases where head (a) or (b) has been held applicable[41]; but a party who makes an unsuccessful plea of undue influence or fraud usually has to pay the costs of the successful party.

(4) *EXECUTOR'S RIGHT TO COSTS OUT OF THE ESTATE.* An executor who proves a will in solemn form is entitled, unless the court orders otherwise, to take his costs of the probate action out of the estate.[42] He does not need an order of the court for this purpose.[43] The court may order otherwise if the executor has acted unreasonably—for instance, by carelessly losing the original will.[44] If the executor unsuccessfully propounds a will the rules of practice already considered apply: costs follow

---

[34] *Goodacre v. Smith* (1867) L.R. 1 P. & D. 359; *Orton v. Smith* (1873) L.R. 3 P. & D. 23; *In the Estate of Osment* [1914] P. 129 (conduct of legatees).

[35] *Smith v. Smith* (1865) 4 Sw. & Tr. 3.

[36] *Mitchell v. Gard* (1863) 3 Sw. & Tr. 257, 278.

[37] *Tippett v. Tippett* (1865) 1 P. & D. 54: see also *Ferrey v. King* (1861) 3 Sw. & Tr. 51 (conflicting evidence of attesting witnesses).

[38] *Spiers v. English* [1907] P. 122, 124.

[39] *ibid.*; *Re Cutcliffe's Estate* [1959] P. 6 (not special circumstances if T misled persons into false hopes of benefiting by his will).

[40] See Chap. 3 pp. 56–58.

[41] *e.g.* costs out of the estate in *Mitchell v. Gard* (1863) 3 Sw. & Tr. 75 and 275 (undue influence and three other pleas failed); *Orton v. Smith* (1873) L.R. 3 P. & D. 23 (undue influence, fraud, and other pleas failed): no order as to costs in *Smith v. Smith* (1866) L.R. 1 P. & D. 239 (undue influence and two other pleas failed).

[42] Ord. 62, r. 6(2): see *In the Estate of Plant* [1926] P. 139 (executors proved will but failed on codicil); *Re Barton* [1977] C.L.Y. 3182.

[43] He is better off without an order, which necessitates taxation of his costs. *In the Estate of Cole* (1962) 106 S.J. 837.

[44] *Burls v. Burls* (1868) 1 P. & D. 472.

the event[45] unless head (a) or (b) applies.[46] To protect himself against the risk of being condemned in costs, a person appointed executor may find it advisable before he propounds the will to insist on an indemnity from the beneficiaries interested in upholding it.

II. THE REVOCATION OF GRANTS

A. Grounds for Revocation

A personal representative may be removed *either* by the revocation of his grant (which is considered in this section) *or* by the appointment of a substituted personal representative or by the termination of his appointment (which is considered later[1]).

The jurisdiction of the High Court to revoke a grant of probate or letters of administration is exercised by the Family Division as regards non-contentious or common form business, and by the Chancery Division as regards revocation actions.[2] The county court also has jurisdiction (limited in amount) over revocation actions.[3] In the Family Division a district judge or registrar may order a grant to be revoked or amended, but only on the application or with the consent of the person to whom the grant was made unless there are exceptional circumstances.[4] The court has power to revoke a grant of its own volition where the grant ought not to have been made or contains an error.[5] But if the person to whom the grant was made opposes revocation, a revocation action is normally necessary.

The main grounds for revocation of a grant may be classified in two categories.

1. Grant wrongly made

Usually a grant is wrongly made as a result of a false statement by the grantee, whether made fraudulently or in ignorance of the truth. For example, revocation is ordered where the "deceased" is found to be still alive;[6] where a will is discovered after a grant of simple administration has been made, or a later will is discovered after an earlier will has been proved; where an invalid or revoked will has been proved; where a grant has been made to an infant on the basis that he is of full age; where administration has been granted to a person who falsely claimed to be

---

[45] *Twist v. Tye* [1902] P. 92.
[46] *e.g.* costs out of the estate in *Boughton v. Knight* (1873) L.R. 3 P. & D. 64.
[1] *Post*, p. 507.
[2] *Ante*, p. 320.
[3] *Ante*, p. 322.
[4] N.C. Prob. Rules 1987, r. 41; see also r. 26(2).
[5] Supreme Court Act 1981, s. 121: the court may also cancel the resealing of a grant, s. 121(3); for resealing see *ante*. p. 325.
[6] *In the Goods of Napier* (1809) 1 Phill. 83 (left for dead on the field of battle and appeared personally in court on revocation of probate).

the deceased's surviving spouse,[7] or next of kin;[8] or where administration has been granted to the Treasury Solicitor and next of kin are disovered. Occasionally a grant is wrongly made as a result of an official error. For example, revocation is ordered where a grant has been made without special leave before the minimum time has elapsed from the deceased's death,[9] or where a grant has been made whilst a *caveat* was in force.[10]

2. Subsequent events

A grant which was properly made may be revoked by reason of the occurrence of subsequent events.

(1) *GRANTEE BECOMES INCAPABLE.* If there are at least two executors and one or more of them becomes incapable of managing his affairs by reason of mental or physical incapacity, the grant of probate is revoked. In *In the Goods of Galbraith*[11] a grant of probate made six years previously to two executors was revoked because both had become unfit to act in their old age, owing to their physical and mental infirmity. Instead the court made a grant of letters of administration *de bonis non* with the will annexed. If only one of the executors had become incapable, the court would have revoked the original grant and made a fresh grant of probate to the other executor, with power for the incapable executor to take probate if he recovered.[12]

Similarly, if there are at least two administrators and one or more of them becomes incapable, the grant of administration is revoked and a new grant made.[13]

But if there is a sole, or sole surviving, executor or administrator and he becomes incapable, the grant to him is not revoked. Instead a grant of letters of administration *de bonis non* and for the use and benefit of the incapable grantee, limited during his incapacity, is made and the court impounds the original grant so that it does not remain at large.[14]

(2) *GRANTEE WISHES TO BE RELIEVED OF DUTIES.* A grant may be revoked if a grantee wishes to be relieved of his duties for some good reason, such as advanced age.[15]

---

[7] *In the Goods of Moore* (1845) 3 N.C. 601 ("widow" not married to deceased); *In the Estate of Evon* (1963) 107 S.J. 893.

[8] *In the Goods of Bergman* (1842) 2 N. of C. 22: see also *In the Goods of Morris* (1862) 2 Sw. & Tr. 360 (grant to elected guardian of minors revoked as there was testamentary guardian).

[9] *Ante*, p. 349.

[10] See *Re Davies* [1978] C.L.Y. 3095.

[11] [1951] P. 422.

[12] *In the Estate of Shaw* [1905] P. 92.

[13] *In the Goods of Newton* (1843) 3 Curt. 428.

[14] *In the Goods of Cooke* [1895] P. 68; the original grant is not impounded if the new grant is made to a person authorised by the Court of Protection; see *ante*, p. 343. For enduring powers of attorney see *Practice Direction (Powers of Attorney)* [1986] 1 W.L.R. 419.

[15] *In the Goods of Thacker* [1900] P. 15 (grant to receiver in bankruptcy revoked after debts paid); *In the Goods of Hoare* (1833) 2 Sw. & Tr. 361 and *cf. In the Goods of Heslop* (1846) 1 Rob. Eccl. 457. A personal representative may not simply have a grant in his favour revoked because he has become bored with the administration. For reform to allow personal representative to retire for good cause see Law Reform Committee, 23rd Report, *The powers and duties of trustees*, Cmnd. 8733 (1982), pp. 53 and 67.

(3) *GRANTEE DISAPPEARS.* If a grantee disappears and the estate has not been fully administered, the grant is revoked and a new grant is made.[16] As Sir Francis Jeune P. put it in *In the Goods of Loveday*[17] where the administratrix had disappeared,

> "the real object which the Court must always keep in view is the due and proper administration of the estate and the interests of the parties beneficially entitled thereto; and I can see no good reason why the Court should not take fresh action in regard to an estate where it is made clear that its previous grant has turned out abortive or inefficient."

(4) *GRANTEE COMMITS BREACH OF DUTY.* If the grantee commits a serious breach of his duties, probably his grant will be revoked and a new grant made where this is appropriate so as to secure the proper administration of the estate. This ground for revocation appears to be supported by the words already quoted of Sir Francis Jeune in *In the Goods of Loveday*.[18]

B.   EFFECT OF REVOCATION

A grant of probate or letters of administration is in a sense a precarious title because the grant is liable to be revoked at some later date. The deceased may die apparently intestate so that a grant of simple administration is made, and years later a will appointing executors may be found. Or the deceased may die leaving a "will" which is proved by the executors, but which years later is discovered to have been a forgery. In the meantime, before the revocation of the first grant, the personal representative may have administered the estate.

1.   Purchaser from the former personal representative

A purchaser from a personal representative to whom a grant has been made is protected by two statutory provisions.

(1) *CONVEYANCE VALID DESPITE REVOCATION OF GRANT.* Section 37 of the Administration of Estates Act 1925 provides that a conveyance of any interest in real or personal estate made to a purchaser by a person to whom probate or letters of administration has been granted is valid, notwithstanding any subsequent revocation or variation of the

---

[16] *In the Goods of Loveday* [1900] P. 154 (widow obtained administration and later disappeared); *In the Goods of Covell* (1890) 15 P.D. 8; *In the Goods of Bradshaw* (1888) 13 P.D. 18 (creditor administrator absconded): see also *In the Estate of Thomas* [1912] P. 177 (administrator emigrated to New Zealand but his address was ascertainable: grant revoked).

[17] [1900] P. 154, 156.

[18] But see *In the Estate of Cope* [1954] 1 W.L.R. 608, 609, where Collingwood J. said that "those words must be read with regard to the facts" of *In the Goods of Loveday*.

grant.[19] The section has a wide application because "conveyance" is so widely defined by the Act—the expression includes:

> "a mortgage, charge by way of legal mortgage, lease, assent, vesting declaration, vesting instrument, disclaimer, release and every other assurance of property or of an interest therein by any instrument, except a will."[20]

But, to be protected under section 37, a purchaser must have acquired the interest in the property in good faith and for valuable consideration, which includes marriage but not a nominal consideration in money.[21]

Section 37 does not apply to a disposition of property to a purchaser by a personal representative unless it was made by a "conveyance".[22] Most sales of goods by personal representatives will probably fall outside section 37 because the property in the goods is transferred without any written instrument. If this is so, the principle laid down in 1914 by the Court of Appeal in *Hewson v. Shelley*[23] applies. The effect of applying *Hewson v. Shelley* is much the same as section 37. In *Hewson v. Shelley* a widow took a grant of simple administration to her husband's estate, believing that he had died intestate. The administratrix sold and conveyed the deceased's land to a purchaser. Eleven years later a will of the deceased was found in the back of a bureau, the letters of administration were revoked, and probate was granted to the plaintiffs as executors. The plaintiffs sued the purchaser for the return of the land, but the Court of Appeal held that the purchaser had a good title because he had bought the land in good faith.

(2) *GRANT CONCLUSIVE AS AN ORDER OF THE COURT.* A purchaser is also protected by section 204(1) of the Law of Property Act 1925 which reads:

> "An order of the court under any statutory or other jurisdiction shall not, as against a purchaser, be invalidated on the ground of want of jurisdiction, or of want of any concurrence, consent, notice, or service, whether the purchaser has notice of any such want or not."

A grant of probate[24] or letters of administration[25] is of course an order of the court and is, therefore, conclusive. Again, section 204(1) only protects a purchaser in good faith and for valuable consideration, which includes marriage but not a nominal consideration in money.[25]

The two statutory provisions were considered in *Re Bridgett & Hayes' Contract.*[27] In that case land was settled on B for life and after her death

---

[19] s. 37 applies whenever the conveyance was made, or the grant was revoked or varied, or the testator or intestate died, but without prejudice to any order of the court made before 1926, s. 37(1) and (2). As to contracts made by a personal representative see Administration of Estates Act 1925, s. 39(1) and the Law of Property (Misc Provs) Act 1994, s. 16, *post* p. 392.

[20] s. 55(1)(ii).

[21] s. 55(1)(xviii).

[22] *e.g.* It does not apply to oral leases.

[23] [1914] 2 Ch. 13.

[24] *Re Bridgett & Hayes' Contract* [1928] Ch. 163.

[25] *Hewson v. Shelley* [1914] 2 Ch. 13, 29–30 and 33.

[27] *Supra*: see also *In the Estate of Taylor* [1929] P. 260, 263.

upon trust for sale. At B's death in 1926 the legal estate was vested in her as tenant for life and T was the sole trustee of the settlement. A general grant of probate was made to B's executor C, who contracted to sell the land to a purchaser. The purchaser objected to C's title on the ground that the legal estate was vested in T as B's special executor. Romer J. held that C could make a good title. Even assuming that the legal estate vested in T at B's death, the legal estate vested in C as from the date of the general grant of probate, and the purchaser was protected by section 204(1) of the Law of Property Act 1925. Romer J. added that if this grant of probate were subsequently revoked, the purchaser would be protected by section 37 of the Administration of Estates Act 1925—it could hardly be doubted that if the purchaser took a conveyance from C he would be acting in good faith.[28]

2. Payments made to the former personal representative

Section 27(2) of the Administration of Estates Act 1925 provides that, where a grant of probate or letters of administration is revoked, all payments and dispositions made in good faith to a personal representative under the grant before its revocation are a valid discharge to the person making them. Thus, if the deceased's debtor pays his debt in good faith to the deceased's personal representative under a grant before it is revoked, the debtor is discharged.

3. Payments made by the former personal representative

Section 27(2) of the Act also enacts that a personal representative who acted under a grant before its revocation may retain and reimburse himself in respect of any payments or dispositions made by him, which the person to whom representation is afterwards granted might have properly made. The former personal representative should reimburse himself in this way before delivering the balance of the assets to the new personal representative.

4. Indemnity of former personal representative

Section 27(1) of the Administration of Estates Act 1925 provides that:

"Every person making or permitting to be made any payment or disposition in good faith under a representation shall be indemnified and protected in so doing, notwithstanding any defect or circumstance whatsoever affecting the validity of the representation."

Presumably the section applies to any payment or disposition made in good faith by the former personal representative before his grant was revoked, whether in discharging the deceased's funeral, testamentary and administration expenses, debts and liabilities, or in distributing the deceased's estate to the beneficiaries entitled under the former grant. In

---

[28] Romer J. also decided that anyway T was not entitled to a grant of probate limited to settled land, because the land ceased to be settled land at B's death, see *ante* pp. 337 *et seq.*

In the Estate of Bloch[29] a grant of letters of administration made to X and Y in 1952 was revoked by the court in 1959 because the "deceased" was still alive. Y was held entitled to an indemnity under section 27(1), but the court refused an indemnity to X who had not acted in good faith, having withheld material evidence when application was made for leave to swear death prior to the grant.

Apart from any protection afforded by section 27(1), a personal representative who receives notice of a claim which casts doubt on the validity of the grant made to him, and subsequently makes payments in disregard of that claim, is liable to the deceased's estate if his grant is later revoked. Thus in a New Zealand case an executor, who obtained probate of a will and, knowing that next of kin were contemplating an action for revocation on the ground that the testatrix lacked testamentary capacity, paid pecuniary legacies to beneficiaries under the will, was held liable by the Privy Council to the deceased's estate for the sums so paid, after probate had been revoked.[30] The same result would follow under English law unless an honest belief by the executor that the testatrix had testamentary capacity and that the action for revocation would fail suffices for "good faith," so that the executor is protected by section 27(1).

5. Distribution to wrong beneficiary

If the former personal representative made a distribution to a beneficiary entitled under the former grant but not under the new grant, the beneficiary is not protected. The remedies available against him are considered later.[31]

---

[29] *The Times*, July 2, 1959: the report does not state the nature of the payments made by X and Y.

[30] *Guardian Trust & Executors Company of New Zealand Ltd. v. Public Trustee of New Zealand* [1942] A.C. 115; see p. 123 where the Privy Council referred to "what befell another executor who paid the legacies given by a will that was afterwards declared to be invalid, and whose sad story was told by him to Sam Weller when they were fellow inmates of the Fleet prison," (*Pickwick Papers*, Chap. XLIV).

[31] *Post*, pp. 510 *et seq.*

CHAPTER 16

COLLECTION, REALISATION AND MANAGEMENT OF THE ESTATE

A personal representative has a statutory duty to "collect and get in the real and personal estate of the deceased and administer it according to law."[1] This Chapter explains part of this process of administration. The next chapter deals with the payment of the deceased's funeral, testamentary and administration expenses, debts and liabilities, and Chapter 20 deals with the distribution of the estate to the persons entitled under the deceased's will or intestacy. Normally the administration of the deceased's estate is carried out by the personal representatives out of court. If need be, the personal representatives may ask the court to decide any matters of difficulty which arise.[2] Very occasionally the general administration of the estate is carried out under the direction of the court in an administration action.[3]

I. DEVOLUTION ON PERSONAL REPRESENTATIVES

1. Devolution of property on a death before 1926

At common law a deceased's entire personal estate, including leaseholds (which are known as *chattels real*), devolved on his personal representatives. This included personalty held on trust by the deceased, unless the deceased was survived by one or more co-trustees who held the personalty jointly with the deceased, in which case the personalty remained vested in the co-trustees by virtue of the right of survivorship. A deceased's realty did not, however, vest in his personal representatives, at common law, but passed directly to the devisee under his will or to his heir entitled on intestacy. But if the deceased died after 1897, the Land Transfer Act 1897 made the deceased's realty (including realty over which he exercised a general power of appointment by his will)

---

[1] Administration of Estates Act 1925, s. 25 as amended by Administration of Estates Act 1971, s. 9.
[2] *Post*, pp. 507–508.
[3] *Post*, pp. 503 *et seq.*

vest in his personal representatives.[4] After 1897 the deceased's personal representatives also became his real representatives.

2. Devolution of property on a death after 1925

On a death after 1925 the deceased's entire personal estate continues to devolve on his personal representatives. As to the deceased's land, section 1(1) of the Administration of Estates Act 1925 provides that "real estate to which a deceased person was entitled for an interest not ceasing on his death shall on his death ... devolve from time to time on the personal representative of the deceased" in the same manner as chattels real (*i.e.* leaseholds) devolved before 1926. The personal representatives represent the deceased in regard to this real estate as well as in regard to his personal estate.[5]

(1) *"REAL ESTATE" WHICH DEVOLVES.* The "real estate" which devolves is defined to include chattels real (*i.e.* leaseholds), and land in possession, remainder, or reversion, and every interest in or over land to which the deceased was entitled at his death.[6] It includes:

(i) Land held on trust by the deceased, including settled land.[7] This head is only applicable where the deceased held the land at his death as the sole trustee, *e.g.* as the last surviving trustee of land held on trust for sale, or as the sole tenant for life of settled land. It is not applicable where the deceased is survived by one or more co-trustees who held the land jointly with the deceased and who therefore remain entitled following his death by operation of the right of survivorship. Again it is not applicable where the deceased held the land at his death in his capacity as a personal representative and not as a trustee.[8]

(ii) Land held by the deceased by way of mortgage or security.[9]

(iii) Land appointed by the deceased in his will under a general power of appointment.[10] By way of contrast, pure personalty appointed by the deceased in his will under a general power of appointment has never devolved on his personal representatives.[11]

(iv) Land in which the deceased held an entailed interest which was barred by his will and which passes under a gift contained in the deceased's will: if not, the entailed interest does not devolve on the deceased's personal representatives.[12]

---

[4] s. 1: s. 1 did not apply to legal estates in copyholds or customary freeholds but it did apply to equitable interests therein, Re Somerville & Turner's Contract [1903] 2 Ch. 583. On a death after 1881 real estate held by the deceased on trust or by way of mortgage vested in his personal representative. Conveyancing Act 1881, s. 30.

[5] Administration of Estates Act 1925, s. 1(3).

[6] *ibid.* ss. 3(1)(i) and 55(1)(xxiv).

[7] *ibid.* s. 3(1)(ii). But see *ante* p. 337 for grants to settled land.

[8] *Ante*, p. 340.

[9] *ibid.* s. 3(1)(ii).

[10] *ibid.* s. 3(2). For the exercise by will of a general power of appointment see *ante*, pp. 211 et seq.

[11] *O'Grady v. Wilmot* [1916] 2 A.C. 231. But both real and personal estate appointed by the deceased in his will under a general power of appointment are assets for payment of his debts, *post* p. 409.

[12] Administration of Estates Act 1925, s. 3(2) and (3); Law of Property Act 1925, s. 176; see *ante*, p. 213.

(2) *INTEREST CEASING ON DEATH.* An interest of the deceased which ceases on his death does not devolve on his personal representatives. Again, the interest of the deceased under a joint tenancy does not devolve where another joint tenant survives the deceased and remains entitled following his death by operation of the right of survivorship.[13] On the other hand, the interest of the deceased as an equitable tenant in common does devolve, unless it was a life interest. It is, therefore, necessary to ascertain the interests of the deceased and his co-owner, both at law and in equity.[14] The deceased may have been a legal joint tenant and equitable tenant in common: in that case his co-owner takes at law by operation of the right of survivorship but the deceased's equitable undivided share devolves on his personal representatives. For instance, the deceased and his wife may have held the legal fee simple in Blackacre as joint tenants upon an express (or statutory[15]) trust for sale and to stand possessed of the proceeds of sale and the income until sale upon trust for the deceased and his wife absolutely as tenants in common in equal shares. At the death of the deceased his wife takes the legal fee simple estate by operation of the right of survivorship, but the deceased's equitable half-share as tenant in common devolves on his personal representatives. This equitable half-share, being an interest under a trust for sale of land, devolves on the deceased's personal representatives as personalty, not as realty.[16]

(3) *PROTECTED, STATUTORY AND ASSURED TENANCIES.* The Housing Act 1988 came into force on January 15, 1989[17] and different succession rules apply according to whether a tenancy was created, and/or whether the relevant death occurred, before, or on or after, that date.

(i) *Protected Tenancies.* A tenancy entered into before January 15, 1989 is a protected tenancy for the purposes of the Rent Act 1977 if a dwelling-house is let as a separate dwelling.[18] Where the contractual tenancy still subsists at the tenant's death, the statutory succession provisions discussed below in relation to statutory tenancies apply,[19] and the right of the statutory successor takes precedence over that of the person upon whom the contractual tenancy (which is suspended) devolves.[20]

(ii) *Statutory Tenancies.* After the termination of a Rent Act protected tenancy, the person who was the protected tenant becomes the statutory tenant and remains so if and so long as he occupies the dwelling-house as his residence.[21] A statutory tenancy gives the tenant no estate or prop-

---

[13] Administration of Estates Act 1925, s. 3(4).
[14] See *Snell's Equity* (29th ed., 1990), pp. 36–38; *Re Caines* [1978] 1 W.L.R. 540 (possible severance of equitable joint tenancy)
[15] Law of Property Act 1925, ss. 34(2) and 35.
[16] Administration of Estates Act 1925, s. 3(1)(ii).
[17] Housing Act 1988, s. 141(3).
[18] Rent Act 1977, s. 1. The Act contains a number of exceptions to this general rule.
[19] Rent Act 1977, s. 2(1)(*b*), Sched. 1 para 1.
[20] *Moodie v. Hosegood* [1952] A.C. 61.
[21] Rent Act 1977, s. 2(1)(*a*).

erty but merely confers upon him a right to retain possession or "a status of irremovability."[22]

On the death of a protected or a statutory tenant ("the original tenant"), there may be a transmission of the tenancy to a person who becomes either a statutory tenant or an assured tenant by succession. The status of the successor depends upon whether the death occurs before, or on or after, January 15, 1989.[23]

Where the original tenant's death occurs on or after January 15, 1989, the surviving spouse,[24] if residing in the dwelling-house immediately before the death of the original tenant, becomes the statutory tenant and remains so for as long as he or she occupies the dwelling-house as his or her residence.[25] If there is no surviving spouse, a person who was a member of the original tenant's family[26] and was residing with him at the time of and for two years immediately preceding his death becomes entitled to an assured tenancy by succession.[27]

If the first successor is still a statutory tenant at his or her death (i.e. he or she was the spouse of the original tenant), a second succession is possible in favour of a person who was a member both of the original tenant's family and of the first successor's family and who was residing in the dwelling house at the time of and for two years immediately before the first successor's death. Such a person becomes entitled to an assured tenancy by succession.[28] No second succession is possible where the first successor is an assured tenant by succession.[29] On the death of such a first successor, the assured tenancy passes under his or her will or on his or her intestacy, but the landlord has a mandatory ground for possession.[30]

---

[22] *Keeves v. Dean, Nunn v. Pellegrini* [1924] 1 K.B. 685, 686; *Jessamine Investment Co v. Schwartz* [1978] Q.B. 264, 272–73.

[23] This is as a result of amendments made to the Rent Act succession rights by the Housing Act 1988, which curtails those rights.

[24] A person who was living with the original tenant as his or her wife or husband is treated as the spouse: Rent Act 1977, Sched. 1 para 2(2). This expression was held in *Harrogate Borough Council v. Simpson* [1986] 2 F.L.R. 91 (a case relating to the Housing Act 1980) not to cover a lesbian relationship.

[25] Rent Act 1977, Sched. 1 para 2(1) (substituted by the Housing Act 1980, s. 76(1); renumbered by virtue of the Housing Act 1988 s. 39(2), Sched. 4 para 2).

[26] The expression is broadly construed, the test being whether an ordinary person would regard the person as a member of the tenant's family: see *Brock v. Wollams* [1949] 2 K.B. 388; *Dyson Holdings Ltd v. Fox* [1976] Q.B. 503.

[27] Rent Act 1977, Sched. 1 para 3 (amended by the Housing Act 1988 Sched. 4 para 4). Where the death occurs before 15 January 1989, the period is six months and the successor becomes a statutory tenant if and so long as he occupies the dwelling house as his residence: Rent Act 1977, Sched. 1 para 3.

[28] Rent Act 1977, Sched. 1 paras 5 and 6(1) (amended and substituted by the Housing Act 1988 Sched. 4 paras 5 and 6)

[29] Where the first successor (whether a spouse or a qualifying family member) died before 15 January, 1989 and was still a statutory tenant at his or her death, a second succession was possible in favour of a spouse or a qualifying family member, subject to the same conditions having to be satisfied as applied on the first succession. On a second succession, the family member had to be a member of the first successor's family, as opposed to the original tenant's family: *Sefton Holdings Ltd v. Cairns* [1988] 1 E.G.L.R. 99, (CA)

[30] Housing Act 1988 Sched. 2 Pt 1, Ground 7. Proceedings for the recovery of possession have to be begun not later than 12 months after the death of the former tenant, or, if the court so directs, the date on which, in the opinion of the court, the landlord became aware of the former tenant's death.

(iii) *Assured Tenancies.* In general, a tenancy of a dwelling-house let as a separate dwelling on or after January 15, 1989 is an assured tenancy under the Housing Act 1988.[31]

When a fixed-term assured tenant dies, the tenancy will vest in his personal representatives and will devolve under his will or on his intestacy. When, however, a periodic assured tenant[32] dies, the tenancy will not devolve under his will or on his intestacy if the tenant is survived by his spouse[33] who immediately before the tenant's death was occupying the dwelling-house as his or her only or principal home.[34] In such a case, provided that the tenant is not himself a successor,[35] the tenancy will vest in the spouse.[36] If the assured periodic tenancy does not vest in the spouse, it will pass under the assured tenant's will or on his intestacy, but a mandatory ground of possession is available to the landlord.[37]

(4) *CORPORATION SOLE.* On the death of a corporation sole (such as a bishop) his interest in the corporation's real and personal estate devolves on his successor and not on his personal representatives.[38]

3. Devolution on personal representatives for the time being

The deceased's estate, both real and personal, devolves on the deceased's personal representatives for the time being.[39] If any change occurs in the deceased's representives, the deceased's estate automatically devolves on the new personal representatives.

Of course, if there are different personal representatives for different parts of the estate, the estate devolves in separate parts on the appropriate personal representatives.[40]

4. Causes of action

The general rule laid down by the Law Reform (Miscellaneous Provisions) Act 1934 is that any causes of action vested in the deceased

---

[31] Housing Act 1988, s. 1. The Act contains a number of exceptions and exclusions (s. 1(1)(c)) and also provides for certain transitional cases (s. 34).

[32] Whether contractual, or statutory following the expiration of a fixed term tenancy: Housing Act 1988, s. 5(2).

[33] This includes a person living with the tenant as his or her wife or husband: Housing Act 1988, s. 17(4).

[34] Housing Act 1988, s. 17(1).

[35] As defined in Housing Act 1988, s. 17(2). The definition is broad and includes not only a person in whom the tenancy vested by virtue of the statutory provisions or under the will or intestacy of a previous tenant, but also the survivor of joint tenants.

[36] The rule in *Moodie v. Hosegood* [1952] A.C. 61 under the Rent Acts has no application in these circumstances.

[37] Housing Act 1988 s. 7(3) (as amended), Sched. 2 Pt 1, Ground 7. Ground 7 is not available where the tenancy has vested in the spouse by virtue of s. 17. For the succession provisions in relation to secure tenancies under the Housing Act 1985, see ss. 87 to 90. The rules are similar to those in the Housing Act 1988, save that there may be a succession in favour of another member of the tenant's family (as defined in s. 113) where there is no spouse.

[38] Administration of Estates Act 1925, s. 3(5).

[39] *ibid.* ss. 1(1) and 55(1)(xi).

[40] *Ante*, p. 337. As to timber, emblements and fixtures see Williams, Mortimer and Sunnucks, *Executors, Administrators and Probate* (17th ed, 1993), pp. 500–506 and 510–514.

at his death survive for the benefit of his estate. Similarly, any causes of action subsisting against him survive against his estate.[41] Where a cause of action survives for the benefit of the deceased's estate two special rules as to damages apply:

(i) the damages recoverable never include any exemplary damages or any damages for loss of income in respect of the "lost years" after death[42]; and

(ii) where the deceased's death has been caused by the act or omission which gives rise to the cause of action, the damages recoverable must be calculated without reference to any loss or gain to his estate consequent on his death, except that a sum in respect of funeral expenses may be included.[43] Thus the damages recoverable must be calculated without reference to the *loss* arising in respect of the cost of administration of his estate, or the liability of his estate to inheritance tax; or the *gain* arising from the proceeds of an insurance policy on his life.[44]

(1) *CONTRACT.*[45] The deceased's personal representatives may enforce a contract made by the deceased with X in his lifetime and obtain damages for X's breach[46] or, if appropriate, an injunction or specific performance.[47] The personal representatives may also carry out the performance of such a contract and then recover the contract price from X.[48] Conversely the personal representatives are liable to X (to the extent of the deceased's assets) for any breach of contract committed before or after the deceased's death.[49]

A contract for personal services is exceptional because it comes to an end by an implied condition on the death of either party. As Willes J.

---

[41] Law Reform (Miscellaneous Provisions) Act 1934, s. 1(1): a cause of action is treated as subsisting against the deceased at his death though the damage necessary to complete the cause of action occurs at or after death, s. 1(4): see *R. v. Criminal Injuries Compensation Board, ex p. Tong* [1976] 1 W.L.R. 1237; *Ronex Properties Ltd v. John Laing Construction Ltd* [1983] Q.B. 398 (contribution); *Re Lanc* [1986] 1 F.L.R. 283 (order on divorce). For claims under the Inheritance (Provision for Family and Dependants) Act 1975 see *ante*, p. 115, n. 7.

[42] Law Reform (Miscellaneous Provisions) Act 1934, s. 1(2)(*a*), as amended by Administration of Justice Act 1982, s. 4(2).

[43] Law Reform (Miscellaneous Provisions) Act 1934, s. 1(2)(*c*); *Hart v. Griffiths-Jones* [1948] 2 All E.R. 729 (funeral expenses include embalming of the body but not monument costing £225); *Stanton v. Ewart F. Youldon Ltd.* [1960] 1 W.L.R. 543 (funeral expenses include simple gravestone but not marble memorial set up as a sign of love and affection); *Grammell v. Wilson* [1982] A.C. 27 (funeral expenses include £595 headstone).

[44] *Gammell v. Wilson* [1982] A.C. 27, 46–47, 69, 74 and 77–78.

[45] See P.M. North (1966) 116 N.L.J. 1364–1366.

[46] *Otter v. Church, Adams, Tatham & Co.* [1953] Ch. 280.

[47] *Beswick v. Beswick* [1968] A.C. 58.

[48] *Marshall v. Broadhurst* (1831) 1 Cr. & J. 403 (executors carried out contract for construction work).

[49] *Wantworth v. Cock* (1839) 10 Ad. & El. 42 ("like any ordinary case of goods ordered by a testator, which the executor must receive and pay for"); *Cooper v. Jarman* (1866) L.R. 3 Eq. 98 (administrators liable on intestate's contract). For special defences of personal representatives see *post*, p. 509.

put it in *Farrow v. Wilson*,[50] where a farm bailiff's contract of employment was held to have come to an end on his employer's death,

"Generally speaking, contracts bind the executor or administrator, though not named. Where, however, personal considerations are of the foundation of the contract, as in cases of principal and agent, and master and servant, the death of either party puts an end to the relation; and, in respect of service after the death, the contract is dissolved, unless there be a stipulation express or implied to the contrary. It is obvious that, in this case, if the servant had died, his master could not have compelled his representatives to perform the service in his stead, or pay damages, and equally by the death of the master the servant is discharged of his service, not in breach of the contract, but by implied condition."

But, even in the case of a contract for personal services, any causes of action subsisting at the death of either party survive for the benefit of, or against, the deceased's estate. The employer's personal representatives are therefore liable to the employee (to the extent of the employer's assets) for any arrears of wages due from the employer at his death.[51]

(2) *TORT.* The general rule that any causes of action vested in, or subsisting against, the deceased survive for the benefit of, or against, his estate is applicable to all torts with the exception of defamation.[52] The damages recovered by the personal representatives in respect of any cause of action vested in the deceased form part of his estate for all purposes. The special rules as to the damages recoverable have already been mentioned.[53]

A cause of action which was vested in the deceased and which survives for the benefit of his estate must be sharply distinguished from a cause of action for damages under the Fatal Accidents Act 1976.[54] Under this Act the personal representatives may recover damages on behalf of certain dependants of the deceased where the death of the deceased was caused by a wrongful act in respect of which the deceased could have sued if he had not died.[55] The damages belong to the dependants for whose benefit they are awarded and are designed to compensate the dependants for the loss of their "breadwinner."[56] Under this Act the per-

---

[50] (1869) L.R. 4 C.P. 744, 746; see also *Graves v. Cohen* (1930) 46 T.L.R. 121 (contract by jockey to ride owner's horses discharged by owner's death).

[51] *Stubbs v. The Hollywell Railway Co.* (1867) L.R. 2 Ex. 311 (engineer's personal representative entitled to recover arrears of salary due at engineer's death).

[52] Law Reform (Miscellaneous Provisions) Act 1934, s. 1(1); Law Reform (Miscellaneous Provisions) Act 1970, ss. 4–5: a claim for bereavement under Fatal Accidents Act 1976, s. 1A does not survive for the benefit of a person's estate on his death, Law Reform (Miscellaneous Provisions) Act 1934, s. 1(1A), as amended by Administration of Justice Act 1982, s. 4(1).

[53] *Ante*, p. 373. Damages for loss of expectation of life are never recoverable, but damages for pain and suffering take account of suffering caused to the injured person by awareness of his reduced expectation, Administration of Justice Act 1982, s. 1.

[54] Consolidating the Fatal Accidents Acts 1846–1959.

[55] Fatal Accidents Act 1976, ss. 1 and 2–4, as amended by Administration of Justice Act, 1982, s. 3(1).

[56] Damages may also be awarded in respect of the deceased's funeral expenses if incurred by the dependants: Fatal Accidents Act 1976, s. 3(5), as amended.

sonal representatives may also recover £3,500 damages for bereavement for the benefit of the deceased's wife or husband, or the deceased's parents if the deceased was an unmarried minor.[57] Damages recovered under the Fatal Accidents Act form no part of the deceased's estate.[58]

5. Tax

The personal representatives are liable for income tax and capital gains tax chargeable on the deceased.[59]

II.   COLLECTION AND PRESERVATION OF THE ESTATE

1. Collection of the estate

The personal representatives must carry out their statutory duty to "collect and get in the real and personal estate of the deceased" with reasonable diligence.[1]

(1) *UNSECURED DEBTS.* Personal representatives should therefore require payment of any unsecured debts due to the deceased and, if need be, bring legal proceedings in order to recover payment. In *Caney v. Bond*[2] the testator died, having lent £500 to X on a promissory note. His executor failed to call in the debt. X repaid £100 to the executor and would have repaid the whole debt if he had been pressed to do so. The balance of £400 was lost when X died insolvent two years after the testator. The court held that the executor was personally liable to make good the loss. But a personal representative who has taken no steps to enforce a debt will not be liable if he can prove that there were reasonable grounds for believing that the debtor could not pay.[3]

(2) *SECURED DEBTS.* Personal representatives are not under any duty to call in and realise loans made by the deceased on mortgages of land which are authorised investments under the deceased's will, unless the

---

[57] *ibid. s.* 1A: the specified sum of £3,500 damages may be varied by the Lord Chancellor by statutory instrument, s. 1A(5).

[58] In assessing damages under the Fatal Accidents Act 1976, benefits accruing to any person from the deceased's estate or otherwise as a result of his death are disregarded, s. 4, as amended.

[59] Taxes Management Act 1970, ss. 74(1) and 77(1).

[1] Administration of Estates Act 1925, s. 25, as amended by Administration of Estates Act 1971, s. 9; *Re Tankard* [1942] Ch. 69 (personal representatives' duty to pay debts with "due diligence"): see *post*, p. 413.

[2] (1843) 6 Beav. 486: see also *Lowson v. Copeland* (1787) 2 Bro. C.C. 156 (sum due on bond); *Powell v. Evans* (1801) 5 Ves. 839 (sums due on bond: "debts due upon personal security are what executors without great reason ought not to permit to remain longer than is absolutely necessary"); *Tebbs v. Carpenter* (1816) 1 Madd. 290 (executor failed to collect rents); *Stiles v. Guy* (1848) 16 Sim. 230, 1 M. & G. 422 (executors failed to compel their co-executor to account and pay the balance he owed).

[3] *Clack v. Holland* (1854) 19 Beav. 262, 271–272; *Stiles v. Guy, supra* (onus on executors to prove debtor could not pay); *Re Brogden* (1888) 38 Ch.D. 546.

money is needed for the payment of funeral and testamentary expenses, debts and pecuniary legacies.[4]

(3) *STATUTORY POWERS*. Under section 15 of the Trustee Act 1925, a personal representative has power to allow time for the payment of any debt, to accept composition or any real or personal security for any debt or property claimed, and to compromise, abandon or settle any debt or claim relating to the deceased's estate.[5] If the personal representative exercises this wide power[6] in good faith, he is not responsible for any consequential loss. But the personal representative is only protected by the section if he exercises an active discretion. In *Re Greenwood*[7] the testator died, having lent £1,000 to X during his lifetime. By his will the testator gave his estate to his executors upon the usual trusts for conversion and investment. The executors did not collect the debt, even though it was unsecured and ought to have been got in at an early stage. Seven years later, at the instance of the beneficiaries, the executors issued a writ for the debt, but by then X was insolvent and part of the debt was not recovered. Eve J. held the executors liable to the beneficiaries for the loss. The executors would have been protected by section 15[8] if they had given time to the debtor after a full consideration by them of all the circumstances. But here the giving of time resulted from the passive inactivity of the executors, who simply let the matter drift.

2. The inventory and account

If required to do so by the court, the personal representative has a statutory duty to "exhibit on oath in the court a full inventory of the estate and when so required render an account of the administration of the estate to the court."[9] Any person interested[10] in the deceased's estate may apply to the court[11] for an order requiring such an inventory and account from the personal representative. An order may be made against a former administrator whose grant has been revoked by the court in a probate action.[12] Lapse of time is not in itself a bar but the court has a discretion to refuse such an order.[13]

---

[4] *Re Chapman* [1896] 2 Ch. 763, esp. at pp. 773 and 778.
[5] For the statutory powers in relation to reversionary interests, see Trustee Act 1925, ss. 22 and 68(1)(17).
[6] See *Re Earl of Strafford* [1980] Ch. 28.
[7] (1911) 105 L.T. 509.
[8] Actually, it was s. 21 of the Trustee Act 1893 (s. 15's predecessor).
[9] Administration of Estates Act 1925, s. 25, as amended by Administration of Estates Act 1971, s. 9.
[10] *Myddleton v. Rushout* (1797) 1 Phillim. 244 ("any kind of interest" suffices); *Hackman v. Black* (1755) 2 Lee 251 (creditor); *Kenny v. Jackson* (1827) 1 Hag. Ecc. 105 (residuary legatee).
[11] Application is made to a registrar, N.C. Prob. Rules 1987, r. 61(2).
[12] *In the Estate of Thomas* [1956] 1 W.L.R. 1516; *Taylor v. Newton* (1752) 1 Lee 15 (order made against former administrator whose grant had expired). Apparently an order may be made against the executors of a deceased administrator with the will annexed, *Ritchie v. Rees* (1822) 1 Add. 144, 153, and against the executor of a deceased executor though the other original executor is still alive, *Gale v. Luttrell* (1824) 2 Add. 234.
[13] *Burgess v. Marriott* (1843) 3 Curt. 424, 426; *Ritchie v. Rees, supra,* (administration granted in 1777: application in 1822 for inventory and account refused as estate fully

Compared with an administration action[14] an application for an inventory and account is a relatively cheap procedure but the scope of the remedy is limited. In essence it enables the applicant to obtain information from the personal representative as to the property comprised in the estate (the inventory) and the manner in which the administration has been carried out (the account).

3. Time for realisation of unauthorised investments

Personal representatives have a duty to realise any investment, which it is not proper for them to retain, within a reasonable time, which prima facie means within the executor's year, *i.e.* within a year from the date of death. In *Grayburn v. Clarkson*[15] the testator held company shares with unlimited liability and by his will he directed his executors to convert his estate with all convenient speed. The court held that the executors were liable for the loss caused by their failure to sell the shares within the executor's year. The executors were entitled to exercise a reasonable discretion as to when they sold, but they had failed to show any reason why they had not sold within the executor's year. "It certainly was the duty of the executors with all convenient speed, and, indeed, as early as possible, to sell shares involving such [an unlimited] liability."[16] But the executors are not liable if, in the honest exercise of the reasonable discretion allowed them, they decide to postpone the sale beyond the end of the executor's year.[17]

4. Preservation of the estate

Personal representatives are under a duty to take reasonable care in preserving the deceased's estate.[18] If they take reasonable care, they are not liable for the loss of the testator's goods which are destroyed by an accidental fire,[19] or which are taken by a thief from the possession of the personal representatives or their agent, such as their solicitor or banker.[20]

(1) *POWER TO INSURE.* A personal representative has power under the Trustee Act 1925 to insure any building or other insurable property[21] against loss or damage by fire to any amount not exceeding three-quarters of its value. The premiums may be paid out of the income of the insured property or of any other property subject to the same trusts

administered); *Scurrah v. Scurrah* (1841) 2 Curt. 919; *Pitt v. Woodham* (1828) 1 Hag. Ecc. 247; *Bowles v. Harvey* (1832) 4 Hag. Ecc. 241.
[14] See *post*, pp. 503 *et seq.*
[15] (1868) 3 Ch. App. 605: see also *Hughes v. Empson* (1856) 22 Beav. 181.
[16] *Grayburn v. Clarkson* (1868) 3 Ch. App. 605 at p. 608: see also *Sculthorpe v. Tipper* (1871) L.R. 13 Eq. 232: *cf. Re Norrington* (1879) 13 Ch.D. 654.
[17] *Buxton v. Buxton* (1835) 1 My. & Cr. 80 (Mexican bonds sold 19 months after death); *Marsden v. Kent* (1877) 5 Ch.D. 598; *Re Chapman* [1896] 2 Ch. 763.
[18] *Job v. Job* (1877) 6 Ch.D. 562 (*per* Jessel M.R., "an executor or administrator is in the position of a gratuitous bailee"); *Re Gunning* [1918] 1 Ir.R. 221.
[19] *Executors of the Lady Croft v. Lyndsey* (1676) 2 Freem.Ch. 1.
[20] *Jones v. Lewis* (1751) 2 Ves.Sen. 240 (administratrix not liable for loss of assets taken by robbery from her solicitor).
[21] *Re Earl of Egmont's Trusts* [1908] 1 Ch. 821 (heirlooms are insurable property).

without obtaining the consent of any person entitled to the income.[22] This power is not applicable if the deceased's will expresses a contrary intention,[23] or if the personal representative is bound forthwith to convey the property absolutely to any beneficiary upon being requested to do so,[24] in which case it is left to the beneficiary to insure.

But a personal representative is not under any *duty* to insure unless the deceased's will imposes such a duty on him.[25]

(2) *DEPOSIT OF DOCUMENTS.* If a personal representative (not being a trust corporation) retains, or invests in, any securities payable to bearer,[26] such securities *must*, until they are sold, be deposited for safe custody and collection of income with a banker or banking company.[27] The personal representative is not responsible for any loss incurred by reason of the deposit and any cost incurred is payable out of the income of the trust property.[28] Apart from this duty to deposit securities payable to bearer, any documents held by a personal representative *may* be deposited with a banker or a company whose business includes the undertaking of the safe custody of documents and any cost incurred is payable in the same way.[29] Such documents may also be deposited with the personal representative's solicitor or other agent for the purpose of transacting business required in the administration of the deceased's estate.[30]

III. REALISATION OF THE ESTATE

Personal representatives often hold either the whole, or part, of the deceased's estate upon trust for sale. If the deceased died wholly or partly intestate, section 33 of the Administration of Estates Act 1925 imposes a trust for sale on each asset (other than money) as to which the deceased died wholly intestate.[1] Again, it is common for a testator by his will to direct his executors to hold his residuary estate upon trust

---

[22] Trustee Act 1925, ss. 19(1) and 68(1)(17): as to the application of insurance money see s. 20.

[23] *ibid.* s. 69(2).

[24] *ibid.* s. 19(2).

[25] *Re McEacharn* (1911) 103 L.T. 900 (no duty to exercise the statutory power); *Bailey v. Gould* (1840) 4 Y. & C.Ex. 221 (uninsured factory burnt down: executors not liable); *Fry v. Fry* (1859) 27 Beav. 144: but see *Garner v. Moore* (1855) 3 Drew. 277 and Williams, Mortimer and Sunnocks, *Executors, Administrators and Probate* (17th ed., 1993), p. 733–734. For possible reform see Law Reform Committee's, 23rd Report, *The powers and duties of trustees,* Cmnd. 8733 (1982), pp. 41–43 and 66.

[26] If a security is payable to bearer, the person in possession is entitled to demand payment; that is *why* great care must be taken with any such security; a security payable to bearer is much like cash.

[27] Trustees Act 1925, ss.7(1) and 68(17): for the power to retain or invest in such securities see s. 7(1).

[28] *ibid.* s. 7(2).

[29] *ibid.* ss.21 and 68(17): see *Re Sisson's Settlement* [1903] 1 Ch. 262.

[30] *Field v. Field* [1894] 1 Ch. 425 (deeds in custody of trustees' solicitors): see also Trustee Act 1925, ss.23 and 30 and *Re Vickery* [1931] 1 Ch. 572, *post*, pp. 396 *et seq.*

[1] *Ante*, pp. 31 (total intestacy) and 47 (partial intestacy).

for sale. Generally, however, personal representatives do not make title to a purchaser under such a trust for sale. Instead, the personal representatives sell and make title under the ample powers which attach to the office of personal representative.[2] These powers to sell, mortgage and lease must now be considered.

1. Powers to sell

Powers of sale are conferred both (1) at common law and in equity, and (2) by statute.

(1) *COMMON LAW.* Both at common law and in equity a personal representative has power to sell the deceased's personal estate (including leaseholds) for the purpose of carrying out the administration of the deceased's estate. An unpaid creditor of the deceased,[3] or a beneficiary under his will or intestacy,[4] cannot reclaim the property sold from the purchaser; if this were not the rule, no one would ever buy from a personal representative.

Under section 2(1) of the Administration of Estates Act 1925 a personal representative has the same powers with respect to real estate[5] as were in force before 1926 with respect to leaseholds.[6]

(2) *STATUTE.* A personal representative also has a statutory power of sale under section 39(1) of the Administration of Estates Act 1925. This section provides that in dealing with the deceased's real and personal estate his personal representatives shall have all the powers conferred on trustees for sale of land. These include all the powers of a tenant for life and trustees of a settlement under the Settled Land Act 1925[7]; for instance, power to sell or exchange land, or any part thereof, or any easement, right or privilege of any kind over or in relation to the land,[8] and power to sell or exchange the surface and the minerals separately.[9] Personal representatives have power to enter into a contract to make such a sale or exchange[10] and any contract is binding on, and enforceable by, the personal representatives for the time being of the deceased.[11]

The powers conferred by section 39(1) are exercisable for purposes of administration (as was the case at common law) and also "during a

---

[2] As to the powers exercisable under a grant of administration *ad colligenda bona* or limited to an action see *ante*, pp. 344 and 346.

[3] *Nugent v. Gifford* (1738) 1 Atk. 463; *Whale v. Booth* (1784) 4 T.R. 625.

[4] *Ewer v. Corbet* (1723) 2 P.Wms. 148.

[5] See Administration of Estates Act 1925, s.3, and *ante*, p. 369.

[6] The Land Transfer Act 1897, s.2(2) had the same effect on a death after 1897. And see *Re Chaplin & Staffordshire Potteries Waterworks Co. Ltd's Contract* [1922] 2 Ch. 824 (personal representatives may sell the surface and minerals of the deceased's freehold land separately).

[7] Law of Property Act 1925, s.28(1) (as amended by Law of Property (Amendment) Act 1926).

[8] Settled Land Act 1925, s.38; for the regulations respecting sales and exchanges see ss.39 and 40.

[9] *ibid.* s.50: see also Trustee Act 1925, s.12(2).

[10] Settled Land Act 1925, s.90(1): see also Trustee Act 1925, s.12(1).

[11] Administration of Estates Act 1925, s.39(1) (iii); for power to raise capital money see Trustee Act 1925, s.16.

minority of any beneficiary or the subsistence of any life interest, or until the period of distribution arrives."[12] The reference to a minority of any beneficiary or the subsistence of any life interest appears to have been inserted to cover the case of the deceased dying intestate leaving a widow or infant next of kin.[13]

2. Powers to mortgage

(1) *COMMON LAW.* At common law and in equity a personal representative has power to raise money required for purposes of administration by mortgaging[14] or pledging[15] (as may be appropriate) any of the deceased's personal estate.

(2) *STATUTE.* Under section 39(1) of the Administration of Estates Act 1925 this common law power "including power to raise money by mortgage or charge (whether or not by deposit of documents)" may be exercised by personal representatives over both the real and personal estate of the deceased. Again, because under section 39(1) personal representatives have all the powers conferred on trustees for sale of land, they have all the powers to raise money by legal mortgage of a tenant for life[16] under the Settled Land Act 1925.[17]

Personal representatives also have power, for the purpose of paying inheritance tax for which they are liable on any property (or raising the amount of it when paid), to raise the amount of the tax by sale or mortgage of, or a terminable charge on, the property.[18]

3. Powers to lease

(1) *COMMON LAW.* At common law and in equity a personal representative has power to grant a lease for purposes of administration.[19] For instance, if the deceased's estate includes a leasehold interest for which the personal representative cannot find a purchaser or negotiate a surrender to the landlord, he may grant an underlease. This common law

---

[12] Administration of Estates Act 1925, s.39(1): for the meaning of minority see Family Law Reform Act 1969, s.1 and Sched. 3, para. 6.

[13] *Re Trollope's W.T.* [1927] 1 Ch. 596, 603–605.

[14] *Mead v. Orrery* (1745) 3 Atk. 235, 239–240; *Scott v. Tyler* (1788) Dick. 712, 725; *M'Leod v. Drummond* (1810) 17 Ves. 152, 154; *Earl Vane v. Rigden* (1870) L.R. 5 Ch. 663 ("it is a very common practice for an executor to obtain an advance from a banker for the immediate wants of the estate by depositing securities. It would be a strange thing if that could not be done").

[15] *Russell v. Plaice* (1854) 18 Beav. 21, 28–29.

[16] Though the powers of a tenant for life to mortgage are limited—see S.L.A. 1925 s. 71(1).

[17] Law of Property Act 1925, s.28(1) (as amended); Settled Land Act 1925, ss.49(1)(c), 69–71 and 90. For extensions of s.71 see *inter alia* Landlord and Tenant Act 1927, s.13(1); Landlord and Tenant Act 1954, s.8(5) and Sched. 2, para. 6, and Leasehold Reform Act 1967, s.6(5) and Sched. 2, para. 9(1). For the power of personal representatives to demise land for a term to trustees to raise money for giving effect to beneficial interests see Administration of Estates Act 1925, s.40: see also Trustee Act 1925, s.16.

[18] Inheritance Tax Act 1984, s.212(1) and (4) (tax includes interest and costs properly incurred in respect of tax).

[19] Oceanic Steam Navigation Co. (v.) Sutherberry (1880) 16 Ch.D. 236, 243.

power now applies to the deceased's real estate as well as to the deceased's leaseholds.[20]

(2) *STATUTE.* As already mentioned, under section 39(1) of the Administration of Estates Act 1925 personal representatives have all the powers of a tenant for life under the Settled Land Act 1925, which include powers to lease[21] and to accept a surrender of a lease.[22]

4. Protection of purchaser

(1) *PROPRIETY OF THE DISPOSITION.* At common law a purchaser or mortgagee was entitled to presume that the sale or mortgage to him by the personal representative was made for purposes of administration.[23] But the purchaser or mortgagee was not protected if he knew that the disposition was made by the personal representative other than for purposes of administration.[24]

Section 36(8) of the Administration of Estates Act 1925 now provides greater protection for a purchaser of a legal estate in land. It provides that:

"a conveyance[25] of a legal estate by a personal representative to a purchaser shall not be invalidated by reason only that the purchaser may have notice that all the debts, liabilities, funeral and testamentary or administration expenses, duties, and legacies of the deceased have been discharged or provided for."

For section 36(8) to apply, the purchaser (or mortgagee or lessee[26]) must have acquired a legal estate in land[27] in good faith[28] and for money or money's worth.[29]

(2) *APPLICATION OF THE PURCHASE MONEY.* Again, at common law a purchaser or mortgagee was not concerned to ensure that the personal representative applied the purchase, or mortgage, money properly. As Lord Thurlow put it in *Scott v. Tyler,*[30]

"It is of great consequence that no rules should be laid down here,

---

[20] Administration of Estates Act 1925, s.2(1).
[21] Settled Land Act 1925, ss. 41–48; but the powers are limited, for example, the general rule is that a tenant for life cannot grant a lease for more than 50 years; for proposals for reform see the Law Reform Committee's 23rd Report, *The powers and duties of trustees,* Cmnd. 8733, para 8.6: and for the grant of an option see s. 51.
[22] Settled Land Act 1925, s. 52: for the power to enter into contracts see s. 90(1) and Administration of Estates Act 1925, s. 39(1)(iii).
[23] *Re Venn & Furze's Contract* [1894] 2 Ch. 101.
[24] *Re Verrell's Contract* [1903] 1 Ch. 65; *Wilson v. Moore* (1834) 1 M. & K. 337.
[25] "Conveyance" includes *inter alia* a mortgage, charge by way of legal mortgage, and a lease: see Administration of Estates Act 1925, s. 55(1)(iii).
[26] Administration of Estates Act 1925, s. 55(1)(xviii): s. 36(8) applies to conveyances made after 1925, whenever the deceased died, s. 36(12).
[27] *ibid.* s. 55(1)(vii).
[28] *ibid.* s. 55(1)(xviii).
[29] *ibid.* s. 36(11): *quaere* whether a nominal consideration in money suffices, see s. 55(1)(xviii); *Midland Bank Trust Co. Ltd. v. Green* [1981] A.C. 513, 531–532.
[30] (1788) Dick. 712, 725: see also *M'Leod v. Drummond* (1810) 17 Ves. 152, 154.

which may impede executors in their administration, or render their disposition of the testator's effects unsafe, or uncertain to the purchaser; his title is complete by sale and delivery; what becomes of the price, is no concern of the purchaser. This observation applies equally to mortgages or pledges . . ."

This common law rule has now been enacted in section 14 of the Trustee Act 1925 which provides that the receipt in writing of a personal representative[31] for any money, securities or other personal property payable or transferable to him under any trust or power shall be a sufficient discharge to the person paying or transferring the same and "shall effectually exonerate him from seeing to the application or being answerable for any loss or misapplication thereof." The statutory protection of the purchaser cannot be excluded by a contrary direction in the deceased's will.[32]

(3) *GOOD FAITH ESSENTIAL.* Good faith on the part of the purchaser is always essential, whether the conveyance is of a legal estate in land (so that section 36(8) applies) or of an equitable interest in land or any interest in pure personalty (to which section 36(8) is not applicable). If the purchaser knows that the disposition to him is a breach of duty on the part of the personal representative, the purchaser's bad faith vitiates the disposition.[33] If the transaction is vitiated by bad faith on the part of the purchaser, a creditor or a beneficiary entitled under the deceased's will[34] or intestacy may have the transaction set aside unless the creditor or beneficiary is barred by laches.[35]

(4) *PREVIOUS ASSENT.* A personal representative's powers are exercisable over the property for the time being vested in him in his capacity as personal representative. He cannot exercise his powers over property which he has already transferred to the trustees or the beneficiary entitled under the deceased's will or intestacy.[36] Prior to 1926 this principle sometimes gave rise to difficulty, particularly in a case where the deceased had settled property by his will and the trustees were the same persons as the executors.

Since 1925, section 36(6) of the Administration of Estates Act 1925 provides some protection for a purchaser (or mortgagee or lessee[37]) of a legal

---

[31] Trustee Act 1925, s. 68(1)(17)

[32] *ibid.* s. 14(3): see also ss. 17 and 68(1), (7) and (17).

[33] *Doe d. Woodhead v. Fallows* (1832) 2 Cr. & J. 481. In *Scott v. Tyler* ((1788) Dick 712, 715) Lord Thurlow gave some instances of bad faith on the part of the purchaser. He said that the transaction was vitiated if the purchaser "concerts with an executor...by obtaining the testator's effects at a nominal price, or at a fraudulent undervalue, or by applying the real value to the purchase of other objects for his own behoof, or in extinguishing the private debt of the executor."

[34] *Hill v. Simpson* (1802) 7 Ves. 152; *M'Leod v. Drummond* (1810) 17 Ves. 152, 169–170; *Wilson v. Moore* (1834) 1 M. & K. 337.

[35] *Elliot v. Merriman* (1740) 2 Atk. 41; *Andrew v. Wrigley* (1792) 4 Bro. C.C. 125.

[36] *Attenborough v. Solomon* [1913] A.C. 76 (see *post,* pp. 392–393).

[37] Administration of Estates Act 1925, s. 55(1)(xviii): s. 36(6) applies to assents and conveyances made after 1925, whenever the deceased died, s.36(12).

estate in land[38] in good faith[39] and for money or money's worth.[40] Suppose that P contracts to purchase the legal estate in Blackacre from a personal representative V. If V has previously made an assent or conveyance of Blackacre to the trustees or beneficiary entitled under the deceased's will or intestacy, the latter may require that notice of the assent or conveyance be placed on or annexed to the probate or letters of administration.[41] If this has been done, P will ascertain from his inspection of the probate or letters of administration that V cannot make title to Blackacre as personal representative. But if this has not been done, section 36(6) protects P by providing:

    (i) "A statement in writing by a personal representative that he has not given or made an assent or conveyance in respect of a legal estate shall, in favour of a purchaser,. . .be sufficient evidence"[42] of this[43]; and

    (ii) "A conveyance by a personal representative of a legal estate to a purchaser accepted on the faith of such a statement shall. . .operate to transfer or create the legal estate expressed to be conveyed in like manner as if no previous assent or conveyance had been made by the personal representative."

Thus, where section 36(6) applies, P acquires the legal estate in Blackacre, despite the previous assent or conveyance made by V in favour of the trustees or beneficiary entitled under the deceased's will or intestacy. But section 36(6) operates "without prejudice to any previous disposition made in favour of another purchaser deriving title mediately or immediately under the personal representative." It follows that it does not protect the purchaser against a previous purchaser for money or money's worth,[44] whether the latter took directly from the personal representative, or took from the trustees or beneficiary in whose favour the personal representative made a previous assent or conveyance.

(5) *REVOCATION OF GRANT.* The protection of a purchaser from a personal representative against any subsequent revocation of the latter's grant has already been considered.[45]

IV.   CARRYING ON THE DECEASED'S BUSINESS

On the death of the sole proprietor of a business, the assets of the business which were vested in the deceased devolve on his personal

---

[38] *ibid*. s. 55(1)(vii).

[39] *ibid*. s. 55(1)(xviii).

[40] *ibid*. s. 36(11).

[41] *ibid* s. 36(5). In the case of registered land this precaution appears unnecessary, see Ruoff & Roper, *Registered Conveyancing* (6th ed., 1991), 27–12.

[42] Sufficient but not conclusive evidence, see *Re Duce & Boots Cash Chemists (Southern) Ltd.'s Contract* [1937] Ch. 642 (on the construction of s. 36(7)).

[43] In practice such a statement is invariably inserted in a conveyance of unregistered land by a personal representative.

[44] Administration of Estates Act 1925, ss. 36(11) and 55(1)(xviii).

[45] *Ante*, pp. 364 *et seq*.

representatives. On the death of a partner, the assets of the partnership which were vested in the deceased (other than as a joint tenant[1]) devolve on his personal representatives: but such assets remain partnership assets and the surviving partner or partners may deal with them for the purposes of the partnership.[2] If the deceased was a shareholder in an incorporated company which owned the business, the deceased's shares, but not the assets of the business, devolve on his personal representatives. If the shares are unauthorised investments, the personal representatives should sell them within a reasonable time.[3]

1. Authority to carry on business

The general rule is that personal representatives have no authority to carry on the deceased's business.[4] Similarly on the death of a partner, his personal representatives are generally under a duty to call in the deceased's share in the partnership business and they ought not to permit the deceased's share to be left outstanding in the business.[5] For instance, if under the partnership agreement (or under a contract made with the personal representatives after the deceased's death) the surviving partners are bound to purchase the deceased's share, the personal representatives should require payment of the price due to the deceased's estate: if the surviving partners are not so bound, and if the surviving partners do not have an option to purchase the deceased's share,[6] the personal representatives should require the business of the partnership to be wound up.[7]

There are certain exceptions to the general rule that personal representatives have no authority to carry on the deceased's business.

(1) *PROPER REALISATION.* Personal representatives have authority to carry on the deceased's business with a view to the proper realisation of his estate; for example, to carry out the deceased's obligations under a contract made by him,[8] or to enable the business to be sold as a going concern.[9] Thus, if selling the deceased's business as a going concern is a proper method of realisation, his personal representatives may carry

---

[1] Land vested in the partners can only be held by them as legal joint tenants, Law of Property Act 1925, s. 34, but in equity the partners are presumed to be tenants in common, *Re Fuller's Contract* [1933] Ch. 652.

[2] *Re Bourne* [1906] 2 Ch. 427.

[3] *Ante*, p. 377. For the duty of personal representatives who are majority shareholders see *Re Lucking's W.T.* [1968] 1 W.L.R. 866, 874–875; *Barclays Bank Trust Co. Ltd. (No. 1)* [1980] Ch. 515, 530–535 (trust corporation has higher duty of care).

[4] *Barker v. Parker* (1786) 1 T.R. 287, 295; *Kirkman v. Booth* (1848) 11 Beav. 273.

[5] *Kirkman v. Booth, supra.*

[6] It is not improbable that, under the terms of the partnership agreement, the surviving partners will either have a duty to purchase the deceased partner's share, or an option to purchase it. There may be tax implications in relation to business property relief, I.H.T.A. ss. 103–114, see Chap. 12 pp. 276–277.

[7] Parnership Act 1890, ss. 33(1), 38–39 and 42: see *Barclays Bank Trust Co. Ltd. v. Bluff* [1982] Ch. 172.

[8] *Marshall v. Broadhurst* (1831) 1 Cr. & J. 403 ("if a man makes half a wheelbarrow or a pair of shoes, and die, the executors may complete them"); *Edwards v. Grace* (1836) 2 M. & W. 190.

[9] *Dowse v. Gorton* [1891] A.C. 190, 199; *Garrett v. Noble* (1834) 6 Sim. 504.

on the business for such a reasonable period of time as is necessary to enable them to effect the sale. Normally this period is not much longer than the executor's year.[10]

(2) *AUTHORITY IN THE WILL.* The personal representatives have authority to carry on the deceased's business if they are directed, or empowered, to do so by the deceased in his will. If a testator wishes to direct, or empower, his personal representatives to do so, it is desirable that he should insert a suitable express provision in his will. If, however, the personal representatives are empowered to postpone the sale of the deceased's business, they have by implication authority to carry on the business during the period of postponement.[11] It is desirable that a testator should specify in his will which assets of his estate may be employed by his personal representatives in carrying on his business.[12]

Section 33(1) of the Administration of Estates Act 1925, in imposing a trust for sale and conversion on an intestacy, confers on the personal representatives power to postpone such sale and conversion for such a period as they may think proper. The personal representatives probably have, by implication, authority to carry on the deceased's business during the period of postponement.[13]

Personal representatives who carry on the deceased's business without authority are liable to make good any losses they incur. If personal representatives consider it expedient to carry on the deceased's business but lack the authority to do so, it may be advisable for them to apply to the court for an order authorising them to do so,[14] or to seek an indemnity from the beneficiaries (if they are ascertained and *sui juris*).

2. Liability of personal representative for debts incurred

A personal representative is personally liable on every contract which he makes in carrying on the deceased's business—"he is liable for every shilling on every contract he enters into.[15] It is immaterial that he is expressed to make the contract as personal representative[16]—he is still personally liable. Thus, if the personal representative incurs a debt in carrying on the deceased's business, the creditor may sue the personal representative personally and enforce the judgment against the latter's assets. The creditor is not entitled at common law to payment out of the deceased's assets because the debt was not due from the deceased.[17] The

---

[10] *Re Crowther* [1895] 2 Ch. 56, 60. Though what is reasonable must, to some extent, depend on general economic conditions and on the nature of the business.

[11] *Re Crowther* [1895] 2 Ch. 56: *cf. Re Smith* [1896] 1 Ch. 171; *Re Chancellor* (1884) 26 Ch.D. 42, 46.

[12] *e.g. Cutbush v. Cutbush* (1839) 1 Beav. 184 (assets employed in the business at the testator's death); *Re Slater* (1915) 113 L.T. 691 (power to employ a sufficient amount of deceased's other capital not employed in the business); *M'Neillie v. Acton* (1853) 4 De G.M. & G. 744.

[13] Applying the reasoning of *Re Crowther, supra.*

[14] See Trustee Act 1925, s. 57.

[15] *Owen v. Delamere* (1872) L.R. 15 Eq. 134, 139.

[16] *Labouchere v. Tupper* (1857) 11 Moo.P.C. 198; *Liverpool Borough Bank v. Walker* (1859) 4 De G. & J. 24.

[17] *Re Morgan* (1881) 18 Ch.D 93, 99: see also *Farhall v. Farhall* (1871) 7 Ch.App. 123.

creditor may, however, be entitled in equity to payment out of the deceased's assets by subrogation to the personal representative's own right of indemnity out of those assets.

3. Indemnity of personal representative

To what extent is a personal representative who incurs liabilities in carrying on the deceased's business entitled to be indemnified out of the assets of the deceased's estate? The personal representative may be entitled to such an indemnity:

(1) because he had authority to carry on the business; or,

(2) because one or more creditors of the deceased have assented to the carrying on of the business by the personal representative.

(1) *EFFECT OF AUTHORITY TO CARRY ON THE BUSINESS.* Under this head the extent of the personal representative's right of indemnity depends on the nature of the authority he exercised to carry on the business.

(a) *Proper realisation.* If the personal representative carried on the business with a view to the proper realisation of the deceased's estate, his right of indemnity may be exercised against both the deceased's creditors and the beneficiaries.[18] In this case his right of indemnity takes priority over the claims of the deceased's creditors.

(b) *Other authority.* If, on the other hand, the personal representative carried on the business under an authority in the will but not with a view to proper realisation, his right of indemnity may be exercised against the beneficiaries but not against the deceased's creditors.[19] The reason for this distinction is that the beneficiaries are bound by the terms of the will but the creditors are not. Of course, under this right of indemnity the personal representative may only resort to assets which the will authorised him to employ in carrying on the business.[20]

(2) *EFFECT OF ASSENT BY CREDITOR.* If one of the deceased's creditors has assented to the carrying on of the business, the personal representative is entitled to be indemnified out of the deceased's assets in priority to that creditor.[21] This rule applies whether or not the personal representative had authority under the will to carry on the business.[22] If, on the other hand, a creditor of the deceased has not assented to the carrying on of the business, and the business has not been carried on with a view to proper realisation, that creditor may treat the continuance of the business as improper: if he does so, he is entitled to be paid out

---

[18] *Dowse v. Gorton* [1891] A.C. 190, 199 (realisation by selling the deceased's business as a going concern).

[19] *Dowse v. Gorton, supra; Re Millard, ex p. Yates* (1895) 72 L.T. 823; *Re East* (1914) 111 L.T. 101.

[20] *Ex. p. Garland* (1804) 10 Ves. 110; *Cutbush v. Cutbush* (1839) 1 Beav. 184.

[21] *Dowse v. Gorton* [1891] A.C. 190. The assets out of which the personal representative is entitled to be indemnified include any assets acquired in carrying on the business.

[22] *Re Brooke* [1894] 2 Ch. 600.

of the value of the assets which existed at the deceased's death and the personal representative has no right to be indemnified in priority to him.[23]

A creditor does not assent to the carrying on of the business if he merely knows of it and does nothing to stop it.[24] "It is necessary . . . to show an active affirmative assent. Mere standing by with knowledge and doing nothing is not sufficient."[25]

4. Creditor's right of subrogation

If in carrying on the deceased's business the personal representative incurs a debt[26] in respect of which he is entitled to indemnity out of the assets, then, by subrogation to the personal representative, his creditor is entitled to claim the benefit of his right of indemnity. The creditor is therefore entitled in equity to stand in the personal representative's shoes and obtain payment out of the deceased's assets.[27]

The creditor may obtain payment out of the assets to exactly the same extent as the personal representative is entitled to be indemnified out of the assets.

This right of subrogation is most important to the creditor if the personal representative becomes insolvent. In that event, by invoking his right of subrogation, the creditor may be able to obtain payment in full out of the deceased's assets.

5. Assets and profits of the business

Any assets acquired and any profits made by the personal representative in carrying on the deceased's business belong to the deceased's estate.[28] But a creditor of the deceased who is entitled to treat the continuance of the business as improper may not be entitled to invoke this principle. Such a creditor has a choice:

    (i) If he treats the continuance of the business as improper, he may only make the personal representative accountable for the value of the assets which existed at the deceased's death: in that event the personal representative has no right to be indemnified in priority to him.[29]

---

[23] *Re Oxley* [1914] 1 Ch. 604; *Re East* (1914) 111 L.T. 101.

[24] *Re Oxley, supra.*

[25] *Re Oxley, supra,* at p. 616.

[26] Or a liability for damages for a tort, *Re Raybould* [1900] 1 Ch. 199 (letting down the surface in the course of carrying on the deceased's colliery business in a reasonable manner).

[27] *Ex p. Edmonds* (1862) 4 De G.F. & J. 488, 498; *Re Johnson* (1880) 15 Ch.D. 548; *Re Evans* (1887) 34 Ch.D. 597; *Re Owen* (1892) 66 L.T. 718; *Re Frith* [1902] 1 Ch. 342.

[28] *Abbott v. Parfitt* (1871) L.R. 6 Q.B. 346 (price due for bread sold by personal representatives carrying on deceased's bakery business was asset of deceased's estate); *Moseley v. Rendell* (1871) L.R. 6 Q.B. 338; *Gibblett v. Read* (1744) 9 Mod. 459.

[29] *Per* Lord Macnaghten in *Dowse v. Gorton* [1891] A.C. 190, 203–204 (such creditors may "make the executors accountable for the value of the assets used in carrying on the business, and they may also follow the assets and obtain a charge on the business in the hands of the executors for the value of the assets misapplied, with interest thereon; and they may enforce the charge, if necessary, by means of a receiver and a sale').

(ii) If, on the other hand, he treats the business as properly continued, the personal representative is accountable to him for assets acquired and profits made in carrying on the business, but the personal representative is entitled to be indemnified in priority to him against liabilities incurred in carrying on the business. Such a creditor "cannot approbate and reprobate in one breath."[30]

V. THE DECEASED'S LEASEHOLDS

On the death of a tenant, his leasehold interest devolves on his personal representatives[1] without their having to enter the property.[2] The personal representatives cannot refuse the leasehold interest, because they cannot renounce part of their office.[3] This is so even if the tenant's interest is worthless because the rent exceeds the value of the land. If the lease contains a covenant prohibiting any assignment by the tenant without the landlord's consent, there is no breach of covenant when the leasehold interest devolves by operation of law on the tenant's personal representatives.[4]

When considering the liability of a personal representative for rent or breach of the other covenants in a lease, it is vital to distinguish between two types of liability:

(1) liability as personal representative (representative liability), which arises from his office; and
(2) personal liability as assignee of the deceased's leasehold interest, which arises if the personal representative enters into possession of the demised premises.

1. Liability as personal representative

The personal representative is liable as such for rent due from the deceased at his death and for any subsisting breach of other covenants in the lease.[5] Similarly, the personal representative is liable as such for rent falling due and for any breach of covenant committed during the period for which he is liable after the deceased's death.[6] This "liability period" ends, of course, with the determination of the lease. If the deceased was an assignee of the lease (and so liable under privity of

---

[30] *ibid.* at p. 204.
[1] *Ante,* p. 368.
[2] *Wollaston v. Hakewill* (1841) M. & G. 297.
[3] *Billinghurst v. Speerman* (1965) 1 Salk. 297; *Rubery v. Stevens* (1832) 4 B. & Ad. 241, 244. For renunciation by a personal representative of his office in regard to settled land if he is not a trustee of the settlement, see Administration of Estates Act 1925, s. 23(1), and *ante,* p. 339.
[4] *Parry v. Harbert* (1539) 1 Dyer 45b.
[5] If the deceased was the original lessee, under privity of contract all the covenants in the lease were binding on him, even if he had assigned the tenancy during his lifetime, but if he was an assignee of the lease, under privity of estate only covenants which touched and concerned the land were binding on him: see Megarry and Wade, *The Law of Real Property* (5th ed., 1984), pp. 742 *et seq.*
[6] *Youngmin v. Heath* [1974] 1 W.L.R. 135 (weekly tenancy of furnished rooms).

estate but not privity of contract), this liability period also ends with an assignment of the lease by the personal representative. But if the deceased was the original tenant, his personal representative remains liable as such for rent and any breach of the other covenants during the entire unexpired term of the lease, despite any assignment of the lease by the tenant during his lifetime or by the personal representative.[7]

(1) *EXTENT OF REPRESENTATIVE LIABILITY.* In his representative capacity the personal representative is liable only to the extent of the deceased's assets.[8] He does not incur any personal liability unless he enters into possession of the demised premises.[9] But a constructive entry into possession suffices: for example, a personal representative enters into possession if he accepts rent from a sub-tenant.[10]

(2) *PROTECTION AGAINST REPRESENTATIVE LIABILITY.* If the deceased was an assignee of the lease, the personal representative may end the liability period by assigning the lease. If the lease is onerous (the rent exceeding the value of the land), the personal representative should try to end the liability period as soon as possible by negotiating a surrender of the lease to the landlord or an assignment of the lease to a third party.[11]

If the deceased was the original tenant, an assignment by the personal representative does not end the liability period, but section 26 of the Trustee Act 1925 provides protection for the personal representative against any representative liability after he has assigned the lease to a purchaser or a beneficiary entitled to it.[12]

2. Personal liability

If the personal representative[13] (as is usual)[14] enters into possession of the demised premises, he becomes personally liable as an assignee of the deceased's leasehold interest.[15] A personal representative who enters is personally liable for rent falling due and any breach of the other coven-

---

[7] *Coghill v. Freelove* (1690) 3 Mod. 325; *Pitcher v. Tovey* (1692) 4 Mod. 71, 76: and despite any assignment of the lease by the deceased during his lifetime, *Brett v. Cumberland* (1619) Cro.Jac. 521.

[8] *Wilson v. Wigg* (1808) 10 East 315 (personal representative may plead *plene administravit*, whether breach of covenant was by the deceased or after his death); *Helier v. Casebert* (1665) 1 Lev. 127; *Lydall v. Dunlapp* (1743) 1 Wils. 4.

[9] *Rendall v. Andreae* (1892) 61 L.J.Q.B. 630; *Wollaston v. Hakewill* (1841) 3 M. & G. 297, 320–321.

[10] *Mayor, Aldermen and Burgesses of Stratford-upon-Avon v. Parkes* [1914] 2 K.B. 562, 569.

[11] *Rowley v. Adams* (1839) 4 My. & Cr. 534: *cf. Rendall v. Andreae, supra,* at p. 631.

[12] s. 26 does not prejudice the right of the landlord to follow the deceased's assets into the hands of persons amongst whom they have been distributed, s. 26(2): for this remedy see *post,* pp. 510 *et seq.* The section also protects the personal representative against representative liability for a rentcharge or under an indemnity covenant, see s. 26(1) and (3).

[13] The rule does not apply to an *executor de son tort* because the deceased's leasehold interest does not devolve on him. *Mayor, Aldermen & Burgesses of Stratford-upon-Avon v. Parker* [1914] 2 K.B. 562; see *post* p. 519, n. 50.

[14] Constructive entry suffices, see *supra.*

[15] *Mayor, Aldermen & Burgesses of Stratford-upon-Avon v. Parker, supra* at p. 567; *Tilney v. Norris* (1700) 1 Ld.Raym. 553.

ants which touch and concern the land[16] and which are committed after his entry into possession and so long as the lease is vested in him.[17] He is not personally liable as assignee for breaches committed after he has assigned the lease.

(1) *EXTENT OF PERSONAL LIABILITY.* There is an unusual upper limit on his personal liability for rent. The personal representative may, by proper pleading, limit his liability for rent to the actual value of the premises, *i.e.* the amount he received or might by the exercise of reasonable diligence have received from the premises during his period of liability as assignee.[18] It seems that this upper limit is meant to prevent hardship to the personal representative in a case where the rent reserved exceeds the actual value of the premises. But, illogically, this upper limit appears not to be applicable to his personal liability for breach of other covenants, so that a personal representative who enters is apparently fully liable for breach of a repairing covenant in the lease, even though the lease is onerous.[19]

(2) *PROTECTION AGAINST PERSONAL LIABILITY.* Section 26 of the Trustee Act 1925 provides protection for a personal representative against his representative liability but not against his personal liability.[20] A personal representative who incurs personal liability by entering into possession is entitled:

    (i) to have a proper indemnity from the beneficiaries[21] (*e.g.* the beneficiaries may give security); or,
    (ii) to set aside an indemnity fund out of the deceased's estate.[22]

The indemnity fund is for the protection of the personal representative and not of the lessor.[23] It is distributable to the beneficiaries when all possible claims against the personal representative have either been satisfied, or become statute-barred by lapse of time since the determination, or assignment by the personal representative, of the lease.[24] If the personal representative assigns the lease to the beneficiary entitled without taking a proper indemnity from him, the personal representative is not

---

[16] If they touch and concern the land, they are binding on him as assignee under privity of estate. Examples of covenants which touch and concern the land are coventants to repair, to insure, and not to assign without the landlord's consent.

[17] *Whitehead v. Palmer* [1908] 1 K.B. 151.

[18] *Rendall v. Andreae* (1892) 61 L.J.Q.B. 630, 633; *Re Bowes* (1887) 37 Ch.D. 128 (for form of pleading see p. 132); *Hornidge v. Wilson* (1841) 11 Ad. & E. 645 (executor liable for value he might have received if he had complied with covenant to repair); *Hopwood v. Whaley* (1848) 6 C.B. 744. See also *Minford v. Carse* [1912] 2 Ir.R. 245 (receiver in possession: executors not liable for rent).

[19] *Rendall v. Andreae, supra,* at p. 633; *Tremeere v. Morison* (1834) 1 Bing.N.C. 89; *Sleap v. Newman* (1862) 12 C.B.(N.S.) 116: but see *Reid v. Lord Tenterden* (1833) 4 Tyr. 111, 118 and 120.

[20] *Re Owers* [1941] Ch. 389.

[21] *Simmons v. Bolland* (1817) 3 Mer. 547; *Dobson v. Carpenter* (1850) 12 Beav. 370; *Hickling v. Boyer* (1851) 3 Mac. & G. 635; *Dean v. Allen* (1855) 20 Beav. 1.

[22] *Re Owers, supra.*

[23] *King v. Malcott* (1852) 9 Hare 692.

[24] *Re Lewis* [1939] Ch. 232.

then entitled to set aside an indemnity fund out of the deceased's estate.[25]

VI. EXERCISE OF POWERS BY PERSONAL REPRESENTATIVES

1. Sole personal representative

A sole personal representative has the same powers as two or more personal representatives. This is so where a single personal representative was appointed initially or where only one of several personal representatives survives.[1] In particular, a sole personal representative, acting as such, may give a valid receipt for, or direct the application of, the proceeds of sale of land[2]: by way of contrast, a sole trustee may not do so unless the sole trustee is a trust corporation.[3]

A sole personal representative may contract in his representative capacity with himself as an individual[4]: normally a person cannot make a contract with himself.

2. Joint personal representatives

The general rule is that joint executors have joint *and several* authority: the act of one of them in exercise of their powers is therefore binding on the other executors and the deceased's estate.[5] This rule may also apply to joint administrators, though there is no decisive authority.[6] So:

  (i) A sale or other disposition of a chattel comprised in the deceased's estate by one of the executors is valid.[7]
  (ii) One executor may pay a debt due from the deceased,[8] or accept payment of[9] or release[10] a debt due to the estate, or settle an account with a person liable to the estate.[11]

(1) *STATUTORY EXCEPTIONS.* This general rule is subject to significant statutory exceptions.

---

[25] *Re Bennett* [1943] 1 All E.R. 467; *Shadbolt v. Woodfall* (1845) 2 Coll. 30; *Smith v. Smith* (1861) 1 Dr. & Sm. 384.
[1] Administration of Estates Act 1925, s. 2(1) and (2). For survivorship of powers see *post,* p. 393.
[2] Law of Property Act 1925, s. 27(2) as amended by Law of Property (Amendment) Act 1926, Sched.
[3] *ibid.*; Settled Land Act 1925, s. 18(1); Trustee Act 1925, s. 14.
[4] *Rowley, Holmes & Co. v. Barber* [1977] 1 W.L.R. 371 (solicitor's executor employed himself as legal executive).
[5] *Jacomb v. Harwood* (1751) 2 Ves.Sen. 265, 267; *Attenborough v. Solomon* [1913] A.C. 76. For possible reform see Law Reform Committee's 23rd Report, *The powers and duties of trustees,* Cmnd. 8733 (1982), pp. 55–56 and 68.
[6] *Fountain Forestry Ltd. v. Edwards* [1975] Ch. 1, 10–14 (where Brightman J. reviewed the case law)
[7] *Kelsack v. Nicholson* (1596) Cro. Eliz. 478 and 496; *Jacomb v. Harwood, supra.*
[8] *Jacomb v. Harwood, supra,* at pp. 267–268.
[9] *Charlton v. Earl of Durham* (1869) 4 Ch. App. 433.
[10] *Herbert v. Pigott* (1834) 2 Cr. & M. 384.
[11] *Smith v. Everett* (1859) 27 Beav. 446.

(a) *Interests in land.* The rule does not apply to any "conveyance"[12] of freehold or leasehold land[13]: such a conveyance must not be made without the concurrence of all the personal representatives (still living) to whom a grant has been made in respect of the land conveyed, or without an order of the court.[14]

A contract to sell land is not a "conveyance" and before the enactment of section 16 of the Law of Property (Miscellaneous Provisions) Act 1994[15] it seemed that one of two or more executors could enter into a contract to sell land to a purchaser and that this contract would be binding on the deceased's estate; though he could not convey the land to the purchaser without the concurrence of his co-executors or an order of the court.[16] Section 16 now requires the concurrence of all personal representatives in any contract to convey real estate, as well as for the conveyance itself. The section applies to contracts made on or after July 1, 1995.[17]

(b) *Shares and stock.* If a company is regulated by the Companies Acts, its articles usually require a transfer of its shares to be executed by all the personal representatives.[18] The Bank of England may decline to give effect to a transfer of government stock unless it is executed by all the personal representatives.[19]

(2) *AUTHORITY OF TRUSTEES.* By contrast, trustees, as opposed to executors, must always act jointly.[20] This difference between the authority of executors and of trustees may make it essential to decide whether persons appointed to be executors and trustees held particular property as executors or as trustees at the time when one of them sold or otherwise disposed of it. In *Attenborough v. Solomon*[21] T by his will appointed his sons X and Y to be executors and trustees and, after bequeathing certain pecuniary legacies, gave his residuary estate to X and Y upon

---

[12] "Conveyance" is defined to include "a mortgage, charge by way of legal mortgage, lease, assent, vesting instrument, disclaimer, release and every other assurance of property or of an interest therein by any instrument, except a will". Administration of Estates Act 1925, s. 55(1)(iii). A denial of their landlord's title in a pleading on behalf of one of two executors is not a "conveyance" within this definition, *Warner v. Sampson* [1958] 1 Q.B. 404 (reversed on other grounds [1959] 1 Q.B. 297.)

[13] Administration of Estates Act 1925, s. 3(1). If the deceased died before 1926, the general rule applies to his leasehold land, see Administration of Estates Act 1925, s. 54; Land Transfer Act 1897, s. 2(2) and *Anon.* (1536) 1 Dyer 23(b).

[14] Administration of Estates Act 1925, ss. 2(2) and 24.

[15] This section amends section 2(2) of the Administration of Estates Act 1925.

[16] *Fountain Forestry Ltd. v. Edwards* [1975] Ch. 1, 11–12.

[17] Law of Property (Misc Provs) Act 1994 (Commencement No. 2) Order 1995, S.I. 1995 No. 1317.

[18] Companies Act 1985, ss. 8, 182 and 183(3); Companies (Alteration of Tables A etc.) Regulations 1984 (S.I. 1984 No. 1717), Table A, arts. 29–31. If personal representatives are registered as the holders of shares or stock in a company incorporated under the Companies Clauses Acts, a transfer is invalid unless executed by all of them; *Barton v. North Staffordshire Railway Co.* (1888) 38 Ch.D. 458; *Barton v. London and North Western Railway Co.* (1889) 24 Q.B.D. 77.

[19] Goverment Stock Regulations 1965 (S.I. No. 1420), reg. 6(2); Finance Act 1942, s. 47(2) and Sched. 11, Pt. 111.

[20] *Luke v. South Kensington Hotel Ltd* (1879) 11 Ch.D. 121, 125; see Hanbury and Martin, *Modern Equity* (14th ed., 1993) p. 175–476.

[21] [1913] A.C. 76.

trust for sale and distribution as directed by the will. Within one year of T's death X and Y paid all the debts and expenses and legacies and settled the estate accounts. Fourteen years after T's death X (unknown to Y) pledged a silver plate comprised in the residuary estate with a pawnbroker who did not know that X was not its absolute owner. X misapplied the money raised by the pledge. After X's death Y discovered the pledge and sued the pawnbroker for the plate's return. The House of Lords held that the pledge was invalid and the pawnbroker had to return the plate. At the date of the pledge, X and Y held the residuary estate as trustees and not as executors.

3. Powers in the will annexed to an office

By his will a testator may confer powers on the persons who are appointed by him as his executors or his trustees. It is a question of construction whether such a power is intended to be (i) a bare power personal to those persons,[22] or (ii) a power annexed to their office, so as to be exercisable by the holders or holder of the office for the time being.[23]

4. Survivorship of powers

Under section 18(1) of the Trustee Act 1925,[24] where a trust or power is imposed on, or given to, personal representatives jointly, it may be performed, or exercised, by the survivors or survivor of them for the time being. In the absence of any contrary direction in the will,[25] this provision applies to all the statutory and common law powers of personal representatives and to all the powers conferred by will which are annexed to their office.[26]

5. Effect of order for general administration

If in an administration action the court makes an order for general administration (*i.e.* an order for the administration of the deceased's estate under the direction of the court[27]), the personal representatives must not exercise their powers without first obtaining the sanction of

---

[22] *Down v. Worrall* (1833) 1 M. & K. 561; *Forbes v. Forbes* (1854) 18 Beav. 552 (bequest of £2,000 to executors in trust to build a bridge over the river Don, the site "to be chosen by them": Romilly M.R. said power to choose site seemed to have been personal to original executors, who had died without choosing).

[23] *Crawford v. Forshaw* [1891] 2 Ch. 261 (power for "my executors herein named" to select charities held annexed to office of executor: two executors who proved could, but renouncing executor could not, exercise power): see also *Lambert v. Randle* (1863) 3 New Rep. 247 (power for executor acting under his will to carry on testator's business; executor renounced: held power not exercisable by administratrix with will annexed). And see *Re Smith* [1904] 1 Ch. 139, 144.

[24] Applicable to personal representatives, Trustee Act 1925, ss. 68(1)(17) and 69(1).

[25] *ibid.* s. 69(2).

[26] But not to a bare power given to persons by name and not annexed to an office, *Re Harding* [1923] 1 Ch. 182. See also Williams, Mortimer and Sunnucks, *Executors, Administrators and Probate* (17th ed., 1993), pp. 697–698.

[27] For administration proceedings see *post*, pp. 503 *et seq.*

the court.[28] Thus if the personal representatives desire to sell, deal with, or distribute any assets of the deceased's estate, they must first apply for the sanction of the court.[29]

VII. DECEASED A SOLE TRUSTEE

1. Devolution of trust property

If at his death the deceased held property as a sole or last surviving trustee, the property devolves on his personal representatives.[1] To meet this situation section 18(2) of the Trustee Act 1925 provides that:

"Until the appointment of new trustees, the personal representatives or representative[2] for the time being of a sole trustee, or, where there were two or more trustees of the last surviving or continuing trustee, shall be capable of exercising or performing any power or trust which was given to, or capable of being exercised by, the sole or last surviving or continuing trustee, or other the trustees or trustee for the time being of the trust."

This provision applies to any trust unless a contrary intention is expressed in the trust instrument.[3]

2. Personal representative is not bound to act as trustee

The personal representative of such a deceased trustee is not bound to perform the trust—he has "an absolute right to decline to accept the position and duties of trustee if he chooses so to do,"[4] He is only bound, in his capacity as personal representative, to collect and preserve the property of which the deceased was trustee:[5] he is not bound, for instance, to pay the income of that property to the beneficiary entitled to it under the trust. But under section 18(2), the personal representative may, if he chooses, perform the trust or exercise the power. There is only one restriction: under section 18(2) a sole personal representative (who is not a trust corporation) cannot give a valid receipt for the proceeds of sale or other capital money arising under a trust for sale of land or for capital money arising under the Settled Land Act 1925.[6]

---

[28] *Re Viscount Furness* [1943] Ch. 415 (sanction is needed even if the accounts and inquiries ordered are not to be proceeded with except with the leave of the judge in person); *Minors v. Battison* (1876) 1 App.Cas. 428.

[29] See generally A.J. Hawkins (1968) 84 L.Q.R. 64, 68–73.

[1] *Ante*, pp. 368 *et seq*: for grants to settled land see *ante*, pp. 337 *et seq*.

[2] This does not include an executor who has renounced or has not proved, Trustee Act 1925, s. 18(4).

[3] *ibid.* s. 69(1) and (2).

[4] *Re Benett* [1906] 1 Ch. 216, 225: see also *Legg v. Mackrell* (1860) 2 De G.F. & J. 551, *Re Ridley* [1904] 2 Ch. 774. But as to the personal representative of a Settled Land Act trustee appointed by the court see Settled Land Act 1925, s. 34(2).

[5] *Re Benett, supra*, at pp. 227–228: see also Administration of Estates Act 1925, s. 25 as amended by Administration of Estates Act 1971, s. 9.

[6] Trustee Act 1925, ss. 18(3) and 14(2) (as amended by Law of Property (Amendment) Act 1926, ss. 7, 8(2) and Sched.).

3. Appointment of new trustees

The personal representative may only perform the trust or exercise the power under section 18(2) "until the appointment of new trustees." An appointment of new trustees may be made under section 36 of the Trustee Act 1925:[7]

    (i) by the person or persons nominated for the purpose of appointing new trustees by the trust instrument.[8]

    (ii) if there is no person nominated who is able and willing to act, by the personal representative.[9]

The personal representative cannot be compelled to exercise his power to appoint new trustees.[10] If need be, an appointment of new trustees may be made by the court.[11]

VIII. DELEGATION BY A PERSONAL REPRESENTATIVE

The basic rule is that a personal representative cannot delegate unless he has authority to do so.[1] The same rule applies to a trustee.[2] There are a number of statutory provisions which confer authority on a personal representative to delegate to an agent. Taken together these statutory provisions have a wide ambit, but they do not authorise a personal representative to delegate everything to his agent on every occasion. It is necessary to consider each of the three main statutory provisions in turn, with a view to ascertaining in each case:

    (1) the extent of the personal representative's power to delegate (for instance, is the personal representative permitted to delegate the exercise of his powers to the agent?); and

    (2) in what circumstances liability is imposed on the personal representative if loss occurs (for instance, if the agent disappears with assets of the estate).

---

[7] Subject to any contrary intention expressed in the trust instrument, Trustee Act 1925, s. 69(1) and (2).

[8] If the persons nominated make an appointment of new trustees but do not include the personal representative among the new trustees, this operates to displace the personal representative for all purposes from the trust, *Re Routledge's Trusts* [1909] 1 Ch. 280.

[9] Trustee Act 1925, s. 36(1) and (4): for appointment by a renouncing executor see s. 36(5). An executor who has not proved may appoint under section 36(1), but his title to appoint can only be proved by production of a grant of probate or letters of administration with the will annexed, *Re Crowhurst Park* [1974] 1 W.L.R. 583, 593–594. The personal representative may include himself among the new trustees he appoints; if he does not do so, his own appointment of new trustees displaces him for all purposes from the trust.

[10] *Re Knight's Will* (1884) 26 Ch.D. 82.

[11] Trustee Act 1925, s. 41(1) and Settled Land Act 1925, s. 34.

[1] See generally on delegation, G.H. Jones (1959) 22 M.L.R. 381; W.S.H. (1931) 47 L.Q.R. 463; Law Reform Committee's 23rd Report, *The powers and duties of trustees*, Cmnd. 8733 (1982), pp. 34–41 and 65–66.

[2] *Pilkington v. Inland Revenue Commissioners* [1964] A.C. 612, 639; *Turner v. Corney* (1841) 5 Beav. 515, 517.

The three main statutory provisions[3] are all contained in the Trustee Act 1925. They are:

(1) section 23(1), which confers a general power to employ an agent;
(2) section 23(2), which confers a power to appoint an agent in respect of any property forming a part of the deceased's estate in any place outside the United Kingdom; and
(3) section 25, which confers a power of temporary delegation by power of attorney.

1. General power to employ an agent

Section 23(1) of the Trustee Act 1925 contains the power most commonly exercised by personal representatives. It reads as follows:

"Trustees or personal representatives may, instead of acting personally, employ and pay an agent, whether a solicitor, banker, stockbroker or other person, to transact any business or do any act required to be transacted or done in the execution of the trust, or the administration of the testator's or intestate's estate, including the receipt and payment of money, and shall be entitled to be allowed and paid all charges and expenses so incurred, and shall not be responsible for the default of any such agent if employed in good faith."

(1) *EXTENT OF THE POWER.* Under this provision the personal representative may delegate to the agent any business required to be transacted or any act required to be done in the administration of the estate. There is no requirement (as there was before 1926[4]) that delegation to the agent should be reasonably necessary or in accordance with ordinary business practice. A personal representative:

"is no longer required to do any actual work himself, but he may employ a solicitor or other agent to do it, whether there is any real necessity for the employment or not."[5]

There is, however, one significant limit on the extent of the personal representative's power to delegate under section 23(1)—he may not delegate to the agent the execution of any duty or the exercise of any power or discretion vested in him. Thus the personal representative may employ a solicitor to carry out conveyancing work required on a sale of land, or a stockbroker to sell government stock, but under section 23(1) the personal representative has no power to delegate the decision whether to sell the land or the stock. By contrast, both the other main statutory provisions (about to be considered) expressly authorise delegation of any duty, power or discretion vested in the personal representative.

---

[3] Other provisions include (i) Trustee Act 1925, s. 8 (employment of valuer when lending money on mortgage), (ii) s. 22(4) (audit of accounts by independent accountant), and (iii) Law of Property Act 1925, s. 29 (delegation of powers of management) and Administration of Estates Act 1925, s. 39(1).

[4] *Ex p. Belchier* (1754) Amb. 218; *Speight v. Gaunt* (1883) 22 Ch.D. 727, C.A., (1883) 9 App.Cas. 1 H.L.

[5] *Per* Maugham J. in *Re Vickery* [1931] 1 Ch. 572, 581.

The general power to employ an agent conferred by section 23(1) is supplemented by section 23(3), which deals with the delegation to an agent of the receipt of money (or other valuable consideration) in certain transactions.[6] Section 23(3) authorises a personal representative to appoint a solicitor[7] to be his agent to receive (say) the price due from a purchaser of land, or money payable under an insurance policy, by producing a deed containing a receipt and executed by the personal representative, or the policy of insurance with a receipt signed by the personal representative.

(2) *LIABILITY OF THE PERSONAL REPRESENATIVE FOR LOSS.* The difficulty is that it is not certain which rules govern the liability of the personal representative when loss occurs as a result of delegation to an agent under section 23(1).

(a) *The rules before 1926.* The rules in force before 1926 were well settled. A personal representative or trustee had a duty to act as a prudent man of business, both in selecting and in supervising his agent.[8] So, a personal representative had to employ an agent appropriate to the work to be done[9]—*e.g.* a stockbroker to do stockbrokers' work—and had to take proper care in selecting his agent—selecting a stockbroker who stood in good credit and whose fitness he had no reason to doubt.[10] In addition, a personal representative had to take proper care in supervising his agent—so, if anything occurred which would have aroused the suspicions of a prudent man as to the stockbroker's solvency or honesty, the personal representative had to take steps to protect the estate's assets.[11] Moreover the personal representative must not leave money or other assets of the estate in the hands of his agent for an unreasonable length of time.[12]

The question arises whether these rules have been changed since 1925.

(b) *Effect on liability of section 23(1) and (3).* The final words of section 23(1) state that a personal representative "shall not be responsible for the default of any such agent if employed in good faith." On one construction of these words the personal representative's duty has been reduced from the objective standard of proper care in selection and supervision to the subjective level of employment of the agent in good faith.[13]

But it remains uncertain whether section 23(1) has this effect. It may be that these final words in section 23(1) exempt the personal represent-

---

[6] s. 23(3) applies to a personal representative, ss. 68(1)(17) and 69(1).
[7] Or banker in the case of money payable under an insurance policy, s. 23(3)(*c*).
[8] *Speight v. Gaunt, supra.*
[9] *Fry v. Tapson* (1884) 28 Ch.D. 268.
[10] *Speight v. Gaunt* (1883) 22 Ch.D. 727, 740, 745, 747 and 762.
[11] *Speight v. Gaunt* (1883) 9 App.Cas. 1, 13–15.
[12] *Matthews v. Brise* (1843) 6 Beav. 239 (stockbroker sold Exchequer bills left in his hands and misapplied proceeds: trustee held liable to beneficiaries); *Rowland v. Witherden* (1851) 3 Mac. & G. 568; *Wyman v. Paterson* [1900] A.C. 271.
[13] *Snell's Equity* (29th ed., 1990), p. 266 (it seems the liability of trustees "no longer depends on reasonableness but merely on good faith"): *cf.* the wording of the Trustee Act 1925, s. 15, see *ante*, p. 376.

ative who employs an agent in good faith from any possible *vicarious* liability for his agent's default, but they may leave intact the personal representative's *own duty* to take proper care in the selection and supervision of his agent.[14] The reference in these final words to responsibility for the agent's default are appropriate to the exemption of a principal from vicarious responsibility for his agent's default.

In the absence of any decision on the effect of section 23(1) on the liability of a personal representative, a dictum of Maugham J. in *Re Vickery* provides the only judicial guidance available. Referring to section 23(1) Maugham J. said:

> "No doubt [the personal representative] should use his discretion in selecting an agent, and should employ him only to do acts within the scope of the usual business of the agent ..."[15]

So which construction of section 23(1) does this dictum support?

A proviso to the supplementary power in section 23(3) expressly preserves the pre-1926 liability of a personal representative in case he permits any money (or other valuable consideration) to remain in the hands of the solicitor for a period longer than is reasonably necessary to enable the solicitor to pay it to the personal representative. This proviso is applicable where the personal representative delegates under this supplementary power.[16] If section 23(1) really does reduce a personal representative's duty to the subjective level of employment of the agent in good faith, it is open to a personal representative to minimise his liability by appointing his agent whenever possible under section 23(1) rather than under 23(3).

(c)   *Effect on liability of section 30(1).* Section 30(1) of the Trustee Act 1925 provides as follows:

> "A trustee shall be chargeable only for money and securities actually received by him notwithstanding his signing any receipt for the sake of conformity, and shall be answerable and accountable only for his own acts, receipts, neglects, or defaults, and not for those of any other trustee, nor for any banker, broker, or other person with whom any trust money or securities may be deposited, nor for the insufficiency or deficiency of any securities, nor for any other loss, unless the same happens through his own wilful default."

Section 30(1) certainly applies to a personal representative because "trustee" is defined to include a personal representative.[17]

Section 30(1) was not new in 1925. An almost identical statutory provision had been in force since 1859[18] and the provision in the 1859 Act

---

[14] G.H. Jones (1959) 22 M.L.R. 381, 394–395, Hanbury and Martin, *Modern Equity* (14th ed., 1993), pp. 549–559.

[15] [1931] 1 Ch. 572, 581.

[16] *Re Vickery, supra* at p. 581. The personal representative is not liable under the proviso unless he knew or ought to have known of the solicitor's receipt of the money, *Re Sheppard* [1911] 1 Ch. 50.

[17] Trustee Act 1925, ss. 68(1)(17) and 69(1).

[18] Law of Property Amendment Act (or Lord Cranworth's Act) 1859, s. 31 repealed and re-enacted by Trustee Act 1893, s. 24.

itself reproduced an indemnity clause commonly inserted by draftsmen in trust instruments before 1859.[19] What effect did this statutory provision have before 1926? Lord Selborne L.C. gave the answer in 1884 in *Re Brier*[20]:

> "It does not substantially alter the law as it was administered by Courts of Equity, but gives it the authority and force of statute law, and appears to me to throw the *onus probandi* on those who seek to charge an executor or trustee with a loss arising from the default of an agent, when the propriety of employing an agent has been established."

In *Re Brier* a coal merchant was owed a number of small debts at his death. His executors (acting properly) employed an agent to collect the debts but the money collected was lost owing to the agent's insolvency. The Court of Appeal held that the executors were not liable for this loss unless it occurred through to their wilful default (for instance, because "the executors were negligent"[21]), and the burden of proving this lay on the persons who sought to charge the executors with the loss.

"Wilful default" was (and still is) a technical expression of equity. A personal representative or trustee normally has to account only for assets which he has actually received. But he may be ordered to account upon the footing of wilful default, *i.e.* to account in addition for assets which he would have received but for his own wilful default.[22] In this context wilful default means a breach of duty by the accounting party which caused a loss of assets.[23] Before 1926, the words "wilful default" at the end of this statutory provision were construed in the same sense.[24]

To sum up the effect of this statutory provision before 1926:

(i) the burden of proving wilful default lay on the persons who sought to charge the personal representative with any loss which had arisen following delegation to any agent; and

(ii) wilful default meant a breach of duty by the personal representative which caused the loss—for instance, a breach of his duty to use proper prudence.

In *Re Vickery*,[25] in 1931, Maugham J. put a radically different meaning on the words "wilful default" in section 30(1) of the Trustee Act 1925. The defendant, the deceased's sole executor, employed a local solicitor to wind up the estate. The plaintiffs were the beneficiaries entitled to the residuary estate, which included £214 in the Post Office Savings Bank and £62 in Savings Certificates. The solicitor obtained a grant of probate

---

[19] *Re Brier* (1884) 26 Ch.D. 238, 243. For an instance of such an indemnity clause in a will see *Buxton v. Buxton* (1835) 1 My. & Cr. 80.

[20] *Re Brier, supra*, at p. 243. But *cf.* Romer J.'s explanation of *Re Brier* in *Re City Equitable Fire Insurance Co. Ltd* [1925] Ch. 407, 438–439.

[21] *Re Brier, supra* at p. 243 (an interjection of Lord Selborne L.C. in argument).

[22] *Post*, pp. 496 *et seq.*

[23] *Re Stevens* [1898] 1 Ch. 162, 170 and 175; *Job v. Job* (1877) 6 Ch.D. 562, 564–565; *Re Tebbs* [1976] 1 W.L.R. 924 (*post*, p. 497); *Barclays Bank Trust Co. Ltd. (No. 2)* [1980] Ch. 515, 545–546 (wilful default does not require conscious wrongdoing): see generally J. E. Stannard [1979] Conv. 345: *cf.* J. A. Andrews (1981) 1 Legal Studies, 303, 310–311 and 322.

[24] *Re Chapman* [1896] 2 Ch. 763: see also *Speight v. Gaunt* (1883) 9 App.Cas. 1, 13–14.

[25] [1931] 1 Ch. 572: see also *Re Munton* [1927] 1 Ch. 262, 274–275.

and, with the defendant's authority, collected the £214 and the £62. The defendant then learned for the first time that the solicitor had in the past been suspended for five years by the Law Society, and one of the plaintiffs pressed the defendant to change his solicitor but the defendant did not do so as the solicitor was promising to complete the matter in a very few days. Three months after the defendant had learned of the original solicitor's suspension, he instructed another solicitor and thereafter obtained from the court an order against the original solicitor for an account, but the original solicitor absconded and the sums were lost. Maugham J. held that the defendant was not liable for the loss because he was guilty only of an error of judgment in not changing his solicitor when he was first pressed to do so, and this did not amount to wilful default within section 30(1). To quote from his judgment[26]:

> "I think that, where an executor employs a solicitor or other agent to receive money belonging to the estate in reliance on s. 23, sub-s. 1, of the Trustee Act 1925, he will not be liable for a loss of the money occasioned by the misconduct of the agent unless the loss happens through the wilful default of the executor, using those words as implying ... either a consciousness of negligence or breach of duty, or a recklessness in the performance of a duty."

Maugham J. took this meaning of "wilful default" from a decision of the Court of Appeal in *Re City Equitable Fire Insurance Company, Limited*[27] where a clause in the company's articles exempted the directors and auditors from liability for loss unless it happened through their own "wilful neglect or default." In this case Warrington L.J. warned against the "greater danger of being misled" if one attempted to apply decisions on the duties of trustees in order to determine the liability of auditors under a clause in a company's articles.[28] Maugham J. reversed this process and applied this decision on the duties of auditors under a clause in a company's articles in order to determine the liability of an executor under section 30(1) of the Trustee Act 1925.

If Maugham J.'s construction of "wilful default" in section 30(1) is good law, then a personal representative is not liable for the loss of assets received by an agent appointed under section 23(1) unless the personal representative was conscious that, in doing the act which is complained of or in omitting to do the act which it is said he ought to have done, he was committing a breach of duty, or he was recklessly careless whether it was a breach of his duty or not. Maugham J.'s construction is, however, unlikely to be followed because it is not compatible with the pre-1926 authorities and it does not set an objective standard of prudent conduct for personal representatives. This is not to say, however, that the defendant executor would have been held liable in *Re Vickery* if Maugham J. had applied the pre-1926 rule; he would probably not have been held liable. The problem with *Re Vickery* concerns *obiter dicta*.

---

[26] [1931] 1 Ch. 572 at pp. 583–584.
[27] [1925] 1 Ch. 407, esp. pp. 430–442 (and note Romer J. never referred to *Re Chapman* or *Speight v. Gaunt*) and 516–518, 521–525, and 528–529.
[28] *Re Vickery* [1931] 1 Ch. 572 at pp. 523–524.

(d) *When is wilful default material?* On what occasions does section 30(1) require wilful default (whatever it means) to be established in order to make a personal representative liable? Maugham J. in *Re Vickery* gave a list: losses occasioned by his signing receipts for the sake of conformity, or by reason of the wrongful acts or defaults of another personal representative or of an agent with whom trust money or securities have been deposited, or by the insufficiency or deficiency of any securities, or "some other analogous loss."[29]

In *Re Lucking's Will Trusts*[30] Cross J. discussed the liability of a trustee who employs a manager for a business owned by the trust. He rejected the argument that such a trustee would be liable only for his negligence in supervising the manager if wilful default by the trustee was established: section 30(1) was not applicable because the manager was not a person with whom trust money or securities were deposited. This indicates that the category of "some other analogous loss" is a narrow one.

2. Property outside the United Kingdom

Section 23(2) of the Trustee Act 1925 confers on a personal representative power to appoint any person to act as his agent or attorney in respect of any property forming part of the deceased's estate in any place outside the United Kingdom.

(1) *EXTENT OF THE POWER.* Under this provision the personal representatives may delegate to the agent the collection, sale, or management of this foreign property,[31] and also the execution of any trust (or any duty incident to the office of personal representative[32]) or the exercise of any power or discretion vested in the personal representatives in relation to it.

(2) *LIABILITY OF THE PERSONAL REPRESENTATIVE FOR LOSS.* Section 23(2) concludes with the cryptic statement that the personal representatives "shall not, by reason only of their having made such appointment, be responsible for any loss arising thereby." This appears to leave intact the personal representatives' duty to take proper care in the selection and supervision of the agent. The effect (if any) of section 30(1) on this duty has already been discussed.

3. Temporary delegation by power of attorney

Under section 25 of the Trustee Act 1925[33] a personal representative has a wide power of temporary delegation by power of attorney. In practice, a personal representative is most likely to delegate by this means

---

[29] [1931] 1 Ch. 572, 582.
[30] [1968] 1 W.L.R. 866, 873–874.
[31] And also "executing and perfecting insurances" of it—the word "insurances" being "obviously a misprint for assurances," *per* Eve J. in *Green v. Whitehead* [1930] 1 Ch. 38, 45.
[32] Trustee Act 1925, s. 68(1)(17).
[33] As amended by Powers of Attorney Act 1971, s. 9. Beware of the now misleading marginal note referring to delegation during absence abroad. A power of attorney under s. 25 cannot be an enduring power, Enduring Powers of Attorney Act 1985, s. 2(8).

on the occasion of his absence abroad, but the exercise of the power is
not restricted to any particular occasion.

(1) *EXTENT OF THE POWER.* By power of attorney the personal representative may delegate the execution of any trust (or any duty incident
to the office of personal representative) or the exercise of any power or
discretion vested in him as personal representative, either alone or jointly
with any other person. The delegation must be for a period not exceeding
12 months and, if there are only two personal representatives, must not
be made to the other personal representative, unless a trust corporation.

(2) *LIABILITY OF THE PERSONAL REPRESENTATIVE FOR LOSS.* Section 25(5) makes the personal representative liable for the attorney's acts
or defaults in the same manner as if they were his own. This obviously
makes it important for the personal representative to select a suitable
attorney.

4. Direction in will

These statutory powers of a personal representative to delegate to an
agent apply subject to any contrary intention expressed in the deceased's
will,[34] but such a contrary intention is rarely, if ever, expressed. Sometimes a will contains an express indemnity clause protecting an executor
against any liability for loss unless (to quote the widest form of clause)
the loss has been caused by his own actual fraud. This form of clause
confers an extremely wide protection and many draftsmen would regard
it as inappropriate for any executor who is to be paid for his services.

A direction by a testator in his will that a named solicitor shall be "the
solicitor to my estate and to my said trustees in the management and
carrying out the provisions of this my Will" is not binding on the executors and trustees of his will.[35] They may choose their own agents.

IX. REMUNERATION OF PERSONAL REPRESENTATIVES

The fundamental principle is that a personal representative, like a
trustee, is not entitled to any remuneration for the work he does[1] unless
he is in some way authorised to receive remuneration. If he accepts the
office, then, in so far as he is not authorised to receive remuneration, he
must give his services gratuitously, although he is entitled to reimburse
himself out of the deceased's estate for his out-of-pocket expenses.[2] There
are, however, several different ways in which a personal representative
may acquire authority to receive remuneration for his services. These
will now be considered.

---

[34] Trustee Act 1925, s. 69(2).
[35] *Foster v. Elsley* (1881) 19 Ch.D. 518: see also *Shaw v. Lawless* (1838) 5 Cl. & F. 129.
[1] *Robinson v. Pett* (1734) 3 P. Wms. 249 ("It is an established rule, that a trustee, executor,
    or administrator, shall have no allowance for his care and trouble"); *Brocksopp v. Barnes*
    (1820) 5 Madd. 90; *Re White* [1898] 2 Ch. 217.
[2] *Post*, pp. 412–413.

1. Legacy given to proving executors

The most obvious way is by the testator making a gift by will to each of his executors who proves his will or, alternatively (a wider form) who accepts office.[3] Such a gift encourages an executor to prove the will and not renounce. Such a gift usually takes the form of a pecuniary legacy.

There is a presumption that any specific or general legacy given to a person appointed executor is meant to be conditional on his accepting office.[4] This presumption may, of course, be rebutted[5] and the presumption does not apply to a gift of residue.[6] For the avoidance of doubt, any gift made by will to a person appointed executor should either be expressed as conditional (*e.g.* "if he shall prove this will") or as unconditional (*e.g.* "whether or not he shall prove this will").

2. Charging clause in will

By his will the testator may authorise his executors to charge and be paid remuneration for their services. Such a "charging clause" is a form of gift which is commonly inserted in a will, because otherwise a professional person, such as a solicitor or accountant, is unlikely to be willing to act as executor.

(1) *CONSTRUCTION OF A CHARGING CLAUSE.* Which executors may charge? At what rate? And for what services? The answers to these questions depend on the proper construction of the particular charging clause. Often a charging clause authorises any executor engaged in any profession[7] or business to charge his usual professional or proper charges.[8] But for what services may he charge? The charging clause may authorise him to charge only for work which could not have been done by a layman: if so, an executor who is a solicitor is not entitled to charge for work which a layman could have done for himself.[9] On the other hand, the charging clause may (and in current practice usually does) authorise the executor to charge both for professional services and for work which a layman could have done for himself.[10] It has been said

---

[3] *Ante,* p. 303.

[4] *Re Appleton* (1885) 29 Ch.D. 893; *Stackpoole v. Howell* (1807) 13 Ves. 417. See generally *Hawkins and Ryder on The Construction of Wills* (1965), pp. 398–400.

[5] *Bubb v. Yelveston* (1871) 13 Eq. 131 (gift of £1,000 to each executor "as a remembrance": held executor who did not act was entitled); *Cockrell v. Barber* (1826) 2 Russ. 585.

[6] *Griffiths v. Pruen* (1840) 11 Sim. 202; *Christian v. Devereux* (1841) 12 Sim. 264; *Re Maxwell* [1906] 1 I.R. 386: but see *Barber v. Barber* (1838) 3 My. & Cr. 688.

[7] *Re Werthiemer* (1912) 106 L.T. 590 (executor who was British Museum keeper of antiquities entitled to charge for professional services in selling testator's works of art).

[8] *Re Fish* [1893] 2 Ch. 413 (one trustee cannot settle charges of other solicitor-trustee so as to bind beneficiaries); *Willis v. Kibble* (1839) 1 Beav. 559; *Re Wells* [1962] 1 W.L.R. 874.

[9] *Re Chapple* (1884) 27 Ch.D. 584; *Re Chalinder & Herington* [1907] 1 Ch.58; *Harbin v. Darby* (1860) 28 Beav. 325: see also *Clarkson v. Robinson* [1900] 2 Ch. 722.

[10] *Re Ames* (1883) 25 Ch.D. 72; *Re Fish, supra.* An example (from *Hallet's Conveyancing Precedents* (1965), p. 1044) reads, "Any of my Executors or my Trustees who shall be an individual engaged in any profession or business may be employed by my Executors or my Trustees and shall be entitled to charge and be paid all professional or other reasonable and proper charges for any business done or services rendered or time spent by him or his firm in connection with the administration of my estate or the trusts powers or provisions of this Will or any codicil hereto whether or not within the usual scope of his

that a charging clause "has always received a strict interpretation from the courts."[11]

The form of charging clause which is appropriate to an executor engaged in a profession or business does not empower a trust corporation (such as a bank appointed as executor) to charge its scale fees.[12] For this purpose, a charging clause appropriate to a trust corporation is needed.[13]

(2)   *A CHARGING CLAUSE IS A LEGACY.* A charging clause in a will constitutes a conditional legacy to the executor, just as a gift by will of £100 to the executor for his trouble if he proves the will is a conditional legacy. A charging clause is therefore subject to the rules which govern legacies in a will.[14]

(a)   *Executor or spouse an attesting witness.* Section 15 of the Wills Act 1837 deprives an attesting witness, and his or her spouse, of any benefit under a legacy in the will.[15] It follows that if a solicitor-executor (or his spouse) attests the will, the solicitor is not entitled to any remuneration for his services under a charging clause in the will.[16]

(b)   *Insolvent estate.* If the deceased's estate is insolvent, his funeral, testamentary and administration expenses, debts and liabilities must be paid so far as possible.[17] No legacy can be paid because no part of the estate is left after payment of expenses, debts and liabilities. Thus, if the deceased's estate turns out to be insolvent, an executor is not entitled to any remuneration under a charging clause in the will.[18]

(c)   *Abates as a pecuniary legacy.* If the deceased's estate is solvent but there are insufficient assets available to pay his pecuniary legacies in full, then the pecuniary legacies abate rateably.[19] For instance, if there are only sufficient assets available to pay one-third of the total amount of the pecuniary legacies, then each legatee receives only one-third of the amount of his pecuniary legacy. The sum payable to an executor as

---

profession or business and although not of a nature requiring the employment of a professional or business person."

[11] *Per* Harman J. in *Re Gee* [1948] Ch. 284, 292; *Re Orwell's W.T.* [1982] 3 All E.R. 177, 179. A clause authorising an executor to retain directors's fees may also be available: see *Re Llewellin's W.T.* [1949] Ch. 225.

[12] *Re Cooper* (1939) 160 L.T. 453; *In the Estate of Campbell* [1954] 1 W.L.R. 516.

[13] Each bank or insurance company undertaking such business is ready to supply its own recommended current form of charging clause. Usually the charges include both an acceptance fee and a withdrawal fee (payable out of capital) and an income fee. For an instance see *Re Waterman's W.T.* [1952] 2 All E.R. 1054.

[14] But remuneration under a charging clause may be "earned" for tax purposes, *Dale v. I.R.C.* [1954] A.C. 11.

[15] *Ante*, p. 232.

[16] *Re Pooley* (1888) 40 Ch. D. 1: *cf. Re Royce's W.T.* [1959] Ch. 626 (solicitor appointed trustee of will after testator's death may rely on charging clause though an attesting witness).

[17] *Post*, pp. 438 *et seq.*

[18] *Re White* [1898] 1 Ch. 297, [1898] 2 Ch. 217; *Re Salmen* (1912) 107 L.T. 108. But the court may authorise remuneration in a proper case, *post*, p. 406. For possible reform see Law Reform Committee's 23rd Report, *The powers and duties of trustees*, Cmnd. 8733 (1982), pp. 27 and 64.

[19] For the abatement of pecuniary legacies see *ante* pp. 253 *et seq.* and *post* p. 425.

remuneration under a charging clause is a pecuniary legacy[20] and abates rateably with the other pecuniary legacies,[21] unless there is a provision in the will giving the executor priority over the other pecuniary legatees.[22]

If an executor is disqualified under these rules from relying on a charging clause, he is nevertheless entitled by virtue of his office of personal representative to reimbursement out of the estate for his out-of-pocket expenses.

(3) *SOLICITOR-EXECUTOR WITH NO CHARGING CLAUSE.* In the absence of a charging clause on which he can rely or any other authority to receive remuneration, a solicitor-executor, like any other executor, is entitled to no remuneration for his services, only to reimbursement for his out-of-pocket expenses.[23] The rule is just as applicable if the solicitor-executor employs the firm in which he is a partner to perform the services: the firm is not entitled to remuneration for its services because the solicitor-executor is, in effect, acting as his own solicitor.[24]

A solicitor-executor may, of course, employ another solicitor to act for him. A solicitor-executor may therefore employ his partner (as opposed to the firm which includes himself) to act for him and may pay his partner's proper charges, provided that it has been expressly agreed between him and his partner that he shall not derive any benefit from the charges.[25]

3. Contract with beneficiaries

A personal representative may contract with beneficiaries entitled under the deceased's will or intestacy (provided they are *sui juris*) for remuneration to be paid to him for his services out of the assets to which they are entitled. A personal representative may presumably make a similar contract with the deceased's creditors. To be valid, such a contract must not be made as a result of undue influence by the personal representative.[26] Moreover, unless the contract is made by deed, it must be supported by valuable consideration: if (say) letters of administration have already been granted to the personal representative he may well

---

[20] Administration of Estates Act 1925, s. 55(1)(ix).
[21] *Re Brown* [1918] W.N. 118 (amount due to solicitor under charging clause to be ascertained when work done and to abate rateably); *Commissioner of Stamp Duties of New South Wales v. Pearse* [1954] A.C. 91, 113. For possible reform see Law Reform Committee's 23rd Report, *supra*.
[22] Which, in professionally drawn wills, there often is.
[23] *Moore v. Frowd* (1837) 3 My. & Cr. 45; *Todd v. Wilson* (1849) 9 Beav. 486.
[24] *Re Corsellis* (1887) 34 Ch. D. 675; *Re Gates* [1933] Ch. 913 (rule applies though solicitor-executor agrees with partners not to share in profit costs); *Re Hill* [1934] Ch. 623 (rule applies though solicitor-executor is a salaried partner); *Christophers v. White* (1847) 10 Beav. 523 (rule applies though other partners do the work).
[25] *Clack v. Carlon* (1861) 30 L.J. Ch. 639 (*quoad* the transaction the solicitor-executor and his partner must not be in partnership); *Re Doody* [1893] 1 Ch. 129, 134; *Re Hill, supra*, at pp. 631 and 633–634.
[26] *Gould v. Fleetwood* (1732) 3 P.Wms. 251, n. [A] (executor agreed with residuary legatees to act in return for 100 guineas but died before completing his task; held not entitled and the court said, "all bargains of this kind ought to be discouraged, as tending to eat up the trust"); *Aycliffe v. Murray* (1740) 2 Atk. 58 (court would be "extremely cautious and wary" in upholding such a contract).

not furnish consideration by promising to perform, or by performing, his existing duty to administer the estate according to law.[27]

4.   Order of the court

The court may authorise remuneration for a personal representative (or a trustee) in the exercise of its inherent jurisdiction to secure the competent administration of the estate.[28] Remuneration may be authorised for his past[29] and future[30] services, and the remuneration authorised by a charging clause in the will may be increased, whether or not he has already accepted office.[31] The court only authorises remuneration in a proper case,[32] where it is in the interests of the creditors[33] or the beneficiaries[34] to do so.

The court has a statutory jurisdiction to authorise remuneration for a corporation (other than the Public Trustee[35]) where the court appoints the corporation to be a personal representative, either solely or jointly with another person.[36] Thus, on granting letters of administration to a bank, the court may authorise the bank to charge for its services.[37] The court may also authorise a person appointed as a substituted personal representative to charge remuneration for his services.[38] Again, if the court appoints a judicial trustee under the Judicial Trustees Act 1896, the court may assign remuneration to him.[39] The court may in its discretion appoint a judicial trustee so as to provide a remedy in a case where the administration of the deceased's estate by his executor or administrator has broken down and it is not desired to put the estate to the expense of a general administration by the court.[40] Similarly, the court may assign reasonable remuneration to an administrator pending suit.[41]

---

[27] See A. L. Goodhart (1956) 72 L.Q.R. 490.
[28] Re Duke of Norfolk's S.T. [1982] Ch. 61 (reviewing the cases): see also Forster v. Ridley (1864) 4 De G.J. & S. 452 (executors remunerated for managing deceased's leaseholds and carrying on business); Re Freeman's S.T. (1887) 37 Ch.D. 148 (remuneration for trustee). For possible reform see Law Reform Committee's 23rd Report, The powers and duties of trustees, Cmnd. 8733 (1982), pp. 29–30 and 64 (Professional persons acting as administrators).
[29] Re Macadam [1946] Ch. 73 (trustees holding company shares remunerated for exceptional work as directors); Re Masters [1953] 1 W.L.R. 81 (bank remunerated for acting as administrator and trustee); Re Keeler's S.T. [1981] Ch. 156 see also Boardman v. Phipps [1967] 2 A.C. 46, 104 and 112.
[30] Re Duke of Norfolk's S.T., supra, (future services of trust corporation).
[31] ibid.
[32] Re Worthington [1954] 1 W.L.R. 526 (remuneration refused to solicitor-administrator in absence of exceptional circumstances); Re Barbour's S.T. [1974] 1 W.L.R. 1198, 1203.
[33] Re Duke of Norfolk's S.T. supra, at p. 77 (order of court authorising remuneration binds creditors of insolvent estate); Re Worthington, supra.
[34] Re Duke of Norfolk's S.T. supra, at p. 79.
[35] The Public Trustee has statutory authority to charge fees, Public Trustee Act 1906, s. 9, as amended by Public Trustee (Fees) Act 1957 and fees orders made thereunder.
[36] Trustee Act 1925, ss. 42, 68(1), (17) and 69(1).
[37] In the Estates of Young [1934] W.N. 106; Re Masters, supra.
[38] Administration of Justice Act 1985, s. 50(3): see post, p. 507.
[39] Judicial Trustees Act 1896, s. 1(5); Judicial Trustee Rules 1983 (S.I. 1983 No. 370), reg. 11.
[40] Re Ridsdel [1947] Ch. 597, 605: see also Re Ratcliff [1898] 2 Ch. 352 and Re Wells [1968] 1 W.L.R. 44: see post, p. 506.
[41] Supreme Court Act 1981, s. 117(3): see also Re Howlett [1950] P. 177: see ante, p. 346.

5. The Rule in *Cradock v. Piper*

Under the Rule in *Cradock v. Piper*[42] a solicitor who is a personal representative (or his firm) is entitled to profit costs for work done in connection with litigation on behalf of the personal representatives jointly, except so far as the costs have been increased by his being one of the parties. The Rule applies whether the litigation is hostile (*e.g.* an action by or against the personal representatives) or friendly (*e.g.* an application in chambers for the maintenance of an infant[43]). But the Rule does not apply to work done on behalf of the solicitor alone[44]—he must have acted on behalf of himself and his co-executor or co-administrator jointly. Moreover the Rule has no application at all to non-litigious work[45] and is therefore of relatively narrow ambit. The Rule "must be taken as settled but it is exceptional and anomalous and not to be extended."[46]

6. Foreign remuneration received without volition

In Re Northcote's Will Trusts[47] the deceased died domiciled in England and his executors took an English grant of probate. Then, in accordance with an undertaking given by them to the Inland Revenue, they obtained a grant in New York State in respect of the deceased's American assets. Under the law of that state they were entitled to a commission on the American assets. Harman J. held that the executors might keep this commission, which never formed part of the English assets, and which came to them without their volition because they were under an obligation to carry out their undertaking. The ambit of this rule appears to be very narrow.

7. Reform proposals

The Committee of Enquiry into the Public Trustee Office recommended legislation enabling all professional or corporate trustees to charge for their services, whether or not the will includes a charging clause.[48] If implemented this recommendation would confer on those personal representatives who are members of a profession, such as solicitors or accountants, or who are corporations, a general authority to charge for their services.

At present only the Public Trustee enjoys such a general authority.[49]

---

[42] (1850) 1 Mac. & G. 664.
[43] *Re Corsellis* (1887) 34 Ch.D. 675.
[44] *Lyon v. Baker* (1852) 5 De G. & Sm. 622.
[45] *Re Corsellis, supra; Broughton v. Broughton* (1855) 5 De G.M. & G. 160.
[46] *Re Worthington* [1954] 1 W.L.R. 526, 529; see also *Re Corsellis, supra*, at pp. 682–683, 687–688 and 689; *Re Doody* [1893] 1 Ch. 129, 141–142.
[47] [1949] 1 All E.R. 442. See also *Denton v. Davy* (1836) 1 Moo. P.C. 15 and *Campbell v. Campbell* (1842) 13 Sim. 168.
[48] 1972 Cmnd. 4913, App. 2: *cf.* Law Reform Committee's 23rd Report, *The powers and duties of trustees*, Cmnd. 8733 (1982), p. 28 (statutory provision for professional trustees to charge not recommended).
[49] See p. 406 n. 35.

CHAPTER 17

PAYMENT OF EXPENSES AND DEBTS

I. ASSETS, EXPENSES AND DEBTS

A. WHAT ARE ASSETS?

Consideration has already been given to the property which devolves on personal representatives.[1] We are now concerned with the property which constitutes assets for the payment of the deceased's debts and liabilities. Section 32(1) of the Administration of Estates Act 1925 defines two categories of property which constitute assets.

1. Deceased's estate to the extent of his beneficial interest

The first category mentioned in section 32(1) is "the real and personal estate, whether legal or equitable, of a deceased person, to the extent of his beneficial interest therein." Thus the entire real[2] and personal estate of the deceased constitutes assets to the extent of the deceased's beneficial interest in it. If at his death the deceased held property as a sole or last surviving trustee so that the property devolves on his personal representatives, this trust property is not assets,[3] though any beneficial interest of the deceased therein (not ceasing on his death) constitutes assets.

The following property constitutes assets in the hands of a personal representative, whether or not it falls within section 32(1).

(1) *TRANSACTIONS DEFRAUDING CREDITORS.* If the deceased during his lifetime entered into a transaction which is set aside after his death as defrauding his creditors,[4] any property recovered by his personal representatives constitutes assets in their hands.[5]

(2) *INCOME AND ASSETS ARISING AFTER DEATH.* Income arising

---

[1] *Ante*, pp. 368 *et seq.*
[2] Real estate means real estate, including chattels real, which devolves on the personal representative, Administration of Estates Act 1925, s. 55(1)(xix) and see *ante*, p. 369.
[3] *Re Webb* [1941] Ch 225; *Re Gordon* [1940] Ch. 851; *Hassall v. Smithers* (1806) 12 Ves. 119.
[4] Insolvency Act 1986, ss. 423–425.
[5] For the operation of Law of Property Act 1925, s. 172 (now repealed) see *Re Eichholz* [1959] Ch. 708, 723–724; *Shears v. Rogers* (1832) 3 B. & Ad. 362: see also *Cadogan v. Cadogan* [1977] 1 W.L.R. 1041.

after death from the deceased's beneficial interest in his real and personal estate is assets. Thus the income of the deceased's residuary estate arising after his death is assets.[6] So, too, are assets "by increase," such as the lambs born to the deceased's sheep after his death.[7] Again, any property acquired and any profits made by the personal representative in carrying on the deceased's business after his death are assets.[8]

(3) *BENEFITS FOR WHICH PERSONAL REPRESENTATIVE IS ACCOUNTABLE.* A personal representative, like a trustee, is accountable for benefits received by him by virtue of his position as personal representative and such benefits constitute assets for the payment of the deceased's debts and liabilities. For instance, under the Rule in *Keech v. Sandford*,[9] if a personal representative obtains a renewal of a lease of property which was vested in him as personal representative, he holds the new lease for the benefit of the deceased's estate[10] and the new lease therefore constitutes assets.

2. Property appointed by will under a general power

The second category of property mentioned in section 32(1) is realty and personalty of which the deceased "in pursuance of any general power[11] (including the statutory power to dispose of entailed interests) disposes by his will."

(1) *ENTAILED INTEREST.* If at his death the deceased is tenant in tail in possession of Blackacre and disposes by will of the fee simple in Blackacre pursuant to his statutory power,[12] then under section 32(1) the fee simple in Blackacre constitutes assets and (as has already been noted) devolves on the deceased's personal representatives.[13] On the other hand an unbarred entail is not assets for the payment of the debts of the deceased tenant in tail.[14]

(2) *APPOINTMENT BY WILL.* Section 32(1) applies only if the

---

[6] *Re Tong* [1931] 1 Ch. 202 (C.A.).
[7] *Re Tong* [1930] 2 Ch. 400, 404 (Clauson J.).
[8] For this rule and its limits see *ante*, p. 387.
[9] (1726) Sel. Cas. t. King 61: see generally Cretney (1969) 33 Conv. (N.S.) 161. The Rule in *Keech v. Sandford* applies to an executor *de son tort*, *Mulvany v. Dillon* (1810) 1 Ball & B. 409. For another instance see *Re Edwards' W.T.* [1982] Ch. 30.
[10] *Bromfield v. Chichester* (1773) 2 Dick. 480 (executrix renewed leases held by deceased: court declared she held renewed leases for benefit of deceased's estate: *James v. Dean* (1805) 11 Ves. 392; *Re Thompson* [1930] 1 Ch. 203: *cf. Re Biss* [1903] 2 Ch. 40 (landlord refused renewal to administratrix of deceased tenant and granted new lease to one of next of kin: latter was held entitled to retain lease).
[11] *Re Phillips* [1931] 1 Ch. 347: see A.D. Hughes (1962) 26 Conv. (N.S.) 25, esp. at pp. 32–34; Williams, Mortimer and Sunnucks, *Executors, Administrators and Probate* (17th ed., 1993), p. 596.
[12] Law of Property Act 1925, s. 176: the will must refer specifically to Blackacre, or to the instrument under which it was acquired, or to entailed property generally: see *ante*, pp. 213–214.
[13] *Ante*, p. 369.
[14] Law of Property Act 1925, s. 176(2).

deceased by his will exercises a general power of appointment.[15] If he does not do so, the person who takes in default of appointment takes the settled property and it does not constitute assets for the payment of the deceased's debts and liabilities.[16]

3. Property appointed by deed under a general power[17]

Before 1926, a creditor was entitled in equity to resort, not only to property appointed by will under a general power, but also, in the last instance, to property appointed by the deceased *by deed* under a general power, provided the appointment was made in favour of a volunteer and took effect only at the deceased's death.[18]

Section 32(1) does not specifically mention property appointed by deed. There is nothing in the Administration of Estates Act 1925 to deprive a creditor of the equitable right he had before 1925 and so, on a death after 1925, a creditor is still entitled to resort, in the last instance, to property appointed by the deceased by deed under a general power provided:

    (i) the appointment was made in favour of a volunteer; and
    (ii) the appointment took effect only on the deceased's death.[19]

Such property appointed by the deceased by deed under a general power does not devolve on his personal representatives. A creditor may bring proceedings to "intercept" the appointed property.[20]

Property appointed by the deceased by will or deed under a special power[21] is never assets[22] unless the deceased makes a valid appointment of it to himself.[23]

4. Donatio mortis causa

Property given by *donatio mortis causa* is liable for the debts of the donor, but only in the last resort on a deficiency of the assets of his estate.[24] If the donor makes the *donatio* by an "incomplete" delivery or

---

[15] As to the exercise by will of a general power of appointment see Wills Act 1837, s. 27, *ante*, pp. 211 *et seq.*

[16] *Holmes v. Coghill* (1802) 7 Ves. 499, (1806) 12 Ves. 206. But it forms part of the deceased donee (of the power)'s net estate under the Inheritance (Provision for Family and Dependants) Act 1975, s. 25(1): see *ante*, p. 150.

[17] For a discussion of the difference between general, special and intermediate powers, see Hanbury and Martin, *Modern Equity* (14th ed., 1993) pp. 171–172.

[18] *O'Grady v. Wilmot* [1916] 2 A.C. 231; *Townshend v. Windham* (1750) 2 Ves.Sen. 1; *George v. Milbanke* (1803) 9 Ves. 190; *Pack v. Bathurst* (1745) 3 Atk. 269; *Troughton v. Troughton* (1747) 3 Atk. 656.

[19] *Re Phillips* [1931] 1 Ch. 347.

[20] *Re Phillips, supra.*

[21] For a discussion of the difference between general, special and intermediate powers, see Hanbury and Martin, *Modern Equity* (14th ed., 1993) pp. 171–172.

[22] *Townshend v. Windham* (1750) 2 Ves.Sen. 1, 9–10.

[23] *Re Penrose* [1933] Ch. 793. If the deceased may make a valid appointment to himself, it may be classifiable as a general power

[24] *Smith v. Casen* (1718) 1 P.Wms. 406; *Ward v. Turner* (1752) 2 Ves.Sen. 431, 434; *Tate v. Leithead* (1854) Kay 658, 659; *Re Korvine's Trust* [1921] 1 Ch. 343, 348: *cf. Warnock-Smith* [1978] Conv. 130. See *ante*, p. 30. Property given by *d.m.c.* is part of the deceased's "net estate" for the purposes of the Inheritance (Provision for Family and Dependants) Act 1975, see *ante* p. 151.

transfer, the legal title to the property remains vested in the donor's personal representative. On the other hand, if the *donatio* vests the donor's title in the donee, presumably a creditor may bring proceedings against the donee for payment of his debt out of the property.

It is probable that property to which the Rule in *Strong v. Bird* applies is liable for the donor's debts.[25]

B. Funeral, Testamentary and Administration Expenses

1. Funeral expenses

The law relating to the corpse of a testator has already been discussed.[26] Now two matters must be considered:

(1) when is a personal representative personally liable for the deceased's funeral expenses? and

(2) what funeral expenses are payable out of the deceased's estate?

(1) *PERSONAL LIABILITY OF PERSONAL REPRESENTATIVE.* The personal liability of a personal representative for funeral expenses may arise under contract or quasi-contract:

(i) A personal representative who orders the funeral is personally liable in contract to the undertaker for the contract price or, if no price is fixed, on a *quantum meruit* for a reasonable price for the funeral which is ordered.[27] If another person orders the funeral and the undertaker gives credit to that person, the latter is liable in contract to the undertaker, but the personal representative is not liable to the undertaker.[28]

(ii) If no other person is liable in contract to the undertaker, a personal representative is personally liable in quasi-contract to the undertaker for reasonable funeral expenses. It is immaterial that another person ordered the funeral; if no other person is liable in contract, the law imposes an obligation on the personal representative to pay the reasonable expenses of a funeral conducted in a manner suitable to the deceased's position and circumstances.[29] The personal representative is, however, only liable so far as he has available assets of the deceased to meet the expenses.[30]

---

[25] *Ante*, p. 318. As to property subject to a statutory nomination see *Bennett v. Slater* [1899] 1 Q.B. 45, 52.

[26] *Ante*, pp. 6–7.

[27] *Corner v. Shaw* (1838) 3 M. & W. 350, 356; *Brice v. Wilson* (1834) 8 Ad. & E. 349, n.(c) (executor ratified contract with undertaker).

[28] *Green v. Salmon* (1838) 8 Ad. & E. 348, 350, explaining *Brice v. Wilson, supra.*

[29] *Rogers v. Price* (1829) 3 Y. & J. 28; *Tugwell v. Heyman* (1812) 3 Campb. 298 ("the dead body could not remain on the surface of the earth"); *Corner v. Shaw, supra*, at pp. 355–356; *Rees v. Hughes* [1946] K.B. 517, 524–525 and 528.

[30] In *Sharp v. Lush* (1879) 10 Ch.D. 468, 472 Jessel M.R. said *obiter*, "Even if the executor never receives assets to the amount of the funeral expenses, he is liable to pay, although he did not order the funeral"; *Re Walter* [1929] 1 Ch. 647, 655. Probably the personal representative is liable to pay to the extent of the assets.

(2) *FUNERAL EXPENSES PAYABLE OUT OF THE DECEASED'S ESTATE.* Reasonable funeral expenses are payable out of the deceased's estate to the personal representative if he incurs liability to the undertaker in contract or quasi-contract. Similarly, another person who orders and pays for the funeral may recover reasonable funeral expenses from the personal representative out of the deceased's estate[31] unless that person paid for the funeral as an act of bounty.[32] But if the personal representative (or another person) incurs funeral expenses in excess of what is reasonable, he must bear the excess himself.

The reasonableness of the funeral expenses is a question of fact to be decided having regard to all the circumstances of the particular case.[33] The following factors may be material:

(i) the insolvency of the deceased's estate which makes a lower scale of expenses appropriate[34];
(ii) the deceased's position in life[35]; and
(iii) the deceased's religious beliefs[36] and any wishes expressed by him as to his funeral.

Social fund payments to meet funeral expenses are recoverable by the D.S.S. out of the deceased's estate, as if they were funeral expenses.[37]

2. Testamentary and administration expenses

The Administration of Estates Act 1925 uses the expression "testamentary and administration expenses" in connection with the administration of solvent estates[38] but does not define its meaning. The same expression is used in connection with the administration of insolvent estates, again without defining its meaning.[39] Recourse must be had to the decided cases which are concerned with the meaning of similar expressions in wills.

The expression "testamentary and administration expenses" means, in general, expenses incident to the proper performance of the duties of an

---

[31] *Green v. Salmon, supra.*

[32] *Colely v. Colely* (1866) 12 Jur. (N.S.) 496; *cf. Williams v. Williams* (1882) 20 Ch.D. 659. See also *Shallcross v. Wright* (1850) 12 Beav. 505.

[33] *Goldstein v. Salvation Army Assurance Society* [1917] 2 K.B. 291 (funeral expenses recoverable under assurance policy may include tombstone). See also *Hart v. Griffiths–Jones* [1948] 2 All E.R. 729 (embalming of body but not monument costing £225); *Stanton v. Ewart F. Youldon Ltd* [1960] 1 W.L.R. 543 (simple gravestone but not marble memorial set up as a sign of love and affection); *Gammell v. Wilson* [1982] A.C. 27 (£595 headstone)—all cases decided under Law Reform (Miscellaneous Provisions) Act 1934. Reasonable funeral expenses are deducted from the value of the estate for inheritance tax purposes; see Inheritance Tax Act 1984 s. 172 and see also Inland Revenue Statement of Practice, SP 7/87.

[34] At any rate if the personal representative knows of, or has any reason to anticipate, the insolvency: *Edwards v. Edwards* (1834) 2 Cr. & M. 612; *Hancock v. Podmore* (1830) 1 B. & Ad. 260; *Bissett v. Antrobus* (1831) 4 Sim. 512; *Stag v. Punter* (1744) 3 Atk. 119.

[35] *Stag v. Punter, supra; Re Walter* [1929] 1 Ch. 647, 655.

[36] *Gammell v. Wilson* [1982] A.C. 27, 43.

[37] Social Security Act 1986, s. 32(4): for these payments see Social Fund (General Regulations) 1987 (S.I. 1987 No. 481), para. 7).

[38] Administration of Estates Act 1925, s.34(3): see *post*, p. 420.

[39] Administration of Insolvent Estates of Deceased Persons Order 1986 (S.I. 1986 No. 1999), paras. 4(2) and 5(2): see *post*, p. 438.

executor or administrator.[40] By way of example the expression includes the following, if properly incurred:

(i) the expense of obtaining probate or letters of administration[41];
(ii) the costs of obtaining legal advice as to the administration of the estate[42];
(iii) the cost of an administration action or other proceedings instituted for a proper purpose[43];
(iv) the expense incurred in collecting and preserving the assets of the deceased's estate[44]; and
(v) the expense incurred in ascertaining the deceased's debts and liabilities (including the cost of advertisements).

Testamentary and administration expenses also include any inheritance tax payable in respect of the deceased's death on his property situated in the United Kingdom which vests in his personal representatives.[45]

C. DEBTS AND LIABILITIES

1. Personal representatives' duty to pay debts

Personal representatives must carry out their duty to pay the deceased's debts with due diligence.

(1) *NATURE OF THE DUTY.* To quote the classic statement of this duty by Uthwatt J. in *Re Tankard*[46]:

"It is the duty of executors, as a matter of the due administration of the estate, to pay the debts of their testator with due diligence having regard to the assets in their hands which are properly applicable for that purpose, and in determining whether due diligence has been shown regard must be had to all the circumstances of the case. . . . The duty is owed not only to creditors, but also to beneficiaries, for the ultimate object of the administration of an estate is to place the beneficiaries in possession of their interest and that object cannot be fully achieved unless all debts are satisfied."

Thus if personal representatives fail to pay a debt of the deceased with due diligence, even though they have assets in hand properly applicable

---

[40] *Sharp v. Lush* (1879) 10 Ch.D. 468 (in a will "executorship expenses" are "expenses incident to the proper performance of the duty of the executor in the same way as testamentary espenses are, neither more nor less"); *Re Taylor's Estate* [1969] 2 Ch. 245 (in the construction of wills "testamentary expenses" and "administration expenses" are prima facie synonymous).

[41] *Re Clemow* [1900] 2 Ch. 182 and *cf. Re Prince* [1898] 2 Ch. 225. For costs of a probate action see *ante*, p. 361.

[42] *Sharp v. Lush, supra.*

[43] *Sharp v. Lush, supra; Miles v. Harrison* (1874) L.R. 9 Ch.App. 316; *Harloe v. Harloe* (1875) L.R. 20 Eq. 471; *Re Hall-Dare* [1916] 1 Ch. 272.

[44] *Peter v. Stirling* (1878) 10 Ch.D. 279, 284; *Re Goetze* [1953] Ch. 96, 111–113; *Re Sebba* [1959] Ch. 166.

[45] See, *post*, pp. 433 *et seq.*

[46] [1942] Ch. 69, 72.

for that purpose, they are liable not only to creditors but also to the beneficiaries for any consequent loss. A loss may result because the debt bears interest[47] or because the creditor brings proceedings to obtain payment.[48]

(2) *TIME FOR PAYMENT*. To quote Uthwatt J. again in *Re Tankard*[49]:

"There is, in my opinion, no rule of law that it is the duty of executors to pay ... debts within a year from the testator's death. The duty is to pay with due diligence. Due diligence may, indeed, require that payment should be made before the expiration of the year, but the circumstances affecting the estate and the assets comprised in it may justify non-payment within the year, but, if debts are not paid within the year, the onus is thrown on the executors to justify the delay."

The personal representatives may well be able to justify non-payment of a debt within the executor's year. For example, the personal representatives may never have had assets in their hands properly applicable for payment of the debt.[50] Again, if the deceased's estate is insolvent, or if it may turn out to be insolvent, the personal representatives may need more than one year in order to ascertain the assets and the extent of the debts, and to determine which debts are payable under the order of priority applicable to an insolvent estate.[51]

In this last quotation Uthwatt J. was referring to debts due from the deceased at his death. If the debt does not fall due for payment until some time after the deceased's death, the personal representatives' duty (assuming the estate is solvent) is to pay the debt with due diligence once it has become due.

(3) *MODIFICATION OF THE DUTY BY WILL*. Quoting again from Uthwatt J's judgment.[52]

"As against creditors, the provisions of the testator's will which relate to the realisation of his assets or otherwise bear on the payment of debts are irrelevant. As against beneficiaries, the position is different. Beneficiaries take their interest under the will only on the terms of the will. As respects them full effect has to be given to any provisions which, either in express terms or by implication, modify the executor's duty of paying debts with due diligence."

In *Re Tankard* T by his will gave his residuary estate to his executor (a trust company) upon the usual trust for sale and, after payment of his debts, funeral and testamentary expenses, to hold the balance for the beneficiaries. The will empowered the executor to retain any part of T's estate in the form of investment existing at his death for so long as the executor in its absolute discretion might think fit, without being respons-

[47] *ibid.* at pp. 72–73; *Hall v. Hallett* (1784) 1 Cox. 134; *Re Stevens* [1898] 1 Ch. 162, 168–169.
[48] *ibid.* at p. 73
[49] *ibid.*
[50] *Re Stevens, supra.*
[51] *Post,* pp. 441 *et seq.*
[52] [1942] Ch. 69, 74.

ible for any loss occasioned thereby. At his death T owed over £9,000 to a creditor. The executor did not sell sufficient of T's assets to clear the debt during the executor's year. After the end of the executor's year the assets fell in value and the executor had to sell more of the assets to clear the debt than would have been necessary on a sale during the year. Uthwatt J. held that the beneficiaries' action for damages against the executor failed, because the executor had duly exercised the power conferred on him by the will to retain assets. As against the beneficiaries, the will had modified the executor's duty to pay the deceased's debts with due diligence.

Of course, if the *creditor* had suffered loss from any breach by the executor of his duty to pay the deceased's debts with due diligence, the power to retain assets conferred by the will would have been irrelevant.

2. Debts unknown to personal representatives

Personal representatives who distribute assets to the beneficiaries remain liable for the unpaid debts and liabilities of the deceased to the extent of the assets which would have been properly applicable for their payment, even though the personal representatives had no notice of such debts and liabilities when they made the distribution to the beneficiaries.[53] But personal representatives may protect themselves against this liability (1) by advertising for claims in accordance with section 27 of the Trustee Act 1925, or (2) by obtaining the leave of the court to distribute on the footing that all the deceased's debts and liabilities have been ascertained.

(1) *ADVERTISING FOR CLAIMS.* Under section 27 of the Trustee Act 1925[54] personal representatives may give notice of their intention to distribute, requiring any person interested to send in particulars of his claim[55] to the personal representatives within a stated time, not being less than two months. The notice is to be given:

  (i) by advertisement in the *London Gazette*; and
  (ii) by advertisement in a newspaper circulating in the district in which land to be distributed is situated (this requirement is not applicable if no land is to be distributed); and
  (iii) by "such other like notices, including notices elsewhere than in England and Wales,[56] as would, in any special case, have been directed by a court of competent jurisdiction in an action for administration."[57]

---

[53] *Knatchbull v. Fearnhead* (1837) 3 My. & Cr. 122 (executors distributed without notice of deceased's liability for his breach of trust); *Norman v. Baldry* (1834) 6 Sim. 621. For the defence of limitation see *post*, p. 500.

[54] As amended by Law of Property (Amendment) Act 1926, ss. 7, 8(2) and Sched.

[55] This includes a claim to be a beneficiary under the deceased's will or intestacy as well as a claim to be a creditor, *Re Aldhous* [1955] 1 W.L.R. 459, see *post*, pp. 470–471. It is desirable for the notice to refer to both a creditor and a beneficiary (*e.g.* "any person having any claim against or any interest in" the deceased's estate), *ibid.* at p. 462.

[56] *Re Holden* [1935] W.N. 52: *cf. Re Achillopoulos* [1928] Ch. 433.

[57] Trustee Act 1925, s. 27(1). See R.S.C., Ord. 44, r. 5; *Re Bracken* (1889) 43 Ch.D. 1. For advertisement for beneficiaries under the deceased's will or intestacy see *Newton v.*

Section 27(2) provides that nothing in the section

> "frees the ... personal representatives from any obligation to make searches or obtain official certificates of search similar to those which an intending purchaser would be advised to make or obtain."

The meaning of this provision is not clear. In order to be certain of the protection of section 27, before distributing land personal representatives should probably carry out the same searches as an intending purchaser of land would be advised to make in the Land Registry, or the Land Charges Registry, and the local land charges registry. It is possible to suggest that before distributing any asset, personal representatives should search in bankruptcy against the deceased and against any beneficiary to whom the distribution is to be made.

After the expiration of the stated time for claims to be sent in, the personal representatives may distribute to the persons entitled, having regard only to the claims (whether formal or not) of which the personal representatives then have notice. Thus, if the personal representatives first satisfy the requirements as to advertising and making searches, and then distribute the deceased's assets, they are not, in respect of the distributed assets, liable for any debt or liability of the deceased[58] of which they did not have notice at the time of distribution.[59] It is advisable for personal representatives to advertise and make searches at an early stage in the administration of the deceased's estate, because section 27 does not protect them in respect of assets which they have already distributed before these requirements are satisfied.[60]

Section 27 does not protect personal representatives against any debt or liability of which they have had notice at the time of distribution, even though the claimant did not respond to the advertisement.[61] Nor does section 27 protect personal representatives against a person who claims that they have "no right to administer the estate at all"[62]—for instance, against the next of kin entitled on intestacy, who claim that the grant of probate of the deceased's will to the executors should be revoked on the ground that the deceased lacked testamentary capacity.

A testator cannot by his will deprive his personal representatives of their protection under section 27.[63]

Sherry (1876) 1 C.P.D. 246, 256 (advertise in foreign country if claimant may be residing there). It is important for the personal representatives to satisfy this requirement because otherwise they lose the protection of section 27.

[58] Or to an unknown beneficiary under the deceased's will or intestacy, *Re Aldhous* [1955] 1 W.L.R. 459: see *post*, pp. 470–471.

[59] Trustee Act 1925, s. 27(2); *Clegg v. Rowland* (1866) L.R. 3 Eq. 368 (executor has the same protection as if he had distributed under an order of the court); *Re Frewen* (1889) 60 L.T. 953. For notice where a personal representative is acting for the purpose of more than one estate see Trustee Act 1925, s. 28.

[60] *Re Kay* [1897] 2 Ch. 518 (some assets distributed before advertisement to widow in need: personal representatives not protected, but relief against liability granted under Judicial Trustees Act 1896, s. 3—now Trustee Act 1925, s. 61): see *post*, pp. 502–503.

[61] *Re Land Credit Company of Ireland* (1872) 21 W.R. 1351.

[62] *Guardian Trust & Executors Company of New Zealand Ltd. v. Public Trustee of New Zealand* [1942] A.C. 115, 125 (a Privy Council decision on the New Zealand equivalent of s. 27): see *ante*, p. 367.

[63] s. 27(3).

(2) *LEAVE OF THE COURT TO DISTRIBUTE.* If the court gives personal representatives leave to distribute on the footing that all the deceased's debts and liabilities have been ascertained, this protects the personal representatives against any unknown debts and liabilities. In *Re Gess*[64] the deceased, who was of Polish nationality, died domiciled in England in 1939 and the administrators of his estate were unable to advertise for creditors in Poland owing to the wartime occupation of Poland by Germany. The court gave them leave to distribute without advertising in Poland and on the footing that all the debts and liabilities of the estate had been ascertained.

Neither section 27 of the Trustee Act 1925, nor the leave of the court to distribute, prejudices the remedy of an unpaid creditor against a recipient of the deceased's assets.[65] This remedy is considered later.[66]

3. Future debts and liabilities

A debt or liability of the deceased may not fall due for payment until long after the deceased's death. For example, the deceased may have been the original tenant of a lease, which he assigned to a third party long before his death: his personal representatives will remain liable as such for rent and for any breach of covenant during the entire unexpired term of the lease. There is no problem as long as the assignee and his assigns continue to pay the rent and perform the covenants in order to avoid forfeiture of the lease. But if the assignee becomes insolvent, the liability of the original tenant for the rent and for other breaches of covenant can be onerous. Recent market conditions in relation to commercial leases have made this a serious problem for the personal representatives of deceased former original tenants.

If there is any possible future debt or liability of which the personal representatives have notice (so that they are not protected by advertising for claims in accordance with section 27 of the Trustee Act 1925), and to which section 26 does not apply, what courses of action are open to the personal representatives?

(1) *ORDER OF THE COURT.* The safest course is for the personal representatives to apply to the court for directions. If the personal representatives make a full disclosure of all the information they have, and act in accordance with the order of the court, the personal representatives are fully protected.[67] The court generally authorises the estate to be distributed without making any provision for future contingent liabilities.[68] This protects the personal representatives and leaves the unpaid creditor (if the contingent liability arises) to pursue his remedy against a recipient

---

[64] [1942] Ch. 37: see also *Re Benjamin* [1902] 1 Ch. 723 (missing beneficiary) and *post*, p. 471.

[65] Trustee Act 1925, s. 27(2); *Re Gess*, [1942] Ch. 37, at p. 39.

[66] *Post*, pp. 510 *et seq.*

[67] *Re King* [1907] 1 Ch. 72 where Neville J. reviewed the case law (possible future liability on deceased's company shares not fully paid up: order of the court directing distribution to residuary beneficiaries exonerates personal representatives from liability to company); *Re Nixon* [1904] 1 Ch. 638, (leases formerly held by deceased: distribution directed and personal representatives not liable on leases thereafter).

[68] *Re King, supra; Re Johnson* [1940] W.N. 195; *Re Sales* [1920] W.N. 54.

of the deceased's assets.[69] This practice is not, however, appropriate if there is a reasonable probability that a liability will arise.[70]

(2) *DISTRIBUTON WITHOUT AN ORDER OF THE COURT.* If the personal representatives distribute the assets of the estate without first applying to the court and acting in accordance with its order, and later the contingent liability arises, the personal representatives are liable to the unpaid creditor to the extent of the assets they distributed.[71] If this happens, the personal representatives may claim repayment from a beneficiary of the capital value of the assets which they distributed to him, unless at the time of distribution they knew that the claim had already fallen due for payment.[72] This right to claim repayment permits the personal representatives to distribute the assets of the estate provided the contingent liability is remote.[73].

In order to secure more protection without incurring the expense of an application to the court, personal representatives:

(i) may obtain a proper indemnity from the beneficiaries before distributing the assets (e.g. a beneficiary may give security[74] to repay his share of the assets if the contingent liability arises); or

(ii) may set aside an indemnity fund out of the deceased's estate.[75]

Which of these different courses of action should be chosen by the personal representatives may depend on several factors, including the nature and extent of the possible future debt or liability, the value of the deceased's estate and the financial position of each beneficiary.

4. Statute-barred debts

Personal representatives have a duty to rely on all proper defences to a claim being made by a creditor and they commit a breach of duty (or *devastavit*) if they pay a debt which need not be paid.[76] To this general rule there is a single well-established exception: personal representatives may plead the Limitation Acts as a defence, but they are not under any duty to do so if the Acts have only barred the claimant's remedy and not extinguished his claim. Thus, if they think fit, personal representat-

---

[69] *Post*, pp. 510 *et seq.*

[70] *Re Arnold* [1942] Ch. 272: *cf. Re Johnson, supra.*

[71] *Taylor v. Taylor* (1870) L.R. 10 Eq. 477 (executors liable for unexpected calls on company shares made after death); *Knatchbull v. Fearnhead* (1837) 3 M. & C. 122; *Re Bewley's Estate* (1871) 24 L.T. 177. For the defence of limitation see *post*, p. 500.

[72] *Jervis v. Wolferstan* (1874) L.R. 18 Eq. 18 (repayment of ·capital but not of intermediate income received by beneficiary); *Whittaker v. Kershaw* (1890) 45 Ch.D. 320.

[73] *Jervis v. Wolferstan, supra,* at pp. 25–26; *Whittaker v. Kershaw, supra,* at pp. 326 and 329.

[74] A personal representative may, as a condition of giving an assent, require security for the discharge of a liability: Administration of Estates Act 1925, s. 36(10).

[75] *Simmons v. Bolland* (1817) 3 Mer. 547; *Fletcher v. Stevenson* (1844) 3 Hare 360; *Dobson v. Carpenter* (1850) 12 Beav. 370; *Hickling v. Boyer* (1851) 3 Mac. & G. 635; *Dean v. Allen* (1855) 20 Beav. 1.

[76] *Re Rownson* (1885) 29 Ch. D. 358, 363–364; *Midgley v. Midgley* [1893] 3 Ch. 282, 289, 299 and 304. For their statutory powers in relation to debts (including power to pay or allow any debt or claim on any evidence that they think sufficient) see Trustee Act 1925, s. 15 and *ante*, p. 376.

ives may pay a statute-barred debt of the deceased.[77] But this exception is anomalous and will not be extended.[78] There are limits to the scope of the exception:

(1) *DEBT ALREADY DECLARED STATUTE-BARRED.* If the court has already declared the debt to be statute-barred, the personal representatives have a duty to rely on the defence of *res judicata* and they must not pay the debt.[79]

(2) *ORDER FOR ADMINISTRATION.* If the court makes an order for the administration of the estate, any creditor or beneficiary is entitled to raise the defence of limitation against a creditor who comes in under the order to prove his debt, notwithstanding the refusal of the personal representatives to raise this defence.[80] But, exceptionally, creditors and beneficiaries are not permitted to raise this defence against a creditor who was himself the plaintiff in the administration proceedings. The personal representatives did not raise this defence against the time-barred plaintiff-creditor, and another creditor or beneficiary, who has got the benefit of the administration order, cannot be permitted to raise it.[81]

(3) *INSOLVENT ESTATE.* If the deceased's estate is insolvent only debts provable in bankruptcy may be claimed and a statute-barred debt is not provable in bankruptcy.[82]

If a claimant sues for his debt and one of the personal representatives pleads limitation in his defence, but the other personal representative does not, the court acts on the defence as being more for the advantage of the estate.[83] Whether one personal representative may pay a statute-barred debt of the deceased if the other personal representative objects has never been decided[84]; perhaps one executor may do so under the rule that executors have joint and several authority.[85]

5. Interest on debts

If a debt of the deceased carries interest, it is payable by the personal representatives as part of the sum due from the estate. If a debt does

---

[77] *Norton v. Frecker* (1737) 1 Atk. 524, 526; *Stahlschmidt v. Lett* (1853) 1 Sm. & G. 415; *Hill v. Walker* (1858) 4 K. & J. 166; *Midgley v. Midgley, supra,* at pp. 289, 297 and 304. See Limitation Act 1980 ss. 5, 8 and 20 (debt not extinguished) and *cf.* s. 17 (title to land extinguished).

[78] *Re Rownson, supra,* at pp. 363–365; *Midgley v. Midgley, supra,* at p. 299 (this anomalous exception "is to be confined within the limits of its own anomaly").

[79] *Midgley v. Midgley, supra.*

[80] *Shewn v. Vanderhorst* (1831) 1 Russ. & M. 347 (residuary legatee raised defence of limitation); *Moodie v. Bannister* (1859) 4 Drew. 432; *Fuller v. Redman (No. 2)* (1859) 26 Beav. 614 (creditor raised defence of limitation). But the court does not raise this defence on behalf of an absent beneficiary, *Alston v. Trollope* (1866) L.R. 2 Eq. 205.

[81] *Briggs v. Wilson* (1835) 5 De G.M. & G. 12, 21; *Fuller v. Redman (No. 2)* (1859) 26 Beav. 614, 617–619.

[82] Administration of Insolvent Estates of Deceased Persons Order 1986 (S.I. 1986 No. 1999); *Ex p. Dewdney and ex p. Seaman* (1809) 15 Ves. 479. *Ex p. Roffey* (1815) 19 Ves. 468.

[83] *Midgley v. Midgley* [1893] 3 Ch. 282, 298 and 302.

[84] *ibid.* at pp. 297 and 301–302.

[85] *ibid.* p. 297: see *ante,* p. 391.

not carry interest but the court directs an account of the deceased's debts to be taken, then, unless the court orders otherwise, interest is allowed on the debt at the rate payable on judgment debts from the date of the judgment directing the account.[86] But if the estate is insolvent, the bankruptcy rules as to interest on debts are applicable.[87]

II. SOLVENT ESTATES

The deceased's estate is solvent if the assets are sufficient to pay all his funeral, testamentary and administration expenses, debts and liabilities.[1] In that event these expenses, debts and liabilities are payable in full and any balance of the deceased's estate is distributable to the beneficiaries entitled under his will or intestacy. So the beneficiaries are concerned as to which assets of the estate are liable to bear the burden of the expenses, debts and liabilities. It is in each beneficiary's interest to claim that the burden should not fall on assets to which he is entitled. This means that rules are needed to regulate the burden of the expenses, debts and liabilities and these rules as to incidence regulate "competition" between the beneficiaries.

Creditors are not concerned with the rules regulating the burden of the deceased's expenses, debts and liabilities: a creditor is not even bound by them and may obtain payment out of any assets regardless of these rules.[2] If a creditor is paid out of an asset which is not, under these rules, liable to bear the burden of his debt, the matter can be adjusted between the beneficiaries in the personal representatives' final accounts and, if need be, the doctrine of marshalling (which is explained later[3]) provides a remedy for the disappointed beneficiary.

All the rules as to incidence now to be considered have one common feature—they may be varied by a contrary intention on the part of the deceased. It is, however, necessary to consider the expression of such a contrary intention separately in relation to each of the incidence rules.

A. THE STATUTORY ORDER OF APPLICATION OF ASSETS

Section 34(3) of the Administration of Estates Act 1925 provides that, where the deceased's estate is solvent, his real and personal estate shall, subject to any provisions contained in his will, be applicable towards the discharge of the funeral, testamentary and administration expenses, debts and liabilities payable thereout in the order mentioned in Part II of the First Schedule to the Act. Special rules are applicable to debts

---

[86] R.S.C., Ord. 44, r. 9. See also Supreme Court Act 1981, s. 35A, as amended by Administration of Justice Act 1982, s. 15(1) and Sched. I, Pt. I.
[87] *Post*, pp. 441 and 443–444.
[1] *Re Leng* [1895] 1 Ch. 652, 658: see *post*, p. 438.
[2] *Re Tong* [1931] 1 Ch. 202, 212; Administration of Estates Act 1925, s. 35(3).
[3] *Post*, pp. 436–438.

charged on the deceased's property and to the incidence of inheritance tax: these special rules are considered later.[4]

The statutory order of application of assets set out in Part II of the First Schedule is as follows:

"1. Property of the deceased undisposed of by will, subject to the retention thereout of a fund sufficient to meet any pecuniary legacies.[5]

2. Property of the deceased not specifically devised or bequeathed but included (either by a specific or general description) in a residuary gift, subject to the retention out of such property of a fund sufficient to meet any pecuniary legacies, so far as not provided for as aforesaid.[6]

3. Property of the deceased specifically appropriated or devised or bequeathed (either by a specific or general description) for the payment of debts.

4. Property of the deceased charged with, or devised or bequeathed (either by specific or general description) subject to a charge for the payment of debts.

5. The fund, if any, retained to meet pecuniary legacies.

6. Property specifically devised or bequeathed, rateably according to value.

7. Property appointed by will under a general power, including the statutory power to dispose of entailed interests, rateably according to value.

8. The following provisions shall also apply—
    (a) The order of application may be varied by the will of the deceased."

This statutory order applies on the death of any person after 1925[7] unless the order is varied by the deceased's will.

In this statutory order no distinction is made between realty and personalty. The Schedule refers repeatedly to "property," which is defined in the Administration of Estates Act 1925 as including any interest in real or personal property.[8] All the real and personal property falling within a particular paragraph is therefore liable rateably for the expenses, debts and liabilities.[9]

Take an example of the operation of the statutory order. By his will T gives his freehold house, Blackacre, to A; his shares in JKL Ltd. to B; legacies of £10,000 to C and £4,000 to D (which legacies T directs to be paid out of his residuary personal estate); his residuary real estate to E; and his residuary personal estate to F.

T dies in 1995 and all the beneficiaries survive him. None of T's property is undisposed of by his will so paragraph 1 of the statutory order

---

[4] *Post,* pp. 428 and 433.

[5] For the incidence of general pecuniary legacies, see *post,* pp. 446 *et seq.*

[6] For the incidence of general pecuniary legacies, see *post,* pp. 446 *et seq.*

[7] Administration of Estates Act 1925, s. 54; *Re Gates* [1930] 1 Ch. 199 (order applies on death intestate after 1925 of pre-1926 lunatic).

[8] s. 55(1)(xvii)

[9] *Re Harland-Peck* [1941] Ch. 182, 187–189; *Re Anstead* [1943] Ch. 161 (the headnote is wrong).

is not applicable. The first step to take is to set aside out of the residuary personal estate a fund to satisfy the general pecuniary legacies of £10,000 and £4,000.[10] T's estate is applicable towards the discharge of expenses, debts and liabilities in the following order:

(i) Both T's residuary real estate (given to E) and his residuary personal estate (given to F) fall within paragraph 2. This property is primarily liable for expenses, debts and liabilities and it must be exhausted before any other property is touched. The residuary real estate and residuary personal estate bear this burden rateably in proportion to their respective values. Thus, if the residuary real estate is valued at £60,000 and the residuary personal estate (after setting aside £14,000 to pay the pecuniary legacies) is valued at £20,000, the residuary real estate bears three-quarters, and the residuary personal estate one-quarter, of the burden of the expenses, debts and liabilities.

(ii) None of T's property falls within paragraphs 3 or 4, so the pecuniary legacy fund is liable next under paragraph 5. If (say) one-half of the (£14,000) pecuniary legacy fund is needed to meet expenses, debts and liabilities, then each pecuniary legacy abates proportionally: in that event, C and D each receive only one-half of their respective legacies.

(iii) Both Blackacre (realty specifically devised to A) and T's shares in JKL Ltd. (personalty specifically bequeathed to B) fall within paragraph 6 and bear expenses, debts and liabilities rateably according to their respective values. Thus if Blackacre is valued at £100,000 and the JKL shares at £50,000, Blackacre bears two-thirds and the JKL shares one-third of the burden of any expenses, debts and liabilities falling on paragraph 6 property.

In this example T has not by his will varied the statutory order or given priority to a particular pecuniary legacy. T might, for instance, have directed that the legacy to C should be payable in priority to the legacy to D: in that event D's legacy would abate before C's legacy.[11]

Paragraph 1—property undisposed of by will

It is necessary to consider:

(1) what property falls within paragraph 1; and
(2) what provisions in a will vary the statutory order so that property falling within paragraph 1 is not primarily liable.

(1) *PROPERTY NOT EFFECTIVELY DISPOSED OF BY WILL FALLS WITHIN THIS PARAGRAPH.* Paragraph 1 is not confined to property which the deceased does not attempt to dispose of by will, but includes

---

[10] *Re Anstead, supra*, (unlike the example in the text, the will did not contain a direction to pay legacies out of residuary personalty); *Re Wilson* [1967] Ch. 53, 70. For the classification of legacies and devises, see *ante*, pp. 170 *et seq*.

[11] But C would not have been entitled to interest on his legacy in priority to the legacy to D, in the absence of express direction to this effect; *Re Wyles* [1938] Ch. 313.

property of which he attempts, unsuccessfully, to dispose. In *Re Lamb*[12] T by his will directed his debts and expenses to be paid by his executors as soon as possible after his death and, after making certain gifts, directed the residue of his estate to be equally divided between W, X, Y and Z. The words of severance in this direction created a tenancy in common. W predeceased T and so his quarter share of residue lapsed[13] and went to T's next-of-kin entitled under the intestacy rules. The court held that this quarter share was "property of the deceased undisposed of by will" and was therefore primarily liable under paragraph 1 for T's expenses and debts. If W, X, Y and Z had all survived T and each had taken his quarter share, T's residue as a whole would have been primarily liable under paragraph 2 for T's expenses and debts.

Similarly, if a testator by his will gives his residuary estate upon trusts which do not effectively dispose of all the income arising after his death, any undisposed of income is "property of the deceased undisposed of by will".[14]

(2) *VARIATION OF THE STATUTORY ORDER.* The testator may vary the statutory order by his will. If he varies it, property falling within paragraph 1 is not primarily liable. Variation of the statutory order may either be by express provision or by implication. There should be relatively little difficulty where the testator has expressly provided that the statutory order should be varied. But the problem is to decide, as a question of construction, whether the testator has impliedly varied the order. Most of the decided cases deal with lapsed shares of residue; the cases fall into two groups:

(i) In one group of cases the testator varies the statutory order *by directing expenses and debts to be paid out of residue as a whole,* thereby charging residue as a whole with their payment. In *Re Harland-Peck*[15] T made certain gifts by her will and then provided that: "Subject to the payment of my funeral and testamentary expenses . . . and debts . . . I devise and bequeath all the rest and residue of my property" to X and Y in equal shares as tenants in common. Y predeceased T and his half share lapsed and went to Z who was T's next-of-kin entitled on her intestacy. The Court of Appeal held that the provision in the will varied the statutory order and so expenses and debts were payable out of residue as a whole, not primarily out of Y's lapsed share under paragraph

---

[12] [1929] 1 Ch. 723: see also *Re Tong* [1931] 1 Ch. 202; *Re Worthington* [1933] Ch. 771; *Re Sanger* [1939] Ch. 238.

[13] For the doctrine of lapse (and the exceptions to it), see *ante*, pp. 234 *et seq.*

[14] *Re Tong, supra,* (gift of income to X failed as X's spouse attested the will: income liable under para. 1) *cf.* the earlier decision in *Re Cruse* [1930] W.N. 206 (gift of income effective but gift in remainder partially failed: debts held payable out of residue as a whole).

[15] [1941] Ch. 182: see also *Re Petty* [1929] 1 Ch. 726 (gift of residue to trustees upon trust for sale and out of the proceeds to pay expenses and debts); *Re Kempthorne* [1930] 1 Ch. 268 (personal estate "subject to and after payment of . . . expenses and debts" to be divided among residuary legatees); *Re Berrey's W.T.* [1959] 1 W.L.R. 30 ("after all my debts, and funeral, and expenses are paid I give" residue to named beneficiaries). See also *Re Atkinson* [1930] 1 Ch. 47 and *Re Martin* [1955] Ch. 698.

1. The result was that X and Z each suffered part of the burden of the expenses and debts.

(ii) In the other group of cases the testator directs expenses and debts to be paid *but does not specify out of what property they are to be paid*. This is construed as a direction to pay them in due course of administration pursuant to the statutory order. Expenses and debts are therefore payable primarily out of any lapsed shares of residue under paragraph 1. *Re Lamb*[16] (which has already been considered) falls within this group of cases. The result in *Re Lamb* was that the next-of-kin suffered the primary burden of the expenses and debts.

It has been suggested[17] that it is difficult to distinguish between, on the one hand, a gift of residue subject to and after payment of expenses and debts (which falls within the first group of cases) and, on the other hand, a direction to pay expenses and debts followed by a gift of residue (which falls within the second group of cases). There appears, however, to be a distinction, though arguably it is a fine one—in the first group of cases the testator directs expenses and debts to be paid out of residue as a whole; in the second group of cases he does not direct out of what property the expenses and debts are to be paid.

Paragraph 2—property included in a residuary gift.

Paragraph 2 is worded so that property falls within it if it is not specifically devised or bequeathed but is included (either by a specific or general description) in a residuary gift. As already explained, gifts by T's will of "my freehold house Blackacre" to A and "my shares in JKL Ltd." to B (followed by gifts of T's residuary real estate to E and residuary personal estate to F) are examples of a specific devise and a specific bequest. Blackacre and the shares both fall within paragraph 6 and T's residuary real and residuary personal estate both fall within paragraph 2. If, on the other hand, after making these gifts of Blackacre and the shares, T had given "my residuary real estate including my freehold house Whiteacre" to E and "my residuary personal estate including my Rover car" to F, both Whiteacre and the Rover car would have fallen within paragraph 2, as property included in a residuary gift by a specific description.

A general gift by the testator in his will of all his real estate, or of all his personal estate, may be a residuary gift within paragraph 2. In *Re Wilson*[18] T by her will, after giving a number of specific and pecuniary legacies, gave "all my real estate and the residue of my personal estate" to D absolutely. Pennycuick J. held that T's real estate (as well as her residuary personal estate) fell within paragraph 2, even though there was no previous devise of any other realty in the will. He said that "in

---

[16] [1929] 1 Ch. 723: see also *Re Tong, supra, Re Worthington, supra; Re Sanger, supra.*

[17] *Per* Simonds J. in *Re Sanger, supra,* at pp. 248–249.

[18] [1967] Ch. 53: *cf. dicta* in *Re Rowe* [1941] Ch. 343, 348 and *Re Ridley* [1950] Ch. 415, 420–422: for the pre-1926 rule that "all devises were by their nature specific" see *Hensman v. Fryer* (1867) 3 Ch.App. 420 and *Lancefield v. Iggulden* (1874) 10 Ch.App. 136, and *ante,* p. 173.

ordinary language today lawyers would, I think, not inaptly describe such a gift as a residuary devise. They would certainly not describe it as a specific devise."[19]

Paragraph 3—property specifically appropriated
Paragraph 4—property charged

(1) *PROPERTY FALLING WITHIN PARAGRAPHS 3 AND 4.* Property of the deceased falling within these paragraphs is liable for the deceased's expenses, debts and liabilities because the property was specifically appropriated or devised or bequeathed for the payment of debts (paragraph 3), or because the property was charged with, or devised or bequeathed subject to, a charge for the payment of debts (paragraph 4).

By his will a testator often appropriates his residuary estate for the payment of debts or charges his residuary estate with the payment of debts. Paragraphs 3 and 4 do not, however, apply to property included in a residuary gift, because such property falls within the earlier paragraph 2.[20]

(2) *VARIATION OF THE STATUTORY ORDER.* Assuming that the statutory order applies, property falling within paragraph 3 or 4 is liable only after property undisposed of by the will (paragraph 1) and property included in a residuary gift (paragraph 2) have been exhausted. But the statutory order may be varied by the will. Thus if a will appropriates, or charges, property for, or with, the payment of expenses and debts, it is necessary to decide (i) whether the will varies the statutory order so as to make that property primarily liable for expenses and debts, or (ii) whether that property merely falls within paragraph 3 or 4. As Upjohn J. said in *Re Meldrum*[21] it is "essentially a matter of construction of the will in each case whether the provisions of the schedule apply, or whether they have been varied by the terms of the will."[22]

Paragraph 5—the pecuniary legacy fund

The expression "pecuniary legacy" is widely defined in section 55(1)(ix) of the Administration of Estates Act 1925 and:

> "includes an annuity, a general legacy, a demonstrative legacy so far as it is not discharged out of the designated property, and any other general direction by a testator for the payment of money, including all death duties free from which any devise, bequest, or payment is made to take effect."

The distinction between a general legacy, a demonstrative legacy, and a

---

[19] *Re Wilson* [1967] Ch. 53 at p. 68.
[20] *Re Kempthorne* [1930] 1 Ch. 268.
[21] [1952] Ch. 208.
[22] [1952] Ch. 208, 212. *Re Meldrum* is an example of a case where it was held that the statutory order had been varied, it may be contrasted with *Re Gordon* [1940] Ch. 769 where the statutory order was held applicable; see also *Re Kempthorne*.

specific devise or specific legacy is important in applying paragraphs 5 and 6 of the statutory order: this was considered in Chapter 7.[23]

If part of the pecuniary legacy fund is needed to meet expenses and debts, all the pecuniary legacies abate rateably unless by his will the testator has shown an intention that one or more pecuniary legacies are to have priority.

Paragraph 6—property specifically devised or bequeathed

Under paragraph 6 property specifically devised or bequeathed bears the burden of expenses and debts "rateably according to value."

(1) *RATEABLY ACCORDING TO VALUE.* In applying paragraph 6 the relevant value is the value of each property to the testator at his death. *Re John*[24] provides a classic illustration. By his will T gave Blackacre (subject to a mortgage created by T during his lifetime) to X and Whiteacre (subject to certain legacies given by T's will) to Y. Farwell J. held that Blackacre and Whiteacre were liable to bear the burden of expenses and debts rateably according to the value of each property at the testator's death. In the case of Blackacre this was the probate value of T's equity of redemption (*i.e.* the value of Blackacre less the mortgage debt), and in the case of Whiteacre the probate value of Whiteacre but without making any deduction for the legacies to be paid thereout.[25]

(2) *OPTION GIVEN BY WILL.* T may by his will give X an option to purchase property comprised in T's estate, from T's personal representatives, at a stated price. For instance, in *Re Eve*[26] T by his will gave X an option to acquire 1,000 of T's shares in a named company at £1 per share, which was less than their market value at T's death. X gave notice of his intention to exercise the option. T's residue was insufficient to pay expenses and debts in full and the question was whether the shares subject to the option had to bear any part of the expenses and debts. Roxburgh J. said that, "The shares are not bequeathed subject to a charge or condition. An option to purchase cannot be a specific bequest of shares"[27] and the benefit given to X (*i.e.* the difference between the option price and the market value) was not a specific bequest. He decided that property subject to an option given by will did not fall anywhere within the statutory order. He concluded that:

"the property subject to an option is the last to be available for the payment of debts. For, indeed, in so far as the property subject to the option is required for the payment of debts, the option over that property cannot be exercised at all, and the benefit of it is totally destroyed by operation of law. But so long as the purchase price stated in the

---

[23] *Ante*, pp. 170 *et seq.* As to abatement of annuities see *post*, pp. 255–256 *et seq.*
[24] [1933] Ch. 370: see also *Re Cohen* [1960] Ch. 179 (probate values, and not later sale values).
[25] Subject to the provisions of the will, the legatees take priority over Y and the legacies only abate if Whiteacre (after bearing its share of expenses and debts) is insufficient to pay them in full, *Re Saunders–Davies* (1887) 34 Ch.D. 482; *Re Bawden* [1894] 1 Ch. 693.
[26] [1956] Ch. 479.
[27] *ibid.* at p. 482.

will is, with the other available assets, sufficient for the payment of debts, it, and not the shares, constitutes the fund available for that purpose."[28]

If the principles enunciated in *Re Eve* are good law, an option is destroyed if any sum, however small, is required from the property (in addition to the option price) for the payment of expenses and debts. The destruction of the option frees the option property to meet expenses and debts (normally as part of the residuary estate), and thereby benefits a beneficiary under the will who was given other property which was liable for expenses and debts before the option property. The decision in *Re Eve* treats X as a person with a right to purchase the shares if available for sale, and not as a beneficiary whose benefit under the will is liable to abatement.[29] But X acquired his right to purchase the shares by virtue of the gift of the option to him in the will and it is arguable that X is really a beneficiary and, as such, his benefit ought to be liable to abatement.

If X takes as a beneficiary under a conditional specific gift in the will, the property falls within paragraph 6 and the gift abates with the other specific devises or bequests. Thus if by his will T gives his property Blackacre to X if X pays £1,000 to Y, Blackacre is property specifically devised and falls within paragraph 6. Does it make any difference if X is required to pay the £1,000 to T's estate and not to Y? If on the true construction of T's will X takes as a beneficiary, it makes no difference and the property falls within paragraph 6.[30]

Paragraph 7—property appointed by will under a general power.

Paragraph 7 is the last paragraph in the statutory order. "Property appointed by will under a general power, including the statutory power to dispose of entailed interests"[31] falls within paragraph 7 and is liable for expenses and debts rateably according to value.

Under section 27 of the Wills Act 1837 a general gift includes property over which the testator has a general power of appointment, unless the will shows a contrary intention.[32] Accordingly, such property passes under a residuary gift without any express appointment, unless the will shows a contrary intention. Alternatively, but with the same effect, the testator may make a gift of his residuary estate "including any property over which I have a general power of appointment."

Before 1926, if a residuary bequest in a will included personal property over which the testator had a general power of appointment (either by virtue of section 27 or by such express inclusion), the appointed property was liable for expenses and debts as if it formed part of the testator's

---

[28] *ibid.* at p. 483; but *cf. Re Kerry* [1889] W.N. 3.
[29] *cf. Re Fison's W.T.* [1950] Ch. 394, esp. at p. 407 (effect of Administration of Estates Act 1925, s.35(1) on option) and see *post*, pp. 431–432; *Re Lander* [1951] Ch. 546 (incidence of estate duty on an option) and see *post*, p. 435.
[30] Probably, if X is required to pay the £1,000 to T's estate, the burden of debts and expenses falling on Blackacre ought to be borne so far as possible by the £1,000 paid by X: *cf. ante*, n. 25.
[31] *Ante*, p. 409.
[32] *Ante*, pp. 211–213.

residuary personalty.[33] It has been suggested that since 1925, if a residuary gift includes real or personal property over which the testator has a general power of appointment (either by virtue of section 27 or by express inclusion), the appointed property is liable for expenses and debts under paragraph 2, and not under paragraph 7, of the statutory order.[34] If this is so, it must be because the will has thereby varied the statutory order, as paragraph 2 applies only to property of the deceased.

Assets not included in the statutory order

As already explained, property which is subject to an option given by the testator's will was held in *Re Eve* to fall outside the statutory order. Again, property appointed by deed under a general power and property given by *donatio mortis causa* are liable for the deceased's debts in the last resort,[35] though neither is mentioned in the statutory order: there is no case-law on the order of application of these assets *inter se*.

B.   Debts charged on the Deceased's Property

Under section 35 of the Administration of Estates Act 1925 a special rule applies to any debt charged on the deceased's property. A common instance is a mortgage debt due to a bank or building society and charged on the deceased's house. Under this rule, the property charged is primarily liable for the payment of the debt, unless the deceased has shown a contrary intention. If by his will the deceased gives his house to his widow, she takes it subject to the mortgage debt and is not entitled to have the mortgage debt discharged out of the deceased's other assets unless the deceased has shown a contrary intention.

Section 35(1), which is applicable on the death of any person after 1925,[36] provides as follows:

"Where a person dies possessed of, or entitled to, or, under a general power of appointment (including the statutory power to dispose of entailed interests) by his will disposes of, an interest in property, which at the time of his death is charged with the payment of money, whether by way of legal mortgage, equitable charge or otherwise (including a lien for unpaid purchase money), and the deceased has not by will deed or other document signified a contrary or other intention, the interest so charged shall, as between the different persons claiming through the deceased, be primarily liable for the payment of

---

[33] *Re Hartley* [1900] 1 Ch. 152.
[34] *Hawkins and Ryder on the Construction of Wills* (1965), p. 361.
[35] *Ante*, pp. 410–411.
[36] Administration of Estates Act 1925, s.54. On a death before 1926 the Real Estate Charges Act 1854 (Locke King's Act) and the Real Estate Charges Acts 1867 and 1877 (all together called Locke King's Acts) applied this special rule to any debt charged on realty or leaseholds, but not on pure personalty.

the charge; and every part of the said interest, according fo its value, shall bear a proportionate part of the charge on the whole thereof."

1. Property charged at death

For section 35(1) to apply there must be an interest in property which is charged with the payment of money at the time of the deceased's death.

(1) *INTEREST IN PROPERTY.* Section 35(1) applies to any interest in any property, whether real or personal[37];

    (i) if the deceased is possessed of or entitled to it at his death[38]; or

    (ii) if by his will the deceased disposes of it under a general power of appointment (including the statutory power to dispose of entailed interests).[39]

Usually the property charged is an interest in land but section 35(1) also applies to pure personalty—for example, to the deceased's company shares which under the articles of association are subject to an equitable charge for money owing to the company by the deceased at his death.[40]

(2) *CHARGED WITH THE PAYMENT OF MONEY AT DEATH.* The section applies to any charge "whether by way of legal mortgage, equitable charge or otherwise (including a lien for unpaid purchase money)." It is not confined to charges created by act of parties[41] but extends to charges created by statute, such as the charge imposed by a court on the property of a judgment debtor.[42]

But the interest in property must be charged with the payment of money at the time of the deceased's death. In *Re Birmingham*[43] T contracted to buy Blackacre from V for £3,500 and paid V a deposit of £350. Before completion of the purchase, T died. After T's death her solicitors completed their work in connection with the purchase and became entitled to their costs. By her will T gave Blackacre to her daughter D and gave her residuary estate to E and F. The court held that under section 35(1) D took Blackacre subject to V's lien for the unpaid balance of the purchase price: this lien arose when the contract was made and before T's death. So, if the market value of Blackacre was £3,500, D only

---

[37] Administration of Estates Act 1925, s. 55(1)(xvii).

[38] *Re Coxen* [1948] 2 All E.R. 492 (motor car ordered by, but no particular car appropriated to, deceased: s. 35 not applicable to unpaid price as deceased not entitled at death).

[39] *Ante*, p. 409. On a death before 1926 the Acts did not apply to entails, *Re Anthony* [1893] 3 Ch. 398.

[40] *Re Turner* [1938] Ch. 593: see also *Re Coxen, supra*, at p. 496.

[41] *Pembrooke v. Friend* (1860) 1 J. & H. 132 (equitable mortgage by deposit of title deeds— though it may not be possible to create such a mortgage after 1989, see *United Bank of Kuwait v. Sahib, The Times*, July 7, 1994); *Re Hawkes* [1912] 2 Ch. 251 (memorandum of charge securing an overdraft); *Re Kidd* [1894] 3 Ch. 558 and *Re Fraser* [1904] 1 Ch. 726 (vendor's lien).

[42] Charging Orders Act 1979, ss. 1–3: see *Re Anthony* [1892] 1 Ch. 450 (charge created by Judgments Act 1838, s. 13).

[43] [1959] Ch. 523

benefited to the extent of the £350 deposit. On the other hand, the court held that the solicitors' costs did not fall within section 35(1), but were payable out of T's residue as an ordinary debt, because, at T's death, Blackacre was not charged with the payment of the solicitors' costs.[44]

2. Incidence of the charge under section 35

Assuming that the deceased has not shown a contrary intention then "as between the different persons claiming through the deceased' the charged property is made primarily liable for the payment of the charge. The section regulates the incidence of the charge as between the different beneficiaries claiming through the deceased.[45]

(1) *TWO PROPERTIES (CHARGED TOGETHER) GIVEN TO DIFFER-ENT BENEFICIARIES.* Suppose that at his death T is entitled to the Whiteacre Estate (which comprises Greater Whiteacre and Lesser Whiteacre) in fee simple subject to a mortgage securing a loan of £100,000 by M to T. By his will T gives Greater Whiteacre to X and his residuary estate (including Lesser Whiteacre) to Y. Under section 35(1) each part of the property charged, according to its value at the date of T's death, must bear a proportionate part of the charge. Thus X takes Greater Whiteacre and Y takes Lesser Whiteacre subject (in each case) to a rate-able proportion of the mortgage debt. In *Re Neeld*[46] the Court of Appeal held that the fact that part of the mortgaged property is specifically devised and the other part falls into residue does not signify a contrary intention so as to exclude the application of section 35(1).

(2) *TWO PROPERTIES (CHARGED SEPARATELY) GIVEN TO THE SAME BENEFCIARY.* Consider next a different situation, involving two charges, each on a different property. At his death T is entitled in fee simple to (i) Blackacre subject to a mortgage securing a loan of £50,000 to T, and (ii) Greenacre subject to another mortgage securing a loan of £30,000 to T. By his will T gives Blackacre and Greenacre by two separate gifts to B and his residuary estate to C. Under section 35(1) B takes Black-acre subject to the £50,000 mortgage and Greenacre subject to the £30,000 mortgage. If Blackacre is worth less than the mortgage debt secured on it (as, in times of "negative equity", it may easily be) the amount of the deficiency falls on the fund liable for T's unsecured debts (in this example his residuary estate); section 35(1) does not impose on B an obligation to make up the deficiency out of the equity of redemption of Greenacre.[47]

---

[44] *ibid.* at p. 531: the court pointed out that, if the conveyance had been completed in T's lifetime, the solicitors would have received the title deeds in the normal course and at T's death would have had an equitable lien on the deeds for their unpaid costs.

[45] Including the Crown taking property as *bona vacantia* on an intestacy, Administration of Estates Act 1925, ss. 46(1)(vi) and 57(1).

[46] [1962] Ch. 643, where the authorities are reviewed and *Re Biss* [1956] Ch. 243 is overruled. In *Re Biss* it was held that lesser Whiteacre, which fell into residue, was primarily liable for the whole mortgage debt.

[47] *Re Holt* (1916) 115 L.T. 73 (pre-1926 intestacy under which B took Blackacre and Green-acre as heir: the balance of the mortgage debt secured on Blackacre fell on the deceased's personalty as the fund then liable for unsecured debts, and not on Greenacre).

T may, however, by his will show an intention that B is to take Black-acre and Greenacre as a whole subject to the burden of both the mortgages: in that event, the amount of the deficiency in respect of Blackacre falls primarily on the equity of redemption of Greenacre.[48]

3. Section 35 confined to regulating incidence between beneficiaries

Section 35 is concerned only with regulating the incidence of the charge as between the different beneficiaries.

(1) *CHARGEE'S RIGHTS REMAIN THE SAME.* Section 35(3) makes it clear that the rights of the chargee (*i.e.* the person entitled to the charge) are not in any way affected. If the deceased was personally liable to the chargee for the debt, the chargee may obtain payment out of the deceased's other assets. If he does so, the doctrine of marshalling applies, so that the debt falls ultimately on the charged property.[49] And a beneficiary entitled to the charged property under the deceased's will or intestacy does not become personally liable to the chargee for the debt,[50] but if the beneficiary fails to make the payments due under the charge, the chargee is likely to enforce his remedies (such as the power of sale) against the property.

(2) *DEBT NOT FALLING ON PROPERTY CHARGED WITH IT.* If the charged property of the deceased is not primarily liable for the debt, section 35 is relevant only so far as the debt cannot be discharged by the person, or from the property, primarily liable. In *Re Ritson*[51] T, who carried on a business in partnership with his brother, charged his own freehold property to secure a partnership debt to the bank. At T's death, the partnership assets were sufficient to pay all the partnership debts in full, including the debt to the bank. The Court of Appeal held that the debt to the bank must be paid out of the partnership assets. It did not fall on T's freehold property or on any other asset of his estate, and therefore no question arose as to the incidence of this debt as between the different beneficiaries entitled to T's estate.

(3) *OPTION GIVEN BY WILL.* Does section 35(1) apply if by his will T gives X an option to purchase particular property comprised in T's estate at a stated price from T's personal representatives and the property is charged with a debt at T's death? The answer depends on the construction of T's will. If X is to be regarded as a person with a right to purchase (even though on favourable terms), then section 35(1) does not apply and if X exercises the option he is entitled to a transfer of the property free from incumbrances. On the other hand, if X is to be regarded as a

---

[48] *Frewen v. Law Life Assurance Society* [1896] 2 Ch. 511; Re Baron Kensington [1902] 1 Ch. 203.
[49] Post, pp. 436–438.
[50] *Syer v. Gladstone* (1885) 30 Ch.D. 614 (the headnote is misleading).
[51] [1899] 1 Ch. 128: see also Re Holland [1907] 2 Ch. 88 and Re Hawkes [1912] 2 Ch. 251, 255 (if T charges his property as surety, and after T's death the principal debtor pays off the debt, no question arises as to its incidence between T's beneficiaries).

beneficiary under the will, then under section 35(1) X can only take the property subject to the charge.[52]

4. Contrary intention

The deceased's contrary or other intention (excluding or modifying the operation of section 35(1)) may be shown by will, deed or other document. In practice, if a testator wishes to give particular property free from charges, it is desirable for him to show his intention clearly in his will.

(1) *DIRECTION IN WILL FOR PAYMENT FROM PERSONAL OR RESIDUARY ESTATE.* Under section 35(2) a general direction by a testator for the payment of debts out of his general personal estate, or his residuary estate, or his residuary real estate, is not enough to exclude the operation of section 35(1). There must, in addition, be words which, expressly or by necessary implication, refer to the charge. For example, by his will T makes a specific devise of Whiteacre to X, and at T's death Whiteacre is charged with a mortgage debt due from T. Whiteacre will be relieved of the primary burden of the mortgage debt if by his will T directs payment out of residue of all his debts, "including the mortgage debt charged on Whiteacre" *or* "including all my mortgage debts." Similarly Whiteacre will be relieved of this burden if by his will T directs payment out of residue of all his debts "except mortgage debts, if any, charged on Brownacre": these words by necessary implication show T's intention that the mortgage debt on Whiteacre is to be paid out of residue.[53]

(2) *DIRECTION IN WILL FOR PAYMENT FROM SPECIAL FUND.* On the other hand a direction by T for the payment of his debts out of a special fund, (not being his general personal estate, residuary real and personal estate, or residuary real estate) is sufficient to show his intention that any debt charged on Whiteacre is to be paid out of the special fund; in this case there need be no express or implied reference to the charge on Whiteacre. Thus, if T directs payment of his debts out of his Barclays Bank account, or out of the proceeds of sale of his property, Greenacre, this shows his intention that any debt charged on Whiteacre is to be paid out of this account or out of these proceeds.[54]

If, however, the special fund is inadequate to pay off the whole of the debt charged on Whiteacre, Whiteacre remains primarily liable under section 35(1) for the payment of the unsatisfied balance.[55]

(3) *DOCUMENT OTHER THAN DECEASED'S WILL.* In order to show a contrary intention (excluding or modifying the operation of section

---

[52] *Re Fison's W.T.* [1950] Ch. 394, esp. 407 (reviewing previous authorities).
[53] *Re Valpy* [1906] 1 Ch. 531. See also *Re Fleck* (1888) 37 Ch.D. 677 ("trade debts" to be paid from residuary personalty included trade debt secured by equitable mortgage); *Re Nevill* (1889) 59 L.J.Ch. 511 Cf. *Re Beirnstein* [1925] Ch. 12 (direction to pay sums secured on mortgage does not apply to unpaid purchase money secured by vendor's lien).
[54] *Re Fegan* [1928] Ch. 45.
[55] *ibid*; and see *Re Birch* [1909] 1 Ch. 787.

35(1)) in a non-testamentary document, the deceased must indicate how he intends the burden of the charge to be borne as between the beneficiaries after his death. Thus, if T contracts to buy Blackacre from V and sends to his solicitors a letter enclosing a cheque and stating "Cheque enclosed for balance of purchase money," this letter merely indicates T's intention as to the payment of the unpaid balance of the purchase price in his lifetime. If T dies before completion of the purchase, the letter does not indicate how the burden of V's lien for the unpaid balance of the purchase price is to be borne as between the beneficiaries under his will.[56] Again in *Re Birmingham* (which has already been discussed[57]) T, having contracted to buy Blackacre from V, wrote to her solicitors stating that she wished to leave Blackacre to her daughter D, and T subsequently executed a codicil to this effect. The court held that T had not signified a contrary intention because neither the letter nor the codicil indicated how the burden of V's lien was to be borne as between the beneficiaries under T's will.

C. INCIDENCE OF INHERITANCE TAX

Rules are needed to determine the incidence of inheritance tax payable by personal representatives in respect of the deceased's death. There are two basic rules:

(1) Inheritance tax on the deceased's free real and personal estate[58] in the United Kingdom is a testamentary and administration expense[59] and is payable in accordance with the statutory order of application of assets.
(2) Inheritance tax on any other property falls on that property and must be borne by the beneficiary who takes it.[60]

Both these rules apply subject to any contrary intention shown by the deceased in his will. It is convenient to refer to such a contrary direction as a "free of inheritance tax" provision.

1. Inheritance tax as a testamentary expense

Inheritance tax payable by personal representatives is a testamentary and administration expense if it is payable in respect of the deceased's death on his free real and personal estate in the United Kingdom, *i.e.* on "the value of property in the United Kingdom which (a) vests in the deceased's personal representatives, and (b) was not immediately before the death comprised in a settlement."[61] Thus, if by his will T makes spe-

---

[56] *Re Wakefield* [1943] 2 All E.R. 29: see also *Re Nicholson* [1923] W.N. 251 (T served six months' notice on mortgagee of her intention to pay off mortgage but died before doing so: held letter showed no contrary intention excluding s. 35(1)).
[57] *Ante*, p. 429.
[58] "free estate" is explained below, see *infra*, n. 61.
[59] Inheritance Tax Act 1984, s. 211(1).
[60] *ibid.* s. 211(3).
[61] Inheritance Tax Act 1984, s. 211(1).

cific gifts to his son of his freehold house in London and of his BP shares, any inheritance tax payable in respect of his death on the value of these assets is a testamentary expense and is payable in accordance with the statutory order of application of assets, unless there is a contrary direction in the will. As these gifts are specific, the house and the shares fall within paragraph 6 of the statutory order and are only liable for expenses and debts after property in paragraphs 1 to 5 has been exhausted.

Certain items of property are conditionally exempted from inheritance tax on death. For instance, pictures, books, works of art, scientific collections or other things which appear to the Treasury to be of national, scientific, historic or artistic interest are exempted from inheritance tax if an undertaking is given to keep them in the United Kingdom and to take steps for their preservation and for securing reasonable access to the public.[62] If these undertakings are broken, or if the object is disposed of, a charge to inheritance tax arises.[63] This inheritance tax is not, however, a testamentary expense: it is borne by the persons who would be interested in the proceeds of sale of the objects,[64] or who disposed of the objects.[65] Similar provisions apply to land which in the opinion of the Treasury is of outstanding scenic or historic or scientific interest, and to buildings for the preservation of which special steps should in the opinion of the Treasury be taken by reason of their outstanding historic or architectural interest.[66]

2. Inheritance tax borne by the beneficiary

Inheritance tax which is payable in respect of the deceased's death on any property other than the deceased's free real and personal estate in the United Kingdom falls on that property and must be borne by the beneficiary who takes it. This rule is contained in section 211(3) of the Inheritance Tax Act 1984 and the section also applies to all property movable or immovable outside the United Kingdom. It also applies to property which does not vest in the deceased's personal representatives, such as property given by *donatio mortis causa*[67] or statutory nomination,[68] and the deceased's severable share of property held jointly (which vests by survivorship in the other joint tenant). In each case, under the second rule, the personal representatives are entitled to claim repayment of any inheritance tax they have paid, from the person in whom the property is vested. In practice, in the case of property outside the United Kingdom, the personal representatives may experience difficulty in obtaining repayment.

Section 211(3) also applies to any land (whether freehold or leasehold) which was settled land at the death of the deceased.[69]

---

[62] *ibid.* ss. 30–31, as amended by Finance Act 1985, Sched. 26.
[63] *ibid.* ss. 32 and 33: certain disposals do not make tax chargeable, s. 32(4) and (5).
[64] *ibid.* s. 207(1) (breach of undertaking).
[65] *ibid.* s. 207(2) (disposal).
[66] *ibid.* ss. 31–33, as amended by Finance Act 1985, Sched. 26.
[67] *Re Hudson* [1911] 1 Ch. 206 (estate duty on a *d.m.c.* is not a testamentary expense): the bare legal title to the subject matter of a d.m.c. may vest in the personal representatives but the equitable interest vests in the donee, see *ante*, p. 29.
[68] *Re Walley* [1972] 1 W.L.R. 257 (estate duty on a statutory nomination not a testamentary expense).
[69] Even if, on his death, it ceases to be settled.

3. Incidence of inheritance tax on a pecuniary legacy

In the absence of any contrary direction in T's will, the two basic rules outlined above[70] regulate the incidence of inheritance tax on any immediate pecuniary legacy given by T's will.

(1) *PROPERTY FROM WHICH IMMEDIATE PECUNIARY LEGACY IS PAYABLE.* The incidence of inheritance tax on an immediate pecuniary legacy therefore depends on the nature of the property from which it is payable. This is determined by the provisions of T's will, or by the general rules as to the incidence of pecuniary legacies.[71] If under the provisions of T's will, or these general rules, the pecuniary legacy is payable out of T's free real and personal estate in the United Kingdom, any inheritance tax is a testamentary expense. On the other hand, so far as the pecuniary legacy is payable out of T's property outside the United Kingdom, the pecuniary legacy bears its own inheritance tax.

(2) *DEFERRED PECUNIARY LEGACY.* The position is different in the case of a deferred pecuniary legacy given by T's will. Say T by his will gives property on trust for P for life, and after P's death on trust to pay a pecuniary legacy to Q and subject thereto for R absolutely. When P dies Q and R must bear the inheritance tax payable on the property in respect of P's death rateably according to the respective values of Q's legacy and R's residue.[72]

4. Incidence of inheritance tax on an option

If T by his will gives X an option to purchase from T's personal representatives at a stated price particular property comprised in T's estate, how is the inheritance tax to be borne? If the option property is real or personal estate in the United Kingdom, the inheritance tax is payable as a testamentary expense in accordance with the statutory order of application of assets, subject, of course, to any contrary direction in his will.

5. "Free of inheritance tax" provisions

(1) *THE NEED FOR VARIATION.* The rules which govern the incidence of inheritance tax payable in respect of a deceased's death are unsatisfactory because they do not carry out the likely intentions of the deceased. How many testators would wish inheritance tax to be borne by one beneficiary who takes a specific gift of shares in a foreign company, but not by another beneficiary who takes a specific gift of shares in an English company? Again, how many testators would wish inheritance tax to be borne by a pecuniary legatee in so far as his legacy is payable from property outside the United Kingdom, but not other-wise?

While these incidence rules remain in force, a testator needs to con-

---

[70] *Ante,* p. 433.
[71] *Post,* pp. 446 *et seq.*
[72] See *Berry v. Gaukroger* [1903] 2 Ch. 116. Probably Q's legacy does not bear inheritance tax payable in respect of T's death even though it falls on the property. see *Re McNeill* [1958] Ch. 259 and *Re Maryon-Wilson's W.T.* [1968] Ch. 268.

sider very carefully what "free of inheritance tax" provisions he wishes to insert in his will. A testator may vary these incidence rules by his will as he chooses.[73] Of course, if the testator wishes to relieve one beneficiary of the burden of the tax which he would otherwise be liable to bear, the testator needs to consider which other beneficiary is to bear the burden of that tax.[74]

(2) *CONSTRUCTION.* The Inheritance Tax Act 1984 provides that so far as any provision in any document, whenever executed, refers (in whatever terms) to estate duty or death duties, it shall have effect, so far as may be, as if it also referred to inheritance tax chargeable on death.[75] Similarly any reference to capital transfer tax in any document has effect as a reference to inheritance tax.[76]

The construction of a "free of inheritance tax" provision always depends on the precise words of the particular provision, which must be read in the context of the will as a whole. The existing case law on "free of duty" (*i.e.* free of estate duty) provisions does, however, give some guidance to the likely construction of "free of inheritance tax" provisions. On the basis of this case law the court will probably adopt the following approach:

   (i) The court will presume that a "free of inheritance tax" provision is intended by the testator to apply only to tax payable in respect of his own death and not to tax payable in respect of any other event, such as the subsequent death of a beneficiary who takes a life interest under the testator's will.[77]
   (ii) A direction in a will to pay "testamentary expenses" out of residue will apply to inheritance tax only so far as it is a testamentary expense, and will not apply to inheritance tax payable on property outside the United Kingdom.[78] On the other hand, a direction in a will to pay "all inheritance tax" out of residue will include tax payable on property outside the United Kingdom[79] in respect of the dispositions made by the will.[80]

D.   MARSHALLING AS BETWEEN BENEFICIARIES

1. Need for marshalling

A creditor of the deceased may obtain payment out of any of the

---

[73] Administration of Estates Act 1925, s. 34(3) and Sched. 1, Pt. II, para. 8(*a*) (as to testamentary expenses); Inheritance Tax Act 1984, s. 211(2) and (3).
[74] But an exempt gift of a share of residue (such as to a spouse or to a charity) can never bear inheritance tax attributable to a non-exempt share of residue, Inheritance Tax Act 1984, s. 41.
[75] Sched. 6, para. 1; Finance Act 1986, s. 100(1).
[76] Finance Act 1986, s. 100(1).
[77] *Re Shepherd* [1949] Ch. 117; *Re Embleton's W.T.* [1965] 1 W.L.R. 840.
[78] *Re Owers* [1941] Ch. 17.
[79] *Re Pimm* [1904] 2 Ch. 345; *Re Neeld (No. 2)* [1965] 1 W.L.R. 73, 76.
[80] *Re Walley* [1972] 1 W.L.R. 257 (on construction of will, estate duty direction extended to statutory nomination but not *inter vivos* gifts)

assets, regardless of the rules as to the incidence of the deceased's expenses and debts as between the beneficiaries entitled under his will or intestacy or any variation of these rules by the deceased.[81] If a creditor is paid out of an asset which, as between the beneficiaries, is not liable to bear the burden of his debt, the doctrine of marshalling provides a remedy for the disappointed beneficiary. The doctrine ensures that the incidence rules, and not the choice of a creditor or of the personal representatives, finally prevail as between the beneficiaries.[82]

2. Effect of marshalling

Under the doctrine of marshalling equity adjusts the remaining assets so as to compensate B, the disappointed beneficiary. Suppose that the creditor has obtained payment out of Blackacre, which was specifically devised to B by the deceased in his will and which therefore falls within paragraph 6 of the statutory order of application of assets. If the deceased did not vary the statutory order by his will, any property falling within paragraphs 1 to 5 of the statutory order is liable for expenses and debts before Blackacre. So B is entitled to compensation out of any property falling within paragraphs 1 to 5.

> "The general principle of marshalling is that if any beneficiary is disappointed of his benefit under the will through a creditor being paid out of the property intended for the beneficiary, then to the extent of the disappointment the beneficiary may recoup or compensate himself by going against any property which ought to have been used to pay the debts before resorting to his property."[83]

Again, if other property was specifically devised or bequeathed by the deceased in his will, B is entitled to insist that it must contribute rateably to the payment of the debt.[84]

3. Assessment of compensation

Compensation is assessed so as to make good to the disappointed beneficiary what he has lost. In *Re Broadwood*[85] T by his will gave all his shares in a named company to his son if he attained the age of 21 years. T's executors sold some of the shares at 17s. 6d. each in order to pay T's debts. Later T's son attained 21 years and under the doctrine of marshalling became entitled to compensation (from the fund retained to meet T's pecuniary legacies) for his disappointment in not receiving the shares which had been sold. When T's son attained 21 years. the shares were worth only 5s. each. The court held that the compensation must be measured by the loss to the son at the date when he attained 21 years and

---

[81] *Ante,* p. 420.

[82] *Aldrich v. Cooper* (1803) 8 Ves. 382, 396; *Re Cohen* [1960] Ch. 179, 190. See also Administration of Estates Act 1925, s. 2(3).

[83] *Snell's Principles of Equity* (25th ed., 1960), p. 337, quoted in *Re Matthews' W.T.* [1961] 1 W.L.R 1415, 1419. See also *Re Wilson* [1967] Ch. 53, 72.

[84] *Tombs v. Roch* (1846) 2 Coll. 490; *Gervis v. Gervis* (1847) 14 Sim. 654: see also *Re Cohen, supra.*

[85] [1911] 1 Ch. 277.

became entitled to a transfer of the shares—*i.e.* 5s., and not 17s. 6d., per share.[86]

III. INSOLVENT ESTATES

The deceased's estate is insolvent if the assets, when realised, will be insufficient to meet in full all his funeral, testamentary and administration expenses, debts and liabilities.[1] Solvency or insolvency is a question of fact.[2] If there is doubt as to the solvency of the deceased's estate, the prudent course is for the personal representatives to administer the estate in accordance with the rules applicable to an insolvent estate and make no distribution to the beneficiaries, until it becomes certain that the estate is solvent.

If the deceased's estate is insolvent but is not being administered in bankruptcy,[3] certain provisions of the law of bankruptcy are applicable in the administration of the deceased's estate. These provisions are specified in the Administration of Insolvent Estates of Deceased Persons Order 1986[4] and, unlike the incidence rules applicable in the case of a solvent estate, they cannot be varied by a contrary intention on the part of the deceased.[5] The provisions regulate "competition" between the creditors as to which of them shall be paid—the creditors cannot all be paid in full and, of course, nothing is distributable to the beneficiaries.

Under the Administration of Insolvent Estates of Deceased Persons Order 1986:

(i) The reasonable funeral, testamentary, and administration expenses have priority over preferential debts.[6]

(ii) The bankruptcy rules apply to the administration of the estate "with respect to the respective rights of secured and unsecured creditors, to debts and liabilities provable, to the valuation of future and contingent liabilities and to the priorities of debts and other payments."[7]

Thus some, but by no means all, of the bankruptcy rules are applicable to the administration of the deceased's insolvent estate by personal representatives.

The administration of a deceased's insolvent estate may be carried out in three different ways—*i.e.*:

---

[86] Plus any dividends paid in respect of the period since T's death.

[1] Insolvency Act 1986, s. 421(4); see *Re Leng* [1895] 1 Ch. 652, 658.

[2] *Re Pink* [1927] 1 Ch. 237, 241–242: see also *Re Smith* (1883) 22 Ch.D. 586, 592 (the court may direct an inquiry whether the estate is insolvent) and *George Lee & Sons (Builders) Ltd* v. *Olink* [1972] 1 W.L.R. 214 (inquiry ordered).

[3] The deceased may have been adjudicated bankrupt before his death, in which case the estate continues to be administered in bankruptcy

[4] S.I. 1986 No. 1999, made under the Insolvency Act 1986, s. 421.

[5] *Re Rothermere* [1943] 1 All E.R. 307; *Turner* v. *Cox* (1853) 8 Moo. P.C. 288.

[6] *Post*, pp. 442 *et seq.*

[7] Administration of Insolvent Estates of Deceased Persons Order 1986 (S.I. 1986 No 1999) Art. 4(1).

(i) by the personal representatives out of court (this is the usual method);

(ii) under the directions of the court in an administration action[8]; or

(iii) in bankruptcy, after an insolvency administration order has been made by the bankruptcy court for the administration in bankruptcy of the deceased's estate.

Under the Insolvency Act 1986, an insolvency administration order may be made upon the petition of the personal representatives or of a creditor whose debt would have been sufficient to support a bankruptcy petition against the deceased if still alive.[9] If such an order is made, the official receiver acts as receiver of the deceased's estate[10] until the appointment of a trustee in bankruptcy,[11] in whom the deceased's estate vests on his appointment.[12] The trustee carries out the administration in bankruptcy of the deceased's estate. But the same rules as to payment of funeral, testamentary and administration expenses and debts apply, irrespective of the way in which the administration of the deceased's insolvent estate is carried out.[13]

A. ASSETS, EXPENSES AND DEBTS

1. What are assets?

The question what property constitutes assets for the payment of the deceased's debts and liabilities was considered at the beginning of this chapter.[14] The special rules of bankruptcy, which in certain circumstances add the property of third persons to a bankrupt's assets for the benefit of his creditors, apply only if an insolvency administration order has been made by the bankruptcy court for the administration in bankruptcy of the deceased's estate: these special rules cover, for instance, transactions entered into by the deceased at an undervalue,[15] preferences by the deceased,[16] and extortionate credit transactions between the deceased

---

[8] *Post*, pp. 503 *et seq*. The court in which proceedings for administration have been commenced may, if satisfied the estate is insolvent, transfer proceedings to the bankruptcy court, Insolvency Act 1986, s. 271, as modified by the Order (S.I. 1986 No. 1999), para. 3 and Sched. 1. References to this Act "as modified" mean as modified by this Order.

[9] ss. 264, 267, 269, and 271–273, as modified; the "bankruptcy level" is currently £750, s. 267(4); for other persons who may petition see s. 264(1)(c) and (d).

[10] ss. 287–289 and 291, as modified.

[11] ss. 292–297, as modified: the official receiver may become the trustee, *ibid*.

[12] s. 306.

[13] ss. 305, 328–329 and 386–387 and Sched. 6, as modified. Exceptionally s. 347(1) (right of landlord to distrain for only six months' rent accrued due before the date of the insolvency administration order) applies in an administration in bankruptcy of the deceased's estate, but not otherwise, *Re Fryman's Estate* (1888) 38 Ch.D. 468; *Re Wells* [1929] 2 Ch. 269.

[14] *Ante*, pp. 408 *et seq*. On an administration of the deceased's estate in bankruptcy, such clothing, bedding, furniture, household equipment and provisions as are necessary for satisfying the basic domestic needs of the deceased's family are excluded from the deceased's estate, Insolvency Act 1986, s. 283(2), as modified; see also ss. 308–309. As to the deceased's dwelling-house see ss. 313 and 336–337.

[15] ss. 339 and 341–342, as modified.

[16] ss. 340–342, as modified.

and a creditor.[17] In *Re Palmer*,[18] the Court of Appeal held that an insolvency administration order, made after the deceased's death, took effect at the moment of his death and caused all property vested in him at the moment of his death to become vested in his trustee in bankruptcy, but that it did not operate to include in the estate any interest in property which had ceased at the moment of his death. Accordingly, the deceased's interest in a joint tenancy which ceased at the moment of his death, accrued by right of survivorship to his surviving joint tenant and did not form part of the "estate of a deceased person" over which the insolvency administration order had effect. This meant that the deceased's interest was not available to his creditors.

2. Funeral, testamentary and administration expenses

These expenses (so far as they are reasonable) take priority over the deceased's preferential debts.[19] In all probability the deceased's funeral expenses[20] retain their long-established priority over the testamentary and administration expenses.[21]

3. Debts and liabilities

The bankruptcy rules apply with respect to the debts and liabilities provable in the administration of the deceased's insolvent estate.

(1) *DEBTS AND LIABILITIES PROVABLE AT THEIR VALUE.* All debts and liabilities of the deceased, present or future, certain or contingent, are provable against his insolvent estate. It is immaterial whether the amount of a debt or liability is fixed or liquidated, or is capable of being ascertained by fixed rules or as a matter of opinion.[22] Again it is immaterial whether the liability arises under an enactment, a breach of trust, a contract, a tort,[23] a bailment, or out of an obligation to make restitution.[24]

If a debt or liability of the deceased does not bear a certain value, by reason of its being subject to any contingency or for any other reason, its value must be estimated.[25]

(2) *SET-OFF.* Where there have been mutual dealings between the

---

[17] s. 343, as modified.
[18] [1994] Ch. 316.
[19] *Post,* pp. 442 *et seq.*
[20] *Ante,* pp. 411–412.
[21] *R. v. Wade* (1818) 5 Price 621, 627; *Re Walter* [1929] 1 Ch. 647 (funeral expenses of bankrupt).
[22] Insolvency Act 1986, s. 382(1) and (3). A statute-barred debt is not provable, *Ex p. Dewdney, ex p. Seaman* (1809) 15 Ves. 479, (1815) 19 Ves. 467: and counsel's fees are not provable against a deceased solicitor's insolvent estate, *Re Sandiford (No. 2)* [1935] Ch. 681.
[23] *Ante,* pp. 374–375.
[24] Insolvency Act 1986, s. 382(2) and (4).
[25] Insolvency Act 1986, s. 322(3): any person dissatisfied with the estimate may apply to the court, which may assess its value, s. 303. As to the value of contingent debts or liabilities see *Hardy v. Fothergill* (1888) 13 App.Cas. 351; *Re Bridges* (1881) 17 Ch.D. 342; *Re McMahon* [1900] 1 Ch. 173 (company may prove for estimated value of liability of deceased insolvent shareholder for future calls).

deceased and another person, an account must be taken and the sum due from the one party must be set off against that due from the other, and only the balance of the account is to be claimed.[26]

(3) *INTEREST ON DEBTS.* If a debt bears interest, arrears of interest are provable as part of the debt for any period up to the date of the insolvency administration order.[27] Probably, in an administration out of court or under the directions of the court in an administration action, interest borne by a debt ought to be calculated up to the date of death of the deceased.[28]

B. ORDER OF PRIORITY OF DEBTS

The order of priority of debts in the administration of a deceased's insolvent estate is governed by the bankruptcy rules.[29]

1. Debts of secured creditors

A secured creditor holds security for his debt (whether a mortgage, charge, lien or other security) over property of the deceased.[30] A typical instance is a bank or building society holding a mortgage on the deceased's house. Under the bankruptcy rules the rights of a secured creditor are as follows:

(i) He may rely on his security and not prove for his debt.[31] This is a safe course if his security is adequate.

(ii) He may realise his security and prove for the balance of his debt.[32] This is a possible course if his security is inadequate.

(iii) He may set a value on his security and prove for the balance of his debt as an unsecured creditor.[33] This is a possible course if his security is inadequate, but he values it at his own risk. If he values it too low, the personal representatives (or trustee in bankruptcy)

---

[26] Insolvency Act 1986, s. 323; *Watkins v. Lindsay & Co.* (1898) 67 L.J.Q.B. 362; *Re D.H. Curtis (Builders) Ltd.* [1978] Ch. 162.

[27] Insolvency Act 1986, s. 322(2), as modified. This reference to the date of the insolvency administration order is a drafting error: it should refer to the date of death of the deceased debtor, so as to be consistent with ss. 328(4) and 329(2), as modified, which provide for interest since the date of death, see *post*, pp. 443–444.

[28] The bankruptcy rule applies (*Re Bush* [1930] 2 Ch. 202; *Re Theo. Garvin Ltd.* [1969] 1 Ch. 624) but cannot be applied literally: see also *Re Sagor* [1930] W.N. 149 (interest allowed to date of order by court for administration).

[29] Administration of Estates of Deceased Persons Order 1986 (S.I. 1986 No 1999) Arts. 3 and 4.

[30] Insolvency Act 1986, s. 383(2): a lien on documents is disregarded unless the documents are held as giving a title to property, s. 383(4).

[31] *ibid.* s. 285(4).

[32] *ibid.* s. 322(1); Insolvency Rules 1986 (S.I. 1986 No. 1925), rr. 6.109 and 6.119.

[33] Insolvency Rules 1986, rr. 6.96 and 6.98. The creditor has a limited power to alter his valuation, r. 6.115; *Re Becher* [1944] Ch. 78.

will exercise their right to redeem the security at his value.[34] If he values it too high, he will prove for too small a balance.[35]

(iv) He may surrender his security and prove for the whole debt.[36] This course is not advisable if his security has any value.

In so far as a secured creditor obtains the payment of his debt by realising his security, he enjoys priority over the deceased's funeral, testamentary and administration expenses and unsecured creditors. On the other hand, in so far as a secured creditor proves for his debt, he is in the same position, and entitled to the same priority, as an unsecured creditor.

The deceased's reasonable funeral, testamentary and administration expenses take priority over the debts of unsecured creditors. The latter are payable according to the following order of priority, under which four classes of debts exist, *i.e.* specially preferred, preferential, ordinary and deferred debts.

2. Specially preferred debts

The first class is specially preferred debts. These are:

(i) *money or property belonging to any friendly society*, which was in the possession of the deceased as an officer of the society[37]:

(ii) *proper expenses incurred by the trustee under a deed of arrangement* which has subsequently been avoided by the bankruptcy of the debtor,[38] or incurred as expenses of the administration of a voluntary arrangement under the Insolvency Act 1986.[39]

These specially preferred debts[40] must be met out of the deceased's insolvent estate before any of his other debts are paid.[41]

3. Preferential debts

The preferential debts are next payable, ranking equally between themselves, so that if there are insufficient assets to pay them all in full they must all abate proportionately.[42] The preferential debts are listed in Schedule 6 to the Insolvency Act 1986.[43] The categories of preferential debts are as follows:

(i) *Money owed to the Inland Revenue for income tax deducted at source*: this category covers sums due at death[44] from the deceased on

---

[34] Insolvency Rules 1986, r. 6.117: alternatively they may insist on sale, r. 6.118.
[35] *Re Hopkins* (1881) 18 Ch.D. 370.
[36] Insolvency Rules 1986, r. 6.109(2).
[37] Friendly Societies Act 1974, s. 59.
[38] Deeds of Arrangement Act 1914, s. 21; see *Re Geen* [1917] 1 K.B. 183.
[39] Insolvency Act 1986, ss. 264(1)(c) and 276.
[40] See Regimental Debts Act 1893, s. 2 (preferential debts of persons dying while subject to military law); Ley (1971) 35 Conv.(N.S.) 420: see also Insolvency Act s. 348(4).
[41] Insolvency Act 1986, s. 328(6).
[42] Insolvency Act 1986, s. 328(1) and (2).
[43] *ibid.* s. 386.
[44] *ibid.* s. 387(6), as modified. If at death an interim receiver has been appointed under s. 286, the date on which the interim receiver was first appointed is the relevant date, and not the date of death, throughout Sched. 6.

account of PAYE income tax deductions from his employees' remuneration paid during the period of 12 months before his death.[45]

(ii) *VAT, car tax, betting and gaming duties.* This category covers VAT referable to the period of six months before death[46]; car tax which became due within 12 months before the death; and certain betting and gaming duties due within the same period.[47]

(iii) *Social Security Contributions.* This category covers certain Social Security contributions due within the 12 months before death.[48]

(iv) *Certain Pension scheme contributions.*[49]

(v) *Remuneration of employees.* This covers any amount owed by the deceased to an employee or former employee by way of remuneration[50] in respect of the period of four months before his death, but not exceeding £800 (being the limit currently prescribed by order by the Secretary of State[51]).

If any person has distrained on the goods of the deceased within three months before an insolvency administration order is made, the distrained goods, or their proceeds of sale, are charged for the benefit of the deceased's estate with the specially preferred and preferential debts of the deceased to the extent that the deceased's estate is insufficient to meet these debts.[52]

4. Ordinary debts

Next in order of priority come the ordinary debts, *i.e.* all other debts except the deferred debts (considered below).

All the ordinary debts rank equally between themselves and if they cannot be paid in full they must all abate proportionately.[53] A creditor does not obtain any priority over the other creditors by obtaining judgment for his debt against the personal representatives.[54]

5. Interest on preferential and ordinary debts since death

Next in order of priority, interest is payable on all the preferential and ordinary debts in respect of the periods during which they have been outstanding since the death of the deceased. Interest on these debts ranks

---

[45] And in respect of deductions required to be made by the deceased for that period under Income and Corporation Taxes Act 1988, s. 559 (sub-contractors in the construction industry).

[46] Insolvency Act 1986, Sched. 6, para. 3.

[47] Betting and Gaming Duties Act 1981, s. 12(1), s14 and Sched. 2.

[48] Under Social Security Contributions and Benefits Act 1992.

[49] Being a sum to which Pension Schemes Act 1993, Sched. 4 applies (imposing 4 or 12 months' time limits).

[50] This is widely defined in Insolvency Act 1986, Sched. 6, paras. 13–15 so as to include certain sums due under the Employment Protection (Consolidation) Act 1978 and the Trade Union and Labour Relations (Consolidation) Act 1992.

[51] Insolvency Proceedings (Monetary Limits) Order 1986 (S.I. 1986 No. 1996), para. 4.

[52] Insolvency Act 1986, s. 347(3): the person distraining ranks as a preferential creditor to the extent that the charge operates, *Ibid.* s. 347(4)

[53] *ibid.* s. 328(3).

[54] *Pritchard v. Westminster Bank Ltd.* [1969] 1 W.L.R. 547.

equally, irrespective of the priority accorded to the debts themselves.[55] The rate of interest payable on a debt is whichever is the greater of (i) the rate specified in section 17 of the Judgments Act 1838[56] at the death (currently 8 per cent.[57]), and (ii) the rate applicable to that debt apart from the bankruptcy.[58]

6. Deferred debts

Deferred debts come last in the order of priority. They include debts owed in respect of credit provided by a person who was the spouse of the deceased at the latter's death.[59]

C.   FAILURE TO OBSERVE THE ORDER OF PRIORITY OF DEBTS

1. Liability for payment of inferior debt

A personal representative is under a duty to administer a deceased's insolvent estate in accordance with the statutory rules as to the payment of debts.[60] He is therefore liable for a breach of this duty (constituting a *devastavit*) if he fails to observe the order of priority of debts. Thus the personal representative incurs liability if he applies the deceased's assets in paying an inferior debt (*e.g.* a deferred debt) which he ought not to have paid, and leaves unpaid a superior debt (*e.g.* a preferential or ordinary debt) which he ought to have paid because he had notice of it. His payment of the inferior debt constitutes an admission by him that he has assets sufficient to satisfy all debts of which he then has notice and which have priority over the inferior debt: if the deceased's assets are not sufficient, the personal representative is personally liable to pay all such debts.[61] But the personal representative does not incur liability if, acting in good faith and without undue haste, he pays an inferior debt without notice of a superior debt.[62]

2. Duty to pay debts of the same class *pari passu*

Formerly a personal representative had a right of preference, *i.e.* a right to prefer one creditor of the same class to another, and a right of retainer,

---

[55] Insolvency Act 1986, s. 328(4), as modified.
[56] As amended by Administration of Justice Act 1970, s. 44.
[57] Judgment Debts (Rate of Interest) Order 1993 (S.I. 1993 No. 564).
[58] Insolvency Act 1986, s. 328(5), as modified.
[59] *ibid.* s. 329, as modified.
[60] Administration of Estates Act 1925, s. 25 as amended by Administration of Estates Act 1971, s. 9; Insolvency Act 1986, s. 421; Administration of Insolvent Estates of Deceased Persons Order 1986 (S.I. 1986 No. 1999).
[61] 2 Bl. Comm. 511: see *Britton v. Batthurst* (1683) 3 Lev. 113; *Rock v. Layton* (1700) 1 Ld. Raym. 589.
[62] *Harman v. Harman* (1686) 2 Show. 492; *Re Fludyer* [1898] 2 Ch. 562 ("Since the case of *Harman v. Harman* it has been considered settled law that an executor who pays creditors without notice of the existence of a creditor of higher degree is not liable to account for the sums so paid at the instance of that creditor"). Contrast the position of a personal representative who distributes to *beneficiaries* without notice of an unpaid debt of the deceased, *ante*, p. 415.

i.e. a right to pay his own debt in full in preference to other creditors of the same class as himself. These ancient common law rights of preference and retainer were abolished by section 10(1) of the Administration of Estates Act 1971 as from January 1, 1972.[63] A personal representative is generally under a duty to pay all debts of the same class *pari passu*.[64]

3. Personal representative having no reason to believe estate insolvent

Section 10(2) of the Administration of Estates Act 1971 provides *partial* protection for a personal representative who pays a debt when he has no reason to believe that the deceased's estate is insolvent. Under section 10(2) a personal representative who, in good faith and at a time when he has no reason to believe that the deceased's estate is insolvent, pays the debt of any creditor (including himself, unless he took letters of administration in his capacity as creditor) is not liable to account to creditors of the same class as the paid creditor if it subsequently appears that the estate is insolvent. This does not protect the personal representative against creditors of a superior class, to whom the personal representative is liable to account if he had notice of them.[65] Section 10(2) was introduced to enable a personal representative to pay tradesmen's bills at an early stage in the administration.[66] But it does not provide any protection to a personal representative if he has any reason to believe that the deceased's estate is insolvent because, for instance, a particular asset is of dubious value or a particular liability is of dubious extent.[67]

---

[63] s. 14(2): and see Law Com. No. 31, paras. 5 and 7–9: for criticism see Sunnucks (1972) 122 New L.J. 26.

[64] *Pari passu* is a Latin expression meaning "on an equal footing" or "proportionately to their respective claims".

[65] *cf.* Law Com. No. 31, para. 8, esp. n. 16.

[66] Law Com. No. 31, para. 8.

[67] For the court's power to relieve a personal representative from liability see Trustee Act 1925, ss. 61, 68(1)(17) and 69(1), *post*, pp. 502–503.

CHAPTER 18

INCIDENCE OF GENERAL LEGACIES

The classification of legacies as specific, general or demonstrative was explained in Chapter 7.

In Chapter 17 there was a discussion as to the incidence of debts where an estate is solvent.[1]

This Chapter deals with the incidence of general legacies.[2]

The rules which govern the incidence of general legacies (including general annuities)[3] cannot be stated with any certainty.[4] Obviously rules are needed in order to determine:

(a) which assets are applicable for the payment of general legacies; and

(b) the order in which such assets are to be applied for this purpose.

The rules in force on the death of a testator before 1926 were clear and well settled, though perhaps in need of reform. Unfortunately, it is not certain to what extent the Administration of Estates Act 1925 has altered them where the testator dies after 1925. The primary responsibility for the present uncertainty rests with the draftsman of the Act but the judicial decisions since 1925 are themselves in a state of confusion.[5] To avoid possible litigation, any draftsman of a will needs to consider inserting in it an express provision as to the incidence of general legacies.

A. THE RULES BEFORE 1926

Before 1926, general legacies were payable only out of the testator's general personal estate, *i.e.* that part of his personal estate which was

---

[1] *Ante*, pp. 420.
[2] There is no problem with the incidence of legacies where the estate is insolvent—if it is insolvent, no legacies are paid.
[3] For Annuities, see Chap. 7.
[4] See generally E.C. Ryder [1956] C.L.J. 80; *Theobald on Wills* (15th ed., 1993), pp. 807 *et seq.*
[5] Ryder, *loc. cit.* p. 100; Theobald, *op. cit.* p. 809; *Re Taylor's Estate* [1969] 2 Ch. 245, 253 ("it is not unlikely that in some future [case] the riddle will go before some higher court to which the problem of interpreting the Act and reconciling the authorities may seem simpler that it appears to me. Failing that it may conceivably be considered for a measure of aggiornamento at the hands of the Law Commission and the Legislature").

not the subject of an effective specific legacy.[6] This rule applied unless any contrary intention was shown by the testator in his will.

1.   General personal estate alone applicable

Thus, before 1926, personal estate which was the subject of an effective specific legacy was exempt from the payment of general legacies. So, too, was all the testator's realty. The exemption of specific legacies probably gave effect (and would today still probably give effect) to most testators' likely intention.[7] It appears improbable, however, that by 1925 the exemption of all the testator's realty gave effect to his likely intention[8]: in this respect the pre-1926 rules probably needed reform, so as to make the testator's general real estate (which was not the subject of an effective specific devise) liable for the payment of general legacies.

2.   General personal estate liable *pari passu*

Before 1926 every part of the testator's general personal estate was liable *pari passu* for the payment of general legacies, whether or not it was effectively disposed of by will or passed on intestacy. If T by his will gave his residuary personal estate to X and Y as tenants in common in equal shares, and X pre-deceased T so that his share lapsed and went on intestacy to T's next-of-kin, the burden of T's general legacies fell *pari passu* on Y's share and the next-of-kin's share of T's residuary personal estate.

3.   Contrary intention shown by will

The testator was free to direct by his will that his general legacies should be paid out of any property he chose to specify. Thus the rule that general legacies were payable only out of the testator's general personal estate was subject to any contrary intention shown by the testator in his will.[9] In this connection two well-known rules of construction became established.

(1)   *THE RULE IN GREVILLE V. BROWN.* Under the rule in *Greville v. Brown*,[10] if a testator by his will gave general legacies and gave the residue of his real and personal property as one mass, this charged the realty with the legacies in aid of the personalty: accordingly the legacies were payable primarily out of the personalty, but were payable out of the realty so far as the personalty proved to be insufficient. The justification for the rule was that, by giving the residue of his real and personal property as one mass, the testator showed that he intended the legacies

---

[6] *Robertson v. Broadbent* (1883) 8 App.Cas 812. But see *ante*, pp. 212–213.
[7] *ibid.* at p. 815.
[8] For a discussion of the reasons why realty was exempt see Theobald, *op. cit.* p. 808.
[9] For the case law on contrary intention see *Hawkins and Ryder on the Construction of Wills* (1965), pp. 367 *et. seq.*
[10] (1859) 7 H.L.C. 689: see also *Elliott v. Dearsley* (1881) 16 Ch. D. 322; *Re Boards* [1895] 1 Ch. 499.

to be treated as a deduction from the entire mass.[11] It was immaterial how the residuary gift was worded provided that there was in substance a single gift, comprising both residuary realty and residuary personalty, to the same person or persons, and it did not matter whether they took beneficially or as trustees.[12]

(2) *THE RULE IN ROBERTS V. WALKER.* Under the rule in *Roberts v. Walker*,[13] if a testator by his will *directed* payment of legacies out of a mixed fund of realty and personalty, the legacies were payable rateably out of the realty and personalty in proportion to their respective values. This rule applied in the common case of a gift by a testator of his residuary real and personal estate[14] to trustees upon trust for sale and conversion, and upon trust to pay the legacies given by his will out of the moneys arising from the sale and conversion of his residuary real and personal estate: accordingly in this case the legacies were payable rateably out of the residuary realty and residuary personalty.[15]

B. THE RULES AFTER 1925

So to what extent has the Administration of Estates Act 1925 altered these pre-1926 rules where the testator dies after 1925? The only provisions of the Act which need to be considered are section 33, in relation to the administration of assets on a partial intestacy, and section 34(3) which refers to the statutory order of application of assets set out in Part II of the First Schedule.

1. Effect of section 33

The effect on the incidence of general legacies of section 33 of the Act is material only if the testator dies partially intestate. Section 33(1) provides that "on the death of a person intestate as to any real or personal estate" such estate (if not already money) shall be held by his personal representatives upon trust for sale and conversion into money. Section 33(2) must be quoted in full:

"Out of the net money to arise from the sale and conversion of such real and personal estate (after payment of costs), and out of the ready

---

[11] (1859) 7 H.L.C. 689 at p. 697.

[12] *Greville v. Brown* (1859) 7 H.L.C. 689 ("all the rest, residue and remainder of any property I may die possessed of or entitled to, of what nature soever"); *Re Bawden* [1894] 1 Ch. 693 ("all the real and personal estate to which at my death I shall be beneficially entitled . . . and not otherwise disposed of": rule applicable—the testator need not use the word "residue").

[13] (1830) 1 R. & My. 752; see also *Allan v. Gott* (1872) L.R. 7 Ch. App. 439; *Re Spencer Cooper* [1908] 1 Ch, 130.

[14] Or of all his real and personal estate, *Stocker v. Harbin* (1841) 3 Beav. 479; *Salt v. Chattaway* (1841) 3 Beav. 576.

[15] *Re Spencer Cooper, supra.* The rule was also applicable where a power to sell realty and personalty was conferred on trustees provided the testator showed an intention to create a mixed fund for the payment of legacies, *Allan v. Gott,* supra: *cf. Boughton v. Boughton* (1848) 1 H.L.C. 406 and *Tench v. Cheese* (1855) 6 De G.M. & G. 453.

money of the deceased (so far as not disposed of by his will, if any), the personal representative shall pay all such funeral, testamentary and administration expenses, debts and other liabilities as are properly payable thereout having regard to the rules of administration contained in this Part of this Act, and out of the residue of the said money the personal representative shall set aside a fund sufficient to provide for any pecuniary legacies bequeathed by the will (if any) of the deceased."

The special rule applicable to debts charged on the deceased's property under section 35 of the Act is, of course, not affected by section 33(2). Finally, section 33(7) enacts that section 33 has effect subject to the provisions contained in the testator's will.

(1) *SECTION 33(2) MAKES UNDISPOSED-OF PROPERTY PRIMARILY LIABLE.* If a testator dies after 1925 partially intestate, and section 33(2) applies in respect of the property undisposed of by his will, then under section 33(2) the net money arising from the sale and conversion of that property and the testator's ready money (if undisposed of by his will) are first to be applied in payment of the testator's expenses, debts and liabilities, and next a pecuniary legacy fund is to be set aside out of the residue of that money. Thus section 33(2), where it applies, has altered the old rules as to the incidence of general legacies by throwing their burden primarily on the undisposed-of property, whether it is realty or personalty or both.

In *Re Worthington*[16] T by her will gave general legacies and gave all the residue of her estate both real and personal to A and B in equal shares. A predeceased T, and so A's share lapsed and went as on T's intestacy. If the pre-1926 rules had still applied, the incidence of the legacies would have been governed by the rule in *Greville v. Brown*, and they would have been payable primarily out of the residuary personalty (whether or not it went as on intestacy), with residuary realty only liable in aid. But the Court of Appeal held in *Re Worthington* that the legacies were payable primarily out of the lapsed share of residue. It follows that, where section 33(2) is applicable, the old rules have clearly been altered so as to make the undisposed-of property primarily liable for legacies.

(2) *WHEN IS SECTION 33(2) APPLICABLE?* If section 33(2) is applicable, its effect on the incidence of general legacies is clear. Unfortunately there is some uncertainty as to when section 33(2) applies. First consider two situations where section 33(2) applies:

(i) T dies wholly intestate as to one or more assets of his estate: each such asset (if not already money) is held upon the statutory trust for sale and conversion imposed by section 33(1),[17] and section 33(2) applies to the net money arising from the sale and to any of T's undisposed-of ready money.[18]

---

[16] [1933] Ch. 771; followed in *Re Berrey's W.T.* [1959] 1 W.L.R. 30.

[17] *cf. Re McKee* [1931] 2 Ch. 145, 159, 160 and 165–166; *Re Plowman* [1943] Ch. 269.

[18] *Re Martin* [1955] Ch. 698 (intestacy as to realty so that s. 33(1) and (2) applicable: but legacies held payable out of realty under para. 1): see *post*, pp. 454–455.

(ii) T dies wholly intestate as to a share in his residuary estate (e.g. A's share of T's residuary estate which lapsed and went as on T's intestacy in *Re Worthington*): such share is held upon the statutory trust for sale and conversion imposed by section 33(1). Again section 33(2) applies to the net money arising from the sale.[19]

But a different situation arises where T creates an effective trust for sale by his will and some beneficial interest thereunder (e.g. a life interest or a share of capital) fails. Suppose that T by his will makes certain gifts, including general legacies, and gives his residuary real and personal estate to trustees upon trust for sale and conversion, and to hold the money arising from such sale and conversion upon trust for his nieces X and Y as tenants in common in equal shares. T dies after 1925. X predeceases T, and so X's share lapses and goes as on T's intestacy. The express trust for sale in T's will remains effective, and this express trust for sale excludes the statutory trust for sale imposed by section 33(1) (because there cannot be two subsisting trusts for sale at the same time, and section 33 is expressly made subject to the provisions contained in T's will.[20]) But does section 33(2) still apply to X's share which goes as on T's intestacy? In all probability section 33(2) does not apply to X's share because section 33(2) appears to apply only to the net money arising from the *statutory* trust for sale and to any of T's undisposed-of ready money.[21]

If, however, the express trust for sale in T's will fails owing to the *complete* failure of its objects (e.g. because, in the above example, both X and Y predeceased T and both their shares lapsed), then the statutory trust for sale imposed by section 33(1) applies, and section 33(2) applies to the net money arising from the sale.

2. Effect of section 34(3) and the statutory order

The effect on the incidence of general legacies of section 34(3) and the statutory order of application of assets needs to be considered in several different situations:

(i) if the testator dies partially intestate and section 33(2) applies, but the legacies cannot be paid in full out of the pecuniary legacy fund set aside out of the undisposed-of property falling within section 33(2)—this undisposed-of property is first applied in payment of the testator's expenses, debts and liabilities;

(ii) if the testator dies partially intestate but section 33(2) does not apply; and

[19] *Re Berrey's W.T.* [1959] 1 W.L.R. 30 (gift of residue by T to A, B, C and D equally; B predeceased T, causing B's share to lapse and go as on T's intestacy: held s. 33(1) and (2) applied to B's share, and general legacies were payable primarily out of B's share).
[20] *Re McKee, supra*, esp. at pp. 159 and 165–166; *Re Taylor's Estate* [1969] 2 Ch. 245.
[21] *Re McKee, supra*, at pp. 165–166 (on the meaning of "real and personal estate" in s. 33); *Re Taylor's Estate, supra*; *Re Beaumont's W.T.* [1950] Ch. 462 as explained in *Re Berrey's W.T., supra*, at p. 40. But *cf.* Albery (1969) 85 L.Q.R. 464, 467 who suggests that "ready money" in s. 33(2) includes the proceeds of sale arising under an express trust for sale in T's will; *sed quaere*.

(iii) if the testator dies fully testate—in this case section 33 never applies.

Section 34(3) of the Administration of Estates Act 1925 provides that the testator's real and personal estate shall, subject to any provisions contained in his will, be applicable towards the discharge of "the funeral, testamentary and administration expenses, debts and liabilities payable thereout" in the statutory order mentioned in Part II of the First Schedule. Under that statutory order the testator's undisposed-of property "subject to the retention thereout of a fund sufficient to meet any pecuniary legacies" is primarily liable under paragraph 1, and the testator's property included in a residuary gift "subject to the retention out of such property of a fund sufficient to meet any pecuniary legacies, so far as not provided for as aforesaid" is next liable under paragraph 2. As has been noted already, no distinction is made between realty and personalty in the statutory order, and all the realty and personalty falling within any particular paragraph is liable rateably for the testator's expenses, debts and liabilities.[22]

Under paragraphs 1 and 2 the order of resort is different from that specified in section 33(2)—under both paragraphs 1 and 2 the pecuniary legacy fund is set aside *first*, and the *balance* of the undisposed-of property, or property included in a residuary gift, is liable for expenses, debts and liabilities.[23] Probably the different order of resort specified in section 33(2) is due to a drafting error. Unfortunately different orders of resort may well produce different practical results: for instance, as regards the incidence of inheritance tax on the legatees if the undisposed-of property is not sufficient to pay all the expenses, debts and liabilities and legacies in full, and resort has to be made to property of a different nature included in a residuary gift.

The effect on the incidence of general legacies of section 34(3) and the statutory order depends on their proper construction, as to which there appear to be two main views.

(1) *FIRST CONSTRUCTION—THE OLD RULES STILL APPLY.* One view is that section 34(3) and the statutory order have not altered the old rules as to the incidence of general legacies. If this view is correct, a pecuniary legacy fund is to be retained out of the testator's undisposed-of property under paragraph 1 only if and so far as this property is answerable for legacies under the old rules. Similarly, a pecuniary legacy fund is to be retained out of the testator's property included in a residuary gift under paragraph 2 only if and so far as this property is answerable for legacies under the old rules. In effect this view construes paragraphs 1 and 2 as if they read, "subject to the retention . . ." *if and so far as appropriate under the rules as to the incidence of legacies* "of a fund sufficient to meet any pecuniary legacies."[24] This view is supported by at least two first instance decisions on the construction of paragraph 2, *Re Thompson* and *Re Anstead*, and by two more first instance decisions

---

[22] *Ante*, p. 421.
[23] *Re Anstead* [1943] Ch. 161 (the headnote is wrong); *Re Wilson* [1967] Ch. 53, 70.
[24] *Re Taylor's Estate, supra*, at pp. 251–253.

on the construction of paragraph 1, *Re Beaumont's Will Trusts* and *Re Taylor's Estate*.

In *Re Thompson*[25] T by his will gave general legacies and gave all his real and personal estate not otherwise disposed of to certain charities. If the old rules still applied on a death after 1925, the incidence of his general legacies was governed by the rule in *Greville v. Brown*. In order to determine the incidence of death duties, it was necessary to decide whether the general legacies were payable (i) rateably out of residuary realty and residuary personalty, or (ii) primarily out of the residuary personalty, the residuary realty only being liable in aid under the rule in *Greville v. Brown*. Clauson J. decided in favour of the latter alternative on the ground that section 34(3) and paragraph 2 of the statutory order had not altered the old rules as to the incidence of general legacies. In his judgment he said[26]:

> "It is suggested that the effect of that provision is to alter the law, and to provide that the fund which is to be retained out of residuary realty and personalty in order to meet pecuniary legacies is to be retained in the following way: that a proportionate part is to be retained out of realty and personalty pro rata of the amount of the realty and personalty respectively. The provision does not say so, and the provision is not concerned with any such matter. The provision is concerned with the way in which funeral testamentary and administration expenses, debts and liabilities are to be met. There is no indication there that there is any intention of altering the law. . ." (as to the incidence of general legacies).

The absence of any reference to legacies in section 34(3) must be regarded, at the least, as a strong indication that the statutory order deals only with the incidence of the testator's expenses, debts and liabilities. Whether or not the statutory order was meant to alter the rules as to the incidence of legacies, the references to the pecuniary legacy fund in paragraphs 1, 2 and 5 of the statutory order were unavoidable: the statutory order had to indicate at what point the pecuniary legacy fund became liable for the testator's expenses, debts and liabilities.[27] Moreover, the words in paragraphs 1 and 2, "subject to the retention. . .," are "a curious formula" to have used if the legislature intended to impose an obligation to retain a pecuniary legacy fund regardless of the old rules.[28]

In *Re Anstead*[29] it was again necessary to decide which assets were applicable for the payment of general legacies in order to determine the incidence of death duties. T by his will gave general legacies and gave the residue of his real and personal estate upon certain trusts. The will

---

[25] [1936] Ch. 676. See also *Re Rowe* [1941] Ch. 343 where Farwell J. (perhaps *obiter*) agreed with *Re Thompson*: in *Re Rowe* T's will read. "I devise all my real estate and bequeath all the residue of my personal estate" to X and Y equally: held a specific devise and realty was not liable for legacies. But "I devise all my real estate" may be a general devise, *Re Wilson* [1967] Ch. 53: see *ante*, p. 424.

[26] [1936] Ch. 676, 682.

[27] Ryder, *loc. cit.* pp. 84–85 and 98.

[28] *Re Taylor's Estate* [1969] 2 Ch. 245, 252.

[29] [1943] Ch. 161 (the headnote is wrong): in *Re Anstead* T directed his trustees to provide for an annuity given by his will out of his residuary personal estate: no question arose as to this. See also *Re Wilson* [1967] Ch. 53, 71.

contained no direction as to the incidence of general legacies, and if the old rules still applied on a death after 1925 their incidence was governed by the rule in *Greville v. Brown*. Uthwatt J. decided that under paragraph 2 of the statutory order the first thing to be done was to set aside a pecuniary legacy fund out of residue—this was to be set aside primarily out of the residuary personalty, the residuary realty only being liable in aid if the residuary personalty proved insufficient (for which Uthwatt J. cited *Re Thompson*). The testator's expenses, debts and liabilities were then payable out of the balance of the residuary estate under paragraph 2, and the pecuniary legacy fund only became liable for expenses, debts and liabilities under paragraph 5. Thus Uthwatt J. decided that the pecuniary legacy fund was to be retained out of residue under paragraph 2 in accordance with the old rules, and not rateably out of the residuary realty and residuary personalty.

The other two decisions which support this view were on the construction of paragraph 1, which refers to the retention of a pecuniary legacy fund in similar language to paragraph 2. In *Re Beaumont's Will Trusts*[30] T by her will gave pecuniary legacies free of duty, and gave all her real estate and her personal estate not otherwise disposed of to trustees upon trust for sale and conversion, and, after payment of her expenses and debts, to stand possessed of the residue for A, B, C, and D equally. C predeceased T, and so C's share lapsed and went as on T's intestacy and fell within paragraph 1 of the statutory order. In his judgment Danckwerts J. said that section 34(3) of the Act "has in effect made no provision with regard to such things as legacies...the position of the legacies depends on the old law"[31] (and he cited *Re Thompson*). Accordingly he decided that the legacies (and the duty on them, which had the effect of an additional legacy) were payable out of the whole estate before division into four equal parts,[32] and not primarily out of C's lapsed share under paragraph 1 of the statutory order.

The same situation arose in *Re Taylor's Estate*[33] (a case decided in the Durham Chancery Court) and again the court held that the legacies were payable out of the residuary estate as a whole in accordance with the old law, and not primarily out of the lapsed share under paragraph 1 of the statutory order.

(2)　*SECOND CONSTRUCTION—PARAGRAPHS 1 AND 2 OF THE STATUTORY ORDER DETERMINE INCIDENCE.* The other view is that section 34(3) and the statutory order have altered the old rules as to the incidence of general legacies. According to this view, a pecuniary legacy fund must be retained out of the testator's undisposed-of property under paragraph 1, irrespective of whether it would have been answerable for legacies under the old rules. Logically this view also requires that a pecuniary legacy fund (so far as not provided for out of any undisposed-of property) should be retained out of the testator's property included in

---

[30] [1950] Ch. 462: see also *Re Berrey's W.T.* [1959] 1 W.L.R. 30.
[31] [1950] Ch. 462, at p. 466.
[32] Under the rule in *Greville v. Brown* the burden fell primarily on T's personalty, with realty liable in aid.
[33] [1969] 2 Ch. 245 (the Chancellor considered the construction of the statutory provisions at pp. 250–253).

a residuary gift under paragraph 2, irrespective of whether it would have been answerable for legacies under the old rules. All the decisions supporting this view have turned on the wording of paragraph 1, not paragraph 2, but it appears unlikely that the reference to the retention of a pecuniary legacy fund in paragraph 2 is to be construed differently from the similar reference in paragraph 1.[34] Assuming that this is correct, if the undisposed-of property within paragraph 1 (or the property included in a residuary gift within paragraph 2) includes both realty and personalty, it is not clear whether the legacies are payable primarily out of the personalty within that paragraph, the realty within that paragraph being only liable in aid, or whether the legacies (like the expenses and debts) are payable rateably out of the realty and the personalty within that paragraph.[35] The latter alternative seems more likely to be adopted.

Now for the cases which support this view. The clearest decision is *Re Midgley*.[36] T by her will gave pecuniary legacies and gave her residuary real and personal estate to trustees upon trust for sale and, after payment of her expenses and debts, to hold the residue upon trust for six named persons equally. By a codicil T revoked the gift to one of these persons, and consequently that person's one-sixth share went as on T's intestacy and fell within paragraph 1 of the statutory order. Harman J. held that paragraph 1 required the legacies to be paid out of his one-sixth share. He asked,[37] "What, then, is to be done with the fund which has been retained thereout?" (*i.e.* out of the undisposed-of property under paragraph 1).

> "The answer, it seems to me, is that it must be used to meet the pecuniary legacies, because it has been retained for that purpose. It is, if I may say so, a tortuous way of legislating . . ."

Of course no one challenges the proposition that a fund retained to meet pecuniary legacies should be used to pay them (unless the fund becomes liable for expenses and debts under paragraph 5). The crucial difference between the two views is over the *retention* of a fund. According to the first view, a fund is to be retained out of the undisposed-of property only if and so far as this property is answerable for legacies under the old rules. On the other hand, according to Harman J. in *Re Midgley*, a fund must be retained out of the undisposed-of property irrespective of whether it would have been answerable for legacies under the old rules.

Of the other cases which support this view, *Re Gillett's Will Trusts*[38] is weaker authority because counsel for the next-of-kin entitled on intestacy conceded that under paragraph 1 the legacies must be paid out of the testator's undisposed-of property unless the will showed a contrary intention. *Re Martin*,[39] is another decision of Danckwerts J. By his will T

---

[34] See *Re Wilson* [1967] Ch. 53, 70.
[35] *Re Martin* [1955] Ch. 698, 704–705; Ryder, *loc. cit.* pp. 99–100 suggests that under para. 2 the personalty is primarily liable.
[36] [1955] Ch. 576.
[37] *Ibid.* at p. 583.
[38] [1950] Ch. 102: see *Re Berrey's W.T.* [1959] 1 W.L.R. 30, 35.
[39] [1955] Ch. 698. See also *Re Lamb* [1929] 1 Ch. 723 (assumed, without argument, para. 1 applied) and *Re Worthington* [1933] Ch. 771 (para. 1 cited as well as s.33(2)—both were cases where s.33(2) applied.

gave pecuniary legacies, gave all his real estate to X, and gave his residuary personal estate to trustees upon certain trusts which did not fail. By a codicil T revoked the gift of his real estate to X, and so the realty went on T's intestacy and section 33(1) and (2) applied to it. The legacies were therefore payable out of the realty pursuant to section 33(2).[40] Danckwerts J. decided that the legacies were payable out of the realty, but he based his decision on paragraph 1 of the statutory order, construing paragraph 1 as if it required a pecuniary legacy fund to be retained out of the undisposed-of realty, regardless of the old rules under which the legacies were payable out of the general personal estate. Danckwerts J's earlier decision in *Re Beaumont's Will Trusts*[41] ("the position of the legacies depends on the old law") appears to be incompatible with his reasoning in *Re Martin*.

The unhappy conclusion to be drawn from this review of the statutory provisions and of more than half a century's case law on their construction is that the effect of the Administration of Estates Act 1925 has been to produce lasting uncertainty as to what rules govern the incidence of general legacies. It is unfortunate that no appellate court has ever had to decide between the two constructions of section 34(3) and the statutory order.

3. Express provision in a will as to incidence of legacies

There is, however, one comfort to be drawn from a study of the statutory provisions: they take effect subject to the provisions contained in the testator's will.[42] Accordingly the draftsman of a will may (and should) insert in the will an express provision as to the incidence of general legacies and thereby exclude whatever rules would otherwise apply. By his will a testator often gives his residuary real and personal estate to trustees upon trust for sale and conversion, and directs that out of the proceeds of such sale and conversion and his ready money they are to pay his funeral, testamentary and administration expenses and debts, and the general legacies given by his will or any codicil thereto. Such a direction ensures that, if some beneficial interest in his residuary estate fails, the general legacies are payable out of the whole residuary estate.[43]

A direction in a will as to the incidence of general legacies can remove the uncertainty which the Administration of Estates Act 1925 has produced. A "free of inheritance tax" provision in a will can avoid the trap set for testators by the rule that property outside the United Kingdom bears its own inheritance tax.[44]

---

[40] See *Re Berrey's W.T., supra* and *ante,* p. 450, n. 19, where Danckwerts J. regarded the C.A. decision in *Re Worthington* as binding authority.

[41] *Ante,* p. 453.

[42] ss. 33(7) and 34(3); Sched. 1, Pt. II, para. 8(a): see *Re Wilson* [1967] Ch. 53 (gift of specific and general legacies; gift of "all my real estate and the residue of my personal estate" to X: held will showed intention that legacies were to be paid exclusively from personal estate—real estate not liable for general legacies but liable for expenses and debts under para. 2); *Re Taylor's Estate* [1969] 2 Ch. 245, 250; *Re Feis* [1964] Ch. 106, 116–117.

[43] *cf.* Form 8 of the Statutory Will Forms 1925 (prescribed under Law of Property Act 1925, s. 179 and which may be incorporated in a will); Form 8 makes the legacies payable primarily out of personality.

[44] See *ante,* p. 435.

CHAPTER 19

INCOME AND INTEREST

This chapter covers the rules governing the income or interest carried by gifts by will. By his will the testator may make a gift of property (i) to a person beneficially or (ii) to trustees upon trust for persons in succession (*e.g.* upon trust for A for life and subject thereto for B absolutely). In each case the question arises what income or interest does the gift by will carry? But in the case of the trust for persons in succession, a second question also arises; what constitutes income to be paid to the life tenant and what constitutes capital of the trust? The answer to this second question forms part of the law of trusts and is not discussed in this book.[1]

A. SPECIFIC LEGACIES AND DEVISES

1. Immediate specific gifts

A specific legacy or specific devise which takes effect immediately carries with it all the income or profits accruing from its subject matter after the testator's death. For instance, under a specific legacy of company shares the legatee is entitled to the dividends after the testator's death.[2] Similarly, under a specific devise of Blackacre which is subject to a tenancy at the testator's death, the devisee is entitled to the rent after the testator's death.

(1) *APPORTIONMENT OF INCOME.* In order to ascertain the amount

---

[1] The rule in *Allhusen v. Whittell* (1867) L.R. 4 Eq. 295, which relates to administration is considered at the end of this Chapter. For the duty to convert under the rule in *Howe v. Earl of Dartmouth* (1802) 7 Ves. 137 (applicable to unauthorised investments comprised in a residuary bequest of personalty to be enjoyed by persons in succession), and the duty to apportion under this rule (or the rule in *Gibson v. Bott* (1802) 7 Ves. 89), the rule in *Re Earl of Chesterfield's Trusts* (1883) 24 Ch.D. 643, and the rule in *Bouch v. Sproule* (1887) 12 App.Cas. 385, see *Snell's Equity* (29th ed., 1990), pp. 226–231 and 375–379, or Hanbury and Martin *Modern Equity* (14th ed., 1993) pp. 526–539, or Pettit, *Equity and the Law of Trusts* (7th ed., 1993), pp. 404–418. The rule in *Bouch v. Sproule* was *not* followed in the recent case of *Sinclair v. Lee* [1993] Ch. 497 on the basis that strict application of the rule would have produced a result manifestly inconsistent with the testatrix's presumed intention.

[2] *Re West* [1909] 2 Ch. 180 (specific legacy of company shares carried dividends from death of testatrix); *Re Marten* [1901] 1 Ch. 370: see also *Chester v. Urwick* (1856) 23 Beav. 420 (specific legacy of one or other stocks at discretion of executors: held legatee entitled to dividends from testator's death) and *cf. Re Collins' W.T.* [1971] 1 W.L.R. 37, 42–43.

of income accruing after the testator's death it may be necessary to apportion income under section 2 of the Apportionment Act 1870. This section provides that:

"All rents, annuities, dividends, and other periodical payments in the nature of income. . .shall, like interest on money lent, be considered as accruing from day to day, and shall be apportionable in respect of time accordingly".

(a) *Effect of Apportionment Act 1870.* Consider first the specific devise of Blackacre to X by the testator T. If at his death T has a cause of action against the tenant of Blackacre for rent already due, this cause of action is an asset of his estate at his death and (like rent paid to T before his death) falls into his residuary estate.[3] If, on the other hand, rent falls due for payment after T's death, under section 2 of the Act it is apportionable in respect of the period for which it is paid: if this period overlaps T's death, X is entitled to so much of the rent as is apportioned to the time after T's death but any rent apportioned to the time before T's death falls into T's residuary estate.[4]

The Apportionment Act applies to the dividends[5] of all companies registered under the Companies Acts, whether public or private in the company law sense,[6] provided the dividend is declared in respect of some definite, though not necessarily regularly recurring, period, so that the dividend can be apportioned in respect of that period.[7]

A testator may (and usually will) exclude the operation of the Apportionment Act by words expressly so stating or requiring that conclusion by necessary implication,[8] but not by any general inference from his will.[9]

(b) *Apportionment Act not applicable.* Occasionally the Apportionment Act 1870 is not applicable—for instance, it does not apply to the profits accruing from the testator's own business of which he was the proprietor,[10] or from a share in a private partnership.[11] In these cases the profits

---

[3] *Ellis v. Rowbotham* [1900] 1 Q.B. 740; *Re Aspinall* [1961] Ch. 526 (T died at 8.30 a.m. on Xmas day: held at his death T had no cause of action for rent payable on Xmas day because cause of action accrued later at midnight)

[4] *Re Aspinall, supra.*

[5] Defined in s.5 of the Act to include "all payments made by the name of dividend, bonus, or otherwise out of the revenue of trading or other public companies. . ." but not "payments in the nature of a return or reimbursement of capital": see also *Re Griffith* (1879) 12 Ch.D. 655 (bonus on company shares out of surplus profits distributable every five years apportionable under the Act).

[6] *Re Lysaght* [1898] 1 Ch. 115; *Re White* [1913] 1 Ch. 231. See also *Re Griffith, supra* (Act applies to unincorporated life assurance society with power to sue or be sued under special Act of Parliament).

[7] *Re Jowitt* [1922] 2 Ch. 442.

[8] Apportionment Act 1870, s. 7: see *Re Lysaght* [1898] 1 Ch. 115 (specific legacy of company shares, with declaration that "every share. . .shall carry the dividend accruing thereon at my death": held Act excluded and legacy carried whole dividend for year in which testator died without apportionment); *Re Meredith* (1898) 78 L.T. 492: *cf. Re Edwards* [1918] 1 Ch. 142. See for possible reform Law Reform Committee's 23rd Report, *The powers and duties of trustees,* Cmnd. 8733 (1982), pp. 25 and 64 (recommending Act should not apply, subject to any contrary intention in the will).

[9] *Re Joel's W.T.* [1967] Ch. 14, 23–24.

[10] *Re Cox's Trusts* (1878) 9 Ch.D. 159.

[11] *Jones v. Ogle* (1872) 8 Ch. App. 192; *Re Lynch-White* [1937] 3 All E.R. 551.

are treated as having accrued entirely on the final day of the period for which they are declared.[12]

(2) *LIABILITIES.* A legatee or devisee taking under an immediate specific legacy or devise must bear the liabilities incident to the subject matter of the gift after the testator's death.[13] Consider again the specific devise of Blackacre to X by the testator T, if at T's death Blackacre is let to a tenant under a lease containing a covenant by the landlord to keep the exterior of the demised premises in repair, X must bear the expense of repairing in accordance with this covenant after T's death.[14] There are, however, two limits to the burden which X must bear:

(i) If in his lifetime T entered into a binding contract to have certain building work done at Blackacre, X as devisee is entitled to have this work carried out for his benefit after T's death at the expense of T's estate.[15]

(ii) If the covenant in the lease relates to something which was to be done by T (the landlord) preparatory to the complete establishment of the relation of landlord and tenant, then the burden of the covenant falls on T's estate and not on X. An example is a covenant to repair where the object of the covenant was to ensure that the premises were put initially into a condition fit for the occupation of the tenant.[16]

Of course, if Blackacre is subject to a mortgage debt at T's death, section 35 of the Administration of Estate Act 1925 applies and Blackacre is primarily liable for the payment of the mortgage debt, unless T has shown a contrary intention.[17]

2. Contingent or deferred specific gifts

A specific legacy or specific devise may be contingent (*e.g.* "to X if he attains the age of 30 years"), or deferred to a future date which must come sooner or later (*e.g.* "to X after the death of my wife A"), or both contingent and deferred (e.g. "to X, after the death of my wife A, if he attains the age of 30 years").

Section 175 of the Law of Property Act 1925 applies to contingent or

---

[12] *Ibbotson v. Ogle* (1866) L.R. 1Eq. 188; *Browne v. Collins* (1871) 12 Eq. 586; *Re Robbins* [1941] Ch. 434.

[13] The outgoings must be apportioned if income is apportioned, *Re Joel's W.T.* [1967] Ch. 14, 30–31. As to expenses incurred by the personal representatives in the upkeep and preservation of the subject matter of a specific devise or specific legacy, see *ante* p. 177.

[14] *Re Day's W.T.* [1962] 1 W.L.R. 1419 (X liable on covenants "of a kind incident to the relationship of landlord and tenant"); *Mansel v. Norton* (1883) 22 Ch.D. 769. As to the liabilities to be borne by a specific legatee of a leasehold see *Theobald on Wills* (15th ed., 1993), p. 820.

[15] *Re Rushbrooks's W.T.* [1948] Ch. 421: *cf. Re Day's W.T., supra,* (no binding contract to carry out any particular work).

[16] *Re Day's W.T., supra:* see also *Eccles v. Mills* [1898] A.C. 360 (covenant by landlord to finish laying down land in grass: held burden fell on his estate and not on specific devisee); *Re Hughes* [1913] 2 Ch. 491; *Re Smyth* [1965] I.R. 595.

[17] *Ante,* pp. 428 *et seq.*

deferred specific gifts in a will coming into operation after 1925. It provides as follows:

"(1) A contingent or future specific devise or bequest of property, whether real or personal, and a contingent residuary devise of freehold land, and a specific or residuary devise of freehold land to trustees upon trust for persons whose interests are contingent or executory shall, subject to the statutory provisions relating to accumulations, carry the intermediate income of that property from the death of the testator, except so far as such income, or any part thereof, may be otherwise expressly disposed of.

(2) This section applies only to wills coming into operation after the commencement of this Act."

Section 175 mentions a contingent or deferred specific devise or bequest ("future" in the section means deferred[18]), and a specific devise to trustees upon trust for persons whose interests are contingent or deferred (again "executory" in the section appears to mean deferred[19]), but the section does not mention a specific bequest to trustees upon trust for persons whose interests are contingent or executory. The omission is puzzling but such a specific bequest to trustees probably falls within the earlier reference to "a contingent or future specific. . .bequest."[20]

Where it applies, section 175 makes a contingent or deferred specific gift of property carry the intermediate income of that property, but subject to the rule that the income can only be accumulated and added to the capital for as long as the statutory rule against accumulations permits.[21] Section 175 does not, of course, apply where the intermediate income is otherwise expressly disposed of.[22]

Section 175 probably accords with the likely intentions of a testator who makes a contingent specific gift, but the same cannot be said of the deferred specific gift. If a testator makes a specific gift "to X after the death of my wife A," it seems reasonable to assume that he does not wish X to have any income which accrues before A's death. Unfortunately section 175 applies to a deferred, as well as to a contingent, specific gift.

Where there is a beneficiary living who is contingently entitled, section 31 of the Trustee Act 1925 often governs the destination of the intermediate income carried by the special gift. Under this section the personal representatives have power during the infancy of the beneficiary to apply the whole or part of the income for his maintenance, education or

---

[18] *Re McGeorge* [1963] Ch. 544, 550–552.
[19] *ibid.*
[20] See P. V. Baker (1963) 79 L.Q.R. 184, 186. For the rules applicable to wills coming into operation before 1926 see *Hawkins and Ryder on the Construction of Wills* (1965), p. 78.
[21] *Re McGeorge, supra,* (deferred specific devise, which was vested subject to being divested, held to carry intermediate income under s. 175 for permitted accumulation period): for the rule against accumulations see Law of Property Act 1925, ss. 164–166, as amended by Perpetuities and Accumulations Act 1964, s. 13.
[22] *Re Hatfield* [1958] Ch. 469 (specific devise by T to A for life, remainder to his sons successively in tail male, remainder to B for life, remainder to his sons successively in tail male, remainder to C in fee simple; T died, A died without issue, and B disclaimed his life interest; B had no son: held until the birth of a son to B the income was payable to C, and was expressly disposed of, and s. 175(1) did not apply).

benefit (accumulating any surplus income), and after the beneficiary has attained his majority the personal representatives must pay the whole income to him until he either attains a vested interest, or dies, or his interest fails.[23] Section 31 applies so far as a contrary intention is not expressed in the will.[24] The section is not applicable to intermediate income carried by a deferred specific gift, and such income must be accumulated and added to the capital for as long as the statutory rule against accumulations permits.[25]

B.   GENERAL LEGACIES

The rules now to be considered governing the interest carried by general legacies also apply to demonstrative legacies but (as has already been explained) do not apply to general annuities.

1.   Interest runs from time for payment

The basic principle is that a general legacy carries interest from the time at which it is payable. Unless the testator directs otherwise, the appropriate rate of interest is 6 per cent per annum[26] and it is simple, not compound, interest. The justification for this rule is that the interest payable compensates the legatee for any delay in paying him his legacy.

The rule is not confined to a general legacy of a sum of money but applies, for instance, to a general legacy of company shares.[27]

2.   Time for payment

The time for payment of a legacy (1) may be fixed by the testator in his will and, if not, (2) has to be fixed by rules of law.

(1)   *TIME FIXED BY THE TESTATOR.* If by his will a testator directs a legacy to be paid "immediately after my death," the legacy carries interest from the date of the testator's death because the testator has fixed this date as the time for payment.[28] Similarly, a legacy directed to be paid to X at the age of 21 years bears interest from X's 21st birthday,

---

[23] Trustee Act 1925, ss. 31(1) and (2) and 68(17), as amended by Family Law Reform Act 1969, s. 1(3) and (4), Sched. 1, Pt. I and Sched. 3, para. 5(1). See generally *Snell's Equity* (29th ed., 1990), pp. 274 *et seq.*

[24] s. 69(2); *Re Turner's W.T.* [1937] Ch. 15.

[25] *Re McGeorge, supra.*

[26] R.S.C., Ord. 44, r. 10. The rate was increased from 5 per cent, by R.S.C. (Amendment No. 2) 1983 (S.I. 1983 No. 1181), which came into operation on October 1, 1983.

[27] *Re Hall* [1951] 1 All E.R. 1073.

[28] *Re Riddell* [1936] W.N. 252; *Re Pollock* [1943] Ch. 338; *cf. Webster v. Hale* (1803) 8 Ves. 410 (legacy to be paid "as soon as possible": held no date fixed for payment, and interest payable from one year after testator's death). For the effect of Administration of Estates Act 1925, s. 44, see *post,* p. 469.

whether the legacy is vested or contingent.[29] Again, a legacy directed to be paid on the death of a tenant for life carries interest from the death of the tenant for life.

(2) *TIME FIXED BY RULES OF LAW.* If no time for payment is mentioned in the will, the time for payment of a general legacy is fixed by rules of law.

(a) *Immediate general legacy.* The normal rule is that an immediate legacy is payable one year after the testator's death, *i.e.* at the end of the executor's year. This rule has been adopted for the sake of convenience: it may well be impracticable for the personal representatives to pay the legacy at the end of the executor's year but it is treated as payable at that time, so that the legacy carries interest from that time until the legacy is actually paid.[30] The rule is applicable even though the testator's estate does not produce any income[31]—for instance, because it consists mainly of a reversionary interest which cannot be sold to advantage.[32]

The same rule applies to a general legacy upon trust for A for life and subject thereto for B absolutely. The legacy carries interest from the end of the executor's year and A is not entitled to any interest in respect of the executor's year.[33]

A legacy which is vested but is liable to be divested in a certain event (*e.g.* given to a child X, with a gift over to Y in the event of X dying under the age of 21) also carries interest from the end of the executor's year.[34]

(b) *Contingent or deferred general legacy.* A general legacy which is contingent or deferred (or both) carries interest from the time at which it becomes payable. Such a general legacy is not mentioned in section 175 of the Law of Property Act 1925 and accordingly does not carry intermediate income under that section,[35] as does a contingent or deferred specific gift.

It follows that a general legacy to an unborn child carries interest only from the birth of the child,[36] and a general legacy to X if he attains the age of 18 years carries interest only from X's 18th birthday.[37] Again, a general legacy given to a person appointed executor and conditional on

---

[29] *Heath v. Perry* (1744) 3 Atk. 101; *Crickett v. Dolby* (1795) 3 Ves. 10; *Tyrrell v. Tyrell* (1798) 4 Ves. 1; *Lord v. Lord* (1867) L.R. 2 Ch. 782 (legacies to be paid when certain litigation ended: held interest ran from end of litigation 18 years after death of testatrix); *Holmes v. Crispe* (1849) 18 L.J.Ch. 439 (legacies to be paid when testator's estate sufficient: held interest ran from then). But if X attains 21 years before T's death the legacy is payable one year after T's death, *Re Palfreeman* [1914] 1 Ch. 877.

[30] *Wood v. Penoyre* (1807) 13 Ves. 325a, 333–334.

[31] *Pearson v. Pearson* (1802) 1 Sch. & Lef. 10.

[32] *Re Blachford* (1884) 27 Ch.D. 676 (T died in 1869; her main asset was a reversionary interest which fell into possession in 1881: held legatee was entitled to interest on his legacy from one year after T's death); *Walford v. Walford* [1912] A.C. 658.

[33] *Re Whittaker* (1882) 21 Ch.D. 657.

[34] *Taylor v. Johnson* (1728) 2 P.Wms. 504.

[35] *Re Raine* [1929] 1 Ch. 716.

[36] *Rawlins v. Rawlins* (1796) 2 Cox. 425.

[37] *Re George* (1877) 5 Ch.D. 837; *Re Dickson* (1885) 29 Ch.D. 331; *Re Inman* [1893] 3 Ch. 518.

his accepting the office carries interest only from the time he accepts the office.[38]

(c) *Legacy directed to be severed.* A legacy which the testator directs to be severed from his general estate may carry interest for a beneficiary from the end of the executor's year, even though his beneficial interest in the legacy is contingent or deferred. Whether it does so depends on the purpose for which severance is directed. Thus a general legacy given to trustees upon trust to invest and hold the legacy, and the investments representing it, upon trust for X if he attains the age of 18 years is treated under the general rule as payable by the executor to the trustees at the end of the executor's year, and the legacy carries interest from the end of the executor's year. The same result follows if T by his will directs that the legacy be severed (or set apart) by his executor from his general estate and held for the benefit of X if he attains the age of 18 years: in that case the legacy is treated as severable by the executor at the end of the executor's year and it carries interest from the end of the executor's year.[39] But if by his will T directs that the legacy be set apart merely for convenience of administration (*e.g.* so as to enable the rest of his estate to be distributed) and not for some purpose connected with the legacy, or if without any such direction the executor in fact sets the legacy apart, the legacy carries interest for X only from his 18th birthday, and meanwhile the interest accruing from the fund which has been set apart falls into T's residuary estate.[40]

3. Interest runs from death under four exceptional rules

There are four exceptional rules under which a general legacy carries interest from the date of the testator's death.

(1) *SATISFACTION OF A DEBT.* A legacy to a creditor of the testator, which operates as a satisfaction of his debt, carries interest from the testator's death and not from the end of the executor's year.[41] This rule is not applicable if by his will the testator fixed a time later than his death for payment of the legacy.[42]

(2) *LEGACY CHARGED ONLY ON REALTY.* A legacy which is charged only on realty carries interest from the date of the testator's death if the legacy is vested.[43] Again this rule is not applicable if by his

[38] *Angermann v. Ford* (1861) 29 Beav. 349; *Re Gardner* (1893) 67 L.T. 552 (legacy given to infant as executor: held interest ran from time he accepted office after attaining full age). As to accepting office see *Lewis v. Matthews* (1869) L.R. 8. Eq. 277.

[39] *Re Medlock* (1886) 55. L.J.Ch. 738; *Johnston v. O'Neill* (1879) 3 L.R.Ir. 476 ("the rule that the interest follows the capital prevails and the legatee gets his legacy with its interim accretions"); *Re Couturier* [1907] 1 Ch. 470; *Re Pollock* [1943] Ch. 338.

[40] *Festing v. Allen* (1844) 5 Hare 573; *Re Judkin's Trusts* (1884) 25 Ch.D. 743; *Re Inman* [1893] 3 Ch. 518.

[41] *Clark v. Sewell* (1744) 3 Atk. 96, 98–99; *Re Rattenberry* [1906] 1 Ch. 667: for satisfaction of a debt by a legacy see *ante*, pp. 224–225.

[42] *Adams v. Lavender* (1824) M'Cl. & Y. 41.

[43] *Maxwell v. Wettenhall* (1722) 2 P. Wms. 26; *Shirt v. Westby* (1808) 16 Ves. 393: the rule does not apply if a legacy is charged on realty in aid of the personalty, *Freeman v. Simpson* (1833) 6 Sim 75.

will the testator fixed a later time for payment of the legacy and the rule has a narrow area of operation. It does not apply to a legacy directed to be paid out of the proceeds of sale of realty devised upon trust for sale— in that case the legacy has been held to carry interest from one year after the testator's death, when the sale might reasonably have been effected.[44]

(3) *TESTATOR'S INFANT CHILD.* If a testator gives a legacy to his infant child, or to an infant to whom he stands *in loco parentis,* the legacy carries interest from the date of the testator's death in order to provide maintenance for the child.[45] This rule is very old and it originated from the court presuming that the legacy was intended by the testator to carry interest in order to provide for the child's maintenance if the will made no other provision for maintenance.[46] The rule is not applicable if the testator has by his will made some other provision for the child's maintenance.[47] Moreover, the rule applies only where the legacy is given directly to the child, and it is not applicable if the legacy is given to trustees upon trust for the child.[48]

The rule applies even though the legacy to the child is not payable until the child attains full age, or is contingent upon his attaining full age or previously marrying.[49] But the rule does not apply if the specified contingency has no reference to the child's infancy.[50]

The rate of interest carried is 5 per cent per annum if the income available is sufficient.[51] The interest may be applied for the child's maintenance, either under the statutory power of maintenance[52] or pursuant to an order of the court. Any surplus interest not applied for the child's maintenance is accumulated and added to the capital of the legacy.[53]

(4) *INTENTION TO PROVIDE FOR MAINTENANCE OF INFANT.* If a testator gives a legacy to an infant and shows in his will an intention to

---

[44] *Turner v. Buck* (1874) L.R. 18 Eq. 301; *cf. Re Waters* (1889) 42 Ch.D.517.

[45] *Re Bowlby* [1904] 2 Ch. 685 (infant child); *Wilson v. Maddison* (1843) 2 Y. & C.C.C. 372 (testator *in loco parentis* to child). If the child is *en ventre sa mere* at the testator's death, the legacy carries interest only from the child's birth, *Rawlins v. Rawlins* (1796) 2 Cox. 425.

[46] *Harvey v. Harvey* (1722) 2 P. Wms. 21 (father gave legacies to his children payable at 21: "it should be presumed that the father who gave these legacies, intended they should carry interest . . . for everyone must suppose it to have been the intention of the father, that his children should not want bread during their infancy"); *Heath v. Perry* (1744) 3 Atk. 101, 102; *Wynch v. Wynch* (1788) 1 Cox 433.

[47] *Hearle v. Greenbank* (1749) 3 Atk. 695, 716; *Donovan v. Needham* (1846) 9 Beav. 164; *Re George* (1877) 5 Ch.D. 837. If a share of residue is also given to the child contingently on attaining 21, the statutory power of maintenance (now in Trustee Act 1925, s. 31) out of the income of this share of residue does not exclude this exceptional rule, *Re Moody* [1895] 1 Ch. 101: *sed quaere* and *cf. Re Abrahams* [1911] 1 Ch. 108, 114.

[48] *Re Pollock* [1943] Ch. 338 (legacy by T to trustees upon trust for T's son if he attains 25: held legacy was severed and carried interest from end of executor's year).

[49] *Re Bowlby* [1904] 2 Ch. 685.

[50] *Re Abrahams* [1911] 1 Ch. 108: see also *Re Jones* [1932] 1 Ch. 642 and the exceptional rule considered in (4) below.

[51] Trustee Act 1925, s. 31(3) (5 per cent. "subject to any rules of court to the contrary"): *cf.* R.S.C., Ord. 44, r. 10 (6 per cent.).

[52] Trustee Act 1925, ss. 31 and 68(1)(17), as amended by Family Law Reform Act 1969, s. 1(3) and (4), Sched. 1 Pt. I and Sched. 3, para. 5(1).

[53] *ibid.*: see *Re Bowlby, supra.*

provide for the infant's maintenance,[54] the legacy carries interest from the date of the testator's death,[55] unless the testator has by his will made some other provision for the infant's maintenance.[56] Under this rule the legatee need not be the child or quasi-child of the testator, but the legatee must be an infant.[57]

This rule, unlike the previous one, applies to a legacy which is contingent upon an event having no reference to the legatee's infancy.[58]

To sum up the effect of these technical rules in the case of a contingent legacy given by T to an infant who is not T's child—*e.g.* given by T "to my nephew James if he attains the age of 18 years." Such a legacy carries interest from the time at which the contingency is satisfied and the legacy becomes payable,[59] except in the following cases:

(i) it carries interest from the end of the executor's year if T by his will directs the legacy to be severed from his general estate for some purpose connected with the legacy; and

(ii) it carries interest from the date of T's death, unless by his will he makes some other provision for the legatee's maintenance, if he stands *in loco parentis* to the legatee (and the other requirements of exception (3) are satisfied) or if he shows in his will his intention to provide for the infant's maintenance (so that exception (4) applies).

It may well be preferable for the draftsman of a will to insert an express direction as to the date from which a general legacy to an infant is to carry interest, rather than leave these technical rules to apply.

C.   RESIDUARY GIFTS

1.   Immediate residuary gifts

A residuary bequest of personalty or residuary devise of realty[60] which takes effect immediately carries with it all the income or profits accruing from its subject matter after the testator's death.

In examining the effects of contingent or deferred residuary gifts, it is necessary to consider residuary bequests and residuary devises separ-

---

[54] Or education, *Re Selby-Walker* [1949] 2 All E.R. 178.

[55] *Re Churchill* [1909] 2 Ch. 431 (legacy by T to infant grand-nephew, to vest at 21; power for trustees to apply legacy for his benefit whilst under 21: held legacy carried interest from T's death as T intended to provide for maintenance): see also *Re Stokes* [1928] Ch. 716 (statutory power to maintain applicable and treated as showing intention to provide for infant's maintenance).

[56] *Re West* [1913] 2 Ch. 345.

[57] *Raven v. Waite* (1818) 1 Sw. 553.

[58] *Re Jones* [1932] 1 Ch. 642 (the headnote is wrong).

[59] *Re Raine* [1929] 1 Ch. 716 (legacy to godchild S if he should attain 21; held legacy carried interest only from date S attained 21).

[60] Rents accruing before death from part of the testator's personal estate, *Constable v. Constable* (1879) 11 Ch. D. 681 (rent apportioned to period prior to death under Apportionment Act 1870 passed as personalty, not realty).

ately, because section 175 of the Law of Property Act 1925 does not apply to residuary bequests.

2. Contingent or deferred residuary bequests

(1) *CONTINGENT RESIDUARY BEQUESTS.* A residuary bequest of personalty which is contingent (but not otherwise deferred) carries intermediate income with it, provided the intermediate income is not otherwise disposed of by the will.[61] Thus, whilst the contingent event on which vesting depends remains undecided, any intermediate income not otherwise disposed of is either:

    (i) dealt with in accordance with section 31 of the Trustee Act 1925 if there is a beneficiary living who is contingently entitled;[62] or

    (ii) accumulated and added to capital for as long as the statutory rule against accumulations permits.[63]

At the end of the permitted accumulation period, any income subsequently accruing whilst the event remains undecided goes as on the testator's intestacy.[64]

(2) *DEFERRED RESIDUARY BEQUESTS.* By contrast, a residuary bequest of personalty which is deferred to a future date which must come sooner or later does not carry with it intermediate income arising between the testator's death and that date; if this intermediate income is not disposed of by the will, it goes as on the testator's intestacy. The rule applies to any deferred residuary bequest, whether it is vested[65] (*e.g.* a gift "to X after A's death"), vested subject to divesting[66] (*e.g.* a gift "to X after A's death, but if X dies before A to X's children equally"), or contingent[67] (*e.g.* "to X after A's death if X attains 30 years of age"). As Cross J. put it in *Re Geering*[68]:

"The very fact that a testator defers a gift to a future date is itself prima facie an indication that he does not intend the legatee to have the income of residue accruing before that date."

3. Contingent or deferred residuary devises

Section 175 of the Law of Property Act 1925 (which applies to wills coming into operation after 1925[69]) provides that:

---

[61] *Green v. Ekkins* (1742) 2 Atk. 473; *Trevanion v. Vivian* (1752) 2 Ves. Sen. 430 (gift of residuary personalty to A if he attains 21: held gift carried intermediate income which must be accumulated); *Bective v. Hodgson* (1864) 10 H.L.C. 656.

[62] *Ante,* pp. 459–460.

[63] *Re Geering* [1964] Ch. 136, 144.

[64] *Re Taylor* [1901] 2 Ch. 134. For the statutory rule against accumulations see Law of Property Act 1925, ss. 164–166, as amended by Perpetuities and Accumulations Act 1964, s. 13.

[65] *Berry v. Geen* [1938] A.C. 575; *Re Oliver* [1947] 2 All E.R. 162, 166.

[66] *Re Gillett's W.T.* [1950] Ch. 102: *cf. Re Nash's W.T.* [1965] 1 W.L.R. 221.

[67] *Re Geering* [1964] Ch. 136, not following *Re Drakeley's Estate* (1854) 19 Beav. 395 and *Re Lindo* (1888) 59 L.T.

[68] *Re Geering* [1964] Ch. 136. at p. 145.

[69] For the rules applicable to wills coming into operation before 1926 see *Hawkins and Ryder on the Construction of Wills* (1965), p. 78.

"a contingent residuary devise of freehold land, and a . . . residuary devise of freehold land to trustees upon trust for persons whose interests are contingent or executory shall, subject to the statutory provisions relating to accumulations, carry the intermediate income of that property from the death of the testator, except so far as such income, or any part thereof, may be otherwise expressly disposed of."

(1) *CONTINGENT RESIDUARY DEVISES.* A residuary devise of realty which is contingent (but not otherwise deferred) falls within section 175, whether made directly to the devisee or to trustees upon trust for a beneficiary whose interest is contingent. Thus a contingent residuary devise, like a contingent residuary bequest, carries intermediate income unless the income is otherwise expressly disposed of by the will.

(2) *DEFERRED RESIDUARY DEVISES.* Section 175 does not mention a deferred residuary devise but it does apply to a residuary devise to trustees upon trust for persons whose interests are "executory," and this appears to mean deferred.[70]

To sum up, section 175 of the Law of Property Act 1925 has produced some useful, and some unfortunate, effects:

    (i) A residuary bequest which is contingent (but not otherwise deferred) has always carried intermediate income. Section 175 makes a specific legacy, a specific devise, and a residuary devise if each is contingent (but not otherwise deferred) carry intermediate income if the will came into operation after 1925. This reform probably accords with the likely intentions of a testator, and moreover each type of contingent gift now has the same effect.

    (ii) A residuary bequest which is deferred does not carry intermediate income. Unfortunately section 175 makes a specific legacy, a specific devise, and some (if not all) types of residuary devise carry intermediate income though they are deferred. This reform frustrates the likely intentions of a testator, and moreover the different types of deferred gift do not all have the same effect.

There is a strong case for amending section 175 to make it accord with the likely intentions of a testator. It would also be helpful if the section codified the rules, stating in clear language which types of gift do, and which do not, carry intermediate income.[71]

D. THE RULE IN *ALLHUSEN* v. *WHITTELL*

1. The object of the rule

If by his will T settles his residuary estate for persons in succession—e.g. on trust for A for life and subject thereto for B absolutely—it is presumed that T intends each of these persons successively to enjoy the

[70] *Re McGeorge* [1963] Ch. 544, 550–552.
[71] P.V. Baker, (1963) 79 L.Q.R. 184, 186–187.

same property, *i.e.* his net residuary estate after payment of his funeral and testamentary expenses, debts and liabilities, and legacies. It follows that A is not entitled to receive the income accruing from the portion of T's estate needed for the payment of these outgoings. Under the rule in *Allhusen v. Whittell*[72] these outgoings are treated as having been paid partly out of capital and partly out of the income accruing from that portion of the capital during the period between T's death and the payment of these outgoings by the personal representatives. Consider an example. Suppose that T has given general legacies amounting to £11,000 and that his personal representatives pay these legacies one year after his death. If T's estate has yielded income during that year at the rate of 10 per cent. after deduction of income tax, these legacies are treated as having been paid out of £10,000 capital and out of £1,000 income. The tenant for life is not entitled to the £1,000 income accruing from the £10,000 capital needed for the payment of the general legacies.

The rule in *Allhusen v. Whittell* "was founded on the broad equitable principle that where residue was limited to persons in succession, their successive enjoyment should be an enjoyment of the same fund."[73] The rule is to be applied in a common-sense manner so as to give effect to this equitable principle. "The actual accountancy will not be difficult so long as the true object is borne in mind".[74]

2. Outgoings within the rule

If a debt or liability itself carries interest (as does unpaid inheritance tax), the outgoing consists of the total amount paid by the personal representatives, whether in respect of the debt or liability or the interest carried by it. This total amount ought to be paid partly out of capital and partly out of the income accruing from that portion of the capital in accordance with the rule.[75]

A contingent debt or liability of T falls within the rule—such as an annuity for life payable by T under a covenant made by T during his lifetime. Accordingly, when T's personal representatives pay such an annuity, each instalment is to be paid partly out of capital and partly out of the income accruing from that portion of the capital during the period between T's death and the payment of that instalment.[76] Each successive instalment includes more accruing income and less capital

---

[72] (1867) L.R. 4 Eq. 295: the rule applies to residuary realty. *Marshall v. Crowther* (1874) 2 Ch.D. 199. The rule has been held not to apply to an absolute gift to A which is liable to be divested by a gift over to B on a certain event, *Re Hanbury* (1909) 101 L.T. 32.

[73] *Per* Sargant J. in *Re McEuen* [1913] 2 Ch. 704, 713.

[74] *Ibid.* at p. 717. *Cf.* Law Reform Committee's 23rd Report, *The powers and duties of trustees*, Cmnd. 8733 (1982), p. 22 (witnesses described the rule "as complex, fiddlesome and resulting in a disproportionate amount of work and expense"); for possible reform see *ibid.*, pp. 24–25 and 64. In practice, the rule will be excluded, because it is "complex, fiddlesome etc. . .".

[75] *Re Wills* [1915] 1 Ch. 769, 779 (but "in the case of small estates or estates of moderate size it might very often be a good rough and ready rule to allow the interest on the estate duty to be paid out of income, and the capital to be paid out of capital"); *Re McEuen* [1913] 2 Ch. 704, 717.

[76] *Re Perkins* [1907] 2 Ch. 596; *Re Poyser* [1910] 2 Ch. 444; *Re Berkeley* [1968] Ch. 744; *cf. Re Darby* [1939] Ch. 905 (rule not applicable if T took property on which annuity charged, but T not under any personal liability to pay annuity).

than the previous instalment. A payment made by the personal representatives to X in consideration of X accepting an assignment of T's onerous leaseholds also falls within the rule.[77] On the other hand (and rather illogically), a contingent legacy given by T in his will has been held to fall outside the rule, on the ground that the fund to pay the legacy remains part of residue yielding income for the tenant for life until the contingency occurs.[78]

3. Period for calculation of income

If the outgoings are paid at about the end of the executor's year, the outgoings are treated as having been paid partly out of capital and partly out of the income accruing from that portion of the capital during the executor's year. But if any substantial outgoing is paid some time before,[79] or some time after,[80] the end of the executor's year, the period for calculation of the accruing income is the period from T's death until such outgoing is paid or satisfied.

The rule does not require "extremely elaborate and minute calculations" to be made in every case.[81]

4. Excluded by contrary intent in the will

The rule in *Allhusen v. Whittell* may be, and often is, excluded by the testator showing a contrary intent in his will[82]—*e.g.*:

> "I direct that the rule known as the rule in *Allhusen v. Whittell* shall not apply in the administration of my estate and the execution of the trusts of this Will and any codicil hereto."[83]

---

[77] *Re Shee* [1934] Ch. 345.
[78] *Allhusen v. Whittell* (1867) L.R. 4 Eq. 295, 303–304; *Re Fenwick's W.T.* [1936] Ch. 720.
[79] *Re McEuen* [1913] 2 Ch. 704.
[80] *Re Wills* [1915] 1 Ch. 769.
[81] *Re McEuen* [1913] 2 Ch. 704, 716.
[82] See the Statutory Will Forms 1925, Form 8(7)(c) (which authorises trustees to adjust as they think fit the incidence, as between capital and income, of payments made in due course of administration).
[83] The common form clause excluding apportionment of income under the rule in *Howe v. Earl of Dartmouth* (1802) 7 Ves. 137 does not exclude the rule in *Allhusen v. Whittell*, *Re Ullswater* [1952] Ch. 105.

CHAPTER 20

DISTRIBUTION OF THE ESTATE

In its narrower sense, the process of administration of the deceased's estate is complete when the personal representatives have got in the estate and paid, or made provision for the payment of, the expenses, debts, and liabilities of the deceased, and any inheritance tax payable in respect of his death. In its wider (and probably more accurate[1]) sense, administration embraces the culmination of this process—the distribution of the estate by the personal representatives to the persons entitled under the deceased's will or intestacy. These persons may be beneficially entitled to the distributed assets or they may hold the distributed assets as trustees.

A. DISTRIBUTION TO THE PERSONS ENTITLED

1. Time for distribution

Section 44 of the Administration of Estates Act 1925 provides that a personal representative is not bound to distribute the deceased's estate before the expiration of one year from the death.[2] As already explained, a different rule governs the time for payment of the deceased's debts. A personal representative has a duty to pay the deceased's debts with due diligence, and due diligence may require that payment should be made before the expiration of one year from the death.[3]

Accordingly, a personal representative cannot be compelled to pay a legacy before the expiration of one year from the death, even though by his will the testator directed the legacy to be paid within (say) six months after his death.[4] This rule may produce hardship if the legatee (*e.g.* the deceased's widow) is in immediate need of money. The court has power to make an interim order in favour of an applicant under the Inheritance (Provision for Family and Dependants) Act 1975 if the applicant is in immediate need of financial assistance.[5]

---

[1] See *Harvell v. Foster* [1954] 2 Q.B. 367.
[2] s. 44 is expressed to be "subject to the foregoing provisions of this Act": this may refer to ss. 36(10) and 43(2) of the Act, for which see *post*, pp. 485–486.
[3] *Ante*, pp. 413–414.
[4] See *Pearson v. Pearson* (1802) 1 Sch. & Lef. 10, 12; *Brooke v. Lewis* (1822) 6 Madd. 358. But the legacy carries interest from the time for payment fixed by the testator in his will, *ante*, p. 460.
[5] See *ante*, pp. 156–157.

A personal representative is free to pay a legacy, or to distribute the residuary estate, before the expiration of the executor's year if he chooses.[6] And section 43(1) of the Administration of Estates Act 1925 empowers a personal representative to permit a person entitled to land to take possession of it (or receive the rents payable by tenants[7]) prior to an assent or conveyance in his favour; this does not prejudice the right of the personal representative to resume possession or to convey the land.

On the other hand, a personal representative is not bound to distribute the deceased's estate at the expiration of one year from the death—it may take longer than this to complete the administration of the estate.

2. Ascertaining the persons entitled

Personal representatives are under a duty to distribute to the persons properly entitled under the deceased's will or intestacy.[8] It is, therefore, important for personal representatives to ascertain all the persons properly entitled, or at any rate to protect themselves against liability in case they fail to do so. If doubt arises as to the proper construction of the will, the personal representatives may apply to the court for this to be determined.[9] Again, it may be advisable to ask the court to conduct an inquiry to ascertain the beneficiaries. For example, such an inquiry may be needed if the deceased died intestate at an advanced age, and the class of next-of-kin entitled under the intestacy rules are his uncles and aunts of the whole blood on the statutory trusts, so that the class includes the issue of each deceased uncle or aunt, taking *per stirpes*.

What other protection is there for personal representatives in case they fail to ascertain all the persons properly entitled?

(1) *ADVERTISING FOR CLAIMS.* Under section 27 of the Trustee Act 1925[10] personal representatives may give notice of their intention to distribute and require any person interested to send in particulars of his claim to the personal representatives within a stated time, not being less than two months. The requirements imposed by this section as to advertising this notice and making searches have already been considered in relation to ascertaining the debts and liabilities of the deceased.[11] If the personal representatives satisfy these requirements, they may distribute to the persons entitled having regard only to the claims (whether formal or not) of which the personal representatives then have notice. In that event, the personal representatives are not, in respect of the distributed assets, "liable to any person of whose claim the . . . personal representatives have not had notice at the time of . . . distribution."[12]

---

[6] *Pearson v. Pearson, supra; Angerstein v. Martin* (1823) 1 Turn & R. 232, 241; *Re Palmer* [1916] 2 Ch. 391, 398 and 401.
[7] Administration of Estates Act 1925, s. 55(1)(xii).
[8] *Re Diplock* [1948] Ch. 465, 503: *Re Hayes' W.T.* [1971] 1 W.L.R. 758, 765.
[9] *Post*, p. 508.
[10] As amended by Law of Property (Amendment) Act 1926, ss. 7, 8(2) and Sched.
[11] *Ante*, pp. 415 *et seq.*
[12] Trustee Act 1925, s. 27(2).

In *Re Aldhous*[13] T died partially intestate and T's executor gave notice in accordance with the requirements of section 27; the executor received no claims from any person claiming to be entitled as T's next-of-kin and, believing that there were no next-of-kin, the executor paid the assets undisposed of by T's will to the Treasury Solicitor on behalf of the Crown as *bona vacantia*. In fact, unknown to the executor, there were next-of-kin of T who were entitled to these assets under the intestacy rules. Danckwerts J. said he thought it was plain that, if proceedings were brought by the next-of-kin against the executor in respect of this payment to the Treasury Solicitor, the executor would be protected by section 27—this protection is:

"effective not only in respect of claims of creditors but in respect of the claims of next-of-kin of a deceased person or, I suppose, of persons entitled under the will of a deceased person to share in the estate of that person."[14]

There seems little reason to doubt that section 27 protects personal representatives against the claims of unknown beneficiaries entitled under the deceased's will or intestacy, as well as against the claims of unknown creditors.[15]

Section 27 does not prejudice the remedy of an unpaid beneficiary against a recipient of the deceased's assets. This is considered later.[16]

(2) *LEAVE OF THE COURT TO DISTRIBUTE*. The court may make a "Benjamin Order" giving the personal representatives leave to distribute on a particular footing set out in the order, *e.g.* on the footing that a missing beneficiary under the testator's will was unmarried and predeceased the testator without issue,[17] or that a son who died in the lifetime of the testatrix left no child who survived her.[18] The particular footing set out in the order is, of course, based on probable inferences from the proved facts, but the order does not constitute a positive declaration of rights[19] and, accordingly, it does not prevent any missing beneficiary (if he subsequently appears) from pursuing his remedy against a recipient

---

[13] [1955] 1 W.L.R. 459: see also *Newton v. Sherry* (1876) 1 C.P.D. 246 (personal representative protected against claim of unknown next of kin by Law of Property Amendment Act 1859, s. 29, now replaced by Trustee Act 1925, s. 27, which is worded differently); *Re Letherbrow* [1935] W.N. 34 and 48 (advertisements for next of kin); *Re Ward* [1971] 1 W.L.R. 1376.

[14] [1955] 1 W.L.R. 459 at p. 462.

[15] See Law Reform Committee's 19th Report, *Interpretation of Wills*, Cmnd. 5301 (1973), paras. 51 and 65(8), which recommended s. 27 should be amended to put this "beyond argument."

[16] *Post*, pp. 510 *et seq.*

[17] *Re Benjamin* [1902] 1 Ch. 723 (P disappeared in September 1892; P's father died in June 1893 and by his will gave P a share of residue; despite inquiries and advertisements nothing heard of P: order that trustees be at liberty to distribute upon the footing P did not survive his father): see also *Re Taylor's Estate* [1969] 2 Ch. 245; *Re Lowe's W.T.* [1973] 1 W.L.R. 882, 887; *Re Green's W.T.* [1985] 3 All E.R. 455.

[18] *Re Beattie*, unreported, see Mosse (1936) 81 L.J. News. 163.

[19] *Hansell v. Spink* [1943] Ch 396, 399; *Re Green's W.T., supra* at p. 462 ("The true view is that a *Re Benjamin* order does not vary or destroy beneficial interests. It merely enables trust property to be distributed in accordance with the practical probabilities . . .").

of the deceased's assets.[20] Sometimes a Benjamin Order is made after an inquiry by the court has proved inconclusive,[21] but such an order may be made without any prior inquiry by the court if suitable advertisements for a missing beneficiary produce no claims,[22] or even without any advertisements if the inference from the proved facts is irresistible.[23]

A Benjamin Order protects personal representatives, who distribute on the footing set out in the order. Unlike section 27 of the Trustee Act 1925, the protection is not conditional on the personal representatives having complied with statutory requirements as to advertising and making searches.[24] Before making a Benjamin Order the court itself decides what further advertisements (if any) ought to be made. Such an order is also advantageous to the known beneficiaries, or the next of kin, as the share of the missing beneficiary becomes distributable amongst them, subject to the (usually remote) possibility of the missing beneficiary appearing and recovering his share from them.

(3) *ADOPTION.* The duty of personal representatives to distribute to the persons properly entitled is modified by statute in cases where an adoption could affect entitlement. A personal representative is not under a duty to enquire whether any adoption has been effected or revoked before he distributes any property, though that fact could affect entitlement to the property.[25] The personal representative is not liable if he distributes the property without regard to that fact if he has not received notice of it before the distribution; this protection of the personal representatives does not prejudice the remedy of the true beneficiary against a recipient of the deceased's assets.[26]

3. Beneficiary owes money to the estate

Suppose that B, as a beneficiary under T's will or intestacy, is entitled to money from T's estate; and B also owes money to T's estate. In this situation B is not permitted to take any money out of the estate until he has made good the money which he owes to it.[27] Accordingly, T's per-

---

[20] *Post,* pp. 510 *et seq.*

[21] As in *Re Benjamin, supra,* (Master unable to certify whether P alive or dead, or, if dead, when he died); *Re Lowe's W.T., supra.*

[22] As in *Re Beattie, supra,* (advertisements to ascertain if deceased son left any child); *Re Taylor's Estate, supra.*

[23] As in *Re Green's W.T., supra* (by her will T, who died in 1976, gave her estate to her son B; B had been a gunner in a bomber which went missing in a raid on Berlin in 1943; nothing ever heard of the bomber or its crew: irresistible inference crew perished, though T believed when she died that B was still alive).

[24] *Ante,* p. 415.

[25] Adoption Act 1976, s. 45(1): see also Legitimacy Act 1976, s. 7(1)—no duty to enquire whether any person is illegitimate or has been adopted by one of his natural parents, and could be legitimated (or, if deceased, be treated as legitimated). Family Law Reform Act 1969, s. 17 conferred similar protection on personal representatives as regards illegitimacy but has been repealed by Family Law Reform Act 1987, ss. 20 and 33(4) and Sched. 4.

[26] Adoption Act 1976, s. 45(2) and (3); Legitimacy Act 1976, s. 7(2) and (3). For the remedy against a recipient see *post,* pp. 510 *et seq.*

[27] *Re Rhodesia Goldfields Ltd* [1909] 1 Ch. 239, 247 ("the rule is of general application that . . . where a fund is being distributed, a party cannot take anything out of the fund until

sonal representatives have the right to apply any money due to B as a
beneficiary in satisfaction of any money due from B to the estate.[28]

(1) *MONEY PAYABLE TO B.* This right of "retainer" can be exercised
by T's personal representatives only if B is entitled to a sum of money
from T's estate. It cannot be exercised if B is entitled to a specific legacy
of something other than money, such as government stock.[29]

(2) *MONEY PAYABLE BY B.* The other requirement is that B owes
money[30] to T's estate. If the debt owed by B is payable by instalments,
the personal representatives may retain any instalments already due, but
they are not entitled to retain future instalments not yet due out of a
legacy presently payable.[31] This requirement is also not satisfied if the
debt due to T's estate is owed by B and another person jointly.[32]

The right of retainer is exercisable against the beneficiary B in respect of
money which B owes to T's estate, but not in respect of money which
anyone else owes to T's estate. It follows that if T by his will makes a gift to
his children living at his death, and provides that the children of any
deceased child shall take "such share as their parent would have taken if
living", T's personal representatives cannot retain a debt due to T's estate
from a deceased child out of the share payable to that child's children.[33]

(3) *EFFECT OF LIMITATION OR BANKRUPTCY.* If T's personal representatives could have recovered from B all the money due from him
to T's estate, this right of retainer merely saves them the bother of
obtaining and enforcing judgment against B. But the right of retainer is
exercisable by T's personal representatives in circumstances where they
could not have recovered from B all the money due. For instance, it is
exercisable:

   (i) where the debt due from B was statute-barred at T's death[34]; or
   (ii) where B goes bankrupt after he has become entitled as a beneficiary
        under T's will or intestacy to money from T's estate.[35] But if T's per-
        sonal representatives prove in B's bankruptcy for the money due

---

he has made good what he owes to the fund"). See generally B. S. Ker (1954) 18
   Conv.(N.S.) 176.
[28] *Re Melton* [1918] 1 Ch. 37: *Turner v. Turner* [1911] 1 Ch 716.
[29] *Re Savage* [1918] 2 Ch. 146 (specific legacy of colonial stock: rule not applicable—"you
   must have money payable against money payable"); *Re Taylor* [1894] 1 Ch. 671 (specific
   legacy of profits of business to B: held executors had right to retain profits as against
   debt due from B to T's estate): *cf. Re Eiser's W.T.* [1937] 1 All E.R. 244 (executors need
   not retain income payable under discretionary trust).
[30] It suffices if B is liable in damages to T's estate, *Re Jewell's Settlement* [1919] 2 Ch. 161,
   173–177 (damages equal to surrender value of lapsed insurance policy).
[31] *Re Abrahams* [1908] 2 Ch. 69.
[32] *Turner v. Turner* [1911] 1 Ch. 716 (debt due to T's estate from two partners jointly: held
   executors not entitled to retain legacy given to one partner); *Re Pennington and Owen
   Ltd.* [1925] Ch. 825.
[33] *Re Binns* [1929] 1 Ch. 677; but it is different in the case of an advancement to T's deceased
   child because an advancement is a payment on account of that child's share, at pp. 682–
   685; and see *Re Bruce* [1908] 2 Ch. 682.
[34] *Courtenay v. Williams* (1844) 3 Hare 539, affirmed (1846) 15 L.J.Ch. 204 (debt still exists
   though remedy by action barred); *Re Akerman* [1891] 3 Ch. 212.
[35] *Re Watson* [1896] 1 Ch. 925; *Re Melton* [1918] 1 Ch. 37; *Re Lennard* [1934] Ch. 235.

from B, they cannot then exercise the right of retainer.[36] Moreover, if B was an undischarged bankrupt when he became entitled as a beneficiary, T's personal representatives may prove in B's bankruptcy, but they cannot exercise the right of retainer because there was never a time when there were cross-obligations to pay in full.[37]

4. Beneficiary an infant

As a general rule, an infant (*i.e.* a person who is under 18 years of age[38]) cannot give a valid receipt for money or securities to which he is entitled as a beneficiary under a will[39] or intestacy, and neither can his parents,[40] guardian,[41] or adult spouse on his behalf.

(1) *RECEIPT BY MARRIED INFANT FOR INCOME.* The first exception to this general rule is statutory. Under section 21 of the Law of Property Act 1925 a married infant[42] has power to give valid receipts for all income (but not capital) to which the infant is entitled, including statutory accumulations of income made during the minority.[43]

(2) *PROVISION IN WILL.* The testator may by his will authorise payment of a legacy or share of residue to an infant beneficiary at a fixed age (*e.g.* at 17 years of age) or on marriage, or (alternatively) direct that the receipt of an infant beneficiary who has attained a fixed age or married shall be a good discharge.[44], Another common provision is to authorise payment to the parents or guardians of an infant beneficiary. Under such provisions personal representatives have a discretion (which they may surrender to the court) to decide whether in all the circumstances payment would be for the infant's benefit.[45]

(3) *APPOINTMENT OF TRUSTEES.* Instead of making a gift by will direct to an infant, a testator may (and often does) make the gift to one or more trustees upon trust for the infant[46]; in that case the receipt of the trustees is a good discharge to the personal representatives.[47]

---

[36] *Stammers v. Elliott* (1868) 3 Ch. App. 195.
[37] *Cherry v. Boultbee* (1839) 4 My. & Cr. 442 ("there never was a time at which the same person was entitled to receive the legacy and liable to pay the entire debt"); *Re Hodgson* (1878) 9 Ch.D. 673.
[38] Family Law Reform Act 1969, s. 1(1) and (2). See *Re Hellmann's Will* (1866) L.R. 2 Eq. 363 (legacy may be paid when infant comes of age according to English law or law of domicil, whichever first happens) and *Re Schnapper* [1928] Ch. 420; and see Dicey and Morris, *The Conflict of Laws* (12th ed., 1993), p. 1028.
[39] *Harvell v. Foster* [1954] 2 Q.B. 367, 377 and 383.
[40] *Dagley v. Tolferry* (1715) 1 P.Wms. 285 (£100 legacy to B, an infant, paid to B's father: executor held liable to pay legacy again to B's trustee in bankruptcy); *Rotheram v. Fanshaw* (1748) 3 Atk. 628, 629.
[41] *Re Cresswell* (1881) 45 L.T. 468.
[42] *i.e.* an infant who is over the age of 16 but under the age of 18.
[43] See Trustee Act 1925, s. 31(2)(i).
[44] *Re Somech* [1957] Ch. 165.
[45] *ibid.*
[46] In practice, a personal representative may also be a trustee and/or may be appointed testamentary guardian of the testator's infant children: see specimen will on pp. 165 et seq.
[47] *Cooper v. Thornton* (1790) 3 Bro.C.C. 96 (legacy of £100 given to X to be divided between himself and his family: held X took the legacy as trustee and payment to X discharged the executor).

If, under the will (if any) of the deceased, the gift is not made to trustees for the infant, the personal representatives have power under section 42(1) of the Administration of Estates Act 1925 to appoint a trust corporation, or two or more individuals not exceeding four (whether or not including one or more of the personal representatives), to be the trustee or trustees of the property for the infant. Section 42(1) applies whenever the deceased died. This power is, however, only exercisable where the infant is absolutely entitled under the will or on intestacy to a devise, or a legacy, or to the residue of the estate or any share therein. So, if the deceased died intestate, the power can only be exercised (i) if the infant is *absolutely* entitled as the deceased's surviving spouse, or (ii) if there is no preceding life interest and the infant has married, so as to become absolutely entitled under the statutory trusts.[48] If, pursuant to section 42(1), personal representatives duly appoint trustees and vest the infant's property in them, the personal representatives, as such, are discharged from all further liability in respect of that property.[49] Henceforth each of the personal representatives is liable, as a trustee, only if he was appointed one of the trustees of the infant's property.

(4) *PAYMENT INTO COURT.* Personal representatives may pay money or securities to which an infant is entitled into court; the receipt or certificate of the proper officer is a sufficient discharge to the personal representatives.[50] But since 1925 payment into court is seldom necessary because (as is explained below) personal representatives now have a wide power of appropriation under section 41 of the Administration of Estates Act 1925.

(5) *MAINTENANCE AND ADVANCEMENT.* Finally, personal representatives may make payments of income or capital for the benefit of an infant pursuant to any express power contained in the testator's will, the statutory powers of maintenance and advancement,[51] or any order made by the court.[52]

B. APPROPRIATION

Prior to 1926 a personal representative had no adequate power to appropriate assets so as to be entitled (for instance) to make an appropriation to satisfy a vested pecuniary legacy given to an infant. Such an appropriation was not binding on the infant because he was not compet-

---

[48] *Re Yerburgh* [1928] W.N. 208; *Re Wilks* [1935] Ch. 645, 650: see also *Re Kehr* [1952] Ch. 26 (s. 42 applies where infant absolutely entitled under intestacy rules of deceased's German domicil). For the statutory trusts see *ante,* p. 40.

[49] Administration of Estates Act 1925, s. 42(1); see *Harvell v. Foster* [1954] 2 Q.B. 367, 384, and *post,* p. 490.

[50] Trustee Act 1925, ss. 63 and 68(1)(17): see R.S.C., Ord. 92, r. 2.

[51] Trustee Act 1925, ss. 31, 32, and 68(1)(17) (s. 31 as amended by Family Law Reform Act 1969, s. 1(3) and (4), Sched. 1, Pt. 1 and Sched. 3 para. 5(1)); Administration of Estates Act 1925, s. 47(1)(ii).

[52] See generally *Snell's Equity* (29th ed., 1990), pp. 274 *et seq.*

ent to consent to it.[53] Since 1925 a personal representative has a wide power of appropriation under section 41 of the Administration of Estates Act 1925. The section applies whenever the deceased died.[54] If a personal representative exercises this power, two main consequences follow:

(i) henceforth the beneficiary's interest is in the appropriated assets: if they increase in value he gets the benefit, if they diminish in value he bears the loss[55]; and

(ii) the appropriation clears the other assets for distribution to the other beneficiaries.

1. Statutory power of appropriation

Section 41 applies whether the deceased died testate or intestate.[56] Under the section the personal representative may appropriate any part of the deceased's real or personal estate,[57] in its actual condition at the time of appropriation, in or towards satisfaction of any legacy or any other interest or share in the deceased's property, whether settled or not. An appropriation must not, however, affect prejudicially any specific devise or bequest[58]; so the subject matter of a specific devise or bequest must not be appropriated in satisfaction of a general legacy or a share of residue.

(1) *WHEN CONSENT REQUIRED.* Whether the personal representative needs the consent of any person to the appropriation depends on which of the following three alternatives is applicable.

(a) *Beneficiary absolutely entitled.* If the appropriation is made for the benefit of a person absolutely and beneficially entitled in possession, the consent of that person is required.[59] Thus, a beneficiary who is absolutely entitled to an immediate legacy of £1,000 may insist on payment in cash, and refuse to take company shares in satisfaction of his legacy. If the beneficiary is an infant, the consent may be given on his behalf by his parents, guardian, or by the court.[60]

---

[53] *Re Salomons* [1920] 1 Ch. 290 (before 1926 advisable to pay infant's legacy into court or obtain order of court approving appropriation in an administration action). Land Transfer Act 1897, s. 4 gave a power of appropriation, but s. 4 was never put into effective operation as the power to prescribe provisions for valuation was never implemented.

[54] s. 41(9).

[55] *Ballard v. Marsden* (1880) 14 Ch.D. 374, 376; *Re Richardson* [1896] 1 Ch. 512; *Re Marquis of Abergavenny's Estate Act Trusts* [1981] 1 W.L.R. 843, 846.

[56] s. 41(9).

[57] Including property over which a testator exercises a general power of appointment, including the statutory power to dispose of entailed interests, s. 41(9).

[58] s. 41(1), proviso (i).

[59] s. 41(1), proviso (ii). At common law executors may appropriate to one of themselves, *Re Richardson* [1896] 1 Ch. 512, and an administrator may appropriate to himself, *Barclay v. Owen* (1889) 60 L.T. 220.

[60] ss. 41(1), proviso (ii) and (1A) and 55(1)(iv), as amended by County Courts Act 1984, s. 148(1) and Sched. 2, para. 13; if the beneficiary is mentally incapable see s. 41(1), provisos (ii) and (iv) as amended by Mental Health Act 1959, s. 149(1) and Sched. 7, Pt. I and Mental Health Act 1983, s. 148(1) and Sched. 4, para. 7. An infant surviving spouse may require, or consent to, the appropriation of the matrimonial home comprised in an

(b) *Settled Interest.* An appropriation may be made in or towards satisfaction of a settled legacy, share or interest, *i.e.* any legacy, share or interest to which a person is not absolutely entitled in possession at the date of appropriation.[61] This includes, for example, a contingent or deferred legacy.

If the appropriation is made in respect of any settled legacy, share or interest, the consent of either the trustee thereof, if any (not being the personal representative), or the person who may for the time being be entitled to the income is required.[62] Again, the consent of an infant may be given on his behalf.[63]

(c) *No consent required.* No consent to the appropriation is required if, independently of the personal representative, there is no trustee of a settled legacy, share or interest, and no person of full age and capacity entitled to the income thereof. But in this case the appropriation must be of an investment authorised by law or by the deceased's will,[64] whereas under heads (a) and (b) above this is not necessary.[65]

(2) *PROTECTION OF NON-CONSENTING PERSONS.* In making the appropriation, the personal representative must have regard to the rights of any person not yet born, or who cannot be found or ascertained, and of any other person whose consent is not required (*e.g.* a person entitled in remainder to a settled legacy).[66] An appropriation duly made binds all the persons interested in the deceased's property whose consent is not required.[67]

(3) *VALUATION.* An appropriation is made at the value of the appropriated assets as at the date of the appropriation, and not as at the deceased's death.[68]

For the purpose of appropriation the personal representative may ascertain and fix the value of the respective parts of the deceased's estate (and of the deceased's liabilities) as he may think fit, and for this purpose the personal representative must employ a duly qualified valuer where this is necessary.[69]

---

intestate's residuary estate, see Intestates' Estates Act 1952, Sched. 2, para. 6(2); if the surviving spouse is mentally incapable see para. 6(1).

[61] s. 41(8). This includes an annuity; s. 419 authorises the setting apart of a fund to answer an annuity by means of the income of that fund or otherwise—presumably an appropriation under s. 41 with the annuitant's consent clears the other assets for distribution to the other beneficiaries: *cf.* the effect of an appropriation not made under s. 41, *ante*, p. 179.

[62] s. 41(1), proviso (ii).

[63] See *supra*, n. 60.

[64] s. 41(1), proviso (v).

[65] s. 41(1), proviso (ii) and s. 41(2); but if the beneficiary is mentally incapable see s. 41(1), proviso (iv).

[66] s. 41(5).

[67] s. 41(4). For the protection of a purchaser of land from a person to whom it has been appropriated see ss. 41(7) and (8) and 55(1)(xix).

[68] *Re Charteris* [1917] 2 Ch. 379, 386; *Re Collins* [1975] 1 W.L.R. 309 ("a rule of administration too well established to require further discussion").

[69] s. 41(3): *cf. Re Bythway* (1911) 104 L.T. 411 (executrix not entitled to appropriate to herself unquoted company shares at her own valuation).

2. Express power in will

Section 41 does not prejudice any other power of appropriation conferred by law[70] or by the deceased's will.[71]

C. ASSENTS

1. Right of beneficiary during administration

What is the true status of a beneficiary under a will or intestacy during the administration of the deceased's estate?

(1) *NO EQUITABLE INTEREST IN UNADMINISTERED ASSETS.* As a general rule, a beneficiary under a will or intestacy has no legal or equitable proprietary interest in the unadministered assets of the deceased's estate.[1] The entire ownership of the unadministered assets is in the deceased's personal representative. Whatever property comes to a personal representative by virtue of his office comes to him "in full ownership without distinction between legal and equitable interests. The whole property [is] his."[2] The personal representative holds this property for the purpose of carrying out the administration of the deceased's estate. Of course, equity imposes on him fiduciary duties (sometimes called "trusts"), *e.g.* to get in the estate, to preserve the assets, to deal properly with them, and to apply them in due course of administration for the benefit of creditors and beneficiaries.[3] But equity does not treat the unadministered assets as if they constituted a trust fund held upon trust for the beneficiaries. For equity to have done so:

"would have been in plain conflict with the basic conception of equity that to impose the fetters of a trust upon property, with the resulting creation of equitable interests in that property, there had to be specific subjects identifiable as the trust fund. An unadministered estate was incapable of satisfying this requirement ... until administration was complete no one was in a position to say what items of property would need to be realised for the purposes of that administration or of what the residue, when ascertained, would consist or what its value would be."[4]

---

[70] See Law of Property Act 1925, s. 28(3) and (4) (power to partition land held in undivided shares) and Administration of Estates Act 1925, s. 39(1); Trustee Act 1925, s. 15(b) (power to sever and apportion blended trust funds or property): as to the common law power of appropriation see *Re Lepine* [1892] 1 Ch. 210; *Re Beverley* [1901] 1 Ch. 681.

[71] See the Statutory Will Forms 1925, Form 6. It is common in practice to include a power to appropriate without obtaining the consent of the beneficiary.

[1] *Commissioner of Stamp Duties (Queensland) v. Livingston* [1965] A.C. 694 (gift of share of all real and residuary personal estate: the judgment of the P.C. analyses the case law); *Lord Sudeley v. Att.-Gen.* [1897] A.C. 11 (gift of share of residuary real and personal estate); *Dr. Barnardo's Homes National Incorporated Association v. Commissioners for Special Purposes of the Income Tax Acts* [1921] 2 A.C. 1 (gift of residuary estate); *Eastbourne Mutual B.S. v. Hastings Corporation* [1965] 1 W.L.R. 861 (interest as sole next-of-kin on intestacy).

[2] *Commissioner of Stamp Duties (Queensland) v. Livingston, supra*, at p. 707.

[3] *ibid.* at p. 707: see also *Re Hayes' W.T.* [1971] 1 W.L.R. 758, 764–765.

[4] Commissioner of Stamp Duties (Queensland) v. Livingston [1965] A.C. 694 at p. 708.

(2) *BENEFICIARY HAS A CHOSE IN ACTION TO ENSURE DUE ADMINISTRATION.* The true status of a beneficiary under a will or intestacy is that he has a chose in action to have the deceased's estate properly administered.[5] He may, for instance, bring an action to have the estate administered by the court, or for some other less sweeping remedy.[6] His remedies are considered in Chapter 21.

This chose in action is transmissible by the beneficiary. In *Re Leigh's Will Trusts*[7] T by her will made a specific gift to B of "all shares which I hold and any other interest ... which I may have" in S Ltd. T never had any shares or other interest in S Ltd., but, both at the date of her will and her death, she was the sole administratrix and sole beneficiary of the unadministered estate of her husband, who had died intestate. His estate included some shares in, and a debt due from, S Ltd. Buckley J. held that the specific gift to B was effective.

The obligations of the executors in administering the estate can be varied by a direction given by all the relevant legatees and such variations are frequently effected in order to save tax.[8] In the recent case of *Crowden v. Aldridge*[9] there was a dispute as to whether memoranda which had been signed by all the legatees were effective to vary the devolution of the estate. The variation in this case was not for the purpose of saving tax, but was to benefit the deceased's housekeeper; the memoranda stated that the signatories were "prepared to enter into a deed to formalise this gift". Some of the beneficiaries, having signed the memoranda, refused to execute the deed. It was held[10] that the variation by the memoranda was effective because, although the exact juridical analysis of the transaction was obscure,[11] it operated in the same way as a unanimous direction to trustees by all the relevant beneficiaries under a trust. The decision gives rise to a number of problems and has been criticised.[12] The case appears to decide that "beneficiaries under an unadministered estate have a much wider power to make informal gifts than other persons have.[13]

(3) *SPECIFIC GIFT BY WILL.* There may be a single exception to the general rule that the entire ownership of the unadministered assets is in the deceased's personal representative. It has been said that a beneficiary entitled under a specific bequest or devise takes an equitable interest in

---

[5] *ibid.* at p. 717. But see also *Crowden v. Aldridge infra.*
[6] A pecuniary or residuary legatee (or a creditor) may follow and recover assets improperly abstracted from the estate, but he does so on behalf of the estate, so that the assets are restored to the estate for use in due course of administration; the remedy "asserts the estate's right of property, not the property right of creditor or legatee," *ibid.* at pp. 713–714. For this remedy see *post*, p. 515.
[7] [1970] Ch. 277: see P.V.B. (1970) 86 L.Q.R. 20.
[8] *Ante* pp. 285 *et seq.*
[9] [1993] 1 W.L.R. 433.
[10] By Jonathan Sumption QC, sitting as a Deputy Judge of the High Court.
[11] [1993] 1 W.L.R. 433, 439.
[12] By J.G. Ross Martyn in [1994] Conv. 446.
[13] *ibid.* at p. 449. The variation was not made by deed and the person in whose favour it was made (the housekeeper) had supplied no consideration. The decision could, also, be described as being "undesirable as a matter of policy" *ibid.* at p. 452.

the subject matter of the gift at the death of the testator,[14] although the legal estate vests in the personal representative, who may, of course, resort to the property for payment of the deceased's expenses, debts and liabilities. But this exception appears to be of doubtful validity as it is not consistent with the principle that:

"whatever property came to the executor *virtute officii* came to him in full ownership, without distinction between legal and equitable interests. The whole property was his."[15]

It may well be that, until a personal representative assents to a specific gift, the specific legatee or devisee (like any other beneficiary) has, during the period of administration, only a chose in action to have the deceased's estate properly administered.[16]

2. Assent in respect of pure personalty

At common law, an assent by a personal representative merely indicates that he does not require certain property of the testator for purposes of administration and that the property may pass under the testator's will.

(1) *SUBJECT MATTER OF ASSENT.* Originally the common law power to assent applied to bequests of leaseholds, as well as of pure personalty, and it was extended to devises of realty by the Land Transfer Act 1897.[17] But section 36 of the Administration of Estates Act 1925 introduced different provisions which are applicable to an assent to the vesting of an estate or interest in land, whether freehold or leasehold. Assents in respect of land are considered later. The Administration of Estates Act 1925 did not affect the common law power to assent in respect of pure personalty and this is considered first.

At common law an executor[18] (and probably an administrator[19]) may assent in respect of any gift of pure personalty by will, whether the gift is specific, general, or residuary. It is said that an administrator cannot assent in respect of pure personalty which passes on intestacy, though there appears to be no case law authority for this.[20]

(2) *FORM OF ASSENT.* At common law an assent is not required to be (and in practice seldom is) made in writing. It may be made expressly

---

[14] *I.R.C. v. Hawley* [1928] 1 K.B. 578, 583; *Re Neeld* [1962] Ch. 643, 687–688 and 691: see also *Williams v. Holland* [1965] 1 W.L.R. 739, 743–44; *Re K* [1986] Ch. 180, 188.

[15] *Commissioner of Stamp Duties (Queensland) v. Livingston* [1965] A.C. 694, 707 and see p. 712: see *Kavanagh v. Best* [1971] N.I. 89, 93–94.

[16] *Re Hayes' W.T.* [1971] 1 W.L.R. 758, 764 (*per* Ungoed-Thomas J., "no legatee, devisee or next-of-kin has any beneficial interests in the assets being administered").

[17] s. 3 (not applicable to copyholds, s. 1(4)).

[18] An assent by one executor binds the other executors, even where the bequest is to himself, *Townson v. Tickell* (1819) 3 B. & Ald. 31, 40; see *ante*, pp. 391 *et seq.*

[19] *i.e.* an administrator with the will annexed: see Williams, *Law Relating to Assents* (1947), p. 96 citing *Gundry v. Brown* (1678) Rep. temp. Finch 370.

[20] See Williams, *op cit.* pp. 4 and 122–123; *cf.* Garner (1964) 28 Conv.(N.S.) 298, 300–301.

(*e.g.* by a few informal words spoken by the executor[21]), or it may be implied from the conduct of the executor. Whether there has been an assent is generally a question of fact.[22] A useful instance of the implication of an assent is the case of *Attenborough v. Solomon*,[23] which has already been considered.[24]

(3) *EFFECT OF ASSENT.* An assent indicates that the executor does not require certain property for administration purposes and that the property may pass under the testator's will. The assent in effect activates the gift of the property by the testator's will. "The will becomes operative so far as its dispositions of personalty are concerned only if and when the executor assents to those dispositions."[25] If the property is given by the will to the executor himself, either beneficially or as trustee, after he has assented to the gift the property is vested in him as beneficiary or trustee (as the case may be), and not as personal representative.

Moreover, in the case of a specific legacy, but not of a general legacy or of a residuary bequest, three other consequences follow from an assent:

(i) After the executor has assented to a specific legacy, the legatee may bring an action at common law to recover possession of the subject matter of the legacy from the executor[26] or a third party.[27] A beneficiary cannot enforce his claim to a general legacy,[28] or a share of residue, or his rights on intestacy,[29] by an action at common law. But even in the case of a specific legacy, the *legal* title to the subject matter may not be capable of assignment by an assent. For instance, company shares are only transferable in the manner provided by the articles of the company,[30] *i.e.* by entering the name of the transferee in the register of members of the company.[31] After an executor has assented to a specific legacy of company shares, he holds the shares as trustee for the legatee until the legal title is duly transferred to the legatee.[32]

(ii) An assent to a specific legacy relates back to the death of the testator and the legatee becomes entitled to the income or profits accruing from its subject matter since the testator's death.[33]

---

[21] *Doe d. Sturges v. Tatchell* (1832) 3 B. & Ad. 675; *Barnard v. Pumfrett* (1841) 5 My. & Cr. 63, 70.

[22] *I.R.C. v. Smith* [1930] 1 K.B. 713 (an outstanding mortgage does not necessarily prevent inference of an assent to a residuary gift): an assent to a gift of a life interest operates as an assent to the gift in remainder (and vice versa), *Stevenson v. Mayor of Liverpool* (1874) L.R. 10 Q.B. 81. See generally Williams, *op. cit.* pp. 102 *et seq.*

[23] [1913] A.C. 76: see also *Wise v. Whitburn* [1924] 1 Ch. 460.

[24] *Ante*, pp. 392–393.

[25] *Attenborough v. Solomon* [1913] A.C. 76, *per* Lord Haldane at p. 82.

[26] *Doe d. Lord Saye and Sele v. Guy* (1802) 3 East. 120; *Re Culverhouse* [1896] 2 Ch. 251; *Re West* [1909] 2 Ch. 180, 185.

[27] *Stevenson v. Mayor of Liverpool* (1874) L.R. 10 Q.B. 81; *Re West* [1909] 2 Ch. 180.

[28] *Deeks v. Strutt* (1794) 5 T.R. 690.

[29] *Jones v. Tanner* (1827) 7 B. & C. 542.

[30] Companies Act 1985, s. 182(1).

[31] See, *ibid.* s. 183(1) and (3).

[32] *Re Grosvenor* [1916] 2 Ch. 375, 378.

[33] *Re West* [1909] 2 Ch. 180: see also *I.R.C. v. Hawley* [1928] 1 K.B. 578 and *cf. Dr Barnardo's Homes National Incorporated Association v. Commissioners for Special Purposes of the Income Tax Acts* [1921] 2 A.C. 1, 8 and 11 (an assent to a residuary bequest does not relate back to death).

(iii) After an executor has assented to a specific legacy, the costs of transferring its subject matter to the legatee must be borne by the legatee.[34] A testator may, of course, exclude this rule by a direction in his will that the costs of transferring the subject matter of a specific legacy shall be paid out of his residuary estate.[35]

3. Assent in respect of land

Section 36(1) of the Administration of Estates Act 1925 confers power on a personal representative to "assent to the vesting, in any person who (whether by devise, bequest, devolution, appropriation or otherwise) may be entitled thereto, either beneficially or as a trustee or personal representative, of any estate or interest' in land, whether freehold or leasehold.[36] Section 36 applies to any assent (or conveyance) made after 1925, whenever the testator or intestate died.[37]

This statutory power to assent in respect of land may be exercised by any personal representative,[38] whether the deceased died testate or intestate. The reference in section 36(1) to an assent in favour of a person entitled by "devolution" covers the case of a beneficiary entitled under the intestacy rules. Again, an assent may be made in favour of a personal representative of a beneficiary who is entitled under the deceased's will or intestacy but who dies before distribution, or (alternatively) who predeceased the deceased but nevertheless takes under the deceased's will under an exception to the doctrine of lapse.[39] The reference to a person "otherwise" entitled apparently authorises an assent in favour of a purchaser, at any rate if the assent carries out a contract for sale made by the deceased in his lifetime.[40] It remains uncertain whether section 36(1) authorises an assent in favour of a purchaser from a beneficiary.[41]

(1) *SUBJECT MATTER OF ASSENT.* The statutory power to assent applies to any estate or interest in freehold or leasehold land "to which the testator or intestate was entitled . . . and which devolved upon the personal representative."[42] The land devolving upon a personal representative includes land appointed by the deceased in his will under a general power of appointment, and an entailed interest in land, provided

---

[34] *Re Grosvenor* [1916] 2 Ch. 375 (assent to specific legacies of company shares: held costs of transfer to be borne by legatees); *Re Sivewright* [1922] W.N. 338: *Re Leech* [1923] 1 Ch. 161. As to specific gifts of foreign assets see *Re Fitzpatrick* [1952] Ch. 86 and authorities cited.

[35] Such a direction may extend to expenses incurred by the personal representative in the upkeep and preservation of the subject matter of a specific legacy, see *ante*, p. 177.

[36] Administration of Estates Act 1925, s. 55(1)(xix).

[37] *ibid.* s. 36(12).

[38] *ibid.* s. 55(1)(xi) provides that "personal representative" means the executor, original or by representation, or administrator for the time being of the deceased. All the personal representatives (still living) to whom a grant has been made in respect of the land must concur in an assent, ss. 2(2) and 24, and see *ante*, p. 392.

[39] *Ante*, pp. 239 *et seq.*

[40] *G.H.R. Co. Ltd. v. I.R.C.* [1943] K.B. 303.

[41] See Williams, *op. cit.* pp. 13 *et seq.*

[42] Administration of Estates Act 1925, s. 36(1).

it has been barred by and passes under a gift contained in the deceased's will.[43]

It follows that the statutory power to assent is not applicable to land which is conveyed to the personal representative after the death of the deceased, because the land did not devolve upon the personal representative.[44] In this case the personal representative should convey the land to the person entitled by deed.

(2) *FORM OF ASSENT.* An assent to the vesting of an equitable interest in land is not required to be made in writing. A personal representative may assent orally, or impliedly by his conduct, to the vesting of an equitable interest in land.[45] The rule is, however, different for an assent to the vesting of a legal estate in land, with respect to which section 36(4) provides as follows:

"An assent to the vesting of a legal estate shall be in writing, signed by the personal representative, and shall name the person in whose favour it is given and shall operate to vest in that person the legal estate to which it relates; and an assent not in writing or not in favour of a named person shall not be effectual to pass a legal estate."

Apart from this provision, no particular form of assent is prescribed except in the case of registered land.[46]

Plainly an assent by a personal representative to the vesting of a legal estate in land in *another person* (whether beneficially, or as a trustee, or as a personal representative of another deceased person) must be made in signed writing, and the person in whose favour the assent is given must be named in the assent. If an assent does not comply with this rule, it is not effectual to pass the legal estate.

Does the same rule apply to an assent by a personal representative to the vesting of a legal estate in land in. *himself* (whether beneficially, or as a trustee, or as a personal representative of another deceased)? In *Re King's Will Trusts*[47] Pennycuick J. held that the same rule applies. In that case T by her will appointed A and B to be executors and trustees and made a specific devise of Blackacre to them upon trust. A and B obtained probate, A died, and B appointed X to be a trustee of the will. B then died, and B's executor C became executor by representation of T. X appointed Y to be a trustee of the will, and X then died. None of them, A, B or C, ever made any written assent to the vesting of the legal estate in Blackacre. Pennycuick J. held that the legal estate in Blackacre was still vested in C as executor by representation of T, and he rejected the

---

[43] *Ibid.* ss. 1(1), 3, 36(1) and 55(1)(xix): see *ante,* pp. 368 *et seq*

[44] *Re Stirrup's Contract* [1961] 1 W.L.R. 449 (assent under seal took effect as conveyance): but see Elphinstone (1961) 25 Conv.(N.S.) 490.

[45] *Re Edwards' W.T.* [1982] Ch. 30, 40 (W owned Blackacre and died intestate, leaving H solely entitled; H obtained letters of administration and occupied Blackacre for 20 years until H died; no assent in writing by H in his own favour: held H had assented by his conduct to vesting of equitable interest in himself, so that it passed to H's executors).

[46] See Land Registration Act 1925, s. 41(4); Land Registration Rules 1925, r. 170 and Sched., Forms 56 and 57.

[47] [1964] Ch. 542: see *Re Edward's W.T., supra,* at pp. 33 and 40; *Beebe v. Mason* (1980) 254 E.G. 987.

argument that, prior to the appointment of X, the legal estate had become vested in B in his capacity as trustee.

Pennycuick J.'s construction of section 36(4) has been criticised on the ground that a legal estate does not "pass" if a personal representative merely assents in his own favour, so as to alter the capacity in which he holds the legal estate; accordingly it is argued that such an assent need not be in writing, but can be made orally or impliedly by conduct.[48] But Pennycuick J.'s construction seems to accord both with the wording and the object of section 36(4).[49] And even if the criticism is technically justified and the decision in *Re King's Will Trusts* is overruled at some future date, a signed written assent by a personal representative in his own favour (whether beneficially, or as a trustee, or as a personal representative of another deceased) will still remain highly desirable, so as to provide documentary evidence of the title to the legal estate.

The person in whose favour an assent (or conveyance) of a legal estate is made by a personal representative may (and should for his own protection) require that notice of it be written on, or endorsed on, or permanently annexed to, the probate or letters of administration at the cost of the deceased's estate; he may also require that the probate or letters of administration be produced to prove that this has been done.[50] This provision protects him against the possibility that the personal representative may execute another assent or conveyance in respect of the same property.[51]

The question whether a personal representative can cease to hold property in that capacity and start to hold it in the capacity of trustee *without any assent or conveyance in his own favour* is considered later in this Chapter.[52]

(3) *EFFECT OF ASSENT.* An assent in respect of land is a form of conveyance.[53] Section 36(4) provides that an assent to the vesting of a legal estate in land shall operate to vest the legal estate in the person named in whose favour it is given.[54] On the other hand, an assent in respect of pure personalty activates the gift of the property by the testator's will, so that the property passes under the will and not under the assent.

Section 36 regulates the effect of an assent in respect of land as follows:

> (i) An assent relates back to the death of the deceased unless a contrary intention appears.[55] As has already been noted, at common

---

[48] For criticisms see Garner (1964) 28 Conv. (N.S.) 298; R. R. A. Walker (1964) 80 L.Q.R. 328. See also Farrand, *Contract and Conveyance* (2nd ed., 1973), pp. 111 *et seq.* analysing the previous meagre case law. *Re King's Will Trusts* was *not* followed in the recent Irish case of *Mohan v. Roche* [1991] 1 I.R. 560, which is noted by J.A. Dowling in [1992] Conv 383.

[49] Ryder (1976) 29 C.L.P. 60, 63.

[50] Administration of Estates Act 1925, s. 36(5).

[51] *ibid.* s. 36(6) and (7): see *ante*, pp. 382–383.

[52] *Post*, pp. 490–492.

[53] See Law of Property Act 1925, s. 52. The statutory covenants for title may be implied in an assent, Administration of Estates Act 1925, s. 36(3) and Law of Property Act 1925, s. 76(1)(F) and Sched. 2, Pt. VI.

[54] See also s. 36(2), which also applies to an assent to the vesting of an equitable interest.

[55] *ibid.*

law only an assent to a specific legacy relates back to the death of the testator.

(ii) Section 36(7) provides that an assent or conveyance by a personal representative in respect of a legal estate is, in favour of a purchaser for money or money's worth,[56] "sufficient evidence that the person in whose favour the assent or conveyance is given or made is the person entitled to have the legal estate conveyed to him and upon the proper trusts, if any." The purchaser is protected in this way unless notice of a previous assent or conveyance affecting that legal estate has been placed on or annexed to the probate or administration. But an assent is only "sufficient," and not conclusive, evidence. In *Re Duce and Boots Cash Chemists (Southern) Ltd.'s Contract*[57] the assent to X by T's executor contained a recital which showed that Blackacre was settled land under T's will, and ought to have been vested in the tenant for life and not in X. Bennett J. said that the effect of section 36(7) is that "a purchaser when investigating title may safely accept [an assent] as evidence that the person in whose favour it has been made was the person entitled to have the legal estate conveyed to him unless and until, upon a proper investigation by a purchaser of his vendor's title, facts come to the purchaser's knowledge which indicate the contrary.[58] Accordingly Bennett J. decided that the purchaser was entitled to object to the title.

(iii) Normally, an assent made in signed writing requires no stamp duty,[59] and an assent made by deed no longer requires a 50p deed stamp.[60] If any assent or conveyance is made for value it must be stamped *ad valorem*.[61]

As already explained, after an executor has assented to a specific legacy of pure personalty the costs of transferring its subject matter to the legatee must be borne by him. Probably the costs of an assent to the vesting of freehold or leasehold land in a specific devisee or legatee are payable as a testamentary expense, and do not have to be borne by the devisee or legatee[62]; but the costs of a vesting assent by personal representatives under the Settled Land Act 1925 fall on the settled property.[63]

(4) *PROTECTION OF PERSONAL REPRESENTATIVE.* A personal representative has power to give an assent subject to any legal estate or charge by way of legal mortgage,[64] *e.g.* an assent in respect of the deceased's house subject to a mortgage or charge securing the deceased's debt to a building

---

[56] *ibid.* s. 36(11): see *ante*, p. 381, n. 29.

[57] [1937] Ch. 642.

[58] *ibid.* at p. 650.

[59] Administration of Estates Act 1925, s. 36(11); *Kemp v. I.R.C.* [1905] 1 K.B. 581: see also Settled Land Act 1925, s. 14(2).

[60] Finance Act 1985, s. 85(1) and Sched 24; see also Finance Act 1985 s. 87 and The Stamp Duty (Exempt Instruments) Regulations 1987 (S.I. 1987, 516).

[61] *G.H.R. Co. Ltd. v. I.R.C.* [1943] K.B. 303; *Jopling v. I.R.C.* [1940] 2 K.B. 282.

[62] Williams *op. cit.* p. 44.

[63] Settled Land Act 1925, s. 8(2).

[64] Administration of Estates Act 1925, s. 36(10): *Williams v. Holland* [1965] 1 W.L.R. 739, 743–744.

society.[65] As a condition of giving an assent or making a conveyance, a personal representative may require security for the discharge of any duties, debt, or liability to which the property is subject.[66] An instance is unpaid inheritance tax, payable in respect of the testator's death, to which his freehold house is subject under a direction in the will.[67] In order to protect himself the personal representative needs to insist on proper security being given for the discharge of this tax before he assents to the vesting of the house in the person entitled.[68] But an assent or conveyance by the personal representative does not, except in favour of a purchaser of a legal estate for money or money's worth, prejudice the right of the personal representative to be indemnified out of the property against any such duties, debt or liability.[69]

(5) *COMPELLING THE PERSONAL REPRESENTATIVE TO ASSENT.* The personal representative is not entitled to postpone the giving of an assent merely by reason of the subsistence of any such duties, debt or liability if reasonable arrangements have been made for discharging them.[70]

Under section 43(2) any person who, as against the personal representative, claims possession of land which devolved on the personal representative, or an assent or conveyance in respect of it, or to be registered as proprietor of it under the Land Registration Act 1925, may apply to the court for directions, and the court may make such vesting or other order as may be deemed proper. But such a person is not entitled to require the personal representative to execute an assent in his favour before the end of the executor's year.[71] Moreover, even after the executor's year has ended, the personal representative may still be justified in refusing to execute an assent, *e.g.* he may need to sell the property in order to apply the proceeds of sale in payment of the deceased's expenses, debts and liabilities,[72] or there may be doubt as to the construction of the gift of the property by the deceased's will.[73]

D. PERSONAL REPRESENTATIVE OR TRUSTEE?

1. Personal representative holds office for life

After a grant of representation has been made to him, a person holds

---

[65] See Administration of Estates Act 1925, s. 35 which is discussed *ante*, pp. 428 *et seq.*
[66] *ibid.* s. 36(10). See also Settled Land Act 1925, s. 8(3) and (6).
[67] *Ante*, pp. 433 *et seq.*
[68] *cf. Re Rosenthal* [1972] 1 W.L.R. 1273 (specific devise of house to S; house transferred to S without any security for discharge of unpaid estate duty on it; S sold the house, went to live abroad, and failed to pay duty: held trustees not entitled to recoup duty falling on house out of residue, but must bear it themselves).
[69] Or, except in favour of a purchaser of a legal estate for money or money's worth, the right of the personal representative to recover the property, Administration of Estates Act 1925 s. 36(9) and (11): for the right to follow the property see s. 38 and *post*, p. 515. For the definition of purchaser see s. 55(1)(xviii): see also *Re Lander* [1951] Ch. 546, 551–552.
[70] Administration of Estates Act 1925 s. 36(10).
[71] *Re Neeld* [1962] Ch. 643, 688; *cf.* Administration of Estates Act 1925, s. 44 which is expressed to be "subject to the foregoing provisions of this Act."
[72] See *Williams v. Holland* [1965] 1 W.L.R. 739.
[73] *Re Neeld, supra,* at pp. 688–689.

the office of personal representative for the whole of his life,[1] unless the grant was of limited duration,[2] or he is subsequently removed from office.[3] Even though a personal representative has fully administered the deceased's estate, he retains the capacity to represent the estate in any future legal proceedings,[4] or to recover any assets which fall into the deceased's estate on the subsequent death of a testator, whose gift by will to the deceased takes effect under an exception to the doctrine of lapse.[5]

A personal representative continues to hold office as such, even though he no longer holds any property in that capacity.

2. Distinctions between personal representative and trustee

Broadly speaking, the function of a personal representative is to wind up a deceased's estate, whereas the function of a trustee is to hold property on trust. In spite of this basic difference in function, the office of personal representative resembles that of a trustee in many respects. The fiduciary duties of a personal representative are sometimes called "trusts."[6] The provisions of the Trustee Act 1925 apply to a personal representative where the context admits.[7] Moreover, as the Court of Appeal pointed out in *Harvell v. Foster*[8]:

> "the Administration of Estates Act 1925 (the title of which is not without significance), includes in Part III (headed 'Administration of Assets') section 33, which provides that the estate of an intestate is vested in the personal representative 'upon trust' for sale, calling in and conversion, ... and ... Part IV of the same Act, being the part devoted to the devolution of the estates of persons dying intestate and headed 'Distribution of Residuary Estate' is expressed throughout in terms of trusts."

In the case of a partial intestacy, section 49 of the Act even provides that the personal representative "shall, subject to his rights and powers for the purposes of administration, be a trustee" for the persons entitled under the intestacy rules.

But the rules applicable to personal representatives do differ, sometimes significantly, from the rules applicable to trustees. These differences may make it essential to decide whether persons, who were both personal representatives and trustees, were at the relevant time holding the property in question in their capacity of personal representatives or in their capacity of trustees. The following are instances where the rules differ:

---

[1] *Attenborough v. Solomon* [1913] A.C. 76, 83; *Harvell v. Foster* [1954] 2 Q.B. 367, 383.
[2] *e.g.* a grant of letters of administration (with the will annexed) for the use and benefit of a minor, who was appointed executor: the grant terminates when the minor attains 18 years of age or dies.
[3] *Ante*, pp. 362 *et seq.*
[4] *Harvell v. Foster, supra*
[5] *Ante*, pp. 239 *et seq.*
[6] *Commissioner of Stamp Duties (Queensland) v. Livingston* [1965] A.C. 694, 707: see *ante*, p. 478.
[7] Trustee Act 1925, s. 68(1)(17); see also s. 69(1).
[8] [1954] 2 Q.B. 367, 380.

(1) *SEVERAL AUTHORITY OF EXECUTORS.* Joint executors, and perhaps joint administrators, have joint *and several* authority (subject to important exceptions), whereas trustees must always act jointly.[9] This difference (which was crucial in the case of *Attenborough v. Solomon*) has already been considered.[10]

(2) *RECEIPT OF SOLE PERSONAL REPRESENTATIVE.* A sole personal representative, acting as such, may give a valid receipt for, or direct the application of, the proceeds of sale of land.[11] A sole trustee may not do so, unless the sole trustee is a trust corporation.[12]

(3) *PERSONAL REPRESENTATIVE'S DUTY IS TO THE ESTATE.* A trustee "has a duty to hold the balance evenly between the beneficiaries to whom the property belongs and for whom the trustee holds it."[13] On the other hand, a personal representative's duty during the administration of the deceased's estate is to consider the interest of the estate as a whole.

In *Re Hayes' Will Trusts*[14] T by his will appointed P, Q, R and S to be the executors and trustees of his will, devised Blackacre to them upon certain trusts, and conferred on them power to sell Blackacre to S at its estate duty valuation. During the administration of T's estate the executors agreed the estate duty valuation with the district valuer, and then contracted to sell Blackacre to S at this agreed valuation. Ungoed-Thomas J. said that their power to agree a valuation was a "purely personal representative administration power."[15] In agreeing the estate duty valuation, the executors were not under a duty to hold the balance evenly between S (who benefited from a low valuation) and the other beneficiaries (who benefited from a high valuation); their duty as executors was to consider the interest of the estate as a whole.

(4) *DEATH OF SOLE REPRESENTATIVE.* If a sole (or last surviving) personal representative dies without having fully administered the deceased's estate, and there is no chain of representation through proving executors, a grant of administration *de bonis non* is made in respect of the deceased's unadministered estate, so as to enable the administration of the estate to be completed.[16] But if at his death the deceased held property as a sole (or last surviving) trustee, the property devolves on the trustee's personal representatives.[17]

(5) *SURETY'S GUARANTEE.* A surety's guarantee covers a breach by an administrator of his duties as administrator, but not of his duties as

---

[9] Trustees must act jointly *unless* the trust instrument provides otherwise.
[10] *Ante*, pp. 392–393.
[11] Law of Property Act 1925, s.27(2) as amended by Law of Property (Amendment) Act 1926, Sched.
[12] *Ibid.*; Settled Land Act 1925, s.18(1); Trustee Act 1925, s.14.
[13] *Re Hayes' W.T.* [1971] 1 W.L.R. 758, 764.
[14] *Supra*: see also *Re Charteris* [1917] 2 Ch. 379.
[15] *Supra*, at p. 764.
[16] *Ante*, p. 340.
[17] *Ante*, pp. 368 *et seq.*

a trustee. This difference (and the decision in *Harvell v. Foster*) has already been explained.[18]

(6) *LIMITATION PERIOD APPLICABLE.* In general, the period of limitation in respect of any claim to the personal estate of a deceased,[19] or in respect of an action to recover any land of a deceased,[20] whether under a will or intestacy, is 12 years, whereas the period of limitation for an action by a beneficiary to recover trust property, or in respect of any breach of trust, is six years.[21]

(7) *TAX.* There are differences in the tax treatment of personal representatives and trustees—particularly in relation to the capital gains tax annual exempt amount. Personal representatives are entitled to a full annual exempt amount[22] for the tax year of the deceased's death and the two subsequent tax years,[23] whereas active trustees are entitled to only half this[24] and gains made by bare trustees count not as their gains but as gains made by the beneficiaries on whose behalf they hold.[25] The Scottish case of *Cochrane's Executors v. I.R.C.*[26] suggests that where there is a doubt as to whether disposals have been made by personal representatives acting as personal representatives, or acting as bare trustees, it will be held that the disposals have been made by them as personal representatives. Whether this will be to the advantage of the personal representatives, or to the advantage of the Revenue, will depend on the facts of the particular case.

3. Transition from personal representative to trustee.

Three different situations need consideration.

(1) *PERSONAL REPRESENTATIVE NOT A TRUSTEE UNDER THE WILL.* In general, a personal representative does not become a trustee of property which T by a gift in his will (whether specific, general or residuary) gives to B absolutely, without creating any trust for B by his will. In that case it is the duty of the personal representative (acting as such) to distribute the property to B.[27]

---

[18] *Ante*, p. 357.
[19] Limitation Act 1980, s.22 (but the period of limitation for an action to recover arrears of interest on a legacy is six years): no limit applies in case of fraud or property retained or converted to his own use by the personal representative, s.21(1) and (2). For limitation see *post*, pp. 500 *et seq*.
[20] *ibid*. s.15(1) and (6) and Sched. 1, para. 2.
[21] *ibid*. s.21(3): again no limit applies in case of fraud or property retained or converted to his own use by the trustee, s.21(1) and (2).
[22] Which is £6,000 p.a. for the tax year 1995–96
[23] Taxation of Chargeable Gains Act 1992 s.3(7).
[24] *ibid*. s.3(8) and Sched. 1.
[25] *ibid*. s. 60.
[26] (1974) 49 T.C. 299.
[27] See *Re Richardson* [1920] 1 Ch. 423 (gift of residuary estate to B); *Re Mackay* [1906] 1 Ch. 25; *Re Barker* [1892] 2 Ch. 491 (postponed legacy): and *cf. Re Oliver* [1927] 2 Ch. 323. But an executor who has assented to a specific legacy of company shares holds the shares as trustee for the legatee until the legal title is duly transferred to the legatee, *Re Grosvenor* [1916] 2 Ch. 375 and see *ante*, p. 481.

If B, to whom T makes a direct gift by his will, is an infant, so that immediate distribution is impossible, it is the duty of the personal representative (acting as such) to retain the property in trust for B and to transfer it to B once he attains full age.

In *Harvell v. Foster*[28] T by his will gave all his estate to his daughter absolutely and appointed her sole executrix. At T's death she was an infant, and letters of administration with the will annexed were granted to her husband for her use and benefit until she should attain full age. After T's debts and expenses had been paid, the husband disappeared with most of the assets. The Court of Appeal, in giving judgment, said that:

> "the duty of an administrator, as such, must at least extend to paying the funeral and testamentary expenses and debts and legacies (if any) and where, as here, immediate distribution is impossible owing to the infancy of the person beneficially entitled, retaining the net residue in trust for the infant. At least until the administrator can show that he has done this, it cannot, in our judgment, be said of him that he has duly administered the estate according to law."[29]

Moreover the Court of Appeal said that the administrator remains liable for the net residue in his capacity of personal representative until he transfers it to the infant after she has attained full age.[30] The administrator retains the net residue "in trust" for the infant in his capacity as personal representative, and he does not thereby become a trustee in the proper sense.[31]

Again, in general, a personal representative does not become a trustee of property which T by a gift in his will gives to other persons X and Y upon trust. In that case it is the duty of the personal representative (acting as such) to distribute the property to X and Y. The claim of the beneficiaries under the trust is against X and Y.[32]

(2) *PERSONAL REPRESENTATIVE A TRUSTEE UNDER THE WILL.*
A personal representative becomes a trustee of property under T's will because:

> (i) a trust of the property is created by the will (often the trust is for beneficiaries taking successive interests in the property under the will[33]); and

---

[28] [1954] 2 Q.B. 367. See also *Re Davis* [1891] 3 Ch. 119; *Re Mackay, supra.*
[29] [1954] 2 Q.B. 367. At p. 383.
[30] *ibid.* at p. 384. Alternatively the personal representative may appoint trustees for the infant under s.42(1) of the Administration of Estates Act 1925, see *ante,* p. 475.
[31] *Re Davis, supra,* at p. 124 (*per* Lindley L.J.—"an executor was always in a loose sense a trustee for creditors and legatees").
[32] *Re Oliver* [1927] 2 Ch. 323, 330–331. For the effect of an assent to a specific legacy of company shares see *ante,* n. 27.
[33] *Phillipo v. Munnings* (1837) 2 My. & Cr. 309 (£400 legacy held on trust); *Re Swain* [1891] 3 Ch. 233 (residue held on trust); *Re Timmis* [1902] 1 Ch. 176; *Re Oliver* [1927] 2 Ch. 323 (£2,000 legacy held on trust). See also *Re Claremont* [1923] 2 K.B. 718 (trust to sell residuary personalty and apply proceeds for benefit of T's two nieces): Law of Property Act 1925, s. 34(3) (gift of land to tenants in common operates as gift to trustees of will for purposes of Settled Land Act 1925, or to personal representatives, upon the statutory trusts).

(ii) the personal representative is appointed to be a trustee of the property by the will or (alternatively) no effective appointment of any other trustee of the property is made by the will.[34]

When a personal representative assents in his own favour as trustee, he changes his capacity from personal representative to trustee. The decision of the House of Lords in *Attenborough v. Solomon*[35] is a classic instance of this occurring. T by his will appointed X and Y to be executors and trustees, and gave his residuary estate to X and Y upon trust for sale and distribution as directed by the will. The same principle applies where T by his will makes a specific gift of property on trust,[36] or a gift of a general legacy on trust.[37]

The question arises whether a personal representative may cease to hold property in that capacity, and start to hold it in the capacity of trustee of the will, without any assent or conveyance in his own favour.[38] There is some case law authority for the principle that, as soon as a personal representative has cleared the estate by discharging all the deceased's expenses, debts and liabilities, and legacies, he automatically begins to hold the residuary estate as a trustee on the trusts declared by the will. In *Re Cockburn's Will Trusts*[39] Danckwerts J. felt "no doubt about the matter at all."

The principle that a personal representative may change his capacity from personal representative to trustee without any assent or conveyance in his own favour cannot, however, be regarded as settled law. Apart from the cases of *Re Ponder*[40] and *Re Yerburgh*,[41] which are mentioned later because they both relate to intestacy, the other cases usually cited in support of the principle (*i.e. Eaton v. Daines*,[42] *Re Pitt*,[43] and *Re Cockburn's Will Trusts*[44]) were all decisions on whether personal representatives had power to appoint new trustees of the will. In each of these cases the personal representatives may already have assented in their own favour by their conduct[45]: indeed, the fact that the personal representatives had cleared the estate was evidence of such an assent and the reports of these cases do not state that there had been no assent. There

---

[34] *Re Cockburn's W.T.* [1957] Ch. 438.

[35] [1913] A.C. 76: see *ante*, pp. 292–293 and 481.

[36] *Wise v. Whitburn* [1924] 1 Ch. 460 ("the effect of the assent was to strip the executors of their title as executors and to clothe them with a title as trustees"); *Dix v. Burford* (1854) 19 Beav. 409.

[37] *Phillipo v. Munnings* (1837) 2 My. & Cr. 309: see also *Clegg v. Rowland* (1866) L.R. 3 Eq. 368, 372–373; *O'Reilly v. Walsh* (1872) 6 I.R.Eq. 555, 7 I.R.Eq. 167.

[38] See generally Ryder (1976) 29 C.L.P. 60; Stebbings [1984] Conv. 423.

[39] [1957] Ch. 438, 439.

[40] [1921] 2 Ch. 59.

[41] [1928] W.N. 208.

[42] [1894] W.N. 32.

[43] (1928) 44 T.L.R. 371 (T died in 1917; administratrix cleared the estate and in 1927 appointed trustees of the will in her place: held appointment valid).

[44] [1957] Ch. 438, [1957] 2 All E.R. 522 (T died in 1947; administrators cleared the estate and made partial distribution to a residuary beneficiary: held administrators had power to appoint new trustees of the will).

[45] Assuming (as is probable) that an administrator with the will annexed may assent at common law, see *ante*, p. 480. In *Re Cockburn's W.T.*, *supra*, the property included land as well as pure personalty (as reported in [1957] 2 All E.R. 522), but the administrators may at least have assented in respect of pure personalty.

is also some authority against the principle. In *Attenborough v. Solomon*, Lord Haldane said that "the will becomes operative so far as its dispositions of personalty are concerned only if and when the executor assents to those dispositions."[46]

In the present state of the authorities it is not safe to assume that personal representatives, who have cleared the estate, cease to hold land comprised in the testator's residuary estate in their capacity of personal representatives, and start to hold the land in their capacity as trustees, even though they have made no written assent or conveyance in their own favour.[47] In order to put their change of capacity beyond doubt, personal representatives should make a written assent in their own favour as trustees.

(3) *INTESTACY.* The decision in *Re Ponder*[48] concerned the estate of X, who died intestate in 1919, leaving a widow and two infant sons. His widow obtained letters of administration, paid his expenses and debts, and invested each son's share of X's personalty in her name. Sargant J. held that the widow had ceased to hold these assets as administratrix and instead held them as a trustee; it followed that the court had jurisdiction to appoint the Public Trustee to be a trustee of these assets jointly with the widow. If this decision was good law, it involved the implication that the administratrix had become a trustee, though the pre-1926 intestacy rules applicable to personalty did not declare any trust for the next of kin. It seems doubtful, however, whether the case was rightly decided. Probably the widow held these assets as administratrix in trust for the sons.[49] She had a duty as administratrix to distribute each son's share to him when he attained full age, and she was not a trustee of these assets so as to be entitled (for instance) to appoint new trustees in place of herself and retire from the trust.

As has already been pointed out, the provisions of the Administration of Estates Act 1925 applicable on a death intestate after 1925 do refer to personal representatives holding on trust.[50] Two questions therefore arise:

    (i) Do personal representatives ever become trustees in the proper sense under these provisions, so (for instance) as to be entitled to appoint new trustees in their place and to retire from the trust?[51]

    (ii) If so, do the personal representatives automatically cease to hold the deceased's estate in that capacity, and start to hold it as trustees, as soon as they have paid the expenses debts and legacies (or "cleared the estate" as it is sometimes called)?

The case law is meagre. In *Re Yerburgh*[52] X died intestate in 1926, leaving

---

[46] [1913] A.C. 76, 82–83: see also *Re Trollope's W.T.* [1927] 1 Ch. 596, 605.

[47] In *Re King's W.T.* [1964] Ch. 542 (which was considered *ante* pp. 483–484) the devise was specific: see Ryder, *loc. cit.* pp. 71–73.

[48] [1921] 2 Ch. 59.

[49] See *Harvell v. Foster* [1954] 2 Q.B. 367, 379–380 and 382–384: *cf. Re Cockburn's W.T.* [1957] Ch. 438, 440. As to realty of an intestate who died before 1926, see *Re Ponder, supra,* and Toates [1926] 2 K.B. 30.

[50] *Ante,* p. 487.

[51] Under Trustee Act 1925, s. 36(1).

[52] [1928] W.N. 208: see also *Re Cockburn's W.T., supra,* at p. 439.

a widow and two infant children. His administrators cleared the estate and applied to the court for directions. Romer J. is reported as saying:

> "that s. 33 of the Administration of Estates Act had imposed certain duties on legal personal representatives under which they became trustees when the estate had been fully administered. They ceased to be legal personal representatives and became trustees at a particular date ... the old law applied and determined the time when [they] ceased to be legal personal representatives and became trustees for sale. At the moment when that event happened they ought to make a vesting assent under s. 36, vesting the property in themselves as trustees."

This brief judgment answers "yes" to the first question,[53] but Romer J.'s answer to the second question is not clear. Did he mean that an assent was *desirable* to evidence an automatic change in capacity, or (alternatively) was it *essential* to effect the change in capacity? Perhaps more case law is needed on both these questions.

---

[53] But see *Re Trollope's W.T.* [1927] 1 Ch. 596, 603–605 (on the effect of Administration of Estates Act 1925, s. 39); *Harvell v. Foster* [1954] 2 Q.B. 367, 384 (on the effect of s. 42(1) where an infant is absolutely entitled); *Re Wilks* [1935] Ch. 645, 650–651.

Chapter 21

REMEDIES

A. Liability of Personal Representative

1. Devastavit

If a personal representative commits any breach of the duties of his office, causing a loss of assets, he is said to commit a *devastavit*, *i.e.* a wasting of the assets of the deceased's estate. A personal representative is personally liable to the deceased's creditors and beneficiaries for any loss caused by his *devastavit*.

(1) *NATURE OF A DEVASTAVIT.* Occasionally the duties of the office of personal representatives are termed "trusts"[1] and a breach of those duties is referred to as a "breach of trust."[2] The will of the testator may contain a gift of his residuary estate to his executors "upon trust" to carry out one or more of those duties, *e.g.* to pay the testator's expenses and debts. But it is sometimes important to distinguish between a *devastavit* and a breach of any trust created by the testator's will. For instance, a personal representative by virtue of his office has a duty to pay the deceased's debts with due diligence, having regard to the assets in his hands which are properly applicable for that purpose. This duty may be modified by the testator's will as against the beneficiaries, but not as against the creditors.[3] If the personal representative commits a breach of this duty, he is liable to the creditors for any loss suffered by them as a result of his *devastavit*, irrespective of his liability under any trust or power contained in the testator's will.

The following are instances of a breach by a personal representative of the duties of his office, which, if it causes loss to the deceased's creditors or beneficiaries, renders the personal representative personally liable for a *devastavit*:

  (i) any breach by a personal representative of his duty to collect and get in the deceased's estate with reasonable diligence[4];
  (ii) any breach of his duty to take reasonable care in preserving the deceased's estate[5];

---

[1] *Commissioner of Stamp Duties (Queensland) v. Livingston* [1965] A.C. 694, 707.
[2] *Re Marsden* (1884) 26 Ch. D. 783.
[3] *Re Tankard* [1942] Ch. 69, 72 and 74: see *ante*, p. 414.
[4] *Hayward v. Kinsey* (1701) 12 Mod. Rep. 568, 573: see *ante* p. 375.
[5] *Ante*, pp. 377–378.

(iii) any breach of his duty to deal properly with the assets of the deceased's estate, *e.g.* improperly converting the assets to his own use[6];

(iv) any breach of his duty to pay the debts of the deceased with due diligence[7];

(v) any breach of his duty to protect the estate against unenforceable claims, *e.g.* paying a debt which he need not pay[8];

(vi) any breach of his duty to administer the deceased's estate, if it is insolvent, in accordance with the statutory rules as to the payment of debts[9]; and

(vii) any breach of his duty to distribute the estate to the persons properly entitled under the deceased's will or intestacy.[10]

(2) *DEVOLUTION OF PERSONAL REPRESENTATIVE'S LIABILITY FOR A DEVASTAVIT.* If a personal representative commits a devastavit, and dies, his liability for the devastavit devolves on his personal representative, to the extent of his available assets.[11]

(3) *EFFECT OF ACQUIESCENCE IN A DEVASTAVIT.* If a creditor or beneficiary acquiesced in a *devastavit*, the personal representative is not, in general, liable to him. The same principle applies if a person acquiesced in a breach of trust.[12] The onus of proving acquiescence in the *devastavit* lies on the personal representative.[13] In order to satisfy this onus, the personal representative must show that the creditor or beneficiary acquiesced in the *devastavit* with full knowledge of all the facts.[14] There is, however, no hard and fast rule that he must also have had knowledge of the legal consequences of those facts.[15]

Acquiescence by one creditor or beneficiary does not affect the rights of any other person who has not acquiesced. If the personal representative is liable for his *devastavit* to any other person, then, under section 62 of the Trustee Act 1925,[16] the court may, in its discretion, impound all or any part of the interest of a beneficiary who has instigated, requested,[17] or consented in writing to the breach of duty by the personal representative,[18] by way of indemnity to the personal representative. The

---

[6] *Marsden v. Regan* [1954] 1 W.L.R. 423 (executrix gave away the deceased's furniture: held a *devastavit*).

[7] *Ante*, p. 413.

[8] *Re Rownson* (1885) 29 Ch. D. 358, 363–364; *Midgley v. Midgley* [1893] 3 Ch. 282, 284, 299 and 304: for payment of statute-barred debts see *ante*, pp. 418–419.

[9] *Ante*, pp. 444–445.

[10] *Hilliard v. Fulford* (1876) 4 Ch. D. 389: see *ante*, p. 470.

[11] Administration of Estates Act 1925, s. 29: s. 29 also applies to an executor *de son tort* who commits a *devastavit*: see *post*, p. 517.

[12] *Fletcher v. Collis* [1905] 2 Ch. 24: see generally *Snell's Equity* (29th ed., 1990), pp. 294 *et seq.*

[13] *Re Marsden* (1884) 26 Ch. D. 783, 790.

[14] *ibid.*

[15] *Holder v. Holder* [1968] Ch. 353, approving *Re Pauling's S.T. (No. 1)* [1962] 1 W.L.R. 86, 108 (affirmed [1964] Ch. 303); *Re Freeston's Charity* [1978] 1 W.L.R. 741, 754–755.

[16] As amended by Married Women (Restraint upon Anticipation) Act 1949, s. 1(4) and Sched. 2.

[17] *Griffith v. Hughes* [1892] 3 Ch. 105 (the instigation or request may be oral).

[18] Trustee Act 1925, s. 62 applies to a breach of the duties incident to the office of a personal representative, as well as to a breach of trust, s. 68(1)(17). Apart from s. 62, equity has

court does not impound the interest of a beneficiary under this section unless the beneficiary knew the facts which rendered what he was instigating, requesting, or consenting to in writing, a breach of duty by the personal representative, though the beneficiary need not know that those facts amounted in law to a breach of duty.[19]

2. Liability to account

As already explained, a personal representative has a statutory duty to exhibit on oath a full inventory of the estate, and render an account of the administration of the estate, when required to do so by the court.[20] He must also keep clear and accurate accounts and permit the interested parties to inspect them free of charge.[21] By this means they may ascertain how the personal representative has carried out the administration.

But in equity the liability of the personal representative to account does not merely provide the interested parties with information as to how the personal representative has carried out the administration. It also provides a means of remedying many breaches of duty by a personal representative in the conduct of the administration. A personal representative may be ordered by the court to account in an administration action or (alternatively) in an action for specific relief.[22] A personal representative generally has to account for (1) his receipts and (2) his payments.

(1) *ACCOUNTING FOR RECEIPTS.* Under the form of order to account which is usually made against a personal representative (called an order for "a common account"), the personal representative must bring in an account showing the assets of the deceased's estate which he or his agent actually received. An executor, who owes a debt to the deceased's estate, is treated as having paid the debt to himself as executor, and he must therefore account for the amount of the debt as an asset of the estate which he received.[23] An administrator, who owes a debt to the deceased's estate, must account in the same way.[24]

Sometimes a personal representative is ordered by the court to account upon the footing of wilful default, *i.e.* to account, not only for assets which he or his agent actually received, but also for assets which he

---

jurisdiction to impound the interest of a beneficiary who instigated a breach of trust, to the extent to which he benefited by the breach, *Raby v. Ridehalgh* (1855) 7 De G.M. & G. 104.

[19] *Re Somerset* [1894] 1 Ch. 231, 270 and 274.

[20] Administration of Estates Act 1925, s. 25, as amended by Administration of Estates Act 1971, s. 9: for application for an inventory and an account see *ante*, pp. 376–377.

[21] *Freeman v. Fairlie* (1812) 3 Mer. 29, 43–44; *Ottley v. Gilby* (1845) 8 Beav. 602 (legatee entitled to inspect, but not to a copy of the accounts at the expense of the estate); *Re Bosworth* (1889) 58 L.J. Ch. 432.

[22] *Post*, pp. 503 *et seq.*

[23] *Ingle v. Richards (No. 2)* (1860) 28 Beav. 366 (debt which executor owed to T was asset in his hands, for which he must account as asset of T's estate); *Re Bourne* [1906] 1 Ch. 697; *Jenkins v. Jenkins* [1928] 2 K.B. 501; *Commissioner of Stamp Duties v. Bone* [1977] A.C. 511, 518.

[24] Administration of Estates Act 1925, s. 21A (added by Limitation Amendment Act 1980, s. 10 and amended by Limitation Act 1980, s. 40(2) and Sched. 3): s. 21A also applies to an executor by representation.

would have received but for his own wilful default. In this context wilful default means a breach of duty by the personal representative which caused a loss of assets. The breach of duty may constitute a *devastavit*[25] or a breach of trust.[26] Wilful default does not require conscious wrongdoing by the personal representative.[27]

The personal representative may be ordered to account upon the footing of wilful default in respect of the whole estate or (alternatively) in respect of a particular asset or transaction. In *Re Tebbs*[28] the executors of T's will sold T's land to a company pursuant to an option to purchase conferred on the company by the will. The sale was made four years after T's death at the probate value of the land, instead of at its (higher) current market value as required by the option. This was a breach of trust by the executors. A residuary beneficiary sought an order against the executors for an account to be taken upon the footing of wilful default in respect of T's whole estate. The court ordered an account upon the footing of wilful default in respect of this land, but ordered a common account in respect of the rest of T's estate. The court had jurisdiction to make an order for an account upon the footing of wilful default in respect of T's whole estate,[29] but Slade J. said that the test to apply was to ask, "is the past conduct of the trustees such as to give rise to a reasonable prima facie inference that other breaches of trust[30] not yet known to the plaintiff or the court have occurred?"[31] The evidence before the court did not give rise to such a prima facie inference.

(2) *ACCOUNTING FOR PAYMENTS.* The personal representative must discharge himself as regards the assets he received by showing that he dealt with them in due course of administration. For instance, he may show that he applied the assets in paying expenses and debts of the deceased which were properly payable by him, or that he distributed the assets pursuant to an order of the court. He can also discharge himself by showing that the assets were lost in some way for which he was not responsible.[32]

But if the personal representative has made a wrongful application of the assets, this is disallowed when the court takes the account of his payments.[33] For example, if it is found that the personal representative

---

[25] *Re Stevens* [1898] 1 Ch. 162.
[26] *Re Tebbs* [1976] 1 W.L.R. 924: see also *Re Wrightson* [1908] 1 Ch. 789, 799–800 (active breach of trust: no "roving inquiry" ordered to ascertain other breaches); *Bartlett v. Barclays Bank Trust Co. Ltd. (No. 2)* [1980] Ch. 515, 546 (wilful default means a "passive" as distinct from an "active" breach of trust): but surely an "active" breach, as much as a "passive" breach, may give rise to a reasonable prima facie inference that other breaches have occurred.
[27] *Bartlett v. Barclays Bank Trust Co. Ltd. (No. 2), supra*: see J.E. Stannard [1979] Conv. 345; *cf.* J.A. Andrews (1981) 1 Legal Studies 303, 310–311 and 322.
[28] *Supra.*
[29] *Sleight v. Lawson* (1857) 3 K. & J. 292; *Re Youngs* (1885) 30 Ch. D. 421, 431–432.
[30] Or *devastavits*: the test appears equally applicable whether the breaches of duty constitute breaches of trust or *devastavits*.
[31] *Re Tebbs* 1976 1 W.L.R. 924 at p. 930. *Cf Re Wrightson, supra,* and *Bartlett v. Barclays Bank Trust Co. Ltd., supra.*
[32] *Job v. Job* (1877) 6 Ch. D. 562; see *ante,* pp. 377–378. As to loss of assets in the hands of an agent see *ante,* pp. 395 *et seq.*
[33] *Re Stevens* [1898] 1 Ch. 162, 169–170 and 172.

has paid £1,000 to a person as a creditor, who in fact was not a creditor of the deceased, this payment is disallowed and the personal representative must replace the £1,000 which he misapplied.[34]

3. Liability for co-representative

Under section 30(1) of the Trustee Act 1925, a personal representative is chargeable only for money and securities received by him notwithstanding his signing any receipt for the sake of conformity and is answerable and accountable only for his own acts, receipts, neglects, or defaults, and not for those of any other personal representative "unless the same happens through his own wilful default."[35] This provision (and the decision in *Re Vickery*[36] on the meaning of wilful default) has already been considered in relation to the liability of a personal representative in case loss occurs following delegation to an agent. In all probability, this provision did not alter the established rules of equity relating to the liability of a personal representative for his co-representative.[37]

Under these rules of equity, an executor, X, is not vicariously liable for his co-executor, Y, if Y commits a *devastavit* or a breach of trust.[38] Nevertheless, X is fully liable for his own devastavit or breach of trust. The following are instances of X's liability:

(i) X is liable for his own breach of "the duty of all executors to watch over, and, if necessary, to correct the conduct of each other."[39] Thus, in *Styles v. Guy*,[40] X was held liable for a *devastavit* because he failed to compel his co-executor Y to pay a debt which was due from Y to the testator T; six years after T's death Y became bankrupt and the debt was lost.

(ii) X is liable for his own breach of the duty of executors to deal properly, and in the ordinary course of business, with the assets of the deceased's estate. To quote Lord Cottenham in *Terrell v. Matthews*,[41] "If money be required for the payment of debts or legacies, one executor is safe in joining in the sale of stock or other property, and permitting another executor to receive the proceeds for that purpose . . ."[42]; but if he joins in such sales when the money is not required, and he had not reasonable grounds for believing that it was so required, he is liable for the money so received by his co-executor."[43]

---

[34] *Re Stuart* (1896) 74 L.T. 546, 547.

[35] s. 30(1) applies to a personal representative, ss. 68(1)(17) and 69(1).

[36] [1931] 1 Ch. 572; see *ante*, pp. 398 *et seq.*

[37] *Re Brier* (1884) 26 Ch. D. 238, 243 (discussed *ante*, pp. 399): *cf. Re Munton* [1927] 1 Ch. 262, 274–275. As to the effect of an express indemnity clause see *Mucklow v. Fuller* (1821) Jacob 198.

[38] *Hargthorpe v. Milforth* (1594) Cro. Eliz. 318; *Styles v. Guy* (1849) 1 Mac. & G. 422, 429 (*devastavit*); *Williams v. Nixon* (1840) 2 Beav. 472.

[39] *Styles v. Guy, supra* at p. 433.

[40] *Supra*; see also *Booth v. Booth* (1838) 1 Beav. 125 (liable as stood by, knowing co-trustee was committing a breach of trust); *Williams v. Nixon* (1840) 2 Beav. 472; *Candler v. Tillett* (1855) 22 Beav. 257.

[41] (1841) 1 Mac. & G. 433n., 434–435.

[42] *Terrell v. Matthews, supra.*

[43] *Chambers v. Minchin* (1802) 7 Ves. 186; *Shipbrook v. Hinchinbrook* (1810) 16 Ves. 477; *Underwood v. Stevens* (1816) 1 Mer. 712. *Re Gasquoine* [1894] 1 Ch. 470: *cf. Lowe v. Shields* [1902] 1 I.R. 320 and *Clough v. Bond* (1838) 2 My. & Cr. 490.

These rules of equity relating to the liability of an executor are also applicable to the liability of an administrator for his co-administrator.[44]

4. Defence of limitation

When is limitation a defence to a claim made against a personal representative:

(1) by a creditor of the deceased? and
(2) by a beneficiary under the deceased's will or intestacy?

(1) *CLAIM BY CREDITOR.* A personal representative may plead the defence of limitation to a claim by any person in respect of a cause of action which accrued during the lifetime of the deceased, in just the same way as the deceased might have done if he were still alive.[45] Time continues to run against the claimant during the interval between the death and the grant of representation to the deceased's estate.[46] Moreover, time still continues to run if the claimant becomes the executor or administrator of his debtor.[47]

(a) *Charge by will for payment of debt.* Consider the situation where T at his death owes a simple contract debt to C, and T by his will charges a particular asset of his estate with the payment of this debt. C's action against T's personal representative, if founded on the simple contract debt, is barred after six years from the date on which his cause of action accrued,[48] but C's action to enforce the charge (whether on real or personal property) is only barred after 12 years from the date when his right to receive the money accrued.[49] Accordingly, it may be important to decide whether T, in providing by his will for the payment of his debts, has merely directed their payment or has created a charge for their payment.

In *Scott v. Jones*[50] T by his will gave all his personal estate to his executors for the payment of his debts. T died in 1816. The House of Lords held that this direction did not amount to a trust or charge so as to give C, who was T's simple contract creditor, the benefit of any longer period of limitation; at T's death his executors took T's personalty subject to a liability under the general law to pay his debts, and this direction added nothing to that liability. Since 1925 no distinction is made between realty and personalty in relation to liability for T's debts.[51] Accordingly, since 1925, if T by his will gives all his real and personal estate to his executors for the payment of his debts, this direction probably creates no charge

---

[44] *Lees v. Sanderson* (1830) 4 Sim. 28; *Clough v. Bond, supra,* at pp. 496–498.
[45] In general, a personal representative may, if he thinks fit, pay a statute-barred debt of the deceased, see *ante,* pp. 418 *et seq.*
[46] *Rhodes v. Smethurst* (1838) 4 M. & W. 42, (1840) 6 M. & W. 351 ("if the statute begins to run it must continue to run"); *Boatwright v. Boatwright* (1873) 17 Eq. 71.
[47] *Bowring-Hanbury's Trustee v. Bowring-Hanbury* [1943] Ch. 104.
[48] Limitation Act 1980, s. 5; *Barnes v. Glenton* [1899] 1 Q.B. 885. An action founded on a specialty debt (*i.e.* a debt contracted by deed) is barred after 12 years, *ibid.* s. 8.
[49] Limitation Act 1980, s. 20(1).
[50] (1838) 4 Cl. & F. 382: see also *Freake v. Cranefeldt* (1838) 3 My & Cr. 499. *Cf.* a pre-1926 direction to pay debts out of realty, which did create a charge, *Re Stephens* (1889) 43 Ch.D. 39; *Re Balls* [1909] 1 Ch. 791; *Re Raggi* [1913] 2 Ch. 206.
[51] *Ante,* p. 421.

capable of giving simple contract creditors the benefit of a 12-year period of limitation.[52] The result is probably the same if T by his will gives all his real and personal estate to his executors upon trust for sale and to pay his debts out of the proceeds of sale.[53]

(b) *Devastavit.* If a personal representative commits a *devastavit* by distributing assets without providing for payment of a debt, the creditor's action against the personal representative personally for the *devastavit* is barred after six years from the date of distribution.[54] The same period of limitation applies where the creditor claims an account against the personal representative so as to remedy his devastavit.[55]

(2) *CLAIM BY BENEFICIARY.* We now turn to the defence of limitation to a claim made by a beneficiary under the deceased's will or intestacy.

(a) *Pure personalty.* Section 22 of the Limitation Act 1980 provides that:

(i) "no action in respect of any claim to the personal estate[56] of a deceased person or to any share or interest in any such estate (whether under a will or on intestacy) shall be brought after the expiration of twelve years from the date on which the right to receive the share or interest accrued;" and

(ii) "no action to recover arrears of interest in respect of any legacy, or damages in respect of such arrears, shall be brought after the expiration of six years from the date on which the interest became due."

In all probability, the right of a legatee to receive an immediate general legacy accrues at the testator's death though he cannot recover the legacy until the end of the executor's year; accordingly, the 12 years' limitation period runs from the testator's death,[57] at any rate if there are assets applicable for the payment of the legacy.[58] In the case of a residuary legatee under a will, or a beneficiary entitled on intestacy, if an asset falls into the deceased's estate many years after his death, the 12 years' limitation period in respect of that asset runs from the date on which it came into the personal representative's hands.[59]

---

[52] See generally Williams, Mortimer and Sunnucks, *Executors, Administrators and Probate* (17th ed., 1993), pp. 900–902.

[53] See *Scott v. Jones, supra,* at pp. 397–398: but *cf.* Williams, Mortimer and Sunnucks, *op. cit.* p. 902.

[54] Limitation Act 1980, s. 2: *Re Gale* (1883) 22 Ch.D. 820 (immaterial creditor receives interest on his mortgage from beneficiaries after the *devastavit*); *Lacons v. Warmoll* [1907] 2 K.B. 350 (contingent debt); *Re Blow* [1914] 1 Ch. 233.

[55] Limitation Act 1980, s. 23: see *Re Blow, supra; Re Lewis* [1939] Ch. 232: the defence of limitation must be raised before the court directs the account to be taken, *Re Williams* [1916] 2 Ch. 38.

[56] Personal estate excluding the deceased's leaseholds, Limitation Act 1980, s. 38(1).

[57] *Waddell v. Harshaw* [1905] 1 Ir.R. 416; *Re Deeney* [1933] N.I. 80: the right to receive a contingent legacy accrues when the contingency is satisfied, *Rudd v. Rudd* [1895] 1 Ir.R. 15.

[58] *Re Ludlam* (1890) 63 L.T. 330, 332; *Bright v. Larcher* (1859) 27 Beav. 130 (on appeal, 4 De G. & J. 608).

[59] *Re Johnson* (1884) 29 Ch.D. 964 (next-of-kin entitled on intestacy held not barred in respect of reversionary interest which fell into deceased's estate within limitation period before action); *Adams v. Barry* (1845) 2 Coll. 285 (residuary legatee).

(b) *Land.* An action by a beneficiary to recover any land is barred after the expiration of 12 years from the date on which his right of action accrued.[60] For this purpose land includes any legal estate or equitable interest in land, a rentcharge, and any interest in the proceeds of sale of land held upon trust for sale.[61]

(c) *No limitation period applicable.* There are two important exceptions to the rules so far considered which are applicable to a claim by a beneficiary to pure personalty or land. Under section 21(1) of the Limitation Act 1980[62] no period of limitation applies to an action by a beneficiary:

(i) in respect of any fraud,[63] or fraudulent breach of trust, or fraudulent breach of the duties incident to the office of a personal representative, to which the personal representative was a party or privy; or

(ii) to recover from the personal representative property or the proceeds thereof in his possession, or previously received by him and converted to his use.[64]

If either of these exceptions is applicable, so that no period of limitation applies, the equitable doctrine of *laches*[65] may be available as a defence for the personal representative.

(3) *EXTENSION OF LIMITATION PERIOD.* The disability of the claimant,[66] or fraud, concealment, or mistake[67] may extend or postpone the period of limitation. Again, if a personal representative acknowledges[68] the claim of a creditor to recover any debt or other liquidated money claim, or the claim of a beneficiary to the deceased's personal estate or any share or interest therein, the claimant's right of action is deemed to have accrued on the date of the acknowledgment.[69] In order to be effective, an acknowledgment must be made in signed writing by the personal representative (or his agent) to the claimant (or his agent).[70] Similarly, if a personal representative (or his agent) makes any payment to the claim-

---

[60] Limitation Act 1980, s. 15(1): see *ibid.* s. 15(6) and Sched. 1, para. 2.

[61] *ibid.* s. 38(1); see also s. 18(1).

[62] For definition of "trust" and "trustee" see Limitation Act 1980, s. 38(1) and Trustee Act 1925, s. 68(1)(17).

[63] *Re Sale Hotel and Botanical Gardens Co. Ltd.* (1897) 77 L.T. 681 (moral fraud not required), reversed on another point, (1898) 78 L.T. 368: *cf. Collings v. Wade* [1896] 1 Ir.R. 340 (fraud must amount to dishonesty).

[64] *Re Howlett* [1949] Ch. 768 (trustee, chargeable with occupation rent for his own use of trust property, is treated as still having it in his own pocket, and no period of limitation applies): see also *Re Timmis* [1902] 1 Ch. 176. If the personal representative, acting honestly and reasonably, has made a distribution to himself as beneficiary, his liability is limited to the excess over his proper share, Limitation Act 1980, s.21(2).

[65] Limitation Act 1980, s.36(2): for *laches* see *Lindsay Petroleum Oil Co. v. Hurd* (1874) L.R. 5 P.C. 221, 239–240.

[66] Limitation Act 1980, ss.28, 38 (infancy or of unsound mind).

[67] *ibid.* s.32.

[68] The personal representative must acknowledge an existing liability, *Re Flynn (No. 2)* [1969] 2 Ch. 403; *Bowring-Hanbury's Trustee* v *Bowring-Hanbury* [1943] Ch. 104. For an acknowledgment in a will see *Howard v. Hennessey* [1947] Ir.R. 337.

[69] Limitation Act 1980, ss.29(5) and 38(9). As to an acknowledgment of the title of the person entitled to a right of action to recover land, see *ibid.* ss.29 and 31(1).

[70] *ibid.* s.30: see *Bowring-Hanbury's Trustee v. Bowring-Hanbury, supra.*

ant (or his agent) in respect of such a claim, the claimant's right of action is deemed to have accrued on the date of the payment.[71] An acknowledgment of, or payment in respect of, any claim to the deceased's personal estate or any share or interest therein by one of several personal representatives is binding on the deceased's estate[72] Any acknowledgment, or payment, makes the relevant period of limitation start to run afresh but cannot revive any right of action already barred by limitation.[73]

5. Power of court to grant relief from liability

Under section 61 of the Trustee Act 1925,[74] the court has power, in its discretion,[75] to relieve a personal representative either wholly or partly from personal liability for any breach of trust,[76] or any breach of the duties incident to the office of a personal representative, if it appears to the court that the personal representative:

   (i) "has acted honestly and reasonably;" and
   (ii) "ought fairly[77] to be excused for the breach ... and for omitting to obtain the directions of the court in the matter in which he committed such breach."

The onus of proving that he acted honestly and reasonably rests on the personal representative.[78] If this first requirement is made out, the court considers whether the personal representative ought fairly to be excused, looking at all the circumstances of the particular case.[79] One material circumstance is whether the personal representative is a trust company,[80] or a professional man,[81] undertaking the office in return for remuneration; if so, the court is less likely to grant relief to such a personal representative than to one who acts gratuitously.

Each case depends on its own particular circumstances, but it may be helpful to consider one instance where partial relief was granted. In *Re Kay*[82] T died in June, having by his will given to his widow an immediate

---

[71] Limitation Act 1980, ss.29(5), 30(2) and 38(9): as to payment of part of the interest due, see s.29(6).

[72] *ibid.* s.31(8). As to an acknowledgment of, or payment in respect of, a debt by one of several personal representatives, see s.31(6), (7) and (9): *Re Macdonald* [1897] 2 Ch. 181 (on effect of Lord Tenterden's Act 1828, s.1, now repealed).

[73] Limitation Act 1980, s.29(7).

[74] For definition of "trust" and "trustee" see Trustee Act 1925, s. 68(1) (17): see *Re Kay* [1897] 2 Ch. 518; *Marsden v. Regan* [1954] 1 W.L.R. 423.

[75] *Marsden v. Regan, supra,* at p. 437 ("this matter of relief is essentially one for the judge in his discretion").

[76] *Re Rosenthal* [1972] 1 W.L.R. 1273 (s. 61 does not apply to breach of trust merely contemplated by trustees).

[77] *Marsden v. Regan, supra,* at p. 434 ("in fairness to the executor and to other people who may be affected").

[78] *Re Stuart* [1897] 2 Ch. 583 (onus on trustee to show he acted reasonably).

[79] *National Trustees Company of Australasia Ltd. v. General Finance Company of Australasia Ltd.* [1905] A.C. 373, 381.

[80] *ibid.* (trust company made wrong distribution, on its solicitors' bad advice: P.C. refused relief); *Re Pauling's S.T.* [1964] Ch. 303, esp. at pp. 338–339.

[81] *Re Windsor Steam Coal Co.* (1901) Ltd. [1929] 1 Ch. 151, 164–165.

[82] [1897] 2 Ch. 518. See also *Re Lord de Clifford's Estate* [1900] 2 Ch. 707 (executors paid sums for administration purposes to their solicitors, who became bankrupt); *Re Roberts* (1897) 76 L.T. 479 (executor failed to get in debt due to testator's estate); *Re Grindey*

legacy of £300, and a life interest in the remainder of his estate. He left assets of £22,000, and debts believed to amount to not more than £100. His executor X, believing T's estate to be solvent with substantial assets, paid the £300 legacy to the widow, and allowed her to receive the income from the estate for her household expenses. In August, Y made a rather indefinite claim against T's estate for rents collected by T on Y's behalf. In November, X published the usual advertisements for creditors. In December, Y issued a writ claiming an account of these rents. X, being advised (wrongly) that there was a complete defence to this action, continued to allow the widow to receive the income until two years later, when the action came to trial, and ultimately Y obtained judgment against T's estate for more than £26,000. It followed that T's estate was insolvent and that X had committed a devastavit by distributing assets to the widow. The court relieved[83] X from his liability to Y for this devastavit in respect of the £300 legacy and the income paid to the widow before Y issued the writ. Romer J. said that X had acted reasonably in making these payments to the widow until T's debts could be fully ascertained. Admittedly "a prudent and reasonable executor ought to advertise for creditors as soon as possible after his testator's death,"[84] but X's delay in advertising had not affected Y's claim. Romer J. refused, however, to grant relief to X in respect of the income paid to the widow after Y issued the writ, because this disclosed a serious and substantial claim against T's estate. Thereafter X had not acted reasonably—he neither ascertained the extent of Y's claim nor applied to the court for directions.

B. ADMINISTRATION PROCEEDINGS

1. Nature of administration proceedings

Administration proceedings include:

(1) Actions for the administration of the deceased's estate by the court. If the court makes an order for administration, the whole or some part of the administration may be carried out under the direction of the court.

(2) Actions for specific relief, such as the determination of a particular question arising in the administration of the deceased's estate.

There is no rigid dividing line between actions for administration and actions for specific relief. As will be explained, in an action for administration the court may order specific relief instead. Again, the plaintiff in an action for specific relief usually applies, in addition, for an order for the administration of the deceased's estate if and so far as this is necessary.

Administration proceedings are often non-contentious, in the sense that they are commenced so as to obtain the guidance of the court on

---

[1898] 2 Ch 593; *Marsden v. Regan* [1954] 1 W.L.R. 423. For a survey of the cases see L.A. Sheridan (1995) 19 Conv. (N.S.) 420.

[83] Under Judicial Trustees Act 1896, s. 3 (the repealed predecessor of Trustee Act 1925, s. 61).

[84] *Re Kay, supra,* at p. 522.

difficulties arising in the administration of the estate. A personal representative is always entitled to seek the guidance of the court in matters of difficulty.

2. Actions for administration

(1) *JURISDICTION OVER ADMINISTRATION.* In the High Court an action for the administration of the estate of a deceased person is assigned to the Chancery Division.[1] Such an action may be commenced by writ or by originating summons,[2] although an originating summons is not appropriate to a claim based on an allegation of fraud,[3] or where there is likely to be a substantial dispute of fact.[4]

The following also have jurisdiction over the administration of a deceased's estate:

   (i) the county court, if the estate does not exceed £30,000 in amount or value[5];
   (ii) the Public Trustee, if the estate is solvent, its gross capital value is less than £1,000, and the persons beneficially entitled are persons of small means[6]; and
   (iii) the bankruptcy court, if the deceased died insolvent.[7]

Henceforth this consideration of administration proceedings concentrates on proceedings in the Chancery Division.

(2) *PARTIES TO AN ADMINISTRATION ACTION.* An administration action may be commenced by the personal representatives, by a creditor of the deceased[8] (suing either on his own behalf,[9] or on behalf of himself and all other creditors), or by any beneficiary interested in the deceased's estate under his will or intestacy.[10]

No order for the administration of the deceased's estate can be made until a personal representative has obtained a grant of representation to

---

[1] Supreme Court Act 1981, s. 61 and Sched. 1, para. 1.
[2] R.S.C., Ord. 5, r. 1; Ord. 85, r. 4.
[3] *ibid.* Ord. 5, r. 2(b).
[4] *ibid.* Ord. 5, r. 4(2).
[5] County Courts Act 1984, ss. 23 and 147: County Courts Jurisdiction Order 1981 (S.I 1981 No. 1123):if the estate exceeds £30,000, the parties may confer jurisdiction on a specified county court by a signed memorandum, County Courts Act 1984, s. 24.
[6] Public Trustee Act 1906, ss. 2(4) and 3(1); *Re Devereux* [1911] 2 Ch. 545 (gross capital value at date of application to Public Trustee). As to transfer from the court to the Public Trustee, see *ibid.* s. 3(5). For the powers of the Public Trustee see Public Trustee Rules 1912 (S.R. & O. 1912 No. 348), rr. 14–15.
[7] *Ante,* p. 439: see *Re Bradley* [1956] Ch. 615. No petition can be presented to the bankruptcy court after proceedings for administration have been commenced in another court, but that court may transfer the proceedings to the bankruptcy court if satisfied that the estate is insolvent, Insolvency Act 1986, s. 271 as modified by Administration of Insolvent Estates of Deceased Persons Order 1986 (S.I. 1986 No. 1999).
[8] *Re Hargreaves* (1890) 44 Ch.D. 236 (annuitant, whose annuity is not in arrear, is not entitled to bring administration action). A business creditor of a personal representative, entitled by subrogation to payment out of the deceased's assets, may obtain an administration order, *Re Shorey* (1898) 79 L.T. 349.
[9] *Re James* [1911] 2 Ch. 348.
[10] *Peacock v. Colling* (1885) 54 L.J.Ch. 743 (a beneficiary contingently entitled may bring administration action): *cf. Clowes v. Hilliard* (1876) 4 Ch.D. 413.

the estate,[11] and the personal representative (or each of them, if more than one) must be made a party to the action.[12] Thus an order for administration cannot be made against an executor *de son tort*,[13] though he may be compelled to account for the assets of which he has taken possession.[14]

If no grant of representation has been made, a creditor[15] or beneficiary[16] may apply to the court for the appointment of a receiver of the deceased's estate (and, if necessary, a manager of his business), so as to preserve the assets until a grant of representation is made. But, if a probate action has already begun, it is usually preferable to apply for the appointment of an administrator pending suit, who has the wider rights and powers of a general administrator, other than the right of distributing the residue of the estate after payment of the deceased's debts and expenses.[17]

(3) *ORDER FOR ADMINISTRATION.* As already explained, if the court makes an order for general administration, the personal representatives must not exercise their powers without first obtaining the sanction of the court.[18] An order for administration (but not the mere commencement of an administration action) also stops time running under the Limitation Act against the claims of creditors of the deceased.[19] After the court has made an order for administration, a further order may be made for the transfer to the same court of any other pending High Court action brought by, or against, the personal representatives.[20]

The court is not bound to make an order for administration unless, in the opinion of the court, the questions at issue between the parties cannot properly be determined otherwise than under such an order.[21] Thus, if a testator by his will directs his executors to take proceedings to have his estate administered by the court, the court is not bound to make an order for administration.[22] If the court does make an order for administration, and orders the whole administration to be carried out under the direction of the court, the costs incurred are likely to be considerable.[23] For instance, in a beneficiary's action against an executor the usual form

---

[11] *Rowsell v. Morris* (1873) L.R. 17 Eq. 20; *Re Sutcliffe* [1942] Ch. 453. A creditor may obtain an order for administration against an administrator *pendente lite*, *Re Toleman* [1897] 1 Ch. 866: *cf. Dowdeswell v. Dowdeswell* (1878) 9 Ch.D. 294 (order for general administration cannot be made against administrator *ad litem*).

[12] R.S.C., Ord. 85, r. 3(1).

[13] *Rowsell v. Morris, supra,* (order for administration cannot be made against personal representative of executor de son tort): *cf. Re Lovett* (1876) 3 Ch.D. 198.

[14] *Coote v. Whittington* (1873) L.R. 16 Eq. 534: see *post*, p. 517.

[15] *Re Sutcliffe* [1942] Ch. 453 (creditor may have to undertake, if required, to take a grant of representation himself).

[16] *Re Oakes* [1917] 1 Ch. 230.

[17] *Ante*, pp. 344–346.

[18] *Ante*, pp. 393–394.

[19] *Re Greaves* (1881) 18 Ch.D. 551.

[20] R.S.C., Ord. 4, r. 4.

[21] R.S.C., Ord. 85, r. 5(1): see *Re Blake* (1885) 28 Ch.D. 913.

[22] *Re Stocken* (1888) 38 Ch.D. 319.

[23] See Law Reform Committee's, 23rd Report, *The powers and duties of trustees*, Cmnd. 8733 (1982), p. 56 ("an extremely clumsy, costly and time consuming procedure and in practice it is only in wholly exceptional cases that its use can be recommended").

of order[24] directs the following accounts and inquiries to be taken and made:

> (i) An account of the property not specifically devised or bequeathed by the testator come to the hands of the defendant, the executor of the will of the testator, or to the hands of any other person or persons by the order or for the use of the defendant.[25]
>
> (ii) An account of the testator's debts and funeral and testamentary expenses, or, where the deceased died more than six years before judgment, an inquiry whether there is any debt or funeral or testamentary expense of the testator remaining unpaid.
>
> (iii) An account of legacies and annuities.
>
> (iv) An inquiry what parts if any of the testator's property are outstanding or undisposed of, and whether any part of such property so outstanding or undisposed of is subject to any and what incumbrances.

Ultimately, after the Chancery master has certified the result of the accounts and inquiries ordered, the court makes an order for payment or distribution to the beneficiaries entitled.

Instead of ordering the whole administration to be carried out under the direction of the court, the court may make a limited order. Here are some instances:

> (i) The court may order such particular accounts or inquiries as are needed, or otherwise determine the particular questions which arise in the administration. Thus the court may order appropriate specific relief in an action for administration.
>
> (ii) If the plaintiff (being a creditor or a beneficiary) alleges that no accounts, or insufficient accounts, have been furnished by the personal representatives, the court may order that proceedings in the action be stayed for a specified period, and that in the meantime the personal representatives shall furnish the plaintiff with proper accounts.[26] In addition, in order (if necessary) to prevent proceedings by other creditors or beneficiaries, the court may make an order for administration and direct accounts and inquiries, but at the same time order that no proceedings are to be taken under the order for administration, or under the accounts and inquiries, without the leave of the judge in person.[27]

3. Appointment of a judicial trustee

On the application of a personal representative or beneficiary, the Chancery Division may, in its discretion, appoint a person to be a judicial

---

[24] See Chancery Masters' Practice Forms (in *The Supreme Court Practice*, Vol. 2), Form No. 10: the usual form of order in a creditor's action is Form No. 11.

[25] If the will gives a life interest in residue, *add* distinguished between capital and income. If an account on the footing of wilful default is ordered, *add* or which without the wilful neglect or default of the defendant might have come to his hands.

[26] R.S.C., Ord. 85, r. 5(2).

[27] *Ibid.*: see *Re Viscount Furness* [1943] Ch. 415.

trustee to complete the administration of the deceased's estate.[28] A judicial trustee may be appointed to act alone, or jointly with any other person, and, if sufficient cause is shown, in place of the existing personal representatives.[29] The appointment of a judicial trustee provides "a middle course"[30] in cases where the administration of the estate by the personal representatives out of court has broken down, and it is not desired to put the estate to the expense of the whole administration being carried out under the direction of the court. A judicial trustee, as an officer of the court, "acts in close concert with the court and under conditions enabling the court to supervise his transactions,"[31] but, unlike the position of a personal representative after an order for general administration has been made, a judicial trustee may exercise his powers without first obtaining the sanction of the court.[32]

4. Appointment of a substitute for, or removal of, a personal representative

The Chancery Division also has power in its discretion:

(i) to appoint a substituted personal representative in place of all or any of the existing personal representatives of the deceased; or
(ii) if there are two or more existing personal representatives, to terminate the appointment of one or more (but not all) of them.[33]

The power is exercisable on an application relating to the deceased's estate by a personal representative of the deceased or a beneficiary under the deceased's will or intestacy.[34] This provides an alternative course to the appointment of a judicial trustee[35] in cases where an exercise of the power is appropriate in order to secure the proper administration of the deceased's estate out of court.

5. Actions for specific relief

Instead of bringing an action for the administration of the deceased's estate by the court, a personal representative, creditor, or beneficiary may bring an action for specific relief, *i.e.* for the determination of any question, or for any relief, which could be determined, or granted, in an

---

[28] Judicial Trustees Act 1896, ss. 1 and 2 (as amended by Administration of Justice Act 1982, s. 57); Judicial Trustee Rules 1983 (S.I. 1983 No. 370). As to remuneration of a judicial trustee, see *ante*, p. 406.

[29] Judicial Trustees Act 1896, ss. 1 and 2; *Re Ratcliff* [1898] 2 Ch. 352, 355–356. A judicial trustee cannot be appointed in respect of only part of the estate vested in executors, *Re Wells* [1968] 1 W.L.R. 44.

[30] *Re Ridsdel* [1947] Ch. 597, 605.

[31] *ibid.*: see Judicial Trustees Act 1896, s. 1(3) and (4).

[32] *Re Ridsdel* [1947] Ch. 597.

[33] Administration of Justice Act 1985, s. 50(1) and (2): see *ante*, p. 297. As to remuneration of a substituted personal representative, see *ante*, p. 706.

[34] Administration of Justice Act 1985, s. 50(1) and (5).

[35] On an application under section 50 the court may appoint a judicial trustee, *ibid.* s. 50(4), and on an application for a judicial trustee the court may exercise its powers under section 50, Judicial Trustees Act 1896, s. 1(7) as amended by section 50(6).

administration action.[36] Such an action for specific relief is nearly always begun by originating summons. The personal representative (or each of them, if more than one) must be made a party.[37] Often the personal representative is the plaintiff, seeking the guidance of the court in particular matters of difficulty which arise in the course of the administration of the deceased's estate out of court. In such an action the personal representative has a clear duty to lay before the court all the relevant facts which are within his knowledge.[38]

Here are a few examples[39] of the specific relief which may be sought in such an action:

(i) The determination of any question arising in the administration of the deceased's estate, *e.g.* the question whether upon the true construction of the testator's will the rule in *Allhusen v. Whittell*[40] is applicable.

(ii) The determination of any question as to the composition of any class of beneficiaries.[41]

(iii) The determination of any question as to the rights or interest of a person claiming to be entitled under the deceased's will or intestacy, *e.g.* the question whether a specific gift has been adeemed,[42] or from what date a particular general legacy carries interest.[43]

(iv) An order requiring a personal representative to furnish and, if necessary, verify accounts.[44]

(v) An order directing a personal representative to do, or not to do, a particular act, *e.g.* directing whether he should carry on the deceased's business.[45] or whether he should take, or defend, legal proceedings on behalf of the estate.[46] If, without the direction of the court, a personal representative takes, or defends, legal proceedings, he is not allowed his costs out of the estate unless the costs were properly incurred for the benefit of the estate.[47]

[36] R.S.C., Ord. 85, r. 2. The court's jurisdiction to construe a will, or control the administration of a deceased's estate, cannot be ousted by the terms of the will, *Re Wynn* [1952] Ch. 271.

[37] R.S.C., Ord. 85, r. 3(1).

[38] *Re Herwin* [1953] Ch. 701, 708–709 and 714–715.

[39] For other examples see R.S.C., Ord. 85, r. 2(2) and (3).

[40] (1867) L.R. 4 Eq. 295: see *ante*, pp. 466 *et seq.* For power of court to authorise action by personal representatives to be taken in reliance on opinion of counsel of 10 years' standing on question of construction see Administration of Justice Act 1985, s. 48.

[41] See Chancery Masters' Practice Forms, Form No. 7. If the inquiry proves inconclusive the court may make a Benjamin Order, see *ante*, p. 471.

[42] *Ante*, pp. 247 *et seq.*

[43] *Ante*, pp. 460 *et seq.*

[44] A legatee is entitled to inspect the accounts at the expense of the estate, but he must normally pay any expenses incurred in furnishing him with a copy, *Ottley v. Gilby* (1845) 8 Beav. 602; *Re Bosworth* (1889) 58 L.J. Ch. 432: *cf. Re Skinner* [1904] 1 Ch. 289 (executors' gross neglect to account).

[45] *Ante*, pp. 383 *et seq.*

[46] For the practice where the proposed legal proceedings are against a beneficiary see *Re Mortiz* [1960] Ch. 251; *Re Eaton* [1964] 1 W.L.R. 1269; and where the proposed defence is against an adverse claim to the entire estate, *Re Dallaway* [1982] 1 W.L.R. 756; *Re Evans* [1986] 1 W.L.R. 101.

[47] *Re Beddoe* [1893] 1 Ch. 547; *Stott v. Milne* (1884) 25 Ch.D. 710.

6. Costs in administration proceedings

A personal representative is entitled to the costs of administration proceedings (in so far as they are not recovered from, or paid by, any other person) out of the estate as a matter of course.[48] The court may only order otherwise on the ground that the personal representative has acted unreasonably, or has in substance acted for his own benefit rather than for the benefit of the estate.[49] The costs of all other parties to administration proceedings are in the discretion of the court.[50]

In the case of an action begun by originating summons for specific relief (*e.g.* to determine the proper construction of the testator's will), the costs of all parties[51] are normally allowed out of the estate where there is some difficulty which justifies the application to the court.[52]

C. DEFENCES OF PERSONAL REPRESENTATIVE TO CREDITOR'S ACTION

Instead of commencing administration proceedings, a creditor of the deceased may bring an action against the personal representative to recover a debt due from the deceased.[53] In general, the personal representative may plead any defence to the action which would have been open to the deceased, and in addition the personal representative may plead certain special defences:

1. Plene administravit

This defence is to the effect that the personal representative has fully administered all the assets of the deceased which have come to his hands. If the plaintiff creditor joins issue on this plea, the burden of proof lies on him to show that the personal representative still has, or ought to have, assets in his hands.[54]

If the personal representative's defence of *plene administravit* succeeds, the plaintiff (assuming that he is otherwise successful in the action) may obtain judgment only against future assets, *i.e.* against assets of the deceased coming to the personal representative's hands after the date of the judgment.[55] So far as the personal representative's defence of *plene administravit* fails, the plaintiff (on the same assumption) may obtain judgment against the personal representative as such for a sum equal to

---

[48] R.S.C., Ord. 62, r. 6(2). His costs are taxed on the indemnity basis, *ibid.* r. 14.
[49] *ibid.*
[50] Supreme Court Act 1981. s. 51(1).
[51] The costs of the personal representative on the indemnity basis, and of other parties on the standard basic, R.S.C., Ord. 62, rr. 12 and 14.
[52] *Re Buckton* [1907] 2 Ch. 406: *cf. Re Halston* [1912] 1 Ch. 435 (adverse litigation).
[53] For causes of action against the deceased which survive against his estate, see *ante*, pp. 372 *et seq.*
[54] *Giles v. Dyson* (1815) 1 Stark. 32; *Reeves v. Ward* (1835) 2 Bing. N.C. 235.
[55] Called a judgment of assets *quando acciderint* or *in futuro*: for leave to issue execution on such a judgment see R.S.C., Ord. 46, r. 2(1)(c).

the amount of the unadministered assets proved against him, but as to any balance only against future assets.[56]

2. Plene administravit praeter

This defence is to the effect that the personal representative has fully administered all the assets of the deceased which have come to his hands, except assets of a stated amount which he admits are still in his hands. If this defence succeeds, the plaintiff (on the same assumption) may obtain judgment against the personal representative as such for a sum equal to the amount of the assets admitted, but as to any balance only against future assets.

3. Existence of debts having priority over the plaintiff's debt[57] and no assets ultra.

If this defence succeeds, the plaintiff may only obtain judgment against future assets.

"The law as regards the consequences of a failure to plead *plene administravit* bears very hardly on a personal representative."[58] If a personal representative fails to plead these special defences, and the plaintiff obtains judgment against him, the personal representative thereby conclusively admits that at the date of judgment he had sufficient assets to satisfy the claim.[59] Accordingly, if the plaintiff levies execution but the judgment is not satisfied, a presumption arises that the personal representative has committed a *devastavit* in the interval between judgment and execution.[60] The personal representative is personally liable to the plaintiff for this *devastavit* unless the personal representative is able to rebut this presumption in some way, *e.g.* by proving that during this interval he handed over the assets to a receiver appointed by the court.[61]

D.   LIABILITY OF RECIPIENT OF ASSETS

1. Two equitable remedies

At the outset it is essential to distinguish between two different equitable remedies:

(1) First, there is the equitable right to claim a refund from a person to whom the deceased's assets have been wrongly paid by the personal representative. This remedy is available against the recipient

---

[56] *Jackson v. Bowley* (1841) Car. & M. 97.
[57] For the order of priority of debts see *ante*, pp. 441 *et seq.*
[58] *Midland Bank Trust Co. v. Green (No. 2)* [1979] 1 W.L.R. 460, 469.
[59] *Batchelar v. Evans* [1939] Ch. 1007; *Marsden v. Regan* [1954] 1 W.L.R. 423 (personal representative does not thereby admit that he had sufficient assets to satisfy judgment for costs to be taxed); *Midland Bank Trust Co. v. Green (No. 2), supra*; *I.R.C. v. Stannard* [1984] 1 W.L.R. 1039, 1041.
[60] *Leonard v. Simpson* (1835) 2 Bing.N.C. 176.
[61] *Batchelar v. Evans, supra:* cf. *Marsden v. Regan, supra,* (presumption not rebutted, but relief from liability granted under Trustee Act 1925, s.61).

of the assets and he is not excused from repayment because he has spent the assets wrongly paid to him. But, as in the case of any personal claim, this remedy is only fully effective if the defendant is solvent.

(2) Secondly, there is the equitable right to trace and recover property from its holder, whether or not he was the recipient from the personal representative. If the property has become mixed with other property, the appropriate remedy may be a declaration of charge on the mixed fund. The equitable right to trace, being a proprietary claim, remains effective despite the insolvency of the holder of the property. But the right to trace is lost if the property ceases to be identifiable, and there is no right to trace against a bona fide purchaser of the property for value without notice.

Each of these remedies may be available in a case where the deceased's assets have been wrongly distributed by the personal representative. The first remedy (claiming a refund) was created by the Court of Chancery in the seventeenth century as it gradually wrested from the ecclesiastical courts jurisdiction over the administration of the estates of deceased persons.[1] This first remedy is certainly applicable in the administration of estates, though it may not be applicable in the execution of trusts,[2] and it must now be more fully considered. The second remedy (tracing) is a more general remedy, which is not confined to the administration of estates, and only certain rules, which are particularly applicable to tracing as a remedy in the administration of estates, are considered here.[3]

Unfortunately, a word of warning is needed on terminology. Even though these two remedies are markedly different, each of them is sometimes referred to as the remedy of "following the assets" and on occasion this phrase appears to be used in a sense embracing both these remedies at once.[4]

2. Right of creditor, legatee or next-of-kin to claim refund

If D's personal representative wrongly pays assets to Y, instead of to X who, as creditor, legatee, or next-of-kin of D, is properly entitled to them, X has an equitable right to claim a refund from Y[5] of such an amount as X cannot recover from the personal representative. This claim against Y does not carry interest.[6]

(1) *BASIS OF LIABILITY.* As Lord Simonds put it in *Ministry of Health*

---

[1] *Per* Lord Simonds in *Ministry of Health* v *Simpson* [1951] A.C. 251, 266: see also *Re Diplock* [1948] Ch. 465, 489.

[2] *Ministry of Health v. Simpson* [1951] A.C. 251 at pp. 265–266: see also *Butler v. Broadhead* [1975] Ch. 97.

[3] *Post*, p. 515. For the remedy of tracing generally see *Snell's Equity* (29th ed., 1990), pp. 297 *et seq.*, or Hanbury and Martin, *Modern Equity* (14th ed., 1993), pp. 643 *et seq.*

[4] The right to "follow" the assets is referred to in Administration of Estates Act 1925, s. 38(1); Trustee Act 1925, ss. 26(2) and 27(2); Legitimacy Act 1976, s. 7(3); and Adoption Act 1976, s. 45(3).

[5] Or, if Y has died, from Y's personal representative or legatee, *March v. Russell* (1837) 3 My. & Cr. 31.

[6] *Re Diplock* [1948] Ch. 465, 506–507. Interest may be recoverable under the equitable right to trace, *ibid.* at pp. 557–558.

v. Simpson,[7] this remedy was developed "by the Court of Chancery in the administration of assets of a deceased person to avoid the evil of allowing one man to retain money legally payable to another." It is immaterial whether the money is legally payable to X as an unpaid or underpaid creditor, legatee or next-of-kin of D. The evil to be avoided, and the remedy applicable, is the same. The defendant Y "has no great reason to complain that he is called upon to replace what he has received against his right."[8]

If X is D's creditor, X is entitled to payment out of any of D's assets regardless of the rules regulating the burden of D's debts as between the beneficiaries, and therefore X may generally claim a refund from any of the beneficiaries. But, as the creditor's remedy is equitable, the court may order the beneficiaries to refund upon such terms (*e.g.* as to the order of refunding) as the court deems it equitable to impose, so as to regulate the burden of the debt as between them.[9]

The leading authority on this remedy is the decision of the House of Lords in *Ministry of Health v. Simpson*. In 1936 Caleb Diplock died intestate as to his residuary estate. He left a will by which he purported to dispose of his residuary estate by directing his executors to apply it for such "charitable or benevolent" objects in England as they might in their absolute discretion select. The executors, acting in good faith, distributed over £200,000 from the residuary estate among 139 charities before the next-of-kin challenged the validity of the residuary gift, which was held by the House of Lords to be void for uncertainty.[10] The next-of-kin exhausted their primary remedy against the executors in respect of the wrongful distribution of the estate,[11] and claimed to recover the balance from the wrongly paid charities. The claim against the charities was made under two alternative heads, *i.e.* (i) under the equitable right to claim a refund and (ii) under the equitable right to trace. In *Re Diplock*[12] the Court of Appeal held that both these remedies were applicable. An appeal by one charity (a hospital) against its liability under head (i) was unanimously rejected by the House of Lords in *Ministry of Health v. Simpson*. The House of Lords held that, as the next-of-kin had exhausted their primary remedy against the executors, the next-of-kin were entitled to claim a refund from the hospital in respect of the money wrongly distrib-

---

[7] [1951] A.C. 251, 268. As to a creditor's claim, Lord Davey said in *Harrison v. Kirk* [1904] A.C. 1, 7, "the Court of Chancery, in order to do justice and to avoid the evil of allowing one man to retain what is really and legally applicable to the payment of another man, devised a remedy by which, where the estate had been distributed either out of court or in court without regard to the rights of a creditor, it has allowed the creditor to recover back what has been paid to the beneficiaries or the next-of-kin who derive title from the deceased testator or intestate."

[8] *David v. Frowd* (1833) 1 My. & K. 200, 211.

[9] *National Assurance Co v. Scott* [1909] 1 I.R. 325 (creditor held entitled to refund from residuary legatees and, if need be, from pecuniary legatees). But if D's estate was administered by the court, and the creditor failed to prove for his debt, the creditor may only recover from each beneficiary the sum he was properly liable to bear, *Gillespie v. Alexander* (1827) 3 Russ. 130, 138; *Greig v. Somerville* (1830) 1 R. & M. 338; *Davies v. Nicolson* (1858) 2 De G. & J. 693, 702; *Todd v. Studholme* (1857) 3 K. & J. 324, 336–337.

[10] *Chichester Diocesan Fund and Board of Finance v. Simpson* [1944] A.C. 341: see *ante*, pp. 257–258.

[11] The executors paid £15,000 under a compromise approved by the court.

[12] [1948] Ch. 465 (reviewing the case law).

uted to it by the executors. The hospital had spent this money on erecting new buildings, so that the next-of-kin had lost their right to trace, but the hospital was nevertheless under a personal liability to refund.[13]

(2) *TWO REQUIREMENTS*. The equitable right to claim a refund is applicable if two requirements are satisfied.

(a) *Wrongful Payment by Personal Representative*. The first requirement is that the personal representative must have wrongly paid assets of the deceased's estate to Y. This requirement is satisfied if the personal representative distributed assets to Y, who had no title at all and was a stranger to the estate.[14]

In order to determine whether Y received more assets than he was properly entitled to receive, it may be necessary to ascertain the extent of the available assets at the time of the distribution to Y.[15]

Y's liability to refund does not depend upon his knowledge, or assumed knowledge, that he is not properly entitled. In *Ministry of Health v. Simpson* the hospital received and spent the money in good faith, believing that it was properly entitled, but was nevertheless held liable to refund the money.[16]

(b) *Any remedy against personal representative exhausted*. The second requirement is that X must exhaust his primary remedy (if any) against the personal representative in respect of his wrongful payment to Y. This second requirement certainly has to be satisfied if X claims as D's legatee or next-of-kin[17] and probably the same rule applies if X claims as D's creditor.[18]

X's claim against Y for a refund is limited to the amount which X cannot recover from the personal representative.[19] Sometimes X cannot recover anything from the personal representative and in that event X may claim a refund from Y of the whole amount which was wrongly paid to Y. This situation arises, for instance:

(i) if the personal representative is liable to X for a *devastavit* but is wholly without assets; or

(ii) if the personal representative is protected from liability to X because the personal representative acted under an order of the court in paying Y, *e.g.* under a Benjamin Order giving the personal representative leave to distribute on the footing that X, a missing beneficiary, predeceased D.

[13] *Ministry of Health v. Simpson* [1951] A.C. 251, 276: *cf.* G.H. Jones (1957) 73 L.Q.R. 48, 61 et seq.

[14] *Re Diplock* [1948] Ch. 465, 502: see *Re Lowe's W.T.* [1973] 1 W.L.R. 882, 887 (wrong payment to Crown).

[15] *Fenwick v. Clarke* (1862) 4 De G.F. & J. 240 (accidental loss of other assets when bank unexpectedly failed); *Re Winslow* (1890) 45 Ch.D. 249. *Peterson v. Peterson* (1866) L.R. 3 Eq. 111; *Re Lepine* [1892] 1 Ch. 210.

[16] *Fenwick v. Clarke* (1862) 4 De G.F. & J. 240.

[17] *Orr v. Kaines* (1750) 2 Ves.Sen. 194 (X an underpaid legatee); *Re Diplock* [1948] Ch. 465, 503–505; *Ministry of Health v. Simpson* [1951] A.C. 251, 267–268.

[18] *Hodges v. Waddington* (1684) 2 Vent. 360; *Hunter v. Young* (1879) 4 Ex.D. 256.

[19] *Re Diplock, supra,* at pp. 503–505 (X may issue a writ against Y for a refund before exhausting his remedy against the personal representative).

(3)   *DEFENCES.* X's claim against Y for a refund is liable to be defeated by the defence of limitation. If X claims as a legatee or next-of-kin entitled to D's pure personalty, section 22 of the Limitation Act 1980 is applicable and the period of limitation is 12 years from the date when X's right to receive his share or interest accrued.[20] Thus the same period of limitation applies to X's claim against Y for a refund as applies to X's claim against the personal representative.[21] If X claims as a creditor of D, X must bring his action within six years from the accrual of his cause of action.[22]

Again, if X acquiesces in the distribution to Y by the personal representative and thereby releases X's claim in respect of the assets paid to Y, X cannot thereafter claim a refund from Y.[23]

3.   Right of personal representative to claim refund

In general, a personal representative cannot exercise the equitable right to claim a refund from Y, a beneficiary to whom he distributed the deceased's assets.[24] Exceptionally, a personal representative is entitled to claim a refund from Y if a debt, of which the personal representative had no notice at the time of the distribution, is afterwards discovered and the personal representative is obliged to pay it.[25] The personal representative is not entitled to a refund from Y if the personal representative had notice of the debt at the time of distribution.[26] It is, however, immaterial that at the time of distribution the personal representative had notice of the existence of a contingent liability of the deceased, *e.g.* for possible calls on unpaid company shares. If this liability arises and the personal representative is obliged to discharge it, he may claim repayment from Y of the capital value of the assets distributed to him, unless at the time of distribution the personal representative knew that the claim had already fallen due for payment.[27]

A personal representative who, by a mistake of law (and not a mistake of fact), has overpaid one beneficiary Y cannot obtain repayment from Y[28]; the personal representative must make good the sum overpaid from

---

[20] *Re Diplock* [1948] Ch. 465, 507–516; affirmed *Ministry of Health v. Simpson* [1951] A.C. 251, 276–277: for s. 22, see *ante*, p. 500.

[21] *Re Diplock, supra,* at p. 514; *Ministry of Health v. Simpson, supra,* at p. 277.

[22] Limitation Act 1980, s. 5: if X claims a specialty debt, the period is 12 years, *ibid.* s. 8.

[23] *Blake v. Gale* (1886) 32 Ch.D. 571: see *Ridgway v. Newstead* (1861) 3 De G.F. & J. 474 (legatee's position altered) and *cf. Re Eustace* [1912] 1 Ch. 561 (mere delay).

[24] *Orr v. Kaines* (1750) 2 Ves. Sen. 194; *Hodges v. Waddington* (1679) 2 Cas. in Ch. 9.

[25] *Nelthrop v. Hill* (1669) 1 Cas. in Ch. 135, 136; *German v. Lady Colston* (1678) 2 Rep. Ch. 137: for the effect of advertising for claims, see *ante*, pp. 415–416. A personal representative may also be entitled to claim a refund from Y if he distributed to Y under a court order: *Newman v. Barton* (1690) 2 Vern. 205; *Noell v. Robinson* (1686) 2 Ventr. 358.

[26] *Jervis v. Wolferstan* (1874) L.R. 18 Eq. 18, 25.

[27] *Jervis v. Wolferstan, supra,* (repayment of capital but not of intermediate income received by beneficiary); *Whittaker v. Kershaw* (1890) 45 Ch.D. 320: see *ante*, p. 418.

[28] *Re Diplock* [1948] Ch. 465, 479–480, "as regards common law claims for money had and received the action will not lie where the money has been paid under a mistake of law". But recovery of payments made by mistake of law is under review; see Law Com No 227 *Restitution: Mistakes of Law and Ultra Vires Public Authority Receipts and Payments* (1994). See also *Woolwich Equitable Building Society v. I.R.C.* [1993] A.C. 70.

his own pocket so that the other beneficiaries are paid in full.[29] But the personal representative is entitled to deduct the sum overpaid from any other sum falling due to Y from the personal representative,[30] unless in the particular circumstances this would be inequitable.[31]

4. Right to trace

Legatees, devisees and next-of-kin are all entitled to exercise the equitable right to trace and recover property from the holder of it, other than a bona fide purchaser for value without notice or any person deriving title under him.[32] An unsatisfied creditor of the deceased is also entitled to exercise the equitable right to trace for the purpose of obtaining payment,[33] except against such a purchaser or any person deriving title under him.[34] The Administration of Estates Act 1925[35] provides that an assent or conveyance by a personal representative in respect of any property does not prejudice the equitable right of any person to trace the property in this way.

X may exercise his equitable right to trace, even though he has not exhausted his remedy (if any) against the personal representative in respect of his wrongful payment to Y. But in so far as X has already recovered from the personal representative, he loses his equitable right to trace.[36]

E. EXECUTOR DE SON TORT

The term *executor de son tort* (or executor in his own wrong[37]) is applied to a person who is not an executor or administrator but who nevertheless acts in some way as if he were an executor. Such a person is called an *executor* (and not an administrator) *de son tort* even though the deceased left no will.

A person appointed executor by the testator in his will can establish

---

[29] *Hilliard v. Fulford* (1876) 4 Ch.D. 389, 394 (the personal representatives "who have made the error will have to pay for it"): see Goff and Jones, *The Law of Restitution* (4th ed., 1993), Chap. 4.

[30] *Livesey v. Livesey* (1827) 3 Russ. 287 (overpayments of annuity deductible from future payments of annuity); *Dibbs v. Goren* (1849) 11 Beav. 483; *Re Musgrave* [1916] 2 Ch. 417.

[31] *Re Horne* [1905] 1 Ch. 76: cf. *Re Musgrave, supra*, at p. 425 and *Re Ainsworth* [1915] 2 Ch. 96, 104–106.

[32] *Re Diplock* [1948] Ch. 465.

[33] *Salih v. Atchi* [1961] A.C. 778, 793; *Davies v. Nicolson* (1858) 2 De G. & J. 693.

[34] *Dilkes v. Broadmead* (1860) 2 De G.F. & J. 566 (marriage consideration); *Spackman v. Timbrell* (1837) 8 Sim. 253; *Salih v. Atchi, supra*, at 793—though the creditor "cannot follow the property against the purchaser, he can follow the purchase price in the hands of the [beneficiary]," or rely on his equitable right to claim a refund from the beneficiary: see also Administration of Estates Act 1925, s. 32(2).

[35] Administration of Estates Act 1925, ss. 38(1), (3) and 55(1)(xviii): see also s. 36(9) and (11).

[36] *Re Diplock* [1948] Ch. 465, 556–557.

[37] Administration of Estates Act 1925, s. 28.

his title only by means of a grant of probate.[38] If such a person acts in some way as executor without any grant of probate, he is treated by the court as an *executor de son tort* (and not as an executor) because he cannot establish his title as executor.[39] On the other hand, once probate has been granted, this establishes his title as executor as from the testator's death. Logically he ought then to be regarded as an executor (and not as an *executor de son tort*) as from the testator's death.[40]

1.   Acts creating liability as *executor de son tort*

Section 28 of the Administration of Estates Act 1925 provides as follows:

"If any person, to the defrauding of creditors or without full valuable consideration, obtains, receives or holds any real or personal estate of a deceased person or effects the release of any debt or liability due to the estate of the deceased, he shall be charged as executor in his own wrong to the extent of the real and personal estate received or coming to his hands, or the debt or liability released, after deducting—

(a) any debt for valuable consideration and without fraud due to him from the deceased person at the time of his death; and

(b) any payment made by him which might properly be made by a personal representative."

Probably the section made no material change in the rules in force before 1926 specifying what acts made a person liable as *executor de son tort*.

(1)   *INTERMEDDLING.* If a person intermeddles with any of the deceased's assets in England or Wales[41] as if he were an executor, this makes him liable as *executor de son tort*. The rule applies to intermeddling with the deceased's realty[42] as well as his personalty. Examples include carrying on the deceased's business,[43] selling his goods,[44] and receiving payment of debts due to him.[45] Again, the act of transferring title to foreign personal representatives constitutes an intermeddling with the deceased's English estate.[46] In *I.R.C. v. Stype Investments* (Jersey) Ltd.[47] at C's death a Jersey company held English land on trust for C in fee simple, with the benefit of a contract for the sale of the land to P for £20 million. After C's death the company completed the sale and directed P to pay the price to its Jersey bank account. In an action by the Inland Revenue Commissioners claiming capital transfer tax, the Court of Appeal held

---

[38] *Ante*, pp. 328–329.

[39] *Att.–Gen. v. The New York Breweries Co. Ltd.* [1898] 1 Q.B. 205, affirmed [1899] A.C. 62.

[40] *Sykes v. Sykes* (1870) L.R. 5 C.P. 113 (the headnote is misleading): *cf. Webster v. Webster* (1804) 10 Ves. 93.

[41] *Beavan v. Lord Hastings* (1856) 2 K. & J. 724 (intestate's brother obtained representation in Belgium but did not intermeddle with English assets: not *executor de son tort*).

[42] Administration of Estates Act 1925, s. 28.

[43] *Padget v. Priest* (1787) 2 T.R. 97; *Hooper v. Summersett* (1810) Wightw. 16.

[44] *Read's Case* (1604) 5 Co. Rep, 33b; *Nulty v. Fagan* (1888) 22 L.R. Ir. 604.

[45] *Sharland v. Milldon* (1846) 5 Hare 469.

[46] *New York Breweries Co. Ltd. v. Attorney-General* [1899] A.C. 62.

[47] [1982] Ch. 456.

that the company was an *executor de son tort* because it had diverted £20 million, part of C's English assets, to Jersey out of the reach of C's personal representatives when constituted in England.[48]

(2) *AS IF HE WERE AN EXECUTOR.* To become liable as *executor de son tort* a person must intermeddle as if he were an executor. If he intermeddles out of humanity or necessity, this does not make him an *executor de son tort.*[49]

2. Liability of *executor de son tort*

(1) *LIABILITY TO CREDITORS AND BENEFICIARIES.* In general an *executor de son tort* is liable to creditors and beneficiaries of the deceased as if he were the lawful executor.[50] But under section 28 of the Administration of Estates Act 1925 he is only liable "to the extent of the real and personal estate received or coming to his hands."[51] Unlike a personal representative, an *executor de son tort* is not under any duty to collect and get in the deceased's assets.[52]

Under section 28, in determining the extent of the liability of an *executor de son tort*, two deductions are to be made from the assets for which he is liable. These two deductions are as follows:

(i) Any debt for valuable consideration and without fraud due to the *executor de son tort* from the deceased at death. Thus an *executor de son tort* may apparently "retain" for his own debt as against another creditor, even though the other creditor is of a higher degree[53] and even though the *executor de son tort* has reason to believe that the deceased's estate is insolvent. In this respect, surprisingly, an *executor de son tort* is treated more favourably than a personal representative.[54]

(ii) Any payment made by the *executor de son tort* which might properly be made by a personal representative. An *executor de son tort* may therefore deduct payments made by him in discharge of the deceased's funeral expenses and debts in due course of administration of the deceased's estate.[55] "In many cases it may

---

[48] *Ibid.* at p. 474 ("the act of transferring title from English personal representatives to Jersey personal representatives constituted an intermeddling with the English estate").

[49] This is not expressed in Administration of Estates Act 1925, s. 28 but is probably still the law. *Camden v. Fletcher* (1838) 4 M&W. 378. *Harrison v. Rowley* (1798) 4 Ves. 212, 216. *Peters v. Leeder* (1878) 47 L.J.Q.B. 573. In *Pollard v. Jackson* (1994) 67 P. & C.R. 327, the Court of Appeal held that a tenant who continued to occupy property after his landlord's death was *not* an *executor de son tort.*

[50] Unlike an executor, in the absence of liability by estoppel, an *executor de son tort* is not personally liable to the lessor for breach of covenant in respect of the deceased's leasehold of which he has taken possession, because the lease is not vested in him, *Mayor, Aldermen and Burgesses of Stratford-upon-Avon v. Parker* [1914] 2 K.B. 562.

[51] Or, if he effected the release of any debt or liability due to the deceased's estate, to the extent of the debt or liability released.

[52] For duty of a personal representative see Administration of Estates Act 1925, s. 25 as amended by Administration of Estates Act 1971, s. 9; *ante,* p. 375.

[53] *Ante,* pp. 442 *et seq.*

[54] *Ante,* pp. 444–445. Before 1926 an *executor de son tort* was not permitted to retain for his own debt, *Curtis v. Vernon* (1790) 3 T.R. 587.

[55] *Oxenham v. Clapp* (1831) 2 B. & Ad. 309.

be very convenient, and even necessary, that an *executor de son tort* should dispose of the assets of the deceased in due course of administration."[56]

The liability of an *executor de son tort* to a creditor or beneficiary ceases if, before they bring an action against him, he delivers or accounts for all the assets received by him to the lawful personal representative of the deceased.[57] By this means an *executor de son tort* may purge his wrongdoing in receiving the assets.

An *executor de son tort* may be cited by a creditor or beneficiary to take probate if he has been duly appointed as executor[58] but he cannot be compelled to take a grant of letters of administration.[59]

(2) *LIABILITY FOR INHERITANCE TAX.* An *executor de son tort* is liable for the inheritance tax attributable to the value of any property with which he intermeddles. He is treated as a person in whom such property is vested and in that capacity he is personally liable for inheritance tax chargeable in respect of the death of the deceased.[60] He is not liable for tax beyond the extent of such property.[61]

(3) *LIABILITY TO THE PERSONAL REPRESENTATIVES.* An *executor de son tort* is liable to the lawful personal representatives under the general law (*e.g.* in tort[62] or quasi-contract) for his acts of interference with the deceased's assets.[63] The *executor de son tort* may, however, mitigate the damages awarded against him by showing that he has made payments in due course of administration of the deceased's estate: the lawful personal representatives would have been bound to make these payments and to this extent the deceased's estate has suffered no loss.[64]

---

[56] *Per* Lord Tenterden C.J. in *Oxenham v. Clapp, supra*, at p. 313.

[57] Again this is not expressed in Administration of Estates Act 1925, s. 28 but is probably still the law: *Anon.* (1702) 1 Salk. 313; *Padget v. Priest* (1787) 2 T.R. 97; *Curtis v. Vernon* (1790) 3 T.R. 587, 2 H.Bl. 18; *Hill v. Curtis* (1865) L.R. 1 Eq. 90.

[58] *Ante*, p. 304.

[59] *Ante*, p. 314.

[60] Inheritance Tax Act 1984, ss. 199(4) and 200(1) and (4): see *I.R.C. v. Stype Investments (Jersey) Ltd.* [1982] Ch. 456, 466; *I.R.C. v. Stannard* [1984] 1 W.L.R. 1039. An *executor de son tort* may also be liable for inheritance tax on a chargeable transfer made by an *inter vivos* disposition of the deceased, s. 199(1) and (4) and see s. 406(6). If owing to the wide definition of "personal representatives" in s. 272 an *executor de son tort* is also liable as a personal representative under s. 200(1), then probably under s. 204(1) no liability arises for assets which he might have received but for his own neglect or default, because he is under no duty to get in assets.

[61] Inheritance Tax Act 1984, s. 204(3).

[62] *Whitehall v. Squire* (1703) Carth. 103 (conversion of deceased's horse); *Fyson v. Chambers* (1842) 9 M. & W. 460 (conversion of deceased's household goods).

[63] See *I.R.C. v. Stype Investments (Jersey) Ltd., supra*, at pp. 476–477; *Official Solicitor v. Stype Investments (Jersey) Ltd.* [1983] 1 W.L.R. 214.

[64] *Whitehall v. Squire, supra; Padget v. Priest* (1787) 2 T.R. 97, 100; *Mountford v. Gibson* (1804) 4 East. 411, 450 and 454. If an *executor de son tort* pays a creditor of the deceased in due course of administration, the creditor is not liable to the lawful personal representatives if the creditor reasonably believed that the *executor de son tort* was the lawful personal representative, *Thomson v. Harding* (1853) 2 E. & B. 630, and *cf. Mountford v. Gibson* (1804) 4 East 441.

INDEX